PENGUIN CLASSICS

PENGUIN POETS IN TRANSLATION
GENERAL EDITOR: CHRISTOPHER RICKS

DANTE IN ENGLISH

DANTE ALIGHIERI was born in Florence in 1265 and belonged to a noble but impoverished family. He followed a normal course of studies, possibly attending university in Bologna, and when he was about twenty he married Gemma Donati, by whom he had three children. He had first met Bice Portinari, whom he called Beatrice, in 1274, and when she died in 1290 he sought distraction by studying philosophy and theology and by writing the *Vita Nuova*. During this time he became involved in the strife between the Guelfs and the Ghibellines; he became a prominent White Guelf and when the Black Guelfs came to power in 1302 Dante, during an absence from Florence, was condemned to exile. He took refuge first in Verona and after wandering from place to place, as far as Paris and even, some have said improbably, to Oxford, he settled in Ravenna. While there he completed the *Divine Comedy* which he had begun in about 1308, if not later. Dante died in Ravenna in 1321.

ERIC GRIFFITHS was born in Liverpool and grew up there in a Welsh-speaking, chapel-going family. He studied at the universities of Cambridge and Princeton, and learned Italian in the house of a parish priest not far from Ferrara. He teaches at Trinity College, Cambridge, and is the author of *The Printed Voice of Victorian Poetry* (1989).

MATTHEW REYNOLDS studied at Trinity College, Cambridge and at the Scuola Normale Superiore in Pisa. He now teaches at Oxford where he is Times Lecturer and a fellow of St Anne's College. He is author of *The Realms of Verse: English Poetry in a Time of Nation-Building* (2001) and co-editor of Manzoni's *The Betrothed* (199'

T0315611

Dante in English

Edited by
ERIC GRIFFITHS *and* MATTHEW REYNOLDS

PENGUIN BOOKS

In memory of Marjorie Ballard (1902–1984) and Bruno Minghetti (1921–1992).

PENGUIN BOOKS

Published by the Penguin Group
Penguin Books Ltd, 80 Strand, London WC2R ORL, England
Penguin Group (USA) Inc., 375 Hudson Street, New York, New York 10014, USA
Penguin Group (Canada), 10 Alcorn Avenue, Toronto, Ontario, Canada M4V 3B2
(a division of Pearson Penguin Canada Inc.)
Penguin Ireland, 25 St Stephen's Green, Dublin 2, Ireland
(a division of Penguin Books Ltd)
Penguin Group (Australia), 250 Camberwell Road,
Camberwell, Victoria 3124, Australia (a division of Pearson Australia Group Pty Ltd)
Penguin Books India Pvt Ltd, 11 Community Centre,
Panchsheel Park, New Delhi – 110 017, India
Penguin Group (NZ), cnr Airborne and Rosedale Roads, Albany,
Auckland 1310, New Zealand (a division of Pearson New Zealand Ltd)
Penguin Books (South Africa) (Pty) Ltd, 24 Sturdee Avenue,
Rosebank 2196, South Africa

Penguin Books Ltd, Registered Offices: 80 Strand, London WC2R ORL, England

www.penguin.com

First published 2005
003

Editorial material and selection copyright © Eric Griffiths and Matthew Reynolds, 2005
All rights reserved

The moral right of the editors has been asserted

Set in 10.25/12.25 pt PostScript Adobe Sabon
Typeset by Rowland Phototypesetting Ltd, Bury St Edmunds, Suffolk
Printed in England by Clays Ltd, St Ives plc

ISBN 978-0-14-042388-4

www.greenpenguin.co.uk

ALWAYS LEARNING

PEARSON

Contents

Editors' Note

We refer throughout to Dante's last poem as the *Commedia* without the '*Divina*' which crept into its title in the sixteenth century; whether or not the work deserves to be called 'divine', it was an enthusiastic publisher who gave it that praise, not its author.

In the body of the anthology, we have revised each other's work so frequently that each of us now blames the other (and with some reason) for such errors as remain. We also collaborated on the prefatory material, but responsibility for the Introduction rests with Eric Griffiths, for Dante's Life with Matthew Reynolds.

We are grateful to all those who helped us put this book together, in particular to: Laura Barber; Jane Birdsell; Colin Burrow; Kate Clanchy; Richard Finn; Christopher Jenkins; Alistair Jones; Robin Kirkpatrick; Lino Leonardi; Tom Lubbock; Raphael Lyne; John Marenbon; Jessica Martin; Gabriele Minghetti and all the Federzoni-Minghetti family; Robert Ombres; Ralph Pite; Rachel Polonsky; Michael, Gabriel and Theodore Reynolds; Christopher Ricks; Stephen Ryan; Allan White; and, above all, Jeremy Maule.

Dante's Life

Dante Alighieri was born, in May or June 1265, in Florence, then one of the four most populous cities in what is now Italy; only Milan, Venice and Genoa equalled its population of about 100,000. Florence was prosperous through trade in textiles (see Dante's evocation of elaborate fabrics in *Inferno* 17) and financial services (the 'florins' mentioned at *Inferno* 30.89 take their name from the city which introduced them in 1252), but had long been riven by conflicts between groups of aristocratic clans known as Guelfs and Ghibellines. The factions gave allegiance, respectively, to the Papacy and the Holy Roman Empire, but since neither of those great powers was able to exert much control at a distance (in this respect, each resembled rather the United Nations than the United States), the daily reality of Guelf–Ghibelline strife was recurrent warfare with other Tuscan towns (Siena, Lucca, Pistoia) and recurrent squabbles in the debating chambers and on the streets of Florence. The Alighieri were Guelfs of aristocratic status, though not especially grand ones: Dante could boast a famous ancestor, Cacciaguida (celebrated in *Paradiso* 15), but his father, who made his living as a businessman and small landowner, was not prominent enough to be exiled with the Guelf leaders after the terrible battle of Montaperti in 1260, nor to assume a public position when they returned to power following the battle of Benevento in 1266: he was, however, one of the 20 per cent of adult male Florentines who had the right to vote in municipal elections. The Guelfs (themselves soon at odds with one another) remained uneasily dominant in Florence throughout Dante's life.

Like every Florentine born in the preceding year, Dante will have been christened on 26 March 1266 in the baptistery referred to in *Inferno* 19 as 'my beautiful San Giovanni'; later documents suggest that the original spelling of his first name was 'Durante', although there is no indication that he ever used this form himself. His given name has no Christian significance: this was usual in the thirteenth century when only about a quarter of Italian children were named after saints (a proportion which rises to two-thirds over the next hundred years; Dante followed this trend in naming his own children). Nothing is known of his mother, Bella, except that she died sometime between 1270 and 1275 having given birth to a daughter: Dante's father soon remarried; another son and daughter were born. The first documentary evidence of Dante's existence is his betrothal, on 9 January 1277, to Gemma Donati, scion of a powerful Guelf clan: later, probably in 1285, the couple were married. That there is no explicit mention of Dante's wife or immediate family in his extant writings is more likely a sign of his discretion than of the unhappiness which Boccaccio attributed to the marriage: the many acute references to mother–child relations in the *Commedia* show his interest in at least this aspect of family life.

The woman to whom Dante vowed his imagination had entered his life before his betrothal. According to the *Vita Nuova* (probably compiled 1293–5) he first met Beatrice when he was nine and she was eight; nine years later – in 1283 – they renewed their acquaintance and a flowering of love lyrics followed. Since his childhood, Dante had been studying Latin with a tutor and reading the works by Virgil, Ovid, Lucan, Statius and Horace which were to be so great an influence on the *Commedia*; now he also came to grips with contemporary French culture, perhaps under the guidance of his mentor Brunetto Latini (see *Inferno* 15), drawing two verse sequences, *Il Detto d'Amore* and *Il Fiore*, from the *Roman de la Rose*. His friendship with the avant-garde poet Guido Cavalcanti (see *Inferno* 10) likewise dates from these early years, and in 1286–7 it is probable that he spent a few months in the university city of Bologna: certainly he was affected by the Bolognese verse of

Guinizelli, father of the *dolce stil nuovo* (sweet new style), to whom he pays tribute in *Purgatorio* 26.

Beatrice married in 1287 and died in 1290. By his own account Dante sought consolation (for either or both of these events) in philosophy: he certainly read Cicero, Boethius, Aquinas and Albertus Magnus, and probably attended the lay schools held at the Franciscan church of Santa Croce and the Dominican Santa Maria Novella. There he will have encountered the difficult theological problems to which he returns in *Paradiso*: according to *Convivio* he studied so hard that his eyes were temporarily damaged. Not that his mind was entirely on higher things: from the 1290s date his scurrilous exchange of sonnets (or *tenzone*) with Forese Donati (see *Purgatorio* 23) and his poems of bitter love for the '*donna pietra*'; her identity, like those of the other objects of his literary and perhaps actual affections, the '*pargoletta*' and the two 'screen women' of the *Vita Nuova*, is unknown.

Sometime between 1281 and 1283 Dante's father had died, leaving him at the head of his family at a time of growing conflict between the great families (*grandi*) on the one hand, and the artisans and small traders (*popolo*) on the other, although a temporary equilibrium was established when Paolo Malatesta (the Paolo of *Inferno* 5) was Capitano del Comune in 1282–3. Dante's detailed knowledge of life in the countryside (the *Commedia* makes frequent reference to such matters as the maintenance of hedges and the movement of sheep) suggests that he was closely involved in the running of his family's modest lands: certainly he takes a landlord's view of the peasantry, neglecting to mention the ferocity with which taxes were extracted from them or the amino-starvation from which many of them suffered. The Italian weather in this period was not kind to farmers: there had been three major floods in the first ten years of Dante's life, and there were serious crop-failures in 1272, 1273 and 1285, as well as bizarre infestations of caterpillars (1282) and gnats (1287). Tuscan politics was no calmer, and (as the *Commedia* again makes clear) Dante played his part in Florence's frequent wars. It is possible that he joined in a small military expedition to aid Siena in 1285–6; probably he

careful, conceptual subdivisions', to Virgil, who knew the Latin verb '*divido*' (I separate, distribute, divide) but could not have known the new application the word received more than a thousand years after his death.

Similarly, Dante has Virgil not only quote but also parodically invert one of the most solemn hymns of the Church to which the Roman poet never belonged, when in the first line of *Inferno* 34 he alerts Dante to the figure of Lucifer with the words '*Vexilla regis prodeunt inferni*' ('The banners of the king come forth – the king of Hell, that is'). Venantius Fortunatus's hymn dates from the late sixth century CE and is sung in the Latin rite on Good Friday when the presanctified host is carried in procession to the altar. Virgil skews its opening words by adding '*inferni*' so they become apt in reverse to the presence of the devil; in doing so, he displays an insider's knowledge of Catholic liturgy and also exercises a freedom with regard to that liturgy when, it might be piously thought, only an outsider would take such liberties. Making his allusion, Virgil is both inside and outside the Church; his joke and the position it implies for him focus all Dante's sorrowful inquiry throughout the *Commedia* about the fate of this virtuous pagan and the worth of the classical culture for which he stands.

The Latin of the *Commedia* is both 'classical' and 'medieval', both 'pagan' and 'Church', and is thus for Dante a time-machine in which he travels through cultures and compares them. He is intensely comparative and fiercely combative as well, militant for the dignity of thinking people such as himself who were not in holy orders (he has some claim to be considered a founding father of the Lay Pride movement which would have such large consequences in the centuries to follow). So he takes sardonic pleasure in turning the prestige of Latin against those greasy eminences who may have wished to reserve its lustre for themselves. When he meets Pope Adrian V in *Purgatorio* 19, the pontiff raises his head from the cobbles to which it is pressed in purgation of his avarice, promises to explain why he's being punished, but insists first on trying to save face: '*ma prima / scias quod ego fui successor Petri*' ['but first / let it be known unto thee that I was successor to Saint Peter'] – around the

The moment Virgil appears in the *Commedia*, the poem's Italian is set once and for all beside Latin; the first word Dante speaks to Virgil, even before he knows who Virgil is, is Latin, though in a construction which Virgil when living would not have felt quite at home with: '*Miserere*' (Latin), 'have pity', not the Italian '*abbi pietà*', but then '*di me*' (Italian) not '*mei*' (Latin). The *Commedia* is throughout a purposefully and inquiringly bilingual poem, bringing into consideration as it moves between *gramatica* and *volgare* the reciprocal abrading and support between universalizing culture and local authenticities. Composing poems or hymns in both Latin and in their mother-tongues came naturally to educated poets, for they had become bilingual in the process of becoming educated. When William Langland's *Piers Plowman* in the last quarter of the fourteenth century splices Latin and English, it sometimes does so to mark out the stages of acculturation through which the poet and his poem have come into being, stages which result in the self having two vocabularies for itself, the first vernacular and, in the full sense of the term, 'familiar', the second adoptive, more accurate and polished but always retaining about it the quality of an overlay:

> 'What are ye called,' quoth I, 'in that court among Christ's
>   people?'
> 'The whiles I quick the corpse,' quoth he, 'called am I *anima*; . . .
> And for that I can and know called am I *mens*;
> And when I make moan to God *memoria* is my name;
> And when I deem dooms and do as truth teacheth,
> Then is *ratio* my right name, reason in English . . .'[33]

The *Commedia* too knows its way round the technical vocabulary of what was then the cutting edge (Latin was the language of scientific speculation as well as of theology and cult) – witness '*imaginativa*' (*Purgatorio* 17.13) or '*dividendo*' (*Purgatorio* 17.112), among many others. That last instance, though, opens out an extra dimension to the poem's Latinisms, for Dante gives the word '*dividendo*', a term from the procedures of scholasticism which roughly means 'proceeding by

'*etterno essilio*' ('eternal exile', *Inferno* 23.126) whereas
Heaven for Beatrice is '*loco ove tornar disio*' ('the place to
which I desire to return', *Inferno* 2.71, cf. also 2.84) and the
blessed are '*quanto di noi là sù fatto ha ritorno*' ('as many of
us as have made our way back up there', *Paradiso* 30.114). If
Dante's work ever chances to overcome his cruel banishment,
'*ritornerò poeta*' ('I shall return as a poet', *Paradiso* 25.8) to
Florence, though when he tells his Florentine literary father,
Brunetto Latini, that Virgil is 'leading me back home'
('*reducemi a ca*', *Inferno* 15.54), he means 'heaven' by 'home'.[27]
Anna Akhmatova (1889–1966) maybe remembered all this,
enfolded in that dropped '*n*', when she wrote thrillingly in 1936
from Leningrad about Dante and his walled and fractured home
town: 'He from hell to her sent a curse / And in heaven could
not her forget'.[28] The phrase which the *Vita Nuova* applies to
Florence after Beatrice's death – '*città dolente*' ('city of lamenta-
tion')[29] – resurfaces in *Inferno* 3.1 as a proper name for Hell.

The account Dante gives in the *Convivio* of his debt to the
vulgar tongue recognizably describes the 'linguistic construc-
tion of the self', though he speaks in humane, imaginatively
particular terms of nurture and reciprocity rather than in the
unexamined idiom of 'construction' which some intellectuals
at present take for granted. Italian has emphatic priority for
Dante as his *first* language in both time and rank, because it
was 'by itself throughout my mind before any other language';[30]
what's more, it was for him the gateway to '*gramatica*', the
parlance of the literate, the learned domain, for it was 'through
Italian that I entered upon Latin'. The '*volgare*' was for him a
first Virgil because '*fu introduttore di me nella via di scienza*'
('it was my sponsor on the road of knowledge').[31] Here we
should recall what is often forgotten: most European literatures
began as post-colonial literatures, and the *Commedia* has some
title to be considered the first masterpiece by a post-colonial
writer, for most Europeans were once Roman subjects and, in
the words of Donald Davie's fine reminder, 'however used we
may be to regarding ourselves as *colons* (colonists) [we have]
also been *colonisés* (the colonized). The evidence of that is in
our language, as soon as we set it beside Latin.'[32]

Commedia maintains the same of Dante and the Florentines who gave him speech. The blessed souls in the heaven of the sun, after hearing Solomon's discourse on the resurrection of the body, speak the dialect of Dante's home town:

> *Tanto mi parver subiti e accorti*
>   *e l'uno e l'altro coro a dicer 'Amme!',*
>   *che ben mostrar disio d'i corpi morti;*
> *forse non pur per lor, ma per le mamme,*
>   *per li padri e per li altri che fuor cari*
>   *anzi che fosser sempiterne fiamme.*
>   (*Paradiso* 14.61–66)

[Both choirs seemed to me so prompt and keen to utter 'Amen' to what he said that they clearly showed longing for their dead bodies; and perhaps not only on their own account, but for the sake of their mothers and of their fathers and of the others who were dear to them before they became sempiternal flames.]

The Dante of *De vulgari eloquentia* thought it was '*propter amentiam suam*' ['because they are demented'] that Tuscans believed their own '*turpiloquio*' ['dirty utterance']²⁵ to be the best Italian, but Dante enskied lends a more kindly ear to the loppings and slurrings of his fellow citizens. They drop the final 'n' from '*Ammen*' and, doing so, retain the vocal physique of Florentines, though each awaits reunion with his or her larynx along with the rest of each individual's past frame; they also provide him with the impetus to rhyme from their unregenerate speech habits through '*mamme*' ['mothers'] to '*fiamme*' ['flames']. From earthly and still beloved '*mamme*' to the ecstatic '*fiamme*' of the blessed in contemplation – the whole *Commedia* sparks between those two poles. He had written in the *Convivio* that 'the supreme desire of each existing thing ... is to return to its beginning';²⁶ the treatise names God as that beginning, but the poem is less clear-cut and more candid about his desires, for in the *Commedia* Dante has throughout a double domicile, in God and in Florence. Hence the richly pivotal character of 'return' ('*tornare*', '*ritornare*') in the poem: Hell is

> 'O animal grazioso e benigno
> che visitando vai per l'aere perso
> noi che tignemmo il mondo di sanguigno . . .'

['O gracious and kindly creature, you who come through the
dark air to visit us who stained the world with our blood . . .']

As Dante begins to elicit voices from the lost people, the rhyth-
mic signal comes through with an apt faintness, as from a
short-wave radio almost out of range amid a storm of inter-
ference. The first line can be heard as having either nine, ten or
the expected eleven syllables of the poem's hendecasyllabic
norm, depending on whether '*grazioso*' has three or four syl-
lables, and whether the voice slides together either, neither or
both of the proximate open vowels at '*O ani-*' and '*-ioso e*'.
Costanzo di Girolamo has rightly remarked that Francesca's
greeting would 'only with extreme difficulty be interpreted and
heard as a hendecasyllable, did it not appear in a continuous
body of hendecasyllables . . . many of which are rhythmically
unambiguous, and were we not, what's more, familiar with
Dante's characteristic versification, which is flexible and vari-
ous in its use of certain metrical devices (here: *dialefe*, dieresis,
and *sinalefe*)'.[23] The haziness as to whether we have, at some
points in the line, one or two syllables matches our temporary
uncertainty as to how many people are responding to Dante.
They have always been referred to in the plural before they
speak ('*quei due . . . 'nsieme . . . li . . . i . . . ei . . . li . . . cotali*'),
and when they speak, speak as a 'we' until the feminine ending
of a past participle ten lines into the reply – '*nata fui*' ['I was
born'] – reveals that Dante, Virgil and we are listening to a
woman's voice alone, that of Francesca da Rimini, to whom
we are (at '*nata*') at last tuned in, though the absence of any
speech-marker to single her out has made us hear her in implicit
duet with her Paolo, '*questi, che mai da me non fia diviso*' ['this
man who is inseparable from me'], as she calls him in a claim
whose tone cannot be fathomed, though it is a claim that the
acoustic Dante lends her voice for a while bears out.[24]
   Not even God has put Paolo and Francesca asunder; the

because it is most united with him. And just as a man's mother-tongue is most close to him, so it is most united with him, for it alone is in his mind before he learns any other language, and not only is it essentially united with him but also contingently united with him, insofar as it is linked for him with the people who are most close to him, such as his kin, his fellow citizens, his own people. Such is a man's mother-tongue, something not only close but most especially close to every man. And so, if, as I said above, closeness is the seed of friendship, it is clear that such closeness has been one of the causes of the love I bear my mother-tongue, for it is closer to me than any other.[20]

The intense repetitions of his prose swell with affection for the language in which he utters them (it was through repeating he first learned to speak), as for the birthplace from which he was in exile when he wrote that it was closest to him of all the world because there he '*tiene se medesimo*', literally 'has his self' – across the fact of his banishment from Florence, the present tense is poignant. He says at one point his native Tuscan assisted at his conception, and does not mean this as a metaphor.[21] The kinship of such formulations with his poetic practice in the *Commedia* comes out in many ways. One sign the *Commedia* is written in no grand or 'tragic' style is its gravitation, often at key moments, to idioms of affiliation or community which in his *De vulgari eloquentia* he had looked down on as unfitted for the high-flown;[22] the *Convivio*'s emphasis on '*prossimitate*' ('closeness') as formative of the self may also be traced in the crowded sociability of Dante's afterlife. In the *Commedia*, even Hell, a realm it makes some sense to picture as an abyss of isolation and self-imprisonment, bustles with interchange – needling, ripostes and empty threats. 'Neighbours from Hell', it seems, reading the poem, is a new phrase for an old fact.

Not that all his infernal proximities are sheerly abrasive. The first time the damned speak to Dante is when he calls a pair of souls from out the 'flock where Dido was'; the wind bears them to him and then the words come:

natural for both religious and secular experts to adopt; it is not, though, the only angle from which the *Commedia* views the process, for in the poem Dante is a pupil – extremely gifted, no doubt, and diligent but still at times distracted during lessons, alert to the moments when teacher is flustered, and always both growing out of and outgrowing what he is told, as an independent-minded student should.

Boccaccio makes Dante seem extremely civic-minded in the reasons he gives why the *Commedia* was written in Italian; the poem sounds like a worthy project for adult education or an exercise in 'outreach'. Dante did have an exalted sense of political mission, yet public-spiritedness alone is an unlikely motor for so intimate, so searching a poem as the *Commedia*, with all its rancours and longing. A remarkable passage in Dante's *Convivio* helps explain how the poem brings together, though it does not always harmonize, broad, theologico-political concerns and a keenly individual focus. The *Convivio*, which he wrote between 1304 and 1307, just before it is thought he started on *Inferno*, offers a series of commentaries on some of his earlier poems and, because commentary was a learned kind of writing, Dante feels the need to explain why he glosses his own works in Italian rather than Latin as would have been expected. He speaks of his *'perfettissimo amore'* ['most entire love'] for his native tongue and, citing Aristotle and Cicero, tries to say where such love comes from:

> closeness and kindness are the natural causes which bring love into being; benefits gained, study, and custom are the causes which make it grow. And all these causes brought into being and strengthened the love I bear to my mother-tongue, as I shall briefly show.
>
> The closer something is to a man, the more (as compared with all other things of the same kind) it is united with him: thus, of all men a son is closest to his father; of all arts, medicine is closest to the doctor, and music to the musician, because these arts are more united with them than other arts; of all lands, that land where he has his being [*tiene se medesimo*] is closest to a man,

beginning of civilization'.[17] This must be so because human beings have to teach, learn, discover and develop their beliefs, and do so according to the diversity of their talents. Understanding comes along a path of misunderstandings; to every creed and every science there belongs its own troop of attendant howlers. Garbling is a venerable feature of human cultures, and it may not be anachronistic to let ourselves be guided in imagining how religious messages then went awry by recalling the lurid superstitions which at present hover, so prompt and rife, about the field of 'popular science'. It is not clear that DNA and its implications are more widely understood now than the Scriptures and their implications were then (the transfer of the honorific metaphor 'book of life' from sacred writings to the human genome might imply a continuity, of mis-taking as of illumination).[18] Bernard Hamilton suggests such a comparison when he remarks: 'The gulf between the highly articulate and intellectual faith of trained theologians and the simple beliefs of the mass of the laity in the later Middle Ages was almost unbridgeable.'[19]

Only *almost* unbridgeable, though: all trained theologians had once been 'simple' and had crossed the 'gulf', though some preferred to forget the fact. The *Commedia* strains to be a bridge between these disparities, rather a daunting rope bridge perhaps, over a vertiginous drop, and with some slats missing, but a bridge nonetheless, approachable from either end. As such a bridge, it is particularly susceptible to wresting by those firmly planted on one or other side of the chasm it spans, so that it has been and still is tugged by some until it looks gleamingly orthodox, while it is touted by others as forming, more or less surreptitiously, a subversive vanguard, whether Protestant, free-masonic, folkloric or, recently, Bakhtinian/deconstructionist. All these tidyings strip the poem of the dynamism which makes it so attractive, even to its tidiers, for if the *Commedia* had no friction at its heart it would not stir them to supply it with the neatness of their choice. Such interpretations of the poem concentrate on what they suppose it teaches and pay less heed to how it teaches. That is a teacher's-eye view of what counts in the process of learning, such as has been through the ages

as it is with the cleaner lines of encyclicals and canon law.
Whatever contribution it makes to or takes from Christian
theology, the *Commedia* is – in the volatility of its rhythmic
pulse, its narrative intricacies and the crannies of its dictions –
a primer of Christian anthropology.

And what the Church then taught, its official doctrine, is by
no means identical with what was everywhere understood as
its teaching. Pious women in the diocese of Lyons revered
St Guinefort, a holy greyhound; the Bishop of Pamiers was
disquieted when young Grazide Lizier replied to his question
about the Creator: 'I do not believe that God made wolves,
flies, lizards and other creatures harmful to men; nor do I
believe that he made the Devil'; 'the masses in the West . . .
often misunderstood or considered a kind of disgrace . . . the
mystery of the Incarnation'.[15] As late as the sixteenth century,
by which time the Church had made strenuous efforts to
sharpen up its magisterial act, a puzzle-headed miller who had
read a bit could not make out the crucifixion: 'it seemed a
strange thing to me that a lord would allow himself to be taken
in this way, and so I suspected that since he was crucified he
was not God.'[16] He died in and for his perplexity, unprotected
by the patron of orthodoxy, Saint Dominic, for whom he had
been named. Some people are now charmed – and at least as
many are repelled – by a picture of Dante's time as culturally
unanimous: everybody believed much the same thing in much
the same way, and what the Pope said went. In those days there
was an 'age of faith' and now we live in different times which
are so plural and complex we can't even agree on a name for
them. Whichever response this picture provokes, it should be
recognized what kind of picture it is – a cartoon, which stands
in the same relation to historical actualities as Tom and Jerry
to the behaviour and anatomy of cats and mice. What seems
the consensus of a past epoch is often a trick of the written
record: we read only a narrow sample of what was written in
the past; that sample is itself the work of that narrower band
of people who could then read and write; the unanimity we
pine for or deplore is the product of these factors. Whereas in
fact 'belief itself has been in constant mutation . . . from the

making cheap loans to farmers, draining marshes, mediating in disputes, advising parishioners 'that they should never put their children in bed with them in case through negligence they should roll over and smother them',[14] ministry makes up the flesh and bone of actual Christianity (and takes up a good deal of the time of parish priests) in a way which historians of the Church largely ignore because of their preoccupation with theology and 'high' politics. Many historians of religion, both the pro- and the anti-clerical, write as if they had never seen the inside of a church. By which I do not mean to criticize the ways in which they spend their Sundays but to indicate a certain thinness in their descriptions. If you look merely at the church buildings of Dante's time, you see those churches might have been required to perform the functions of what we now call look-out towers, granaries, trading standards offices, public service broadcasting, bomb shelters, bank vaults, tourist information centres, catwalks, museums, weather stations and camps for refugees, to name a few: they were, in the eloquent French phrase for what English drably terms 'village halls', *salles polyvalentes*. It would be foolish to suppose, though devout to hope, that this dense ambiguity of purpose never resulted in confusion of role, let alone cross-purpose and strife. Even today, if you walk round an old but still serving church, you may light on a rich jumble: the statue of a saint whose cult has subsided, lacking an arm; a pile of cyclostyled pastoral letters; plasticene oxen, asses and cribs; the various wherewithal of flower-arrangers; in my experience, there is also often (usually behind the altar along with inexplicable quantities of papier mâché) a mineral-water bottle containing a virulently green liquid. Such clutter bears witness not only to the fads and makeshifts through which over the years fervour passes, but also to one level of the actual processes known by theologians as 'the incarnation of the Word', though these relics and detritus are rarely touched on in exegeses of John's gospel, chapter 1, verses 1–18. Dante's poem feeds off and responds to this bric-a-brac that clusters round a faith: it is as conversant with bugbears, false hopes, self-aggrandizement in the guise of custodianship and all the other interstitial lichen of a lived religion

precedent, did not lose the opportunity of being understood by the educated, showed the beauty of our native tongue and his skill in it, and brought pleasure and self-understanding to the simple who had been left behind in neglect by every other writer.[9]

Most people in Dante's world could neither read nor write and few were literate in both Italian and Latin (probably less than 10 per cent).[10] Illiteracy has been, in historical fact, literature's darkest and most persistent blind spot, and not only literature's but also the Church's. I as I write and you as you read forget the hours and pains it took us to form and follow the alphabet; the processes through which our skill was acquired drop out of our consideration while we exercise the skill. What's true of individuals is true of epochs too: the present passes over the civilizing process through which it came to be itself. So, though a scholar such as Christopher Kleinhenz assures us that 'when he wrote the *Divine Comedy*, Dante did not – indeed, he could not – imagine a reader as biblically illiterate'[11] as many in our day are said to be, this is true only in the sense that I do not, perhaps cannot, imagine my own hand when I hold it before my eyes. Imagination is of the absent. Dante did not imagine people ignorant of the Scriptures; he saw and heard them round him all the time. Before the invention of printing, few parish churches owned copies of the sacred writings; the clergy in rural areas were themselves often barely able to read from their lectionaries. Church councils lamented the Church's failure to exercise its *magisterium* [teaching authority]; synods enacted that priests should change their lax ways and expound the Gospel, at least on Sundays and feast days; Humbert of Romans, the Dominican expert on preaching, noted that 'the poor rarely go to church and rarely to sermons, so that they know little of what pertains to their salvation.'[12] Even the few laypeople who could read Latin did not much read the Scriptures.[13]

The ministry of the Church may have been widespread then, but from this it does not follow that its teaching was pervasive. Ministry is distinct from teaching. In such vital matters as

Many wondered, and among the many several of the learned, what on earth could have led Dante to abandon this opening in the elevation of Latin ('*gramatica*') and opt to write on such a high theme '*in volgare*', in the idiom of the common people. A century later, one troubled cleric, the Franciscan Giovanni Bertoldi da Serravalle, at the urging of a cardinal and a couple of English bishops, redressed Dante's self-impaired dignity by translating the poem 'back' into Latin where it was thought more properly to belong.[8]

This discarded snippet of a Latin *Commedia* sits oddly, both with itself and with the poem Dante eventually wrote. The spring in its rhythm is out of kilter with the staid gestures of epic exordium ('*canam*'); the hints of rhyme in these hexameters – '*fluvido . . . mundo*', '*lata patent*' – might jangle on an ear attuned to Virgil, for rhyme came to prominence in Western verse with Christianity. On the other hand, an orthodox Christian scrutineer might be differently vexed, by the sense rather than the tune. Dante speaks of 'realms' without mention of their ruler, and to describe God's realms as '*contermina*' – sharing their borders – with earthly kingdoms of flux could mislead a reader into thinking those realms are governed by laws which are predictable extensions of human laws, a risky thought which might, if unqualified, be pursued through possible implications of 'according as each has deserved' to the conclusion that the afterlife is just a merit award, leaving divine grace no part to play in the final destiny of individuals. The wavering in status and direction of these lines, strung between imperial and ecclesial Latins, is that of Christendom at Dante's time and, so far as those two Latins may stand for, respectively, 'the things which are Caesar's' and 'the things that are God's' (Matthew 22:21), at any time.

Boccaccio gives several reasons why Dante gave up Latin:

> so he could be more useful to his fellow Florentines and to other Italians, for he knew that had he written in Latin verse, as the poets of the past wrote, he would have benefited only the educated but, writing in the vernacular, he created a work without

teaches. One of the most faithful renderings of Dante into
English, for example, comes from Beckett when the last words
of his 'ninth text for nothing' literally translate the last words
of *Inferno*, though this passage of Beckett's writing is far from
a word-for-word rendering of anything in Dante. It is something
more than that, it is a continuing of why Dante wrote as well
as a recognition of how he wrote. It could even be said that
Beckett here brings over for a while into English 'the whole
thing' which the *Commedia* is:

> The graveyard, yes, it's there I'd return, this evening it's there,
> borne by my words, if I could get out of here, that is to say if I
> could say, There's a way out there, there's a way out somewhere,
> to know exactly where would be a mere matter of time, and
> patience, and sequency of thought, and felicity of expression. But
> the body, to get there with, where's the body? It's a minor point,
> a minor point. And I have no doubts, I'd get there somehow, to
> the way out, sooner or later, if I could say, There's a way out
> there, there's a way out somewhere, the rest would come, the
> other words, sooner or later, and the power to get there, and the
> way to get there, and pass out, and see the beauties of the skies,
> and see the stars again.[6]

II DANTE'S DOUBLE TONGUE:
'*GRAMATICA*' AND '*VOLGARE*'

Dante first translated himself. According to Boccaccio, the
Commedia once began:

> *Ultima regna canam, fluvido contermina mundo,*
> *spiritibus que lata patent, que premia solvunt*
> *pro meritis cuicunque suis*

> [I will sing the last realms, which edge our flowing world, exten-
> sive realms full of spirits who receive their dues, according as
> each has deserved][7]

of translations by many hands, ordered according to the chronology of the translators' lives not according to the poem's own intricately looping schemes of temporality. For example, our anthology begins at the beginning of Dante-in-English, with Chaucer's version of a speech from *Inferno* 33. Yet Ugolino, however prime a position he has held in English responses to the *Commedia*, is evidently not where Dante's poem starts, nor even a major stopping-off point on the poem's way. Trying to explicate what is involved in rendering one line – *Inferno* 20.28 – took us back to *Inferno* 4 and would take us on to at least *Purgatorio* 30–31, not to mention *Paradiso* 18 and 20. Our introduction sketches some dimensions of the *Commedia*'s own timing which get lost when the poem is dispersed through the history of its English versions. In particular we have stressed the centrality of *Purgatorio* to Dante's work in the hope of encouraging more readers on beyond *Inferno*, to which for some reason modern imaginations cling.

We have annotated the individual translations closely, oppressively closely some readers may feel as they follow us through our footnotes which repeatedly point out that an English phrase is 'not in Dante' or give literal versions of phrases the translators have rendered more freely. The Italian poet Eugenio Montale (1896–1981), himself a translator of Shakespeare, Hardy, Eliot and others, has an anecdote of how he bumped into Auden at one of Milan's airports: 'he takes a snapshot of me, he once again tells me how greatly he admires Dante, a poet whom the English cook up according to their own tastes (and how right they are to do so)' ['*poeta che gl'Inglesi cucinano a modo loro (e hanno ragione)*'].[5] Far be it from us to criticize English cooking, but we thought it worth indicating some occasions when the ingredients have been changed. As our notes persistently recall Dante's words and point out where English versions depart from them, they may come to read like an aggrieved catalogue of infidelities. This is not our intention and we hope it is not our tone. We do think faithfulness a virtue in translators but it is not the only virtue they can and must exercise, and, anyway, faithfulness is a complex process of growth and adaptation, as the *Commedia* itself

Sometimes the poem has suffered from the clamour and attitudinizing that attends on our disagreements with each other. Dante was hailed by some and hated by others (with equal implausibility) as a proto-Protestant; his work has been both straw man for the fervent anti-Christian and standard-bearer for zealots of another persuasion. As in Dante's hell, there has been more heat than light about many of these quarrels. But the *Commedia* has come through such storms because it represents them: they are at its heart and not just accidents which happened to it. Centred on the story of an individual's development, and setting that story amid broader quandaries about religious and cultural development, the poem survives with added lustre and a curious equanimity into the present when, it is often said, Dante's beliefs are being super-seded much as Virgil's were when Dante met him, when we mean by the *'altre stelle'* ('other stars') on which his poem closes stars far other than he imagined. Which is not to claim that the *Commedia* is timeless (it is too soon to say that) but only to observe how frequently and diversely it has in the past managed to be timely, and so given us reason to suppose it may in future manage to be so again.

These features of the poem – the closeness of its lexical weave across long spans of historical change and of reading-time, its cultic and cultural self-consciousness, its extreme specificity of reference and its equally extreme scope of implication – govern the shape of this anthology. Its 'Introduction' is an introduction in English to Dante, not an introduction to Dante-in-English. That is, the introduction tries to enable an English-speaker who has little or no Italian to develop some sense of what Dante's original is like, and indeed of why it matters that the poem was written first in what we now call 'Italian'. Though we provide many samples of Dante's writing outside the *Commedia*, we concentrate on his last poem because we, along with most of his readers, are drawn to him most strongly through that poem and only secondarily because of his other works. He is for us the poet of the *Commedia*, both the person who wrote that poem and the person who figures in it. But the integrity of the *Commedia* and its author are difficult to represent in a series

> From Love's due Rites, Nuptial embraces sweet,
> And with desire to languish without hope,
> Before the present object languishing
> With like desire, which would be miserie
> And torment less then none of what we dread,
> Then both our selves and Seed at once to free
> From what we fear for both, let us make short,
> Let us seek Death[4]

Virgil described the unrequited love of the lost pagans for God – 'without hope we live in desire' – quite demurely, and only from the pagans' point of view. Eve in her despair piles on the agony by explicitly voicing the reciprocal ache between two lovers each of whom sees the other feeling the lack of 'Nuptial embraces sweet', by the oscillating presence/absence of her prepositions ('with ... without ... with'), and by extending the Dantescan internal rhymes across a greater span of longing from 'sweet' through 'be miserie' and 'we' and 'Seed' and 'free' and 'we fear' to 'seek Death'.

Piercing as the allusion is, and provoking as is the analogy it suggests between sexual frustration and the yearning of the virtuous pagans for a good eternally beyond them, the question of God's conduct to those pagans is not Milton's subject here, but it is Dante's subject in the line Milton remembers from the *Commedia*. According to Judaeo-Christianity, God has revealed his will for human beings in, through and over time; those like Virgil who lived, geographically or chronologically, out of reach of that revelation might have some grounds for wondering about God's justice when they find themselves cut off from him by the sheer facts of their date and place of birth. The *Commedia*, both through explicit statement and through innumerable details of its shaping, responds to such worries and so involves itself with the histories of religions; it is integrally a work of comparative religion as well as of comparative literature. Unsurprisingly, then, the poem's own future, what happened to it after 1321 when Dante died, has been entangled with the religious and the irreligious history which followed.

A reader might first notice Virgil's unprecedented insistence –
'I'd like to make it clear to you, before you go any further' –
on spelling out the exact charge against this group, where
previously he had tended to briskness about particular fates
('I'll tell you very briefly' (*Inferno* 3.45); 'let's not dwell on
them, take a look and pass on' (*Inferno* 3.51); 'you'll find out
later' (*Inferno* 3.76–8)). Then we discover that, though he
speaks for some time of the unbaptized as a third-personal
'they' from whom we might suppose he is distinct ('*ei* ...
peccaro ... *elli hanno* ... *ebber* ... *furon* ... *adorar*'), he is in
fact one of 'them' and must give up the grammatical distance
he has kept, switching to a first-personal 'we' ('*semo perduti*').
Virgil comes out as a virtuous pagan on the words '*son io
medesmo*' ('am I myself'); Dante makes his word '*medesmo*'
('myself') rhyme with the words which name the reason for
Virgil's sad exclusion ('*battesmo* ... *cristianesmo*', 'baptism ...
Christianity'), maximally confronting the lost individual with
the formulae of his loss. Once he has, with whatever reluc-
tance, admitted where he belongs, Virgil's lines are suffused
with internal rhyme on his form of 'we are' ('*semo* ... *speme
vivemo*'), a wistful solidarity among the words themselves. And,
though Virgil stresses that he and his like suffer only the pain
of having lost out on God and not also the quasi-physical
torments of damned sinners ('*sol di tanto offesi* ...'), Dante
implicitly queries that 'only' by internally rhyming on it himself
when he tells us how sharply he felt for Virgil's plight ('*sol* ...
Gran duol', 'only ... A great sorrow').

As it happens, Milton also questioned Virgil's 'only' when,
having heard the densely affectionate drama in this passage, he
alluded to it at the point in *Paradise Lost* where Eve proposes
suicide to Adam as a way out of their fallen predicament and
its consequences:

> Childless thou art, Childless remaine:
> So Death shall be deceav'd his glut, and with us two
> Be forc'd to satisfie his Rav'nous Maw.
> But if thou judge it hard and difficult,
> Conversing, looking, loving, to abstain

its pagan fathers (not to mention its standing with regard to Mother Church). And it does not leave these deep and testing questions of translation, of religious and cultural transition, to come sidelong into a reader's mind from a hint here or a subtlety there: it dramatizes and upfronts them, incorporates them into its tissues and structure, gives them the force of human encounter, of a sore point unwittingly touched upon or of separation and its pangs.

For instance, when Virgil tells Dante why pagans, however exemplary, can't get to heaven, Dante stages the explanation with a minute care which is at once poignant and wry:

> *Lo buon maestro a me: 'Tu non dimandi*
> *che spiriti son questi che tu vedi?*
> *Or vo' che sappi, innanzi che più andi,*
> *ch'ei non peccaro; e s'elli hanno mercedi,*
> *non basta, perché non ebber battesmo,*
> *ch'è parte de la fede che tu credi.*
> *E se furon dinanzi al cristianesmo,*
> *non adorar debitamente a Dio:*
> *e di questi cotai son io medesmo.*
> *Per tai difetti, non per altro rio,*
> *semo perduti, e sol di tanto offesi,*
> *che sanza speme vivemo in disio.'*
> *Gran duol mi prese al cor quando lo 'ntesi* (4.31ff.)

[The good master to me: 'You don't ask, then, what spirits these are whom now you see? I'd like to make it clear to you, before you go any further, that they did not sin; and such merits as they have don't tip the balance, because they have not been baptized, which is an element of the faith you hold. And as they lived before Christianity, they did not worship God as is due: and of these I myself am one. For such shortcomings, and not for any other guilt, we are lost, and are punished only in that without hope we live in desire.' A great sorrow seized my heart when I heard him]

> *Ed elli a me: 'L'angoscia de le genti*
> *che son qua giú, nel viso mi dipigne*
> *quella pietà che tu per tema senti . . .'*
> (*Inferno* 4.19–21)

[And he to me: 'The anguish of the people down there colours
my face with that pity which you take for fear . . .']

Nothing is said in the *Commedia* to explain why turning pale
with pity counts for virtue while weeping for pity does not. The
pagans are not as severely judged as the prognosticators, but
if Virgil can pity their assigned place without impiety, what
prohibits Dante from doing the same for others later in the
poem? The apparent inconsistency may be Virgil's alone: Dante
might be exposing, however delicately, Virgil's tender self-pity
which co-exists with a doctrinal tough-mindedness about what
other people deserve (Virgil would not be unique in such double
standards). Or Dante could be the sole source of this contradic-
tion, because he forgot in *Inferno* 20 what he had written in
Inferno 4, or because he has his own form of the duplicity, of the
dilemma, which speaks in Virgil's divergent senses of *'pietas'*. A
third way of reading this crux would be to hear the *Commedia*'s
senses of pity, and the time taken in the poem to move between
those senses, as testimony to the ambiguities of the long process
we call, for the sake of conciseness, 'Christianization'.

Problems such as what to do with different systems of gram-
matical gendering, how to negotiate the exigencies of rhyme or
other formality, whether to explicate semantic knots, face any
alert translator of any complex writing. They are, though, high-
lighted in the *Commedia* because the poem itself so concentrates
on translation and transvaluation, principally in the encounter
between Virgil and Dante but also in hundreds of vivid details
– narrative, lexical and allusive – even after the two poets part.
Scholars speak of 'comparative literature' and mean 'comparing
works from the literature of two languages', as when a passage
of Milton is compared with an analogue in Ovid, but the *Com-
media* is in itself a work of comparative literature, already
engaged in a searching assay of its debt to and distance from

'altogether dead' and my 'good and dead' give different readings of the temperature in this exchange between Dante and Virgil; it matters less which, if either, reading is correct than that we recognize how mercurial the linguistic atmosphere is and have the instruments to register its fluctuations.

Ciaran Carson's 'Here piety is true when pity's dead' clarifies *Inferno* 20.28 more thoroughly than either Cary's or Single-ton's version and explicates the 'superb pun' on which it hinges, but maybe it is not absolutely necessary to clarify the line. Even 'absolutely necessary not to clarify it' because it is purposefully dark. Carson's version is admirably clear, but clear to whom? To a reader – yet Virgil, who speaks the line, is not addressing the reader. He is rebuking Dante, who has wept on seeing the punishment meted out to false prophets, fortune tellers and other assorted expert forecasters. His claim in this line is that to pity those who suffer just punishment implies a doubt about the justice of their punishment, and, as God is the competent judicial authority concerned, such pity would entail impiety. Readers have disagreed over Virgil's logic, and over whether and how Dante was impressed by his reproof. Dante seems to have foreseen such potential for dissent, for he encourages his reader to think for himself (*'or pensa per te stesso'*) half a dozen lines before Virgil's strictures; helpful as Carson is, he may have done more than he should to spare a reader the trouble of thinking for himself as Dante had to think.

Dante and Virgil might not mean the same thing by 'pity' or by 'piety'. Indeed, Virgil himself did not always mean the same thing by the Latin word he had for what English separates out into these two nouns: Colin Burrow observes in *'pietas'* as Virgil uses it a 'duplicity of the term, spreading from an urgent pang of ethical identification to an austerely impersonal concern for the emergence of an empire'.[3] Perhaps Dante too noticed this about Virgil. He certainly arranges his poem so that, long before Virgil comes down on Dante's compassionate tears, the Latin poet himself has been moved to a physical sign of pity by the lot of one group in the underworld – his own lot in fact, the virtuous pagans in their perpetual limbo:

slighting its precursors and the Reformation sought to demon-
strate its own righteousness through chanting the abuses per-
petrated by the unreformed. The *Commedia* underwent these
European convulsions: it more or less disappeared while they
lasted – the poem was rarely seen or heard in these islands
between Chaucer and Milton, and much the same is true of its
fate on the mainland. Coming to the poem when it revived
after this interval of four hundred, faction-packed years, the
eighteenth-century translators of Dante need not be blamed for
attributing to the poem itself qualities which they lent it because
of the angle from which they saw and heard it, but nor should
they be praised for confusing their own historicity with that of
the work, as if only the *Commedia* and not they themselves too
were dated.

Charles Singleton renders *Inferno* 20.28 into English prose
and so is not burdened by some of a verse-translator's obliga-
tions. No syllable-count restrains him from accurately and
expansively translating '*ben morta*' as 'altogether dead'. 'Good
and dead' might be closer to the densely suggestive colloquial-
ism which Dante gives here to Virgil (Italians ask for a coffee
'*ben caldo*', 'good and hot', when they want it steaming and
freshly expressed). Yet the slight officialese of 'altogether dead'
does not sound out of place in Virgil's mouth. The *Commedia*
is a dramatic poem: it consists largely of interviews between
Dante and more or less major celebrities of his time and earlier
times. We should not speak only of 'Dante's style in the *Comme-
dia*', for he changes his tune in response to the people he's
talking to and their idioms. Virgil is co-host rather than guest
for most of the first two *cantiche*, but he and Dante share a
vital double act – electric with swells of affection and estrange-
ment, like that of parent and child – not merely a simulacrum
of chumminess, both 'talking from the same script'. That double
act between the poets, and between the affiliated but distinct
worlds they stand for, generates throughout the poem an
intense pondering in its verbal details, so that a reader asks of
the poem as of a friend's behaviour from moment to moment,
'Now what did she mean by putting it like that?' Singleton's

the party game in which one player has to convey the title of a book, film or play to others. There are two extremes of method: the player may try in one set of gestures to get 'the whole thing' across; or he or she may proceed in small steps, word by word, even syllable by syllable (perhaps employing the conventional sign for 'sounds like'). It is, though, not forbidden and may be wise to switch methods – if you have tried unsuccessfully to do 'the whole thing' of *Anna Karenina*, you might be advised to backtrack and start again with 'sounds like "spanner"'. Cary's 'most doth' grates on the voice but this is less to be regretted than the impression the archaism gives that Dante wrote in an Italian which would have sounded two hundred years old to his first readers; he didn't, he wrote and revelled in a sweet new style. Cary's 'doth' for 'does' exemplifies a 'backdating' tendency in many Englishings of the *Commedia*, a tendency which corresponds to a sense of the poem as a curio from a more or less superseded world. The small instance of Cary's 'doth' can serve as an emblem of the complex ways in which people's beliefs about the past have refracted their image of the poem. As the *Commedia* is a work intent on trying to understand its own past, it's fitting that it has in turn become part of that same process for its later readers, but such a fit is not always neat, let alone comfortable; we fight over our pasts as well as coo over them and Dante's poem has often been caught in our cross-fire.

Dante died a generation before the catastrophe of the Black Death to which maybe a quarter, maybe a third of Europe's population fell victim, proportionally far more than in all the twentieth century's wars. ('The best modern estimates . . . give a probable average mortality of around 47 per cent [in Britain, where mortality was highest][2] from *Yersinia pestis*.) Historians have disputed how wide and grave were the effects of these many deaths, but it's likely that images of the plague and its horrors helped shade more sombrely the picture that came to be drawn of Dante's time; 'Black Death' came into the English language in the mid eighteenth century, about the same time we began to hear of the 'Dark Ages'. Polemic had already thickened the shadows when the Renaissance flattered itself by

is true when pity's dead' (by, respectively, Henry Cary (1812), Charles Singleton (1970) and Ciaran Carson (2002)).

Italian consistently inflects words to show their grammatical gender as English does not: so Cary's 'herself' and 'she' (responding to the article '*la*' and the termination of '*morta*') are faithful in one respect but also misleading because they make Dante's '*pietà*' sound as if she were a female deity, like Keats's Melancholy with 'her sovran shrine', whereas '*pietà*' is just a feminine noun. A grammatical glitch, a different system of gender inflection, gives birth to a discrepancy of style between Dante and Cary. The whole *Commedia* is an allegory of sorts but the poem rarely resorts to personified concepts like Melancholy or Error. Such walking, talking abstractions figured in poetry long before Dante and continued their pantomime long after him but his masterpiece mostly does without them, for reasons of artistic manner and of theological discretion.

And then there is Cary's furry-tongued mouthful 'most doth' which answers to nothing in Dante's clean-cut line. The archaizing verb-form 'doth' marks for Cary a 'poeticality' he rightly hears in the original but which arises there not from pastiche antiquation like Cary's 'doth' but, most evidently, through structural rhyme ('*morta*' comes between '*scorta*' and '*comporta*'), from which his blank verse translation abstains. The rights or wrongs of rhymed or unrhymed versions of the *Commedia* have long been debated by translators, as the body of this anthology shows; the issue is not likely to be settled by a preface. Each side of the argument has some right on its side. Different responsibilities, different priorities, face a translator who works primarily for a monoglot or primarily for a bilingual audience: a reader who has Italian, for example, gains little from even the most felicitous 'dubbing' of Dante's phonological patterns into English. The shadowing of an original's form by a translation may or may not be a matter of principle but any translating, however it handles the physique of the original, is an exercise of skill in bringing about recognitions, and must, like many skills, involve a measure of opportunism, of knowing when to insist on a principle and when to go easy on it. Translating for an audience which cannot read the original resembles

Introduction

I PITY AND HISTORY

A translator of Dante might be forgiven for giving up hope. In the case of Signorina Adriana Ottolenghi, the Neapolitan teacher in Samuel Beckett's first story, 'Dante and the Lobster', a settled despondency resulted from her long years of trying to convey the Florentine to English-speakers:

> 'It occurred to me' she said 'apropos of I don't know what that you might do worse than make up Dante's rare movements of compassion in Hell. That used to be' her past tenses were always sorrowful 'a favourite question'.
>
> He assumed an expression of profundity.
>
> 'In that connexion' he said 'I recall one superb pun anyway: "qui vive la pietà quando è ben morta . . ." [*Inferno* 20.28].'
>
> She said nothing.
>
> 'Is it not a great phrase?' he gushed.
>
> She said nothing.
>
> 'Now' he said like a fool 'I wonder how you could translate that?'
>
> Still she said nothing. Then:
>
> 'Do you think' she murmured 'it is absolutely necessary to translate it?'[1]

Inferno 20.28 is a tricky line, as some attempts on it make clear: 'Here pity most doth show herself alive, / When she is dead'; 'Here pity lives when it is altogether dead'; 'Here piety

1314 he composed a letter urging the return of the Papacy from Avignon to Rome. In the same year, Ghibelline forces commanded by Uguccione della Faggiola were in the ascendant in Tuscany. On 19 May 1315, a worried Florence proposed an amnesty – but on grudging terms – to exiles including Dante: he rejected the offer in his stern twelfth Latin letter. That summer, the Black Guelf forces were defeated by Uguccione at Montecatini, but Florence was not then besieged; on 15 October Dante was again condemned to death by his home town.

Dante moved, in 1318, to the quieter and more arty court of Guido Novello at Ravenna. There, he was together with his children (Antonia had become a nun – there is reason to believe she may have taken the name of Beatrice); regarding the presence or otherwise of Gemma there is no evidence. In January 1320 he was in Verona again, where he read out his geological enquiry *Quaestio de aqua et terra* in the church of St Elena. At a time when he was hard at work on *Paradiso* he also wrote his two Latin *Eclogues* as replies to epistolary poems from Giovanni del Virgilio, a professor at Bologna. Experienced diplomat that he was, in the summer of 1321 he took part in an embassy from Ravenna to Venice, and it appears that he fell ill on the journey. On 13 or 14 September 1321, Dante died. *Paradiso* appeared soon after.

Guelf policy. By June 1304 the exiles' hopes had foundered. Dante's whereabouts for the next two years are unknown: wherever he was, he finished his treatise on poetic language, *De vulgari eloquentia* (begun in about 1303), started his philosophical work *Convivio* (abandoned *c.*1308), and wrote the *canzoni* 'Tre donne' and 'Doglia mi reca'. In October 1306, documented history catches sight of him again, engaged in conflict-resolution for the Malaspina family in northern Tuscany; in 1307 he was in the Casentino Valley, east of Florence (see the exquisite souvenir of its landscape in *Inferno* 30.64–6), and in 1308 possibly at Lucca. At around this time he began work on *Inferno*. Early biographers speak of a sojourn in Paris but there is no firm evidence for this, let alone for the English myth, dear to Gladstone, that he visited Oxford.

On 1 May 1308 Albert, the Holy Roman Emperor, was assassinated; his successor Henry was determined to increase the Empire's power in Italy, an ambition in which he was at first supported by Pope Clement V (1305–14), who was French and, as he was exiled in Avignon, more or less detached from Italian politics. Dante's hopes were raised again. On Henry's arrival in Italy in 1310 Dante wrote a letter in Latin welcoming the potentate; at some stage, probably when the Emperor was in Milan for his coronation in 1311, he did him homage in person. In March 1311, from the Casentino, where he was now staying with Count Guido Novello di Batifolle, Dante issued an epistle denouncing Florence; on 17 April he wrote again, urging Henry to besiege the city. In early 1312 Henry travelled through Pisa (Dante may have gone there) to Rome where he underwent his final coronation in the absence of the Pope. Later that year he did at last lay siege to Florence, but without success. On 24 August 1313 Henry died, and with him such hopes of political stability as Dante may have nourished.

By now, Dante was probably at Can Grande's court in Verona, where he stayed until 1318. In 1314 *Inferno* began to be circulated, and in 1315 *Purgatorio*; around the same time *Monarchia*, a work of pro-Imperial political theory, was written, and *Paradiso* begun. Public events continued to engage Dante's attention. Following the death of Pope Clement V in

34.96), he indicates – by reference to the canonical hours of a Church to which he was never joined – that it is 19.30 in the northern hemisphere and so 07.30 in the Antipodes where they are about to emerge; before the invention of luminous watches, this is an astonishing feat of chronometry. The poem itself shares Virgil's acute attention to the simultaneity of different time zones, conscious as it is of complex relations between the narrating instance (the time in which Dante writes the poem) and the narrated events (the time during which he went on his journey). Its fourth line jams past and present tenses together as Dante now experiences how difficult it is to express how harsh his experience in the bitter wood was then: 'Ahi quanto^a dir qual era^e cosa dura' ['Alas how much saying what it was is a hard thing']. This splicing of tenses ('era^e') recurs in the Commedia's frequent souvenirs of his trip through the afterlife, vivid flashbacks which he usually emphasizes with an 'ancora' ('again' and 'still'): his mind still now bathes him in sweat at how the ground then shook (Inferno 3.132); merely the recollection of the wounds he saw then again pains him now (Inferno 16.12); by the ice of lowest hell, he saw a thousand, dog-like faces contorted with the cold and now he has, and always will have, a phobia of frozen ponds (Inferno 32.70–72); Casella sang so sweetly that the sweetness resounds in Dante still (Purgatorio 3.113–14); his climactic vision has almost completely gone from him, yet there still distils within his heart a sweetness born of what he saw (Paradiso 33.61–3).

Some commentators have believed that a sharp distinction should be drawn between 'Dante poeta', the man who, having had the vision, now writes the poem, and 'Dante personaggio', the figure in the poem who represents the poet's past self, a sinful figure in utter contrast to the current writer of the poem, whom we must regard as he regarded himself, as a poeta cleansed of defect by what he has learned in rapture. The poem is to be read, according to this schematism, as written by a man possessed of the authority which flows from having experienced the beatific vision (whatever that authority is supposed to be); this man stages, for the reader's delight and instruction, the

The invulnerable stasis of geometrical postulate ('*punto*') and the impetus ('*punto*') of desire, whether afflictive or rejoiced, consort in her rhyme, a rhyme which doesn't amount to an argument that what Dante longs to say about God can truly be said. And yet the arrangement of his and her words is a sign of his hope, hope which, like his poem, is a creature of time, necessarily abandoned in heaven as in hell.[129] Mandelstam heard how timely Dante's poem is in its vast and intricate semantic orbiting:

> Any given word is a bundle, and meaning sticks out of it in various directions, not aspiring toward any single official point. In pronouncing the word 'sun', we are, as it were, undertaking an enormous journey to which we are so accustomed that we travel in our sleep. What distinguishes poetry from automatic speech is that it rouses us and shakes us into wakefulness in the middle of a word. Then it turns out that the word is much longer than we thought, and we remember that to speak means to be forever on the road.[130]

This is what happened to Dante and what he can make happen in a reader – woken into a vision, awakened to words, '*nel mezzo del cammin*' at every word, even or especially what seems to be the last. 'Let us therefore so look as men who are going to find, and so find as men who are going to go on looking. For *when a man has finished, then it is that he is beginning* [Ecclesiasticus 18:7].'[131]

The *Commedia* has many ways of telling the time, notably in *Purgatorio*, where Dante achieves some of his most sublime effects by measuring events and intervals on a twenty-four-hour clock, as at *Purgatorio* 4.136–9. But even in hell, as timeless a zone as paradise, a sense of time goes with them as they pass through it (another paradox here, for it could rightly be said, 'If you're passing through it, it ain't hell'). At *Inferno* 34.68, Virgil, in the absolute dark around the figure of the fallen Lucifer, knows that it is sunset in Italy: twenty-four hours have passed in the first thirty-four *canti*. A few lines later (*Inferno*

been self-consciously composed through and over time, and in the dimension of composed time his contradictions are not solved but 'wondrously sustained'.[127]

As in the case of the word '*punto*' ['point']. It marks the coordinates of physical space (*Inferno* 6.114; *Purgatorio* 2.3) and time (*Inferno* 1.11; *Paradiso* 33.94) as also that 'point' unextended in either dimension on which the created world depends (*Paradiso* 17.17–18). It is a 'point' about prayer which Virgil made well in his *Aeneid* and which Dante would understand perfectly if he read closely with a clearer mind (*Purgatorio* 6.40) and also a 'passage' in the less reliable fiction which brought Paolo and Francesca low (*Inferno* 5.132). Dante twice recalls Francesca's words for their enflamed downfall – '*ma solo un punto fu quel che ci vinse*' ['but there was just one bit which overcame us'] – when writing of how he himself, in a distinct but continuous ardour, was exceeded in heaven (*Paradiso* 29.8–9 and 30.11). In consecutive sections of the *Convivio*, he resorts to the word, first as a verb when describing how he was so pierced by grief that he was inconsolable – '*io rimasi di tanta tristizia punto, che conforto non mi valeva alcuno*' – then as a noun when defining the geometrical notion of a 'point' – '*lo punto per la sua indivisibilitade è immensurabile*' ['a geometrical point, because it is indivisible, cannot be measured'].[128] As befits the simultaneity of heaven, Beatrice rhymes these two divergent senses with each other while explaining the motions of the stars:

> '*Da quel punto*
> *depende il cielo e tutta la natura.*
> *Mira quel cerchio che piú li è congiunto;*
> *e sappi che 'l suo mover è sí tosto*
> *per l'affocato amore ond'elli è punto.*'
> (*Paradiso* 28.41–5)

['On that point depend the skies and all nature. Look at that sphere which is most nearly joined to it and realize that its motion is so swift because of the flaming love which points it on.']

'Each thing which moves is in some respect lacking and does not possess its whole being at one time.'[124] The Dominican Dante scholar Kenelm Foster offers no comfort to those who hope that the work's swarming mobility of surface may be calmed down and cleared up at a more abstract level: 'the *unity* of this Dantean world is poetic rather than philosophical. Analysed philosophically it turns out, I think, to be a rather uneasy synthesis of Neoplatonist and Aristotelian elements'.[125] Even an 'uneasy synthesis' can have an intelligible sense, though one no grander sometimes than the desire to keep one's cake and eat it too. In the *Convivio*, Dante's Neoplatonic strain makes itself most heard: all distinct objects of desire align like arrows to point to one good, the desired of all desiring, to which each desiring subject longs – just *by* longing – to be united. In the *De monarchia*, he goes to a different tune: there exist both an Aristotelian 'good for man', an authentic finality and dignity in the created world (which Dante feverishly supposes to be the concern of emperors) and a second 'final end' in eternity (of which the Pope is curate). The particular instance of Dante's two-mindedness is quite widely generalizable. It can seem as if human desire is inherently Platonic in its drive to unify all desiring and point it in one direction, whereas human knowing is constitutively Aristotelian in its recognition of a plurality of sciences. This complicates the task of assessing our desire to know as also of attaining a knowledge of our desires. Mary Midgley has observed of the notion of 'good': 'It is, as Plato rightly said, a central notion, because it expresses our belief that all the other things we call good do in some way at some remote point *converge* – that our nature, in spite of its conflicts, is not radically and hopelessly and finally plural, but essentially one.'[126] If a person's thought and conduct were to alternate between the desirous and the knowing model as with the ticking of a clock, the incoherence would be such we could barely say he or she thought or acted at all, but Dante's poem is as big as a life and it is not unusual for a life to be strung out between two such poles (as we conceptualize them). His poem has the added advantage over most lives of having

The Franciscan chronicler Salimbene de Adam manages a
Dantescan amplitude in his account of the mass anti-war move-
ment of the flagellants who swept through Europe in the decade
when Dante was born:

> all men, of both high and low estate, noble soldiers and common
> men, went naked in procession through the cities whipping them-
> selves, headed by bishops and clerics. And they made peace, and
> men restored what they had wrongly taken ... If, however,
> anyone would not whip himself, he was considered to be worse
> than the devil, and everybody pointed the finger at him as a
> strange and diabolic man.[122]

Here we have a more honest record of a group dynamic: the
unanimity of even a peace movement can turn nasty, the soli-
darity of the contrite leads them to demonize anyone who
won't join their band, fingers get pointed at a guilty other; the
conditions are ripening for war to make yet another comeback.
Truth to sad facts such as these, discordant though they are with
any rapid, improving message, is a condition of that dialogue
between writing and the world's pressures which Montale iden-
tified in Dante's comic style, a dialogue which is inherent in
all 'culture patterns' – whether collective, like the flagellants'
penitence, or individual, like Dante's penitential *Commedia* –
as Clifford Geertz describes such patterns: 'Unlike genes, and
other nonsymbolic information sources, which are only models
for, not models *of*, culture patterns have an intrinsic double
aspect: they give meaning, that is, objective conceptual form,
to social and psychological reality both by shaping themselves
to it and by shaping it to themselves.'[123]

The *Commedia*'s own patterns have shown distinct facets to
several commentators. Its novel rhyme-scheme, *terza rima* (*aba
bcb cdc ...*), impresses some by its threefold, self-enclosing
nature, which is taken as apt to the work's Trinitarian theology;
others are struck rather by the scheme's essential intermin-
ability, how it endlessly prompts itself to further tercets as if in
quest of something it lacked, in accord with the formulation

well: he studied with them in the 1290s when they were starting
on their magnificent new church. The brothers were at odds
with each other about the building: Ubertino da Casale, who
was living in the friary while the church was under construc-
tion, denounced its splendours as the work of the Antichrist,
violently inconsistent with the teachings and example of the
Poverello of Assisi. As John White notes, 'it is typical of the
paradox and the tension, indeed the dualism, present not merely
in the Franciscan order but also in Florentine society as a whole
during this period of the birth of capitalism, that S. Croce was
also the favoured church of the great banking families of the
Bardi, Alberti, Peruzzi, and Baroncelli'.[120] The great families
who bankrolled the Franciscans may have had much to repent
of, but the 'paradox and tension' of penitence were not a
capitalist monopoly. Ordinary people also joined in penitential
church-building, like the thousands who hauled wagonloads of
Berchères stone (it is particularly heavy) to build the towers of
Notre-Dame-de-Chartres after the town had been wasted by
fire in 1134. Haimon, abbot of St Pierre-sur-Dives, was edified
by the sight and clearly hoped to edify his readers, for he
tidied his account of this straining multitude into miraculous
unanimity: 'they go forward in such silence that no voice, no
murmur is heard . . . When, again, they pause on the way, then
no other voice is heard but confession of guilt, with supplication
and pure prayer to God that he may vouchsafe pardon for their
sins . . .'[121] I hope I may be forgiven for not believing this, but I
feel sure that someone from time to time must also have said,
'Left a little', or 'Keep your end up, can't you?' The good abbot
is so keen to encourage community service that, unlike Dante,
he conveys no sense of how togetherness may come at a high
price, even the loss of self into indiscriminacy. The world and
its events shrink and conform themselves into a mere pretext
for the cleric's message – another case where the 'what' of
doctrine takes precedence over the 'how' of teaching, over the
discrepant world where teaching is supposed to take place.
Even Dante's 'other world' is more worldly than the abbot's
Chartres, but this contrast should not be allowed to harden
into an antithesis between lay and clerical writing and attitudes.

Ma guarda fiso là, e disviticchia
col viso quel che vien sotto a quei sassi:
già scorger puoi come ciascun si picchia.
(*Purgatorio* 10.115–20)

[The heavy nature of their punishment so cramps them down to earth that my eyes too at first debated with each other about what they were. But look carefully there, and disintricate with your gaze what comes along under those stones: you can make out how each one beats his breast.]

Nervous jokes flicker along the lines: he calls their plight '*grave*' much as the bystanders sigh the pun 'A heavy sight', when the dying Antony is hauled aloft to Cleopatra;[119] he compares the puzzlement of distinguishing these people from their burdens to a '*tencione*', a war of words – a formalized, literary dispute such as Dante actually conducted with Forese Donati (as if the spectacle of the proud were a game like one of those 'how many elephants are hidden in this picture?' teasers); his rhyme of '*rannicchia*' and '*disviticchia*' is far-fetched, finicky even. This edgy humour arises in part from Virgil's awkward confrontation with the '*humilitas*' in which the penitent are being schooled; it is not a virtue he was familiar with on earth. The proud look comic because their separate identities are so packed together by their toil that they become, from one angle, a collective 'what' ('*quel che vien*') where once they had thought themselves distinct individuals well worthy of regard. Only in their confessional breast-beating can each one of them ('*ciascun*') now be discerned.

Dante would not have had to look far to find models for his proud mass toting stones: the construction industry, both civic and ecclesiastical, was experiencing a boom. Town councils improved the supply of water and of justice with hydraulic engineering works and *palazzi della ragione* [courthouses]; they cooperated with Church authorities in the aggrandisement of cathedrals. Even those religious orders which were less in step with secular power – the Franciscans, for instance – had their projects. Dante knew the Franciscans at Santa Croce in Florence

wind which blows against it (*Purgatorio* 5.14–15), but also remembers the fury of self-assertion which caused towers to be built, as when Dante compares his sight of the heaven-defying giants through mist to the turrets of Monteriggione, which were raised as a defence against Florentine assault in the decade of Dante's birth (*Inferno* 31.34–45). A tower is a Mr Big; hence the painful recesses of irony when Count Ugolino, a towering figure on the political scene of his day, is starved to death with his sons inside a tower and says that, while in there, he 'turned to stone inside' (*Inferno* 33.49). So too Dante after his banishment in 1302 may have felt more ambivalently about Florence's security system than he had while within its walls; walls which tightened round the city as its prosperity grew, which were extended in the twelfth century for the first time since the Romans, then again in the mid thirteenth century, and for a third time between 1310 and 1328 – six feet thick and thirty feet high, to protect the Florentines from, among other perils, Dante Alighieri. Among the fixed stars he recalled those walls as embodying

> *la crudeltà che fuor mi serra*
> *del bello ovile ov'io dormi agnello.*
> (*Paradiso* 25.4–5)

[the cruelty which shuts me out from the lovely fold where I slept when a lamb.]

He compares Florence to a sheepfold in a line lavish with internal rhyme (*del, bello, agnello, ovile, ov'io*), its words nuzzling each other, but there is a tough glint in all this fond swell, for Dante knew that Florence's wealth, which supplied and demanded its walls, was built on trade in wool.

Or take the penitents lugging massive stones on the terrace of pride: Virgil explains how to look on them:

> *La grave condizione*
> *di lor tormento a terra li rannicchia,*
> *sí che' miei occhi pria n'ebber tencione.*

line-end, he switches from Italian to Latin, hoicking his utterance back up as best he can to a lost, official dignity he's not yet quite relinquished (though he has done his time on the terrace of the proud). As Dante travels the strata of his own speech, he sets out on an enterprise like the one which Chinua Achebe (1930–) found proper to African writers in the twentieth century, 'a tremendously potent and complex human reinvention of self – calling, as it must do, on every faculty of mind and soul and spirit; drawing as it must, from every resource of memory and imagination and from a familiarity with our history, our arts and culture; but also from an unflinching consciousness of the flaws that blemished our inheritance'.[34]

Dante had the ample and contradictory attitude to Latin that for ages characterized the Western Church's stance towards the language which ruled the world into which Christ was born. None of the Church Fathers went to a 'Church school'; most were taught pagan letters and ever after lived out the conflicting loyalties which such an education instilled, conflicting loyalties which continued to surface for more than a thousand years in the phantasmagoria which surrounded the figure of Virgil: St Odo of Cluny had to be supernaturally warned to cut down on reading Virgil, whose poetry appeared to him in a dream as a beautiful ship full of serpents; in Ravenna, a man was seduced into heresy by 'demons in the likeness of the poets Virgil, Horace and Juvenal'. Yet in Virgil's home town, Mantua, the faithful sang until the end of the Middle Ages a setting of the Mass of Saint Paul which 'contained the legend that the apostle had visited the grave of Virgil in Naples and had wept over not having come soon enough to find him alive'.[35] Latin was to Dante the language apt for conceptual articulation of any subject – politics, science, the faith – because 'Latin can make clear many concepts formed in the mind which the common tongue cannot'; he wrote his treatises on vernacular eloquence and on secular authority in that language for it better secured the truths he sought to expound, as Latin '*è perpetuo e non corruttibile, e lo volgare è, non stabile e corruttibile*' ['is permanent and incorruptible, whereas our common tongue is unstable and corruptible'].[36] Yet this very imperturbable loftiness made Latin stand to the living individual Dante somewhat as the English of the Raj stood to the diversity of an India it governed but comprehended only remotely. Dante says '*lo latino non è conoscente de lo volgare*', which might be translated as 'Latin is not acquainted with the common tongue', as if one language said to the other, 'I don't think we've been introduced.' He thought Latin knew the vernacular in the abstract but not in its particularity;[37] peculiar though this sounds, anybody who speaks a second language with less than perfect fluency will recognize what he means – you tailor your thoughts to the straitened outlines of your competence, bleach away nuances which only a native coloquialism would convey, and hear yourself come out correct, perhaps, but schematized. As Dante understood it, he had a vernacular self, shaped through innumerable, contingent relations; he could not make this self entirely heard in the abstracted permanence of Latin.

In his treatises, he sometimes decried the vernacular as unstable and fractious. The *De vulgari* ... notes that the 'common tongue' in Italy has forked in so many directions that speech varies not only on either side of the Apennines but within one city, as in the case of 'the Bolognese of Borgo San Felice and the Bolognese of Strada Maggiore'[38] (about forty minutes' walk apart, on either side of San Petronio). Both the *De vulgari* ... and the *Convivio* suggest a thought-experiment to demonstrate the restlessness of vernaculars: if those who died long ago returned to their native cities, they would think foreigners had taken them over because speech had been so transmuted there.[39] Against this flux, '*gramatica*' was designed to stand firm because '*gramatica nichil aliud est quam quaedam inalterabilis locutionis ydemptitas diversibus temporibus atque locis*' ['*gramatica* is nothing other than a certain unalterable identity of speech across differences of time and place'],[40] which is why, according to Dante, the texts of Latin comedies and tragedies have such staying-power – they elude change.[41] The *Commedia*, on the other hand, is solicitous of change – change from the midlife crisis in which Dante discovers himself at the start of the poem, change from both his exiles; it imagines not how changed the ancient dead would think this world if they returned to it but how someone now living, Dante himself, would find his thinking changed through an encounter with an other world and its '*nuova gente*'.[42] The '*volgare*' and the self which grew up in it seem frail because so easily and often transmuted, but such precariousness is also their big chance, for it opens to them the possibility of being translated, carried over into an other life. Late in the poem, Dante sees himself translated in Paradise ('*e vidimi translato*', *Paradiso* 14.83) but the writing of the *Commedia* starts from an experience of the self as formed in the process of shuttling between Latin and vernacular cultures, and the story it tells is the story of a further translating, of which learning to speak the second language of *gramatica* is imagined to be a foretaste.

III HOW THE STORY IS TOLD

So the *Commedia* now begins:

> *Nel mezzo del cammin di nostra vita*
> *mi ritrovai per una selva oscura*
> *che la diritta via era smarrita.*

[Halfway along the road of our life, I came to myself amid a dark wood where the straight road was lost.]

Comparing this with the way he opens his Latin treatises, *De vulgari eloquentia* (probably written 1303–5) and *De monarchia* (*c.* 1310–15) brings into sharper relief the distinctiveness of his poem:

> *Cum neminem ante nos de vulgaris eloquentiae doctrina quic-*
> *quam inveniamus tractasse, atque talem scilicet eloquentiam pen-*
> *itus omnibus necessariam videamus . . . Verbo aspirante de celis*
> *locutioni vulgarium gentium prodesse temptabimus*

[Since we find that no one, before ourselves, has dealt in any way with the theory of eloquence in the vernacular, and since we can plainly see that such eloquence is necessary to everyone . . . we

shall try, inspired by the Word that comes from above, to say
something useful about the language of people who speak the
vulgar tongue][43]

*Omnium hominum quos ad amorem veritatis natura superior
impressit hoc maxime interesse videtur: ut, quemadmodum de
labore antiquorum ditati sunt, ita et ipsi posteris prolaborent,
quatenus ab eis posteritas habeat quo ditetur.*

[All men, on whom the Higher Nature has set its seal of love for
truth, are evidently most greatly concerned that, just as they have
been enriched by the work of their ancestors, so too they may
work for their successors, so that their successors may be enriched
by something they have achieved.][44]

Both treatises begin from a universal – 'everyone', 'all men' –
to whom they will be of use or interest (such a universal also
figures in the '*spiritibus*' of the Latin *Commedia*); each thinks
at once of what has preceded it in the intellectual tradition,
even if, in the case of *De vulgari* . . ., what has gone before is
allegedly a blank; neither has a word to be translated as 'I'.
Dante's Italian treatise, the *Convivio*, also begins with a univer-
sal, and with an appeal to the authority of forebears:

*Sì come dice lo Filosofo nel principio de la Prima Filosofia, tutti
li uomini naturalmente desiderano di sapere.*

[As Aristotle says at the start of his *Metaphysics*, all men have a
natural desire for knowledge.][45]

The treatises state at once general principles which they take as
self-evident, and from which they proceed deductively to their
more local arguments, 'since it is required of any theoretical
treatment that it not leave its basis implicit, but declare it
openly'; they define the objects of their study at the outset and
proceed along familiar lines of reasoning, 'since it is quicker
and safer to travel along better-known routes'.[46]

The *Commedia* opens outwith any such orientation. As we
begin to read, we do not know: where its wood is (we never

find this out); when in history the poem begins (at *Inferno* 21.112–14, a devil enables us retrospectively to date its initial sunset); who is speaking (Dante never answers in our earshot when asked his name and is named by Beatrice only and climactically at *Purgatorio* 30.55). It took even longer for us to find out that we are reading the *Divina Commedia*, for the poem added '*Divina*' to its title only in 1555,[47] and then the adjective was probably not a theological precision but a literary-critical gush, for it looks like the culmination of early blurbs in which Dante himself was puffed as '*excelso*' (Milan, 1478) or '*excellentissimo*' (Monza, 1484), and '*divino*' (Venice, 1512).[48] In the first book written about Dante, Boccaccio praises the poem as a '*divina Comedia*', but this is no more the poem's title than are Boccaccio's other terms of endearment for the work, such as '*nostra Comedia*' ['our *Comedy*'].[49] Honoré de Balzac (1799–1850) probably did not realize when he gave his series of novels the would-be polemical title *La Comédie Humaine* that he was retorting to no more than an accidental compound of affectionate overpitch and sales-talk. Where Dante's treatises begin with the timeless present tense of conceptual exposition – '*inveniamus*', '*videtur*', '*desiderano*' – his poem confronts us with a cryptic, storyteller's preterite – '*mi ritrovai*'. That past tense indicates a 'then', a 'before', in which the events of the story happened, and implies by contrast a later 'now', in which we hear about them. The length of the interim between 'then' and 'now' cannot be measured, for it changes each time someone begins to read the *Commedia*. Elemental features of the poem, such as its system of tenses, are as easily neglected as the air we breathe, but they still matter: Dante had to cast his poem as a story because his subject was an ongoing learning process, not the display of a finished product. The *Commedia* was and remains, as Boccaccio said, 'a work without precedent' when it sets off down the '*nuovo e mai non fatto cammino di questa vita*' ['fresh and ever-uncompleted journey of this life'],[50] it being true for Dante, as for each reader new to the poem, that he has never gone this way before.

He started as he meant to go on, for the *Commedia* characteristically explains things only after they have been encountered.

We do not hear about Hell's ground plan until some way into the pit (*Inferno* 11.16ff.), just as the trajectory of desire, and hence the steeps of Purgatory, are laid out after we have been climbing for a while (*Purgatorio* 17.76ff.). Readers have for centuries been struck by the imaginative vivacity of Dante's otherworld and responded to the physical contours they suppose they encounter there, though Dante repeatedly tells us that he alone of all the poem's speakers has a body like ours. Even the gluttonous are lighter than air when Dante and Virgil walk over them, 'setting our feet upon their nullity which seemed to have shape' (*Inferno* 6.35–6); when they embark with damned souls on the ferry across the Styx, only Dante weighs the boat down (*Inferno* 8.27), yet twelve lines later Filippo Argenti clutches its gunwale with his insubstantial hands, and Virgil, who also lacks a body, manages a further four lines on to kiss Dante's face, though he has previously made clear that only at the Last Day will the dead reacquire flesh (*Inferno* 6.97–9). Long after we are more or less accustomed to this fluctuant physicality in the poem, Statius makes an intricate attempt to provide it with a rationale (*Purgatorio* 25.79–108). Dante has greeted his old friend, Forese Donati, who is purging his sins of gluttony, and has lamented the emaciation of Donati's once familiar face; he asks Virgil 'how come he has grown thin since he no longer needs to eat?' and Virgil swiftly hands this puzzler on to Statius – 'but Statius here will lay your desire for knowledge to rest'.[51] Why Statius, who has no better means of knowing than Virgil, is picked on to answer this tricky question is unclear. Perhaps Virgil is paying Statius back for Statius's own forgivable confusion about physicality in the *Commedia*, because when Statius met Virgil in *Purgatorio* 21 he tried to express his love for the elder poet in an embrace, only to be reminded by Virgil (who raised no objection to being embraced by Sordello from *Purgatorio* 6.75 to 7.3) that Virgil has no body to clasp, nor Statius anything to clasp him with.

That comic and touching moment – it is as if Statius had not a 'phantom limb' but an entire phantom body and yet this fact had slipped his mind – with what it conveys about the tenuous persistences of human longing so impressed T. S. Eliot (1888–

1965) that he took it as the epigraph to his first book, *Prufrock and Other Observations*. It stayed with Montale too and provided a source for his wry, elegiac remark to his dead wife: 'it's possible, you know, to love a shadow, shadows that we are.'[52] Commentators have taken less kindly to this aspect of the poem than Eliot and Montale did. Even Natalino Sapegno, usually so patient an editor of Dante, tires of the come and go of physicality in the *Commedia*, and annotates *Purgatorio* 2.79 a shade testily: 'The theory of the aerial body is clearly expounded in *Purgatorio* 25.79–108; but Dante sometimes remembers it and sometimes forgets it, as the imaginative situation demands.' Schlegel could have cited such flickering as evidence for his larger observation that the 'overall plan' of the *Commedia* had only 'hovered' before Dante's 'understanding; he loses sight of it during each individual scene, though he seizes and penetrates each such scene with all the power of his imagination'.[53] I myself have read no poet whose mind is so thoroughly on his job as Dante's is, and don't believe he needs excusing on this account. It all depends, as God might be imagined saying in a moment of exasperated self-exoneration, on what you mean by 'overall plan'.

Having to change our plans is for many of us a frequent experience, but the more general sense of what counts as a plan, of what plans are like, changes more slowly though no less incalculably:

> when things change little by little, we scarcely notice the changes happening, and the longer it takes us to notice how something has changed, the more stable we suppose that thing to be. So we should not be astonished that some people who are scarcely more intelligent than dumb animals suppose that things in their city have always been done in the same, invariable manner[54]

Our road maps, for instance, look different from any map Dante saw, and not only because surveying and draughtsmanship have made great strides, but because the roads are not where they used to be. Maps of Europe now show great axes of interconnection which didn't exist then (many of our roads run alongside rivers on ground which was not drained for human use until the nineteenth century); to imagine Dante's infrastructure, we need to abstract out these arteries and see the B-roads which were his – running on higher slopes, doubled back in hairpins on themselves to comply with uneven terrain, rarely letting a traveller see far straight ahead but shifting angle and vista as they approach their goal. Even the most salient landmark acquires multiple aspects when you come on it after such gradients, by such twists. Take the celebrated fact that each *cantica* of the *Commedia* ends with the word '*stelle*' ['stars']. Very diverse kinds of planning might have brought about this vast symmetry (there are 4,457 lines between the infernal and the purgatorial '*stelle*' and 4,738 from them to the '*altre stelle*' of Paradise): Dante may have had his bright idea long before he wrote his first syllable '*Nel*'; it might have occurred to him at any point on his way; having written as far as *Paradiso* 33.141, he could have reviewed his work and clinched it retrospectively by adding on the interstellar chimes. And we can attach diverse significances to each of these supposed acts of design, from a godlike, transtemporal apprehension of the interlace in his creation, through a craftsman's schooled eye for a natty bit of joinery, to the sheer persistence of an idiosyncrasy, a temperamental fondness for '*stelle*' which Dante himself could hardly control. The fact remains, Dante had stars in his ears, or, as he might have more grandly put it, he resembled the '*astripetam aquilam*' ['star-seeking eagle'] which he took as an emblem of the highest style.[55]

In a spurt of modesty as he sets out, Dante wonders why he has been chosen for a privileged tour of the afterlife even though '*Io non Enea, io non Paulo sono*' ['I am neither Aeneas nor Paul', *Inferno* 2.32]. The standard gloss on this line points out that Aeneas, according to Virgil in *Aeneid* 6, and Saint Paul, according to himself in 2 Corinthians 12, made visionary journeys to the other world; equally standard is a bashfulness about making clear that Dante's journey crucially resembles Aeneas's and not Paul's, because Aeneas and Dante travel in the body while Paul himself couldn't tell whether he was or wasn't embodied when rapt ('*sive in corpore nescio, sive extra corpus nescio*'). The Pauline, the Scriptural, sense of 'body' means something broader than René Descartes (1596–1650) meant by the material as contrasted with the immaterial aspects of a person (that Cartesian disjunction is alien to most Judaeo-Christian thought); it means 'as an embodied individual with an individual's limited comprehension', even 'in human terms'. Dante could have learned, from St Augustine (354–430) as from St Thomas Aquinas (1225–74),[56] about the simultaneous inapplicability and inevitability of such 'human terms', and specifically of physical language and imagery, when talking of God, his attributes and domains. And if the word of these doctors of the Church was not good enough for him, he always had Beatrice to remind him that 'it is only from what is taken in by your senses that you can form notions suitable to your intellect. For this reason, Scripture comes down to the level of your understanding and speaks as if God had hands and feet, though it means something quite other' (*Paradiso* 4.41–5). Beatrice's caution about extending human concepts beyond the horizon of sense-experience in which we learn them applies not only to such terms as 'long', 'white' and 'beard' but – more challengingly – to words like 'just' or 'love', which may be, as we say, 'abstract' but which we have nonetheless abstracted from our experience in this earthly world.

This caution about extending our concepts to the divine is known as 'negative theology'; one of its main sources in Christian tradition is in the writings of the quaintly named Pseudo-Dionysius (*fl.* fifth/sixth century), with whom Beatrice could have discussed such issues because Dante gives him a place high among the blessed in *Paradiso* 28.130. Nor was Dante alone in his admiration: Aquinas quotes Pseudo-Dionysius some 1,700 times and his work was given official sanction at the Fourth Lateran Council in 1215. What stirred up all this admiration are passages like the following in which Pseudo-Dionysius writes of how the human mind can grow in sophistication and prudence about applying its own terms to God:

> as we climb higher we say this. [The supreme Cause] is not soul or mind, nor does it possess imagination, conviction, speech, or

understanding. Nor is it speech per se, understanding per se. It cannot be spoken of and it cannot be grasped by understanding. It is not number or order, greatness or smallness, equality or inequality, similarity or dissimilarity. It is not immovable, moving, or at rest. It has no power, it is not power, nor is it light. It does not live nor is it life.[57]

From this we are not supposed to infer that we should say instead that God is mindless, unimaginative, mute, impotent and dead. Every one of those terms when applied to God is subject to the same reservation as its affirmative counterpart: the point of Pseudo-Dionysius's startling catalogue is not to encourage us to stop characterizing God as loving or just and start characterizing him as hateful and unfair but to slow down the process by which we characterize him in any way at all and assist us to begin recognizing him as, in later words of the same passage, 'beyond assertion and denial'. Pseudo-Dionysius's mystical logic requires and derives from an extreme scepticism about the analogical extension of human terms to the deity: 'we have a habit of seizing upon what is actually beyond us, clinging to the familiar categories of our sense perceptions, and then we measure the divine by human standards and, of course, are led astray by the apparent meaning we give to divine and unspeakable reason.'[58] 'Seizing upon what is actually beyond us' itself felicitously commits something like the intellectual move it reproves, for if the something were really beyond us, we could not seize it. The phrase also fits what happens at moments such as Statius's thwarted clasping. These moments are not symptoms of Dante's intermittent memory for his own creation, nor of his patchy forward-planning; they dramatize as narrative incident what negative theology teaches about logical discretion.

This dramatized logic takes many forms. A physical state may turn into a state of mind (or vice versa), as when, reading Jacopo del Cassero's account of his own last gasps –

'Corsi al palude, e le cannucce e 'l braco
m'impigliar sí, ch'i caddi . . .' (Purgatorio 5.82–3)

['I ran to the marsh, and the reeds and the mud enmeshed me so
much that I fell . . .']

– we should revert to something we heard not long before –
Virgil upbraiding Dante for being so easily distracted by side
issues as they climb the purgatorial steeps:

> 'Perché l'animo tuo tanto s'impiglia,'
>   disse 'l maestro, 'che l'andare allenti? . . .'
>   (*Purgatorio* 5.10–11)

['Why does your spirit so enmesh itself,' my master said, 'that
you slow your pace? . . .']

The verb '*impigliare*' is, as we say, 'metaphorical' when Virgil
uses it and 'literal' from Jacopo del Cassero; both Dante and
his fellow-penitent are equally entangled, though – we should
not align the contrast 'metaphorical'/'literal' with the antithesis
'unreal'/'real'. The *Commedia* perpetually harks back or pre-
echoes in its verbal texture, often, as here, to imply Dante's
fellowship with those he meets. When his scrabble towards
purgatory is barely begun, he tires of it ('*Io era lasso*', 'I was
exhausted' – *Purgatorio* 4.43); Virgil braces him with the
thought that the higher he goes, the easier it gets; then a voice
from someone they can't see drawls a lazy, sceptical remark:
'still, you may need a sit-down before you're through' (*Pur-
gatorio* 4.98–9). Sapegno notes that this voice 'seems to well
up from the poet's own consciousness' and might have con-
firmed his insight by pointing out that when they find the
speaker, lolling in the shade behind a rock, the first thing Dante
observes is that he '*sembiava lasso*' ('seemed exhausted', *Purga-
torio* 4.106), transferring the adjective from himself to, as it
turns out, his old friend, Belacqua. Such a carry-over can be
thought of in psychological terms as a 'projection' of Dante's
state, but that is only one possible optic through which to read
the interanimation between what Dante says and what he sees.

Amid the icy sheen of lower Hell, the poet is accosted by a
sinner:

> *E un ch'avea perduti ambo li orecchi*
> *per la freddura, pur col viso in giùe,*
> *disse: 'Perché cotanto in noi ti specchi? . . .'*
>   (*Inferno* 32.52–4)

[And one who had lost both his ears from the cold, keeping his face down, said: 'Why do you stare at us as if you were staring in a mirror? . . .']

Dante really does see his own reflection in even the most lost, in the sense that he sees in them a condition of sinfulness, of potential for going awry, which he shares whether or not he has committed their particular kinds of sin. The verb '*specchiarsi*' ('to look at oneself in a mirror') returns when he comes to the three steps which form the threshold of Purgatory, the first of which is of marble gleaming like ice:

> *lo scaglion primaio*
> *bianco marmo era sí pulito e terso,*
> *ch'io mi specchiai in esso qual io paio.*
>   (*Purgatorio* 9.94–6)

[the first step was of white marble, so polished and clean that I was mirrored in it exactly as I look.]

Once again, the verbal community, more extended this time because it stretches over a thousand lines between an extreme of damnation and Dante's liminal anxieties as he enters on his visionary purgation, can be understood in terms of a psychological narrative: about to undergo cleansing, Dante thinks back to the irreparable soul and its ice, perhaps with an ill-defined sense of his own culpability, or perhaps to cheer himself in the face of what he dreads is coming by a reflection along the lines of 'there's always someone worse off than you are'.

But psychological sharpness is only part of Dante's design. The interanimation at a verbal level between places and states that are 'far apart' – in the geography of the poem and what that stands for, in the time it takes both poet and reader to get from one to the other – is one more way Dante schools himself and his reader in the discretion needed when analogically extending the terms of this world to convey a vision of this world transformed in God. We habitually assume a disjunction between psychological verities and facts about the world (something must either be 'all in your head' or 'out there'). This disjunction would mislead us about Dante and his tradition of faith. He certainly believed it was a fact about human beings that they desire a good they cannot of themselves achieve; 'God' is his name for that good. But he did not infer from this fact of the human constitution that God was simply a 'projection' of human desire, a wish-fulfilment. On the contrary. For Dante, human beings have such a desire *because* God exists and created them. A passage of Augustine commenting on Psalm 130 (131 in the King James numbering) brings us nearer to the character of Dante's storytelling in which 'inner' and 'outer' may switch places and metaphor is the necessary and insufficient language for the realities he meets:

> For while the soul is in the flesh, people ask it: *Where is your God?* But God is within the soul, 'within' in a spiritual sense, as also high above the soul in a spiritual sense; this is not to be understood in terms of physical distance between places, in the way that some places are higher than others because of the physical distance between them. If this was the kind of 'height' we were in search of, birds would get to God before we did. For the God within *is* the God above, 'above' in a spiritual sense, and nor can the soul come to meet him unless it go beyond itself. So whenever you think of God in physical terms, you go badly wrong.[59]

Augustine's argument incessantly retraces its own terms, winding back on itself and coming on new vistas, as Dante spiralling up the purgatorial terraces catches now his shadow cast at an unprecedented angle, now glimpses of the sea.

Like Aeneas, Dante

corruttibile ancora, ad immortale
secolo andò, e fu sensibilmente. (Inferno 2.14–15)

[subject to corruption still, to the deathless world he went, and
was there in his body.]

The first line here is shaped to take the strain of a paradox: it
spans a contradiction for thought as it begins with the finite
and ephemeral ('*corruttibile*') and yet winds up in the infinite
('*immortale*').[60] In Dante's line, these antithetical terms stand
in earshot of each other: their meanings diverge but their shapes
converge, in the sense that more than half their phonemes
match. An intense force of linguistic cohesion clasps together
two concepts which, intellectually, decline to cohere, and whose
mutual repulsion tweezers apart the grammatical unit 'deathless
world' across the line-end ('*immortale / secolo*'). This small
instance suggests the frame of mind (and body) which governs
the much-prized and rightly praised 'vividness' with which
Dante evokes the 'other' world in human terms, '*sensibilmente*',
for the *Commedia* is a massive foray into self-consciously 'vir-
tual reality', though the point of Dante's 'virtual reality' is not
glamorously technological but theologically sober,[61] which is
not to deny that his vigilance over analogy results over and
again in tremulously lyrical evocations at and of the limits of
the palpable. His readers convince themselves they see an 'other'
world but their imaginings are mostly prompted by similes
drawn from the world we live in now (where else?), so the
perceptual zest they experience in the poem comes actually
from re-encountering things they may have passed perhaps a
hundred times without caring for them till alerted by analogy:
cranes taking their long flight to overwinter on the Nile (*Inferno*
5.46–7 to *Purgatorio* 26.43–4); bioluminescence (*Inferno*
26.25–32); spring floods (*Inferno* 15.7–9); an experiment
with mirrors (*Paradiso* 2.97–105); a set of steps in Florence
(*Purgatorio* 12.100–106).

These similes, perpetually reverting to *this* world, mark
Dante and his readers as having two homes, between which
knowledge shuttles. Dante, like Aquinas, was an empiricist; he

would have agreed with T. S. Eliot 'that Hell, though a state, is a state which can only be thought of, and perhaps only experienced, by the projection of sensory images; and that the resurrection of the body has perhaps a deeper meaning than we understand'.[62] What has appeared to some commentators as absent-mindedness on Dante's part might be better thought of as an alertness in giving us and himself frequent reminders of the discretion needed in this other world of analogies at extreme stretch, this 'dimension', as James Merrill (1926–95) puts it, 'we could neither / Visualize nor keep from trying to'.[63] Dante shows discretion in both relying on the power of language to achieve pattern in excess of rational sense (as in the linking for the ear of '*corruttibile*' and '*immortale*') while also displaying the overreach and torsion of just such movement towards pattern (as in the stretch of '*immortale / secolo*' across the breaking point of the verse-line). As far as discretion is concerned, Dante has not always been well served by his English translators, because the greed for sensuous concretion which is a marked feature of English verse, at least since the time of Shakespeare, has often led them to plump and flesh out what he so delicately etched, as in the long series of vampings-up to which the Ugolino episode was subjected and which climaxes in Heaney's foisting of a 'melon' into the starved Count's mouth,[64] or as in the over-ripe body-heat of Rossetti's 'blessed damozel', who spends so long propping up the 'bar of Heaven' that eventually 'her bosom must have made / The bar she leaned on warm'.[65]

Conversely, Ezra Pound, from his earliest imitations, disembodies Dante – 'My spirit left for a while / this corporal / house of life'[66] – and thus provides for Dante (and procures for himself) an intellectually self-contained certainty. Pound was sure that 'men's inner selves stand visibly before the eyes of Dante's intellect';[67] they do not. Dante has eyes of flesh throughout the poem with the blind spots and self-centred perspectives inherent in the flesh, as Dante understood it; nor does he see 'inner selves', whatever or wherever such Russian dolls are, but individuals and their stretches of time. In the pastiche *Commedia* of Pound's *Cantos* XIV–XVI, Pound introduces himself with a line from *Inferno* 5 ('I came to a place where all light is mute'), though the sinners who follow are not the sexy-to-excess of Dante's fifth canto but sleaze-bags, financial wizards and frauds who come much lower in Dante's hell. For Pound, *Inferno* 5 is less the place where we meet Paolo and Francesca than the zone of Minos, that 'knower of sins';[68] it is such an executive 'knowledge' which Pound, mistaking Dante for a demon, tricks himself out in as he mimics the *Commedia*. A difference of paradigms as well as of temperaments separates the two poets. Pound supposes he has a quasi-clinical expertise at his command when assessing the cases he reviews, the symptoms of cultural malaise: hence the medical terms which point ethical fingers in Pound – 'piles', 'pus', 'crab-lice', 'ossifications', 'cotton wool', 'foetus', 'bile-sweat', 'epileptic', 'tumour', 'pox'[69] – and which are not found in Dante. Pound's false estimate of the visuality of Dante's poem corresponds to another odd feature in Pound's pastiche of the *Commedia* – the absence of dialogue. Nobody talks back to Pound in his 'Hell' cantos, any more than a symptom talks back at a diagnostician; nobody but Pound talks at all.

If the *Commedia* were supposed to be a defence of God's justice or a blueprint for the afterlife, Dante's habit of changing his ground about the extension of his analogical terms would be deplorable, but the poem offers rather an experiential history of what it is to hold, and be held by, some beliefs, not an argued case for adopting them. And 'changing his ground' is something Dante has to do, because his poem takes the form of a journey. It was perhaps this incessant bilocation in the work which prompted the poet Osip Mandelstam (1891–1938) to say 'Dante can be understood only with the help of quantum theory'.[70] At any rate, the *Commedia*'s supposed inconsistencies are of great anthropological interest because, as Clifford Geertz has written, theorists of religion have mostly 'failed to see man as moving more or less easily, and very frequently, between radically contrasting ways of looking at the world, ways which are not continuous with one another but separated by cultural gaps'[71] – gaps such as those which the *Commedia* displays and strives to bridge, between '*gramatica*' and '*volgare*', between the refined jargon of a trained, theological elite and the vivid anecdotes of scriptural narrative or pious legend, between one man's crisis and what he sees when he has been helped out of that.

So, the kind of 'overall plan' the *Commedia* has is one in which occurrence and conceptualization constantly rebound off each other, a learning process. In its recoils between event and explanation, it is *as experienced* a Christian poem, in that all Christian formulations come 'after the event', the event of Incarnation, as theology belatedly attempts to fashion a coherence to its liking from the scriptural narratives. Those who find any religious consideration a hindrance to sympathetic reading of Dante can sideline these suggestions. What the poem needs is for a reader to recognize its exploratory nature, a nature rapidly encapsulated in the brilliant *rima equivoca*[72] with which Virgil rounds off his exposition of love in *Purgatorio* 17:

> *L'amor ch'ad esso troppo s'abbandona,*
> *di sovr'a noi si piange per tre cerchi;*
> *ma come tripartita si ragiona,*
> *tacciolo, acciò che tu per te ne cerchi.*

[The love which gives itself over too much to partial goods weeps itself away above us in three circles; I keep quiet about the rationale of this threefold arrangement, in order that you should search it out for yourself.]

'*Cerchi*', the ordained circles through which Dante and Virgil travel, and '*cerchi*', 'you should search', match in every detail but their meaning; the match itself is meaningful and implies that the reader of this poem, as its author, must try to be like Christ, whom Aquinas described as '*simul viator et comprehensor*' ['at once a traveller and an understander'].[73]

The *Commedia*, that is, tells a story, and has to be understood through the constant adjustment of expectation, slowly unfurled hypotheses and wised-up hindsight which make up the tissue of narratives. Or rather, it tells two stories – the story of Dante's visionary journey, and, implicit in the phrasing and structure of the first story, a second story of how, having had the vision, he wrote it down as Beatrice told him to, for another of Dante's beloved loops is that the *poem* is initiated not in the dark wood where its story begins but in a garden long into that story when she says to him:

> Però, in pro del mondo che mal vive,
>   al carro tieni or li occhi, e quel che vedi,
>   ritornato di là, fa che tu scrive.
>   (*Purgatorio* 32.103–5)

[And so, for the sake of the world lives awry, keep your eyes now fixed on the chariot, and when you have returned back there be sure to write down what you see.]

As St Bonaventure notes, 'narrative modes cannot proceed along the way of rational certainty, because particular facts do not admit of formal proof';[74] this is quite as true of Dante's poem as of the Gospels. Many commentators on Dante do not agree with St Bonaventure and me: they assure us that the *Commedia* is 'encyclopedic', 'a "summa" like the huge works synthesizing Christianity and Aristotelianism conducted by the slightly earlier Thomas Aquinas', and even 'equivalent to Scripture'.[75] One difference between Dante's poem and Aquinas's *Summa Theologiae* is that Aquinas never finished his *Summa*, which begins with theology and breaks off midway through a discussion of penitence, whereas Dante's poem begins with penitence and achieves, for a moment impossible to time, a vision of God. No encyclopedia is complete, but few draw attention to their own omissions so repeatedly as Dante underscores that he is leaving stuff out – because he is too modest (*Inferno* 4.104), because he can't call it to mind (*Inferno* 9.34), because he didn't catch what was said (*Purgatorio* 24.106–7), because he has used up all the paper he'd laid by for the second *cantica* (*Purgatorio* 33.139); *Paradiso* is a continuously enraptured litany of ways of saying 'I can't say'. The *Commedia* 'adds up' to 100 in that it has one hundred subdivisions or *canti*; commentators often point out the replete symmetry of this number, and its self-repose is taken as expressing Dante's entire satisfaction with the all-inclusive 'rightness' of his work, even as a guarantee that he and it have been perfected together. We need not accept this straightforward reading-off of theological coherence (let alone sanctity) from formal cohesion; Jean Leclerq mentions that it was a habit among monastic compilers of *florilegia* 'to signal that there was nothing systematically exhaustive about their works [by adopting for them] a wholly conventional number of chapters, the number one hundred'.[76] There need be nothing metaphysical about even a very round number.

There is a sad irony in the fact that Dante, whom Mandelstam rightly called 'the Descartes of metaphor' with the motto 'I compare, therefore I am',[77] should have had his masterpiece subjected to so many inept analogies. Since the eighteenth century, the *Commedia* has routinely been compared to a Gothic cathedral, where 'Gothic' means the style Ruskin espoused – flamboyant, world-fleeing, death-pestered. If an architectural parallel must be drawn, the Romanesque runs in every respect closer to the *Commedia* in its arches which arise from and return to rest on a massively sensed earth, in the flexible severity with which it historiates stone and makes it catch at light, its drive to interlace and ingenious dramas of reciprocity or conflict between figure and frame. Dante has the art-historical term for sculpted narratives, 'historiated', at *Purgatorio* 10.73 where he's describing the white marble reliefs which exemplify humility for the attention of those on the terrace of pride:

> *Quiv'era storiata l'alta gloria*
> *del roman principato il cui valore*
> *mosse Gregorio a la sua gran vittoria;*
> *i'dico di Traiano imperadore*
> (*Purgatorio* 10.73–6)

[There was sculpted the glorious story of the Roman potentate whose worth impelled Gregory to his great victory; I mean, the emperor Trajan]

The legend of how Pope Gregory I so mourned the fate of
Trajan that he delivered his soul from Hell with his prayers
(and secured him a place among the blessed who loved justice,
see *Paradiso* 20.106ff.) mattered to Dante because it har-
monized with his own perplexed longing that figures like Virgil
or Brunetto Latini (see, respectively, *Inferno* 4.43–5 and
15.79–81) might somehow be enfolded in heaven, whatever
their defects of faith or morals. Dante translates Trajan not
only from one eschatological state to another but from one
artistic manner to another, because, although Imperial Rome
practised narrative sculpture – as, for instance, the scenes of
war against the Dacians on Trajan's own column – the particu-
lar kind of carved ensemble which Dante sees on the terrace of
pride was unknown before the eleventh century CE. For Trajan's
relief in *Purgatorio* is one of three: the first depicts the angel's
annunciation to Mary, the second, David dancing before the
Ark of the Covenant, and the third, Trajan. This tricultural
panorama is Dante's individual development of Romanesque
comparative sculpture, in which Old and New Testament
scenes are arranged in space so that the eye travels between
them as between the stages in time of God's dealings with his
people. Dante knew the reliefs on the façade of San Zeno
Maggiore in Verona where, to the right of the porch, he would
have seen Adam and Eve expelled from the garden of Eden and
then labouring to keep themselves alive, while, at the same level
to the left of the porch, he found Christ's arrest in the garden
of Gethsemane and then his death on the cross. The effect of
parallax between divine dispensations or cultural states intensi-
fied when the procedure was applied to capitals in naves and
cloisters, so that the spectator could move between and around
the scenes in dialogue with each other. That Dante responded
in depth to the shifting perspectives between such historiated
scenes becomes evident when we consider why he chose David's
dancing as a foil for Mary's compliance in the Incarnation. The
scenes are apt to each other not only because their combination
helps us realize that humility is not a specially feminine virtue,
but because of the figure of Michal, David's wife, who scorned
David's cavorting: '*et despexit eum in corde suo*' ('and she

despised him in her heart', 2 Samuel 6:16) when she saw him *'discooperiens se ante ancillas servorum suorum'* ('making a show of himself before the handmaids of his servants', 2 Samuel 6:20). Dante's eyes had moved over the Scriptures as across the façade of San Zeno, for the *'despexit'* and the *'ancillas'* of the Old Testament remained with him as he remembered Mary's gratitude after she had laid herself bare to God:

> *Magnificat anima mea Dominum: . . .*
> *Quia respexit humilitatem ancillae suae.*
> (Luke 1:46, 48)

[My soul proclaims the greatness of God . . . because he has looked upon the lowliness of his handmaid.]

Or we could equally say that the *'respexit'* and *'ancillae'* here reminded him of their ancestors in David's story, for rhyme is a two-way track. He may also have recalled the contrast between Mary's pregnancy as she chanted and the barrenness of Michal's proud contempt: 'And to the day of her death Michal, the daughter of Saul, had no children.' (2 Samuel 6:23; Jerusalem Bible)

Assimilations of the poem to scholasticism and its exercise books, the *summae*, are equally likely to mislead a reader. Scholasticism is a name not for a body of doctrine but for a method of discussion and inquiry; a *summa* is not a smooth block of authoritative pronouncement but the inherently scarred record of historical disputes. Augustine remarked that the Church clarified its beliefs principally when compelled to rebut heresies; the innumerable *'contra Gentiles'* ['against the unbelievers'] or *'adversos haereticos'* ['against heretics'] of Christian tradition bear him out.[78] The very structure of *summae* witnesses to the essentially responsive nature of their doctrinal formulations, for *summae* are set out in *quaestio* – a topic is raised; contradictory opinions about it from previous writers given; and then an attempt is made to reconcile divergences. As John Marenbon has written:

The *quaestio*-technique developed because of the special charac-
teristics of the textbook of theology, the Bible. Everything in the
Bible was accepted by theologians as true, but often scriptural
statements seemed contradictory. The more systematically theo-
logians wished to organize their doctrinal discussions, the less
possible it became to ignore these contradictions; and other con-
tradictions too, between different patristic authors or between
Christian writers and pagan philosophers became evident and
were drawn into the discussion.[79]

The standard phrase for countering opposed views in a *summa*
is '*respondeo dicendum*' ['I reply, saying']. In this respect alone,
the *Commedia* is like a *summa*, besotted as Dante is with the
verb '*rispondere*' in all its forms, so that the poem reads at
times like a string of 'I said to him I said's; so repeated is Dante's
need to say 'and in reply' that he characteristically abbreviates
to 'and he to me' or 'and I to him'. Yet where a *summa* would
just state propositions and objections, Dante's poem dramatizes
even its most rarefied exchanges with a wealth of stage direc-
tions about tone of voice, physical posture or the look in some-
one's eyes. This fleshing-out of debate forms part of the
Commedia's vital concern with the 'how' as well as the 'what'
of teaching, a concern which gets sidelined by comparison of
the poem to scholastic procedures. Scholastic discussion goes
on between the learned, more or less on one cultural level, but
Dante's conversations for at least the first two *cantiche* take
place on a precipitous terrain of uneven attainments and include
not only citations of Aristotle but flattery, gibberish, hair-
pulling and many other varieties of uncharitableness such as
went on in the actual 'Christianization' of Dante's world and
which we hear little about in the quieter disputations of scholas-
ticism. The scholastic's '*respondeo*' is to a proposition, Dante's
'*rispuos' io*' to a person, and hence involves him not only in
intellectual but in ethical interaction. He thought highly enough
of responsiveness to offer as a definition of poetic beauty: 'we
call a poem beautiful when all its voices, as the art demands,
are entirely responsive to each other' ['*intra sé rispondenti*'];[80]
his broader longing for accord led him to paraphrase 'Heaven'

as '*là dove a li'nnocenti si risponde*' ['there where the innocent find a response'] (*Purgatorio* 8.72).

The *Commedia* has, unsurprisingly, some family resemblance to the sacred writings which fathered it, but many scholars who think the poem like the Scriptures have a cloudy notion of what Dante thought the Scriptures are like. That Dante meant his work as 'equivalent to Scripture', even as a 'new Scripture',[81] is improbable; there is no evidence for these claims, again unsurprisingly, because even had he entertained such fancies about his own writing, the instinct of self-preservation would have kept him very quiet about them. One frail reason sometimes adduced for believing he might have intended the poem as quasi-scriptural is that Beatrice's commissioning of him in *Purgatorio* 32 to write down his vision, resembles a similar instruction to the author of Revelation (1:10–11):

> *fui in spiritu in dominica die, et audivi post me vocem magnam tanquam tubae, dicentis: Quod vides, scribe in libro . . .*

> [I was in the spirit on the Lord's day, and I heard behind me a great voice, like a trumpet, saying: What you see, write down in a book . . .]

Beatrice's '*quel che vedi, / ritornato di là, fa che tu scrive*' may distantly recall '*Quod vides, scribe in libro*', but the details of where, how, and by whom the words are said have been completely altered. The 'great voice' of Revelation continued from 'write down in a book' as follows: 'and send it to the seven churches of Asia, to Ephesus and Smyrna . . .' and so on for a complete mailing list; there is nothing like this in Dante. 'To write as an apostle meant to address the church at large, and the intention to address the church at large meant to write as an apostle';[82] Dante is no apostle, he addresses not the 'church at large' but his nameless, individual '*lettor*' ['reader']. Indeed, Beatrice directs him to write neither to, nor as an 'authority' of, the Church but just 'for the sake of the world that lives awry'; she requires of him a form of ministry, not the exercise of the Church's *magisterium*.

The Scriptures have petrified since Dante read them. They have become the subject of drier inquiries than even the Middle Ages made, and also the object of more fierce partisanship than swarmed over them even then. In his time, the sacred writings were not often called 'the Bible' – the term does not appear in the *Commedia* – but rather 'the library' or 'the heavenly library'. Scholars then remembered that '*biblia*' (from the Greek for 'books') is a neuter plural not a feminine singular as it became in late Latin and in modern European languages; remembering that fact should have kept them alert to the long, disparate processes through which this library was collected, as also to the intricacies of its filing system.[83] More people read the Bible in, say, the seventeenth than in the fourteenth century, and not only because more people had learned to read – but size of readership is not the same thing as sophistication in reading. The invention of printing made the Scriptures more widely accessible; it also compacted them, in readers' hands and imaginations, into an apparently unified block. It became easier to feel that you had 'finished' the Bible as you might finish an Agatha Christie, and correspondingly easier to think of the sacred writings as like a puzzle with a single solution or a spiritual 'miracle diet' with a defined set of unambiguous recommendations and vetoes. The Scriptures were ransacked for talismans, 'proof texts' (usually no longer than a verse or two) which might found a sect or serve a political cause. What we now call 'biblical fundamentalism' was born, though from where Dante stood 'superficialism' would be an apter name.

Dante had learned that the Scriptures are in at least one obvious respect not a source of univocally authoritative instruction because they are composed of two Testaments, 'Old' and 'New' in Christian parlance, which are by no means photocopies of each other but stand in the vital, fructive relation known by Christians as 'fulfilment'. God could evidently never go back on His word to the chosen people in the Old Testament; He had, though, according to Christianity, gone forward on it. Patristic and medieval reading of the Scriptures sought the meaning of this historical unfolding of revelation, and understood its own search as participating in the uncompleted process. The search was conducted by theologians through allegorical comparisons of Old and New Testament incidents – the story of Abraham and Isaac, for example, lent its particular dimension of depth to the events at Golgotha. The transpositional habits of thinking which govern such theological studies in development were shown in the design of sculptural groups over Romanesque portals or in cloisters. No one saying or scene had its meaning alone but was inflected by the angle from which you came upon it.[84] We see Dante involved in a related scanning and refocusing on the terraces of Purgatory with their 3D 'compare and contrast' exercises on Judaic, pagan and Christian scenes; Virgil gives him there and then advice which a medieval exegete would have endorsed, and which is also handy for a reader of the *Commedia*: '*non tener pur ad un loco la mente*' ['don't keep your mind fixed on just one place'] (*Purgatorio* 10.46). It is the movement of the eyes which matters. For Dante, a child of his time, the Scriptures were necessarily ambiguous with the ambiguity of any ongoing process, even when that process is believed to be a process of salvation. He had also been schooled in the belief that this process had an end in which all would be revealed, the 'heavenly library' be discovered, for all the density of its cross-references and weirdly unpredictable shelving, as perfectly in accord with itself, when the many books of the '*biblia*' would indeed be legible as a single book. 'Apocalypse' ('uncovering') is the name for that end in which the oneness of Scriptures is unveiled, an end of readings and interpretations which – as it will be the achievement and display of God's meaning throughout all times – can come only in 'the fullness of the times' (Ephesians 1:10). Every time Dante thinks of someone who may in future read his poem – as he continues to do at least until the '*futura gente*' ['people still to come'] of *Paradiso* 33.72 – he shows that his time, the time of his writing, has not yet arrived at that completion. A poem is shaped by the time in which it is written and also shapes the time it takes to read, and so Dante, as he rounds off the *Commedia*, speaks of an apocalyptic moment in which he sees the library of Scriptures and all creation condensed into a one-volume edition:

> *Oh abbondante grazia ond'io presunsi*
> *ficcar lo viso per la luce etterna,*
> *tanto che la veduta vi consunsi!*
> *Nel suo profondo vidi che s'interna*
> *legato con amore in un volume,*
> *ciò che per l'universo si squaderna*
> (*Paradiso* 33.82–7)

[Oh overflow of grace because of which I dared to fix my gaze amid the eternal light so intently that sight itself was there consumed! In that depth I saw that there is gathered and bound with love into one volume everything that is unstitched and scattered across the universe]

He only *saw* that volume; he did not read it, and he did not forget that a vision such as his can as yet be no more than an interim report.

These days we often contrast 'liberal' and 'literal' understandings of the Scriptures: 'literal' readers defend tradition and direct us to the plain sense of scriptural teaching which stands immutably clear of historical change; 'liberals' are a less assured bunch (this is the price they pay for being more in tune with the modern world), much given to a sense of how ambiguously Scripture appears to its various readers as they change with their times. Such a 'literal' / 'liberal' disjunction can only mislead if we read it back into Dante's sense of Scripture and suppose that he too saw authority and ambiguity as opposing powers, in the service of one of which he had to enlist. Once again, we need to sharpen our sense of the actual processes through which a skill – scriptural interpretation, in this case – was learned and conveyed. In Dante's day, the select few who could read rather delighted in the thronging senses of the sacred writings. Responsiveness to their semantic wealth conferred cultural prestige and supplied a reason for, not an objection to, the teaching authority of clerical experts: somebody had to make sense of the texts and who better to do so than those who best registered how alive they still were? Gregory the Great (*c.* 540–604) had described the sacred writings as 'like a river, shallow and deep, in which lambs can walk and elephants swim';[85] he recognized and praised the divergent levels of understanding they made possible. The Scriptures are plural in signification because they are God's word (and so, like Him, uncompounded and inerrant) but God's word *to* His abundant creation (and therefore, like that creation, multiple, self-refracting, ample). Augustine did not contrast authority and ambiguity but identified the '*culmen auctoritas*' ['pinnacle of authority'] in the Scriptures with their ability to speak to many different hearers 'things both true and diverse' ['*vera et diversa*'].[86] Some went further still: not only on every page but in 'every letter of the sacred page, so many precepts fly on wings of virtue, such riches of wisdom are accumulated, that anyone to whom God has granted the means may draw from its fullness'.[87] Not even Roland Barthes, when most flushed with enthusiasm for the *scriptible*, conceived of a text so writerly as to be polysemous 'in every letter'. Yet just because the Scriptures were susceptible of – indeed generated – infinite multiplicity of meanings, the Church considered itself both authorized and bound to inspect, prune, and if necessary lop, the offshoots of the sacred page. Paeans to semantic richness were accompanied by policing cautions to would-be interpreters – 'anyone to whom God has granted the means' implies a requirement for entry into the field of interpretation. In the next sentence, the stipulation becomes bluntly explicit: 'Shall pearls, then, be cast before swine? Shall the Word be given to the ignorant, whom we know to be incapable of receiving it?' Such monopolistic extremes of clericalism were not usual, but they are one grim limit on a spectrum of distaste for and repudiation of the uneducated along which the expert were variously ranged. Much of the Inquisition's energy was taken up with less than kindly treatment of those who had presumed to interpret Scripture without proper schooling; the Church, to whom the task of such schooling had been committed by its founder, showed little compunction about its own share in the responsibility for the heresies it punished, heresies which often sound like those more or less parodic smatterings of information which are a regular by-product of imperfect rapport between teacher and pupil.

The issue of scriptural interpretation is not part of the *Commedia*'s 'intellectual background' but at the heart of its shape, the shape of that learning process through which Dante grows to an understanding of what it might mean for him to be saved. Disparities between levels of understanding Scripture took place not only across the gaps between social classes in medieval Europe; they had long dwelled within individuals, as in the exemplary breast of the African saint, Augustine. In his *Confessions*, Augustine records his struggle to overcome a revulsion from the Judaeo-Christian writings when he read them literally and found in them only 'the fictions of carnal imaginations', such fictions as that 'God is confined within the shape of a human body'. He speaks with biting dryness of hallowed phrases like 'in Abraham's bosom' – 'wherever that is, whatever is meant by that word "bosom"' ['*quidquid illud est, quod illo significatur sinu*'] – and yet reverts to 'bosom' as the right word for a simple reliance on the surface sense of Scripture out of which mature faith is to be built, for the young in faith rest on and grow from the lowly physicality of scriptural language, like children suckling at the breast ['*dum isto humillimo genere verborum tamquam materno sinu eorum gestatur infirmitas*'].[88] Ideally, a full-grown reader of Scripture would remain in touch with his earlier self, its appetite and trust, as Dante integrated his contingently nurtured, perpetually mobile Florentine idiom with a Latin he thought capable of neither growth nor decay. The history of Christianity, though, is not the history of an ideal, and many actual forms of religious life and discourse have set, more or less severely, apart literal and figurative hearings of the Word, and assigned distinct audiences to the divergent hearings. As, for instance, St Bernard of Clairvaux (1090–1153) did in the first words of his sermons to fellow Cistercians on the Song of Songs (sermons in which a breast is never 'merely' a breast): 'To you, brothers, I shall say what I should not say to those who are in the world, or at least I shall say it in a different way.'[89] Religion may have been the opium of the people, but the mystic senses of the Scriptures were the cocaine of some clerics. Dante did not segregate the senses of his poem's words, but he arranged them so that his readers can grow up along with the poem as it develops. The word '*lieto*' ['happy'], for example, can be found throughout the *Commedia*, though its frequency increases (trebles, in fact) from *Inferno* to *Paradiso*. Virgil puts on a 'happy face' [*Inferno* 3.20] to cheer Dante up as they begin their descent; the damned think of life on this earth as a happy life [*Inferno* 19.102] or recall failure to make a wife happy [*Inferno* 26.96]. Two things happen to the word when Dante and Virgil step out of Hell. It becomes a noun (from *Purgatorio* 13 on) and eventually a verb (from *Paradiso* 3 on), rising, as it were, from transient attribute to longer-lasting state to eternal activity. And it begins to apply not only to human happiness but also to the happiness of the divine life, so that God is spoken of as a '*lieto fattore*' ['happy creator', *Purgatorio* 16.89] or, astonishingly, Christ at the moment when he cried 'My God, my God, why hast thou forsaken me?' is called '*Cristo lieto*' ['the happy Christ', *Purgatorio* 23.74]. The higher they climb, the deeper the word seems.

English speakers in particular may come at a tilt to Dante because we have grown accustomed to hearing the King James Bible lauded as an acme of style, a classic of our literature. Whereas for Dante the Bible was not part of what we now call 'literature' but a writing against which all others were measured, and, what's more, a model for his style just because it was not stylish – exalted, mouthable, polished – but rather transfiguratively 'low'. He read the Scriptures in St Jerome's Vulgate, which had itself been when it was composed an exercise in dumbing-down such as the *Commedia* in part aims to be. 'Vulgate' means 'in common speech', as Dante's poem is '*in volgare*'; between Jerome and Dante, what was 'common' had changed, as it continues to change. In 404, when Jerome completed his labours, Latin was a common language throughout the Roman Empire, and it remained close enough to the vernaculars developing in the Italian peninsula to be roughly intelligible to most who lived there until about the year 1000. As compared to classical Latin, from which literary standards of excellence were derived, the Latin of the Vulgate was thought undistinguished, though it formed part of that 'most unexpected and profound renewal of the classical heritage' which began to occur when Ambrose (*c.* 339–97) and Augustine transformed Latin 'by submitting the written style of the [fourth century] intellectual elite to mediation through a spoken message addressed to ... popular audiences'.[90] When Augustine became able to stomach Christianity, his literary tastes, formed in the best imperial mould, also changed: he was taken by the Judaeo-Christian Scriptures, their '*verbis apertissimis et humillimo genere loquendi*' ['extremely accessible words and humble way of speaking'].[91] A transvaluation of literary values breathes through Augustine's praise for a 'humble way of speaking' in writing. E. R. Curtius noted that 'the word *humilitas* first acquires the commendatory meaning "humility" in Church Latin, at the same time keeping the old meaning "low, mean"';[92] Erich Auerbach outlined the dimensions of the word's complex structure when he observed that 'because of its connotations of inferior rank, *humilis* came to be one of the terms most frequently used to designate the low style: *sermo humilis* ... On the other hand (and this is what gives the word [its] semantic force ...), *humilis* became the most important adjective characterizing the Incarnation; in all Christian literature written in Latin it came to express the atmosphere and level of Christ's life and suffering.'[93]

The word, that is, embraced the paradox of Incarnation itself, the earthing of God, as it does on its last appearance in the *Commedia* when St Bernard in *Paradiso* 33.2 hymns Mary as '*umile e alta più che creatura*' ['humble and exalted more than any other creature']. The demands of verse, as often in Dante, yield a theological point here, for the rhythm requires us to say '*umil-ay-alta*', yoking lowliness with height, melding the words through *sinalefe* in our mouths so the phrase has five rather than the possible six syllables. Dante's freedom of movement between words – the latitude he takes now to tweezer them apart with *dialefe*, now to fuse them in *sinalefe* – derives from the everyday speech habits of his community, literate or illiterate. In this respect, his writing approaches lowly neighbourhoods, as when the damned blame everyone and everything but themselves, and Dante apes their quickfire slurs with a run of *sinalefe* (which I mark ^):

> *bestemmiavano Dio^e lor parenti,*
> *l'umana spezie^e 'l loco^e 'l tempo^e 'l seme*
> *di lor semenza^e di lor nascimenti.*
> (*Inferno* 3.103–5)

[they were cursing God 'n' their parents, the human race 'n' the place 'n' the time 'n' the seed which sowed them 'n' which gave them birth.]

The words jostle each other in a complaining crowd, as later they are compacted to mimic granules of the infernal desert-floor at *Inferno* 14.13 – '*Lo spazzo^era^una rena^arida^e spessa*' ['The ground was dry, dense-packed sand']. These vocal condensations, coming on top of Dante's usual conciseness, made translating him hell for many English writers, who were already hampered by the fact that our heroic line is one syllable shorter than its Italian equivalent: hence, the many down-sized 'sprites' who appear for 'spirits' in eighteenth-century versions; hence, the desperate line from Gray's hand: 'When Gaddo at my feet outstretchd, implor'ng'.

By switching from a line which requires each syllable to be sharply discriminated from the next (the first in the following quotation) to a line which puckers up its words together (the second) and then reverting to a line with clear, junctural edges (the third), he paces his narrative with endlessly inventive rubato:

> *Né 'o' sí tosto mai né 'i' si scrisse,*
> *com'el s'accese^e^arse,^e cener tutto*
> *convenne che cascando divenisse*
> (*Inferno* 24.100–102)

[Not an '*o*' nor an '*i*' was ever written so quickly as he catches fire 'n' burns 'n' all-over ash, fittingly, becomes in his fall]

Such moments crackle with vocal opportunities and remind our print-impressed imaginations of what we guess to have been characteristic of storytelling in an oral culture. They bear out at a cellular level of narrating what Piero Camporesi has observed of the broader features of narrative in *Inferno* which brings together 'on the one hand, a legendary folklore culture relating to a subterranean world populated by the symbols of Celtic tradition and fantasy (the well, the bridge, the devouring giant . . .) and, on the other, an elite intellectualizing culture evolved from Graeco-Latin thought (Aristotle, Virgil, St Thomas Aquinas), seeking always to geometrize and classify'.[94] In which of these supposedly disjunct worlds were the Scriptures to be found, you might well ask.

It will not do to speak as if folkloric and elite cultures were reciprocally incommunicado in Dante's day (the same probably goes for any period), just as we cannot cleanly distinguish pagan and Christian cultures. The *Commedia* has often struck commentators as bizarre in its extreme readiness to combine elements from opposed systems of belief, as when the god Neptune pops up in *Paradiso* 33. But neither a culture nor a poem is only a system of beliefs, though it suits those of an intellectualizing bent to pretend otherwise; nor does the actual life of a religious community run unswervingly along the lines laid down by official edict or anathema. At an abstract level, theologians had long debated what use, if any, Christians might properly make of classical culture, and had elaborated subtle justifications for some forms of syncretism. But when we come across sculptures from a pagan temple re-employed in an Apulian crypt, or classical reliefs decorating Christian shrines in the Alps or the Pyrenees, we face not the result of elite cultural theory but early instances of recycling, a sensible use of what was lying around and came in handy. Even the most orthodox believers have other things to do as well as believe orthodoxly. One small indication that such a relaxed practicality is at work in the *Commedia* too is that Dante turns to colloquial *sinalefe* quite as readily when giving voice to St Thomas Aquinas and others of the saved as in his free indirect rendering of underworld allegations, his mimicry of soil structure or turning into ash. The damned were at one in alienated decrying of their own pasts; the penitent are at one in gratitude for the history of deliverance when, at *Purgatorio* 2.46–7, they sing the psalm '*In exitu Israel de Aegypto*' ['When

Israel came out of Egypt'] *'tutti^insieme^ad una voce'* ['all together in one voice'], where the triple emphasis on unanimity in the words is doubly underlined by the liaisons arranged between the words. Dante's Aquinas rounds off a sentence in his account of the Trinity's self-diffusion throughout the universe with the line:

etternalmente rimanendosi^una. (*Paradiso* 13.60)

[eternally remaining-one-with-itself.]

This is a resplendent example of what William Empson thought the prime material of poetry, 'the sort of joke you find in hymns',[95] an intense reach through linguistic cohesion towards a coherence beyond conceptual articulation: the line itself is 3-in-1, because it has three words but makes up one line (with three stresses, on its fourth, eighth and tenth syllables); the verb 'to remain' appears in elaborate, literary form as a reflexive, so that persisting seems an activity of the deity within itself; that 'remaining' is a present participle helps convey that this 'staying-true-to-itself' is, like all God's acts, eternal; the *sinalefe* between *'rimanendosi'* and *'una'* draws the two words into one as by internal attraction within the Trinity; the last word *'una'* is feminine because it qualifies *'luce'* ['light'] from five lines earlier, so its inflectional character creates a small-scale model of self-identity through time; and this 'one' on which the period comes to rest is itself the third rhyme in a triplet.

Yet all this ingenious pliability of idiom, which makes Dante's style *'humilis'* as it adopts the contours of common speech, takes place in accord with the formal requirements of his verse-line, that hendecasyllabic line which, in *De vulgari . . .* 2.5, he had called *'superbius'* above all other Italian lines – 'more magnificent', 'loftier', but also 'more proud', *'superbia'* being the antithesis of *'humilitas'*.[96] This simultaneously double aspect of the writing should remind us again of the fact that there is no such thing as a 'Christian style' any more than there was such a thing as a distinctively 'Christian culture' to mark off the early Christians from their pagan neighbours. The

Scriptures spill out through the mesh of classical literary theory just as Christians were said to be unclassifiable according to ancient social theory: 'there are no more distinctions between Jew and Greek, slave and free, male and female, but all of you are one in Christ Jesus' (Galatians 3:28; Jerusalem Bible). Dispensing with such categories – whether literary or more broadly socio-political – was and is easier said than done (at least for those of us who are not saints), and so Christian writers have had to develop a way of responding to the terms in which good writing has been conceived by those outside their fold.

Some features of this development were described by Victor Hugo (1802–85) with his usual, excitable fondness for neat contrasts between epochs. According to Hugo, Graeco-Roman 'beauty' resulted from an intensely selective idealization of a narrow sample of creation's features, whereas

> Christianity brings poetry back to the real ... Poetry begins to operate like nature itself, intermingling in its creations, but without muddling them up, light and shade, the grotesque and the sublime, in other words, body and soul, the animal and the spiritual ... Grotesquerie, it seems, can serve as a pause for thought, a term of comparison, a stepping-off point from which we launch ourselves towards beauty with refreshed and sharpened senses.[97]

There is reason to hesitate before swallowing whole such schemes as Hugo's by which the messy slowness of historical process is tidied up for ease of summary, and antitheses are marshalled like dominoes about to be played with a triumphant flourish. Yet he brilliantly senses that writing like Dante's arises out of pausing for thought *between* stylistic possibilities and not from espousing one known, approved manner. Dante's terms are all 'terms of comparison', as suits the habits of cultural transposition he acquired when scanning between Old and New Testaments, or turning his gaze from a sculpted mermaid to her contrasting Virgin Mary.

Christianity, thus realized in the conduct of writing with

regard to its own achievements, realized as a reflection on style, or between styles, rather than as a single style intent on its own preservation, permeates the lexical range of the *Commedia* with its profuse familiarity amid 'low' verbal company, and its really Shakespearean leaps across registers. When the generic self-consciousness of antiquity was reasserted in the Renaissance and a neoclassical linguistic segregation came into vogue, the poem suffered an eclipse from which it began to recover only as the eighteenth century tired of what had been promulgated as correctness, a tiring often known as 'Romanticism', for which Hugo's preface to *Cromwell* served as one of many (mutually inconsistent) mission statements. Pietro Bembo spoke for many *cinquecento* neoclassicists when he deplored Dante's verbal frequenting of tax gatherers and whores:

> in order to write on anything which came into his mind, however unsuitable for verse, and however uneasily it sat in this form, he would very often use now Latin words, now foreign ones which have not been accepted in Tuscan, now really old, abandoned ones, at times the out of the ordinary and the coarse, at others, the filthy and the ugly, or the very harsh.[98]

Giovanni Della Casa, for instance, was typical in his Renaissance humanist dismay that Beatrice (of all women!) should cap *Purgatorio* 30 and pronounce on lofty matters in words such as

> *Alto fatto di Dio sarebbe rotto,*
> *se Leté si passasse e tal vivanda*
> *fosse gustata sanza alcuno scotto*
> *di pentimento che lagrime spanda.*

> [The high decree of God would be broken, if he were to pass through Lethe and such a repast were to be tasted before he has cleared his slate with tears such as penitence sheds.]

'*Scotto*' was the offending term here, one of the 'base wordes that come out of the *Tavernes*', in Robert Peterson's translation,

for the word means payment made to 'settle up' at a bar.[99] At
the climax of a canto, in a *distingué* setting of classical allusion
and syntactic refinement, the word carries a real charge, verging
on a humiliation in and of style which is wholly appropriate to
the dramatic shaming of Dante that is taking place at this
point in the story. Henry Cary's nineteenth-century English
still winces away from so characteristic a Dantescan lexical
plummet, rendering the end of *Purgatorio* 30 as

> It were a breaking of God's high decree,
> If Lethe should be past, and such food tasted
> Without the cost of some repentant tear.

where a reminiscence of Milton's 'Lycidas' ('Without the
meed of som melodious tear') smoothes the brunt of Beatrice's
phrase, and heightens the 'tone'. Cary provides Beatrice herself
with a similar, dictional shelter from earthy realities by re-
ferring to her three times in his version of *Purgatorio* 30 as
a 'virgin', though on each occasion Dante, who remembered
– with whatever reluctance – that she had been married, has
the word '*donna*' ('woman', 'lady': see *Purgatorio* 30.32, 64
and 96).[100]

Italian poets are rarely strapped for a rhyme, so the lexical
'knees bend' of '*scotto*' was probably not forced on Dante
because he could think of nothing else to go with '*condotto*'
and '*rotto*'. The sudden vulgarity of the single word has its
place in the larger architecture of the poem, a place which we
can locate by considering the rhyme-word of the next line,
'*spanda*'. The word means 'to pour out'; it appears first in the
poem when Dante discovers he is talking to Virgil and bursts
out in praise of the elder poet as '*quella fonte / che spandi di
parlar sí largo fiume*' ['that spring / which pours forth so broad
a river of speech'] (*Inferno* 1.80); Virgil has the word himself
when noting, in *Inferno* 18.84, that Jason, who stands as a bad
antitype of Virgil's own eloquence, looks regally proud because
'*per dolor non par lagrimar spanda*' ['he pours out no tears on
account of his pain']. Dante returns to the verb in a sarcastic
eulogy of Florence whose fame is not only worldwide but

'gushes throughout Hell' (*Inferno* 26.3); the same verb details the clear water which provokes the purging thirst of the gluttons in *Purgatorio* 22.138. Across sixty-four cantos of the poem, Dante has sprung an arch whose keystone is this speech from Beatrice; this arch stands for a range of considerations about eloquence and honesty which could not be more pertinent to Dante as he stands mute and about to weep before Beatrice and the encircling blessed, harrowed with embarrassment, like a man who convivially declares 'My shout!' and then finds he has forgotten his wallet. '*Scotto*' is perfect for the sense Beatrice wants to awaken in him that his self-esteem is an empty pocket.[101] Dante was a master mason; he worked in all manner of stone, clunch as well as porphyry.

Dante's Scriptures, then, are low in style, infinitely signifying: they generate as well as settle issues. They may offer general rules of conduct, but such rules have still to be brought to life by individuals, brought home within individual lives; Scripture does not and cannot supply a rule for this process of free application – embodiment rather – for reasons which apply to all rules: even those 'given' by God still have to be 'taken' by creatures:

> Since discourse on moral matters even in their universal aspects
> is subject to uncertainty and variation it is all the more uncertain
> if one wishes to descend to bringing doctrine to bear on individual
> cases in specific detail, for this cannot be dealt with by either art
> or precedent. Therefore judgement concerning individual cases
> must be left to the prudence of each person.[102]

The *Commedia* undergoes just such a descent to and through the individual case of Dante Alighieri. It tells us about '*nostra vita*' ('our life') by telling us the story of one individual's self-discovery, '*mi ritrovai*' ('I came to myself'). But *how* exemplary – to what degree, in which respects – Dante is, is left for us to find as we read ourselves into fellowship with him in the course of his poem. Aristotle thought it a mere convention that the protagonists in poetic fictions bear proper names:

the writing of poetry is a more philosophical, a weightier, activity than the writing of history, since poetic statements are of the nature of universals, whereas those of history are particulars. By a 'universal statement' I mean one as to what such and such a kind of man will probably or necessarily do, which is the aim of poetry, though it tacks on proper names to the characters afterwards[103]

Yet when Beatrice says 'Dante' (Purgatorio 30.55), she names a real individual and not a concept with a name more or less felicitously thought up later. So too 'Beatrice' and 'Virgil' are proper names for entities who at least began as historical particulars though they develop a broader scope of implication than most of us acquire. The Commedia is an early instance of what we now call the novel, not a late flowering of philosophical allegory; it belongs with Proust's À la recherche du temps perdu, not with Spenser's The Faerie Queene. We read novels with an operative sense of plausibility which Aristotle well describes ('what such and such a kind of man will probably or necessarily do'), but it is the purpose of at least some novels to elicit from amid the welter of our trusted generalities an imagined encounter with a particular life, a life irresoluble into the categories of expert understanding (what 'kind' of woman is Emma Bovary, or Francesca da Rimini?). As Dante goes on his way of discovery, he keeps meeting groups of people; these groups are categorized under various heads – gluttons, sodomites, the late repentant, backsliders, contemplatives – and the principles governing the categorization are explained to him by his expert guides. These categories and their rationale make up what might be called the 'orthodoxy' of the Commedia, its conceptual scheme, the 'what' of its teaching which Dante too is learning through the poem. But this is only half the story, and not self-evidently the better half. For from each group, Dante singles out an individual or two and engages them in conversation: each such talk starts differently from all the others, has its own landscape and pace, its particular sticky moments, and no two end in the same way. These variations show orthodoxy in the process of becoming actual; they carry

the 'how' of the *Commedia*'s teaching and also help us indi-
viduate the person who is being taught; they introduce us to
Dante as he introduces us to his cast. Dante may assent to
all the official teaching, but only these unforeseeably various
inflections in his staging of his conversations tell us which
doctrines troubled or seized him or left him tepid.

Christendom is macrocosmically as patchy as Christianity is
– for most professed Christians – microcosmically inter-
mittent. Auerbach quietly noted that 'the mimetic content of
the story of Christ required a very long time, more than a
thousand years, to enter into the consciousness of the faithful,
even of the people early converted to Christianity'.[104] Dante
might have shown the truth of that by pointing to the account
books of his Florentine contemporaries, headed as they were, in
spite of the celebrated admonition against serving two masters
(Matthew 6:24; Luke 16:13), '*Al nome di Dio e di guadagno
che Dio ci dia*' ['In the name of God and the profit God may
give us'].[105] Auerbach's phrase, 'the mimetic content of the story
of Christ', rightly suggests that an individual's life of faith is
more like learning a role in a play than like elaborating a
conceptual account of a message supposedly encrypted in the
Gospel narratives. Christianity is not a system of knowledge
but a more or less thoroughly grasped and exercised skill.
The appropriate response to the Gospels' 'mimetic content' is
'*imitatio Christi*' ['the imitation of Christ', where 'imitation'
has the sense of 'following an example'], a perpetuity of re-
hearsal more searching than that *impersonation* of Christ which
has always had more popular appeal, however poor the imper-
sonations, consisting as they often do of noisy self-content and
an unbecoming bossiness. Dante's poem replies to the dramatic
and figurative character of the sacred texts, their foolishness
when regarded with a certain philosophical stringency, by a
process of imitation which engages the self in an activity of
translating at the level of desire and action, of word and cad-
ence, as well as at the level of stated doctrine. William of
St Thierry said the Song of Solomon was written '*in modum
dramatis et stylo comico*' ['in dramatic form and in a comic
style'],[106] where 'dramatic' implies the essential responsiveness

of the Song, its interpersonal acoustic, and 'comic' means a
literary manner answering to Christian 'humility'. So too the
Commedia.

IV THE WORLD OF THE STORY

When Dante started out on *Inferno* some time in the first decade
of the fourteenth century, he was not the only Florentine with
hell in mind. Villani records in his chronicle of the city a
1304 May Day entertainment put on by and for Dante's fellow
citizens who still had access (as the banished poet did not) to
the banks of the Arno:

> it was an old custom of the people from the Borgo San Friano
> to make up the smartest and most various pastimes. So they
> announced that whoever wanted to learn news of the other world
> should come to the Carraia Bridge or the nearby banks of the
> Arno on May Day; and they arranged boats and small craft on
> the Arno, carrying stages on which they performed semblances
> and figurations of hell with fires and other punishments and
> sufferings, with men dressed up as devils, scary to behold, and
> others who had the appearance of naked souls and looked like
> people, and the devils subjected them to a variety of torments
> with extremely loud cries and shrieks and hubbub, hideous and
> terrifying to see and hear; and many citizens came to see this new
> attraction; and the Carraia Bridge, which was at that time made
> of wood, became so laden with the people who were on it that it
> gave way in many places, and fell into the river along with the
> people who were on it, so that many died and drowned there,
> and many were maimed; in this manner, the jest turned to earnest
> and, as had been announced, many did really, through dying
> there, learn news of the other world, with loud lament and sorrow
> throughout the city[107]

These Florentines clustered along their river, delightedly aghast
at first and then really downcast, were kin to the Veronese
gossips who, it is said, pointed at Dante in the street after his

poem had appeared and whispered that you could tell he had been to hell from his unusually deep tan.[108] Yet the spectacle Villani describes took more than credulity to stage: load-bearing pontoons had to be built for the 'figurations of hell'; someone sewed the devils' costumes; someone rehearsed the torments and shrieks; the whole troupe needed coordinating so they would arrive in good time. The audience too did more than gawp. They knew japes like this were an 'old custom' of the San Friano gang and that the first of May was a festival, so came along with informed expectations; they had enough skill as regards fiction to find the show both 'terrifying' and an 'attraction' (they were not so different from the West End audiences who flock to a 'disturbing' play); they distinguished between tales of hell – 'the jest' – and the real trouble which befell the crowd – 'earnest'. Expert mystics of the early four-teenth century such as Meister Eckhart sometimes spoke in amused disdain of simple folk who 'want to see God with the same eyes with which they behold a cow',[109] but reflection on this incident in Florence should dissuade us from adopting a model of the medieval world as neatly segmented into distinct groups, the sophisticated here and the superstitious there. The mindset of Dante's *Commedia* is not different in kind from the disparate thoughts assembled on the banks of the Arno: the poem differs from the fiasco rather in the self-conscious ampli-tude with which it registers and arranges the many attitudes which jostled against each other there.

Disaster follows pastime seamlessly in Villani's long, un-ruffled sentence. That sequence could quite as well be reversed, as the chronicler notes of Florentines as far back as 1177: 'combat between the citizens became so usual that one day they fought each other and the next ate and drank together, exchanging news about the derring-do that one, the prowess that another, had shown in those disputes'.[110] The *Commedia* is a work of documentary realism in this respect: it alternates, like Florentines, spasms of intensity with convivial pauses for thought and recreation, as when, in *Inferno* 11, having made the tricky entrance into the city of Dis, Virgil rests – to take the weightlessness off his feet a while – and Dante suggests they have some instructive conversation 'so that the time will not pass wasted' (*Inferno* 11.14–15). Virgil obliges with an account of hell's layout, and then, edifying done, sets off again with the words '*Ma seguimi oramai, che 'l gir mi piace*' ['But follow me now, I feel like a stroll'].[111] Such nonchalances as Virgil's or the Florentines' puzzle us. We might suppose these are blind spots produced by fixed, medieval staring at the transcendent, a consequence of the fact that, as Jacques Le Goff assures us, 'medieval people had a long way to go before they could penetrate the screen of symbolism and encounter the physical reality of the world in which they lived'.[112] It's a wonder, if Le Goff is right, they managed to carve their symbols so dextrously in stone; it's a wonder they could even feed themselves. But then another expert in the period (and from much the same stable of expertise) thinks they had no trouble seeing the *forêt* for the *correspondances* – quite the contrary: 'in this period people were effectively swallowed up by nature ... Throughout the Middle Ages the natural world dominated existence; people, especially in the countryside, were therefore preoccupied with the workings of nature to a degree that today can seem obsessive.'[113] A third medieval historian, conscious of such truth as there is in each of these discrepant accounts, characterizes the *mentalité* of those days as essentially oxymoronic: 'paradoxicality, strangeness and contradiction were integral organic features of the medieval mind'.[114]

The delight in contrasts which Victor Hugo welcomed as liberatingly ample in 'Christian' art strikes Gurevich as plain freakish when he considers it as a feature of the medieval world: 'The exceptional character of [medieval] culture lies in the strange combination of opposite poles: heaven and earth, spirit and body, gloom and humour, life and death.'[115] Any even mildly complex culture will span many such sets of 'opposite poles' and may do so without provoking bipolar disorder in those whom it frames, though they will usually experience *some* strain. Nor is our own world so smooth and at one that we need find the Middle Ages bizarre in their disparities: global enlightenment has not yet put to flight the *chiaroscuro* of the actual. Now as then, a rounded vision of the world we live in is painful to maintain when glimpsed at all; such stereoscopy seems arduous and remote, sometimes a sheer figment, like what was known as the 'beatific vision' (they are perhaps one and the same). So it is not hard to understand why Dante through Beatrice's mouth calls heaven ''*l paese sincero*' (*Paradiso* 7.130), nor to imagine from out of what experiences of fracture, what intermittences of the heart, he plucked that word to name his desired homeland: '*sincero*' – 'whole', 'entire', 'honest', 'genuine', 'unalloyed', 'integrated', 'ringing true'. Eugenio Montale, at any rate, heard clearly the reciprocity between Dante's writing and the world from which it sprang – in recoil, with an alacrity for return – and found neither the writing nor the reciprocity strange:

> There's been a lot of talk about 'style'. Should style be thought of as expressing 'the writer' or 'the world'? Taking the first option leads to privileging the content of the work, the so-called *Weltanschauung*. From this it follows that poetry can be translated. Form is thought of as a suit of clothes which can be changed, while the body, the cadaver, is left intact. Taking the second option, emphasis falls on the objects which are represented and their function in the context of the work. Tone of voice, the handling of the language, the choice of metaphors – all these too are objects of representation. Man can do nothing without paying heed to the things around him.
>
> In the case when a man is besieged by the things around him . . . his voice can do nothing but engage in dialogue with them, maybe in an attempt to exorcise them. At this stage, there is born the comic style which achieved its greatest triumph in Dante's *Commedia*.[116]

While the state of being besieged by contraries is less peculiar to the Middle Ages than those days' historians at times suggest, a reader now may miss particular details of the contrariness which surrounded Dante. Easter, for example. The *Commedia*'s journey takes place over the days of Easter, 1300. No doubt the main point of dating the fiction from an Easter is to acknowledge that Dante's resurgence from the deathlike impasse in which he finds himself at the start of *Inferno* comes through Christ's self-sacrifice and his victory over the grave at the Resurrection, but Easter Sunday for Dante's fellow citizens had a further, distinctly less uplifting sense, because it was on the morning of Easter Sunday, 1215, that the young aristocrat Bondelmonte de'Bondelmonti, a rising star in one of Florence's main clans, was murdered, 'from which there followed for our city much evil and ruin ... which some think will never end unless God Himself puts a stop to it'.[117] That murder ignited the cycle of vengeance which still raged when Dante was born fifty years later. The Florentine Guelfs, grimly commemorating, chose Easter Sunday, 1267 to expel the Ghibelline families who were party to the feud; Dante was a babe in arms at the time but had probably begun to absorb the venom in the air, venom which spills out when he trades sneers about banishment with the Ghibelline, Farinata, in *Inferno* 10. Farinata died the year before Dante was born, but in citadels of the implacable, such as Florence or Hell, dates set no bounds to hatred. When Farinata's own clan, the Uberti, were thrust out in 1258, their grand towers and houses had been razed to the ground and left in rubble for nearly half a century; Dante walked past this site of derelict pride throughout his youth and early manhood (it is now the Piazza della Signoria), and took office as a Prior in the Palazzo Vecchio, which stands where the Uberti towers stood before their downfall.

Towers into which boss-class families could withdraw when besieged by each other or by popular uprising were ten-a-penny in Dante's Florence: in 1300, when the city's population was about 100,000, there were said to be 150 such fortified retreats. Villani regarded them as an amenity: 'on account of the height of the many towers there were then in Florence, people said that from a distance outside its walls it looked like the loveliest and most burgeoning town that could be found on such a small site'.[118] When you consider such towers arose out of internecine strife, they seem less sure grounds for civic pride, though still pretty 'from a distance'. The *Commedia* finds room to acknowledge the unbowed sublimity of these structures, as when Virgil urges Dante to imitate a tower's fortitude, unconcerned by any

same person. The *Commedia* confesses this in its story and its design: it is truly a 'confessional' poem in the sacramental sense. And this gives a third significance to the fact that the poem takes place over an Easter:

> All the faithful, male or female, shall after they have reached the age of discretion faithfully confess all their sins once a year to their own priest and perform to the best of their ability the penance imposed, receiving reverently at least at Easter the sacrament of the Eucharist[153]

In current, popular imagining of Catholicism, confession bulks oppressively large, but the practice was rarer in Dante's time – the faithful often confessed only on their deathbeds. The Fourth Lateran Council hoped to change all that with its imposition in these words of what Catholics now call their 'Easter duty'. There is little evidence as to whether the Council's hopes were fulfilled in the half-century before Dante's birth but at least the poet was sufficiently impressed to model his poem on the ritual of confession at Easter.

The three *cantiche* of the *Commedia* respond to the three stages of the sacrament: examination of conscience (*Inferno*); confession and penance (*Purgatorio*); reintegration into the community of the faithful, specifically by participation in the Eucharist (*Paradiso*). Had Dante been writing a theological treatise, it would have made sense to begin with God and heaven, for hell consists in irremediable severance from God: the reader in search of information had better be told about God first, the better to realize what losing Him would mean. But the *Commedia* begins with event and experience, rising later to such clarity as it can muster. It has the shape of a sacramental action not of a doctrinal argument, though argument – with oneself as with others – is an element in its action. The poem begins in Hell because that was where Dante was when, unassisted, he thought of his sins. Contemplating its own stains, alone with the demon of conscience, the soul believes its own state irreparable; 'hell' is another name for 'irreparability', as if God might say to you, as your fellow creatures no doubt

wrongs, he should shell out his money [*pecuniam suam solvat*] to those who wronged him, as if they were his benefactors.[151]

We do not know where Dante had got to in the *Commedia* when this chance of pardon came up but the ceremony he repudiates here reads like a parody of the reconciliatory pageant which takes place at the centre of the poem beyond all city walls in *Purgatorio* 29–31. Virgil crowns and mitres Dante (*Purgatorio* 27.142) as if in compensation for the affront his fellow citizens would have offered him with the penal, fool's-cap mitre; Beatrice exacts a figurative '*scotto*' ('settling-up') from him at *Purgatorio* 30.144, though in his Latin letter Dante's self-righteousness peaks and overflows at the thought of handing over cash ('*pecuniam suam solvat*'). *Paradiso* 25 was most probably written some time after he received Florence's poisoned olive branch, but it seems he was still bridling and envisioned for himself quite a different return to the baptistery where he was named: 'I shall return as a poet and at the font where I was baptized I shall take the laurel crown' (*Paradiso* 25.8–9). It was this letter which Anna Akhmatova remembered amid the false accusations and falser clemencies of Stalin's terror when she wrote that Dante did not pass 'barefoot, in a penitential shirt, / With a lighted candle . . . Through his desired Florence'.[152]

Yet when Dante meets Beatrice at last what occurs is a public humiliation, one he not only accepted but created for himself. She baptizes him in the poem, in the sense that she alone and first gives him his name; she not only hears his confession in public but speaks most of it for him. There were indeed 'two Dantes', in Kenelm Foster's phrase: the Dante who, confronted with the secular culture of his time and carrying that culture within himself, could write the word '*humilitas*' in his letter to a Florentine friend as if it named a vice for which, unusually for him, he felt nothing but contempt, and the Dante in whose *Commedia* the word and its cognates on their eighteen occurrences always signify the essential virtue for a human creature, a '*persona umile e peregrina*' ('a humble person on a journey', *Paradiso* 6.135). These two Dantes do not coexist; they are the

which he returns his own (*Paradiso* 22.154) and which at last she turns from him and to the fountain of eternity (*Paradiso* 31.93).

The *Commedia* has so many turns because '*volgere*' is *volgare* for conversion, repentance ('*convertere*', '*metanoia*' in the parlance of *gramatica*). The story is: Dante was so far gone astray he had to be granted his vision and the task of recording it to bring him round. As Virgil says:

> *Questi non vide mai l'ultima sera;*
> *ma per la sua follia le fu sí presso,*
> *che molto poco tempo a volger era.*
> (*Purgatorio* 1.58–60)

[This man never saw his last night but his craziness brought him so close to it that very little time was left for turning.]

Dante went on his visionary pilgrimage, as many pilgrims actually travelled, as an act of penance: 'the sacraments most closely associated with pilgrimage are the Eucharist and penance'.[149] The entire poem is an act of 'turning', of converting the self; this penitential quality is what makes the work '*sacro*'.

In May 1315, Florence offered Dante a pardon and the chance of return, on condition that he served a token prison sentence, paid a fine, '*e dopo quello in alcuna solennità publica fosse misericordievolmente alla nostra principale ecclesia offerto . . .*'[150] ['and then should be pitiably offered up at some public ceremony in our principal church']. There would have been a procession of returnees in sackcloth, carrying candles, with mock mitres on their heads, to San Giovanni, probably on the saint's feast-day (24 June). A letter, which Boccaccio claimed to have transcribed from Dante's manuscript, survives in which Dante indignantly rejects the offer:

> Far be such irrational baseness of heart [*temeraria tantum cordis humilitas*] from a man who is at home with philosophy, that such a man should agree . . . to be offered up, as it were in shackles. Far be it from a man who cries out for justice that, after suffering

devotion in his day, with the fact of pilgrimage during which
'the pilgrim physically traverses a mystical way'.

He has difficulty setting off, though, because no sooner has
he got over being all at sea than a leopard bars his way:

> *e non mi si partía dinanzi al volto,*
> *anzi 'mpediva tanto il mio cammino,*
> *ch'i' fui per ritornar piú volte vòlto.*
> (*Inferno* 1.34–6)

[and it would not budge from before my face, but rather it so
blocked my path that many times I turned round to go back.]

He rhymes a word for 'face' ('*volto*') equivocally with the past
participle of the verb 'to turn' ('*volto*'), and then thickens the
mix by juxtaposing the participle with '*volte*', the Italian for
'times' – as in 'I've told you a thousand times'; '*volta*' and its
plural '*volte*' really do stem, at some distance, from the verb
'*volgere*' as the noun '*volto*' ('face') does not, though his rhyme
hints at a fanciful etymology as if 'face' meant 'that which one
turns'. Dante rarely gets so densely stuck on the word for 'turn'
in what follows but its many recurrences show the intensity
and breadth of his attention to phenomena of turning: the
exasperated Filippo Argenti, who turns his own teeth on himself
(*Inferno* 8.63); the '*Poi si rivolse*' ('then he turned away') with
which both the disdainful angel and the wistful sodomite depart
(*Inferno* 9.100 and 15.121); the triple turning upside down
of Ulysses and his companions in their shipwreck (*Inferno*
26.139); a gambler out of luck who replays the dice-throws
which went against him ('*repetendo le volte*', *Purgatorio* 6.3);
Mary, whose '*Ecce ancilla Dei*' turned the key which opened
the world to incarnate love (*Purgatorio* 10.44, 42); Virgil, to
whom Dante turns so often, as a scared child runs to its mother
(*Purgatorio* 30.43–5), and from his sorrow over whose loss he
is turned by the sound of Beatrice calling 'Dante' (*Purgatorio*
30.62); Constantine, who turned the flight of the imperial eagle
from West to East (*Paradiso* 6.1); Beatrice's lovely eyes, to

the page, repeatedly taking eleven-syllable steps. As, for example, with two of his favourite verbs, in all their forms, transitive, intransitive and reflexive: '*volgere*' and '*rivolgere*', which range as widely in Italian as their equivalent – 'turn' – in English. The first turn we hear of comes appropriately in the poem's first simile, appropriately because similes work by reversion, turning back to a past experience in order to orient the present. Dante somehow gets out of his impasse in the forest:

> *E come quei che con lena affannata*
> *uscito fuor del pelago a la riva*
> *si volge a l'acqua perigliosa e guata,*
> *cosí l'animo mio, ch'ancor fuggiva,*
> *si volse a retro a rimirar lo passo*
> *che non lasciò già mai persona viva.*
> (*Inferno* 1.22–7)

[And like someone who, half-suffocated, escapes from the deep to the shore and turns back to the perilous water and gawps at it, so my mind, though it was still fleeing in panic, turned itself back to gaze again on those straits which nobody has ever passed through alive.]

As so often in the *Commedia*, a verb of motion occurs in both a physical and a figurative sense within a few lines. We may describe this as an inevitable feature of our common tongue, which models psychological 'dimensions' on the dimensions in which our bodies move (we may have something 'on our mind' as 'on our back', we can't 'get over' a bereavement or a chasm, we come 'to' a conclusion as to the sea); we may add that Dante's journey is allegorical and therefore requires verbs of motion to work overtime; we may further recognize here an anticipation of that sophisticated vigilance about analogy which is at the centre of Dante's poetic and theological discretion. So far so true, yet we need also to see that Dante's writing in this respect corresponds with the actuality of

they both run the risks of analogical expression. These issues
have been the focus of much comment on what is 'sacro' about
his poem, to the neglect of its closeness to pilgrimage, a ritual
of movement 'replete with actual objects, "sacra"'. Book 5 of
the *Pilgrim's Guide* tirelessly lists for the pilgrim the bodies of
the saints which '*sunt visitanda*' ('should be visited') on the
roads to Compostela: '*visitandum est*' the body of blessed
Caesarius of Arles, '*visitandum est*' what remains of St Foy at
Conques, St Leonard in the Limousin, St Martin of Tours.[147]
Dante goes and makes his visits too but he animates the relics
and does not confine himself to saints; he goes into more detail
than the *Codex* about how he gets from niche to niche, and
his encounters are more reliably vivid than an actual pil-
grim on a long walk is likely to come across. But that's poetry
for you. Francesca da Rimini calls him a creature '*che visitando
vai per l'aere perso*' ('who goes through the dark air, paying
visits', *Inferno* 5.89); maybe her '*visitando*' shows how in-
congruously she remains a society hostess amid the lost, but
she shares the word not only with the *Pilgrim's Guide* but also
with Beatrice, who introduces St James himself as '*il barone /
per cui là giù si visita Galizia*' ('the great lord for whose sake
down there on earth people pay visits to Galicia', *Paradiso*
25.17–18).

> Pilgrimage may be thought of as extroverted mysticism, just
> as mysticism is introverted pilgrimage. The pilgrim physically
> traverses a mystical way; the mystic sets forth on an interior
> spiritual pilgrimage. For the former, concreteness and historicity
> dominate; for the latter, a phased interior process leads to a goal
> beyond conceptualization.[148]

This is brilliantly said, and yet it needs to be added that a person
in motion will experience not only these polarities in their
distinctness as the Turners lay them out – interior/exterior,
physical/spiritual, 'concreteness and historicity'/'a goal beyond
conceptualization' – but also parallax between them as the eye
realigns them on its travels. Dante is such a person, both as he
imagines traversing all known spheres and as his hand crosses

is the first goal – Jerusalem, Rome, the furthest heaven of the
Commedia. But the shrine is a fulcrum not a terminus. Once
there, the pilgrim turns on himself and begins the way back,
perhaps by routes other than those along which he came, in
Dante's case by writing the poem of his journey. Even as the
vision petered out in *Paradiso* 33, Dante was being turned by
love towards his second destination, the return home to the
'*volgare*'. The last time he mentions pilgrims in the *Commedia*,
he compares himself in Paradise to the new arrival in, say,
Compostela who, even as he takes in the splendours for which
he has travelled, is already thinking how to recount them to
those he left behind (*Paradiso* 31.43–5). The sublime humour
of that simile – the mind flitting from its present devotions to a
picture of the self, surrounded by stay-at-home admirers 'well
I never'-ing at every anecdote – is entirely characteristic of the
poem[144] in its honest amplitude about the varieties of religious
experience.

   Dante's poem is as various and, from a certain point of view,
as patchily 'correct' or single-minded as the *Pilgrim's Guide to
Santiago de Compostela (c.* 1145),[145] which embraces not only
a devout account of the passion of St Eutropius and a note on
the miraculous fountain at Compostela where 'one cannot see
whence the water comes nor can one see whither it goes' but
also curses on boatmen and evil toll-keepers ('may they be
utterly damned!') and warnings against the dangers of horse-
flies, wasps and the Navarrese with their shocking table
manners and less than chaste attitude to mules. Pilgrimage is a
distinctively lay expression of religious impulse and conviction,
and so lacks the consistency requisite from a more clericalized
spirituality; as Edith Turner has written, 'At the heart of the
pilgrimage is the folk, the ordinary people who choose a
"materialist" expression of their religion. In other words, pil-
grimage as a religious act is a kinetic ritual, replete with actual
objects, "sacra", and is often held to have material results, such
as healing.'[146] When Dante calls his work '*sacro*' and '*sacrato*'
(*Paradiso* 25.1 and 23.62), the relevant 'holiness' need not
derive from its forays into theology nor from its concern with
the hermeneutic kinship between Scriptures and poems, because

his being. The fluctuant physicality of the poem is at its height here in the Latinizing pun by which 'spirito' means 'breath', though that materializing of the word which has till now meant 'spirit' is overlain by a hinted relation between this emptying-out of Dante and the blood and water which poured from Christ's side on the cross, and which are in turn symbolized by the wine and water in the eucharistic chalice. The passage is inspired, but it also respires, like the earth itself coming out of shadow into spring. He becomes a river on its way to the sea.

The aqueous mobility of the *Commedia* does not cease in Paradise, though St John had envisioned heaven as the absence of sea (Revelation 21:1 – '*et mare iam non est*', 'and the sea now is no more'). The hieratic courtliness of heaven, as Dante had seen it pictured in the Ravenna mosaics, dissolves in his poem into a place without walls through which runs a river of gems, as if the mosaics had slid their fixings. Dante's heaven is not a relief from motion but a release into motion through absolutely resistless air. In Hell and Purgatory, he plods and scrambles in circles ('*giri*', '*gironi*') where the suffering are spun and buffeted by a motor force beyond themselves, but in Paradise '*girare*' changes from a transitive verb with more or less reluctant objects to a reflexive verb whose whirling is a voluntary, dervish ecstasy, so that, climactically, the three persons of the Trinity appear at *Paradiso* 33.116 as '*tre giri*' ('three circles', 'three spinnings'). For Dante, self-consciousness is gyroscopic in the image of its maker (*Purgatorio* 25.70–75), and heaven is non-stop. Caroline Walker Bynum has stressed how distinct this Dantescan heaven is from the conclusions of many scholastic theologians;[142] there is, on the other hand, a continuity between the poet's temperament and the work of those anonymous designers who placed geometric, whorling labyrinths on the floors or façades of churches which were destinations for pilgrimage,[143] so that the pilgrim, having at last arrived, could trace again the process of journeying, composed and refreshed.

The *Commedia*, like a pilgrim, has at least two destinations, two senses of 'arrival'. A pilgrim begins by exiling himself from his familiar land and travels to a distant sanctuary; the shrine

Hell appear blurred. / You could step across or shake hands.'[141]
He expresses this sense most pervasively in the liquidity of his
poem, its patterns through which words arise and relocate, as
if in the cycle through which water evaporates, is convected,
condenses and precipitates anew (he would certainly have put
'El Niño' in the poem, had he known of it). The human climax
of the poem's story comes when he himself melts:

> Sí come neve tra le vive travi
>   per lo dosso d'Italia si congela,
>   soffiata e stretta da li venti schiavi,
> poi, liquefatta, in sé stessa trapela,
>   pur che la terra che perde ombra spiri,
>   sí che par foco fonder la candela . . .
> lo gel che m'era intorno al cor ristretto,
>   spirito e acqua fessi, e con angoscia
>   de la bocca e de li occhi uscí del petto.
>   (Purgatorio 30.85–90, 97–9)

[Just as snow between the living beams along the spine of Italy
is frozen, blown and made dense by the winds from Slavonia,
then, liquefied, seeps back into itself, merely because the land,
coming out of shadow, is breathing, so that it seems as if a fire
were melting a candle . . . the ice which was condensed around
my heart was made breath and water, and with anguish it came
out through my mouth and my eyes from my breast.]

What frees him up is the compassion the blessed feel for him
under Beatrice's deserved rebuke, a compassion he maps on to
the vast interactions of the globe, as he charts his journey
towards the word 'compatire', occurring uniquely at Purgatorio
30.95 ('lor compatire a me', 'their suffering with me'), a journey
which began in the moment when the Virgin Mary wept for
and with him and sent Beatrice to commission Virgil as his
guide ('si compiange', Inferno 3.94 – also the unique occurrence
of the word in the poem). The Apennines become his ribcage,
his outpouring of contrition the thaw and consequent flood
which irrigates the entire, fractured land of Italy, where he has

> E 'n la sua volontade è nostra pace:
> ell'è qual mare al qual tutto si move
> ciò ch'ella cria o che natura face. (*Paradiso* 3.85–7)

[In His will is our peace; that will is the sea into which all things move, both the things it wills directly and those which nature brings about.]

In that first line, Piccarda may be quoting Saint Augustine, '*in bona voluntate tua pax nobis est*' ['in Your good will is our peace'],[138] but she also sounds like Francesca, who started the notion in the poem that to reach the sea is to find peace, a notion which Piccarda completes by identifying the sea with God's will. The first time we heard of someone '*grazioso*' in the *Commedia* was when Francesca thus complimented Dante; the word's last occurrence comes from Dante at *Paradiso* 3.40, praying Piccarda to do him the kindness ('*grazioso mi fia*') of telling him her name, of becoming for him an individual among the many faces in the moon, as Francesca had become in her more troubled state. Between these two widely separated women, the poem has been awash with water of all kinds. God's will is the sea, according to Piccarda; the empirical manifestations of that will, whether punitive or gracious, are, according to Dante, rain with its differential fall (*Paradiso* 3.90) which spreads out into the poem's vast array of water features – more than fifty rivers (not counting legendary ones), lakes and fountains.[139] And this is because water was the best means of transport in Dante's world, because of 'the centrality of the sea to communications. Despite the obvious dangers, sea transport so far surpassed land communications in ease as to make of the Mediterranean a milieu of interlocking routes on to which the coastlands and harbours faced ... The Mediterranean came indeed to be regarded as like a great river'.[140]

Dante has an ecological sense of the interdependence of God's desiring creatures, a sense such as runs along the patterns of interlace and mutually responsive line which draw together as well as demarcate damned and saved on Romanesque façades, so that 'the many barbed divisions / between Purgatory and

cohere perceptibly, as all creation does inscrutably in God's mind, if God may be said to have a mind.

Thus the cranes which set out in file across the winter skies of *Inferno* 5 don't come to rest until *Purgatorio* 26: they have flown from the circle of the damned carnal sinners to the terrace of the saved carnal sinners. Migratory birds appear in the two *canti* because their homing instincts model the sexual instincts of human beings, both massive forces of orientation on the earth, and because these birds have two homes and find their way between them, unlike Paolo and Francesca, who went astray. Dante is silenced by Francesca's story of how they loved each other; he keeps his head so low so long that Virgil says to him at *Inferno* 5.111 '*Che pense?*' ('What's on your mind?'). Dante is silenced again when Beatrice tells the assembled blessed the story of his infidelities to her memory; she is less patient than Virgil and waits only a moment before snapping '*Che pense?*' (*Purgatorio* 31.10). The analogies between the two silences and the two prompts may acknowledge Dante's closeness to Francesca's sin, though he has travelled far from her circle of incessant storm to the mountain garden where a second woman ties his tongue. Once again, it is the fact of span, and the activity of comparison which measures the span, that matter, for it is interconnection that should be learned here, not antithesis; the poem is a pilgrimage, and 'in pilgrimage . . . the journey is not just a means to an end: pilgrimage makes sacred the whole realm of travel and communications and even the notion of geography itself'.[137]

So too it is peregrination which takes us from Francesca's Ravenna in *Inferno* 5.98–9 – '*la marina dove 'l Po discende / per aver pace co' seguaci sui*' ['the shore to which the river Po descends / in search of peace with all his tributaries'] – along the trembling shores of Purgatory ('*il tremolar de la marina*', *Purgatorio* 1.117) to the sphere of the moon, again to a woman speaking in the first person plural (though with a different extension in her 'we'), the first of the blessed whom we meet in *Paradiso* as Francesca was first in *Inferno*, Piccarda Donati and her lines:

recognizes that he is '*grazioso*', a word which carries both the sense that he is attractive and that he is favoured by God; she attributes goodwill to him ('*benigno*') and regrets she cannot do him the favour of prayer because she is cut off from God. Contrast the greeting he and Virgil get from the last damned soul who speaks to them:

> E un de' tristi de la fredda crosta
> gridò a noi: 'O anime crudeli
> tanto che data v'è l'ultima posta,
> levatemi dal viso i duri veli . . .'
> (*Inferno* 33.109–12)

[And one of the wretches on the frozen crust shouted at us: 'O souls who must be cruel to have been given this lowest placement, take the hard veils from my face . . .']

Paolo and Francesca had come at Dante's call because they responded to the affection in his shout to them ('*affetuoso grido*', *Inferno* 5.87), but there was no kindliness when Frate Alberigo shouted at the poets ('*gridò*'): he cannot tell that one of them is physically alive and the other not, they are both '*anime*' to him; he projects his own damnable cruelty on to them ('*crudeli*'), assuming they have both been assigned to his circle, when neither of them has; he insults them and then demands a service. From the female laywoman who first speaks through to the male member of a religious order who speaks last, the symmetrical contrasts are evident, though assigning values to these symmetries is not straightforward. It seems fair to say she comes better out of the comparison, as might be expected given that she is not so low down in Hell, but how there can be degrees of absolute separation from God is not made any clearer by the sharpness of these contrasts. Moralistic totting-up of 'good points' and 'bad points' for particular figures is not the poem's aim in such characteristic arrangements of coincidence across vast spans; rather the *Commedia* is composed to give a sense of the mystical interconnectivity between such distinct fates, so that the details of the poem

('spirits', 'carnal sinners', 'starlings', 'bad spirits', 'cranes',
'these peoples') (*Inferno* 5.32, 38, 40, 42, 46, 50–51). At
Dante's request, Virgil picks out some classical celebrities from
this crowd:

> *più di mille*
> *ombre mostrommi e nominommi a dito*
> (*Inferno* 5.67–8)

[more than a thousand shades he then showed me, pointing them
out with his finger and naming them]

The thick, phonemic jostling of these lines ('*mi . . . om . . . mo
. . . om . . . mi . . . om . . . mi . . . om . . . mi*') highlights the
swarming multiplicity which Virgil enumerates, but Dante
passes on to his reader only seven of these identifications. His
eye has been caught not by the plethora nor by the legendary
individuals whom Virgil names but by a *pair* ('*quei due*'), one
of whom Dante will, forty-two lines later, call by name,
'*Francesca*', the first of the damned whom he recognizes, as if
picking a woman he knows out on a crowded street, as he
himself in turn will be at long last called by name, individuated,
by Beatrice. Sorting the sinners under categories of sin takes
Minos almost no time, just the one rapidly eliding line ('*dicono^*
e^ odono^, e poi son giú volte', 'they speak, they hear, and
then are turned downwards', *Inferno* 5.15). Meeting a sinner,
though – seeing the individual, as Dante does, *through* the
classification – takes longer, costs more, even the kind of death
which seizes him at the end of the canto. From Virgil's great
exempla to Dante's unhappy couple, the poem leaps more than
a thousand years and also moves from the world renown of
Troy and Rome to a 'human interest' story of the 1280s in a
petty state on the Adriatic, a story which so few people had
taken an interest in that no record of it has been found before
Dante has Francesca tell it.

Hers are the first words a damned soul addresses to him; she
notices his physicality, '*O animal*', his being the kind of creature
who is susceptible to the power of instinct over reason; she

take-up of that '*per me*' over the gate of Hell (*Inferno* 3.1), '*Per me si va nella città dolente*' ['Through me is the entrance to the city of lamentation'], until the sad exclusiveness relents a little when, at *Purgatorio* 22.73, Statius varies '*per me*' in his rush of gratitude to Virgil for what Virgil did for him: '*Per te poeta fui, per te cristiano*' ['Through you I became a poet, through you a Christian']. It is only right that Dante remembered what he owed the earlier poet, and the pagan culture embodied in him, by the way the *Commedia* weaves its own presents into its pasts – here across fifty-three cantos from *Purgatorio* 22 back to *Inferno* 3 – in a long sequence of acts of adhesion.

Dante's love for Virgil is but one, though prime, case of his central concern with '*eros*, natural love, as related to the love of God'.[136] More special pleading than attentive reading has been devoted to this topic, particularly as concerns the episode of Paolo and Francesca, the first of the damned to recognize Dante as among their friends. Leigh Hunt's name leads the list of those who have sugar-coated the lines in their translations; repelled by such Disneyfications, sterner commentators have pored over the episode for clues that Francesca is not as sweet as she sounds. It is supposed that any tenderness in Dante for the damned he meets must imply a more or less articulate dissent from the Church's moral teachings, a dissent which some translators would welcome and others dread. No such implication holds, because of the well-known proviso that God loves sinners but not their sins; there is no reason why Dante, in his measure, should not do the same. These ethical partisan-ships in readers of *Inferno* 5 also suffer from disobeying Virgil's rule of interpretation – 'don't just keep your mind fixed on one place' – and from a consequent neglect of the architectonic interrelations, the thrusts and counterweights, in which Dante places the lost pair.

Inferno 5 begins with the demon Minos, who has no difficulty singling out individuals for appropriate punishment from the dense multitude who pass before him: they are '*molte*' ('many') but he recognizes '*ciascuna*' ('each one') (*Inferno* 5.13–14). Then plurals stream into the lines – '*li spiriti*', '*i peccator carnali*', '*li stornei*', '*li spiriti mali*', '*i gru*', '*quelle / genti*'

> *Com'io divenni allor gelato e fioco,*
> *nol dimandar, lettor, ch'i' non lo scrivo,*
> *però ch'ogne parlar sarebbe poco.*
>   (*Inferno* 34.21–3)

[Don't ask me to tell you, reader, how chilled and faint I then became, because I'm not going to write that down, for anything I said would fall short.]

The state of being '*fioco*' might now be glossed as 'reduced in vitality because cowed by the sight of irreparable loss, of the disfigurement which has befallen as splendid a creature as the archangel once was'. Remembering that the pagan gods about whom Virgil wrote were considered by some medieval commentators to be devils, we could now think that his '*fioco*' appearance conveys the melancholy of cultural supersession; Virgil is a 'faded star' (like Lucifer), a literary 'old flame' about to gutter out through neglect till revived in Dante's admiration. '*Fioco*' last appears in the *Commedia* to express rapt inarticulacy at Dante's vision of the Trinity:

> *Oh quanto è corto il dire e come fioco*
> *al mio concetto!* (*Paradiso* 33.121–2)

[Oh how scant is speech and, as it were, faint to express my conception!]

Now it is not one variety of human discourse that has cast over time another in the shade and made it '*fioco*' but all human speech, specifically Dante's own, which pales in the divine light. The arch of '*fioco*' from the first to the last canto of the poem brings the two poets, divided as they are by the gulf between their creeds, together in a sense that all creeds are tenuous before the reality they try to grasp. There is an equal generosity in the arch Dante springs from Virgil's explanation at *Inferno* 1.126 that he will guide Dante through only the first two realms of the afterlife, because the emperor who reigns in Heaven '*non vuol che 'n sua città per me si vegna*' ['does not wish that entry should be made through me into his city'], across the grating world presses in on him, the day's wickedness perturbs him, the body of this death weighs him down, physical needs [*carnis necessitas*] distract him, the weakness of corruptibility lets him down, and, what is more forceful than any of these, he is called back by brotherly love [*fraterna revocat caritas*].[134]

St Bernard's words re-invoke themselves while they enact the visionary's return to this world, as his '*caritas*' remembers that it comes out of '*car[nis necess]itas*' ('physical needs'), a fellowship in weakness that is also, for writers such as Bernard or Dante, a fellowship in the Lord who said 'my strength is made perfect in weakness'.

V RETURNING AND TELLING

The *Commedia* remembers its own words, and the words of other writers, and integrates these memories into a cohesion of past and present lexical identities as, at a narrative level, it holds together earlier and later Dantes. Virgil stands in the poem for what Virgil in fact was: someone who wrote poetry before Dante but who had so entered into Dante's own writing as to become a past, a very past, self. When Dante first sees him and before he knows who the figure is, he sees '*dinanzi a li occhi . . . / chi per lungo silenzio parea fioco*' (*Inferno* 1.62–3), 'before my eyes . . . someone who on account of long silence seemed *fioco*' – the word is rich and exact and so hard to translate – it means both 'muffled, muted' (of sound) and 'faint, dim' (of light). Because Dante's lines tell us what was before his eyes, 'faint' seems the better choice, but because Virgil's state is the result of 'long silence', 'muted' might be preferred.[135] The synaesthesia of '*fioco*' corresponds to the fact that Dante knew Virgil through evoking a voice from manuscripts of his work, from that especial cooperation of eye and ear known as 'reading poetry'. Dante himself becomes '*fioco*' when he sees the fallen archangel, 'the creature who had been so fair of face':

had been through his vision: addressing his reader, he speaks
of the company of the blessed as

> *quel divoto*
> *triunfo per lo quale io piango spesso*
> *le mie peccata e 'l petto mi percuoto*
> (*Paradiso* 22.106–8)

[that devout exaltation for the sake of which I often bewail my
sins and beat my breast]

The present tenses of penitence ('*piango*', '*percuoto*') are not
vivid conventions of epic narrative: they state what is the case
as he is writing. He writes in the same state as he travelled in
his vision, neither '*poeta*' nor '*personaggio*' but '*peregrino*'
('pilgrim').

Shelley's 'returned to tell' remembers and translates the
moment in which Beatrice gave Dante the specifications for his
poem: he was to write down what he had seen when he had
'*ritornato di là*' ('returned back there', *Purgatorio* 32.105).
Returning to tell the story, Dante returns to human conditions
of speech, to his *volgare* and the self which grew up in that
speech. The *Commedia* itself is part of the fruit the vision bears
in the remainder of the poet's earthly life, as *À la recherche du
temps perdu* is itself a fruit of the learning process Proust goes
through in and for that novel, but it would be a banal error to
identify the *Commedia*'s splendours with supposed perfections
in the man who wrote it. Dante was aware that any vision
amounts to no more than a 'good day', and that a good life is
something more than an unbroken succession of good days, if
such a succession could be sustained. He intimates in many
ways this awareness of the evanescence of vision, for instance
by beginning his final canto with a prayer from St Bernard of
Clairvaux, an adept in raptures and so all the more conscious
that they fade and, indeed, must be relinquished:

And if it should happen that any mortal is rapt for a while or is,
as we put it, for a moment admitted to this union, at once the

spectacle of his own past, unschooled self with all its deplorable weaknesses (such as pity for those who suffer just punishment). But the way past and present bleed into each other through the poem's '*ancora*' suggests some continuity – to put it mildly – between the Dantes 'before', 'during' and 'after' the vision; there *has* to be such continuity for us to see the effect of the poem's process on him.

Shelley called Dante's poem

> the rhyme
>
> Of him whom from the lowest depths of Hell
> Through every Paradise & through all glory
> Love led serene, & who returned to tell
>
> In words of hate & awe the wondrous story
> How all things are transfigured, except Love[132]

Shelley is a better reader of the *Commedia*, and more ortho-dox about rapture, than extreme adherents of the *poeta/personaggio* distinction; his protracting syntax, throughout which Dante, whether passive ('him whom') or active ('& who'), retains his self-identity, is also better tuned in to the poem's nature. Dante writes, in the now of the narrating instance, 'words of hate & awe'; the *Commedia* ripples with unregenerate emotion, for Dante remains a 'spirit unappeased and peregrine'.[133] And then, even St Paul, who had a better class of vision than Dante claims for himself, was not purged of all defect by rapture – quite the contrary, his visions imperilled his humility: 'And lest I should be exalted above measure through the abundance of the revelations, there was given to me a thorn in the flesh, the messenger of Satan to buffet me, lest I should be exalted above measure. For this thing I besought the Lord thrice, that it might depart from me. And he said unto me, My grace is sufficient for thee: for my strength is made perfect in weakness.' (2 Corinthians 12:7–9; King James Bible) Dante himself knew how (at best) partially purged he

129. Compare Aquinas: 'Only in those who are travelling, whether in this life or in purgatory, can there be hope', quoted in Robert Ombres, *The Theology of Purgatory* (Dublin: Mercier Press, 1978), p. 83.

130. Mandelstam, *Complete Critical Prose*, p. 407.

131. St Augustine, *The Trinity*, ed. John E. Rotelle, trans. Edmund Hill (Brooklyn: New City Press, 1991), p. 271.

132. See 'The Triumph of Life' 401–547, in the anthology.

133. T. S. Eliot, *Little Gidding*, II.68, probably itself remembering the '*peregrino spirito*' of *Vita Nuova* 41.11, p. 245.

134. Watkin W. Williams (ed.), *De diligendo Deo* (Cambridge: Cambridge University Press, 1926), X.27, p. 48 (I have slightly modernized the text).

135. Virgil in *Inferno* 1 resembles the figure who appears '*scolorito e fioco*' ('colourless and faint') with news of Beatrice's death in *Vita Nuova* 23.54, p. 340, a passage which often pre-echoes the opening cantos of the *Commedia* and their version of '*smarrimento*' (*Vita Nuova*, 23.35, p. 339).

136. Foster, *The Two Dantes*, p. 37.

137. Peregrine Horden and Nicholas Purcell, *The Corrupting Sea: A Study of Mediterranean History* (Oxford: Blackwell, 2000), p. 446.

138. *Confessiones* 2.390.

139. For some of the *Commedia*'s varieties of rain, see: *Inferno* 6.19, 16.6, 30.95; *Purgatorio* 3.130, 12.42; *Paradiso* 25.78, 32.89.

140. Horden and Purcell, *The Corrupting Sea*, p. 11.

141. Geoffrey Hill, *The Orchards of Syon* (London: Penguin, 2002), LVII. A sculptural instance of this phenomenon can be seen on the tympanum of St Foy at Conques where in the very centre of the lowest register an angel and a demon, each marshalling his or her charges in the apt direction, at the structural cleft of the composition, turn their heads to look over their shoulders at each other; a richly detailed example in the *Commedia* comes in the symbiosis between the words of the lost Guido da Montefeltro (*Inferno* 27) and those of his son, Buonconte, who awaits purgation at *Purgatorio* 5.85–129.

142. See her *The Resurrection of the Body* (New York: Columbia University Press, 1995), p. 304: 'There [in the last cantos of the *Commedia*] Dante finds, not the *requies aeterna* – the stasis – of the scholastic theologians, but the great wheeling motion of love.'

143. As in the nave of Notre-Dame-de-Chartres or on the west front of San Martino in Lucca.

109. Quoted in Edmund Colledge and Bernard McGinn (eds. and trans.), *Meister Eckhart: The Essential Sermons, Commentaries, Treatises and Defence* (Mahwah, NJ: Paulist Press, 1981), p. 61.

110. Villani, *Nuova Cronica*, vol. 2, p. 239.

111. For more on '*girare*' and its cognates, see the last section of this introduction.

112. See his *Medieval Civilization 400–1500* (1964), trans. Julia Burrow (Oxford: Basil Blackwell, 1988), p. 138.

113. Vito Fumagalli, *Landscapes of Fear: Perceptions of Nature and the City in the Middle Ages* (1984–90), trans. Shayne Mitchell (Cambridge: Polity Press, 1994), p. 7.

114. Gurevich, *Medieval Popular Culture*, p. 177.

115. Ibid., p. 176.

116. 'Finché l'assedio dura . . .' (1973), in Giorgio Zampa (ed.), *Il secondo mestiere: Arte, musica, società* (Milan: Mondadori, 1996), pp. 1,502–3.

117. Villani, *Nuova Cronica*, vol. 1, pp. 267–8.

118. Ibid., vol. 1, pp. 151–2.

119. *Antony and Cleopatra*, IV.xvi.42; I quote from Stanley Wells and Gary Taylor (eds.), *William Shakespeare: The Complete Works* (Oxford: Oxford University Press, 1986).

120. John White, *Arts and Architecture in Italy, 1250–1400* (3rd edn., New Haven: Yale University Press, 1993), p. 34.

121. Quoted in Shinners, *Medieval Popular Religion*, pp. 391–2.

122. Ferdinando Bernini (ed.), *Cronica* (2 vols., Bari: Laterza & Figli, 1942), vol. 2, pp. 146–7.

123. Geertz, *The Interpretation of Cultures*, p. 93.

124. (?) Dante, *Epistola* 13.72; I quote from Pier Vincenzo Mengaldo *et al.* (eds.), *Dante Alighieri: Opere Minori* (Milan: Riccardo Ricciardi, 1979), p. 636; the attribution of this letter to Dante is much debated. Two widely diverging, equally thought-provoking accounts of *terza rima* are John Freccero's 'The Significance of *Terza Rima*' in his *The Poetics of Conversion*, ch. 17, and Teodolinda Barolini's in her *The Undivine Comedy: Detheologizing Dante* (Princeton: Princeton University Press, 1992), ch. 2.

125. 'St Thomas and Dante', in his *The Two Dantes and Other Studies* (Berkeley: University of California Press, 1977), p. 57.

126. See her *Beast and Man: The Roots of Human Nature* (rev. edn, London: Routledge and Kegan Paul, 1995), p. 194.

127. Geoffrey Hill, 'Of Coming into Being and Passing Away', in his *Canaan* (Harmondsworth: Penguin, 1996), p. 4.

128. *Convivio* 2.12, p. 117 and 2.13, p. 129.

Dante's and Petrarch's versification, see Emilio Bigi, *Forme e significati nella 'Divina Commedia'* (Bologna: Capelli, 1981), pp. 33–8.

97. Preface to *Cromwell* (1827), in Jean Massin (ed.), *Oeuvres complètes* (16 vols., Paris: Le club français du livre, 1967–72), vol. 3, pp. 50, 54.

98. Pietro Bembo, *Prose della volgar lingua* (1525), as translated in Michael Caesar (ed.), *Dante: The Critical Heritage 1314(?)–1870* (London: Routledge and Kegan Paul, 1989), p. 236.

99. See the extract from his translation of della Casa in the anthology. Social changes may have affected this narrowing of lexical taste, at least as concerns '*scotto*'; the word may not have seemed so improper in the days when a 'priest kept a tavern' and 'beer could also be had at church premises'; I quote from Aron Gurevich, *Medieval Popular Culture: Problems of Belief and Perception* (1981) trans. J. A. Bak and P. A. Hollingsworth (Cambridge: Cambridge University Press, 1988), p. 79.

100. We point out many such ironings-out and starchings-up of Dante's vocabulary in our footnotes.

101. In an equally characteristic symmetry, Dante has '*spandere*' again, most benignly, when Beatrice again makes a sign to him to speak at *Paradiso* 24.56.

102. Aquinas, *Sententia libri Ethicorum* 2.2, as quoted in Davies, *The Thought of Thomas Aquinas*, p. 237; my claim about the application of rules relies on considerations Ludwig Wittgenstein (1889–1951) adduces throughout his later work, for example, in *Philosophical Investigations* trans. G. E. M. Anscombe (2nd edn, Oxford: Blackwell, 1958), Part I, §§198–202, 217–24 and 454.

103. *Poetics* 1451b5–10.

104. Erich Auerbach, *Dante, Poet of the Secular World* (1929) trans. Ralph Manheim (Chicago: University of Chicago Press, 1961), p. 15; we might feel the need to double his 'a thousand years'.

105. Larner, *Italy in the Age of Dante and Petrarch*, p. 192.

106. Quoted in G. R. Evans, *The Mind of St Bernard of Clairvaux* (Oxford: Oxford University Press, 1983), p. 115.

107. Giovanni Villani, *Nuova Cronica*, ed. Giuseppe Porta (3 vols., Parma: Ugo Guanda, 1990), vol. 2, p. 131.

108. Boccaccio, *Opere . . .*, pp. 608–9; Boccaccio claims that Dante overheard the words and went on his way '*sorridendo alquanto*' ['with a bit of a smile'].

in his *The Typological Problem in Dante: A Study in the History of Medieval Ideas* (Helsinki: Societas Scientiarum Fennica, 1958).

85. *Moralia in Job*, quoted in Bernard McGinn, *The Presence of God: A History of Western Christian Mysticism* (London: SCM Press, 1992–), vol. 2, p. 40.

86. *Confessiones* 12.31, 2.367.

87. Walter Map, *De nugis curialium*, quoted and translated in Wakefield and Evans, *Heresies of the High Middle Ages*, p. 203.

88. I quote from *Confessiones* 1.277; 1.310; 2.12; 2.354.

89. *Sermones super Cantica Canticorum* 1, in J. Leclerq *et al.* (eds.), *S. Bernardi Opera* (6 vols., Rome: Editiones Cistercienses, 1957), vol. 1, p. 3.

90. Charles Kannengiesser, 'The Spiritual Message of the Great Fathers', in Bernard McGinn and John Meyendorff (eds.), *Christian Spirituality: Origins to the Twelfth Century* (London: SCM Press, 1986), p. 82. André Vauchez identifies a similar transformation of written style when St Francis 'bridged the gulf which separated lay and clerical cultures, treating Latin as if it were a living language', in his *La spiritualité du Moyen Âge occidental*, p. 138.

91. *Confessiones* 1.284.

92. *European Literature and the Latin Middle Ages* (1948) trans. Willard R. Trask (London: Routledge and Kegan Paul, 1953), p. 408.

93. *Literary Language and its Public in Late Latin Antiquity and in the Middle Ages* (1958) trans. Ralph Manheim (London: Routledge and Kegan Paul, 1965), p. 40.

94. See his *The Land of Hunger* (1978) trans. Tania Croft-Murray (Cambridge: Polity Press, 1996), p. 1.

95. 'Curds and Whey' (1928), in John Haffenden (ed.), *Argufying* (London: Chatto and Windus, 1987), p. 69.

96. Another time warp through which English translators came at Dante results from the fact that many of them heard him through ears accustomed to Petrarch's smoother and more stolid way with the hendecasyllabic line. They found Dante rhythmically impetuous and unpredictable, much as Alexander Pope (1688–1744) found John Donne (1572–1631), whose satires he 'versified'. Dante got caught up in the squabbles and historical parochialism of eighteenth-century prosody, for which see Paul Fussell, *Theory of Prosody in 18th Century England* (New London: Connecticut College, 1954). On the contrast between

72. In a *rima equivoca*, the rhyme-words are identical but distinct in
     sense (as in English, for example, 'creeps' as a present tense
     verb and as a plural noun). The Dante of *De vulgari* ... 2.12
     considered such rhymes beneath the dignity of the high style.
     Other thought-provoking *rime equivoche* occur at *Inferno* 3.8–
     10 on '*duro*' (the difficulty of understanding why Hell is eternal);
     Inferno 7.121–3 on '*fummo*' (the relation between states of the
     soul before and after death); and *Inferno* 34.76–81 on '*anche*'
     (for a moment of narrative suspense).

73. I found this magnificent phrase in Brian Davies, *The Thought of
     Thomas Aquinas* (Oxford: Oxford University Press, 1992),
     p. 316; it comes from *Summa Theologiae* 3a.15.10.

74. *Breviloquium*, Prologue, 5, in *Doctoris Seraphici S. Bona-
     venturae Opera Omnia* (11 vols., Quaracchi: Typographia
     Collegii S. Bonaventurae, 1882–), vol. 5, p. 207.

75. I take all these phrases from Jeremy Tambling's introduction to
     Dante (Harlow: Longman, 1999), pp. 4 and 7; they do not all
     represent Tambling's own views.

76. I translate from his *L'amour des lettres et le désir de Dieu:
     initiation aux auteurs monastiques du Moyen Âge* (1957; third
     edn, Paris: Éditions du Cerf, 1990), p. 177.

77. In the rough notes for the 'Conversation about Dante', in *Com-
     plete Critical Prose*, p. 451.

78. I refer to *Confessiones* 7.19 in the Loeb edition (2 vols.; repr.,
     Cambridge, Mass.: Harvard University Press, 1995), vol. 1,
     p. 392.

79. *Later Medieval Philosophy 1150–1350: An Introduction*
     (London: Routledge and Kegan Paul, 1987), p. 14.

80. *Convivio* 1.5, p. 23; compare the account of human physical
     perfection in terms of responsiveness at *Convivio* 3.8, p. 195.

81. Kleinhenz, 'Dante and the Bible', 89–90.

82. Harry Y. Gamble, *Books and Readers in the Early Church* (New
     Haven: Yale University Press, 1995), p. 107.

83. See Henri de Lubac, *Exégèse médiévale* (1959), trans. as *Medi-
     eval Exegesis* by Mark Sebanc and E. M. Macierowski (2 vols.,
     Grand Rapids: William B. Eerdmans, 1998–), vol. 1, p. 247.

84. De Lubac gives the best guide to this complex matter in the
     preface, introduction and first chapter of *Medieval Exegesis*, but
     see also A. J. Minnis and A. B. Scott (eds.), *Medieval Literary
     Theory and Criticism, c.1100–c.1375* (Oxford: Oxford Univer-
     sity Press, 1988), especially chapters 3, 6 and 9. Johan Chydenius
     discusses Dante's relation to the varieties of allegorical tradition

able exception to scholarly tradition about this matter, pointing out that 'this presence of a body on this journey of the mind marks Dante's poetic originality', in his *Dante: The Poetics of Conversion*, ed. Rachel Jacoff (Cambridge, Mass.: Harvard University Press, 1986), p. 33.

57. *The Mystical Theology* 1045D–1048A, in Colm Luibhed and Paul Rorem (ed. and trans.), *Pseudo-Dionysius: The Complete Works* (New York: Paulist Press, 1987), p. 106.

58. *The Divine Names* 865C, in Luibhed and Rorem, *Pseudo-Dionysius*, p. 106.

59. Franco Gori (ed.), *Enarrationes in Psalmos* (3 vols., Vienna: Österreichischen Akademie der Wissenschaften, 2001), vol. 3, pp. 283–4.

60. Recall that, when speaking of secular culture in the *Convivio*, Dante had characterized Latin as *'perpetuo e non corruttibile'* but, in the religious ambit of the *Commedia*, not even Virgil's Latin can render Aeneas anything but *'corruttibile'*.

61. Some readers may find it helpful to compare the 'now you see it, now you don't' oscillations of the poem with Derrida's employment of concepts *'sous rature'*; Kevin Hart points out similarities between 'negative theology' and Derrida's procedures in his *The Trespass of the Sign: Deconstruction, Theology and Philosophy* (Cambridge: Cambridge University Press, 1989).

62. 'Dante' (1929), repr. in *Selected Essays* (third edn, London: Faber and Faber, 1951), p. 250.

63. See his diffusely Dantescan *The Changing Light at Sandover* (1976–82; one-vol. edn, New York: Alfred Knopf, 1992), p. 16.

64. See Heaney's 'Ugolino' in the anthology.

65. See Rossetti's 'The Blessed Damozel' in the anthology.

66. See Pound's '[From a Notebook]' in the anthology.

67. *The Spirit of Romance* (1910; repr. New York: New Directions, 1968), p. 128.

68. This is the version of *Inferno* 5.9 given in *The Spirit of Romance*, p. 130.

69. Respectively, Cantos XIV.57, 70, 73, 83; XV.2, 19, 34, 39, 55, 57.

70. In the 'Addenda' to his incomparable 'Conversation about Dante', from the text of Jane Gary Harris (ed.), *Mandelstam: The Complete Critical Prose and Letters* (Ann Arbor: Ardis, 1979), p. 446.

71. See his *The Interpretation of Cultures* (1973; repr. London: Fontana Press, 1993), p. 120.

40. *De vulgari* . . . 1.9, p. 20.
41. *Convivio* 1.5, p. 21.
42. *Purgatorio* 2.58 ('the new people' or 'the renewed/refreshed people').
43. I quote Botterill's translation, though I have restored Dante's authorial 'we', which Botterill throughout replaces with an 'I'.
44. I quote from Prue Shaw's edition of the Latin text (Cambridge: Cambridge University Press, 1995), referring to book, section and page number, thus here: 1.1, p. 2; though much in debt to Shaw's translation, the English version here is my own.
45. *Convivio* 1.1, p. 1.
46. Botterill's translation of *De vulgari* . . . 1.1, p. 3 and 1.9, p. 19. Dante's very late (1320) treatise, *Quaestio de aqua et terra*, partly supports and partly eludes my generalization.
47. Dante never referred to his poem as '*divina*'.
48. Dante himself calls Virgil '*divinus poeta noster Virgilius*' ['our own divine poet, Virgil'] in *De monarchia* 2.3, p. 52, where the word can have no implication of Christian orthodoxy, just as '*sacrato*' in Dante's description of the *Commedia* as '*lo sacrato poema*' (*Paradiso* 23.62) probably does not entail the specifically Christian 'sacredness' which some commentators have understood by the phrase, because Dante elsewhere uses the superlative of the word in contexts where it can mean little more than 'extremely venerable', as in the *Convivio*'s outburst of enthusiasm for Cato's '*sacratissimo petto*' ['most estimable breast'] (*Convivio* 4.5, p. 288) or the similar praise of the Decii as '*sacratissime victime*' ['victims who should be highly revered'] in *De monarchia* 2.5, p. 66.
49. Boccaccio, *Opere* . . ., pp. 634 and 647.
50. *Convivio* 4.12, p. 339.
51. *Purgatorio* 25.20–21 and 28–9.
52. *Xenia* 1.13, in *L'opera in versi* (Turin: Einaudi, 1980), p. 293.
53. August Wilhelm von Schlegel (1767–1845), 'Über Zeichnungen', quoted in Ralph Pite, *The Circle of our Vision: Dante's Presence in English Romantic Poetry* (Oxford: Oxford University Press, 1994), pp. 55–6.
54. *De vulgari* . . . 1.9, p. 20.
55. The phrase is from *De vulgari* . . . 2.4, p. 58; Botterill convincingly notes (p. 98) 'the adjective *astripetus* (*astra* "the stars" + *petere*, "to seek") appears to be Dante's own coinage'.
56. See for Augustine *Confessiones* 5.10–6.4 or for Aquinas *Summa Theologiae* 1a.75.6 ad.3 or 1a.98.2. John Freccero is an honour-

and *'greggia'* ['mummy', 'daddy', 'flock']; contrast *Inferno* 32.9, *Purgatorio* 24.73, *Paradiso* 10.94 or 14.64; all references to the *De vulgari* . . . are to the edition of Steven Botterill (Cambridge: Cambridge University Press, 1996) and are given by book and section number followed by the relevant page number; thus in this case: 2.7, p. 66.

23. I translate from his *Teoria e prassi della versificazione* (Bologna: Il Mulino, 1976), p. 98, though di Girolamo is not responsible for the expressive purpose I assign to the rhythmic fact he describes. *'Dialefe'* means the keeping-apart of a terminal and initial vowel which could glide together, *'sinalefe'* the fusion of such vowels; the terms refer to the potential for diphthongs between Italian words where in English we recognize diphthongs mostly only within words (hence our lack of translations for *dialefe* and *sinalefe*).

24. The quotations are from *Inferno* 5.85, 88–90, 97 and 135.

25. *De vulgari* . . . 1.13, pp. 31–2.

26. *Convivio* 4.12, p. 338.

27. The clipped *'a ca'* for *'a casa'* is another touch of reminiscent dialect. Note how rapidly in *De vulgari* . . . 1.6–7, p. 13 Dante moves from his own exile from Florence to humanity's exile from Eden.

28. I quote the literal translation of her 'Dante' which Rachel Polonsky kindly gave me.

29. I quote from the edition of Domenico de Robertis (Milan: Riccardo Ricciardi, 1980), p. 240.

30. *Convivio* 1.12, p. 53.

31. *Convivio* 1.13, p. 57.

32. Donald Davie, *Pound* (London: Fontana, 1975), p. 58.

33. W. W. Skeat (ed.), *The Vision of William concerning Piers the Plowman* . . ., Text B (Oxford: Oxford University Press, 1869), 15.23–28 (modernized).

34. *Home and Exile* (Oxford: Oxford University Press, 2000), p. 79.

35. See respectively: Hamilton, *Religion in the Medieval West*, p. 97; Walter L. Wakefield and Austin P. Evans (eds.), *Heresies of the High Middle Ages* (New York: Columbia University Press, 1969), p. 73; Jaroslav Pelikan, *The Illustrated Jesus Through the Centuries* (New Haven: Yale University Press, 1997), p. 38.

36. Both quotations are from *Convivio* 1.5, pp. 21 and 22–3.

37. *Convivio* 1.6, p. 25.

38. *De vulgari* . . . 1.9, p. 20.

39. Compare *De vulgari* . . . 1.9, p. 21 and *Convivio* 1.5, p. 22.

higher for Dante's Florence, though it is unlikely to have been as high as the 40 per cent which the Florentine chronicler Villani sometimes boastfully claims.

11. See his 'Dante and the Bible: Biblical Citation in the *Divine Comedy*', in Amilcare A. Ianucci (ed.), *Dante: Contemporary Perspectives* (Toronto: University of Toronto Press, 1997), p. 75.

12. Quoted in John Larner, *Italy in the Age of Dante and Petrarch 1216–1380* (London: Longman, 1980), p. 244.

13. See André Vauchez, *La spiritualité du Moyen Âge occidental* (2nd edn, Paris: Éditions du Seuil, 1994), p. 166.

14. William of Pagula (1323), quoted in John Shinners (ed.), *Medieval Popular Religion 1000–1500* (Peterborough, Ontario: Broadview Press, 1997), p. 17.

15. See, respectively: Jean-Claude Schmitt, *The Holy Greyhound: Guinefort, Healer of Children since the Thirteenth Century*, trans. Martin Thom (Cambridge: Cambridge University Press, 1982); Emmanuel Le Roy Ladurie, *Montaillou* (1978) trans. Barbara Bray (Harmondsworth: Penguin, 1990), p. 290; André Vauchez, *The Laity in the Middle Ages: Religious Beliefs and Devotional Practices* (1987) trans. Margery J. Schneider (South Bend, Indiana: University of Notre Dame Press, 1993), p. 6.

16. Carlo Ginzburg, *The Cheese and the Worms* (1976) trans. John and Anne Tedeschi (London: Routledge and Kegan Paul, 1980), p. 63.

17. T. S. Eliot, 'A Note on Poetry and Belief', *The Enemy*, January 1927.

18. Consider Mary Midgley's penetrating accounts of what she mildly calls 'the kinds of thought that can go on in the wide areas that lie outside both official science and official religion' in *Evolution as a Religion* (rev. edn, London: Routledge, 2002), p. viii.

19. *Religion in the Medieval West* (London: Edward Arnold, 1986), p. 11.

20. I translate from *Convivio* 1.12 in the edition of Franca Brambilla Ageno (Florence: Le Lettere, 1995). All further references to this work are to this edition and are given by treatise and section number followed by the relevant page number; thus in this case: 1.12, p. 51.

21. *Convivio* 1.13, p. 57 – '*concorso alla mia generazione*': he is thinking of his parents' pillow-talk.

22. *De vulgari eloquentia* rejects among others '*mamma*', '*babbo*'

in new, even alien, settings, and each translator can hope to return to the poem some of its native freshness as it, in its turn, gave for a while to Christianity again the aspect of a dawn.[157]

NOTES

1. Samuel Beckett (1906–89), *More Pricks than Kicks* (1934; repr. London: Calder and Boyars, 1973), p. 18.

2. Rosemary Horrox (ed.), *The Black Death* (Manchester: Manchester University Press, 1994), p. 3.

3. *Epic Romance: Homer to Milton* (Oxford: Clarendon Press, 1993), p. 47.

4. *Paradise Lost: a Poem written in Ten Books* (1667; repr. Menston: Scolar Press, 1972), 9.989–1001.

5. 'Sulla scia di Stravinskij', in Giorgio Zampa (ed.), *Il secondo mestiere: Arte, musica, società* (Milan: Arnaldo Mondadori, 1996), pp. 410–11; the translation, as throughout this introduction except where otherwise noted, is mine.

6. *Texts for Nothing*, 9 (in French, 1954; translated by the author, 1967), repr. in *Collected Shorter Prose 1945–1980* (London: John Calder, 1986), p. 103. Dante would not have said the body was 'a minor point', as Beckett well knew.

7. *De origine, vita, studiis et moribus viri clarissimi Dantis Aligerii florentini . . .*, in Giovanni Boccaccio (1313–75), *Opere . . .*, ed. Pier Giorgio Ricci (Milan: Riccardo Ricciardi, 1965), p. 637. Boccaccio's account has been doubted by many scholars.

8. See Giuseppe Scalia, 'Dante tradotto in latino', in Enzo Esposito (ed.), *L'opere di Dante nel mondo* (Ravenna: Longo, 1992), pp. 281–7.

9. Boccaccio, *Opere . . .*, p. 636. The immensely consequential relations of Latin and the European vernaculars, particularly as they concern the teaching responsibilities of the Church, are at work here, long before Luther; see Brian Stock's *The Implications of Literacy: Written Language and Models of Interpretation in the Eleventh and Twelfth Centuries* (Princeton: Princeton University Press, 1983), especially his comment that terms such as '*idiotae*' 'contain a double set of values at once recognizing the cultural norms associated with literacy but justifying the sacred simplicity of the illiterate' (p. 27).

10. The percentage for a basic, vernacular literacy may have been

remorse and its scaly fascinations. Many features of his writing show the change: the word '*frate*' ('brother'), for example, which in *Inferno* often sounds formulaic or sarcastically deferential to clerics, becomes genuinely fraternal; other people call Dante their 'brother' and mean it. Hell and the self it enclosed melt, not under Beatrice's rebukes but through the compassion of the blessed – 'with contrition with him, with compassion on him' as Dame Julian said – who surround him, to whom he is joined in his tears: '*peccata mea tamquam glaciem solvisti*' ('you melted away my sins like ice').[156] Augustine's '*solvisti*' is a form of one of the semantically richest Latin verbs – to set free (in a physical sense, from fetters or prison), to set sail, to dissolve an object from what holds it together, to let your hair down, to change into rain, to stream with tears, to absolve, to clear a debt, to cancel the obligation of suffering. Dante had contemptuously steeled himself against the notion that a little cash flow was an acceptable way back to Florence ('*pecuniam suam solvat*') but it is to a form of the same verb, *in volgare*, that he turns for the most humanly ecstatic lines of his poem, as Beatrice opens herself out beyond what he can say:

> *tentando a render te qual tu paresti*
> *là dove armonizzando il ciel t'adombra*
> *quando ne l'aere aperto ti solvesti.*
> (*Purgatorio* 31.143–5)

[trying to render you as you appeared there where the sky in tune shows you forth when into the open air you released yourself.]

It is impossible to replicate the end of *Purgatorio* 31 in English. Only in Italian can we hear how these words are a zenith of eloquence, reintegrating the spectrum of Dante's loves in the light of the beloved figure, *gramatica* herself, responsive and unveiled. And are, at the same time, by the same token, the sound of a child learning the phonemes of his mother-tongue ('*te* ... *ta* ... *te* ... *tu* ... *ti* ... *ta* ... *to* ... *ti* ... *ti*'). Yet because the *Commedia* is a ritual action with 'material results, such as healing', it can be and has actually been re-performed

have done, 'You've gone too far this time'. God, unlike our fellow creatures, must be supposed always to mean what he says. The depths of this state, when the self encounters itself as irreparable, are figured by a mirror of ice, in Dante's master-piece as in the edifying fables collected by Franciscans while he was a child, the *Gesta Romanorum*, which advise us to 'guard our hearts' against 'snow and ice unthawed – crystal, that reflects the awakened and agonized conscience'.[154]

All the sins we encounter in *Inferno* are Dante's, just as he speaks for and through each sinner. Not in that he committed each of these sins, nor in that he dreamed up all the individuals from within himself, but in that he was pierced with that sense of human solidarity which is expressed in the doctrine of 'origi-nal sin' (or in Marx's concept of 'species-being') by virtue of which nothing human is alien to any human and we are known even as we know. Dante is close to Dame Julian of Norwich in his apprehension of the perils of righteousness, whether turned against others or on the self:

> The soule that will be in rest, whan other mannys synne commith [to mynde], he shall fleen it as the peyne of helle, seking into God for remedy, for helpe [agayne] it; for the beholdying of other mannys synnes, it makith as it were a thick myst aforne the eye of the soule, and we may not for the tyme se the fairhede of God, but if we may beholden hem with contrition with him, with compassion on him and with holy desire to God for hem; for withouten this it noyeth and tempestith and lettith the soule that beholdith them . . .[155]

What Dame Julian means by the 'thick myst' which prevents the exacerbated soul from seeing 'the fairhede of God' is expressed by Dante through the fact that in his hell you cannot see the stars.

The air clears as he climbs the purgatorial steeps (there are not only stars to be seen again but fresh, antipodean stars he's never seen before). He issues from the lonely entrapment of conscience despairing over itself into the company of other penitents; only now does contrition begin to loosen the hold of

Further Reading

DANTE'S WRITINGS

An authoritative text of the *Commedia* is established in Giorgio Petrocchi, *La Commedia secondo l'antica vulgata* (4 vols., 2nd edn, Florence: Le Lettere, 1994). Useful annotation can be found in Natalino Sapegno, *La Divina Commedia* (3 vols., rev. edn, Florence: La Nuova Italia, 1985). For readers who need the assistance of a translation, there are facing-page editions of the poem: John Sinclair, *The Divine Comedy of Dante Alighieri* (3 vols., rev. edn, Oxford: Oxford University Press, 1971); and Charles Singleton: *The Divine Comedy* (3 vols., rev. edn, Princeton, NJ: Princeton University Press, 1989).

Christopher Ryan (trans.), *The Banquet* [*Convivio*] (Saratoga: Anma Libri, 1989).

Steven Botterill (ed. and trans.), *De vulgari eloquentia* [facing-page Latin/English] Cambridge: Cambridge University Press, 1996).

Prue Shaw (ed. and trans.), *Monarchia* [facing-page Latin/English] (Cambridge: Cambridge University Press, 1995).

Dino S. Cervigni and Edward Vasta (trans.), *Vita Nuova* (Notre Dame, Ind.: University of Notre Dame Press, 1995).

144. Four of the *Commedia*'s nine references to pilgrimage hinge on the return journey: *Purgatorio* 8.4ff. and 27.110; *Paradiso* 1.51 and here. There is, of course, no reference to peregrination in *Inferno*.

145. Annie Shaver-Crandell and Paula Gerson, ed. and trans. from the *Codex Calixtinus*, Book 5 (London: Harvey Miller Publishers, 1995); I refer to pp. 82–86, 89, 69 and 73.

146. Preface to the paperback edition of Victor and Edith Turner, *Image and Pilgrimage in Christian Culture: Anthropological Perspectives* (New York: Columbia University Press, 1978), p. xiii.

147. *Liber Sancti Jacobi Codex Calixtinus*, transcribed by Klaus Herbers and Manuel Santos Noia (Santiago de Compostela: Xunta de Galicia, 1998), pp. 241, 244, 246.

148. Victor and Edith Turner, *Image and Pilgrimage in Christian Culture*, pp. 33–4.

149. Ibid., p. 32.

150. Boccaccio, *Opere . . .*, p. 624.

151. I translate from Mengaldo *et al.*, *Dante Alighieri: Opere Minore*, p. 596.

152. From Rachel Polonsky's unpublished literal translation of Akhmatova's 'Dante'.

153. *Omnis utriusque sexus*, the twenty-first canon of the Fourth Lateran Council (1215), as quoted in Shinners, *Medieval Popular Religion*, p. 9.

154. Quoted ibid., p. 215.

155. *A Revelation of Love*, ed. Marion Glasscoe (Exeter: University of Exeter Press, 1993), p. 122.

156. St Augustine, *Confessiones* 2.7, vol. 1, p. 88.

157. Compare St Bernard of Clairvaux, *Sermones super Cantica Canticorum* 33: '*Erat ergo aurora, et ipsa suboscura satis, tota illa videlicet Christi conversatio super terram*' ['So Christ's whole experience on earth was a dawn, and a dim one at that'], in *S. Bernardi Opera*, vol. 1, p. 237.

Francis Fergusson, *Dante's Drama of the Mind: A Modern Reading of the* Purgatorio (Westport, Connecticut: Greenwood Press, 1953).

Kenelm Foster, *The Two Dantes and Other Studies* (Berkeley: University of California Press, 1977).

John Freccero, *Dante: The Poetics of Conversion*, ed. Rachel Jacoff (Cambridge, Mass.: Harvard University Press, 1986).

Étienne Gilson, *Dante the Philosopher*, trans. David Moore (London: Sheed and Ward, 1948).

Peter S. Hawkins, *Dante's Testaments: Essays in Scriptural Imagination* (Stanford, Calif.: Stanford University Press, 1999).

Robert Hollander, *Dante: A Life in Works* (New Haven: Yale University Press, 2001).

Rachel Jacoff (ed.), *The Cambridge Companion to Dante* (Cambridge: Cambridge University Press, 1993).

— and Jeffrey T. Schnapp (eds.), *The Poetry of Allusion: Virgil and Ovid in Dante's 'Commedia'* (Stanford, Calif.: Stanford University Press, 1991).

L. Jennaro-MacLennan, *The Trecento Commentaries on the Divina Commedia and The Epistle to Can Grande* (Oxford: Clarendon Press, 1974).

Robin Kirkpatrick, *Dante, The Divine Comedy* (Cambridge: Cambridge University Press, 1987).

—, *Dante's Inferno: Difficulty and Dead Poetry* (Cambridge: Cambridge University Press, 1987).

—, *Dante's Paradiso and the Limitations of Modern Criticism: A Study of Style and Poetic Theory* (Cambridge: Cambridge University Press, 1978).

Richard Lansing (ed.), *The Dante Encyclopaedia* (New York: Garland Books, 2000).

Uberto Limentani, *Dante's Comedy: Introductory Readings of Selected Cantos* (Cambridge: Cambridge University Press, 1985).

— (ed.), *The Mind of Dante* (Cambridge: Cambridge University Press, 1965).

Edward Moore, *Studies in Dante*, First, Second, Third and Fourth Series (Oxford: Clarendon Press, 1896–1917).

CRITICISM AND BIOGRAPHY

Peter Armour, *Dante's Griffin and the History of the World: A Study of the Earthly Paradise (*Purgatorio, *cantos xxix–xxxiii)* (Oxford: Clarendon Press, 1989).

—, *The Door of Purgatory: A Study of Multiple Symbolism in Dante's 'Purgatorio'* (Oxford: Clarendon Press, 1983).

Erich Auerbach, *Dante, Poet of the Secular World* (1929) trans. Ralph Manheim (Chicago: University of Chicago Press, 1961).

John C. Barnes and Cormac ó Cuilleanáin (eds.), *Dante and the Middle Ages* (Dublin: Irish Academic Press, 1995).

Teodolinda Barolini, *The Undivine Comedy: Detheologizing Dante* (Princeton: Princeton University Press, 1992).

Stephen Bemrose, *A New Life of Dante* (Exeter: University of Exeter Press, 2000).

Giovanni Boccaccio, *Life of Dante*, trans. J. G. Nichols (London: Hesperus Press, 2002).

Steven Botterill, *Dante and the Mystical Tradition* (Cambridge: Cambridge University Press, 1994).

Patrick Boyde, *Dante Philomythes and Philosopher: Man in the Cosmos* (Cambridge: Cambridge University Press, 1981).

—, *Dante's Style in his Lyric Poetry* (Cambridge: Cambridge University Press, 1971).

—, *Human Vices and Human Worth in Dante's* Comedy (Cambridge: Cambridge University Press, 2000).

—, *Perception and Passion in Dante's* Comedy (Cambridge: Cambridge University Press, 1993).

Antonio Cippico, Harold E. Goad, Edmund G. Gardner, W. P. Ker, Walter Seton (eds.), *Dante: Essays in Commemoration 1321–1921* (London: University of London Press, 1921).

Alison Cornish, *Reading Dante's Stars* (New Haven: Yale University Press, 2000).

Peter Dronke, *Dante and Medieval Latin Traditions* (Cambridge: Cambridge University Press, 1986).

spelling and punctuation practice among these disparate sources, and have mostly modernized only long ſ and u/v. We hope readers will bear with the resultant variations; they too are a small part of the many idiosyncrasies which Dante has met with in English.

A Note on the Text

All references to the *Commedia* are to the edition of Natalino Sapegno (3 vols., rev. edn, Florence: La Nuova Italia, 1985).

In the body of the anthology, we distinguish four broad categories of relation between Dante and English writers, as follows:

- where a passage translates or substantially derives from Dante, the relevant portion of the original is signalled in square brackets at the head of the passage (thus, in the case of our first extract from Chaucer: [*Inferno* 33.1–90])
- where a passage more freely imitates Dante, the relevant portion of the original is indicated in square brackets at the head of the passage but with a prefatory 'Compare' (thus, in the case of our first extract from Chaucer's *The House of Fame*: [Compare *Purgatorio* 9.19–33])
- where *parts* of a passage translate or substantially derive from Dante, the relevant portion of the original is signalled in the footnotes (thus, in the case of the extract from 'The Wife of Bath's Tale': 20–22 *Purgatorio* 7.121–3)
- where *parts* of a passage more freely imitate or allude to Dante, the relevant portion of the original is signalled in the footnotes but with a prefatory 'compare' (thus, in the case of the first extract from *The House of Fame*: 26–7 compare *Paradiso* 1.61–3)

The English texts in this anthology are drawn from many different kinds of source – manuscripts, early books, modern scholarly editions. We have not tried to produce consistency of

C. H. Sisson, 'On Translating Dante' in *The Divine Comedy: A new verse translation* (Manchester: Carcanet New Press, 1980).

James J. Wilhelm, *Dante and Pound: The Epic Of Judgement* (Orono, Maine: University of Maine Press, 1974).

—, 'Dante' (1929) (repr. in *Selected Essays*, 3rd edn, London: Faber and Faber, 1951).

—, 'What Dante Means to Me' (1950) in *To Criticize the Critic and other Writings* (London: Faber and Faber, 1965).

Steve Ellis, *Dante and English Poetry* (Cambridge: Cambridge University Press, 1983).

Giovanni Giovannini, *Ezra Pound and Dante* (Nijmegen, Utrecht: Dekker & Van de Vegt, 1961).

Seamus Heaney, *The Government of the Tongue* (London: Faber and Faber, 1988).

Stuart Y. McDougal (ed.), *Dante Among the Moderns* (Chapel Hill: University of North Carolina Press, 1985).

—, 'Dreaming a Renaissance: Pound's Dantean Inheritance' in George Bornstein (ed.), *Ezra Pound among the Poets* (Chicago: University of Chicago Press, 1985).

Peter Makin, *Bunting: The Shaping of His Verse* (Oxford: Clarendon Press, 1992).

Osip Mandelstam, 'Conversation about Dante' in *Mandelstam: The Complete Critical Prose and Letters*, ed. Jane Gary Harris (Ann Arbor: Ardis, 1979).

Dominic Manganiello, *T. S. Eliot and Dante* (London: Macmillan, 1989).

Alison Milbank, *Dante and the Victorians* (Manchester: Manchester University Press, 1998).

Akiko Miyake, *Ezra Pound and the Mysteries of Love* (Durham: Duke University Press, 1991).

Howard Nemerov, 'The Dream of Dante' in *Figures of Thought: Speculations on the Meaning of Poetry and Other Essays* (Boston: Godine, 1978).

Ezra Pound, 'Dante' in *The Spirit of Romance* (1910) (repr. New York: New Directions, 1968).

Barbara Reynolds, *The Passionate Intellect: Dorothy L. Sayers' Encounter with Dante* (Kent, Ohio: Kent State University Press, 1989).

Mary T. Reynolds, *Joyce and Dante: The Shaping Imagination* (Princeton, N. J.: Princeton University Press, 1981).

Dorothy L. Sayers, *Introductory Papers on Dante* (New York: Barnes and Noble, 1969).

1700–1832

J. Drummond Bone, 'On "Influence" and on Byron's and
Shelley's use of *Terza Rima* in 1819', *Keats–Shelley Memorial Bulletin* 4, 1981.

Steve Ellis, *Dante and English Poetry* (Cambridge: Cambridge
University Press, 1983).

R. W. King, *The Translator of Dante: The Life, Work and
Friendships of Henry Francis Cary (1772–1844)* (London:
M. Secker, 1925).

Milton Klonsky, *Blake's Dante: The Complete Illustrations to
the Divine Comedy* (New York: Harmony, 1980).

Ralph Pite, *The Circle of our Vision: Dante's Presence in English Romantic Poetry* (Oxford: Oxford University Press,
1994).

V. Tinkler-Villani, *Visions of Dante in English Poetry: Translations of the 'Commedia' from Jonathan Richardson to
William Blake* (Amsterdam: Rodopi, 1989).

Paget Toynbee, 'English Translations of Dante in the Eighteenth
Century' in *Dante Studies* (Oxford: Clarendon Press, 1921),
pp. 281–300.

Timothy Webb, *The Violet in the Crucible: Shelley and Translation* (Oxford: Clarendon Press, 1976).

Frances A. Yates, 'Transformations of Dante's Ugolino' in *Collected Essays* (3 vols., London: Routledge & Kegan Paul,
1982–), vol. 2.

1832–the present

D. Thomas Benediktson and Corinna del Greco Lobner (eds.),
Dante and Modernism, Lectura Dantis 12 (Charlottesville:
University of Virginia, 1993).

Dante, Ezra Pound and the Contemporary Poet, Agenda 34,
3–4, Autumn–Winter, 1996.

Robert Duncan, *The Sweetness and Greatness of Dante's
'Divine Comedy'* (San Francisco: Open Space, 1965).

T. S. Eliot, 'Dante' in *The Sacred Wood* (London: Methuen,
1920).

Oscar Kuhns, *Dante and the English Poets from Chaucer to Tennyson* (New York: H. Holt, 1904).

Paget Toynbee, 'Chronological List of English Translations from Dante from Chaucer to the Present Day' in *Dante Studies* (Oxford: Clarendon Press, 1921), pp. 156–280.

—, *Dante in English Literature from Chaucer to Cary (c. 1380–1844)* (2 vols., London: Methuen, 1909).

David Wallace, 'Dante in English' in Rachel Jacoff (ed.), *The Cambridge Companion to Dante* (Cambridge: Cambridge University Press, 1993).

1300–1700

J. A. W. Bennett, 'Chaucer, Dante and Boccaccio' in P. Boitani (ed.), *Chaucer and the Italian Trecento* (Cambridge: Cambridge University Press, 1983).

Jackson Campbell Boswell, *Dante's Fame in England: References in Printed British Books, 1477–1640* (Newark: University of Delaware Press, 1999).

John G. Demaray, *Cosmos and Epic Representation: Dante, Spenser, Milton and the Transformation of Renaissance Heroic Poetry* (Pittsburgh: Duquesne University Press, 1991).

Richard Neuse, *Chaucer's Dante: Allegory and Epic Theater in 'The Canterbury Tales'* (Berkeley: University of California Press, 1991).

Deborah Parker, *Commentary and Ideology: Dante in the Renaissance* (Durham, North Carolina: Duke University Press, 1993).

Roberta L. Payne, *The Influence of Dante on Medieval English Dream Visions* (New York: Peter Lang, 1989).

Irene Samuel, *Dante and Milton: The 'Commedia' and 'Paradise Lost'* (Ithaca: Cornell University Press, 1966).

Howard H. Schless, *Chaucer and Dante: A Revaluation* (Norman, Okla.: Pilgrim Books, 1984).

Karla Taylor, *Chaucer Reads* The Divine Comedy (Stanford, Calif.: Stanford University Press, 1989).

Victor and Edith Turner, *Image and Pilgrimage in Christian Culture: Anthropological Perspectives* (New York: Columbia University Press, 1978).

André Vauchez, *The Laity in the Middle Ages: Religious Beliefs and Devotional Practices* (1987) trans. Margery J. Schneider (South Bend, Indiana: University of Notre Dame Press, 1993).

John White, *Arts and Architecture in Italy, 1250–1400* (3rd edn, New Haven: Yale University Press, 1993).

DANTE AND LATER WRITING

General

C. P. Brand, 'Dante and the English Poets' in *The Mind of Dante*, ed. U. Limentani (Cambridge: Cambridge University Press, 1965).

Michael Caesar (ed.), *Dante: The Critical Heritage 1314(?)–1870* (London: Routledge & Kegan Paul, 1989).

Glauco Cambon, *Dante's Craft: Studies in Language and Style* (Minneapolis: University of Minnesota Press, 1969).

Gilbert F. Cunningham, *The Divine Comedy in English: A Critical Bibliography* (2 vols., Edinburgh: Oliver and Boyd, 1965–6).

William J. De Sua, *Dante into English* (Chapel Hill: University of North Carolina Press, 1964).

Werner P. Friedrich, *Dante's Fame Abroad, 1350–1850* (Rome: Edizioni di Storia e Letteratura, 1950).

A. B. Giamatti (ed.), *Dante in America: The First Two Centuries* (Binghampton: Medieval and Renaissance Texts and Studies, 1983).

Peter S. Hawkins and Rachel Jacoff (eds.), *The Poets' Dante* (New York: Farrar, Straus and Giroux, 2001).

Robin Kirkpatrick, *English and Italian Literature from Dante to Shakespeare: A Study of Source, Analogue and Divergence* (London: Longman, 1995).

Alison Morgan, *Dante and the Medieval Other World* (Cambridge: Cambridge University Press, 1990).

J. F. Took, *Dante: Lyric Poet and Philosopher: An Introduction to the Minor Works* (Oxford: Clarendon Press, 1990).

Paget Toynbee, *Dante Studies* (Oxford: Clarendon Press, 1921).

Charles Williams, *The Figure of Beatrice: A Study in Dante* (1942; repr. Woodbridge: D. S. Brewer, 1994).

DANTE'S WORLD

Erich Auerbach, *Literary Language and its Public in Late Latin Antiquity and in the Middle Ages* (1958) trans. Ralph Manheim (London: Routledge & Kegan Paul, 1965).

Caroline Walker Bynum, *Fragmentation and Redemption: Essays on Gender and the Human Body in Medieval Religion* (New York: Zone Books, 1991).

—, *The Resurrection of the Body in Western Christianity 200–1336* (New York: Columbia University Press, 1995).

Charles T. Davis, *Dante's Italy and Other Essays* (Philadelphia: University of Pennsylvania Press, 1984).

Cecil Grayson (ed.), *The World of Dante: Essays on Dante and his Times* (Oxford: Clarendon Press, 1980).

George Holmes, *Florence, Rome and the Origins of the Renaissance* (Oxford: Clarendon Press, 1986).

Peregrine Horden and Nicholas Purcell, *The Corrupting Sea: A Study of Mediterranean History* (Oxford: Blackwell's, 2000).

John Larner, *Italy in the Age of Dante and Petrarch 1216–1380* (London: Longman, 1980).

Jacques Le Goff, *The Birth of Purgatory* (1981) trans. Arthur Goldhammer (London: Scolar Press, 1984).

Robert Ombres, *The Theology of Purgatory* (Dublin: Mercier Press, 1978).

Brian Stock, *The Implications of Literacy: Written Language and Models of Interpretation in the Eleventh and Twelfth Centuries* (Princeton: Princeton University Press, 1983).

GEOFFREY CHAUCER (c. 1343–1400)

Chaucer's versions of Dante are among the earliest translations of the poet; the first complete translations were into Castilian (1428) and Catalan (1429). The oldest known manuscript of the *Commedia* dates from Genoa (1336) – as it happens, it was to Genoa that Chaucer travelled on royal business in 1372–3; he also visited Florence, where Dante was by that time revered. He returned to Italy in 1378. He clearly knew the whole *Commedia* well and was impressed not only by its visionary scope and philosophical depth but also by its styles and versification, for he produced in his 'Complaint to his Lady' (not included here) the first known lines of English *terza rima*. J. A. W. Bennett said with justice that 'it is thanks to Chaucer's reading of the *Comedy* that English verse joins the main stream of European poetry'. This reading is unmatched in English until Milton: Chaucer attends to the structure of Dante's poem as well as to its anecdotal vivacity. The second nun quotes the beginning of the end of the *Commedia* before even beginning her tale; the Monk, who is so keen on hunting, carefully omits Ugolino's nightmare of the chase from his homiletic adaptation of the story, and perhaps signals this omission in his last stanza. It may tell us something of Dante's reception in England that, of the three Canterbury pilgrims who refer to the *Commedia* half a century after its author's death, two are clerics and two are women, though Chaucer's own sense of comedy also needs taking into account.

The Monk's Tale   2,407–62 [*Inferno* 33.1–90]

> Off the Erl Hugelyn of Pyze the langour
> Ther may no tonge telle for pitee.
> But litel out of Pize stant a tour,

---

1 *Pyze* Pisa   *langour* suffering   3 *tour* tower

In which tour in prisoun put was he,
And with hym been his litel children thre;
The eldest scarsly fyf yeer was of age.
Allas, Fortune, it was greet crueltee
Swiche briddes for to putte in swich a cage!

Dampned was he to dyen in that prisoun,
For Roger, which that bisshop was of Pize,
Hadde on hym maad a fals suggestioun,
Thurgh which the peple gan upon hym rise
And putten hym to prisoun in swich wise
As ye han herd, and mete and drynke he hadde
So smal that wel unnethe it may suffise,
And therwithal it was ful povre and badde.

And on a day bifil that in that hour
Whan that his mete wont was to be broght,
The gayler shette the dores of the tour.
He herde it wel, but he spak right noght,
And in his herte anon ther fil a thoght
That they for hunger wolde doon hym dyen.
'Allas!' quod he, 'Allas, that I was wroght!'
Therwith the teeris fillen from his yen.

His yonge sone, that thre yeer was of age,
Unto hym seyde, 'Fader, why do ye wepe?
Whanne wol the gayler bryngen oure potage?
Is ther no morsel breed that ye do kepe?
I am so hungry that I may nat slepe.
Now wolde God that I myghte slepen evere!
Thanne sholde nat hunger in my wombe crepe;
Ther is no thyng, but breed, that me were levere.'

---

8 *briddes* birds   9 *dampned* condemned   15 *unnethe* scarcely
24 *fillen* fell   *yen* eyes   27 *potage* soup   28 *breed* bread
31 *wombe* stomach   32 *me were levere* I would prefer

Thus day by day this child bigan to crye,
Til in his fadres barm adown it lay,
And seyde, 'Farewel, fader, I moot dye!'
And kiste his fader, and dyde the same day.
And whan the woful fader deed it say,
For wo his armes two he gan to byte,
And seyde, 'Allas, Fortune, and weylaway!
Thy false wheel my wo al may I wyte.'   40

His children wende that it for hunger was
That he his armes gnow, and nat for wo,
And seyde, 'Fader, do nat so, allas!
But rather ete the flessh upon us two.
Oure flessh thou yaf us, take oure flessh us fro,
And ete ynogh' – right thus they to hym seyde,
And after that, withinne a day or two,
They leyde hem in his lappe adoun and deyde.

Hymself, despeired, eek for hunger starf;
Thus ended is this myghty Erl of Pize.   50
From heigh estaat Fortune awey hym carf.
Of this tragedie it oghte ynough suffise;
Whoso wol here it in a lenger wise,
Redeth the grete poete of Ytaille
That highte Dant, for he kan al devyse
Fro point to point; nat o word wol he faille.

        (c. 1375)

---

34 *barm* lap   37 *say* see   39 *weylaway* alas   40 *wyte* blame on
41 *wende* thought   42 *gnow* gnawed   45 *yaf* gave   49 *starf* died
51 *carf* cut   53 *in a lenger wise* at greater length   55 *highte* is called
56 *o* one

The Prologe of the Seconde Nonnes Tale
29–84 [Paradiso 33.1–20]

And thow that flour of virgines art alle,
Of whom that Bernard list so wel to write,
To thee at my bigynnyng first I calle;
Thou confort of us wrecches, do me endite
Thy maydens deeth, that wan thurgh hire merite
The eterneel lyf and of the feend victorie,
As man may after reden in hire storie.

Thow Mayde and Mooder, doghter of thy Sone,
Thow welle of mercy, synful soules cure,
In whom that God for bountee chees to wone,
Thow humble, and heigh over every creature,
Thow nobledest so ferforth oure nature,
That no desdeyn the Makere hadde of kynde
His Sone in blood and flessh to clothe and wynde.

Withinne the cloistre blisful of thy sydis
Took mannes shap the eterneel love and pees,
That of the tryne compas lord and gyde is,
Whom erthe and see and hevene out of relees
Ay heryen; and thou, Virgine wemmelees,
Baar of thy body – and dweltest mayden pure –
The Creatour of every creature.

₁₀ appears at line "In whom that God for bountee chees to wone,"
₂₀ appears at line "Baar of thy body – and dweltest mayden pure –"

---

1 *flour* flower   2 *Bernard* St Bernard of Clairvaux (1090–1153), Cistercian, abbot, mystic, ecclesiastical networker; he speaks the lines from the *Commedia* on which Chaucer draws *list* delighted   4 *endite* tell
5 *Thy maydens deeth* the martyrdom of St Cecilia, which 'The Second Nonnes Tale' recounts *wan* won   10 *chees* chose *wone* dwell
12 *nobledest so ferforth* ennobled to such an extent
17 *tryne compas* tripartite universe   18 *out of relees* incessantly
19 *heryen* praise *wemmelees* immaculate   20 *baar* bore *dweltest* remained

Assembled is in thee magnificence
With mercy, goodnesse, and with swich pitee
That thou, that art the sonne of excellence
Nat oonly helpest hem that preyen thee,
But often tyme of thy benygnytee
Ful frely, er that men thyn help biseche,
Thou goost biforn and art hir lyves leche.

Now help, thow meeke and blisful faire mayde,
Me, flemed wrecche, in this desert of galle;   30
Thynk on the womman Cananee, that sayde
That whelpes eten somme of the crommes alle
That from hir lordes table been yfalle;
And though that I, unworthy sone of Eve,
Be synful, yet accepte my bileve.

And, for that feith is deed withouten werkis,
So for to werken yif me wit and space,
That I be quit fro thennes that most derk is!
O thou, that art so fair and ful of grace,
Be myn advocat in that heighe place   40
Theras withouten ende is songe 'Osanne,'
Thow Cristes mooder, doghter deere of Anne!

And of thy light my soule in prison lighte,
That troubled is by the contagioun
Of my body, and also by the wighte
Of erthely lust and fals affeccioun;
O havene of refut, O salvacioun

---

28 *leche* physician   30 *flemed* exiled (from heaven)
31 *the womman Cananee* see Matthew 15:22   32 *eten* ate
35 *bileve* faith   36 *deed* dead   37 *yif* give
38 *thennes that most derk is* hell   41 *theras* where   45 *wighte* weight
47 *refut* refuge

Of hem that been in sorwe and in distresse,
Now help, for to my werk I wol me dresse.

50   Yet preye I yow that reden that I write,
Foryeve me that I do no diligence
This ilke storie subtilly to endite,
For bothe have I the wordes and sentence
Of hym that at the seintes reverence
The storie wroot, and folwen hire legende,
And pray yow that ye wole my werk amende.
            (*c.* 1380)

The House of Fame   1.480–508, 2.529–92
        [Compare *Purgatorio* 9.19–33]

When I out at the dores cam,
I faste aboute me beheld.
Then sawgh I but a large feld,
As fer as that I myghte see,
Withouten toun, or hous, or tree,
Or bush, or grass, or eryd lond;
For al the feld nas but of sond
As smal as man may se yet lye
In the desert of Lybye.
10   Ne no maner creature
That ys yformed be Nature
Ne sawgh I, me to rede or wisse.
'O Crist,' thoughte I, 'that art in blysse,
Fro fantome and illusion
Me save!' And with devocion

---

52 *ilke* particular *endite* compose   53 *sentence* meaning   54 *hym* Jacobus
de Voragine, compiler of *The Golden Legend*, the most popular medieval
collection of saints' lives *at the seintes reverence* out of reverence for the
saints

   6 *eryd* cultivated   7 *nas but of sond* consisted only of sand; compare
Inferno 14.8, 13   12 *rede or wisse* advise or instruct

Myn eyen to the hevene I caste.
Thoo was I war, lo, at the laste,
That faste be the sonne, as hye
As kenne myghte I with myn yë,
Me thoughte I sawgh an egle sore,   20
But that hit semed moche more
Then I had any egle seyn.
But this as sooth as deth, certeyn,
Hyt was of gold, and shon so bryghte
That never sawe men such a syghte,
But yf the heven had ywonne
Al newe of gold another sonne;
So shone the egles fethers bryghte,
And somwhat dounward gan hyt lyghte.

*

This egle, of which I have yow told,   30
That shon with fethres as of gold,
Which that so hye gan to sore,
I gan beholde more and more
To se the beaute and the wonder;
But never was ther dynt of thonder,
Ne that thyng that men calle fouder,
That smot somtyme a tour to powder
And in his swifte comynge brende,
That so swithe gan descende
As this foul, when hyt beheld   40
That I a-roume was in the feld.
And with hys grymme pawes stronge,
Withyn hys sharpe nayles longe,
Me, fleynge, in a swap he hente,
And with hys sours ayen up wente,

---

18 *faste be* close to   23 *sooth* sure   26–7 compare *Paradiso* 1.61–3
36 *fouder* bolt of lightning   37 *tour* tower   38 *brende* burned
39 *swithe* quickly   44 *in a swap he hente* at a stroke he seized
45 *sours* soarings

Me caryinge in his clawes starke
As lyghtly as I were a larke,
How high, I can not telle yow,
For I cam up, y nyste how.
For so astonyed and asweved
Was every vertu in my heved,
What with his sours and with my drede,
That al my felynge gan to dede
For-whi hit was to gret affray.

    Thus I longe in hys clawes lay,
Til at the laste he to me spak
In mannes vois, and seyde, 'Awak!
And be not agast so, for shame!'
And called me tho by my name,
And for I shulde the bet abreyde,
Me mette 'Awak,' to me he seyde
Ryght in the same vois and stevene
That useth oon I koude nevene;
And with that vois, soth for to seyn,
My mynde cam to me ageyn,
For hyt was goodly seyd to me,
So nas hyt never wont to be.

    And here-withal I gan to stere,
And he me in his fet to bere,
Til that he felte that I had hete,
And felte eke tho myn herte bete.
And thoo gan he me to disporte,
And with wordes to comforte,
And sayde twyes, 'Seynte Marye,
Thou art noyous for to carye!

50

60

70

---

49 *nyste* don't know   50 *asweved* dazed   51 *heved* head
53 *felynge* senses *dede* go numb   54 *to gret affray* too severe a shock
60 *the bet abreyde* awake more fully   61 *Me mette* I dreamed
62 *stevene* tone   63 *oon I koude nevene* someone I could name (sometimes
identified as Chaucer's wife)   67 *So nas hyt never* as never before
68 *stere* stir   75 *noyous* troublesome

And nothyng nedeth it, pardee,
For also wis God helpe me,
As thou noon harm shalt have of this;
And this caas that betyd the is,
Is for thy lore and for thy prow.   80
Let see! Darst thou yet loke now?
Be ful assured, boldely,
I am thy frend.' And therwith I
Gan for to wondren in my mynde.
'O God,' thoughte I, 'that madest kynde,
Shal I noon other weyes dye?
Wher Joves wol me stellyfye,
Or what thing may this sygnifye?
I neyther am Ennok, ne Elye,
Ne Romulus, ne Ganymede,   90
That was ybore up, as men rede,
To hevene with daun Jupiter,
And mad the goddys botiller.'   (*c.* 1380)

The House of Fame   3.1,091–1,109
     [Compare *Paradiso* 1.13–27]

O God of science and of lyght,
Appollo, thurgh thy grete myght,
This lytel laste bok thou gye!
Nat that I wilne, for maistrye,
Here art poetical be shewed,
But for the rym ys lyght and lewed,
Yit mak hyt sumwhat agreable,
Though som vers fayle in a sillable;
And that I do no diligence
To shewe craft, but o sentence.   10

---

80 *prow* benefit   87 *stellyfye* turn into a star   89–90 compare *Inferno*
2.32   91 *rede* say   92 *daun* Lord
  3 *gye* guide   6 *lewed* unsophisticated   10 *o sentence* solely the meaning

And yif, devyne vertu, thow
Wilt helpe me to shewe now
That in myn hed ymarked ys –
Loo, that is for to menen this,
The Hous of Fame for to descryve –
Thou shalt se me go as blyve
Unto the nexte laure y see,
And kysse yt, for hyt is thy tree.
Now entre in my brest anoon!   (*c.* 1380)

Troilus and Criseyde   5.1,786–1,827
[Compare *Paradiso* 22.133–53]

Go, litel bok, go, litel myn tragedye,
Ther God thi makere yet, er that he dye,
So sende myght to make in som comedye!
But litel book, no makyng thow n'envie,
But subgit be to alle poesye;
And kis the steppes where as thow seest pace
Virgile, Ovide, Omer, Lucan, and Stace.

And for ther is so gret diversite
In Englissh and in writyng of oure tonge,
So prey I God that non myswrite the,
Ne the mysmetre for defaute of tonge;
And red wherso thow be, or elles songe,
That thow be understonde, God I biseche!
But yet to purpos of my rather speche:

10

---

13 *that* what   16 *blyve* quickly   17 *laure* laurel
  7 *Stace* the Neapolitan poet Statius (CE *c.*45–*c.*96) enters the *Commedia*
in *Purgatorio* 21; his elaborate epic, the *Thebaid*, was widely admired in the
Middle Ages   11 *mysmetre* ruin the rhythm   14 *rather* previous

The wrath, as I bigan yow for to seye,
Of Troilus the Grekis boughten deere,
For thousandes his hondes maden deye,
As he that was withouten any peere,
Save Ector, in his tyme, as I kan heere.
But – weilawey, save only Goddes wille,   20
Despitously hym slough the fierse Achille.

And whan that he was slayn in this manere,
His lighte goost ful blisfully is went
Up to the holughnesse of the eighthe spere,
In convers letyng everich element;
And ther he saugh with ful avysement
The erratik sterres, herkenyng armonye
With sownes ful of hevenyssh melodie.

And down from thennes faste he gan avyse
This litel spot of erthe that with the se   30
Embraced is, and fully gan despise
This wrecched world, and held al vanite
To respect of the pleyn felicite
That is in hevene above; and at the laste,
Ther he was slayn his lokyng down he caste,

And in hymself he lough right at the wo
Of hem that wepten for his deth so faste,
And dampned al oure werk that foloweth so
The blynde lust, the which that may nat laste,
And sholden al oure herte on heven caste;   40
And forth he wente, shortly for to telle,
Ther as Mercurye sorted hym to dwelle.   (1382–6)

---

20 *weilawey* alas   21 *slough* slew   24 *spere* sphere
25 *In convers letyng . . .* leaving all material elements on the other side
26 *avysement* perception   27 *erratik* wandering
33 *To respect of* compared with   *pleyn* full   *pleyn felicite* compare *Purgatorio*
28.16   36 *lough* laughed   38 *dampned* condemned   42 *sorted* allotted

Troilus and Criseyde   5.1,856–69

O moral Gower, this book I directe
To the and to the, philosophical Strode,
To vouchen sauf, ther nede is, to correcte,
Of youre benignites and zeles goode.
And to that sothfast Crist, that starf on rode,
With al myn herte of mercy evere I preye,
And to the Lord right thus I speke and seye:

Thow oon, and two, and thre, eterne on lyve,
That regnest ay in thre, and two, and oon,
10   Uncircumscript, and al maist circumscrive,
Us from visible and invisible foon
Defende, and to thy mercy, everichon
So make us, Jesus, for thi mercy, digne,
For love of mayde and moder thyn benigne.
        Amen.   (1382–6)

The Wife of Bath's Tale   1,109–38
[Compare *Convivio*, canzone 3, 21–40]

'But, for ye speken of swich gentillesse
As is descended out of old richesse,
That therfore sholden ye be gentil men,
Swich arrogance is nat worth an hen.
Looke who that is moost vertuous alway,
Pryvee and apert, and moost entendeth ay

---

1 *Gower* John Gower, a poet contemporary with Chaucer
2 *Strode* Radulphus Strode, an Oxford logician
3 *ther* where   5 *sothfast* true   *starf on rode* died on the cross   6 *of* for
8–10 compare *Paradiso* 14.28–30   8 *on lyve* living   11 *foon* enemies
12 *to* of *everichon* each   13 *digne* worthy
    6 *Pryvee and apert* in private and in public

To do the gentil dedes that he kan;
Taak hym for the grettest gentil man.
Crist wole we clayme of hym oure gentillesse,
Nat of oure eldres for hire old richesse.   10
For thogh they yeve us al hir heritage,
For which we clayme to been of heigh parage,
Yet may they nat biquethe for no thyng
To noon of us hir vertuous lyvyng,
That made hem gentil men ycalled be,
And bad us folwen hem in swich degree.
    'Wel kan the wise poete of Florence,
That highte Dant, speken in this sentence.
Lo, in swich maner rym is Dantes tale:
"Ful selde up riseth by his branches smale   20
Prowesse of man, for God, of his goodnesse,
Wole that of hym we clayme oure gentillesse";
For of oure eldres may we no thyng clayme
But temporel thyng, that man may hurte and
        mayme.
    'Eek every wight woot this as wel as I,
If gentillesse were planted natureelly
Unto a certeyn lynage doun the lyne,
Pryvee and apert thanne wolde they nevere fyne
To doon of gentillesse the faire office;
They myghte do no vileynye or vice. . . .'   (c. 1392) 30

SIR DAVID LINDSAY (1486–1555)

Lindsay was educated at St Andrews University and, among
other close connections at court, held office as head of the
Herald's College in Scotland and as Poet Laureate to James V.

---

9 *wole* wills   12 *parage* lineage   18 *highte* is called
20–22 *Purgatorio* 7.121–23, where Dante is speaking through Virgil
20 *Ful selde* very rarely   22 *wole* wills   25 *woot* knows   28 *fyne* cease
30 *myghte* would be able to

He interested himself in Church reform (his reforming sympathies appear in the lukewarm account of Purgatory at lines 59–65 below). *The Dreme*, his first large poem, has broad rather than close resemblances to the *Commedia*, though the parallel at 36–8 is striking.

The Dreme of Schir David Lyndesay, of the Mont
148–82, 216–24, 232–8, 337–50, 596–630

Me thocht ane lady, of portratour perfyte,
Did salus me, with benyng contynance;
And I, quhilk of hir presens had delyte,
Tyl hir agane maid humyl reverence,
And hir demandit, savyng hir plesance,
Quhat wes hir name: scho answerit courtesly:
Dame Remembrance, scho said, callit am I;

Quhilk cummyng is for pastyme and plesoure
Off the, and for to beir the companye,
10 Because I se thy spreit withoute mesoure
So sore perturbit be malancolye,
Causyng thy corps to vaxin cauld and drye;
Tharefor, get up, and gang, anone, with me.
So war we boith, in twynklyng of ane Ee,

Doun throw the eird, in myddis of the centeir,
Or ever I wyste, in to the lawest hell.
In to that cairfull cove quhen we did enter,
Yowtyng and yowlyng wc hard, with mony yell:
In flame of fyre, rycht furious and fell,

---

1 *portratour* figure   2 *salus* greet   3 *quhilk* who   4 *tyl* toward
6 *quhat* what *scho* she   8 *quhilk* whose   9 *beir* keep   12 *vaxin* become
13 *gang, anone* go at once   14 *ane Ee* an eye   15 *eird* earth
16 *Or ever I wyste* before I knew it   18 *yowtyng* yelling
18–21 compare *Inferno* 2.61–6

Was cryand mony cairfull creature,   20
Blasphemand God, and waryand nature.

There sawe we divers Papis and Empriouris,
Withoute recover, mony cairfull kyngis;
Thare sawe we mony wrangous Conquerouris,
Withouttin rycht, reiffaris of otheris ryngis:
The men of kirk lay boundin in to byngis.
Thare saw we mony cairfull Cardinall,
And Archebischopis in thare pontificall,

Proude and perverst Prelattis, out of nummer,
Priouris, Abottis, and fals flattrand freris, –   30
To specifye thame all, it wer ane cummer, –
Regulare channonis, churle monkis, & chartarers,
Curious clerkis, and preistis seculeris:
Thare was sum part of ilk Religioun,
In haly kirk quhilk did abusioun.

*

Rewland that rowte I sawe, in Capis of Bras,
Symone Magus, and byschope Cayphas.

Byschope Annas, and the treatour Iudas,
Machomete, that Propheit poysonabyll,
Choro, Dathan, and Abirone thare was: 40
Heretykis we sawe unnumerabyll.
It wes ane sycht rycht wounderous lamentabyll,

---

21 compare *Inferno* 3.103–5 *waryand* cursing   23 *recover* means of relief
or escape   24 *wrangous* unjust   25 *reiffaris . . .* thieves of other men's
kingdoms   26 *byngis* heaps   28 *pontificall* robes of office
31 *cummer* trouble   32 *chartarers* Carthusians   34 *ilk Religioun* each
religious order   36 *Rewland that rowte* heading that gang
Capis of Bras compare *Inferno* 23.61–5   37–39 the figures named appear
in, respectively, *Inferno* 19.1; 23.115–17; 34.62; 28.31
40 *Choro, Dathan, and Abirone* see Numbers 16:1–35

Quhow that thay lay, in to tha flammis fletyng,
With cairfull cryis, girnyng, and greityng.

*

Full sore wepyng, with vocis lamentabyll,
Thay cryit lowde: O Empriour Constantyne,
We may wyit thy possessioun poysonabyll
Off all our gret punysioun and pyne.
Quhowbeit thy purpose was tyll ane gude fyne,
Thow baneist frome us trew devotioun,
Haiffand sic Ee tyll our promotioun.

*

A lytill above that dolourous doungeoun,
We enterit in ane countre full of cair,
Quhare that we saw mony ane legioun
Greitand and gowland with mony reuthful rair.
Quhat place is this, quod I, of blys so bair?
Scho answerit and said: Purgatorye,
Quhilk purgis Saulis, or that they cum to glorye.

I se no plesour heir, bot mekle paine;
Quharefor, said I, leif we this sorte in thrall:
I purpose never to cum heir agane;
Bot, yit, I do beleve, and ever sall,
That the trew kirk can no waye erre at all.

---

43 *fletyng* fleeing   44 *girnyng, and greityng* snarling and weeping
46–8 compare *Inferno* 19.115–17, referring to the Donation of Constantine
by which it was in Dante's time (and by Dante himself) believed that the
fouth-century emperor had transferred temporal power in the West to the
Pope; Lorenzo Valla proved in 1440 that the document was an
eighth-century forgery   47 *wyit* consider   49 *ane gude fyne* a good
purpose   51 *Haiffand sic Ee* having such concern
55 *Greitand and gowland* weeping and howling *rair* roar   58 *Saulis* souls
or that before   59 *mekle* much   61 contrast *Purgatorio* 2.91–2
62 *sall* shall

Sic thyng to be gret Clerkis dois conclude;
Quhowbeit, my hope standis most in cristis blud.

*

[They rise to the Empyrean, the outermost, motionless heaven
of intellectual light, as does Dante in *Paradiso* 30.]

Quhare to sulde I presume for tyll indyte –
The quhilk Sanct Paule, that doctour sapient,
Can nocht expres, nor in to paper wryte –
The hie excelland worke Indeficient,
And perfyte plesoure, ever parmanent,   70
In presens of that mychtie kyng of glore,
Quhilk was, and is, and sall be ever more!

At Remembrance humilye I did inquyre,
Geve I mycht in that plesour styll remane.
Scho said: aganis reasoun is thy desyre:
Quharefor, my freind, thow mon returne agane,
And, for thy Synnis, be pennance, suffer paine,
And thole the dede, with creuell panis sore,
Or thow be ding to ryng with hym in glore.

Than we returnit, sore aganis my wyll,   80
Doun throw the speris of the hevinnis cleir.
Hir commandiment behuffit I fulfyll,
With sorye hart, wyt ye, withouttin weir.
I wald full faine haif taryit thare all yeir;
Bot scho said to me: thare is no remede:
Or thow remane heir, first thow mon be dede.

---

66 *sulde* should   67–8 see 2 Corinthians 12:3–4; compare *Inferno* 2.31–2
74 *geve* if   78 *thole the dede* be tried for the action   79 *Or* before
ding worthy   82 *behuffit* salutary   83 *weir* doubt

Quod I: I pray yow hartfullye, madame,
Sen we have had sic Contemplatioun
Off hevinlye plesouris, yit or we passe hame,
90   Lat us have sum consideratioun
Off eirth, and of his Situatioun.
Scho answerit and said: that sall be done.
So wer we, boith, brocht in the air, full sone,

Quare we mycht se the Erth all at one sycht,
Bot lyke one moit, as it apperit to me,
In to the respect of the hevinnis brycht.
I have marvell, quod I, quhow this may be:
The eirth semis of so small quantitie,
The leist Sterne fixt in the Firmament
100   Is more than all the eirth, be my Iugment.   (c. 1528)

THOMAS SACKVILLE, 1st EARL OF
DORSET (c. 1536–1608)

Sackville travelled in Italy, c. 1563–6; he had already embarked
on a political career which reached a peak when he became
Lord High Treasurer of England in 1599. He had, unsurpris-
ingly, much sympathy with the mighty, who catalogue their
own woes in the *Myrrour for Magistrates*. Pope classed him in
the 'school of Dante'; this view persisted at least to the time of
Leigh Hunt, who considered him 'a bit of a minor Dante'. Such
persistent comparisons of Sackville to Dante show how little
Dante was read and understood in England from the sixteenth
century to the end of the eighteenth. Almost everything sup-
posed to be Dantescan in this passage derives from *Aeneid* VI
(one of Dante's main sources); the presentation of an after-
life lacks Dante's precise theological inquisitivencss, and the

---

94–6 compare *Paradiso* 22.133–54   95 *moit* speck of dust

allegorical guide, Sorrow, sharply contrasts with the real indi-
viduals who conduct Dante on his journey.

A Myrrour for Magistrates
Induction 484–525

[Conducted into the underworld by the goddess Sorrow, the
speaker sees Troy burning.]

> Herefrom when scarce I could mine iyes withdrawe
> That fylde with teares as doeth the spryngyng well,
> We passed on so far furth tyl we sawe
> Rude Acheron, a lothsome lake to tell
> That boyles and bubs up swelth as blacke as hell.
> Where grisly Charon at theyr fixed tide
> Still ferreies ghostes unto the farder side,
>
> The aged God no sooner Sorowe spyed,
> But hasting strayt unto the banke apace
> With hollow call unto the rout he cryed,   10
> To swarve apart, and geve the Goddesse place.
> Strayt it was done, when to the shoar we pace,
> Where hand in hand as we then linked fast,
> Within the boate we are together plaste.
>
> And furth we launch ful fraughted to the brinke,
> Whan with the unwonted weyght, the rustye keele
> Began to cracke as if the same should sinke.
> We hoyse up mast and sayle, that in a whyle,
> We set the shore, where scarcely we had while
> For to arryve, but that we heard anone   20
> A thre sound barke counfounded al in one.

---

5 *swelth* foul water

We had not long furth past, but that we sawe,
Blacke Cerberus the hydeous hound of hell,
With bristles reard, and with a thre mouthed Jawe,
Foredinning the ayer with his horrible yel.
Out of the diepe darke cave where he did dwell,
The Goddesse strayt he knewe, and by and by
He peaste and couched, while that we passed by.

      Thence cum we to the horrour and the hel,
30   The large great kyngdomes, and the dreadful raygne
Of Pluto in his trone where he dyd dwell,
The wyde waste places, and the hugye playne:
The waylinges, shrykes, and sundery sortes of payne,
The syghes, the sobbes, the diepe and deadly groane,
Earth, ayer, and all resounding playnt and moane.

      Here pewled the babes, and here the maydes unwed
With folded handes theyr sory chaunce bewayled,
Here wept the gyltles slayne, and lovers dead,
That slewe them selves when nothyng els avayled:
40   A thousand sortes of sorrowes here that wayled
With sighes and teares, sobs, shrykes, and all yfere,
That (oh alas) it was a hel to heare.   (1563)

JAMES SANFORDE (fl. 1560)

This extract from Ludovico Guicciardini's *The Garden of
Pleasure* consists, as did many of the works rendered at this
time into English, of 'pleasaunt verses of sundrie Italian Poets'
and 'grave and plesaunt sayings & deedes of divers princes, and
Philosophers' (as Sanforde stated in his dedication to the Earl
of Leicester). Of Sanforde, we know only that he published
translations from Greek, Latin and French as well as Italian and

---

22–8 compare *Inferno* 6.13–22   28 *peaste* fell silent   33–5 compare
Inferno 3.22–7   36 *pewled* cried   41 *yfere* together

so showed he was, as his title-page claims, a 'Gent.' Guicciardini
often quotes wise saws from Dante, always, as here in Virgil's
exposition of the role of Fortune, without heed to their dramatic
setting in the *Commedia*.

Inferno 7   73–96

He that above all wisdome farre ascendes,
The heavens made, and gave to them their guide,
So that eche parte to other brightnesse lendes,
Sundring alyke the light to every side.
He likewise also unto the worlds light,
Makes a minister and a chiefe captaine,
To turne at tymes the vayn wealth of ech wight.
From bloud to bloud, from realme to realme again,
Beyonde the reache of all mens wit and skil:
For one parte rules, and the other downe doth passe,   10
According to hir certayne doome and wil,
That lurketh as an adder in the grasse,
Your wisedome can in no wise hir remove,
She doth forsee, give sentence, and pursue
Hir reigne, as do theirs the other powers above.
Hir sodaine changes have no truces true:
Necessitie doth cause hir to be swifte.
So quick she comes, which doth by course ensue.
This is she that uppon the crosse they lifte
So much, which ought with praises hir pursue,   20
Giving hir blame each where, and misreporte,
But she is blessed and doth not heare this:
Mery among the other chiefest sorte,
She turnes hir sphere, and there abides in blisse.
       (1573; 1576)

ROBERT PETERSON (c. 1550–1610)

Peterson was a lawyer and jobbing translator. His translation of Della Casa exemplifies one way in which Dante's reputation fell in the sixteenth century; such complaints about his impurity of diction became common among the cultivated after Pietro Bembo's attack in 1525 (discussed in the Introduction). Dante was too lexically rangey for Renaissance tastes, rather as Shakespeare began to be considered indecorous and in need of smoothing by some neoclassicizing critics after the Restoration.

Galateo of Maister John della Casa . . . p. 83

A man must not alone beware of unhonest and filthie talke: but also of that whiche is base and vile, and especially where a man talketh & discourseth of greate and highe matters. And for this Cause, perchaunce, woorthely some blame our *Beatrice*, sayeing:

> To passe throughe Lethes floud,
>   the highest Fates would blott,
> Yf man mighte taste the Viandes suche,
>   as there dooe fall by Lott,
> And not paye firste a due
>   repentaunce for his scott.

For, in my conceite, these base wordes that come out of the *Tavernes*, bee verie uncomely for suche a worthy discourse. And when a man hathe like occasion to speake of ye *Sunne*, it shall not be good to call it *The Candell or the Lampe of the world*: bycause such woordes do put us in minde of ye Oyle, and the stuffe of the kitchyn. Neyther should a man that is well advised, say that *Saincte Dominicke* was *Il Drudo della*

5–11 *Purgatorio* 30.142–5; see the discussion of these lines in the Introduction   14–15 *Paradiso* 1.38

Theologia: Nor yet talke, that the glorious *Sainctes* have spoken such base and vile woordes: As for example to say.   20

> *And leave to scratche whereas*
> *the scabs of sinne breake out,*

For they savour of ye dregges, and ye filth of ye common people, as every man may easily see.   (1576)

GEORGE PETTIE (1548–89)

An Oxford graduate, Pettie wrote the bestselling and now for-gotten *A Petite Pallace of Pettie his Pleasure* (1576). He trans-lated Guazzo from a French crib. Guazzo's collection of wise words reveals (briefly, in lines 30–31) that some in the period remained able to hear Dante's verse with pleasure despite his widely deplored 'barbarism'.

The civile Conversation of M. Stephen Guazzo
2.f.71v, 3.ff.142r–142v

ANNIBALE: We must therefore have reverent regard of the trueth, and take heede that we violate not the virginitie thereof in any sort, nor to pull so much as one haire from hir, least we sustaine shame thereby. And I will say unto you more, that the trueth is a thing so tickle, that a man may incurre reprehension, not only by disguising it in some part

---

18–19 *Paradiso* 12.55   18 *Drudo* close friend, lover; the 'low' standing of the word is shown at *Inferno* 18.134 where it is used of a prostitute's regular customer; a modern equivalent of Dante's boldness of phrase might be to call St Dominic 'theology's toyboy'   21–2 *Paradiso* 17.129   23–4 note the assumption that the '*Sainctes*' and the 'common people' are mutually exclusive groups
  5 *tickle* delicate

coulourably, but even by very reporting it simply: which is,
when men tell things which are true, but yet such as fewe
will beleeve to be true.

10 GUAZZO: Of that danger *Dant* expressly speaketh in these
verses.

> *It is not good to tell that truth,*
> *which seemeth like unto a lie:*
> *For though it be no fault in deede,*
> *yet may a man be blamde thereby.*

*

ANNIBALE: As a fruitfull graine sowed in a soyle unfit for it,
bringeth forth no increase, so a childe which is naturally
given to learning, shall never doe well if he be set to warfare,
so much it importeth to finde out in the beginning, whereto
20 he is most inclined. Touching this matter, I remember I have
read certaine verses of *Dant*, which I have now forgotten.
GUAZZO: You shall see I will help you.
ANNIBALE: I pray you doe.
GUAZZO:

> *If that men had more care to follow natures lore,*
> *Of able and accomplisht men, we should have*
> *   greater store,*
> *But contrarie, a Priest of him we use to make,*
> *Who borne is for the warre, wherein he cheefe delight*
> *   doth take,*
> *And him we make a King, whome nature hath*
> *   ordaind,*
> *A lawier for to be, and thus is nature's course restraind.*

ANNIBALE: What pleasure I take in these verses, as well for
their delightfull harmonie, as for that they give mee to know
how good a memorie you are indued withall.   (1581; 1586)

12–15 *Inferno* 16.124–6   24–9 *Paradiso* 8.142–8

EDMUND SPENSER (1552–99)

Spenser shared the contemporary English taste for Italian literature – he translated from Petrarch while at Cambridge University and later wrote a sonnet sequence, *Amoretti* (1595), in the Petrarchan tradition – but there are no definitely identifiable translations or mentions of Dante in his work. Still, there are some grounds for thinking that passages such as lines 24–7 below constitute echoes as well as parallels: the situation in both passages is similar (Dante too is reviving in response to female assistance) and the comparisons to spring flowers resemble each other, though such analogies are also common-or-garden in Petrarch. Spenser's friend Gabriel Harvey and his acquaintance Sir Philip Sidney were well read in Dante, and he probably recognized the importance of the *Commedia* to Ariosto and Tasso, both strong influences on *The Faerie Queene*, as well as Dante's significance for Chaucer, whose 'spirit', he maintained, 'doth in me survive'.

The Faerie Queene   4.12.280–315

[Marinell's mother begs Neptune to provide the cure for her lovesick son.]

> He graunted it: and streight his warrant made,
> Under the Sea-gods seale autenticall,
> Commaunding *Proteus* straight t'enlarge the mayd,
> Which wandring on his seas imperiall,
> He lately tooke, and sithence kept as thrall.
> Which she receiving with meete thankefulnesse,
> Departed straight to *Proteus* therewithall:
> Who reading it with inward loathfulnesse,
> Was grieved to restore the pledge, he did possesse.

---

3 *enlarge* release   4 *which* who   5 *sithence* then   6 *meete* proper

10   Yet durst he not the warrant to withstand,
         But unto her delivered *Florimell*.
         Whom she receiving by the lilly hand,
         Admyr'd her beautie much, as she mote well:
         For she all living creatures did excell;
         And was right joyous, that she gotten had
         So faire a wife for her sonne *Marinell*.
         So home with her she streight the virgin lad,
     And shewed her to him, then being sore bestad.

     Who soone as he beheld that angels face,
20   Adorn'd with all divine perfection,
         His cheared heart eftsoones away gan chace
         Sad death, revived with her sweet inspection,
         And feeble spirit inly felt refection;
         As withered weed through cruell winters tine,
         That feeles the warmth of sunny beames reflection,
         Liftes up his head, that did before decline
     And gins to spread his leafe before the faire sunshine.

     Right so himselfe did *Marinell* upreare,
         When he in place his dearest love did spy;
30   And though his limbs could not his bodie beare,
         Ne former strength returne so suddenly,
         Yet chearefull signes he shewed outwardly.
         Ne lesse was she in secret hart affected,
         But that she masked it with modestie,
         For feare she should of lightnesse be detected:
     Which to another place I leave to be perfected.
                 (1596)

---

13 *mote* might   17 *lad* led   18 *bestad* beset (by misery)   24 *tine* affliction
35 *of lightnesse be detected* be accused of immodesty
36 *perfected* continued and completed

SIR JOHN HARINGTON (*c.* 1561–1612)

Harington, one of Elizabeth I's godchildren, was educated at
Eton College and Cambridge University. The snatch of Dante
in this extract is the first known translation of any part of
the *Commedia* into what looks as if it were about to become
english *terza rima* and so marks an interest in the shape of the
Commedia as well as in some of its sayings. Such an interest
becomes keen and consistent in English readings of Dante only
at the end of the eighteenth century. Harington similarly pre-
serves the *ottava rima* of the original in this influential version
of Ariosto.

Orlando Furioso in English Heroical Verse
Allegorie of the Fourth Book

For the Allegorie of this booke much might be said of *Atlant*,
of his horse and his shield, but I will only touch what I thinke
will be thought most worth the noting and let passe the rest for
each mans private conceipt. *Atlant* by many of his gestures and
actions here specified may signifie Cupid or that fond fancie
that we call love; and whereas he takes up such brave captaines
and souldiers as well as women and weakelings, it seems
consonant to that pretie fantasticke verse of Ovid:

> *Militat omnis armis & habet sua castra Cupido.*
>
> *All lovers warriours are, and Cupid hath his campe.*   10

Furder, the wings of this straunge beast called the Griphith
horse agree with *Petrarks* description of Cupids wings

> *Sopra gli homeri havea sol due grand' ali, di color mille.*
>
> *Upon his shoulders were two mightie wings, of thousand coullers.*

Atlant takes and imprisons those he takes. Love is as close and inextricable a prison as his.

The ways to *Atlants* castell are described to be craggie, head-long, and unpleasant. Such be the wayes of that passion. The castell is said to be placed in the middle of a rockie mountaine
20 cloven in sunder, by which is meant that this folly we speake of possesseth us and dwels in us most of all about the middle of our age, as *Dant* saith:

> *Nel mezzo del camin di nostra vita,*
> *Mi retrovai per una selva oscura,*
> *Che la dritta via era smarrita.*

> *While yet my life was in her middle race*
> *I found I wandred in a darkesome wood,*
> *The right way lost with mine unstedie pace.*

This is that wandring wood of which the dolefull *Petrarke*
30 complaines so often in those his sweet mourning sonets in which he seemes to have comprehended all the passions that all men of that humour have felt.   (1591)

THOMAS HEYWOOD (c. 1574–1641)

Heywood was a professional man of the theatre, who claimed to have contributed to more than 200 plays; his best-known work today is *A Woman Killed With Kindness*. The description of Lucifer below in fact translates (without acknowledgement) rather from Landino's commentary than from *Inferno* itself; it is included as an example of the torrential moralizing through which Dante's poem has often been read.

23–8 *Inferno* I.1–3; the interpretation given here of Dante's dark wood is not widely accepted and seems to be Harington's 'private conceipt'

The Hierarchie of the blessed Angells ...
7.197–206, 234–76 [*Inferno* 34.28–54]

And as in his Creation he was fram'd
More glorious far than others before-namd;
More goodly featur'd, beautifull, and bright,
And therefore had his name deriv'd from Light:
So since his Fall, there's nothing we can stile
So ougly foul, abominably vile;
The putred Fountaine, and bitumenous Well,
From whence all Vice and malefactures swell.
Whose horrid shape, and qualities infest,
Are by the Poet *Dantes* thus exprest: 10

[Heywood quotes here the Italian of *Inferno* 34.28–54]

   In which Description he first notes the place
Where this great Prince of Darkenesse, shut from
     Grace,
Is now tormented, namely, 'a congeal'd Lake.
His mighty stature next, which he doth make
Two thousand cubits. By his Crest is meant
His Envy, Arrogance, and proud ostent.
Three Faces with three sev'rall colours stain'd,
Import in him three Vices still maintain'd:
One, fiery red, Wrath and Exorbitation
Denotes to us, with the Spleenes inflammation.   20
The pale and meagre, Avarice implies.
From the third, blacke and swarthy, doth arise
Unprofitable Sloath. From the two eyes
Which to each face belongs, we may devise

---

1 *his* refers to Lucifer before his fall   4 *name deriv'd from Light* 'Lucifer' from the Latin for 'light-bearer'; the name 'Satan' occurs only once in the *Commedia* (at *Inferno* 7.1)   13 *congeal'd* frozen   15 Heywood draws his statistics from Landino, not from Dante

All Appetites immod'rat. In the growth
Of these three Ills, Ire, Avarice, and Sloath,
Two Wings, two great accitements to those Sinnes
Propose to us: The first of them beginnes
In Turbulence and Fury; from hence grow
The windes of Crueltie that hourely blow.
    Rapacitie and Gripplenesse are they
That to the Misers Avarice obey.
The horrid blasts that hence proceed, include
The most unnat'urall sin, Ingratitude.
Sorrow with Negligence on Sloath attend:
Th'immoderat gusts of Hatred hence ascend.

    Those windes of Wrath, Ingratitude, and Hate,
With fearefull stormes trouble and agitate
Cocitus streames, withall suppressing quite
Those good and godly motions which accite
Either to Faith, or unto Hope and Charity,
Lest any should in them claime singularity.
The greatnesse of his Wings improve th'elation
Of his swel'd heart and proud imagination.
That ev'ry face hath a wide mouth and throat,
So much the Morall doth to us denote,
That all whom such black sinnes contaminate,
His jawes and rav'nous throat ingurgitate.
    His Teares, which he did never yet imploy,
But (as the Crocodile useth) to destroy,
Imports to us, that wretched Sinners state,
Whose slacke Repentance ever comes too late.
    And so far *Dantes*. (1635)

---

31 *Gripplenesse* greed   50 Dante expresses no opinion about the sincerity of Satan's tears

JOHN MILTON (1608–74)

Milton learned Italian at school; influenced perhaps by his friendship with Charles Diodati, he had come to know Dante well before his trip to Italy (1638–9). In Florence he had close contacts with Bonmatthei, the greatest Dante scholar of an age in which the poet's work was disprized. Dante had been popular with anti-Catholic English writers since Jewel and Foxe in 1560–70 embraced him (misleadingly) as a star 'defector' from Rome, but Milton shows from the first more than a propagandist's intimacy with even his anticlerical passages. References to Dante in Milton's prose indicate he had read the epistles and the *De monarchia* as well as the whole *Commedia*; Milton's commonplace book suggests he was re-reading *Purgatorio* after he had begun *Paradise Lost*.

Lycidas   108–31

Last came, and last did go,
The Pilot of the *Galilean* lake,
Two massy Keyes he bore of metals twain,
(The Golden opes, the Iron shuts amain)
He shook his Miter'd locks, and stern bespake,
How well could I have spar'd for thee, young swain,
Anow of such as for their bellies sake,
Creep and intrude, and climb into the fold?
Of other care they little reck'ning make,
Then how to scramble at the shearers feast,   10
And shove away the worthy bidden guest;
Blind mouthes! that scarce themselves know how to hold

---

2 *the Pilot* usually identified as St Peter; see Matthew 16:19   3 compare *Purgatorio* 9.117–18, where the second key is of silver   6–24 compare *Paradiso* 27.40–63, where St Peter's invective against his mercenary and divisive successors has several similarities and also ends with a warning of retribution to come   7 *anow* enough

A Sheep-hook, or have learn'd ought els the least
That to the faithfull Herdmans art belongs!
What recks it them? What need they? They are sped;
And when they list, their lean and flashy songs
Grate on their scrannel Pipes of wretched straw,
The hungry Sheep look up, and are not fed,
But swoln with wind, and the rank mist they draw,
20 Rot inwardly, and foul contagion spread:
Besides what the grim Woolf with privy paw
Daily devours apace, and nothing sed,
But that two-handed engine at the door,
Stands ready to smite once, and smite no more.
    (1638; 1645)

Of Reformation Touching Church-Discipline
in England . . .   p. 26

. . . I will bring you the opinion of three the famousest men for
wit and learning, that *Italy* at this day glories of, whereby it
may be concluded for a receiv'd opinion even among men
professing the Romish faith, that *Constantine* marr'd all in the
Church. *Dante* in his 19. *Canto* of *Inferno* hath thus, as I will
render it you in English blank Verse.

> *Ah* Constantine, *of how much ill was cause*
> *Not thy Conversion, but those rich demaines*
> *That the first wealthy* Pope *receiv'd of thee.*

---

17 *scrannel* thin   18 compare the swollen sheep Beatrice mentions while
denouncing flashy preachers in *Paradiso* 29.106–8   21 *Woolf* plausibly
identified as the Catholic Church but perhaps, like the wolf in *Inferno*
1.49–51, a more general emblem of rapacity

7–9 *Inferno* 19.115–17, referring to the 'Donation of Constantine' by
which it was in Dante's time (and by Dante himself) believed that the
fourth-century emperor had transferred temporal power in the West to the
Pope. Lorenzo Valla proved in 1440 that the document was an
eighth-century forgery. Milton's translation ('how much ill') is exact for
Dante's '*quanto mal*' whereas his gloss exaggerates ('marr'd all')

So in his 20. Canto of *Paradise* hee makes the like complaint,
and *Petrarch* seconds him in the same mind in his 108. Sonnet
which is wip't out by the Inquisitor in some Editions; speaking
of the Roman *Antichrist* as meerely bred up by *Constantine*.
[The third authority cited is Ariosto.]   (1641)   10

To Mr. H. Lawes, on His Aires

Harry whose tunefull and well measur'd Song
   First taught our English Music how to span
   Words with just note and accent, not to scan
   With *Midas* Eares, committing short and long;
Thy worth and skill exempts thee from the throng,
   With praise enough for Envie to look wan;
   To after age thou shalt be writ the man
   That with smooth Aire couldst humour best our
      tongue.
Thou honour'st Verse, and Verse must lend her wing
   To honour thee, the Priest of *Phœbus* Quire,   10
   That tun'st their happiest Lines in hymne or story.
Dantè shall give Fame leave to set thee higher
   Then his *Casella*, whom he woo'd to sing,
   Met in the milder shades of Purgatory.
      (1646; published 1648)

---

10 *Paradiso* 20.55–60

  1 *Harry* Henry Lawes, though a royalist sympathizer, was a friend of
Milton's; this sonnet was first published in Lawes's 1648 collection of
settings of the Psalms   4 *Midas* King Midas was given asses' ears for
preferring Pan's music to Apollo's; see Ovid, *Metamorphoses* 11.146–79
committing putting together wrongly   13 *Casella* in *Purgatorio* 2.76–119,
Dante asks the shade of his friend Casella to sing one of their joint
compositions

Paradise Lost   4.131–193, 223–75

[Satan approaches Eden.]

So on he fares, and to the border comes
Of *Eden*, where delicious Paradise,
Now nearer, Crowns with her enclosure green,
As with a rural mound the champain head
Of a steep wilderness, whose hairie sides
With thicket overgrown, grottesque and wilde,
Access deni'd; and over head up grew
Insuperable highth of loftiest shade,
Cedar, and Pine, and Firr, and branching Palm,
A Silvan Scene, and as the ranks ascend
Shade above shade, a woodie Theatre
Of stateliest view. Yet higher then thir tops
The verdurous wall of Paradise up sprung:
Which to our general Sire gave prospect large
Into his neather Empire neighbouring round.
And higher then that Wall a circling row
Of goodliest Trees loaden with fairest Fruit,
Blossoms and Fruits at once of golden hue
Appeerd, with gay enameld colours mixt:
On which the Sun more glad impress'd his beams
Then in fair Evening Cloud, or humid Bow,
When God hath showrd the earth; so lovely seemd
That Lantskip: And of pure now purer aire
Meets his approach, and to the heart inspires
Vernal delight and joy, able to drive
All sadness but despair: now gentle gales
Fanning thir odoriferous wings dispense

10

20

---

1 *he* Satan   4–5 compare *Purgatorio* 28.101–2   6 compare *Purgatorio*
28.2, 23   14 *our general Sire* Adam   23 compare *Purgatorio* 28.7–9
26 compare *Purgatorio* 28.6, 109–14

Native perfumes, and whisper whence they stole
Those balmie spoiles. As when to them who saile
Beyond the *Cape of Hope*, and now are past   30
Mozambic, off at Sea North-East windes blow
Sabean Odours from the spicie shoare
Of *Arabie* the blest, with such delay
Well pleas'd they slack their course, and many a
            League
Cheard with the grateful smell old Ocean smiles.
So entertaind those odorous sweets the Fiend
Who came thir bane, though with them better
            pleas'd
Then *Asmodeus* with the filthie fume,
That drove him, though enamourd, from the Spouse
Of *Tobits* Son, and with a vengeance sent   40
From *Media* post to *Aegypt*, there fast bound.
    Now to th'ascent of that steep savage Hill
Satan had journied on, pensive and slow;
But further way found none, so thick entwin'd,
As one continu'd brake, the undergrowth
Of shrubs and tangling bushes had perplext
All path of Man or Beast that past that way:
One Gate there onely was, and that look'd East
On th'other side: which when th'arch-fellon saw
Due entrance he disdaind, and in contempt,   50
At one slight bound high overleap'd all bound
Of Hill or highest Wall, and sheer within
Lights on his feet. As when a prowling Wolfe,
Whom hunger drives to seek new haunt for prey,
Watching where Shepherds pen thir Flocks at eeve
In hurdl'd Cotes amid the field secure,
Leaps o're the fence with ease into the Fould:

---

32 *Sabean* of Saba, i.e. Sheba   38 see the Book of Tobit, 6:9–8:8
44 compare *Purgatorio* 28.23–4   53–63 see the extract from 'Lycidas' with
its notes above

Or as a Thief bent to unhoord the cash
Of some rich Burgher, whose substantial dores,
60   Cross-barrd and bolted fast, fear no assault,
In at the window climbes, or o're the tiles;
So clomb this first grand Thief into Gods Fould:
So since into his Church lewd Hirelings climbe.

*

[Satan eventually perches on the Tree of Life.]

Southward through *Eden* went a River large,
Nor chang'd his course, but through the shaggie hill
Pass'd underneath ingulft, for God had thrown
That Mountain as his Garden mould high rais'd
Upon the rapid current, which through veins
Of porous Earth with kindly thirst up drawn,
70   Rose a fresh Fountain, and with many a rill
Waterd the Garden; thence united fell
Down the steep glade, and met the neather Flood,
Which from his darksom passage now appeers,
And now divided into four main Streams,
Runs divers, wandring many a famous Realme
And Country whereof here needs no account,
But rather to tell how, if Art could tell,
How from that Saphire Fount the crisped Brooks,
Rowling on Orient Pearl and sands of Gold,
80   With mazie error under pendant shades
Ran Nectar, visiting each plant, and fed
Flours worthy of Paradise which not nice Art
In Beds and curious Knots, but Nature boon
Powrd forth profuse on Hill and Dale and Plaine,
Both where the morning Sun first warmly smote
The open field, and where the unpierc't shade
Imbround the noontide Bowrs: Thus was this place,

68–70 compare *Purgatorio* 28.121–6   81 compare *Purgatorio* 28.144
84 compare *Purgatorio* 28.69   86 compare *Purgatorio* 28.32–3

A happy rural seat of various view;
Groves whose rich Trees wept odorous Gumms and
    Balme,
Others whose fruit burnisht with Golden Rinde   90
Hung amiable; *Hesperian* Fables true,
If true, here onely, and of delicious taste:
Betwixt them Lawns, or level Downs, and Flocks
Grasing the tender herb, were interpos'd,
Or palmie hilloc, or the flourie lap
Of som irriguous Valley spread her store;
Flours of all hue, and without Thorn the Rose:
Another side, umbrageous Grots and Caves
Of coole recess, o're which the mantling Vine
Layes forth her purple Grape, and gently creeps   100
Luxuriant; mean while murmuring waters fall
Down the slope hills, disperst, or in a Lake,
That to the fringed Bank with Myrtle crownd,
Her chrystall mirror holds, unite thir streams.
The Birds thir quire apply; aires, vernal aires,
Breathing the smell of field and grove, attune
The trembling leaves, while Universal *Pan*
Knit with the *Graces* and the *Hours* in dance
Led on th'Eternal Spring. Not that faire field
Of *Enna*, where *Proserpin* gathring flours   110
Her self a fairer Floure by gloomie *Dis*
Was gatherd, which cost *Ceres* all that pain
To seek her through the world; nor that sweet
    Grove
Of *Daphne* by *Orontes*, and th'inspir'd
Castalian Spring might with this Paradise
Of *Eden* strive . . .   (1667)

91–2 compare *Purgatorio* 28.139–41   105–7 compare *Purgatorio*
28.7–15   109–13 compare *Purgatorio* 28.49–51
110–11 *flours . . . Floure* compare *Purgatorio* 28.41

ANDREW MARVELL (1621–78)

Marvell was well out of England during the Civil War, spending time – 'to very good purpose ... & the gaineing of ... languages', as Milton testified – in Holland, France, Italy and Spain. He returned in 1647 and became Mary Fairfax's tutor around the time he wrote 'Tom May's Death'; he seems to have taught her French and Italian. Dante's view of Brutus and Cassius, gnawed by Satan at Hell's lowest point (alluded to in lines 17–18) had long been politically controversial. Bruni was shocked by it as early as 1402 and it was still irking Dryden at the end of the seventeenth century. Marvell's allusion to the passage in 1650 – the year he wrote 'An Horatian Ode upon Cromwell's Return from Ireland' – has a characteristically ticklish balance of considerations about resistance to rulers.

Tom May's Death   1–40

As one put drunk into the Packet-boat,
Tom May was hurry'd hence and did not know't.
But was amaz'd on the Elysian side,
And with an Eye uncertain, gazing wide,
Could not determine in what place he was,
For whence in Stevens ally Trees or Grass?
Nor where the Popes head, nor the Mitre lay,
Signs by which still he found and lost his way.
At last while doubtfully he all compares,
10   He saw near hand, as he imagin'd *Ares*.

---

2 *Tom May* a translator of Lucan, he was said to have abandoned his royalist sympathies out of pique because he was not made Poet Laureate; he died, allegedly while in a drunken stupor, in 1650   6 *Stevens ally* a street of many pubs – such as the Pope's Head and the Mitre – in Westminster
10 *Ares* the god of war

Such did he seem for corpulence and port,
But 'twas a man much of another sort;
'Twas *Ben* that in the dusky Laurel shade
Amongst the Chorus of old Poets laid,
Sounding of ancient Heroes, such as were
The Subjects Safety, and the Rebel's Fear.
And how a double headed Vulture Eats,
Brutus and *Cassius* the Peoples cheats.
But seeing *May* he varied streight his Song,
Gently to signifie that he was wrong.   20
Cups more then civil of *Emathian* wine,
I sing (said he) and the *Pharsalian* Sign,
Where the Historian of the Common-wealth
In his own Bowels sheath'd the conquering health.
By this *May* to himself and them was come,
He found he was translated, and by whom.
Yet then with foot as stumbling as his tongue
Prest for his place among the Learned throng.
But *Ben*, who knew not neither foe nor friend,
Sworn Enemy to all that do pretend,   30
Rose more then ever he was seen severe,
Shook his gray locks, and his own Bayes did tear
At this intrusion. Then with Laurel wand,
The awful Sign of his supream command,
At whose dread Whisk *Virgil* himself does quake,
And *Horace* patiently its stroke does take,

---

13 *Ben* Jonson, whose beefy appearance may parody by contrast Virgil, who
is pale, thin and hoarse when Dante meets him in *Inferno* 1.61–4; Jonson's
exclusion of May from the company of 'blessed shades' (39) reverses Virgil's
welcome of Dante among the illustrious poets in *Inferno* 4.80–82
17–18 compare *Inferno* 34.55–67 (the Marvell Folio reads 'But' but we
follow E. S. Donno in preferring Cooke's 1772 emendation to 'And')
21–2 Marvell snipes at May's translation of Lucan's *Pharsalia*, which begins,
'Warres more Civill on Aemathian plaines'

As he crowds in he whipt him ore the pate
Like *Pembroke* at the Masque, and then did rate.
Far from these blessed shades tread back agen
40 Most servil' wit, and Mercenary Pen . . .
(written *c.* 1650; published 1681)

JONATHAN RICHARDSON (1665–1745)

In his successful career as a painter, Richardson numbered among his sitters Steele, Prior, and Pope and his dog. His writings on the visual arts were highly regarded: the *Discourse . . . on the Science of a Connoisseur* went through four editions in the eighteenth century and contributed to the contemporary rage for collecting (the *OED* gives Richardson's title as the second known instance in English of 'connoisseur'). His version of the Ugolino episode – Dante's greatest hit in these islands until challenged by Paolo and Francesca – gave a first push to the English vogue for Dante; Richardson also promoted the poet's reputation by comparing him to Michelangelo, with whom his name was thereafter regularly coupled (for example, by Ruskin). Like other promotional campaigns whose success does not always depend on strict accuracy, Richardson's had its drawbacks, as the fabricated 'sublimity' of many eighteenth-century versions of Dante shows.

---

38 *Pembroke* the Earl of Pembroke assaulted May in 1634 and later apologized   40 in the tirade which follows this extract, Jonson compares English political factions with the Guelfs and Ghibellines of Dante's time and poem

A Discourse on the Dignity, Certainty, Pleasure and
Advantage, of the Science of a Connoisseur
pp. 30–33 [*Inferno* 33.1–78]

This great Man (in the 33d Canto of the Ist part of his *Comedia*)
in his Passage thro' Hell, introduces Count *Ugolino* knawing
the Head of this Treacherous, and Cruel Enemy the Archbishop,
and telling his own sad Story. At the appearance of *Dante*.

> *La bocca sollevò dal fiero pasto*
> *Quel peccator,* &c.

He from the Horrid Food his Mouth withdrew,
And wiping with the Clotted, Offal hair
His shudd'ring Lips, raising his Head thus spake.
    You will compel me to renew my Grief
Which e're I speak oppresses my sad Heart;
But if I Infamy accumulate
On him whose Head I knaw, I'le not forbear
To speak tho' Tears flow faster than my Words.
    I know not who you are, nor by what power,
Whether of Saints, or Devils you hither came,   10
But by your Speech you seem a *Florentine*;
Know then that I Count *Ugolino* am,
Archbishop *Ruggieri* this, which known
That I by him Betray'd was put to Death
Is needless to relate, you must have heard;
But what must be unknown to Mortal Men,

---

heading it is not Dante's mere 'appearance' which halts Ugolino's gnawing:
Dante speaks to Ugolino, who is too polite to reply with his mouth full.
Richardson has excised the characteristically Dantescan quality of
responsiveness from the passage, and often changes details so that Ugolino
sounds as if he were soliloquizing   2 *Clotted, Offal* not in Dante
3 *shudd'ring* not in Dante   5 *oppresses* the Italian '*preme*' means 'presses'
or 'squeezes': Richardson is 'raising' Dante's style according to a notion of
epic decorum whose aptness to the *Commedia* is questionable
10 *Whether of Saints, or Devils* not in Dante

The cruel Circumstances of my Death
These I will tell, which Dreadful Secret known
You will conceive how Just is my Revenge.
20   The ancient Tower in which I was confin'd,
And which is now the Tower of Famine call'd,
Had in her Sides some Symptoms of decay,
Through these I saw the first approach of morn,
After a restless night, the first I slept
A Prisoner in its Walls; Unquiet Dreams
Oppress'd my lab'ring Brain. I saw this Man
Hunting a Wolfe, and her four little Whelps
Upon that ridge of Mountains which divides
The *Pisan* Lands from those which *Lucca* claims;
30   With Meagre, Hungry Dogs the Chase was made,
Nor long continued, quick they seiz'd the Prey,
And tore their Bowels with remorseless Teeth.
      Soon as my broken Slumbers fled, I heard
My Sons (who also were confin'd with me)
Cry in their troubled Sleep, and ask for Bread:
O you are Cruel if you do not weep
Thinking on that, which now you well perceive
My Heart divin'd; If this provoke not Tears
At what are you accustomed to weep?
      The hour was come when Food should have been
40   brought,
Instead of that, O God! I heard the noise
Of creaking Locks, and Bolts, with doubled force
Securing our Destruction. I beheld
The Faces of my Sons with troubled Eyes;

---

18 *Dreadful Secret* not in Dante   21–2 Richardson is so occupied
'translating' words not in the original that he here omits a line, *Inferno* 33.24
('and in which [tower] others will be imprisoned'); this line would have
spoiled the spotlit isolation of Richardson's Ugolino   27 *her* the wolf is
male in the original   32 *Bowels* the Italian means 'flanks'
remorseless Dante says only that their teeth were sharp   41 *O God!* not,
unsurprisingly, in the original   41–3 amplified from Dante's 'And I heard
the lower door of the horrible tower being nailed up'

I Look'd on them, but utter'd not a Word;
Nor could I weep; They wept, *Anselmo* said
(My little, dear *Anselmo*) What's the matter
Father, Why look you so? I wept not yet,
Nor spake a Word that Day, nor following Night.
  But when the Light of the succeeding Morn   50
Faintly appear'd, and I beheld my Own
In the four Faces of my Wretched Sons
I in my clenched Fists fasten'd my Teeth:
They judging 'twas for Hunger rose at once,
You Sir have giv'n us Being, you have cloath'd
Us with this miserable Flesh, 'tis yours,
Sustain your Self with it, the Grief to Us
Is less to Dye, than thus to see your Woes.
Thus spake my Boyes: I like a Statue then
Was Silent, Still, and not to add to Theirs   60
Doubled the weight of my Own Miseries:
  This, and the following Day in Silence pass'd.
Why Cruel Earth did thou not open then!
  The Fourth came on; my *Gaddo* at my Feet
Cry'd Father help me; said no more but dy'd:
Another Day two other Sons expir'd;
The next left me alone in Woe; Their Griefs
Were ended. Blindness now had seiz'd my Eyes,
But no Relief afforded; I saw not
My Sons, but grop'd about with Feeble hands   70
Longing to touch their Famish'd Carcasses,
Calling first One, then T'other by their Names,
Till after two days more what Grief could not
That Famine did. He said no more, but turn'd
With baleful Eyes distorted all in haste,
And seiz'd again, and gnaw'd the mangled Head.

... *Michelangelo* was the fittest Man that ever liv'd to Cut,
or Paint, this Story, if I had wish'd to see it represented in

---

46 Richardson omits 'I turned to stone inside'

Sculpture, or Painting I should have fix'd upon this Hand: He
was a *Dante* in his way, and read him perpetually.   (1719)

WILLIAM HUGGINS (1696–1761)

Huggins, a Fellow of Magdalen College, Oxford, published a
translation of Ariosto's *Orlando Furioso* in 1755. He left a
complete version of the *Commedia* in manuscript at his death
(the manuscript is now believed lost). The remaining sample
suggests posterity's loss is calculable, though the original Italian
of this passage has itself been criticized as a stilted paraphrase
of the Lord's Prayer (Matthew 6:9ff.; Luke 11:2ff.).

Dante Il Purgatorio
Canto XI [11.1–21]

As literally as possible.

> Our Father blest, who art in Heav'n above,
> Not circumscrib'd; but thro' consummate love,
> Which to those primal essences you bear,
> Thy name be hallowed; thy power rare,
> By ev'ry creature: as it is but meet,
> All thanks be render'd to thy effluence sweet:
> Advance to us the peace of thy wish'd reign, ⎫
> As, of ourselves, to that we can't attain,   ⎬
> If it comes not, with all our skill humane.   ⎭
>
> 10   As, in the heav'ns, thy angels of their will ⎫
> Make sacrifice, and sing Hosanna still,   ⎬
> So, may, on earth, mankind thy law fulfil.   ⎭

---

2 *consummate* elevated from the Italian, which means 'more' or 'greater'
3 *primal essences* the original means just 'first effects'

> Our daily manna give to us this day,
> Without it, thro' this wild and thorny way,
> Who strives to travel, will more backward stray.
> And, like as we those wrongs, which we receive,
> In others pardon, so thy pardon give
> Benignant: nor survey our merit small,
> And feeble virtue, so propense to fall,
> Suffer not our old enemy to tempt;   20
> But, from his punctures keep us still exempt.
>   *Amen.*   (1760)

CHARLES ROGERS (1711–84)

Rogers was a connoisseur and friend of Sir Joshua Reynolds, whose influential painting of *Count Hugolino and his children* ... (1773) he considered a masterpiece. His blank verse *Inferno* is the first published Englishing of an entire *cantica* of the *Commedia*. It possesses only intermittently the virtue of fidelity for which it was at the time praised: our notes indicate some of the occasions where Rogers 'elevates' Dante's style higher than Dante in this canto thought fit.

Inferno 5

> From the first Circle we descended down
> To that which was of a more narrow space,
> Where Pain from ev'ry one excited cries.
> Horribly grinning Minos, standing there,
> Examines at their entrance each one's crime,

---

14 *wild and thorny way* Huggins does translate quite literally but not 'as literally as possible': the Italian has no 'way', wild or otherwise, but a 'harsh desert' because Dante knew that was where the Israelites received the manna – see Exodus 16   **21** *punctures* goadings; the Italian has the vivid and plain verb for 'to spur'

Tries them, and passes judgment in their turns.
Whene'er a guilty Soul before him comes
It all confesses: He the proper place,
Well knowing, that of Hell's to be their due,
So many times his Tail around him twists,
As the Degrees to which he'd have it cast.
Many before him always ready stand,
Who forward come, and are in order tried;
They plead, they're sentenc'd, and then turned down.
   'O you who to this place of torments come,'
Minos, his office then suspending, said,
'Regard your entrance, and to whom you trust,
'Nor be you by the ample Gates deceiv'd.'
To him my Guide; 'Why do you thus exclaim?
'Prevent his passage not, by Fate ordain'd:
'For who would this, can do what e'er he wills.
'More obstacles it is not fit to raise.'
   Their loud complaining notes I now began
To hear, being at the place of woe arriv'd,
Deprived of all light; which bellows loud
Like the Sea toss'd about by adverse winds.
Th' infernal Storm, which never is allay'd,
The Sprites tormented in its vortex whirls.
When they near the ruinous Gulph approach,
Their Lamentations, and their Shrikes are loud,
Blaspheming e'en Divinity itself.
These who such torments suffered, I learnt,
Were condemn'd to them for their carnal Sins,
Their Reason by their Passion being subdued.
And as the Birds, who at the first approach

The line numbers in the left margin: 10 (at line "So many times his Tail around him twists,"), 20 (at "'Prevent his passage not, by Fate ordain'd:"), 30 (at "Their Lamentations, and their Shrikes are loud,").

7–9 the convoluted syntax is Rogers's contribution   14 here Rogers does
follow Dante's syntax – 'they speak, they hear, and then are turned
downwards' – but the metrical need for a poetical pronunciation of 'turnèd'
corresponds to nothing in the brisk Italian   21 the Italian uses, as often in
Hell, an impersonal construction to avoid direct mention of God: 'it is willed
thus there where everything can be done which is willed'
35 *the Birds* Dante specifies starlings

Of cold, take wing, and gather in thick clouds,
So does the Storm these wretched Spirits drive,
From 'bove, below, and ev'ry side around.
They have no hope of ever being releas'd:
And e'en of lighter punishment despair.   40
Like to the Cranes, who, flying in long trains,
The air disturb with their complaining notes,
These Spirits uttered their moaning griefs.

I therefore said; O Master, who are these
That do so much this dingy Air molest?
The first of these, of whom you would inquire,
He said, was Emperess of many tongues,
And many Nations govern'd; yet so prone
To Leachery become, that she was forc'd
By a new Law to justify her crime: 50
She is Semiramis, the wife belov'd
Of Ninus, and inherited those Lands
O'er which th' unrival'd Sultan now commands.
The next is she who slew herself for Love,
And to her fond Sichæus broke her faith.
Luxurious Cleopatra follows her.
Helen I saw, for whom so long time was
Ill spent in war; the great Achilles next,
Who conquer'd was at last by am'rous charms.
Paris, and Tristan, and a thousand more   60
He shewed me, whom Love had depriv'd of life.
When these were to me nam'd, I was o'ercome
With Pity, and I nearly swoon'd away.

I then; O Poet, willingly I'd speak
To both those who together come this way,

---

45 in the original it is the air which scourges the sinners not they who
'molest' it   51 *belov'd* not in Dante   55 *fond Sichæus* the Italian means
'the ashes of Sichaeus' (Dido was a widow before she fell for Aeneas)
63 *nearly swoon'd away* Dante does not pre-empt the startling effect of his
swoon at the end of the canto; the Italian means 'and I was, as it were, lost'

And seem to move far quicker than the wind.
He thus reply'd; When they shall nearer come,
Requesting by that Love which governs them,
You may that they shall come to you prevail.
70   Soon as the wind them to us wafted had,
I thus to them; 'Unhappy Souls, O now
'With us discourse, if nothing you prevents.'
Like Doves, when they by fond desire are call'd,
With raised wings fly eager to their nests;
So these, leaving both Dido and her band,
Came swiftly tow'rds us through the foggy air;
Such power had with them affection's plea!
'O mortal Man replete with Grace divine,
'Who in this azure region visit us
80   'That have defiled with our blood the world,
'If by the universal King we were
'Befriended, we would to him for you pray:
'Since you commis'rate our unhappy lot,
'We're ready to reply to what you ask;
'Now that the wind is still to favour us.
'The Land where I was born is on the shore
'Plac'd, where the Po and all his rivulets
'Run with their tributes smoothly to the sea.
'Love, which possesses soon a courteous breast,
90   'Seiz'd on my handsome Paramour, whose loss
'I yet lament, reflecting on the act:
'Love, which will always be by love repaid,
'Caus'd me to that great pleasure in him take,
'Which still possesses me, as you perceive.
'Love brought us both to the like fatal end:

---

78 *Grace divine* the original has only '*grazioso*' ('graceful')
83 *commis'rate* the Italian says 'have pity on' as plainly as possible
90–91 the original means 'this man was seized with love for my beautiful
body which has been taken from me': Paolo is right by Francesca as she
speaks   95 *the like fatal end* Dante has 'the same death'

'But Caina him expects who did this deed.'
These suff'ring Shades, when I knew who they were,
I on my breast declin'd my thoughtful head,
'Till Virgil of my meditations ask'd.
I thinking was, alas! on that dire end   100
To which they by their fond amours are brought.
Then to them turning, I, 'Francesca,' said,
'Your torments move my pity, and draw tears:
'But tell me, when your sighs and soft desires
'Were yet uncertain of a due return,
'What caus'd you to unlawful love permit?'
'No greater grief assails us' she replied,
'Than in unhappy hours to recollect
'A better time; and this your Teacher knows.
'But if you still to learn the tender root   110
'Request, from which our am'rous dalliance sprung,
'However irksome, I will it relate.
'Together we, for pleasure, one day read
'How strictly Lancelot was bound by love;
'We then alone, without suspicion, were:
'T'admire each other, often from the book
'Our eyes were ta'en, and oft our colour chang'd;
'That was the point of time which conquer'd us,
'When, reading that her captivating smile
'Was by the Lover she adored kiss'd;   120
'This my Companion, always with me seen,
'Fearful, and trembling, also kiss'd my mouth.
'The Writer, Galeotto, nam'd the Book.
'But from that day we never read in't more.'

---

96 *Caina* part of the ninth circle of hell, where traitors to their families are
punished   99 the Italian gives Virgil direct speech: 'what are you thinking?'
119 *captivating* in Dante the smile is 'desired'   123 *Galeotto* the name of
the go-between who facilitated Lancelot's and Guinevere's adultery;
'Galeotto' is still today an Italian equivalent of 'pandar'. Rogers
misunderstands Francesca, who is not naming the book, nor its writer,
but blaming it for acting for her and Paolo as Galeotto did for their
predecessors

During one Spirit was relating this,
So deeply did the other mourn, that I
With pity swoon'd, and fell like a dead corse.
(1782)

THOMAS GRAY (1716–71)

After leaving Cambridge without a degree, Gray travelled with
his friend Horace Walpole in Italy (1739–40); he returned to
Cambridge in 1742 and eventually held the Regius Chair of
History and Modern Languages. One of the few things he did
in that capacity was to appoint Agostino Isola to teach Italian
(Wordsworth was among Isola's later pupils). He made this
version of the Ugolino episode while studying Italian 'like any
dragon' as an undergraduate, which may account for its lurid
qualities; he never published it. Gray knew Dante's work well,
including the *De vulgari eloquentia*; he acknowledged that *Pur-
gatorio* 8.5–6 helped him towards the opening of the *Elegy
Written in a Country Churchyard*.

Inferno 33   1–78

From his dire food the greisly Fellon raised
His gore-dyed lips, which on the clotter'd locks
Of th' half devoured Head he wiped, & thus
Began; 'Wouldst thou revive the deep despair
The Anguish, that unutter'd nathless wrings

126–7 Dante is for once more emphatic than his translator: he has passed
without dying into the land of the dead but at her words and at Paolo's tears,
'I went faint as if I were dying, and fell as a dead body falls'

  2 *gore-dyed . . . clotter'd* these adjectives are not in Dante, nor are many
of Gray's other incitements to shudder ('ceaseless', 'insatiate', 'direful',
'panting', 'trembling', 'hungry')   5 *nathless* nevertheless; Gray added this
and other archaisms ('rekes', 'amain', 'mought') because he thought them apt
to supposed 'Gothick' qualities in the original

My inmost Heart? yet if the telling may
Beget the Traitour's infamy, whom thus
I ceaseless gnaw insatiate, thou shalt see me
At once give loose to Utterance & to Tears.
   I know not who thou art nor on what errand   10
Sent hither; but a Florentine my ear
Won by thy tongue, declares thee. Know, thou
    seest
In me Count Ugolino, & Ruggieri
Pisa's perfidious Prelate, this: now hear
My Wrongs & from them judge of my revenge.
   That I did trust him, that I was betrayd
By trusting, & by Treachery slain, it rekes not
That I advise Thee; that which yet remains
To thee & all unknown (a horrid Tale)
The bitterness of Death, I shall unfold.   20
Attend, & say if he have injurd me.

   Thro' a small Crevice opening, what scant light
That grim & antique Tower admitted (since
Of me the Tower of Famine hight & known
To many a Wretch) already 'gan the dawn
To send; the while I slumbring lay, A Sleep
Prophetic of my Woes with direful Hand
Oped the dark Veil of fate. I saw methought
Toward Pisa's Mount, that intercepts the view
Of Lucca chas'd by Hell-hounds gaunt & bloody   30
A Wolf full grown; with fleet & equal speed
His young ones ran beside him, Lanfranc there
And Sigismundo & Gualandi rode
Amain, my deadly foes! headed by this

---

14 *Pisa's perfidious Prelate* inserted by Gray who throughout thickens the
alliterative texture of Dante's writing in an attempt at what he takes to be
'period atmosphere' (as at 'slumbring . . . Sleep', 'weakly gleam / And wan',
'struggling Sorrow')   31 *fleet & equal* in the original, these adjectives apply
to the pursuing dogs   32–3 *Lanfranc . . . Sigismuudo & Gualandi* families
hostile to Ugolino; Gray translates as though the names referred to
individuals

The deadliest; he their Chief, the foremost he
Flashed to pursue & chear the eager Cry:
Nor long endured the Chase: the panting Sire
Of Strength bereft, his helpless offspring soon
Oerta'en beheld, & in their trembling flanks
40   The hungry Pack their sharp-set Fangs embrued.
    The Morn had scarce commencd, when I awoke:
My Children (they were with me) Sleep as yet
Gave not to know their Sum of Misery
But yet in low & uncompleated Sounds
I heard 'em wail for bread. oh! thou art cruel
Or thou dost mourn to think, what my poor Heart
Foresaw, foreknew: oh! if thou weep not now,
Where are thy Tears? too soon they had arousd them
Sad with the fears of Sleep, & now the Hour
50   Of timely food approached: when at the gate
Below I heard the dreadful Clank of bars,
And fastning bolts; then on my Children's eyes
Speechless my Sight I fix'd, nor wept, for all
Within was Stone: they wept, unhappy boys!
They wept, & first my little dear Anselmo
Cried, "Father, why, why do you gaze so sternly?
What would you have?" yet wept I not, or answerd
All that whole day, or the succeeding Night
Till a new Sun arose with weakly gleam
60   And wan, such as mought entrance find within
That house of Woe: but oh! when I beheld
My sons & in four faces saw my own
Despair reflected, either hand I gnawed
For Angeuish, which they construed Hunger; straight
Ariseing all they cried, "far less shall be
Our sufferings, Sir, if you resume your gift;

---

36 this line is Gray's invention   51 *dreadful Clank of bars* like Richardson,
Gray turns up the volume from the original's 'I heard them nailing up the
way out'   54 *unhappy boys!* supplied by Gray

These miserable limbs with flesh you cloathed;
Take back what once was yours." I swallowd down
My struggling Sorrow, nor to heighten theirs.
That day & yet another, mute we sate   70
And motionless: O! Earth! couldst thou not gape
Quick to devour me? yet a fourth day came
When Gaddo at my feet outstretchd, implor'ng
In vain my Help, expir'd: ee'r the sixth Morn
Had dawnd, my other three before my eyes
Died one by one; I saw 'em fall: I heard
Their doleful Cries; for three days more I grop'd
About among their cold remains (for then
Hunger had reft my eyesight) often calling
On their dear Names, that heard me now no more: 80
The fourth, what Sorrow could not, Famine did.'
   He finished; then with unrelenting eye
Askaunce he turn'd him, hasty to renew
The hellish feast, & rent his trembling Prey.
     (*c.* 1737–8)

ANON

This odd trifle is one of the first instances of the fondness for
turning excerpts from the *Commedia* into self-contained lyrics
(see the further examples by Peacock and Moore below). The
comparison of frost to despondency and thaw to renewed con-
fidence originally illustrated a moment in Dante's relation to
Virgil and has been sentimentally reapplied by the translator.
His attraction to a Dantescan simile from a natural process
anticipates the enthusiasm for the poet's brilliance with analo-
gies which is a marked feature of his later popularity.

71ff. Gray's frantically run-on blank verse makes Ugolino sound more
declamatory than he does in the painedly formal Italian where Dante as
usual preserves integrity of line   76–7 *I heard / Their doleful Cries* not in
Dante

The Three First Stanzas of the 24th Canto of Dante's Inferna Made Into a Song. In Imitation of the Earl of Surry's Stile. [Inferno 24.1–15]

I

When in the opening of the youthful Year,
 Sol in *Aquarius* bathes his glistering Ray;
In early Morn the Fields all white appear,
 With hoary Frost is cover'd every Spray:
And every Herb and every Grass is shent,
All in the chill Imprisonment ypent.

II

The mean-clad Swain, forth issuing from his Cot,
 Looks sadly all around the whitening Waste;
And grieves that his poor Sheep, by Heaven forgot,
10 Can find no Food, no tender Green to taste:
He beats his Breast as one distract, or mad;
And home returns, with pensive Look and sad.

III

There silent grieves. Then once again looks out,
 And sees the Groves and Meads quite alter'd are.
The Sun has cast his melting Rays about,
 And every Green appears more fresh and fair.
Then Hope returns, and Joy unknits his Brows,
And forth he leads his Flock the tender Grass to brouze.

IV

Thus when my Fair One views me with Disdain,
20 My Heart is sunk within me, sad and dead;
My Spirits yield, and all my Soul's in Pain;

---

5 *shent* spoiled

I sit and sigh, and hang my drooping Head:
But if she smile, my Sadness melts away,
Each gloomy Thought clears up, and I'm all blithe
    and gay. (1746)

CHARLES BURNEY (1726–1814)

Fanny Burney records in her *Memoirs* (1832) of her father
that Dr Burney made a 'sedulous, yet energetic, though prose
translation' of *Inferno* while grieving for the loss of his first
wife in 1761; its whereabouts, if it survives, are unknown. This
version of Dante's meeting with the musician Casella, a meeting
Milton alludes to in 'To Mr. H. Lawes' (see above), was aptly
published in Charles Burney's four-volume *A General History
of Music*.

Purgatorio 2 73–92, 106–17

On me when first these spirits fix their eyes,
They all regard me with a wild surprise,
Almost forgetting that their sins require
The purging remedy of penal fire:
When one of these advanc'd with eager pace,
And open arms, as me he would embrace;
At sight of which I found myself impell'd
To imitate each gesture I beheld.
But vain, alas! was every effort made,
My disappointed arms embrace a shade: 10

19–24 this stanza is Anon's invention

   3–4 the original lacks Burney's satiric archness, saying only 'as if
forgetting to go and make themselves beautiful'; the added irony may stem
from unease with the doctrine of Purgatory (condemned in 1562 as 'a fond
thing vainly invented' by Article 22 of the Anglican Church's Thirty-Nine
Articles)

Thrice did vacuity my grasp elude,
Yet still the friendly phantom I pursued.
My wild astonishment with smiling grace
The spectre saw, and chid my fruitless chace.
The voice and form now known, my fear suspend,
O stay, cried I, one moment with thy friend!
No suit of thine is vain, the vision said,
I lov'd thee living, and I love thee, dead.
But whence this haste? – not long allowed to stay,
20   Back to the world thy Dante takes his way –
Yet let this fleeting hour one boon obtain,
If no new laws thy tuneful pow're restrain,
Some song predominant o'er grief and woe
As once thou sung'st above, now sing below;
So shall my soul, releas'd from dire dismay,
O'ercome the horrors of this dreadful way.
Casella kindly deign'd his voice to raise,
And sung how *Love the human bosom sways*,
In strains so exquisitely sweet and clear,
30   The sound still vibrates on my ravish'd ear;
The shadowy troops, extatic, listening round,
Forgot the past and future in the sound.   (1782)

WILLIAM HAYLEY (1745–1820)

Hayley probably learned his Italian under Agostino Isola at
Cambridge. Though he qualified as a lawyer he devoted himself
mainly to writing plays and widely admired poems such as *The
Triumphs of Temper*. He declined the laureateship in 1790.
Southey said everything about him was good except his poetry;

---

20 the Italian is complex and may be ambiguous; it probably means 'I am on
this journey so that I may return another time here where I am'; Dante makes
a visionary journey to Purgatory so that he will, when he dies, really arrive
there and not in Hell (he doesn't entertain the possibility he might go straight
to Heaven)

Byron, for once in agreement with Southey, ridiculed his work in his poem *English Bards and Scotch Reviewers* (1809). He was, in an eighteenth-century sense, a mediocrity, and has the representative quality of that status: it would be difficult to find a better epitome of the received idea of Dante at this time than he supplies in the first extract below, particularly in the unreflective categorization of the *Commedia* as an 'epic'. His translations of *Inferno* 1–3 are the first extended attempt published in English to translate Dante in his own verse-form; they begin the metrical experimentation with and through Dante which gathers pace in the following century.

An Essay on Epic Poetry . . .   3.79–122

> At length, fair Italy, luxuriant land,
> Where Art's rich flowers in earliest bloom expand,
> Thy daring DANTE his wild Vision sung,
> And rais'd to Epic pomp his native Tongue.
> Down Arno's stream his new-form'd music floats,
> The proud vale echoing with his Tuscan notes.
> See the bold Bard now sink and now ascend,
> Wherever Thought can pierce or Life extend;
> In his wide circuit from Hell's drear abyss,
> Thro' purifying scenes to realms of perfect bliss,   10
> He seems begirt with all that airy throng,
> Who brighten or debase the Poet's song.
> Sublimest Fancy now directs his march
> To opening worlds, through that infernal arch
> O'er whose rough summit aweful words are read,
> That freeze each entering soul with hopeless dread.
> Now at her bidding his strong numbers flow,
> And rend the heart at Ugolino's woe;

---

15 *Inferno* 3.9   17–18 *Inferno* 32 and 33

While Nature's glory-giving tear bedews
20   A tale unrivall'd by the Grecian Muse.
Now to those notes that milder grief inspire,
Pathetic Tenderness attunes his lyre,
Which, soft as murmurs of the plaintive dove,
Tells the sad issue of illicit love.
But all the worse companions of his way
Soon into different sounds his ductile voice betray:
Satiric Fury now appears his guide,
Thro' thorny paths of Enmity and Pride;
Now quaint Conceit his wand'ring steps misleads
30   Thro' all the hideous forms that Folly breeds;
Now Priestly Dullness the lost Bard enshrouds
In cold confusion and scholastic clouds.
Unequal Spirit! in thy various strain,
With all their influence Light and Darkness reign;
In thy strange Verse and wayward Theme alike
New forms of Beauty and Disorder strike;
Extremes of Harmony and Discord dwell,
The Seraph's music and the Demon's yell!
The patient Reader, to thy merit just,
40   With transport glows, and shudders with disgust.
Thy Failings sprung from thy disastrous time;
Thy stronger Beauties from a soul sublime,
Whose vigor burst, like the volcano's flame,
From central darkness to the sphere of fame.   (1782)

---

23 *Inferno* 5, particularly its doves at 82   27–8 Hayley refers to the
factional politics of such *canti* as *Inferno* 10 and 28   31–2 probably
meaning the whole of *Paradiso*   41 *thy disastrous time* a reference to
'medieval barbarism' such as is still popular

An Essay on Epic Poetry ...
Notes to the Third Epistle [Rime 52: 'Guido, i' vorrei ...']

Imitation

Henry! I wish that you, and Charles, and I,
　　By some sweet spell within a bark were plac'd,
　　A gallant bark with magic virtue grac'd,
　　Swift at our will with every wind to fly:
So that no changes of the shifting sky,
　　No stormy terrors of the watery waste,
　　Might bar our course, but heighten still our taste
　　Of sprightly joy, and of our social tie:
Then, that my Lucy, Lucy fair and free,
　　With those soft nymphs on whom your souls are
　　　　bent,   10
　　The kind magician might to us convey,
To talk of love throughout the live-long day;
　　And that each fair might be as well content
　　As I in truth believe our hearts would be.   (1782)

Inferno I   1-75

In the mid season of this mortal strife,
　　I found myself within a gloomy grove,
　　Far wandering from the ways of perfect life:
　　The place I know not, where I chanc'd to rove,

---

1 *Henry ... Charles* Hayley has Englished the names from 'Guido'
[Cavalcanti] and 'Lapo' [Gianni de' Ricevuti]   9 *Lucy* Dante named only
the women loved by his friends, not his own beloved, but Hayley was
probably working from one of the many corrupt texts in which Beatrice's
name does appear
　1 *this mortal strife* Hayley's elevation of Dante's 'our life'
2 *gloomy grove* the Italian means 'dark wood' and was found insufficiently
poetical   3 Dante is less instantly allegorical: his line means 'where the
straight road was lost'

It was a wood so wild, it wounds me sore
But to remember with what ills I strove:
Such still my dread, that death is little more.
But I will tell the good which there I found.
High things 'twas there my fortune to explore:
Yet how I enter'd on that secret ground
I know not to explain; so much in sleep
My mortal senses at that hour were drown'd.
But when I reach'd the bottom of a steep,
That rose to terminate the dreary vale,
Which made cold terrors thro' my bosom creep,
I look'd on high, where breath'd a purer gale,
And saw the summit glisten with that ray
Which leads the wand'rer safe o'er hill and dale.
This soon began to chase those fears away,
Which held my struggling spirit bound so fast
During that night of darkness and dismay:
And, as th' exhausted wretch, by fortune cast
Safe from the stormy deep upon the shore,
Turns to survey the perils he has past,
So turn'd my soul, ere yet its dread was o'er,
Back to contemplate that mysterious strait
Where living mortal never past before.
Arising soon from this repose elate,
Up the rough steep my journey I begin,
My lower foot sustaining all my weight.
Here, while my toilsome way I slowly win,
Behold a nimble Panther springs to sight!
And beauteous spots adorn his motley skin:

10

20

30

---

9 the text from which Hayley translates probably read *'alte'* ('high') for the
now accepted *'altre'* ('other'); the variant suited Hayley's tastes
16 *breath'd a purer gale* not in the original; perhaps an anticipation of the air
of the earthly paradise on the summit of the mountain of Purgatory (see
Purgatorio 28.7)

He at my presence shew'd no signs of fright,
  But rather strove to bar my doubtful way;
  I often turn'd, and oft resolv'd on flight.
'Twas now the chearful hour of rising day;
  The sun advanc'd in that propitious sign
  Which first beheld his radiant beams display
Creation's charms, the work of love divine!   40
  So that I now was rais'd to hope sublime,
  By these bright omens of a fate benign,
The beauteous Beast and the sweet hour of prime.
  But soon I lost that hope; and shook yet more
  To see a Lion in this lonely clime:
With open jaws, athirst for human gore,
  He rush'd towards me in his hungry ire;
  Air seem'd to tremble at his savage roar.
With him, enflam'd with every fierce desire,
  A famish'd She-wolf, like a spectre, came;   50
  Beneath whose gripe shall many a wretch expire.
Such sad oppression seiz'd my sinking frame,
  Such horror at these strange tremendous sights,
  My hopes to climb the hill no longer aim;
But, as the wretch whom lucre's lust incites,
  In the curst hour which scatters all his wealth,
  Sinks in deep sorrow, dead to all delights,
So was I robb'd of all my spirit's health,
  And to the quarter where the sun grows mute,
  Driven by this Beast, who crept on me by stealth.   60
While I retreated from her dread pursuit,
  A manly figure my glad eyes survey'd,
  Whose voice was like the whisper of a lute.

62–3 Hayley's extrapolation from words meaning 'someone who seemed
weak from long silence'

Soon as I saw him in this dreary glade,
    Take pity on me, to this form I cry'd,
    Be thou substantial man, or fleeting shade! –
A man I was (the gracious form reply'd)
    And both my parents were of Lombard race;
    They in their native Mantua liv'd and dy'd:
70 I liv'd at Rome, rich in a monarch's grace,
    Beneath the good Augustus' letter'd reign,
    While fabled Gods were serv'd with worship base.
A Bard I was: the subject of my strain
    That just and pious Chief who sail'd from Troy,
    Sinking in ashes on the sanguine plain.   (1782)

FREDERICK HOWARD, EARL OF
CARLISLE (1748–1825)

Byron quarrelled with Howard, who was his guardian, and
revenged himself by referring to the Earl's poetry as 'paralytic
puling' in his poem *English Bards and Scotch Reviewers* (1809).
Dr Johnson expressed himself more judiciously but he too
found the writing 'not always sufficiently fervid or animated'.
Lord Carlisle made a career in politics, holding such offices as
President of the Board of Trade and Viceroy of Ireland. His
muse had a melancholy bent; as well as this version of the
Ugolino episode, he published poems on the death of Gray and
'on the Fall of a Mountain in Switzerland, which overwhelmed
a large Tract of Country, and by which Six or Seven Hundred
Persons are stated to have been destroyed'.

65ff. the English does not, perhaps could not, convey how Dante's lines
waver between Latin and Italian when he begins to talk to Virgil

Translation from Dante [Inferno 33.1–75]

Now from the fell repast, and horrid food,
The Sinner rose, but first (the clotted blood
With hair depending from the mangled head)
His jaws he wiped, and thus he wildly said:
    Ah! wilt thou then recall this scene of woe,
And teach again my scalding tears to flow?
Thou know'st not how tremendous is the tale,
My brain will madden, and my utterance fail.
But could my words bring horror and despair
To Him whose bloody skull you see me tear,   10
Then should the voice of sweet revenge ne'er sleep,
For ever would I talk, and talking weep.
Mark'd for destruction, I in luckless hour   ⎫
Drew my first breath on the Etruscan shore,   ⎬
And Ugolino was the name I bore.   ⎭
This skull contain'd an haughty Prelate's brain,
Cruel Rugeiro's; why his blood I drain,
Why to my rage he's yielded here below,
Stranger, 'twill cost thee many a tear to know.
Thou know'st perhaps how trusting to this slave   20
I and my children found an early grave.
This thou may'st know, the Dead alone can tell   ⎫
The Dead, the tenants of avenging hell,   ⎬
How hard our fate, by what inhuman arts we fell. ⎭
Through the small opening of the prison's height
One moon had almost spent its waining light.
It was when Sleep had charm'd my cares to rest,
And wearied Grief lay dozing in my breast:

7–8 Carlisle's invention   11 not in Dante   12–13 Carlisle here omits three
lines   13–14, 19, 23, 28 none of these lines is in Dante; instant
personifications such as 'wearied Grief' are not characteristic of the
Commedia

Futurity's dark veil was drawn aside,
30   I in my dream the troubled prospect eyed.
On those high hills, it seem'd, (those hills which hide
Pisa from Lucca,) that, by Sismond's side,
Guland and Landfranc, with discordant cry,
Rouse from its den a wolf and young, who fly
Before their famish'd dogs; I saw the sire
And little trembling young ones faint and tire,
Saw them become the eager blood-hounds prey,
Who soon with savage rage their haunches flay.
I first awoke, and view'd my slumbering boys,
40   Poor hapless product of my nuptial joys,
Scar'd with *their* dreams, toss o'er their stony bed,
And starting scream with frightful noise for bread.

   Hard is thy heart, no tears those eyes can know,
If they refuse for pangs like mine to flow.
My Children wake; for now the hour drew near
When we were wont our scanty food to share.
A thousand fears our trembling bosoms fill,
Each from his dream foreboding some new ill.
With horrid jar we heard the prison door
50   Close on us all, never to open more.
My senses fail, absorb'd in dumb amaze,
Deprived of motion on my boys I gaze:
Benumb'd with fear, and harden'd into stone,
I could not weep, nor heave one easing groan.
My Children moan, my youngest trembling cried,
'What ails my Father?' still my tongue denied
To move; they cling to me in wild affright:
That mournful day, and the succeeding night,

32–3 *Sismond . . . Guland . . . Landfranc* families hostile to Ugolino; like
Gray translates as though the names referred to individuals   40 Dante's
Ugolino does not feel the need to stress that his children are legitimate
42 *scream with frightful noise* supplied by Carlisle

We all the dreadful horrid silence kept:
Fearful to ask, with silent grief they wept.   60
   Now in the gloomy cell a ray of light
New horrors added by dispelling night.
When looking on my boys, in frantic fit
Of maddening grief, my senseless hands I bit.
Alas! for hunger they mistake my rage,
'Let us,' they cried, 'our Father's pains assuage:
' 'Twas he, our Sire who call'd us into day, ⎫
'Clad with this painful flesh our mortal clay, ⎬
'That flesh he gave he sure may take away.' – ⎭
   But why should I prolong the horrid tale?   70
Dismay and silent woe again prevail.
No more that day we spoke! – Why in thy womb
Then, cruel Earth, did we not meet our doom?
Now the fourth morning rose; my eldest child
Fell at his Father's feet; in accent wild,
Struggling with pain, with his last fleeting breath,
'Help me, my Sire,' he cried, and sunk in death.
I saw the others follow one by one,
Heard their last scream, and their expiring groan.
And now arose the last concluding day;   80
As o'er each corse I grop'd my stumbling way,
I call'd my Boys, though now they were no more,
Yet still I call'd, till sinking on the floor,
Pale Hunger did what Grief refus'd to do –
For ever closed this scene of pain and woe.   (1772)

63–4 *in frantic . . . maddening* souped up from Dante's plain '*per lo dolor*'
('in grief' or 'in pain')   85 this line is not in the original, which does not say
what hunger did that grief could not do

HENRY BOYD (c. 1750–1832)

Boyd was born in County Antrim, educated at Trinity College,
Dublin, and ordained as a minister of the Church of Ireland.
He translated Ariosto and Petrarch as well as producing the
first published translation of the whole *Commedia*. As a writer,
Boyd did not lack ambitions of style – witness his verse dramas
on biblical subjects (1793) and his 'Woodman's Tale', written
in Spenserian diction and stanzas (1805). Boyd blamed the
French for delaying recognition of Dante's genius; he thought
them as a nation unsuited to appreciate this 'gloomy and
romantic bard'. An English critic wrote enthusiastically of
Boyd's version: 'the dullness of Dante is often enlivened by Mr
Boyd with profuse ornaments of his own'; it is at least true that
there is much in Boyd that is not in Dante.

Purgatorio 9

I

Aurora, stealing from her Consort's arms,
Shew'd in the glimm'ring East her rising charms;
    The Stars, that form'd the Scorpion's radiant train,
Gemm'd her pale brow; while Night's retiring shade,
Yet o'er the West a partial gloom display'd,
    Measuring the downward Sky with tardy wane.

1–6 Boyd blurs the chronology of the lines. Dante says both that night had
completed almost three of its hours (it is nearly 9 p.m.) and also that dawn is
just beginning (it is about 6 a.m.). Dante is timing by a global clock; when it
is nine at night on the antipodean mount of Purgatory, it is dawn in Italy

II

Then ADAM's gift, my tenement of clay,
To my protracted toils at last gave way
  In MORPHEUS' arms, on grassy couch reclin'd,
Amid my ghostly guard. The hour was come,   10
When gentle PROGNE mourns her ancient doom,
  Her slaughter'd Infant, and her Spouse unkind.

III

But now, from Earth unmoor'd, the mounting Soul
Gave sorrow to the winds, and wing'd the Pole,
  On things immortal, with immortal sight,
Gazing at will. Amid the ample Sky,
Methought an Eagle seem'd his wings to ply,
  With golden gleam, across the fields of Light.

IV

I seem'd to stand upon the PHRYGIAN Plain,
Where GANYMEDE forsook his wond'ring train,   20
  Wafted to Heav'n's Divan with whirlwind speed:
'Fate hovers here,' I cry'd; 'tis hence alone,
The plumy Ranger of th' OLYMPIAN throne,
  Bears off his favour'd prey of mortal breed.

---

9 *MORPHEUS* the classical god of sleep (not mentioned here by Dante)
10–12 another chronological blur: Dante writes that 'at the hour near dawn
when the swallow begins her sad songs', he began to dream; he has fallen
asleep at 9 p.m., slept for nine hours between his lines 12 and 13, and begins
dreaming at 6 a.m. Boyd switches the swallow for a nightingale ('Progne') to
smoothe this leap of time. Nightingale and swallow both come from Ovid,
Metamorphoses 6.412ff.   19 *PHRYGIAN* Trojan
20 *GANYMEDE* kidnapped by Jove, who had assumed the form of an eagle
 21 the Italian means 'when he was snatched to the supreme assembly'
23 *plumy Ranger of th' OLYMPIAN throne* this showy circumlocution for
'eagle' is not in Dante; Chaucer's version of this passage (see the first extract
from *The House of Fame*, above) is closer to the original

V

Not long he linger'd in his station high,
But, like the bolt that fires the angry Sky,
   Sweeping along, he seiz'd me as I stood:
Thence, mounting, to the burning spheres we past,
Whose flames began our blended forms to waste,
30   And lap, with fiery tongues, our seething blood.

VI

Starting in terror from my trance profound
I woke; such fright the young ACHILLES found,
   When first he woke upon the SYRIAN coast:
When, from the CENTAUR's guard, his Mother bore
Her threaten'd Son, to that sequester'd shore,
   Where soon the GREEKS her expectation cross'd.

VII

As the young Warrior woke with sudden start,
Thus fled my slumbers, while, with beating heart
   And icy veins, I gaz'd, distracted round:
40   At length, I spy'd the faithful MANTUAN near,
And now the burning Sun had climb'd the Sphere
   Thrice ten degrees above the wat'ry bound.

VIII

'Fear not,' he cry'd, 'the Point is gain'd at length;
Now, let your Spirit put forth all its strength,
   Fir'd, and expanding to the moment's claim:
Probation's Porch is nigh. – Yon breach behold,
That parts the mural Mound, in ruin roll'd,
   Thither you mounted like ascending Flame.

32–6 ACHILLES ... GREEKS in an attempt to prevent him from enlisting for
the Trojan War, Achilles' mother Thetis kidnapped him while he slept; the
description of his waking alludes to Statius, *Achilleis* 1.247–50
40 *the faithful MANTUAN* Dante here calls Virgil 'my comforter'
41–2 the Italian means 'and the sun was already two hours higher'
45 *Fir'd* an unhappy expression, given the context of the burning dream,
and not in Dante

IX

'Just as the grey dawn usher'd in the Day,
When stretch'd on flow'ry couch, below you lay,   50
  On fleet wing sailing thro' the breaking gloom,
Onward, a Vision came; with fervent plea,
It cry'd, "Resign that slumb'ring Man to me,
  I'll teach his weight to mount on Eagle Plume."

X

'We left the wond'ring Spectres far below,
And as the ruddy East began to glow
  With Orient beams, you rose upon the ray:
The Pageant up the Sky, with easy flight,
Instinctive I pursu'd, and saw you light
  Where yon' fall'n rampires show the rifled way.   60

XI

'She pointed to the pass, and upward soar'd;
The dream departed, and to light restor'd,
  Instant you woke at this important post:'
Like one I stood, in Truth's uncertain light
And doubts involv'd, as Day contends with Night,
  Till ev'ry fear in rising Hope was lost.

XII

This change I felt; and, when I saw the Bard,
With cheerful look and angel-step prepar'd
  The battlements to pass, I soon pursu'd:
Attend, ye Mortals, to the mystic lay,   70
The Song, ascending to the Source of Day,
  Claims, from the daring Muse, a loftier mood.

52–3 *a Vision ... cry'd* the original has simply a woman named Lucia, who
just 'speaks'   57–9 the 'ray' and the 'flight' are all Boyd's own, as is the
inverted syntax   60 *rampires* ramparts   70 *ye Mortals* Dante as usual
addresses his reader ('*lettor*') in the singular and does not imply that as
'mortals' they are a different class of person from him
72 *the daring Muse* there is no Muse of any kind at this point in the original

XIII

To the disparted Mound we came at last,
No ruin now it seem'd, but proudly grac'd
    With a bright portal, and ascending stair:
A Guardian of the Pass was seen above,
With lips fast clos'd, that never seem'd to move;
    Admittance we implor'd with rev'rent air.

XIV

An heav'nly Minister appear'd within,
80   Too bright for mortal eye suffus'd with Sin
    Undazzl'd to behold, a glancing blade,
Far waving in his dexter hand around,
With keen reflection seem'd my sense to wound,
    By this ethereal Habitant dismay'd.

XV

'Keep thy due distance, and declare,' he cry'd;
'What heav'nly Delegate vouchsaf'd to guide
    Your steps? be cautious, lest you meet with harm!'
'A Denizen of Heav'n,' the MANTUAN said,
'Told, where the Gate its shining valves display'd;
90   Soon the bright Sentry own'd the powerful sign.'

XVI

'Mount,' he reply'd; 'then, high distinguish'd soul!
May Saints conduct thee, to that higher goal,
    Where those that pass the test, may claim the Sky:

76–84 Boyd elaborates profusely from words meaning 'I saw, sitting on the
topmost stair, one whose face was such I could not withstand him; and he
had a naked sword in his hand which reflected the sun's rays towards us
so brightly that I turned my gaze on him often but in vain'
88 *A Denizen of Heav'n* Dante's Virgil says 'a woman of the sky'
89 *valves* doors   **91** *high distinguish'd soul!* the angel in the original, though
'*cortese*' ('courteous'), hands out no such accolade

Fear not to scale the stairs.' We venture on;
The lowest step, like Parian marble shone,
   And gave my Form reflected to the eye.

XVII

The second seem'd of dark and sullen hue,
As if from MONZIBEL its birth it drew;
   Its time-worn face was mark'd with many a
      scar:
Deep fissures ran along its inmost grain,   100
Crossing the mass in many a winding vein,
   Like the deep marks of elemental war.

XVIII

The third, a purple radiance flung around,
Like blood, fast spouting from a recent wound,
   The Seraph's feet upon the sanguine floor
Appear'd: upon a throne he sate sublime,
Of chisel'd adamant, defying Time,
   Full in the midst before the massy Door.

XIX

'Your humble hands in supplication rear,'
MARO advis'd; 'that by your potent pray'r   110
   Subdu'd, the Guardian may unlock the Gate.'
Beating my breast, my pliant knees I bent,
The favouring Spirit gave a kind consent,
   But first prepar'd me for my mystic fate.

---

98 *MONZIBEL* the god Vulcan's smithy under Mount Etna; Dante refers to it
in the apt context of *Inferno* 14.56 but not here. Boyd is even more Miltonic
than usual at this point (compare the stanza with the description of Satan at
Paradise Lost 1.599–602) and to even less than usual purpose   109–11 in
the original, Virgil ('MARO') advises Dante simply to 'ask him humbly to
release the bolt'   112 *Beating my breast* not in Dante

XX

Seven deep distinguish'd marks his trenchant blade,
Upon my gore-distilling front pourtray'd;
   'Enter!' he cry'd; 'within the waters flow
That lave such wounds.' My trembling eyes beheld
The sober Vestment which his limbs conceal'd,
120   Of earthy hue, sad sign of guilt and woe!

XXI

Then from beneath his Hermit Garb, he drew
A golden Key, and one of silver hue,
   And turn'd them both. 'If one of these,' he cry'd,
'In this laborious operation fail,
In vain the second wards the Gate assail,
   Altho' by Man, or Angel's hand, apply'd.

XXII

'The one appears of richer metal made,
More skill is in its fellow's frame display'd;
   To these victorious wards the valves unclose:
130 From PETER's hands they came, a charge divine,
Who bade me ne'er to Pity's scale incline,
   Unless her genuine fruit, Repentance shews.'

XXIII

With mighty impulse then, he push'd the Door;
'Enter,' he said; 'you see the Path before:
   But, if you look behind, 'tis instant clos'd,

---

115 *Seven* one for each of the seven deadly sins   122 for the keys, see Matthew 16:19; in later tradition, the golden key stands for the authority to remit punishment for sin granted by Christ to Peter and his successors, the silver for the prudent exercise of that authority   131–2 Dante gives Peter's instruction as 'he told me I should err on the side of opening rather than of shutting, provided the people fall to the ground before me' (falling to the ground is a scriptural sign of recognition of the divine, as for example at Judges 13:20 or John 18:6)

And entrance is deny'd.' With sudden jar
The valves unclose, loud Echo sent afar
    The doubling din, around the rugged Coast.

XXIV

Such angry sounds the great Dictator heard:
So thunder'd the disparting valves, that clear'd   140
    The hallow'd passage to his feet profane;
Where ROME her treasures shew'd, in rich display;
When daring hands the Tribune forc'd away,
    Who strove his impious fury to restrain.

XXV

But these discordant strains were mingled soon
With Hallelujahs, whose harmonious tune
    Mellow'd the movements of the harsher sound:
Confusion sweet! as when the Organ blows,
And choral warblings swell the solemn close,
    The Poet's Art in Melody is drown'd.   (1802)   150

WILLIAM ROSCOE (1753–1831)

Roscoe trained as a lawyer in Liverpool and practised law until
the success of his *Life of Lorenzo de' Medici* (1795) allowed
him to concentrate on literature; he wrote *The Butterfly's Ball*
in verse for children (1806) and edited Pope (1824). Though
his published opinions on Dante are often standard issue – the
Commedia 'compared with the Aeneid ... is a piece of grand
Gothic architecture at the side of a beautiful Roman temple' –

---

139 *the great Dictator* Julius Caesar, whose attempt to plunder the public
treasure was resisted by the tribune Marcellus, whom Caesar then banished
146 *Hallelujahs* Dante is less Handelian than Boyd: his penitents sing the *Te
Deum*   148–50 the original means 'as when singing is accompanied on the
organ and sometimes you can hear the words and sometimes you can't'

he was exceptionally learned about both Italian history and writing. In the letter which includes the following translation, he calls it 'a little detached piece of the celebrated Dante, in which he seems to have sketched the first idea of his Beatrice ... whom he appears to have regarded with a warmth and delicacy of passion far beyond what is found in the writings of any other poet, even of Petrarca himself'. It is doubtful whether the poem does refer to Beatrice. Roscoe is one of the first English translators to show an interest in Dante's lyric poems or 'detached piece[s]'.

From the Italian of Dante Alighieri.
[*Rime* 87: 'Io mi son pargoletta . . .']

'Of loveliest feature and of lightest form,
A stranger here, to glad your sight I come,
With interview of heaven – pleas'd to perform
The task assign'd – then seek my native home –
Scattering delight where'er my course I bend,
That whoso sees me, and refrains from love,
Of love is all insensible, – for when
Nature, from Him whose gracious will did send
Me here, entreated I might be, oh! then
10   To perfect me with beauty all things strove:
The stars rain'd lustre in my eyes, that beam'd
With mild attemper'd light, and heavenly charms
In earthly mould were first to mortals shown:
Yet not alike on all this radiance flam'd;
His heart alone the glow celestial warms,
Who from another's bliss derives his own.' –
This sentence once 't was mine to trace,
Bright beaming from an angel's face,
But by too ardent passion fir'd
20   I nearly at the sight expir'd;

Nor for the deep and hopeless wound,
Sent from those eyes of heavenly blue –
By one whose power too well I knew,
Have I as yet a balsam found.
                    (written 1820; published 1833)

SAMUEL ROGERS (1763–1855)

When his father's death in 1793 released him from his duties
at the family bank, Rogers devoted himself to poetry, con-
noisseurship, travel and elegant socializing. Though his tastes
were formed by the writings of Goldsmith and Johnson – in his
youth he went to visit the great Doctor, but awe overcame him
on the doorstep and he went away without knocking – he knew
later poetic generations well and was often generous to them
financially and critically. He claimed to have brought Cary's
translation of Dante to Wordsworth's and Coleridge's atten-
tion, and to have been instrumental in securing Cary a govern-
ment pension (he also helped the colourful Italianist Ugo
Foscolo, one of the many refugees who spread Dante's fame at
this time). His *Table-Talk* is perhaps more often read these days
than his poetry.

Florence   18–51

On that ancient seat,
The seat of stone that runs along the wall,
South of the Church, east of the belfry-tower,
(Thou canst not miss it) in the sultry time
Would DANTE sit conversing, and with those

---

2 *seat of stone* the 'Sasso di Dante', near the south transept of Santa Maria
del Fiore, on which legend has it Dante used to sit

Who little thought that in his hand he held
The balance, and assigned at his good pleasure
To each his place in the invisible world,
To some an upper region, some a lower;
10   Many a transgressor sent to his account,
Long ere in FLORENCE numbered with the dead;
The body still as full of life and stir
At home, abroad; still and as oft inclined
To eat, drink, sleep; still clad as others were,
And at noon-day, where men were wont to meet,
Met as continually; when the soul went,
Relinquish'd to a demon, and by him
(So says the Bard, and who can read and doubt?)
Dwelt in and governed. – Sit thee down awhile;
20   Then, by the gates so marvellously wrought,
That they might serve to be the gates of Heaven,
Enter the Baptistery. That place he loved,
Loved as his own; and in his visits there
Well might he take delight! For when a child,
Playing, as many are wont, with venturous feet
Near and yet nearer to the sacred font,
Slipped and fell in, he flew and rescued him,
Flew with an energy, a violence,
That broke the marble – a mishap ascribed
30   To evil motives; his, alas, to lead
A life of trouble, and ere long to leave
All things most dear to him, ere long to know
How salt another's bread is, and the toil
Of going up and down another's stairs.   (1830)

---

18 *So says the Bard* in *Inferno* 33.124–38, though strictly it is the damned
Fra Alberigo not Dante who puts forward this wildly unorthodox notion
24 *For when a child* . . . Rogers embroiders the anecdote from *Inferno*
19.16–21   31–4 *Paradiso* 17.55–60

The Campagna of Florence   313–28

But lo, the Sun is setting; earth and sky
One blaze of glory – What we saw but now,
As though it were not, though it had not been!
He lingers yet; and, lessening to a point,
Shines like the eye of Heaven – then withdraws;
And from the zenith to the utmost skirts
All is celestial red! The hour is come,
When they that sail along the distant seas,
Languish for home; and they that in the morn
Said to sweet friends 'farewell,' melt as at parting;   10
When, just gone forth, the pilgrim, if he hears,
As now we hear it – echoing round the hill,
The bell that seems to mourn the dying day,
Slackens his pace and sighs, and those he loved
Loves more than ever. But who feels it not?
And well may we, for we are far away.   (1830)

CHARLES LYELL (1767–1849)

Lyell attributed the 'first idea' of making his translations to the
stimulus he received from the 'remarkable works' of Gabriele
Rossetti, one of those Italian political refugees who so influ-
enced English responses to Dante and to the cause of Italian
unification (the poet was clamorously linked by the nationalists
with their aspirations). Gabriele Rossetti's books are often
described as 'remarkable' by commentators at a loss for a term
at once gentle and just: in them, he expounded with manic
vigour a conspiracy theory of European history, to which
Dante's poems were said to provide the cryptic key. (Ezra Pound
was taken with some of Rossetti's notions.) Lyell, who had
been usefully engaged in the study of New Forest mosses for

7–15 compare *Purgatorio* 8.1–6

several years, was so impressed by this theory that he returned
to his Forfarshire estate in 1826 and turned his energies on
Dante. He is thought also to have translated the prose sections
of the *Vita Nuova* but the manuscript is lost. His *Canzoniere*
(1835) makes the first big step in Victorian enthusiasm for
Dante's lyric poems, an enthusiasm which neatly culminates in
his godson, Dante Gabriel Rossetti's *The Early Italian Poets
from Ciullo d'Alcamo to Dante Alighieri* (1861).

Vita Nuova 3 ['A ciascun'alma presa e gentil core']

> To every captive soul and gentle heart,
>   Into whose sight the present song shall come,
>   Praying their thoughts on what it may portend,
>   Health in the name of Love, their sovereign lord.
> A third part of the hours had almost past
>   Which show in brightest lustre every star,
>   When suddenly before me Love appeared,
>   Whose essence to remember gives me horror.
> Joyful Love seem'd, holding within his hand
>   My heart, and in his arms enfolded lay
>   Madonna sleeping, in a mantle wrapt.
> He then awoke her, and this burning heart
>   Presented humbly, which in fear she ate.
>   That done, I saw him go his way in tears.
>   (1835; revised 1842)

10

Vita Nuova 13 ['Tutti li miei pensier parlan d'Amore']

> My thoughts are all discoursing upon Love,
>   And have in them so great variety,
>   That one persuades me to desire his sway,
>   Another says his power is vanity:

---

11 *Madonna* Beatrice

One sweetly soothes and cheers me while I hope,
   Another ofttimes makes my tears to flow,
   And they alone accord in pity's claim,
   Trembling with fear which is within the heart.
Hence know I not what argument to take,
   And fain would speak, and know not what to say;   10
   Thus do I wander in Love's labyrinth.
And if with all I would accordance make,
   I needs must call upon my enemy,
   Madonna Pity, to be my defence.   (1835; 1842)

JAMES MONTGOMERY (1771–1854)

Montgomery was, in succession, a baker, a clerk, proprietor of the *Sheffield Register*, and a Moravian missionary to Barbados, where he died. His publications were as various as his life: they include *The World Before the Flood: a poem, in ten cantos*; *An Essay on the Phrenology of the Hindoos and Negroes*; a book for chimney-sweeps and 'climbing-boys'; and editions of Cowper and Milton. Eleven of his hymns still figure in *Hymns Ancient and Modern* (the best-known is 'Angels from the realms of glory'). Montgomery shared a growing tendency to regard the *Commedia* primarily as a series of character sketches; he praised in Dante the 'mere hints of narrative or gleams of allusion ... on which a modern versifier or novelist would expend pages'.

Maestro Adamo [*Inferno* 30.49–148]

The hideously comic interview and adventure with Maestro Adamo (Master Adam), the coiner, – in another of the lower rounds of the infernal gulf, where traitors of the baser sort are tormented with unappeasable thirst, in various diseases that excite it, – is thoroughly *Dantesque*, but in the poet's coarser vein. It may form a singular companion piece to the fearfully

sublime, but simply told and tenderly affecting, narrative of
Count Ugolino.

> I saw one shapen like a lute, had he
> Been shorten'd where the man becomes a fork;
> Enormous dropsy (which had swoln his limbs
> With stagnant humours, till his ghastly cheek
> But ill agreed with his unwieldy paunch,)
> Made him, for thirst, gasp like a hectic, – one
> Lip lolling on his chin, upcurl'd the other.
>
>   'Oh! you,' he cried, 'that without pain (though why
> I know not) pass through this unhappy world,
> Hear, and mark well the sorrows of Adamo;
> Living, I had whatever heart could wish,
> And now, alas! I lack a drop of water.
> The murmuring rivulets down the verdant hills
> Of Cassentino, flowing into Arno,
> Which keep their little channels moist and cool,
> Are ever in mine eye; – and not in vain,
> For their sweet images inflame my thirst
> More than the malady that shrinks my visage.
> The rigid justice, which torments me here,
> Even from the place where I committed sin,
> Draws means to mock and multiply my groans;
> Romena stands before me, where I forged
> The lawful coin and Baptist's seal, for which

10

20

1–2 though Dante is usually concise and sometimes crabbed, Montgomery is
responsible for these barely intelligible lines; the original makes clear that
from the groin up Maestro Adamo was distended like the body of a lute
13 *murmuring* the standard-issue epithet has no equivalent in the original
verdant Dante's hills are just plain green (*'verdi'*)   21 *to mock* not in Dante
22–7 'This miserable culprit had been a metallurgist of Brescia, who, at the
instance of Guido, Alessandro, and Aginulpho, three nobles of Romena,
counterfeited the gold florin of Tuscany, which bore the impress of the
Baptist's head. – Branda is a beautiful fountain at Siena.' [*Montgomery's
note*]

I left my wretched body in the flames.
– Yet could I spy the woeful ghost of Guido,
Of Alessandro, or their brother, here,
I would not quit the sight for Branda's fountain!
Somewhere among these pits dwells one, – if truth
Be told by those mad souls that roam at large, –
But what is that to me whose limbs are bound?   30
Oh! were I light enough to move an inch
A century, I had set out ere now
In search of him among the hideous throng,
Through all the eleven long miles of this sad circle,
Which hath not less than half a mile in breadth!
They brought me to this family of fiends,
They tempted me to falsify the florin,
And mix it with three carats of alloy.'

   Then I to him: – 'And who are these two
      wretches,
That smoke like hands in winter plunged through
      snow,   40
Lying close fetter'd on the right of thee?'

   'I found them here, and they have never stirr'd
Since I was dropt into this ditch,' he answered:
'One's the false woman who accused young Joseph,
And t'other Sinon, the false Greek at Troy,
Who, in the excruciate pangs of putrid fever,
Send up such steam.'

---

25 *woeful ghost* the original means 'sad soul'   40 spun from Dante's 'like
wet hands in winter'   42–3 Montgomery omits a line after 'I found them
here' which means 'when I rained down into this trough' – a grotesque
persistence of Adamo's fixation on liquids   44 *the false woman* Potiphar's
wife; see Genesis 39:6–23   45 *Sinon* he tricked the Trojans into bringing the
wooden horse within their walls   44–5 *false . . . false* the insistent repetition
is in the original   46–7 Montgomery refines on Dante's 'coarser vein'; the
original means 'their fever is so sharp they throw out a fug'

That moment one of them,
Wroth to be named so ignominiously,
Struck with the fist on his distended hide,
50   That thunder'd like a drum; – but Master Adam
Repaid the blow upon the assailant's face,
Not less afflictive, with his arm; exclaiming,
'Though reft of locomotion, being so large,
I have a hand at liberty for *that.*'

To whom the other: – 'Thou wert not so prompt,
When thou wast going to the stake; and yet
More prompt than now when thou didst stamp the
        coin.'

'Thou speak'st the truth,' the dropsical replied,
'But didst not so at Troy, when truth was ask'd thee.'

60   'False words I utter'd then, as thou false money;
If for one crime I suffer, thou art damn'd
For more than any demon here,' quoth Sinon.

'Remember! perjured one, the hollow horse,
With its full belly,' Adam cried, 'and stand
Guilty through all the world.'

                                'Stand guilty thou!'
The Greek retorted; 'witness that huge round,
That quagmire, which ingulfs thee in thyself.'

The coiner then: – 'Thy mouth for evil-speaking
Is quite as open as it wont to be;
70   If I have drought while humours swell me up,

51–3 *assailant . . . afflictive . . . locomotion* these grandeurs have no
equivalent in the Italian   66–7 in Dante, Sinon needles Adamo by also
referring to 'the thirst which cracks your tongue'

Thou hast a burning heart and aching head,
And wouldst not need much coaxing to the task
To lap the mirror of Narcissus dry.'

    I stood all fix'd to hear them. – 'Little more
Would make me quarrel with thee; so be warn'd,'
Cried Virgil: – when I heard him speak in warmth,
I turn'd about, and colour'd with such shame,
The very thought brings back the blush upon me.
Like one who dreams of harm befalling him,
And dreaming wishes it may *be* a dream,   80
Desiring that which *is* as though it *were not*,
So I, unable to excuse myself
(For I stood mute), excused myself the more,
Unwittingly. – 'Less shame than thine might make
Atonement for a greater fault than thine,'
My Master said, 'so cast away thy sadness;
And know that I am ever at thy side;
If fortune brings thee where such knaves fall out,
– To love their broils betrays a base-born mind.'
        (1841)

The River of Life [*Paradiso* 30.46–96]

The greater part of the *Paradiso*, – while it exemplifies, almost
beyond example, the power of human language to vary a few
ideas and images in themselves so simple, pure, and hallowed,
that they hardly can be altered from their established associ-
ations without being degraded, – shows also the utter impotence
of any other terms than those which Scripture has employed
'as in a glass darkly,' – and who can *there* add light? – to body

---

73 *the mirror of Narcissus* a pool of water   84–5 in the original, Virgil
continues the run of references to water: 'less shame washes away greater
faults'   89 *base-born* the Italian '*bassa*' does not have so explicit a Yeatsian
scorn for humble origins

forth what eye hath not seen, ear heard, neither hath entered
into the heart of man to conceive. One elaborate specimen
(however defective the translation may be) will elucidate this
failure even in the noble original, which, like its ineffable theme,
in this part is 'dark with excessive bright.' The poet here copies
more directly than he is wont from the sacred Oracles; or, as
in the sublime simile of the rock, illustrates his subject with not
unworthy natural objects; at the same time, with characteristic
ingenuousness, he explains his own feelings on beholding
'things which it is not lawful for a man to utter.'

> As sudden lightning dissipates the sight,
> And leaves the eye unable to discern
> The plainest objects, – living light so flash'd
> Around me, and involved me in a veil
> Of such effulgence, that I *ceased to see*.
> 'Thus Love, which soothes this heaven, all kindly fits
> The torch to take his flame!' – These few, brief words
> Had scarcely reach'd mine ear, when I perceived
> Power from on high diffuse such virtue through me,
> And so rekindle vision, that no flame,
> However pure, could 'scape mine eyes.
>   I saw
> Light, like a river clear as crystal, flowing
> Between two banks with wondrous spring adorn'd;
> While from the current issued vivid sparks,
> That fell among the flowers on either hand,
> Glitter'd like rubies set in gold, and then,
> As if intoxicate with sweetest odours,
> Replunged themselves into the mystic flood,
> Whence, as one disappear'd, another rose.

10

6–7 Beatrice is speaking   12 *clear as crystal* the cliché is not in Dante

'The intense desire that warms and stirs thy
    thoughts   20
To understand what thou beholdest, yields
More joy to me, the more it urges thee;
But ere such noble thirst can be assuaged,
Behoves thee first to drink of this clear fount.'
The sun that lights mine eyes thus spake, and added:
– 'Yon stream, those jewels flitting to and fro,
And all the joyance of these laughing flowers,
Are shadowy emblems of realities,
Not dark themselves, but the defect is thine,
Who hast not yet obtain'd due strength of vision.' 30

Ah! then, no infant, startled out of sleep,
Long past his time, springs to the mother's milk
More eagerly than o'er that stream I bow'd
To make more perfect lustres of mine eyes,
Which, when the fringes of their lids had touch'd it,
Seem'd, from a line, collapsed into a round.
– As maskers, when they cast their visors off,
Appear new persons, stript of such disguise,
The sparks and flowers assumed sublimer forms,
And both the courts of heaven were open'd round
    me. (1841)   40

HENRY CARY (1772–1844)

Anna Seward, the 'Swan of Lichfield', complained of Cary while
he was still at Oxford University that 'his ear has been
debauched by the luscious smoothness of Italian tones'. He
began his translation of the *Commedia* with *Purgatorio*, his
favourite *cantica*, on 16 January 1797, shortly after he was

---

20 the original line has more drive: 'the high desire that inflames you and
urges you on'   25 *The sun* Beatrice   32 *springs* Dante's baby is less
startlingly athletic; it has 'its face turned to the milk'

ordained in the Anglican Church. He worked at the rate of
about three days per canto but stopped after *Purgatorio* 5 and
did not resume the work until May 1800, when he began at the
beginning of *Inferno*. The first *cantica* appeared in Italian/
English facing-page format in 1805–6; the complete translation
followed in 1812. It was mostly ignored until Coleridge lectured
enthusiastically on both Dante and Cary in 1818, after which
the first edition was soon exhausted. Cary's version, in which
Keats and many later writers read Dante, has been continuously
in print since then. Cary was a prolific literary journalist and also
translated Aristophanes (1824), Pindar (1833) and the *Early
French Poets* (1846). He is buried in Westminster Abbey under a
stone marked 'THE TRANSLATOR OF DANTE' and, though
opinions of his version have varied, his right, as far as English is
concerned, to that emphatic 'THE' remains unchallenged.

Inferno 14   16–62

  Vengeance of Heav'n! Oh! how shouldst thou be
        fear'd
By all, who read what here my eyes beheld!
  Of naked spirits many a flock I saw,
All weeping piteously, to different laws
Subjected; for on the'earth some lay supine,
Some crouching close were seated, others pac'd
Incessantly around; the latter tribe,
More numerous, those fewer who beneath
The torment lay, but louder in their grief.
10   O'er all the sand fell slowly wafting down
Dilated flakes of fire, as flakes of snow

---

9 *louder in their grief* for once an English translator is more concise than
Dante who has here the padded line 'but they had their tongues more loosed
in lament'   11 the excellence of this passage may have kept Cary in
Tennyson's mind until 1860 when the phrase 'flakes of fire' appears in
'Tithonus' (1.42)

On Alpine summit, when the wind is hush'd.
As in the torrid Indian clime, the son
Of Ammon saw upon his warrior band
Descending, solid flames, that to the ground
Came down: whence he bethought him with his
        troop
To trample on the soil; for easier thus
The vapour was extinguish'd, while alone;
So fell the'eternal fiery flood, wherewith
The marle glow'd underneath, as under stove   20
The viands, doubly to augment the pain.
Unceasing was the play of wretched hands,
Now this, now that way glancing, to shake off
The heat, still falling fresh. I thus began:
'Instructor! thou who all things overcom'st,
Except the hardy demons, that rush'd forth
To stop our entrance at the gate, say who
Is yon huge spirit, that, as seems, heeds not
The burning, but lies writhen in proud scorn,
As by the sultry tempest immatur'd?'   30
    Straight he himself, who was aware I ask'd
My guide of him, exclaim'd: 'Such as I was
When living, dead such now I am. If Jove
Weary his workman out, from whom in ire
He snatch'd the lightnings, that at my last day
Transfix'd me, if the rest he weary out
At their black smithy labouring by turns
In Mongibello, while he cries aloud;
"Help, help, good Mulciber!" as erst he cried

13–14 *the son / Of Ammon* Alexander the Great   20 *marle* Dante has the
plainest Italian word for 'sand'; Cary may have remembered the 'burning
marl' of *Paradise Lost* 1.296   30 *immatur'd* modern editors prefer '*marturi*'
('martyrs') to '*maturi*' ('matures'), printed in the texts to which Cary had
access   33–6 *If Jove . . . if the rest* Cary preserves the rhetorical bravura of
the original   38 *Mongibello* beneath Mount Etna, where Vulcan had his
smithy; in the next line, Cary, as usual somewhat under the influence of
Milton, prefers the alternative name 'Mulciber' to Dante's 'Vulcano'

40   In the Phlegræan warfare, and the bolts
        Launch he full aim'd at me with all his might,
        He never should enjoy a sweet revenge.'
            Then thus my guide, in accent higher rais'd
        Than I before had heard him: 'Capaneus!
        Thou art more punish'd, in that this thy pride
        Lives yet unquench'd: no torment, save thy rage,
        Were to thy fury pain proportion'd full.'
                (1806; 1814)

                Inferno 26   25–142

        As in that season, when the sun least veils
        His face that lightens all, what time the fly
        Gives way to the shrill gnat, the peasant then
        Upon some cliff reclin'd, beneath him sees
        Fire-flies innumerous spangling o'er the vale,
        Vineyard or tilth, where his day-labour lies:
        With flames so numberless throughout its space
        Shone the eighth chasm, apparent, when the depth
        Was to my view expos'd. As he, whose wrongs
10   The bears aveng'd, at its departure saw
        Elijah's chariot, when the steeds erect
        Rais'd their steep flight for heav'n; his eyes meanwhile,
        Straining pursu'd them, till the flame alone
        Upsoaring like a misty speck he kenn'd;
        E'en thus along the gulf moves every flame,

---

40 *Phlegræan* referring to the valley in Thessaly where Jove fought against
the giants: see Ovid, *Metamorphoses* 1.151–62   44 *Capaneus* one of the
seven kings who fought against Thebes; in his *Thebaid*, Statius attributes to
him the idea that 'fear first created the gods'. He was struck down by a
thunderbolt

    3 *shrill gnat* Cary anglicizes the Italian's 'mosquito'
5 *innumerous spangling* not in Dante; 'innumerous' might be from *Paradise
Lost* 7.455   6 *tilth* ploughed land   7 *numberless* the Italian says just 'so
many flames'; the arithmetical sublime is once again Miltonic ('numberless'
figures nine times in *Paradise Lost*)   9 *As he* Elisha; see 2 Kings 2:11–24

A sinner so enfolded close in each,
That none exhibits token of the theft.
    Upon the bridge I forward bent to look,
And grasp'd a flinty mass, or else had fall'n,
Though push'd not from the height. The guide,
        who mark'd   20
How I did gaze attentive, thus began:
'Within these ardours are the spirits, each
Swath'd in confining fire.' – 'Master, thy word,'
I answer'd, 'hath assur'd me; yet I deem'd
Already of the truth, already wish'd
To ask thee, who is in yon fire, that comes
So parted at the summit, as it seem'd
Ascending from that funeral pile, where lay
The Theban brothers?' He replied: 'Within
Ulysses there and Diomede endure   30
Their penal tortures, thus to vengeance now
Together hasting, as erewhile to wrath.
These in the flame with ceaseless groans deplore
The ambush of the horse, that open'd wide
A portal for that goodly seed to pass,
Which sow'd imperial Rome; nor less the guile
Lament they, whence of her Achilles 'reft,
Deidamia yet in death complains.
And there is rued the stratagem, that Troy
Of her Palladium spoil'd.' – 'If they have power   40
Of utt'rance from within these sparks,' said I,
'O master! think my prayer a thousand fold
In repetition urg'd, that thou vouchsafe

---

29 *Theban brothers* Eteocles and Polynices; see Statius, *Thebaid* 12.429–32
30 *Diomede* Ulysses' companion in arms at Troy; see *Aeneid* 2.162–70
34–6 'The ambush of the wooden horse that caused Æneas to quit the city of Troy and seek his fortune in Italy, where his descendants founded the Roman empire.' [*Cary's note*] Virgil knows the story well, having told it in the *Aeneid*, to which he refers at line 56 below   42–3 Dante is even more emphatic: 'I really pray you, and pray you again, that you count one prayer as a thousand'

To pause, till here the horned flame arrive.
See, how toward it with desire I bend.'
    He thus: 'Thy prayer is worthy of much praise,
And I accept it therefore: but do thou
Thy tongue refrain: to question them be mine,
For I divine thy wish: and they perchance,
50 For they were Greeks, might shun discourse with thee.'
    When there the flame had come, where time and
        place
Seem'd fitting to my guide, he thus began:
'O ye, who dwell two spirits in one fire!
If living I of you did merit aught,
Whate'er the measure were of that desert,
When in the world my lofty strain I pour'd,
Move ye not on, till one of you unfold
In what clime death o'ertook him self-destroy'd.'
    Of the old flame forthwith the greater horn
60 Began to roll, murmuring, as a fire
That labours with the wind, then to and fro
Wagging the top, as a tongue uttering sounds,
Threw out its voice, and spake: 'When I escap'd
From Circe, who beyond a circling year
Had held me near Caieta, by her charms,
Ere thus Æneas yet had nam'd the shore,
Nor fondness for my son, nor reverence
Of my old father, nor return of love,
That should have crown'd Penelope with joy,
70 Could overcome in me the zeal I had
T'explore the world, and search the ways of life,
Man's evil and his virtue. Forth I sail'd

49–50 Dante had no Greek to speak of   58 *self-destroy'd* the Italian reads
'*perduto*' ('lost')   63 *I* Ulysses, though this is not clear until the next line
63–4 *When I escap'd* / From . . . Dante has a more abrupt line-break to
show how impetuously Ulysses' voice is 'thrown out': 'When / I left
Circe . . .'   64 *circling* Cary's addition

Into the deep illimitable main,
With but one bark, and the small faithful band
That yet cleav'd to me. As Iberia far,
Far as Morocco either shore I saw,
And the Sardinian and each isle beside
Which round that ocean bathes. Tardy with age
Were I and my companions, when we came
To the strait pass, where Hercules ordain'd   80
The bound'ries not to be o'erstepp'd by man.
The walls of Seville to my right I left,
On the' other hand already Ceuta past.
'O brothers!' I began, 'who to the west
'Through perils without number now have reach'd
'To this the short remaining watch, that yet
'Our senses have to wake, refuse not proof
'Of the unpeopled world, following the track
'Of Phoebus. Call to mind from whence ye sprang:
'Ye were not form'd to live the life of brutes,   90
'But virtue to pursue and knowledge high.'
With these few words I sharpen'd for the voyage
The mind of my associates, that I then
Could scarcely have withheld them. To the dawn
Our poop we turn'd, and for the witless flight
Made our oars wings, still gaining on the left.
Each star of the' other pole night now beheld,
And ours so low, that from the ocean-floor
It rose not. Five times re-illum'd, as oft
Vanish'd the light from underneath the moon   100
Since the deep way we enter'd, when from far
Appear'd a mountain dim, loftiest methought
Of all I e'er beheld. Joy seiz'd us straight,

---

73 *deep illimitable main* the Italian means 'the high open sea'; Milton
assisted Cary here – 'illimitable ocean, without bound', *Paradise Lost* 2.892
91 *knowledge high* Cary added the 'high'   102 *a mountain dim* the mount
of Purgatory

But soon to mourning chang'd. From the new land
A whirlwind sprung, and at her foremost side
Did strike the vessel. Thrice it whirl'd her round
With all the wave, the fourth time lifted up
The poop, and sank the prow: so fate decreed:
And over us the booming billow clos'd.'
     (1806; 1814)

Purgatorio 30

Soon as the polar light, which never knows
Setting nor rising, nor the shadowy veil
Of other cloud than sin, fair ornament
Of the first heav'n, to duty each one there
Safely convoying, as that lower doth
The steersman to his port, stood firmly fix'd;
Forthwith the saintly tribe, who in the van
Between the Gryphon and it's radiance came,
Did turn them to the car, as to their rest:
And one, as if commission'd from above,
In holy chant thrice shouted forth aloud;
'Come, spouse, from Libanus!' and all the rest
Took up the song. – At the last audit so
The blest shall rise, from forth his cavern each

---

108 *so fate decreed* the Italian translated here means 'as it pleased another';
Ulysses sounds either blank or reticent about what brought him low
109 *booming billow* Dante contented himself with 'the sea'. The canto ends
here; Ulysses is one of the few damned souls to whom Dante allows the last
word (see also *Inferno* 13, 24, 28 and 29)
  1–6 Cary's suspended syntax follows Dante's 7 *the saintly tribe* the
Italian means 'the truthful people' or 'the genuine people' 7–9 this pageant
is described at length in *Purgatorio* 29 8 *the Gryphon* a mythical creature
with the head of a lion and the wings of an eagle; it symbolizes Christ in the
allegorical procession 11 *holy chant* not in Dante 12 '*Come . . .*' in Latin
in the original – see Song of Songs 4:8; the spouse, interpreted by the Church
Fathers as Divine Wisdom, turns out to be Beatrice in what follows

Uplifting lightly his new-vested flesh,
As, on the sacred litter, at the voice
Authoritative of that elder, sprang
A hundred ministers and messengers
Of life eternal. 'Blessed thou! who com'st!'
And, 'O,' they cried, 'from full hands scatter ye   20
Unwith'ring lilies;' and, so saying, cast
Flowers over head and round them on all sides.
    I have beheld ere now, at break of day,
The eastern clime all roseate, and the sky
Oppos'd, one deep and beautiful serene,
And the sun's face so shaded, and with mists
Attemper'd at his rising, that the eye
Long while endur'd the sight: thus in a cloud
Of flowers, that from those hands angelic rose,
And down, within and outside of the car,   30
Fell showering, in white veil with olive wreath'd,
A virgin in my view appear'd, beneath
Green mantle, rob'd in hue of living flame:
And o'er my spirit, that in former days
Within her presence had abode so long,
No shudd'ring terror crept. Mine eyes no more
Had knowledge of her; yet there mov'd from her
A hidden virtue, at whose touch awak'd,
The power of ancient love was strong within me.
    No sooner on my vision streaming, smote   40
The heav'nly influence, which, years past, and e'en

---

15 *new-vested flesh* Dante has a more inquiring phrase, 'the reclothed voice';
just as the dead until the Last Judgement have only quasi-bodies, so they
have only quasi-voices until they re-acquire larynxes   19 *Blessed thou* Dante
has the Latin of the acclamation which greeted Christ on his entry into
Jerusalem; see Matthew 21:9, Mark 11:9, Luke 19:38
20 *from full hands* Dante's angels quote the Latin of *Aeneid* 6.883; in Virgil,
Anchises speaks the words in praise of Marcellus, who died young, like
Beatrice to whom Dante applies them   32 *A virgin* Dante calls her a
'*donna*', a woman

In childhood, thrill'd me, than towards Virgil I
Turn'd me to leftward, panting, like a babe,
That flees for refuge to his mother's breast,
If aught have terrified or work'd him woe:
And would have cried: 'There is no dram of blood,
That doth not quiver in me. The old flame
Throws out clear tokens of reviving fire;'
But Virgil had bereav'd us of himself,
50   Virgil, my best-lov'd father; Virgil, he
To whom I gave me up for safety: nor,
All, our prime mother lost, avail'd to save
My undew'd cheeks from blur of soiling tears.

'Dante, weep not, that Virgil leaves thee: nay,
Weep thou not yet; behoves thee feel the edge
Of other sword, and thou shalt weep for that.'

As to the prow or stern, some admiral
Paces the deck, inspiriting his crew,
When 'mid the sail-yards all hands ply aloof;
60   Thus on the left side of the car I saw,
(Turning me at the sound of mine own name,
Which here I am compell'd to register)

---

42 *In childhood* in the *Vita Nuova* where Dante tells the beginning of the
story of his love for Beatrice, he says he was nine when they first met; some
commentators regard the number as purely symbolic   47 *old flame* Dante
translates from *Aeneid* 4.23 the words in which Dido admits she is in love
with Aeneas   49–51 the Italian is more lucid and plangent; a literal
translation might run: 'But Virgil had left us void of him, Virgil sweetest
father, Virgil to whom for the sake of my well-being I gave myself', though
'salvation' is another possibility for 'well-being'   52 *our prime mother* Eve
53 *soiling tears* a rare misreading from Cary, who is perhaps misled by the
Shakespearean notion that tears are shameful ('soiling') to a man. This idea
is absolutely foreign to Dante, as the sequel shows. The original means: 'all
the delights of the Earthly Paradise, which Eve lost, could not prevent my
cheeks which had been washed in dew [in *Purgatorio* 1] from turning dark
again with tears'   54 *Dante* the first and only time Dante is named in the
Commedia   56 *other sword* the confession and repentance which follow;
the angel's sword had marked Dante's forehead, now Beatrice's reproaches
will pierce him more inwardly – see Luke 2:35

The virgin station'd, who before appear'd
Veil'd in that festive shower angelical.
      Towards me, across the stream, she bent her eyes;
Though from her brow the veil descending, bound
With foliage of Minerva, suffer'd not
That I beheld her clearly; then with act
Full royal, still insulting o'er her thrall,
Added, as one, who speaking keepeth back   70
The bitterest saying, to conclude the speech:
'Observe me well. I am, in sooth, I am
Beatrice. What! and hast thou deign'd at last
Approach the mountain? Knewest not, O man!
Thy happiness is here?' Down fell mine eyes
On the clear fount, but there, myself espying,
Recoil'd, and sought the greenswerd: such a weight
Of shame was on my forehead. With a mien
Of that stern majesty, which doth surround
A mother's presence to her awe-struck child,   80
She look'd; a flavour of such bitterness
Was mingled in her pity. There her words
Brake off, and suddenly the angels sang:
'In thee, O gracious Lord, my hope hath been:'
But went no farther than, 'Thou, Lord, hast set
My feet in ample room.' As snow, that lies
Amidst the living rafters on the back
Of Italy congeal'd, when drifted high
And closely pil'd by rough Sclavonian blasts,
Breathe but the land whereon no shadow falls,   90
And straightway melting it distils away,
Like a fire-wasted taper: thus was I,

---

63 *The virgin* Dante's word is again '*donna*' ('woman')
67 *foliage of Minerva* the olive   72 *in sooth* there is no such poetical
archaism in the original: 'I really am, I really am Beatrice'   76 *espying* the
original has the plain verb 'seeing'   77 *greenswerd* the original specifies
'grass'   84 *In thee* Psalm 31:1–8; the angels, singing Latin on Dante's
behalf, stop before the crucial verse: 'Have mercy upon me, O LORD, for I
am in trouble'   88 *congeal'd* frozen   89 *Sclavonian* from the north-east

Without a sigh or tear, or ever these
Did sing, that with the chiming of the heav'n's sphere,
Still in their warbling chime: but when the strain
Of dulcet symphony, express'd for me
Their soft compassion, more than could the words
'Virgin, why so consum'st him?' then the ice,
Congeal'd about my bosom, turn'd itself
100   To spirit and water, and with anguish forth
Gush'd through the lips and eyelids from the heart.
    Upon the chariot's right edge still she stood,
Immoveable, and thus address'd her words
To those bright semblances with pity touch'd:
'Ye in th'eternal day your vigils keep,
So that nor night nor slumber, with close stealth,
Conveys from you a single step in all
The goings on of life: thence with more heed
I shape mine answer, for his ear intended,
110   Who there stands weeping, that the sorrow now
May equal the transgression. Not alone
Through operation of the mighty orbs,
That mark each seed to some predestin'd aim,
As with aspect or fortunate or ill
The constellations meet, but through benign
Largess of heav'nly graces, which rain down
From such a height, as mocks our vision, this man
Was in the freshness of his being, such,
So gifted virtually, that in him
120   All better habits wond'rously had thriv'd.
The more of kindly strength is in the soil,
So much doth evil seed and lack of culture
Mar it the more, and make it run to wildness.

---

95 *warbling* Cary's tweeness for Dante's 'singing'   98 *Virgin* the original
again has '*donna*'   100–101 *anguish . . . Gush'd* imitating the assonantal
effect of '*angoscia . . . uscî*' in the original   113 *predestin'd* not in Dante
119 *virtually* with virtues

These looks sometime upheld him; for I show'd
My youthful eyes, and led him by their light
In upright walking. Soon as I had reach'd
The threshold of my second age, and chang'd
My mortal for immortal, then he left me,
And gave himself to others. When from flesh
To spirit I had risen, and increase   130
Of beauty and of virtue circled me,
I was less dear to him, and valued less.
His steps were turn'd into deceitful ways,
Following false images of good, that make
No promise perfect. Nor avail'd me aught
To sue for inspirations, with the which,
I, both in dreams of night, and otherwise,
Did call him back; of them so little reck'd him,
Such depth he fell, that all device was short
Of his preserving, save that he should view   140
The children of perdition. To this end
I visited the purlieus of the dead:
And one, who hath conducted him thus high,
Receiv'd my supplications urg'd with weeping.
It were a breaking of God's high decree,
If Lethe should be past, and such food tasted
Without the cost of some repentant tear.'
    (1812; 1814)

Purgatorio 31

'O thou!' her words she thus without delay
Resuming, turn'd their point to me, to whom
They but with lateral edge seem'd harsh before,

---

124 the original means 'For some time I sustained him with my face'
127 *second age* according to Dante, she was twenty-five when she died
141 *The children of perdition* Dante calls the damned 'the lost peoples'
143 *one* Virgil; he recounts his meeting with Beatrice in *Inferno* 2

'Say thou, who stand'st beyond the holy stream,
If this be true. A charge so grievous needs
Thine own avowal.' On my faculty
Such strange amazement hung, the voice expir'd
Imperfect, ere it's organs gave it birth.
    A little space refraining then she spake:
'What dost thou muse on? Answer me. The wave
On thy remembrances of evil yet
Hath done no injury.' A mingled sense
Of fear and of confusion, from my lips
Did such a 'Yea' produce, as needed help
Of vision to interpret. As when breaks
In act to be discharg'd, a cross-bow bent
Beyond its pitch, both nerve and bow o'erstretch'd,
The flagging weapon feebly hits the mark;
Thus, tears and sighs forth gushing, did I burst
Beneath the heavy load, and thus my voice
Was slacken'd on its way. She straight began:
'When my desire invited thee to love
The good, which sets a bound to our aspirings,
What bar of thwarting foss or linked chain
Did meet thee, that thou so should'st quit the hope

10

20

---

4 *Say thou* Dante's Beatrice is more insistent: '*dì, dì*' ('say, say')
6 *avowal* the Italian word is '*confession*' which religious scruples perhaps
inhibited Cary from translating (in his day, confession was a practice
completely in abeyance in the Anglican Church)
10 '*What dost thou muse on?*' she says in Italian '*Che pense?*' ('What are you
thinking about?'), as Virgil does at *Inferno* 5.111 *The wave* of Lethe, the
stream which in the Earthly Paradise washes away memory of sins; Dante
passes through it at 92ff. below 14–15 *as needed . . . interpret* the original
is clearer: 'such a "Yes" that eyes were needed to hear it' – an early reference
to lip-reading 22 *my desire* the Italian is ambiguous between 'my desires'
and 'your desires for me' 24 *foss* ditch; the Italian '*fossi*' was not an
archaism in Dante's time, and still isn't

Of further progress, or what bait of ease
Or promise of allurement led thee on
Elsewhere, that thou elsewhere shouldst rather wait?'
    A bitter sigh I drew, then scarce found voice
To answer, hardly to these sounds my lips   30
Gave utterance, wailing: 'Thy fair looks withdrawn,
Things present, with deceitful pleasures, turn'd
My steps aside.' She answering spake: 'Hadst thou
Been silent, or denied what thou avow'st,
Thou hadst not hid thy sin the more: such eye
Observes it. But whene'er the sinner's cheek
Breaks forth into the precious-streaming tears
Of self-accusing, in our court the wheel
Of justice doth run counter to the edge.
Howe'er that thou mayst profit by the shame   40
For errors past, and that henceforth more strength
May arm thee, when thou hear'st the Syren-voice,
Lay thou aside the motive to this grief,
And lend attentive ear, while I unfold
How opposite a way my buried flesh
Should have impell'd thee. Never didst thou spy
In art or nature aught so passing sweet,
As were the limbs, that in their beauteous frame
Enclos'd me, and are scatter'd now in dust.
If sweetest thing thus fail'd thee with my death,   50
What, afterward, of mortal should thy wish
Have tempted? When thou first hadst felt the dart
Of perishable things, in my departing
For better realms, thy wing thou shouldst have prun'd

26–8 the Italian of these lines has been much debated but Beatrice is
probably saying: 'What easy pickings or hopes of gain appeared in other
women's brows such that you simply had to strut your stuff before them?'
'Strut your stuff' may seem a little racy, but the verb Beatrice uses here,
'*passeggiare*', meant and means 'strolling about to see and be seen'; the
passeggiata still happens most fine evenings in Italian towns   34 *avow'st* the
Italian, as at line 6 above, has the word for 'confess'

To follow me, and never stoop'd again
To 'bide a second blow for a slight girl,
Or other gaud as transient and as vain.
The new and inexperienc'd bird awaits,
Twice it may be, or thrice, the fowler's aim;
But in the sight of one, whose plumes are full,
In vain the net is spread, the arrow wing'd.'

   I stood, as children silent and asham'd
Stand, list'ning, with their eyes upon the earth,
Acknowledging their fault and self-condemn'd.
And she resum'd: 'If, but to hear thus pains thee,
Raise thou thy beard, and lo! what sight shall do!'

   With less reluctance yields a sturdy holm,
Rent from its fibres by a blast, that blows
From off the pole, or from Iarbas' land,
Than I at her behest my visage rais'd:
And thus the face denoting by the beard,
I mark'd the secret sting her words convey'd.

   No sooner lifted I mine aspect up,
Than downward sunk that vision I beheld
Of goodly creatures vanish; and mine eyes,
Yet unassur'd and wavering, bent their light
On Beatrice. Towards the animal,
Who joins two natures in one form, she turn'd,
And, even under shadow of her veil,
And parted by the verdant rill, that flow'd
Between, in loveliness appear'd as much
Her former self surpassing, as on earth
All others she surpass'd. Remorseful goads
Shot sudden through me. Each thing else, the more
Its love had late beguil'd me, now the more

---

64 *self-condemn'd* the original means 'repentant'   67 *holm* oak
69 *Iarbas' land* Libya   77 *the animal* the Gryphon
78 *two natures in one form* the Gryphon's lion/eagle attributes, taken as
symbolizing Christ's simultaneous humanity and divinity
83 *Remorseful goads* Dante specifies 'the nettle of remorse'

Was loathsome. On my heart so keenly smote
The bitter consciousness, that on the ground
O'erpower'd I fell: and what my state was then,
She knows who was the cause. When now my strength
Flow'd back, returning outward from the heart,   90
The lady, whom alone I first had seen,
I found above me. 'Loose me not,' she cried:
'Loose not thy hold;' and lo! had dragg'd me high
As to my neck into the stream, while she,
Still as she drew me after, swept along,
Swift as a shuttle, bounding o'er the wave.

   The blessed shore approaching, then was heard
So sweetly, 'Tu asperges me,' that I
May not remember, much less tell the sound.

   The beauteous dame, her arms expanding, clasp'd   100
My temples, and immerg'd me, where 't was fit
The wave should drench me: and, thence raising up,
Within the fourfold dance of lovely nymphs
Presented me so lav'd, and with their arm
They each did cover me. 'Here are we nymphs,
And in the heav'n are stars. Or ever earth
Was visited of Beatrice, we
Appointed for her handmaids, tended on her.
We to her eyes will lead thee; but the light
Of gladness that is in them, well to scan,   110
Those yonder three, of deeper ken than our's,
Thy sight shall quicken.' Thus began their song;
And then they led me to the Gryphon's breast,
While, turn'd toward us, Beatrice stood.
'Spare not thy vision. We have station'd thee
Before the emeralds, whence love erewhile

---

91 *The lady* Matilda   92 *'Loose me not'* Matilda repeats 'hold me, hold
me'   98 *Tu asperges* Psalm 51:7: 'Purge me with hyssop, and I shall be
clean: wash me, and I shall be whiter than snow'; the Latin is in the original
106 *stars* the four stars of *Purgatorio* 1.22–4   111 *yonder three* the three
theological virtues of faith, hope and charity   116 *emeralds* Beatrice's eyes

Hath drawn his weapons on thee.' As they spake,
A thousand fervent wishes riveted
Mine eyes upon her beaming eyes, that stood
120   Still fix'd toward the Gryphon motionless.
As the sun strikes a mirror, even thus
Within those orbs the twyfold being shone,
For ever varying, in one figure now
Reflected, now in other. Reader! muse
How wond'rous in my sight it seem'd to mark
A thing, albeit steadfast in itself,
Yet in it's imag'd semblance mutable.
        Full of amaze and joyous, while my soul
Fed on the viand, whereof still desire
130   Grows with satiety, the other three
With gesture, that declar'd a loftier line,
Advanc'd: to their own carol on they came
Dancing in festive ring angelical.
        'Turn, Beatrice!' was their song: 'O turn
Thy saintly sight on this thy faithful one,
Who to behold thee many a wearisome pace
Hath measur'd. Gracious at our pray'r vouchsafe
Unveil to him thy cheeks: that he may mark
Thy second beauty, now conceal'd.' O splendor!
140   O sacred light eternal! who is he
So pale with musing in Pierian shades,
Or with that fount so lavishly imbued,
Whose spirit should not fail him in th'essay
To represent thee such as thou didst seem,
When under cope of the still-chiming heaven
Thou gav'st to open air thy charms reveal'd?
            (1812; 1814)

---

118 *fervent* a very mild translation of the Italian, which refers to 'desires
hotter than flame'   124 *muse* Dante just asks his reader to 'think'
139 *second beauty* her mouth   141 *Pierian shades . . . fount* classical
emblems of poetic inspiration

WALTER SAVAGE LANDOR (1775–1864)

Landor believed that 'all that is good in so many hundred pages' of the *Commedia* 'may be included in less than a dozen'. In *The Pentameron* (1836), one of his 'imagined conversations', he disparages Dante through the voice of Petrarch: 'what hatred against the whole human race! what exultation and merriment at eternal and immitigable sufferings! Seeing this, I can not but consider the *Inferno* as the most immoral and impious book that ever was written'. Landor's Boccaccio, though, pleads mitigating circumstances and specifies among the many 'curses' Dante went through particularly 'theology, politics, and that barbican of the *Inferno*, marriage'. Landor's view of Dante's marriage was coloured by his own experience; he had quarrelled irreversibly with his wife in 1835.

[untitled]

They whom blind love hath led to take a wife
Often have changed soft flute for shriller fife,
And felt how different from the pliant maid
She who now trims the brow with horn cockade.
Caesar and Marlboro' bore it in times past,
And Garibaldi will not be the last.
Against the wedded harlot weak men cry,
The braver scorn her and the wiser fly.
Dante soon lost his Beatrice, and fell
From Paradise to Gemma and to Hell.   10
Of ribald lords 'twas hard to mount the stairs,
To climb his own was worse than climbing theirs.

---

5 *Caesar and Marlboro'* Julius Caesar divorced his second wife, Pompeia, after a scandal; the wife of the first Duke of Marlborough was reputed a termagant   6 *Garibaldi* immediately after his second marriage in 1863, the hero of the Risorgimento formed an adverse judgement of his wife's character and left her at once   10 *Gemma* Dante's wife, to whom he was formally betrothed when he was eleven, well before the death of Beatrice

Bitter it seem'd by strangers to be fed,
Bitterest of all he found the household bread.
When Delia was another's more than his,
Tibullus wooed avenging nemesis.
Her hand dispell'd from life its early gloom
And waved away the faithless from his tomb.
In his own land the bones of Albius rest,
Why was the wandering Dante not so blest?   (1863)

ROBERT MOREHEAD (1777–1842)

Morehead was educated at Glasgow, Edinburgh and Oxford,
and ordained in 1802. He was cousin to Francis Jeffrey and so
had an *entrée* to the *Edinburgh Review* for which he wrote
often, notably an essay on Dante in which he accurately
observes: 'he writes like a man employed in a serious business:
and notions and images, which would transport the generality
of poets beyond themselves, seem to pass through his mind like
the common object of his thoughts ... Dante is remarkably
concise, and never uses one word more than is absolutely neces-
sary.' Morehead could not imitate this concision in his Eng-
lishing of *Inferno* 32, having chosen to transpose Dante on to
the lush expanses of the Spenserian stanza.

Inferno 32   1–39

Were my rude rhymes as rugged, rough, and harsh,
As the o'erhanging rocks, whose horror stood
Around the margin of that murky marsh,

---

11 *Paradiso* 17.59–60   13 *Paradiso* 17.58–9   15 *Delia* mistress of the
Roman elegiac poet Albius Tibullus
   1 *rude rhymes ... rugged, rough* for once the English alliterations
correspond to features of the original rather than to the translator's fantasies
about the Middle Ages, though the alliteration in Dante is not on 'r'

Then might I chew, in hope, bright fancy's food;
But, since my purpose cannot be made good,
With fear and trembling each weak verse I frame!
O can it be that one of human blood,
Whose tongue first stammer'd out a parent's name,
Should of that black abyss the secrets strange
    proclaim?

Assist me, then, ye ladies of the lyre;   10
Give to my verse your own dread energy,
E'en as Amphion's ye could once inspire,
Which girded Thebes with towers and turrets high:
So shall my song with its great subject vie!
Ah! wretched race! in that infernal den
(For which in vain appropriate terms I try,)
That next I met; much happier had ye been
Made sheep or goats at first, – or anything but men!

When we had reach'd the low and gloomy pond
Beneath the giant sentinels, whose seat   20
Was on the fencing rock, which still I conn'd
With up-turn'd eyes, – I heard a voice repeat
Beside me, – Take care where you set your feet,
Lest you should crush some wretched brother's head,
And, with hard heels, his face all rudely beat!
I turn'd, and saw before me where was spread
A mighty frozen lake, that seem'd like glass or lead.

2–3 *whose horror . . . murky marsh* spun out of two words in the original,
meaning 'sad hole'   8 *a parent's name* the original means 'a tongue which
calls out "Mummy" or "Daddy"'   10 *ye ladies of the lyre* Dante does not
address the Muses directly nor does he have any equivalent for 'of the lyre'
15 *wretched race* the original is stronger: 'O people who are beyond all
others misbegotten'   27 *or lead* not in Dante

Never as yet did winter's ruffian force
Wrap Austrian Danaw in such mantle bleak,
30   Nor so enchain the Tanais in its course:
Nor, on that lake were massy Tabernique
To fall, or vast Pietrapana's peak,
Would from the margin of its icy floor,
One running rent be heard to growl and creak:
And, (in the season, when, their little store
To heap, the female gleaners o'er the corn fields pour:)

E'en in that season, as a group of frogs,
From green and slimy pool, push forth the snout,
While ceaseless croaking murmurs o'er the bogs:
40   So, with dull livid cheeks, were sticking out,
Above the glassy surface, all about,
Sad faces of the damn'd. Their teeth they gnash'd
Like to the stork's bill clattering, as they lout
With downcast looks: – the cold their lips had gash'd.
And from their weeping eyes despair's black ensigns
      flashed.   (1814)

JOHN HERMAN MERIVALE (1779–1844)

In 1813, Merivale collaborated with Robert Bland on two
well-received volumes of translation from Greek lyric poets; the
following year, he published his *Orlando in Roncesvalles*, a
historical epic in *ottava rima*, on which Byron congratulated
him – 'Your measure is uncommonly well chosen and wielded'
– though Merivale lacks the comic agility which Byron brought
to that form in *Don Juan*. His skill with that Italian stanza may
have encouraged him to make these early attempts at Dante in
Dante's own *terza rima*. Merivale's titles to many of his extracts

---

43 *lout* lower the head

from the *Commedia* show that he too concentrated on Dante's skill in the depiction of characters.

Dante and Farinata [*Inferno* 10]

Now by a secret path our way we find
    Betwixt the wall, and those who, martyr'd, burn;
    My master first – I following close behind –
'Virtue supreme! who dost at pleasure turn
    My steps,' I ask'd, 'amidst those circles dread,
    Speak, and resolve me what I long to learn.
O say, may those who here lie sepulchréd
    Be seen by man? – Already open'd wide
    Are all the lids, and none to guard the dead.'
'– Those tombs again shall close,' he thus replied,   10
    Soon as, from Josaphat they hither hie,
    And bring their bodies, cast till then aside.
On this side of the fiery charnel lie,
    With Epicurus, all his crew profane,
    Who teach that spirits with their bodies die.
Here all thy mind's desire thou shalt obtain;
    Both what in open speech thou cravest to hear,
    And more – the secret wish thy thoughts contain.'
'If all my heart I shew not, 'tis through fear'
    (I said) 'thine ears with needless words to tire;   20
    Following the pattern of thy style severe.'
– 'O Tuscan! thou who, through the city' of fire,
    Of speech so gentle, passest, yet alive,
    Here, may it please thee, rest at my desire.
Thy tongue bears witness that thou dost derive
    Thy being from that glorious native land,
    Wherewith, perchance, I did too rudely strive.'

---

11 *Josaphat* named as the location for the Last Judgement in Joel 3:2

Such, from a tomb's enclosure nigh at hand,
    The sounds that sudden burst; whereat, for fear,
30   I closer to the master took my stand;
Who thus to me – 'Turn back! why press so near?
    Lo, Farinata! His the form you see
    Raised from the waist above the vault appear.'
And now my face on his was fix'd, while he,
    As one who looked on hell with deep disdain,
    Erected stood, with breast and forehead free.
Whereat my ready guide, with might and main,
    Me tow'rds him thrust between those vaults apace,
    And said, 'Take heed thy utter'd words be plain!'
40 When by his tomb I stood, his earnest face
    Scann'd mine awhile: then, in disdainful guise
    He spake; 'Thy fathers who? and what thy race?'
I, prompt to do his will, in brief replies
    His doubts resolved, making disclosure free.
    'Fiercely they stood,' he said, and from his eyes
Raised the proud lids a space, 'opposed to me,
    To me and mine, my lineage and my side;
    And twice like chaff I made their quarrel flee!'
'Nay, and if so it were,' I strait replied,
50   'Tho' scatter'd twice, they twice re-entry made;
    An art thy friends with worse success have tried.'
And now, no lower than the chin display'd,
    A second spirit I beheld arise,
    Kneeling (methought) beside the former shade.
He look'd around me with inquiring eyes,
    As if in hope some other form to see;
    But when he found the search was vain, with sighs

---

32 *Farinata* Farinata degli Uberti, a famously haughty Ghibelline leader;
after many ups and downs of fortune he died in 1264 and was posthumously
convicted of the heresy of denying the immortality of the soul   45 Merivale
is an unusually close translator of Dante, but his effect here, interrupting
Farinata's speech with the narrator's description of gesture, is not in the
original; such 'suspended quotations' are quite rare in the *Commedia*

He said, 'If high exalted genius be
   The guide that leads thee thro' this dungeon blind,
   Where is my son? – and wherefore not with thee?'   60
Then I to him – 'Not by myself I find
   Admittance here; but by one greater led,
   Once held in scorn, perhaps, by Guido's mind.'
Such answer made I to the imprison'd dead,
   Since, in his speech, and in the form of woe
   Endured, I from the first his name had read.
Then, sudden starting up, he ask'd, 'How so?
   Saidst thou, *Once held?* – Is he still living, say,
   Or doom'd no more the blessèd light to know?'
But when he found ensue some brief delay   70
   Ere I made answer to his fond request,
   He dropp'd supine, entomb'd as erst he lay.
Meanwhile, that first heroic spirit possess'd
   Firm, and unmoved, his stand – unchanged in hue,
   Or feature; and these words to me address'd,
Continuing where he left – 'And, grant it true,
   They ill that art have learnt, so keen the thought,
   More tortures thence than from this bed accrue.
Yet ere the queen who reigneth here have caught
   A fiftieth light on her resplendent horn,   80
   That art shalt thou, and that art's worth, be taught;

---

60 *my son* the speaker is Cavalcante dei Cavalcanti, father of the poet Guido
Cavalcanti, Dante's friend and rival; Cavalcanti senior was a political
opponent of Farinata though he was alleged to have shared his epicureanism
68 *still living* Guido was indeed, as Dante eventually reveals at 110–11, 'still
living' at the fictional Easter 1300 of this meeting, though he died a few
months later   69 *blessèd* in the original, the light is 'sweet'; the word for
'blessed' is rarely uttered in Dante's Hell, and never by the damned
77 *that art* of getting back into Florence after banishment
79 *the queen* Proserpina, identified with the moon   80 *fiftieth light* within
four years, that is, 'before 1304'; writing after he had been exiled from
Florence in 1302 on the defeat of the White Guelfs, Dante knew Farinata
would be proved right

And as to the pleasant world thou hopest return,
   The reason of those harsh unequal laws
   Against my race enacted, let me learn.'
– 'Of those most solemn acts,' said I, 'the cause
   Is Arbia's flood, that ran distain'd with red
   By that day's dreadful slaughter.' Here, a pause
He made, and, sadly sighing, waved his head,
   Then spake – 'Yet there I did not singly stand,
90   Nor without cause had join'd that conflict dread.
But singly there I stood, where all our band
   Gave leave that Florence should no longer be;
   And singly, did the fell decree withstand.'
– 'So may thy race at length from ban be free,'
   (I thus adjured him) 'as the doubtful knot
   Thou solvest, which now holds fast my phantasy.
It seems ye view, if I mistake it not,
   Before-hand, things not yet brought forth to light,
   While all the present are like things forgot.'
100   'We view like one that hath distemper'd sight
   Those things,' he said, 'which at a distance lie –
   Such gleams are sent us by the Lord of Might.
But when the far-seen objects press more nigh,
   Our sense is vain; and of your human state
   We nothing know unless from passers by.
Hence mayst thou comprehend how dark the state
   Of all our knowledge from that point of time
   That closes of futurity the gate.'
Repentant then of my unthinking crime,
110   I bade him to that other fallen one say
   His son still breathed in this our mortal clime.

---

87 *that day* the battle of Montaperti   91 *there* at the Council of Empoli,
where Farinata alone opposed the Ghibelline plan to raze Florence
102 *the Lord of Might* Farinata calls God '*il sommo duce*' ('the supreme
leader'), a sort of super-Farinata in fact   105 *passers by* unfortunately the
Italian does not justify Merivale's charming invention of passers-by in hell
109 *my unthinking crime* his failure to answer Cavalcanti's question about
his son

'Tell him, moreover, if I made delay
   In answering, 'twas that I then ponder'd o'er
   A doubt which now thy words have chased away.'
And now my master call'd; whereat the more
   Eager I begg'd the hostile spirit to shew
   Who were his partners on that dismal shore.
'I rest,' he said, ''mid thousands here below.
   The second Frederick yonder tomb doth hold;
   The cardinal this; the rest forbear to know!'   120
Then plunged beneath – I toward that poet old
   My steps address'd, retracing in my mind
   The words that of my fate so darkly told.
Onward he moved, and, moving, in this kind
   Made question, 'Wherefore so disturb'd by fear?'
   Which when I had resolved him, he rejoin'd,
With sage advice, 'Deep in thy bosom bear
   The import of that stern prophetic lore.
   And now these words attend' – (with fingers here
Upraised he spake,) – 'when thou shalt stand before   130
   Her gracious beam, whose bright eye all surveys,
   Thy path of life she will assist to explore.'
Then to the left he turn'd, and through the maze,
   Quitting the wall, a midway path we chose,
   That to a hollow place our steps conveys,
When through the air a noisome stench arose.   (1838)

---

119 *Frederick* Frederick II, Holy Roman Emperor 1214–50, an active ruler
and patron of the arts, twice excommunicated and much admired by Dante
120 *The cardinal* Ottaviano degli Ubaldini; famously worldly, he is reputed
to have said 'if there is a soul, I have sold mine for the Ghibellines'
129 the 'suspended quotation' here *is* in the original   131 *Her* Beatrice's

THOMAS MOORE (1779–1852)

On leaving Trinity College, Dublin, Moore intended to practise law but was diverted into government service in the Bermudas; finding that the duties of his post there were so light as not to require even his presence, he returned to England via Canada (a scandal later blew up about his conduct and he decided to live abroad for a few years). *Irish Melodies* (1807–34) made his name and fortune on both sides of the Irish Sea with their evocation of 'convivial Ireland with the traditional tear and smile' (Yeats); Leopold Bloom hums several of them. *Lalla Rookh* (1817) rode on the crest of a vogue for what Hazlitt considered 'affected orientalism of style'. Moore was, according to his lights, a good friend to Byron, whose *Life . . .* he brought out in 1830. He knew Dante well, though the essential slightness of Moore's creative talent prevented Dante from having more than a slight influence on his writing.

To the Lady Charlotte Rawdon. From the Banks of the St. Lawrence 133–58

Thus have I charm'd, with visionary lay,
The lonely moments of the night away;
And now, fresh daylight o'er the water beams!
Once more, embark'd upon the glitt'ring streams,
Our boat flies light along the leafy shore,
Shooting the falls, without a dip of oar
Or breath of zephyr, like the mystic bark
The poet saw, in dreams divinely dark,
Borne, without sails, along the dusky flood,
10   While on its deck a pilot angel stood,

7–12 *Purgatorio* 2.28–42: the charm of the allusion is to suggest an equivalence of the New World to Purgatory and its 'better waters'; like many souls in Purgatory, though, Moore clings to memories of his former life

And, with his wings of living light unfurl'd,
Coasted the dim shores of another world!

Yet, oh! believe me, mid this mingled maze
Of nature's beauties, where the fancy strays
From charm to charm, where every flow'ret's hue
Hath something strange, and every leaf is new, –
I never feel a joy so pure and still,
So inly felt, as when some brook or hill,
Or veteran oak, like those remember'd well,
Some mountain echo or some wild-flower's smell,   20
(For, who can say by what small fairy ties
The mem'ry clings to pleasure as it flies?)
Reminds my heart of many a silvan dream
I once indulg'd by Trent's inspiring stream;
Of all my sunny morns and moonlight nights
On Donnington's green lawns and breezy heights.
  (1806)

Imitation of the Inferno of Dante   1–47

> 'Così quel fiato gli spiriti mali
> Di qua, di là, di giù, di su gli mena.'
> *Inferno,* canto 5 [42–3]

I turn'd my steps, and lo, a shadowy throng
Of ghosts came flutt'ring tow'rds me – blown along,
Like cockchafers in high autumnal storms,
By many a fitful gust that through their forms
Whistled, as on they came, with wheezy puff,
And puff'd as – though they'd never puff enough.

---

3 Moore parodies Dante's minutely observed similes, especially the autumn cranes and starlings of *Inferno* 5   5 *puff* the joke hinges on a simple pun on 'puff' as 'gust of wind' (the '*fiato*' of the epigraph) and 'puff' as 'hype' (noun and verb)

'Whence and what are ye?' pitying I inquir'd
Of these poor ghosts, who, tatter'd, tost, and tir'd
With such eternal puffing, scarce could stand
10 On their lean legs while answering my demand.
'We once were authors' – thus the Sprite, who led
This tag-rag regiment of spectres, said –
'Authors of every sex, male, female, neuter,
'Who early smit with love of praise and – *pewter*,
'On C—lb—n's shelves first saw the light of day,
'In ——'s puffs exhal'd our lives away –
'Like summer windmills, doom'd to dusty peace,
'When the brisk gales, that lent them motion, cease.
'Ah, little knew we then what ills await
20 'Much-lauded scribblers in their after-state;
'Bepuff'd on earth – how loudly Str—t can tell –
'And, dire reward, now doubly puff'd in hell!'

Touch'd with compassion for this ghastly crew,
Whose ribs, even now, the hollow wind sung through
In mournful prose, – such prose as Rosa's ghost
Still at the' accustom'd hour of eggs and toast,
Sighs through the columns of the *M—rn—g P—t*, –
Pensive I turn'd to weep, when he, who stood
Foremost of all that flatulential brood,
30 Singling a *she*-ghost from the party, said,
'Allow me to present Miss X. Y. Z.

---

14 *pewter* 'The *classical* term for money.' [*Moore's note*]   15 'The reader
may fill up this gap with any one of the *disyllabic* publishers of London that
occurs to him.' [*Moore's note*] Henry Colburn is the leading candidate
25 *Rosa's* 'Rosa Matilda, who was for many years the writer of the political
articles in the journal alluded to, and whose spirit still seems to preside –
"regnat rosa" – over its pages' [*Moore's note*]   31 *Miss X. Y. Z.* 'Not the
charming L. E. L. [Letitia E. Landon], and still less, Mrs F. H. [Felicia
Hemans] whose poetry is among the most beautiful of the present day.'
[*Moore's note*]

'One of our *letter'd* nymphs – excuse the pun –
'Who gain'd a name on earth by – having none;
'And whose initials would immortal be,
'Had she but learn'd those plain ones, A. B. C.

'Yon smirking ghost, like mummy dry and neat,
'Wrapp'd in his own dead rhymes – fit winding-sheet –
'Still marvels much that not a soul should care
'One single pin to know who wrote 'May Fair;' –
'While this young gentleman,' (here forth he drew   40
A dandy spectre, puff'd quite through and through,
As though his ribs were an Aeolian lyre
For the old Row's soft *trade*-winds to inspire,)
'This modest genius breath'd one wish alone,
'To have his volume read, himself unknown;
'But different far the course his glory took,
'All knew the author, and – none read the book.'
　　(1828)

LEIGH HUNT (1784–1859)

Hunt learned Italian at school and translated from it extensively
(Ariosto, Boiardo, Petrarch, Pulci, and many more) as well as
from Greek, Latin (classical and medieval) and French. He was
a journalist of radical sympathies and suffered imprisonment
for his work; his friends included Shelley, Byron and Keats. *The
Story of Rimini* spins 1,706 lines from the sixty or so lines of
its source, proving how right Montgomery was to recognize
the pregnancy of Dante's 'hints of narrative'. In Hunt's work,

---

39 *who wrote 'May Fair;'* George Croly, author of the undistinguished satire
May Fair, In Four Cantos (1827); he makes a 'mystery' of his identity in
lines 53–85   42 *Aeolian lyre* more usually, 'Aeolian harp', a musical
instrument of sorts whose strings resounded when air moved over them; it
had a vogue in the period   43 *the old Row's* Paternoster Row, a
long-established home to the book trade   45 *himself unknown* half this
author's wish has now come true as we have been unable to trace him

translation becomes demonstratively a form of argument with Dante and what are taken to be his views. Thus, Hunt believed that, in the Paolo and Francesca episode, we 'see the whole melancholy absurdity of his theology, in spite of itself, falling to nothing before one genuine impulse of the affections' and translates so as to make this seem true.

The Story of Rimini   3.504–34, 571–608
[Compare *Inferno* 5.82–142]

One day, – 'twas on a summer afternoon,
When airs and gurgling brooks are best in tune,
And grasshoppers are loud, and day-work done,
And shades have heavy outlines in the sun, –
The princess came to her accustomed bower
To get her, if she could, a soothing hour,
Trying, as she was used, to leave her cares
Without, and slumberously enjoy the airs,
And the low-talking leaves, and that cool light
The vines let in, and all that hushing sight
Of closing wood seen through the opening door.
And distant plash of waters tumbling o'er,
And smell of citron blooms, and fifty luxuries more.

She tried, as usual, for the trial's sake,
For even that diminished her heart-ache;
And never yet, how ill soe'er at ease,
Came she for nothing 'midst the flowers and trees.
Yet somehow or another, on that day,
She seemed to feel too lightly borne away, –
Too much relieved, – too much inclined to draw
A careless joy from every thing she saw,
And looking round her with a new-born eye,
As if some tree of knowledge had been nigh,
To taste of nature, primitive and free,
And bask at ease in her heart's liberty.

Painfully clear those rising thoughts appeared,
With something dark at bottom that she feared;
And snatching from the fields her thoughtful look,
She reached o'er-head, and took her down a book,
And fell to reading with as fixed an air,   30
As though she had been wrapt since morning there.

*

Ready she sat with one hand to turn o'er
The leaf, to which her thoughts ran on before,
The other propping her white brow, and throwing
Its ringlets out, under the skylight glowing.
So sat she fixed; and so observed was she
Of one, who at the door stood tenderly, –
Paulo, – who from a window seeing her
Go straight across the lawn, and guessing where,
Had thought she was in tears, and found, that day,   40
His usual efforts vain to keep away.
'May I come in?' said he: – it made her start, –
That smiling voice; – she coloured, pressed her
    heart
A moment, as for breath, and then with free
And usual tone said, 'O yes, – certainly.'
There's apt to be, at conscious times like these,
An affectation of a bright-eyed ease,
An air of something quite serene and sure,
As if to seem so, was to be, secure:
With this the lovers met, with this they spoke,   50
With this they sat down to the self-same book,
And Paulo, by degrees, gently embraced
With one permitted arm her lovely waist;
And both their cheeks, like peaches on a tree,
Leaned with a touch together, thrillingly;
And o'er the book they hung, and nothing said,
And every lingering page grew longer as they read.

As thus they sat, and felt with leaps of heart
Their colour change, they came upon the part
Where fond Genevra, with her flame long nurst,   60
Smiled upon Launcelot when he kissed her first: –
That touch, at last, through every fibre slid;
And Paulo turned, scarce knowing what he did,
Only he felt he could no more dissemble,
And kissed her, mouth to mouth, all in a tremble.
Sad were those hearts, and sweet was that long kiss:
Sacred be love from sight, whate'er it is.
The world was all forgot, the struggle o'er,
Desperate the joy. – That day they read no more.
     (1816)

Paulo and Francesca [*Inferno* 5.82–142]

As doves, that leave some bevy circling still,
Set firm their open wings, and through the air
Sweep homewards, wafted by their pure good will;

So broke from Dido's flock that gentle pair,
Cleaving, to where we stood, the air malign;
Such strength to bring them had a loving prayer.

The female spoke. 'O living soul benign!'
She said, 'thus, in this lost air, visiting
Us, who with blood stained the sweet earth divine;

---

69 Hunts ends his third canto, 'The Fatal Passion', here
   3 *pure good* Hunt's contribution   6 *a loving prayer* Dante describes his
call to them as an 'affectionate cry'; it is Francesca who mentions prayer, a
mention Hunt veils with his 'beseech' at line 11   7 *The female* not in Dante,
where it remains unclear for nine lines which of the pair is speaking
8 *lost* a mistake; '*perso*' is not a form of '*perdere*' ('to lose') but derives from
a medieval Latin word meaning 'dark'   9 *sweet earth divine* Dante's
Francesca lacks the adjectival gush; she just refers to 'the world'

    'Had we a friend in heaven's eternal King,   10
We would beseech him keep thy conscience clear,
Since to our anguish thou dost pity bring.

    'Of what it pleaseth thee to speak and hear,
To that we also, till this lull be o'er
That falleth now, will speak and will give ear.

    'The place where I was born is on the shore,
Where Po brings all his rivers to depart
In peace, and fuse them with the ocean floor.

    'Love, that soon kindleth in a gentle heart,
Seized him thou look'st on for the form and face,   20
Whose end still haunts me like a rankling dart.

    'Love, which by love will be denied no grace,
Gave me a transport in my turn so true,
That lo! 'tis with me, even in this place.

    'Love brought us to one grave. The hand that slew,
Is doomed to mourn us in the pit of Cain.'
Such were the words that told me of those two.

    Downcast I stood, looking so full of pain
To think how hard and sad a case it was,
That my guide asked what held me in that vein.   30

    His voice aroused me; and I said, 'Alas!
All their sweet thoughts then, all the steps that led
To love, but brought them to this dolorous pass.'

---

10 *heaven's eternal King* Francesca calls God 'the king of the universe'; she
says nothing about heaven   22 whatever this line of Hunt's means, it is not
what the Italian means: 'Love which does not permit a beloved person to fail
to reciprocate love'   29 not in the original

Then turning my sad eyes to theirs, I said,
'Francesca, see – these human cheeks are wet –
Truer and sadder tears were never shed.

'But tell me. At the time when sighs were sweet,
What made thee strive no longer? – hurried thee
To the last step where bliss and sorrow meet?'

40   'There is no greater sorrow,' answered she,
'And this thy teacher here knoweth full well,
Than calling to mind joy in misery.

'But since thy wish be great to hear us tell
How we lost all but love, tell it I will,
As well as tears will let me. It befell,

'One day, we read how Lancelot gazed his fill
At her he loved, and what his lady said.
We were alone, thinking of nothing ill.

'Oft were our eyes suspended as we read,
50   And in our cheeks the colour went and came;
Yet one sole passage struck resistance dead.

''Twas where the lover, moth-like in his flame,
Drawn by her sweet smile, kissed it. O then, he
Whose lot and mine are now for aye the same,

---

34 *my sad eyes* not in Dante   **36** Dante does not make this boast about the superior quality of his own tears
39 *the last step where bliss and sorrow meet* this evaluation of the joy of sex is Hunt's   **41** *thy teacher* Virgil   **44** *How . . . love* the original means 'the first root of our love'   **46–7** *how . . . lady said* Hunt's version of words which mean 'how love compelled Lancelot'   **52** *moth-like* the cliché is Hunt's

    'All in a tremble, on the mouth kissed *me*.
The book did all. Our hearts within us burned
Through that alone. That day no more read we.'

    While thus one spoke, the other spirit mourned
With wail so woful, that at his remorse
I felt as though I should have died. I turned   60

    Stone-stiff; and to the ground, fell like a corse.
        (1846)

                Purgatorio I   13–27

The sweetest oriental sapphire blue,
    Which the whole air in its pure bosom had,
    Greeted mine eyes, far as the heavens withdrew;
So that again they felt assured and glad,
    Soon as they issued forth from the dead air,
    Where every sight and thought had made them
        sad.
The beauteous star, which lets no love despair,
    Made all the orient laugh with loveliness,
    Veiling the Fish that glimmered in its hair.
I turned me to the right to gaze and bless,   10
    And saw four more, never of living wight
    Beheld, since Adam brought us our distress;

---

57 *alone* as with 'all' in the previous line, this insistent self-exculpation was
added by Hunt.
    7 *The beauteous star* the planet Venus; Dante says that it 'prompts to
love' not that it 'lets no love despair'   9 *the Fish* the constellation Pisces; the
Italian sounds less like Lewis Carroll and translates as 'veiling Pisces in her
train'   11 *four more* perhaps the stars of the Southern Cross, often
interpreted as symbolizing the four cardinal virtues
12 *since Adam brought us our distress* the Italian says only 'never seen
except by the first people'

Heaven seemed rejoicing in their happy light.
O widowed northern pole, bereaved indeed,
Since thou hast had no power to see that sight!
(1846)

THOMAS LOVE PEACOCK (1785–1866)

Dante's appearance as part of the after-supper entertainment
at Headlong Hall is eloquent of how domesticated he was
becoming in English culture: he was now a genteel fad. The
popularity of *Purgatorio* 8 (see Samuel Rogers above and Byron
below) indicates the growing recognition that he was not the
creator only of *Inferno* but that, as Byron wrote in his journal,
'there is gentleness in Dante beyond all gentleness, when he is
tender' (29 January 1821).

Headlong Hall, Chapter 13
[Compare *Purgatorio* 8.1–6]

Squire Headlong called on Mr. Chromatic for a song; who,
with the assistance of his two accomplished daughters, regaled
the ears of the company with the following

TERZETTO.*

Grey Twilight, from her shadowy hill,
    Discolours Nature's vernal bloom,
And sheds on grove, and field, and rill,
    One placid tint of deepening gloom.

The sailor sighs 'mid shoreless seas,
    Touched by the thought of friends afar,
As, fanned by ocean's flowing breeze,
    He gazes on the western star.

> The wanderer hears, in pensive dream,
> The accents of the last farewell,   10
> As, pausing by the mountain stream,
> He listens to the evening bell.

*Imitated from a passage in the *Purgatorio* of Dante.   (1816)

GEORGE GORDON, LORD BYRON
(1788–1824)

Byron encountered Dante at Harrow School but did not really face his work until he settled in Italy (1817). He sensed a curious interlacing of his own life with passages of the *Inferno* as well as identifying more generally and self-admiringly with Dante as a fellow exile; he wrote to his mistress, Teresa Guiccioli, in 1819 about Paolo and Francesca: 'This story of a fatal love, which has always interested me, now interests me doubly, since Ravenna holds my heart' (the Guicciolis lived in Ravenna; Francesca was born, and Dante is buried, there). He also rented for a while the Lanfranchi palace at Pisa (see *Inferno* 33.32). Sometimes he liked to rail against the *Commedia* – 'Who can read with patience fourteen thousand lines, made up of prayers, dialogues, and questions, without sticking fast in the bogs and quicksands, and losing his way in the thousand turns and windings of the inextricable labyrinths of his three-times-nine circles? and of these fourteen thousand lines, more than two-thirds are . . . defective and bad' – particularly when, as on this occasion, the devout Dantescan, Shelley, was there to writhe in silent protest while he did so. But Dante came alive for Byron as for no English poet of genius since Milton.

Don Juan   2.521–721

'Tis thus with people in an open boat,
     They live upon the love of life, and bear
More than can be believed, or even thought,
     And stand like rocks the tempest's wear and tear;
And hardship still has been the sailor's lot,
     Since Noah's ark went cruising here and there;
She had a curious crew as well as cargo,
Like the first old Greek privateer, the Argo.

But man is a carnivorous production,
10   And must have meals, at least one meal a day;
He cannot live, like woodcocks, upon suction,
     But, like the shark and tiger, must have prey:
Although his anatomical construction
     Bears vegetables in a grumbling way,
Your labouring people think beyond all question,
Beef, veal, and mutton, better for digestion.

And thus it was with this our hapless crew,
     For on the third day there came on a calm,
And though at first their strength it might renew,
20   And lying on their weariness like balm,
Lull'd them like turtles sleeping on the blue
     Of ocean, when they woke they felt a qualm,
And fell all ravenously on their provision,
Instead of hoarding it with due precision.

---

18 *on the third day* compare Byron's relentless marking of time – lines 33,
35, 41, 49, 74, etc. – with *Inferno* 33.53, 65, 67, 72, etc.   22 compare
Ugolino's foreboding when he wakes, *Inferno* 33.41

The consequence was easily foreseen –
   They ate up all they had, and drank their wine,
In spite of all remonstrances, and then
   On what, in fact, next day were they to dine?
They hoped the wind would rise, these foolish men!
   And carry them to shore; these hopes were fine,   30
But as they had but one oar, and that brittle,
It would have been more wise to save their victual.

The fourth day came, but not a breath of air,
   And Ocean slumber'd like an unwean'd child:
The fifth day, and their boat lay floating there,
   The sea and sky were blue, and clear, and mild –
With their one oar (I wish they had had a pair)
   What could they do? and hunger's rage grew wild:
So Juan's spaniel, spite of his entreating,
Was kill'd, and portion'd out for present eating.   40

On the sixth day they fed upon his hide,
   And Juan, who had still refused, because
The creature was his father's dog that died,
   Now feeling all the vulture in his jaws,
With some remorse received (though first denied)
   As a great favour one of the fore-paws,
Which he divided with Pedrillo, who
Devour'd it, longing for the other too.

The seventh day, and no wind – the burning sun
   Blister'd and scorch'd, and, stagnant on the sea,   50
They lay like carcases; and hope was none,
   Save in the breeze that came not; savagely

---

34 the first conjunction in the passage of childhood and nourishment;
compare *Inferno* 33.39   39 dogs surround Ugolino; see *Inferno* 32.70, 105,
108; 33.31, 78   49 it is part of the grim entanglement of this passage with
Judaeo-Christianity that the crew think of cannibalism first on a seventh day,
a sabbath

They glared upon each other – all was done,
    Water, and wine, and food, – and you might see
The longings of the cannibal arise
(Although they spoke not) in their wolfish eyes.

At length one whisper'd his companion, who
    Whisper'd another, and thus it went round,
And then into a hoarser murmur grew,
60   An ominous, and wild, and desperate sound,
And when his comrade's thought each sufferer knew,
    'Twas but his own, suppress'd till now, he found:
And out they spoke of lots for flesh and blood,
And who should die to be his fellow's food.

But ere they came to this, they that day shared
    Some leathern caps, and what remain'd of shoes;
And then they look'd around them, and despair'd,
    And none to be the sacrifice would choose;
At length the lots were torn up, and prepared,
70   But of materials that much shock the Muse –
Having no paper, for the want of better,
They took by force from Juan Julia's letter.

The lots were made, and mark'd, and mix'd, and handed,
    In silent horror, and their distribution
Lull'd even the savage hunger which demanded,
    Like the Promethean vulture, this pollution;
None in particular had sought or plann'd it,
    'Twas nature gnaw'd them to this resolution,
By which none were permitted to be neuter –
80   And the lot fell on Juan's luckless tutor.

53, 56 compare Ugolino's silent staring in *Inferno* 33.47–8
56 *wolfish* Ugolino dreams of a wolf-hunt in *Inferno* 33.28–30
72 *Julia's letter* a goodbye note from Juan's first love; when their adulterous affair is discovered, he is sent from home on this voyage   78 *gnaw'd* the standard-issue word in earlier versions of the Ugolino episode for his eating of Ruggiero's skull

He but requested to be bled to death:
   The surgeon had his instruments, and bled
Pedrillo, and so gently ebb'd his breath,
   You hardly could perceive when he was dead.
He died as born, a Catholic in faith,
   Like most in the belief in which they're bred,
And first a little crucifix he kiss'd,
And then held out his jugular and wrist.

The surgeon, as there was no other fee,
   Had his first choice of morsels for his pains;   90
But being thirstiest at the moment, he
   Preferr'd a draught from the fast-flowing veins:
Part was divided, part thrown in the sea,
   And such things as the entrails and the brains
Regaled two sharks, who follow'd o'er the billow –
The sailors ate the rest of poor Pedrillo.

The sailors ate him, all save three or four,
   Who were not quite so fond of animal food;
To these was added Juan, who, before
   Refusing his own spaniel, hardly could   100
Feel now his appetite increased much more;
   'Twas not to be expected that he should,
Even in extremity of their disaster,
Dine with them on his pastor and his master.

'Twas better that he did not; for, in fact,
   The consequence was awful in the extreme;
For they, who were most ravenous in the act,
   Went raging mad – Lord! how they did
      blaspheme!
And foam and roll, with strange convulsions rack'd,
   Drinking salt-water like a mountain-stream,   110
Tearing, and grinning, howling, screeching,
      swearing,
And, with hyaena laughter, died despairing.

Their numbers were much thinn'd by this infliction,
    And all the rest were thin enough, heaven knows;
And some of them had lost their recollection,
    Happier than they who still perceived their woes;
But others ponder'd on a new dissection,
    As if not warn'd sufficiently by those
Who had already perish'd, suffering madly,
120   For having used their appetites so sadly.

And next they thought upon the master's mate,
    As fattest; but he saved himself, because,
Besides being much averse from such a fate,
    There were some other reasons; the first was,
He had been rather indisposed of late,
    And that which chiefly proved his saving clause,
Was a small present made to him at Cadiz,
By general subscription of the ladies.

Of poor Pedrillo something still remain'd,
130   But was used sparingly, – some were afraid,
And others still their appetites constrain'd,
    Or but at times a little supper made;
All except Juan, who throughout abstain'd,
    Chewing a piece of bamboo, and some lead:
At length they caught two boobies, and a noddy,
And then they left off eating the dead body.

And if Pedrillo's fate should shocking be,
    Remember Ugolino condescends
To eat the head of his arch-enemy
140   The moment after he politely ends

---

135 *boobies* a species of gannet and, by virtue of a pun, a foolish person
noddy 'a soot-coloured sea-bird . . . of tropical regions' (*OED*) and, again by
virtue of a pun, a foolish person   139 *arch-enemy* Ruggiero, who was an
arch-bishop   140 compare *Inferno* 33.76–8, usually omitted by earlier
translators

His tale; if foes be food in hell, at sea
   'Tis surely fair to dine upon our friends,
When shipwreck's short allowance grows too scanty,
Without being much more horrible than Dante.

And the same night there fell a shower of rain,
   For which their mouths gaped, like the cracks of
      earth
When dried to summer dust; till taught by pain,
   Men really know not what good water's worth;
If you had been in Turkey or in Spain,
   Or with a famish'd boat's-crew had your birth,   150
Or in the desert heard the camel's bell,
You'd wish yourself where Truth is – in a well.

It pour'd down torrents, but they were no richer
   Until they found a ragged piece of sheet,
Which served them as a sort of spongy pitcher,
   And when they deem'd its moisture was complete,
They wrung it out, and though a thirsty ditcher
   Might not have thought the scanty draught so sweet
As a full pot of porter, to their thinking
They ne'er till now had known the joys of drinking.   160

And their baked lips, with many a bloody crack,
   Suck'd in the moisture, which like nectar stream'd;
Their throats were ovens, their swoln tongues were
      black,
   As the rich man's in hell, who vainly scream'd
To beg the beggar, who could not rain back
   A drop of dew, when every drop had seem'd
To taste of heaven – If this be true, indeed,
Some Christians have a comfortable creed.

---

144 *horrible* the Italian equivalent is in *Inferno* 33.47; Byron mocks the
frissons much fabricated in earlier Englishings of Ugolino   147–8 compare
Inferno 30.62–3   164 *rich man's in hell* see Luke 16:19–26

There were two fathers in this ghastly crew,
170   And with them their two sons, of whom the one
Was more robust and hardy to the view,
    But he died early; and when he was gone,
His nearest messmate told his sire, who threw
    One glance on him, and said, 'Heaven's will be done!
I can do nothing,' and he saw him thrown
Into the deep without a tear or groan.

The other father had a weaklier child,
    Of a soft cheek, and aspect delicate;
But the boy bore up long, and with a mild
180   And patient spirit held aloof his fate;
Little he said, and now and then he smiled,
    As if to win a part from off the weight
He saw increasing on his father's heart,
With the deep deadly thought, that they must part.

And o'er him bent his sire, and never raised
    His eyes from off his face, but wiped the foam
From his pale lips, and ever on him gazed,
    And when the wish'd-for shower at length was come,
And the boy's eyes, which the dull film half glazed,
190   Brighten'd, and for a moment seem'd to roam,
He squeezed from out a rag some drops of rain
Into his dying child's mouth – but in vain.

The boy expired – the father held the clay,
    And look'd upon it long, and when at last
Death left no doubt, and the dead burthen lay
    Stiff on his heart, and pulse and hope were past,

---

176 *without a tear* compare Ugolino's dry eyes, *Inferno* 33.49
181–4 Ugolino's sons try to alleviate his distress, *Inferno* 33.61–4
186 compare the face-to-face of father and sons in *Inferno* 33.56–7
193 compare *Inferno* 33.72–3, though Ugolino goes blind and cannot see the
bodies he fondles

He watch'd it wistfully, until away
   'Twas borne by the rude wave wherein 'twas cast;
Then he himself sunk down all dumb and shivering,
And gave no sign of life, save his limbs quivering.   200
   (written 1818–19; published 1819)

Don Juan   3.929–60

Sweet hour of twilight! – in the solitude
   Of the pine forest, and the silent shore
Which bounds Ravenna's immemorial wood,
   Rooted where once the Adrian wave flow'd o'er,
To where the last Cesarean fortress stood,
   Evergreen forest! which Boccaccio's lore
And Dryden's lay made haunted ground to me,
How have I loved the twilight hour and thee!

The shrill cicalas, people of the pine,
   Making their summer lives one ceaseless song,   10
Were the sole echos, save my steed's and mine,
   And vesper bell's that rose the boughs along;
The spectre huntsman of Onesti's line,
   His hell-dogs, and their chase, and the fair throng,
Which learn'd from this example not to fly
From a true lover, shadow'd my mind's eye.

Oh Hesperus! thou bringest all good things –
   Home to the weary, to the hungry cheer,
To the young bird the parent's brooding wings,
   The welcome stall to the o'erlabour'd steer;   20
Whate'er of peace about our hearthstone clings,

6–7 see *Decameron* 5.8, translated as 'Theodore and Honoria' by Dryden,
referred to again at 13ff.

Whate'er our household gods protect of dear,
Are gather'd round us by thy look of rest;
Thou bring'st the child, too, to the mother's breast.

Soft hour! which wakes the wish and melts the heart
    Of those who sail the seas, on the first day
When they from their sweet friends are torn apart;
    Or fills with love the pilgrim on his way
As the far bell of vesper makes him start,
30   Seeming to weep the dying day's decay;
Is this a fancy which our reason scorns?
Ah! surely nothing dies but something mourns!
        (written 1819; published 1821)

The Prophecy of Dante 2.15–90

The reader is requested to suppose that Dante addresses him in
the interval between the conclusion of the Divina Commedia
and his death, and shortly before the latter event, foretelling
the fortunes of Italy in general in the ensuing centuries. [from
Byron's preface to the poem]

Hast thou not bled? and hast thou still to bleed,
Italia? Ah! to me such things, foreshown
    With dim sepulchral light, bid me forget
    In thine irreparable wrongs my own;
We can have but one country, and even yet
    Thou'rt mine – my bones shall be within thy breast,
    My soul within thy language, which once set

24–5 Byron may have been moved by thoughts of suckling to the Dante
allusion which immediately follows because of the *Commedia*'s frequent
mentions of mother/child relations   25–30 compare *Purgatorio* 8.1–6
   1ff. Byron refers to this poem as his *'Dante Imitation'* in a letter to his
publisher

With our old Roman sway in the wide West;
   But I will make another tongue arise
   As lofty and more sweet, in which exprest   10
The hero's ardour, or the lover's sighs,
   Shall find alike such sounds for every theme
   That every word, as brilliant as thy skies,
Shall realize a poet's proudest dream,
   And make thee Europe's nightingale of song;
   So that all present speech to thine shall seem
The note of meaner birds, and every tongue
   Confess its barbarism when compared with thine.
   This shalt thou owe to him thou didst so wrong,
Thy Tuscan Bard, the banish'd Ghibelline.   20
   Woe! woe! the veil of coming centuries
   Is rent, – a thousand years which yet supine
Lie like the ocean waves ere winds arise,
   Heaving in dark and sullen undulation,
   Float from eternity into these eyes;
The storms yet sleep, the clouds still keep their
      station,
   The unborn earthquake yet is in the womb,
   The bloody chaos yet expects creation,
But all things are disposing for thy doom;
   The elements await but for the word,   30
   'Let there be darkness!' and thou grow'st a tomb!
Yes! thou, so beautiful, shalt feel the sword,
   Thou, Italy! so fair that Paradise,
   Revived in thee, blooms forth to man restored:

---

20 *banish'd Ghibelline* Dante was Guelf by family allegiance, but his political opinions in the *Commedia* are often Ghibelline in cast (see, for instance, *Inferno* 19.88–133 and *Purgatorio* 6.97–117); Byron draws the phrase from his acquaintance, the poet and editor of the *Commedia* Ugo Foscolo, who calls Dante a '*Ghibellin fuggiasco*' ['banished Ghibelline'] in his 'Dei sepolcri' (1807), 1.174   **21–2** compare *Inferno* 33.27
32ff. compare *Purgatorio* 6.7ff.

Ah! must the sons of Adam lose it twice?
  Thou, Italy! whose ever golden fields,
  Plough'd by the sunbeams solely, would suffice
For the world's granary; thou, whose sky heaven gilds
  With brighter stars, and robes with deeper blue;
40   Thou, in whose pleasant places Summer builds
Her palace, in whose cradle Empire grew,
  And form'd the Eternal City's ornaments
  From spoils of kings whom freemen overthrew;
Birthplace of heroes, sanctuary of saints,
  Where earthly first, then heavenly glory made
  Her home; thou, all which fondest fancy paints,
And finds her prior vision but portray'd
  In feeble colours, when the eye – from the Alp
  Of horrid snow, and rock, and shaggy shade
50 Of desert-loving pine, whose emerald scalp
  Nods to the storm – dilates and dotes o'er thee,
  And wistfully implores, as 'twere, for help
To see thy sunny fields, my Italy,
  Nearer and nearer yet, and dearer still
  The more approach'd, and dearest were they free,
Thou – Thou must wither to each tyrant's will:
  The Goth hath been, – the German, Frank, and Hun
  Are yet to come, – and on the imperial hill
Ruin, already proud of the deeds done
60 By the old barbarians, there awaits the new,
  Throned on the Palatine, while lost and won
Rome at her feet lies bleeding; and the hue
  Of human sacrifice and Roman slaughter
  Troubles the clotted air, of late so blue,
And deepens into red the saffron water
  Of Tiber, thick with dead; the helpless priest,
  And still more helpless nor less holy daughter,
Vow'd to their God, have shrieking fled, and ceased
  Their ministry: the nations take their prey,
70 Iberian, Almain, Lombard, and the beast

And bird, wolf, vulture, more humane than they
   Are; these but gorge the flesh and lap the gore
   Of the departed, and then go their way;
But those, the human savages, explore
   All paths of torture, and insatiate yet,
   With Ugolino hunger prowl for more.
       (written 1820; published 1821)

Francesca of Rimini [*Inferno* 5.97–142]
Translation from the Inferno of Dante, Canto 5.

The reader is requested to consider the following version as an attempt to render *verse* for *verse* the episode in the same metre. Where the same English word appears to be repeated too frequently, he will generally find the corresponding repetition in the Italian; I have sacrificed all ornament to fidelity.

'The Land where I was born sits by the seas,
   Upon that shore to which the Po descends
   With all his followers in search of peace.
Love, which the gentle heart soon apprehends,
   Seized him for the fair person which was ta'en
   From me, and me even yet the mode offends.
Love, who to none beloved to love again
   Remits, seized me with wish to please so strong
   That, as thou seest, yet, yet it doth remain.
Love to one death conducted us along: 10
   But Caina waits for him our life who ended.'
   These were the accents utter'd by her tongue.
Since I first listened to these souls offended

1ff. Byron made two versions of this passage on the same day, of which this is the second. Sending it to his publisher, he wrote 'Enclosed you will find *line for line* in *third rhyme* (*terza rima*) . . . Fanny of Rimini . . . I have done it into *cramp* English . . . to try the possibility'   5 *him* Paolo
11 *Caina* a subdivision of the lowest infernal circle, reserved for those who betrayed their relatives

I bow'd my visage, and so kept it till
'What think'st thou?' said the bard – then I
   unbended
And recommenced, 'Alas! unto such ill
How many sweet thoughts, what strong ecstacies,
Led these their evil fortune to fulfill!'
And then I turned unto their side my eyes,
20   And said, 'Francesca, thy sad destinies
Have made me sorrow till the tears arise.
But tell me, in the season of sweet sighs
By what, and how thy love to passion rose
So as his dim desires to recognize?'
Then she to me – 'The greatest of all woes
Is to recal to mind our happy days
In misery, and that thy teacher knows.
But if to learn our passion's first root preys
Upon thy spirit with such sympathy,
30   I will relate as he who weeps, and says.
We read one day for pastime, seated nigh,
Of Lancelot, how love enchain'd him too;
We were alone, quite unsuspiciously.
But oft our eyes met, and our cheeks in hue
All o'er discolour'd by that reading were;
But one point only wholly us o'erthrew.
When we read the long-sighed-for smile of her
To be thus kiss'd by such a fervent lover,
He, who from me can be divided ne'er,
40   Kiss'd my mouth, trembling in the act all over –
Accursed was the book, and he who wrote;
That day no further leaf we did uncover.'
While thus one spirit told us of their lot
The other wept so, that, with pity's thralls,
I swoon'd, as if by death I had been smote,
And fell down even as a dead body falls.
       (written 20 March 1820; published 1830)

THOMAS MEDWIN (1788–1869) and
PERCY BYSSHE SHELLEY (1792–1822)

Medwin was a friend of Shelley's from childhood on and published his *Life* of the poet in 1847. After serving as a lieutenant in the dragoon guards, he moved for health reasons to Italy, spending much of his time in the company of Shelley and Byron. In 1823 his dramatic poem *Ahasuerus the Wanderer* appeared anonymously. Mary Shelley was unimpressed by his attempt at Dante; '. . . not to say that he fills his verses with all possible commonplaces he understands his author very imperfectly'. Yet the Medwin/Shelley version is notable for its complete excision of the narrative frame, bringing to a culmination the tendencies noted above with reference to Montgomery and Merivale: Ugolino has become the speaker of a dramatic monologue, addressing a characterless interlocutor (Dante and Virgil have disappeared) in a void setting (we cannot tell we are in hell). Medwin also translated Aeschylus's *Agamemnon*.

Inferno 33   22–75

Now had the loophole of that dungeon, still
Which bears the name of Famine's Tower from me,
And where 'tis fit that many another will

Be doomed to linger in captivity,
Shown through its narrow opening in my cell
Moon after moon slow waning, when a sleep,

3–4 This remark of Ugolino's is frequently omitted in earlier versions of this episode   6 *Moon . . .* Medwin distinguishes Shelley's contributions by italics

That of the future burst the veil, in dream
Visited me. It was a slumber deep
And evil; for I saw, or I did seem

10   To see, *that* tyrant Lord his revels keep,
The leader of the cruel hunt to them,
Chasing the wolf and wolf-cubs up the steep

Ascent, that from *the Pisan is the screen*
Of *Lucca*; with him Gualandi came,
Sismondi, and Lanfranchi, *bloodhounds lean*,

Trained to the sport and eager for the game
Wide ranging in his front; but soon were seen
Though by so short a course, with *spirits tame*,

The father and *his whelps* to flag at once,
20   And then the sharp fangs gored their bosoms deep.
Ere morn I roused myself, and heard my sons,

For they were with me, moaning in their sleep,
And begging bread. Ah, for those darling ones!
Right cruel art thou, if thou dost not weep

In thinking of my soul's sad augury;
And if thou weepest not now, weep never more!
They were already waked, as wont drew nigh

The allotted hour for food, and in that hour
Each drew a presage from his dream. When I
30   *Heard locked beneath me of that horrible tower*

---

20 *bosoms* it is their flanks which are bitten in the original
23 *Ah, for those darling ones!* not in Dante   26 *if thou . . . never more!* the
original means 'if this doesn't make you cry, what does?'

The outlet; then into their eyes alone
I looked to read myself, without a sign
Or word. I wept not – turned within to stone.

They wept aloud, and little Anselm mine,
Said – 'twas my youngest, dearest little one, –
'What ails thee, father? Why look so at thine?'

In all that day, and all the following night,
I wept not, nor replied; but when to shine
Upon the world, not us, came forth the light

Of the new sun, and thwart my prison thrown   40
Gleamed through its narrow chink, a doleful sight,
Three faces, each the reflex of my own,

Were imaged by its faint and ghastly ray;
Then I, of either hand unto the bone,
Gnawed, in my agony; and thinking they

'Twas done from sudden pangs, in their excess,
All of a sudden raise themselves, and say,
'Father! our woes, so great, were yet the less

Would you but eat of us, – 'twas *you who clad*
Our bodies in these weeds of wretchedness;   50
Despoil them.' Not to make their hearts more sad,

I *hushed* myself. That day is at its close, –
Another – still we were all mute. Oh, had
The obdurate earth opened to end our woes!

---

35 *my youngest, dearest little one* not in Dante

The fourth day dawned, and when the new sun shone,
Outstretched himself before me as it rose
My Gaddo, saying, 'Help, father! hast thou none

For thine own child – is there no help from thee?'
He died – there at my feet – and one by one,
60   I saw them fall, plainly as you see me,

Between the fifth and sixth day, ere 'twas dawn,
I found *myself blind-groping o'er the three.*
Three days I called them after they were gone.

Famine of grief can get the mastery.
      (written 1821; published 1847)

JOSEPH GARROW (1789–1855)

A devotee of letters, Garrow moved to Florence in 1844 with
his wife and their daughter, Theodosia, who soon married
Trollope's son. There he wrote and had printed his *Early Life
of Dante Alighieri*, the first published translation of the *Vita
Nuova* into English. The Preface notes that 'Dante has been
reproached . . . with a want of tenderness', and suggests that
'this little history of his first love . . . leaves not a doubt upon
the mind, that with a supernatural degree of Intellect he united
a heart of the most sensitive materials'.

56–7 *Outstretched . . . My Gaddo* the inverted syntax is Medwin's
64 *Famine* . . . according to Medwin, Shelley and Byron sharply disagreed
about the implications of this line, Byron confidently declaring it meant
Ugolino ate his sons' corpses, Shelley vehemently denying that it did so

Vita Nuova 9 ['Cavalcando l'altr'ier per un cammino']

As pensive on my tedious journey sped,
   Onwards I rode, the morn 'ere yesterday;
   I did encounter *Love* upon the way, –
   In scanty pilgrim's garments habited. –
In look, he seemed to be one lowly bred,
   And quite bereft of all his lordly sway. –
   Sighing, dejected, he did onwards stray,
   Shunning the folk around, with downcast head –
Soon as he saw, by name he called on me,
   And 'I am come from far,' ('twas thus he spake)   10
   'Where at my bidding dwelt thy heart 'erewhile
'I bring it thence to serve another's smile' –
   Then of his being, I such part did take,
   That straight he vanished; how I could not see.
     (1846)

PERCY BYSSHE SHELLEY (1792–1822)

Shelley began learning Italian in 1813; he applied passages from *Inferno* to the state of his feelings and of his marriage in a notebook for April of that year. In 1817 he tried his hand at *terza rima* in the fragmentary *Prince Athanase* and frequently returned to that form, as in the 'Ode to the West Wind' (whose opening probably owes something to *Inferno* 3.112ff.). Medwin reports that 'though [Shelley] thought highly of Cary's work ... praising the fidelity of the version – it by no means satisfied him. What he meant by an adequate translation was, one in terza rima; for in Shelley's own words, he held it an essential justice to an author, to render him in the same form.' Shelley treats the form with unprecedented skill and subtlety;

---

9 *by name he called on me* Dante characteristically does not give his name though he refers to it

its popularity with later English poets owes much to his example. His efforts to render Dante this formal 'essential justice' cost him dear – witness the fact that most of the pieces which follow were left unfinished at his death (they are printed here from editions of the manuscripts: hence the blanks for missing words and the less than finalized readings in square or angle brackets). He preferred *Purgatorio* and *Paradiso* to *Inferno*, always stressing 'the exquisite tenderness & sensibility & ideal beauty, in which Dante excelled all poets except Shakespeare'. In the *Defence of Poetry* (1821), Dante appears as a proto-Shelley: 'Dante was the first religious reformer . . . Dante was the first awakener of entranced Europe; he created a language in itself music and persuasion, out of a chaos of inharmonious barbarism'.

Sonnet from the Italian of Dante
[*Rime* 52: 'Guido, i' vorrei . . .']

Dante Alighieri to Guido Cavalcanti

Guido, I would that Lapo, thou, and I,
Led by some strong enchantment, might ascend
A magic ship, whose charmèd sails should fly
With winds at will where'er our thoughts might
        wend,
So that no change, nor any evil chance
Should mar our joyous voyage; but it might be,
That even satiety should still enhance
Between our hearts their strict community:
And that the bounteous wizard then would place
10   Vanna and Bice and my gentle love,
Companions of our wandering, and would grace

---

3 *fly* Shelley's boat is more magical than Dante's, which just 'goes on the sea'   10 *Bice* short for 'Beatrice'; Shelley was translating from a poor text, for Dante does not name Beatrice in his poem; the name here should be 'Lagia'

With passionate talk, wherever we might rove,
Our time, and each were as content and free
As I believe that thou and I should be.   (?1815)

'*Voi che'ntendendo il terzo ciel movete*' [*Convivio* 2]

Ye who intelligent the third Heaven move,
Hear the discourse which is within my heart,
Which cannot be declared, it seems so new;
The Heaven whose course follows your power
          and art,
O gentle creatures that ye are, out of
The state in which I find myself, me drew,
And therefore may I dare to speak to you,
Even of the life which now I live – and yet
I pray that ye will hear me when I cry,
And tell of my own heart this novelty,   10
How the lamenting spirit moans in it;
And how a voice there murmurs against her
Who came on the refulgence of your sphere.

A sweet thought, which was once the life within
My heavy heart, many a time and oft
Went up before our Father's feet, and there
It saw a glorious lady throned aloft,
And its sweet talk of her my soul did win
So that it said, 'Thither I too will fare'.
That thought is fled, and one doth now appear   20

---

1 *third Heaven* the heaven of Venus, turned – like the other celestial spheres
in Dante's view – by 'intelligences' or 'angels'   12 *her* a second love of
Dante's after Beatrice   13 *refulgence* traces of an eighteenth-century
'elevation' of Dante's language linger on in Shelley; the Italian word here is
simply '*raggi*' (rays)   17 *a glorious lady* Beatrice

Which tyrannizes me with such fierce stress
That my heart trembles – you may see it leap –
And on another lady makes me keep
Mine eyes, and says, 'Who would have blessedness,
Let him but look upon that lady's eyes,
Let him not fear the agony of sighs.'

This lowly thought, which once would talk with me
Of a bright seraph sitting crowned on high,
Found such a cruel foe, it died, and so
30   My spirit wept – the grief is not even now [gone by] –
And said, 'Alas for me, how swift could flee
That piteous thought which did my life console!'
And the afflicted one questioning
Mine eyes, if such a lady saw they never
And why they would
I said, 'Beneath those eyes might stand for ever
He whom direct regards must kill with awe.'
To have known their power stood me in little stead –
Those eyes have looked on me and I am dead.

40   'Thou art not dead – but thou has\<t> wanderèd,
Thou soul of ours, who thus thyself dost fret,'
A spirit of gentle love beside me said,
'For that fair lady, whom thou dost regret

---

21 *tyrannizes* Shelley slightly overpitches the original's *'segnoreggia'* which has the sense of 'rule' without the implication of oppression   33–7 it looks as though Shelley is struggling, not only to frame in verse, but to make sense of Dante's words, which mean: 'Of my eyes, this afflicted spirit says: "what an hour it was when such a woman saw them, and why didn't they believe me about her? I said: 'I am sure that in her eyes must live he [i.e. Love] who kills spirits such as me'"'   40 *wanderèd* the Italian here is *'ismarrita'*, a form of the word which occurs at the beginning of *Inferno* where the straight way is lost (*'smarrita'*)   43 *that fair lady* Shelley reverses the conclusion of Dante's poem, in which it is the second, powerful lady rather than the first, regretted one who triumphs; in consequence, lines 49–52, which in Dante anticipate the consolations of philosophy, become an intimation of the encounter with Beatrice in *Purgatorio* 30

Hath so transformed the life which once she led,
Thou fearest it – so worthless art thou made.
And see how meek, how pitiful, how staid
Yet courteous in her majesty she is;
And still call her   woman in thy thought
Her, whom if thou thyself deceivest not,
Thou wilt behold decked with such loveliness,   50
That thou wilt cry: 'Only Lord, lo there
Thy handmaiden – do what thou wilt with her!'

My song, I fear that thou wilt find but few
Who fitly shall conceive thy reasoning,
Of such hard matter dost thou entertain;
Whence, if by misadventure, chance should bring
Thee to base company (as chance may do),
Quite unaware of what thou dost contain,
I prithee, comfort thy sweet self again,
My last delight! tell them that they are dull,   60
And bid them own that thou art beautiful.
      (written 1820; published 1862)

Matilda Gathering Flowers [Purgatorio 28.1–51]

Earnest to explore within and all around
The divine wood, whose thick green living woof
Tempered the young day to the sight, I wound

Up the [green] slope, beneath the [forest's] roof,
With slow soft steps, leaving the abrupt steep
And the   aloof.

51–2 *there / Thy handmaiden* see Luke 1:38
   6 there is nothing in the original to suggest how Shelley might have meant
to fill this gap

A gentle air which had within itself
No motion struck upon my forehead bare,
The soft stroke of a continuous wind

10   In which the passive leaves tremblingly were
All bent towards that [part], where earliest
That sacred hill obscures the morning air;

Yet were they not so shaken from their rest
But that the birds, perched on the utmost spray,
[Incessantly] renewing their blithe quest

With perfect joy received the early day,
Singing within the glancing leaves, whose sound
Kept one low burthen to their roundelay,

Such as from bough to bough gathers around
20   The pine forest on bleak Chiassi's shore,
When Aeolus Scirocco has unbound.

My slow steps had already borne me o'er
Such space within the antique wood, that I
Perceived not where I entered any more;

When lo, a stream whose little waves went by,
Bending towards the left the grass that grew
Upon its bank, impeded suddenly

My going on – waters of purest hue
On earth, would appear turbid and impure
30   Compared with this, whose unconcealing dew

---

21 *Aeolus* god of the winds *Scirocco* a hot wind which blows from North Africa over Mediterranean Europe

Dark, dark [yet] clear moved under the obscure
Eternal shades, whose   [glooms]
The rays of moon or sunlight ne'er endure.

I moved not with my feet, but amid the glooms
I pierced with my charmed sight, contemplating
The mighty multitude of fresh May blooms;

And then appeared to me, even like a thing
Which suddenly for blank astonishment
Dissolves all other thought,

A solitary woman, and she went   40
Singing and gathering flower after flower
With which her way was painted and besprent.

Bright lady, who if looks had ever power
To bear <firm> witness of the heart within,
Dost bask under the beams of love, come lower

[Towards] this bank, I prithee let me win
Thus much of thee, that thou shouldst come anear
So I may hear thy song; like Proserpine

Thou seemest to my fancy, singing here
And gathering flowers, at that time when   50
She lost the spring and Ceres her . . . more dear.
    (written 1820)

The Triumph of Life   41–154, 176–292, 401–547

As in that trance of wondrous thought I lay
  This was the tenour of my waking dream.
Methought I sate beside a public way

  Thick strewn with summer dust, & a great stream
Of people there was hurrying to & fro
  Numerous as gnats upon the evening gleam,

All hastening onward, yet none seemed to know
  Whither he went, or whence he came, or why
He made one of the multitude, yet so

10   Was borne amid the crowd as through the sky
One of the million leaves of summer's bier. –
  Old age & youth, manhood & infancy,

Mixed in one mighty torrent did appear,
  Some flying from the thing they feared & some
Seeking the object of another's fear,

  And others as with steps towards the tomb
Pored on the trodden worms that crawled beneath,
  And others mournfully within the gloom

Of their own shadow walked, and called it death . . .
20   And some fled from it as it were a ghost,
Half fainting in the affliction of vain breath.

---

3 *beside a public way* reversing Dante's position, far from any 'straight road'
at the start of the *Commedia*   4–5 compare *Inferno* 3.52–7
6 *gnats* compare *Inferno* 17.50–1   11 *leaves* compare *Inferno* 3.112–14
13–14 compare *Inferno* 9.76–80   17 *trodden worms* compare *Inferno*
3.68–9   18–19 *gloom . . . shadow* compare *Paradiso* 10.71–2

But more with motions which each other crost
Pursued or shunned the shadows the clouds threw
   Or birds within the noonday ether lost,

Upon that path where flowers never grew;
   And weary with vain toil & faint for thirst
Heard not the fountains whose melodious dew

   Out of their mossy cells forever burst
Nor felt the breeze which from the forest told
   Of grassy paths, & wood lawns interspersed   30

With overarching elms & caverns cold,
   And violet banks where sweet dreams brood, but
      they
Pursued their serious folly as of old . . . .

   And as I gazed methought that in the way
The throng grew wilder, as the woods of June
   When the South wind shakes the extinguished
      day. –

And a cold glare, intenser than the noon
   But icy cold, obscured with   light
The Sun as he the stars. Like the young moon

   When on the sunlit limits of the night   40
Her white shell trembles amid crimson air
   And whilst the sleeping tempest gathers might

Doth, as a herald of its coming, bear
   The ghost of her dead Mother, whose dim form
Bends in dark ether from her infant's chair,

---

29 *breeze* compare *Purgatorio* 28.7ff.   39 *young moon* compare *Purgatorio*
29.52–4

So came a chariot on the silent storm
Of its own rushing splendour, and a Shape
So sate within as one whom years deform

Beneath a dusky hood & double cape
50   Crouching within the shadow of a tomb,
And o'er what seemed the head, a cloud like crape,

Was bent a dun & faint etherial gloom
Tempering the light; upon the chariot's beam
A Janus-visaged Shadow did assume

The guidance of that wonder-winged team.
The Shapes which drew it in thick lightnings
Were lost: I heard alone on the air's soft stream

The music of their ever moving wings.
All the four faces of that charioteer
60   Had their eyes banded . . . little profit brings

Speed in the van & blindness in the rear,
Nor then avail the beams that quench the Sun
Or that his banded eyes could pierce the sphere

Of all that is, has been, or will be done. –
So ill was the car guided, but it past
With solemn speed majestically on . . .

The crowd gave way, & I arose aghast,
Or seemed to rise, so mighty was the trance,
And saw like clouds upon the thunder blast

---

46 *a chariot* deriving primarily from Petrarch's *Trionfi* but compare also
Purgatorio 29.107ff.   49 *hood* contrast Beatrice's veil in *Purgatorio* 30.31
53 *Tempering* as A. C. Bradley pointed out, Shelley's fondness for this verb
may owe something to its frequency in Dante, at, for example, *Purgatorio*
28.3   55 *wonder-winged* compare *Purgatorio* 29.94–105

The million with fierce song and maniac dance   70
Raging around; such seemed the jubilee
   As when to greet some conqueror's advance

Imperial Rome poured forth her living sea
   From senatehouse & prison & theatre
When Freedom left those who upon the free

   Had bound a yoke which soon they stooped to
      bear.
Nor wanted here the true similitude
   Of a triumphal pageant, for where'er

The chariot rolled a captive multitude
   Was driven; althose who had grown old in power   80
Or misery, – all who have their age subdued,

   By action or by suffering, and whose hour
Was drained to its last sand in weal or woe,
   So that the trunk survived both fruit & flower;

All those whose fame or infamy must grow
   Till the great winter lay the form & name
Of their own earth with them forever low,

   All but the sacred few who could not tame
Their spirits to the Conqueror, but as soon
   As they had touched the world with living flame   90

Fled back like eagles to their native noon,
   Or those who put aside the diadem
Of earthly thrones or gems, till the last one

71–4 compare the rather different Roman jubilee crowds in *Inferno*
18.28–33; Dante mentions the triumphs of classical Rome in *Purgatorio*
29.115–16   88 *sacred few* perhaps Shelley's version of the elect in
Purgatorio 29.121ff.   91 *eagles* compare *Purgatorio* 9.20ff. and 32.109ff.

Were there; – for they of Athens & Jerusalem
Were neither mid the mighty captives seen
   Nor mid the ribald crowd that followed them

Or fled before . . . Now swift, fierce & obscene
   The wild dance maddens in the van, & those
Who lead it, fleet as shadows on the green,

100   Outspeed the chariot & without repose
Mix with each other in tempestuous measure
   To savage music . . . . Wilder as it grows,

They, tortured by the agonizing pleasure,
   Convulsed & on the rapid whirlwinds spun
Of that fierce spirit, whose unholy leisure

Was soothed by mischief since the world begun,
Throw back their heads & loose their streaming hair,
   And in their dance round her who dims the Sun

Maidens & youths fling their wild arms in air
110   As their feet twinkle; they recede, and now
Bending within each other's atmosphere

Kindle invisibly; and as they glow
Like moths by light attracted & repelled,
   Oft to new bright destruction come & go.

*

97–8 this 'obscene' and 'wild' dance of men and women contrasts with the
decorous all-girl dance at *Purgatorio* 29.121ff.   108 *her who dims* the
moon, as in *Paradiso* 29.97–9   110–12 a phenomenon frequently observed
by Dante in the third *cantica*, as at *Paradiso* 3.109–11

Struck to the heart by this sad pageantry,
Half to myself I said, 'And what is this?
Whose shape is that within the car? & why' –

I would have added – 'is all here amiss?'
But a voice answered .. 'Life' ... I turned & knew
(O Heaven have mercy on such wretchedness!)   120

That what I thought was an old root which grew
To strange distortion out of the hill side
Was indeed one of that deluded crew,

And that the grass which methought hung so wide
And white, was but his thin discoloured hair,
And that the holes it vainly sought to hide

Were or had been eyes. – 'If thou canst forbear
To join the dance, which I had well forborne,'
Said the grim Feature, of my thought aware,

'I will now tell that which to this deep scorn   130
Led me & my companions, and relate
The progress of the pageant since the morn;

'If thirst of knowledge doth not thus abate,
Follow it even to the night, but I
Am weary' ... Then like one who with the weight

Of his own words is staggered, wearily
He paused, and ere he could resume, I cried,
'First who art thou?' ... 'Before thy memory

---

116 *And what ... ?* compare *Purgatorio* 29.21   119 *Life* perhaps an answer
to the 'what' and/or the 'why' of the preceding lines, but perhaps a vocative,
addressed to the 'I' who, like the Dante of the *Commedia*, is the only person
mortally alive in the poem   121 *old root* compare the tree-people of *Inferno*
13   129 *of my thought aware* Virgil and Beatrice frequently read Dante's
mind, which in *Paradiso* becomes an open book to all the blessed

'I feared, loved, hated, suffered, did, & died,
140   And if the spark with which Heaven lit my spirit
      Earth had with purer nutriment supplied

'Corruption would not now thus much inherit
      Of what was once Rousseau – nor this disguise
Stained that within which still disdains to wear it. –

'If I have been extinguished, yet there rise
A thousand beacons from the spark I bore.' –
'And who are those chained to the car?' 'The Wise,

'The great, the unforgotten: they who wore
      Mitres & helms & crowns, or wreathes of light,
150   Signs of thought's empire over thought; their lore

'Taught them not this – to know themselves; their
            might
Could not repress the mutiny within,
      And for the morn of truth they feigned, deep night

'Caught them ere evening.' 'Who is he with chin
      Upon his breast and hands crost on his chain?'
'The Child of a fierce hour; he sought to win

'The world, and lost all it did contain
Of greatness, in its hope destroyed; & more
      Of fame & peace than Virtue's self can gain

---

143 *Rousseau* Jean-Jacques Rousseau (1712–78), the intense delaying of
whose name is very Dantescan; he stands as an emblem of Enlightenment
aspirations and their defeat, and is Shelley's version of Dante's Virgil
146 compare *Purgatorio* 21.95–6   149 *Mitres . . . crowns* compare
Purgatorio 27.142

'Without the opportunity which bore   160
   Him on its eagle's pinion to the peak
From which a thousand climbers have before

'Fall'n as Napoleon fell.' – I felt my cheek
Alter to see the great form pass away
   Whose grasp had left the giant world so weak

That every pigmy kicked it as it lay –
   And much I grieved to think how power & will
In opposition rule our mortal day –

And why God made irreconcilable
Good & the means of good; and for despair   170
   I half disdained mine eye's desire to fill

With the spent vision of the times that were
   And scarce have ceased to be . . . 'Dost thou
      behold,'
Said then my guide, 'those spoilers spoiled, Voltaire,

'Frederic, & Kant, Catherine, & Leopold,
Chained hoary anarch, demagogue & sage
   Whose name the fresh world thinks already old –

---

174 *Voltaire* pseudonym of François-Marie Arouet (1694–1778), one of the chief luminaries of the French Enlightenment; he quarrelled fiercely with Rousseau   **175** *Frederic* Frederick II, 'the Great' (1712–86), King of Prussia 1740–86, friend of Voltaire (briefly); he attempted to introduce universal primary education into Prussia and promoted religious tolerance *Kant* Immanuel Kant (1724–1804); Hegel considered his work 'the French Revolution in philosophy' *Catherine* Catherine II, 'the Great' (1729–96), Empress of Russia 1762–96, friend of Voltaire; her plans for political reform mostly remained just plans *Leopold* Leopold II (1747–92), Grand Duke of Tuscany 1765–90, Holy Roman Emperor 1790–2; he continued his brother's policy of emancipating the peasantry and extending religious liberty

'For in the battle Life & they did wage
　　She remained conqueror – I was overcome
180　By my own heart alone, which neither age

　　'Nor tears nor infamy nor now the tomb
　　Could temper to its object.' – 'Let them pass' –
　　I cried – 'the world & its mysterious doom

　　'Is not so much more glorious than it was
　　　That I desire to worship those who drew
　　New figures on its false & fragile glass

　　'As the old faded.' – 'Figures ever new
　　Rise on the bubble, paint them how you may;
　　　We have but thrown, as those before us threw,

190　'Our shadows on it as it past away.
　　　But mark, how chained to the triumphal chair
　　The mighty phantoms of an elder day –

　　'All that is mortal of great Plato there
　　Expiates the joy & woe his master knew not;
　　　That star that ruled his doom was far too fair –

　　'And Life, where long that flower of Heaven grew
　　　　not,
　　　Conquered the heart by love which gold or pain
　　Or age or sloth or slavery could subdue not –

　　'And near　　　walk the　　　　　　twain,
200　The tutor & his pupil, whom Dominion
　　　Followed as tame as vulture in a chain. –

---

182 *Let them pass* compare Virgil's advice to Dante in *Inferno* 3.51
193 *Plato* contrast his placing in *Inferno* 4.134　194 *his master* presumably
Socrates, though it is not clear what 'joy & woe' Plato knew that Socrates
ignored　200 *tutor & his pupil* Aristotle (see *Inferno* 4.131) and Alexander
the Great (see *Inferno* 14.31–6)

'The world was darkened beneath either pinion
  Of him whom from the flock of conquerors
Fame singled as her thunderbearing minion;

'The other long outlived both woes & wars,
Throned in new thoughts of men, and still had kept
  The jealous keys of truth's eternal doors

'If Bacon's spirit   had not leapt
  Like lightning out of darkness; he compelled
The Proteus shape of Nature's as it slept   210

'To wake & to unbar the caves that held
The treasure of the secrets of its reign –
  See the great bards of old who inly quelled

'The passions which they sung, as by their strain
  May well be known: their living melody
Tempers its own contagion to the vein

'Of those who are infected with it – I
Have suffered what I wrote, or viler pain! –

'And so my words were seeds of misery –
Even as the deeds of others.' – 'Not as theirs,'   220
  I said – he pointed to a company

In which I recognized amid the heirs
  Of Caesar's crime from him to Constantine,
The Anarchs old whose force & murderous snares

---

208 *Bacon* Francis Bacon (1561–1626); he represents the growth of
empirical science which succeeded Aristotelianism as the dominant outlook
of the European intellectual elite   223 *Caesar's crime* Julius Caesar's
ambitions for kingly power

Had founded many a sceptre bearing line
And spread the plague of blood & gold abroad,
   And Gregory & John and men divine

Who rose like shadows between Man & god
   Till that eclipse, still hanging under Heaven,
230   Was worshipped by the world o'er which they strode

                           *

'[. . .]
   And as a shut lily, stricken by the wand
      Of dewy morning's vital alchemy,

'I rose; and, bending at her sweet command,
   Touched with faint lips the cup she raised,
And suddenly my brain became as sand

   'Where the first wave had more than half erased
The track of deer on desert Labrador,
   Whilst the fierce wolf from which they fled amazed

'Leaves his stamp visibly upon the shore
240   Until the second bursts – so on my sight
Burst a new Vision never seen before. –

   'And the fair shape waned in the coming light
As veil by veil the silent splendour drops
   From Lucifer, amid the chrysolite

---

227 *Gregory* presumably Pope Gregory the Great (*c.* 540–604)
John probably either the evangelist John or the John who wrote the Book of
Revelation (for many centuries believed to be the same person)
229 *that eclipse* Shelley means the crucified Christ whose death was marked
by an eclipse: see Matthew 27.45–53   231–2 compare *Inferno* 2.127–30
244 *Lucifer* the morning star, the planet Venus   *chrysolite* Shelley may have
been influenced by the frequent association of planets and precious stones
throughout *Paradiso*

'Of sunrise ere it strike the mountain tops –
    And as the presence of that fairest planet
Although unseen is felt by one who hopes

'That his day's path may end as he began it
In that star's smile, whose light is like the scent
    Of a jonquil when evening breezes fan it,   250

'Or the soft note in which his dear lament
    The Brescian shepherd breathes, or the caress
That turned his weary slumber to content. –

'So knew I in that light's severe excess
The presence of that shape which on the stream
    Moved, as I moved along the wilderness,

'More dimly than a day appearing dream,
    The ghost of a forgotten form of sleep,
A light from Heaven whose half extinguished beam

'Through the sick day in which we wake to weep   260
Glimmers, forever sought, forever lost. –
    So did that shape its obscure tenour keep

'Beside my path, as silent as a ghost;
    But the new Vision, and its cold bright car,
With savage music, stunning music, crost

'The forest, and as if from some dread war
Triumphantly returning, the loud million
    Fiercely extolled the fortune of her star. –

246–8 compare *Inferno* 1.17–18

'A moving arch of victory the vermilion
270   And green & azure plumes of Iris had
Built high over her wind-winged pavilion,

'And underneath aetherial glory clad
The wilderness, and far before her flew
     The tempest of the splendour which forbade

'Shadow to fall from leaf or stone; – the crew
     Seemed in that light like atomies that dance
Within a sunbeam. – Some upon the new

'Embroidery of flowers that did enhance
The grassy vesture of the desart, played,
280   Forgetful of the chariot's swift advance;

'Others stood gazing till within the shade
     Of the great mountain its light left them dim. –
Others outspeeded it, and others made

'Circles around it like the clouds that swim
Round the high moon in a bright sea of air,
     And more did follow, with exulting hymn,

'The chariot & the captives fettered there,
     But all like bubbles on an eddying flood
Fell into the same track at last & were

290   'Borne onward. – I among the multitude
Was swept; me sweetest flowers delayed not long,
     Me not the shadow nor the solitude,

---

270 *Iris* the rainbow; compare *Purgatorio* 29.76–8   **276** *atomies* compare
Paradiso 14.109–17

'Me not the falling stream's Lethean song,
　　Me, not the phantom of that early form
Which moved upon its motion, – but among

　'The thickest billows of the living storm
I plunged, and bared my bosom to the clime
　　Of that cold light, whose airs too soon deform. –

'Before the chariot had begun to climb
　　The opposing steep of that mysterious dell,　　　　300
Behold a wonder worthy of the rhyme

　'Of him whom from the lowest depths of Hell
Through every Paradise & through all glory
　　Love led serene, & who returned to tell

'In words of hate & awe the wondrous story
　　How all things are transfigured, except Love;
For deaf as is a sea which wrath makes hoary

　'The world can hear not the sweet notes that move
The sphere whose light is melody to lovers –
　　A wonder worthy of his rhyme – the grove　　　　310

'Grew dense with shadows to its inmost covers,
　　The earth was grey with phantoms, & the air
Was peopled with dim forms, as when there hovers

　'A flock of vampire-bats before the glare
Of the tropic sun, bringing ere evening
　　Strange night upon some Indian isle, – thus were

---

293 Dante drinks from the stream of Lethe in *Purgatorio* 31.102
294–5 *that early form . . . motion* the phantom resembles Matilda in
Purgatorio 31.95–6 ('she was passing over the water as light as a shuttle')
302 *him whom* Dante

'Phantoms diffused around, & some did fling
    Shadows of shadows, yet unlike themselves,
Behind them, some like eaglets on the wing

320   'Were lost in the white blaze, others like elves
Danced in a thousand unimagined shapes
    Upon the sunny streams & grassy shelves;

'And others sate chattering like restless apes
    On vulgar paws and voluble like fire.
Some made a cradle of the ermined capes

    'Of kingly mantles, some upon the tiar
Of pontiffs sate like vultures, others played
    Within the crown which girt with empire

'A baby's or an idiot's brow, & made
330   Their nests in it; the old anatomies
Sate hatching their bare brood under the shade

    'Of demon wings, and laughed from their dead
        eyes
To reassume the delegated power
    Arrayed in which these worms did monarchize

'Who make this earth their charnel. – Others more
    Humble, like falcons sate upon the fist
Of common men, and round their heads did soar,

    'Or like small gnats & flies, as thick as mist
On evening marshes, thronged about the brow
340   Of lawyer, statesman, priest & theorist,

'And others like discoloured flakes of snow
   On fairest bosoms & the sunniest hair
Fell, and were melted by the youthful glow

  'Which they extinguished; for like tears, they were
A veil to those from whose faint lids they rained
   In drops of sorrow. – I became aware

'Of whence those forms proceeded which thus
      stained
   The track in which we moved; after brief space
From every form the beauty slowly waned,

  'From every firmest limb & fairest face   350
The strength & freshness fell like dust, & left
   The action & the shape without the grace

'Of life; the marble brow of youth was cleft
   With care, and in the eyes where once hope shone
Desire like a lioness bereft

  'Of its last cub, glared ere it died; each one
Of that great crowd sent forth incessantly
   These shadows, numerous as the dead leaves
      blown

'In Autumn evening from a poplar tree –
   Each, like himself & like each other were,   360
At first, but soon distorted, seemed to be

  'Obscure clouds moulded by the casual air;
And of this stuff the car's creative ray
   Wrought all the busy phantoms that were there

---

341 compare *Inferno* 14.28–30   355 *lioness bereft* compare *Inferno*
30.7–8   358–9 compare *Inferno* 3.112–14

'As the sun shapes the clouds – thus, on the way
    Mask after mask fell from the countenance
And form of all, and long before the day

'Was old, the joy which waked like Heaven's
        glance
The sleepers in the oblivious valley, died,
370   And some grew weary of the ghastly dance

'And fell, as I have fallen by the way side,
    Those soonest from whose forms most shadows
        past
And least of strength & beauty did abide.' –

'Then, what is Life?' I said . . . the cripple cast
His eye upon the car which now had rolled
    Onward, as if that look must be the last,

And answered . . . . 'Happy those for whom the fold Of
    (written 1822)

FELICIA HEMANS (1793–1835)

Her parents issued her first *Poems* when she was fourteen; the
book was not well received, except by the young Shelley who
pestered her to correspond with him until, it is said, her mother
asked him to desist. Undaunted by adverse reviews or puppy-
love, she continued to produce volumes, winning a Royal
Society for Literature prize in 1821; her reputation in 1828
may be inferred from Moore's note of that year (see 'Imitation
of the Inferno of Dante' above); 1829 saw the first appearance
of her most celebrated poem, 'Casabianca' ('The boy stood on
the burning deck . . .'). She married Captain Hemans when she

---

366–7 perhaps remembering, and reversing the implications of, *Paradiso*
30.91–6

was nineteen but six years and five children later he 'took a trip to Italy and never returned' (*Cambridge Guide to Women's Writing in English*). She provided for her five sons by the energy of her pen. 'The Maremma' was developed from the six lines devoted to La Pia by Dante, a forty-one-fold expansion of the original. Mrs Hemans had, understandably, great sympathy with the figure of an ill-treated wife, and this distracts her from paying attention to where La Pia appears in the *Commedia* (among the late-repentant) or to how extraordinary Dante's presentation of her is – she exists only as a voice, the third in a sequence whose first two members are men and major political figures (one a Guelf, one a Ghibelline). Dante gives her the last word of her canto.

The Maremma

Nello Della Pietra had espoused a lady of noble family at Sienna, named Madonna Pia. Her beauty was the admiration of Tuscany, and excited in the heart of her husband a jealousy, which, exasperated by false reports and groundless suspicions, at length drove him to the desperate resolution of Othello. It is difficult to decide whether the lady was quite innocent, but so Dante represents her. Her husband brought her into the Maremma, which, then as now, was a district destructive of health. He never told his unfortunate wife the reason of her banishment to so dangerous a country. He did not deign to utter complaint or accusation. He lived with her alone, in cold silence, without answering her questions, or listening to her remonstrances. He patiently waited till the pestilential air should destroy the health of this young lady. In a few months

---

headnote Hemans quotes this passage from a review of the 1818 edition of Cary's Dante; it is an extremely inaccurate account of La Pia's story and of *Purgatorio* 5 (for example, the order in which the spirits speak has been muddled). Dante says nothing, one way or the other, about La Pia's moral character; he says nothing *about* her at all

she died. Some chronicles, indeed, tell us that Nello used the dagger to hasten her death. It is certain that he survived her, plunged in sadness and perpetual silence. Dante had, in this incident, all the materials of an ample and very poetical narrative. But he bestows on it only four verses. He meets in Purgatory three spirits; one was a captain who fell fighting on the same side with him in the battle of Campaldino; the second, a gentleman assassinated by the treachery of the House of Este; the third was a woman unknown to the poet, and who, after the others had spoken, turned towards him with these words:

> 'Recorditi di me; che son la Pia,
> Sienna mi fe, disfecemi Maremma,
> Salsi colui che inanellata pria
> Disposando m'avea con la sua gemma.'
> *Purgatorio*, cant. v [133–6].
>   (*Edinburgh Review*, No. 58 [February 1818])

> 'Mais elle était du monde, où les plus belles choses
>   Ont le pire destin;
> Et Rose elle a vécu ce que vivent les roses,
>   L'espace d'un matin.' – MALHERBE

There are bright scenes beneath Italian skies,
Where glowing suns their purest light diffuse,
Uncultured flowers in wild profusion rise,
And Nature lavishes her warmest hues;
But trust thou not her smile, her balmy breath,
Away! her charms are but the pomp of Death!

Recorditi . . . gemma 'remember me. / I once was Pia. Siena gave me life; / Maremma took it from me. That he knows, / Who me with jewel'd ring had first espoused.' (trans. Cary)   **epigraph** *Mais elle était . . . matin* supplied by Mrs Hemans, from Malherbe's 'Consolation à Monsieur du Périer . . . sur la mort de sa fille'; the lines translate as 'But she was of this world where the loveliest things suffer the harshest fate and, as she was herself a rose, she lived, like roses, no more than a morning.'

He, in the vine-clad bowers, unseen is dwelling,
Where the cool shade its freshness round thee
     throws,
His voice, in every perfumed zephyr swelling,
With gentlest whisper lures thee to repose;   10
And the soft sounds that through the foliage sigh,
But woo thee still to slumber and to die.

Mysterious danger lurks, a siren there,
Not robed in terror or announced in gloom,
But stealing o'er thee in the scented air,
And veiled in flowers, that smile to deck thy tomb:
How may we deem, amidst their deep array,
That heaven and earth but flatter to betray?

Sunshine, and bloom, and verdure! Can it be
That these but charm us with destructive wiles?   20
Where shall we turn, O Nature, if in *thee*
Danger is mask'd in beauty – death in smiles?
Oh! still the Circe of that fatal shore,
Where she, the sun's bright daughter, dwelt of yore!

There, year by year, that secret peril spreads,
Disguised in loveliness, its baleful reign,
And viewless blights o'er many a landscape sheds,
Gay with the riches of the south, in vain,
O'er fairy bowers and palaces of state,
Passing unseen, to leave them desolate.   30

And pillar'd halls, whose airy colonnades
Were formed to echo music's choral tone,
Are silent now, amidst deserted shades,
Peopled by sculpture's graceful forms alone;
And fountains dash unheard, by lone alcoves,
Neglected temples, and forsaken groves.

And there, where marble nymphs in beauty gleaming,
'Midst the deep shades of plane and cypress rise,
By wave or grot might Fancy linger, dreaming
40   Of old Arcadia's woodland deities, –
Wild visions! – there no sylvan powers convene –
Death reigns the genius of the Elysian scene.

Ye, too, illustrious hills of Rome! that bear
Traces of mightier beings on your brow,
O'er you that subtle spirit of the air
Extends the desert of his empire now;
Broods o'er the wrecks of altar, fane, and dome,
And makes the Caesars' ruin'd halls his home.

Youth, valour, beauty, oft have felt his power,
50   His crowned and chosen victims: o'er their lot
Hath fond affection wept each blighted flower
In turn was loved and mourn'd, and is forgot.
But one who perish'd, left a tale of woe,
Meet for as deep a sigh as pity can bestow.

A voice of music, from Sienna's walls,
Is floating joyous on the summer air;
And there are banquets in her stately halls,
And graceful revels of the gay and fair,
And brilliant wreaths the altar have array'd,
60   Where meet her noblest youth, and loveliest maid.

To that young bride each grace hath Nature given,
Which glows on Art's divinest dream, – her eye
Hath a pure sunbeam of her native heaven –
Her cheek a tinge of morning's richest dye;

Fair as that daughter of the south, whose form
Still breathes and charms, in Vinci's colours warm.

But is she blest? – for sometimes o'er her smile
A soft sweet shade of pensiveness is cast;
And in her liquid glance there seems a-while
To dwell some thought whose soul is with the past;   70
Yet soon it flies – a cloud that leaves no trace,
On the sky's azure, of its dwelling-place.

Perchance, at times, within her heart may rise
Remembrance of some early love or woe,
Faded, yet scarce forgotten – in her eyes
Wakening the half-formed tear that may not flow;
Yet radiant seems her lot as aught on earth,
Where still some pining thought comes darkly o'er
     our mirth.

The world before her smiles – its changeful gaze
She hath not proved as yet; her path seems gay   80
With flowers and sunshine, and the voice of praise
Is still the joyous herald of her way;
And beauty's light around her dwells, to throw
O'er every scene its own resplendent glow.

Such is the young Bianca – graced with all
That nature, fortune, youth, at once can give;
Pure in their loveliness – her looks recall
Such dreams, as ne'er life's early bloom survive;
And when she speaks, each thrilling tone is fraught
With sweetness, born of high and heavenly thought.   90

---

65 *that daughter of the south* 'an allusion to Leonardo da Vinci's picture of
his wife Mona Lisa, supposed to be the most perfect imitation of Nature ever
exhibited in painting. – See Vasari in his *Lives of the Painters*' [Hemans'
note: in fact the model for the *Mona Lisa* is unknown]   85 *Bianca* we do
not know where Mrs Hemans found this name for La Pia

And he, to whom are breathed her vows of faith
Is brave and noble – child of high descent,
He hath stood fearless in the ranks of death,
'Mid slaughtered heaps, the warrior's monument:
And proudly marshall'd his Carroccio's way,
Amidst the wildest wreck of war's array.

And his the chivalrous, commanding mien,
Where high-born grandeur blends with courtly grace;
Yet may a lightning glance at times be seen,
100 Of fiery passions, darting o'er his face,
And fierce the spirit kindling in his eye –
But e'en while yet we gaze, its quick, wild flashes
      die.

And calmly can Pietra smile, concealing,
As if forgotten, vengeance, hate, remorse;
And veil the workings of each darker feeling,
Deep in his soul concentrating its force:
But yet he loves – Oh! who hath loved, nor known
Affection's power exalt the bosom all its own?

The days roll on – and still Bianca's lot
110 Seems as an oath of Eden – thou might'st deem
That grief, the mighty chastener, had forgot
To wake her soul from life's enchanted dream;
And, if her brow a moment's sadness wear,
It sheds but grace more intellectual there.

---

95 *Carroccio* chariot   103 *Pietra* Mrs Hemans has been misled by the
Edinburgh Review. La Pia's husband was Nello d'Inghiramo dei
Pannocchieschi; he was lord of the castle of Pietra nella Maremma but this
was not his name.

A few short years, and all is changed – her fate
Seems with some deep mysterious cloud o'ercast.
Have jealous doubts transformed to wrath and hate,
The love whose glow expression's power surpass'd?
Lo! on Pietra's brow a sullen gloom
Is gathering day by day, prophetic of her doom.   120

O! can he meet that eye, of light serene,
Whence the pure spirit looks in radiance forth,
And view that bright intelligence of mien
Form'd to express but thoughts of loftiest worth,
Yet deem that vice within the heart can reign?
– How shall he e'er confide in aught on earth again?

In silence oft, with strange vindictive gaze,
Transient, yet fill'd with meaning strange and wild,
Her features calm in beauty, he surveys,
Then turns away, and fixes on her child   130
So dark a glance, as thrills a mother's mind
With some vague fear, scarce own'd, and undefined.

There stands a lonely dwelling, by the wave
Of the blue deep which bathes Italia's shore,
Far from all sounds, but rippling seas that lave
Gray rocks with foliage richly shadow'd o'er,
And sighing winds, that murmur through the wood,
Fringing the beach of that Hesperian flood.

Fair is that house of solitude – and fair
The green Maremma, far around it spread,   140
A sun-bright waste of beauty – yet an air
Of brooding sadness o'er the scene is shed,
No human footstep tracks the lone domain,
The desert of luxuriance glows in vain.

And silent are the marble halls that rise
'Mid founts, and cypress walks, and olive groves:
All sleep in sunshine 'neath cerulean skies,
And still around the sea-breeze lightly roves;
Yet every trace of man reveals alone,
150   That there life once hath flourished – and is gone.

There, till around them slowly, softly stealing,
The summer air, deceit in every sigh,
Came fraught with death, its power no sign
    revealing,
Thy sires, Pietra, dwelt, in days gone by;
And strains of mirth and melody have flow'd,
Where stands, all voiceless now, the still abode.

And thither doth her Lord, remorseless, bear
Bianca with her child – his alter'd eye
And brow a stern and fearful calmness wear,
160   While his dark spirit seals their doom – to die;
And the deep bodings of his victim's heart,
Tell her, from fruitless hope at once to part.

It is the summer's glorious prime – and blending
Its blue transparence with the skies, the deep,
Each tint of Heaven upon its breast descending,
Scarce murmurs as it heaves, in glassy sleep,
And on its wave reflects, more softly bright,
That lovely shore of solitude and light.

Fragrance in each warm southern gale is breathing,
170   Decked with young flowers the rich Maremma glows,
Neglected vines the trees are wildly wreathing,
And the fresh myrtle in exuberance blows,
And, far and round, a deep and sunny bloom
Mantles the scene, as garlands robe the tomb.

Yes! 'tis *thy* tomb, Bianca! fairest flower!
The voice that calls thee speaks in every gale,
Which o'er thee breathing with insidious power,
Bids the young roses of thy cheek turn pale,
And, fatal in its softness, day by day,
Steals from that eye some trembling spark away.   180

But sink not yet; for there are darker woes,
Daughter of Beauty! in thy spring-morn fading,
Sufferings more keen for thee reserved than those
Of lingering death, which thus thine eye are shading!
Nerve then thy heart to meet that bitter lot;
'Tis agony – but soon to be forgot!

What deeper pangs maternal hearts can wring,
Than hourly to behold the spoiler's breath
Shedding, as mildews on the bloom of spring,
O'er Infancy's fair cheek the blight of death?   190
To gaze and shrink, as gathering shades o'ercast
The pale smooth brow, yet watch it to the last!

Such pangs were thine, young mother! – Thou
        didst bend
O'er thy fair boy, and raise his drooping head;
And faint and hopeless, far from every friend,
Keep thy sad midnight-vigils near his bed,
And watch his patient, supplicating eye,
Fix'd upon thee – on thee! – who could'st no aid
        supply!

There was no voice to cheer thy lonely woe
Through those dark hours – to thee the wind's
        low sigh,   200
And the faint murmur of the ocean's flow,
Came like some spirit whispering – 'He must die!'
And thou didst vainly clasp him to the breast
His young and sunny smile so oft with hope had blest.

'Tis past – that fearful trial! – he is gone!
But thou, sad mourner! hast not long to weep;
The hour of nature's chartered peace comes on,
And thou shalt share thine infant's holy sleep.
A few short sufferings yet – and death shall be
210   As a bright messenger from heaven to thee.

But ask not – hope not – one relenting thought
From him who doom'd thee thus to waste away,
Whose heart, with sullen speechless vengeance
        fraught,
Broods in dark triumph o'er thy slow decay;
And coldly, sternly, silently can trace
The gradual withering of each youthful grace.

And yet the day of vain remorse shall come,
When thou, bright victim! on his dreams shall rise
As an accusing angel – and thy tomb,
220   A martyr's shrine, be hallow'd in his eyes!
Then shall thine innocence his bosom wring,
More than thy fancied guilt with jealous pangs
        could sting.

Lift thy meek eyes to heaven – for all on earth,
Young sufferer! fades before thee – thou art lone –
Hope, Fortune, Love, smiled brightly on thy birth,
Thine hour of death is all Affliction's own!
It is our task to suffer – and our fate
To learn that mighty lesson, soon or late.

The season's glory fades – the vintage-lay
230   Through joyous Italy resounds no more;
But mortal loveliness hath pass'd away,
Fairer than aught in summer's glowing store.
Beauty and youth are gone – behold them such
As Death has made them with his blighting touch!

The summer's breath came o'er them – and they died!
Softly it came to give luxuriance birth,
Called forth young nature in her festal pride,
But bore to them their summons from the earth!
Again shall blow that mild, delicious breeze,
And wake to life and light – all flowers – but these.   240

No sculptured urn, nor verse thy virtues telling,
O lost and loveliest one! adorns thy grave;
But o'er that humble cypress-shaded dwelling
The dew-drops glisten and the wild-flowers wave –
Emblems more meet, in transient light and bloom,
For thee, who thus didst pass in brightness to the
      tomb!   (1820)

JOHN KEATS (1795–1821)

Keats first read Dante in the 1814 three-volume, pocket-sized
edition of Cary's translation (they shared publishers); he told
his brother and sister-in-law that he thought it 'well worth the
while' to learn Italian so he could read the original, and by the
autumn of 1819 he had begun to tackle the poem with Cary as
a crib. It is not certain how much he read (at least *Inferno* 1.9–
15 and 22–27, for he marked them in his copy). His response
to Dante is less sharply local than Shelley's or Byron's and so
less easy to demonstrate, but 'The Fall of Hyperion' often seems
to recall the *Commedia* (in addition to the passage below,
compare the breathless climbing of its opening with *Inferno*
24.31–78).

[*From a letter to the George Keatses*
14 February – 3 May 1819]

The fifth canto of Dante pleases me more and more – it is that
one in which he meets with Paolo and Francesca – I had passed
many days in rather a low state of mind and in the midst of

them I dreamt of being in that region of Hell. The dream was one of the most delightful enjoyments I ever had in my life – I floated about the whirling atmosphere as it is described with a beautiful figure to whose lips mine were joined at it seem'd for an age – and in the midst of all this cold and darkness I was warm – even flowery tree tops sprung up and we rested on them sometimes with the lightness of a cloud till the wind blew us away again – I tried a Sonnet upon it – there are fourteen lines but nothing of what I felt in it – o that I could dream it every night –

> As Hermes once took to his feathers light
> When lulled Argus, baffled, swoon'd and slept
> So on a delphic reed my idle spright
> So play'd, so charm'd so conquer'd, so bereft
> The dragon world of all its hundred eyes
> And seeing it asleep so fled away: –
> Not to pure Ida with its snowcold skies,
> Nor unto Tempe where Jove grieved that day,
> But to that second circle of sad hell,
> Where in the gust, the whirlwind and the flaw
> Of Rain and hailstones lovers need not tell
> Their sorrows – Pale were the sweet lips I saw
> Pale were the lips I kiss'd and fair the form
> I floated with about that melancholy storm –
>   (written 1819)

10

1–2 *Hermes . . . Argus* Hermes saved Io, beloved of Jove, from the many-eyed giant Argus by lulling him to sleep with music: see Ovid's *Metamorphoses* 1.668–720   3 *spright* spirit (a frequent recourse of Dante translators when they are looking to save a syllable)   8 *Tempe* home of Io   9 *second circle* where sins of incontinent appetite are punished; Keats refers particularly to *Inferno* 5 and is exceptional among the many who responded warmly to Paolo and Francesca at this time because he remembers the setting in which Dante places them   10 *flaw* 'a sudden burst or squall of wind' (*OED*)

The Fall of Hyperion   1.233–71

I looked thereon,
And on the pavèd floor, where nigh were piled
Faggots of cinnamon and many heaps
Of other crispèd spice-wood – then again
I looked upon the altar, and its horns
Whitened with ashes, and its languorous flame,
And then upon the offerings again;
And so by turns – till sad Moneta cried:
'The sacrifice is done, but not the less,
Will I be kind to thee for thy good will.   10
My power, which to me is still a curse,
Shall be to thee a wonder; for the scenes
Still swooning vivid through my globèd brain,
With an electral changing misery,
Thou shalt with these dull mortal eyes behold,
Free from all pain, if wonder pain thee not.'
As near as an immortal's spherèd words
Could to a mother's soften, were these last.
But yet I had a terror of her robes,
And chiefly of the veils, that from her brow   20
Hung pale, and curtained her in mysteries,
That made my heart too small to hold its blood.
This saw that Goddess, and with sacred hand
Parted the veils. Then saw I a wan face,

---

1 *thereon* on a temple of Saturn, 'all spared from the thunder of a war /
Foughten long since' – the war between the Titans and the rebellious
Olympian gods   5–6 *horns . . . flame* compare Cary's version of *Inferno*
26.85, above   8 *Moneta* another name for Mnemosyne, 'Memory', the
mother of the Muses; Keats' Moneta is 'sole priestess of [Saturn's]
desolation'   18 *a mother's* Dante several times compares Beatrice's rebukes
to those of a mother – see *Purgatorio* 30.79–81 or 31.64–6

Not pined by human sorrows, but bright-blanched
By an immortal sickness which kills not.
It works a constant change, which happy death
Can put no end to; deathwards progressing
To no death was that visage; it had passed
The lily and the snow; and beyond these
I must not think now, though I saw that face –
But for her eyes I should have fled away.
They held me back, with a benignant light,
Soft-mitigated by divinest lids
Half-closed, and visionless entire they seemed
Of all external things – they saw me not,
But in blank splendour beamed like the mild moon,
Who comforts those she sees not, who knows not
What eyes are upward cast.   (1819)

30

ICHABOD CHARLES WRIGHT

(1795–1871)

Wright resigned his fellowship of Magdalen College, Oxford, on his marriage and returned to work in the family bank at Nottingham (throughout the nineteenth century, Dante attracted bankers and politicians). His translation appeared *cantica* by *cantica* from 1833 to 1840; Thomas Moore thought it 'far exceeded' Cary's, a view which is generous to Wright, because, though often closer to Dante than Cary, he has a less subtle and skilled ear. His version is notable at least for its variant of *terza rima* (Wright rhymes *aba cbc* rather than *aba bcb*), the first of many attempts to convey in English some of the qualities of Dante's *terza rima* without the crushing burden of exact replication. Wright also translated the *Iliad*, into blank verse.

36–9 compare Beatrice's eyes, which Dante sees looking at the sun in *Paradiso* 1.64–6

Inferno 34

'Lo, come the banners of the king of hell!'
    My master said: 'then forward stretch thine eye,
    And, if thou canst – behold the monarch fell.'
Like to a windmill, in the distance seen
    Whirling about, when night enwraps the sky,
    Or dense and murky vapours intervene; –
Such was the structure I now seem'd to view:
    Whereat to shun the blast, behind my guide
    For want of other shelter I withdrew.
Now came we – and I pen the verse with fear –   10
    Where all the shades beneath the frozen tide
    Transparent shone, like straws in crystal clear.
Some prostrate – others upright I observed,
    One on his head, and one upon his feet;
    Another's figure like a bow was curved.
When we had made such progress on our way,
    That to my kind instructor it seem'd meet,
    The Creature, once so beauteous, to display; –
Standing aside, he made me halt, – and cried:
    'Now Dis behold! – be thine, in this dread spot   20
    A heart of firmest courage to provide.'
How hoarse and icy cold I then became –
    Demand not, reader, since I write it not;
    For all description would be weak and tame.
I died not; – nor was life within me left;
    Imagine then, if fancy thou possess,
    What I became, of either state bereft.

---

1 in the original Virgil quotes, in Latin, the processional hymn for Good
Friday, 'Vexilla regis prodeunt' ('the banners of the king advance') and adds
to 'king' 'of hell'   3 *the monarch fell* not in the Italian which has only the
pronoun for 'him'   18 *The Creature* Lucifer, beautiful before his rebellion
and fall   20 *Dis* the Greek name for the king of the underworld; Dante has
'Satan' only once in the *Commedia* (*Inferno* 7.1)

Above the ice uprear'd his bust on high
   The Monarch of that region of distress;
30   And nearer to a giant's height am I,
Than to his arms are giants: – now compute,
   How vast in magnitude the whole must be,
   Which to a portion so immense could suit.
If he were beauteous once, as now debased, –
   Yet in his pride transgressed his Sire's decree,
   Well may all evil unto him be traced.
O what a prodigy he seem'd, to view!
   For on his head three faces were uprear'd;
   The one in front of a vermilion hue:
40 The other two, above each shoulder blade,
   United closely to the first appear'd;
   And at the crest all three a junction made.
Somewhat 'twixt white and yellow was the right;
   The left, to look at, was like those who dwell
   Where Nile descends from Ethiopia's height.
Two mighty wings extended under each,
   Which to a bird so monstrous suited well;
   Nor e'er beheld I sails such distance reach.
Plumes had they none; but in their texture they
50   Were like a bat's; which, flexible and thin,
   Produced three winds by their incessant play,
And froze Cocytus' lowest depth profound.
   The six eyes wept; and o'er his triple chin
   The tears and bloody foam pour'd fast around.
At every mouth his teeth a sinner tore,
   E'en like a mill; so that within his jaws,
   Were three of them at once tormented sore.
To him in front this crushing was but play,
   Compared with what he suffer'd from the claws,
60   Which from his back oft tore the skin away.

28–9 the syntactical inversion is Wright's   35 *his Sire's* God, though Dante
does not call God Satan's 'father' but only his 'maker' ('*fattore*')

'That one above,' to me the master said,
  'Is Judas 'Scariot, doom'd to greater pangs: –
  His feet are quivering, while sinks down his head.
Of the other two, whose heads are plunged below,
  Brutus the one, who from the black throat hangs;
  See how he writhes, yet speaks not in his woe! –
Cassius the other, with such strength endued.
  But night returns; and from the abyss of hell
  'Tis time we went, since all hath now been view'd.'
My master bidding, I his neck ascended;   70
  Then, judging both his time and distance well,
  He, when the pinions were enough extended,
Attach'd him closely to the shaggy side,
  And made from lock to lock his downward way,
  Between the wall of ice, and rugged hide.
When we had reach'd a station where the thigh
  Doth on the swelling of the haunches play,
  My guide with much fatigue and urgency
To where his feet had been, moved round his head,
  And, like to one who mounts, clung to the hair; –   80
  So that to hell again, methought, we sped.
Then panting, as a man forespent with toil –
  My master said: 'Take heed; for by such stair
  Must we escape from this accursed soil.'
Forth issued through a hollow rock my guide,
  And on the brink providing me a seat,
  Sate himself down with caution by my side.
I raised my eyes; – nor change did I expect
  To find in Lucifer; – when lo, his feet,
  That late hung down, were seen in air erect!   90
And how I then with trouble was o'ercast,
  Let grosser minds imagine – not with sense
  Endowed to mark the point which I had past.

---

68 *night returns* Virgil's timing is excellent, for there is no light to measure
by in hell. They have been travelling some twenty-four hours since *Inferno*
2.1; it is twilight on Holy Saturday, 1300

Now spoke the master: 'Rise – no more delay –
  Long is the road and rough that leadeth hence,
  And Phœbus soon will wake the early day.'
No royal path was that on which we were,
  But wrought by nature, savage, rough, and rude;
  Nor was there aught but troublous twilight there.
100 'Ere from the dark abyss we take our way,
  Master,' I said, when on my feet I stood,
  'Some words bestow lest I in error stray,
Where is the ice? – and wherefore is his head
  Fix'd upside down? and tell the reason why
  From night to morn the sun so soon hath sped.'
Then he: 'Thou dost imagine we are still
  On the other side the central point, where I
  Clasped the earth-piercing worm, fell cause of ill.
So far as I continued to descend,
110 That side we kept; but when I turn'd, then we
  Had pass'd the point to which all bodies tend.
Now art thou come to the hemisphere beneath,
  Opposed to that which forms earth's canopy;
  Under whose highest cope pour'd forth his breath
The Man who sinless lived and sinless died.
  Thy feet upon a little sphere are placed;
  Its other front is on Giudecca's side.
Morn rises here, when it is evening there;
  And he, whose locks to aid us we embraced,
120 Remains still fix'd, as when he form'd our stair.

---

96 as Virgil goes on to explain, they are now in the southern hemisphere and
the time has changed accordingly: Jerusalem's sunset on Holy Saturday
corresponds to the dawn of Easter Sunday in the Antipodes. There is no
reference to Phoebus at this point in the original.   115 *The Man* . . . Christ,
who died at Jerusalem, treated by Dante as the 'highest cope' of the northern
hemisphere; Purgatory is at the corresponding point of the southern
hemisphere   117 *Giudecca* the part of the ninth circle that Dante and Virgil
have just left

Hither he fell from heaven, what time forsook
  Its place, through dread of him, the dry land here,
  And 'neath the veil of ocean, refuge took,
And reached our hemisphere: – so, through like
    dread,
  The earth there rising, hence did disappear,
  And sinking down, exalted there its head.
As far from Beelzebub as the profound
  Abyss is deep, a place there is below,
  Not known by sight, but only by the sound
Caused by a rivulet that downward borne   130
  In gentle windings, by its constant flow
  A channel in the stony rock hath worn.'
My guide and I this secret pathway chose,
  To reconduct us to the world of light;
  And up we journeyed, heedless of repose,
He mounting first, while I his steps pursued; –
  Till, through an orifice, heaven's splendours bright
  Burst on mine eyes: – emerging thence, we view'd
The stars once more unfolded to our sight.
    (1833; 1845)

JAMES FORD (1797–1877)

Ford took Anglican orders after graduating from Oxford, and held various posts before retiring on his independent income to Bath; he published several devotional works as well as his version of Dante. William Michael Rossetti, whose blank verse translation of *Inferno* appeared in the same year as Ford's first *cantica*, believed Ford had shown that 'another experiment in terza rima was well worth making'.

121-2 *what time . . . the dry land here* the syntactic inversion is Wright's

Inferno 27

Already was the flame erect, and still,
    From ended speech; already was it gone,
    With the sweet Poet's licence and good will;
Behind it, when another moving on
    Turn'd our regard towards its summit bright,
    By reason of its strange discordant groan.
As the Sicilian bull – so to requite –
    First bellow'd with his cry, whose file with skill
    Its vocal form had so attun'd aright,
10   With the same strange lament kept bellowing still;
    So that, for all 'twas but a brazen frame,
    It seem'd, nathless, susceptible of ill;
Thus lacking outlet, with effect the same,
    The throttled tones of inly smother'd woe
    First sounded forth, as though it were the flame:
But, after they had gain'd the upmost brow,
    Which stirr'd them with the wavy pointed crest,
    As had the tongue, when rising from below,
We heard it thus: 'O thou, toward whom address'd
20   In phrase of Lombardy my voice I turn,
    Who said'st, "Now go, I thee no more molest,"
Though somewhat slow I'm come, of thee to learn,
    Grieve not awhile to pause and converse hold:
    Behold, it grieves me not; and lo! I burn.

---

1 *flame* Ulysses, whose speech ends the previous canto
3 *the sweet Poet* Virgil   4 translatorese for 'when another moving on behind
it'   7 *the Sicilian bull* Phalaris, tyrant of Agrigento, had a hollow bronze
bull made in which he roasted his victims alive; he tried it out first on the
designer who had made it for him   19 *thou* Virgil, a native of Lombardy; in
the original, the snatch of speech quoted in line 21 is not Latin, nor the
Tuscan Italian in which Dante generally represents Virgil's voice, but
Lombard dialect   24 the original is clearer and funnier: 'you see that I don't
mind [stopping to talk], and I'm on fire'

If, of a truth, into this blinded world
   Thou but of late, from that sweet Latium dear
   Whence all my guilt I gather, hast been hurl'd;
Have the Romagnuols, tell me, peace or war?
   For of the heights between Urbino I am,
   And those, where Tiber first unlocks her bar.'   30
Still was I stooping low, with strenuous aim,
   To listen, when my Leader touch'd my side,
   Saying: 'Speak thou; this one from Latium came.'
Without delay, I readily replied,
   As one, whose words were pre-arrang'd with
      care;
   'O spirit! in the flame down yonder hid,
Thine own Romagna is not free from war,
   War in her tyrants' hearts; nor e'er was so:
   But none declar'd and raging left I there.
Ravenna stands, as wont for years to do;   40
   There broods Polenta's Eagle, as to screen
   Under his wings distended Cervia too.
The land of such protracted strife, the scene,
   Which gory heaps of slaughter'd Frenchmen
      knew,
   Lies subject to the Lion's paws of green.
The Mastiffs of Verrucchio, old and new,
   Who evil sway over Montagna bare,
   Follow their wont – their teeth a boring screw.

28–30 the speaker is Guido da Montefeltro, whose native town lies in that
part of Romagna between Urbino and Mount Coronaro where the Tiber has
its source   33 Virgil says in the Italian: 'You do the talking; this one's
Italian', contrasting Guido ('this one') with the Greek Ulysses and Diomedes
of the previous canto, with whom Virgil had conducted the interview for the
Greekless Dante   43 The land Forlì, besieged at Pope Martin V's command
between 1281 and 1283 by French and Italian troops; Guido himself played
a skilful part in their defeat   45 Lion's paws the emblem of the Ordelaffi
family   46 The Mastiffs the Malatesta family, lords of Rimini from 1295

Lamone's, and Santerno's cities fair,
50   To the young Lion argent-fielded bow,
     Who changes sides with seasons of the year.
And she, whose flank washes the Savio,
     As seated 'twixt the mountain and the plain,
     Freedom and thraldom doth alternate know.
Now, who art thou, to tell us kindly deign:
     My willing speech, in thy good turn, repay:
     So may thy name on earth its front maintain.'
After the fire, in its accustom'd way,
     Had somewhat roar'd, it wav'd the sharpen'd crest
60   Now here, now there; and then was heard to say;
'If I believ'd my words to one address'd,
     Who to the earth could possibly return,
     No further shaking should this flame molest;
But, since none ever from this deep-sunk bourn
     Alive retrac'd his steps, if truth I hear,
     I answer thee; nor fear reproach to earn.
A soldier I was first, then Cordelièr:
     In faith, thus girt, my sins to expiate;
     And blessed fruit such faith was sure to bear,
70   But for the Pontiff – cursed be his fate! –
     Who caus'd my wayward feet again to stray:
     And how, and wherefore, I will now relate.
So long as I inform'd the flesh and clay
     My mother gave me, every work I plann'd
     The fox and not the lion did betray.
Ways to detect, to practise underhand –
     I knew them all; and all so well I plied,
     My fame resounding went through every land.

---

49 *Lamone . . . Santerno* the rivers on which stand, respectively, Faenza and Imola   **50** *the young Lion* Maghinardo Pagani da Susinana; he is termed a 'demon' in *Purgatorio* 14.118   **52** *she* the town of Cesena
67 *Cordelièr* after an action-packed life as a Ghibelline chieftain, in the course of which he was excommunicated, Guido da Montefeltro was reconciled to the Church and became a Franciscan (or Cordelier) in 1296, two years before his death   **70** *Pontiff* Boniface VIII, Dante's *prêtre noir*
73 *flesh and clay* the original is more sensible: 'flesh and bones'

When I perceiv'd that of my life the tide
 Was ebbing to that point, when every man   80
 Need lower the sails, and coil the ropes aside,
What was my joy at first now gave me pain:
 I made my shrift and penitential prayer –
 Ah, hapless me! it would have prov'd my gain.
The Prince of our new Pharisees, who near
 The Church of Lateran – nor yet with Jew,
 Nor yet with Saracen, engag'd in war;
Because a Christian was his every foe;
 And none to raze strong Acre's fort had been;
 None merchant to the Soldan's land did go – 90
Nought minded, in himself, the call Divine,
 And his chief Office; nor, in me, that cord,
 Which us'd to make its wearers grow more thin.
But, as Constantine, at Soracte, implor'd
 Sylvester once his leprosy to heal;
 So urg'd he me, and speaking, as my lord,
To cure his pride's inflammatory swell;
 He ask'd my counsel: no reply I made;
 For drunken passion seem'd his words to impel.
"Let not thy heart misgive thee," then he said; 100
 "I now absolve thee: speak; by what design
 May Penestrino in the dust be laid?

---

83 *shrift* an old word for the penance imposed by the priest in confession.
Aversion to the Catholic sacrament of confession may have prompted Ford
to cloud the line and muddle up its order; the Italian runs 'I repented and
made my confession' 85–7 in 1297, Boniface VIII was engaged in civil
strife with the noble Roman family of Colonna 89 *Acre's fort* this last
Christian possession in Palestine fell to the Saracens in 1291
94 *as Constantine* legend had it that gratitude for being cured of leprosy by
Pope Sylvester caused the Emperor Constantine to make his 'Donation' to
the Church 96–7 the meaning of the original is clearer: as Constantine was
cured of leprosy by Sylvester, so Boniface 'asked my expert advice to cure the
fever of his pride' 102 *Penestrino* a Latinizing name for the town of
Palestrina

Heaven's gates to lock, and to unlock, is mine:
    Thou know'st it well; twain, therefore, are the Keys,
    Which were so lightly priz'd by Celestine."
Grave reasons then constrain'd me him to please,
    Where silence was the worst expedient shown:
    I said; "Since, Father, thou dost me release
From that delinquency, to which I'm drawn;
110   Large words of promise, but with scant of deed,
    Shall make thee triumph on the lofty Throne."
When dead, to fetch me, Francis came with speed;
    But "No," said one of the black Cherubin,
    "Bear him not thou; nor wrong me of my meed.
Down deep in Hell, among my slaves, his sin
    Drags him; because he counsell'd false and ill:
    Since then, I have him close my clutch within.
Absolv'd are none, who go on sinning still:
    The rule of contradiction holdeth true –
120   No penitence can stand with lust of will."
O miserable me! how shook I through,
    When, seizing me, he said: "It has, may be,
    Escap'd thee, that so well I logic knew."
He bore me straight to Minos: eight time he
    Twin'd round his scaly back the curling spire;
    Then, having gnaw'd the tip ferociously,
"This wretch," he said, "is for the thieving fire:"
    And so, thou seest me here for aye undone,
    Roaming, with broken heart, in this attire.'
130 His speech thus ended, with a piteous groan
    The flame its parting took, and mov'd away,
    Tossing and beating down the pointed cone.

---

105 *Celestine* Pope Celestine V, who abdicated the papacy (as a result, some
said, of Boniface's intrigues)   112–14 the tortured syntax is Ford's
120 Dante's black angel speaks more lucidly: 'it is not possible to repent of
something and will it at the same time'   124 *Minos* see *Inferno* 5.3–12
128 *for aye undone* Guido says just '*son perduto*' ('I am lost'), Dante's usual
way of referring to damnation   129 *with broken heart* the Italian is less
plangent, meaning 'in bitter regret' or even 'with a grudge against myself'

I and my Chief pass'd on: our ascent lay
   Over the reef to where the arch spans o'er
   Another chasm, in whose inclosure they,
Who heap up guilt by discord, quit the score.   (1865)

JOHN DAYMAN (1802–71)

After a period as a Fellow of Corpus Christi College, Oxford, Dayman became a parish priest in Cumberland, where he lived till his death. The *Athenaeum* greeted his translation as 'a sincere, earnest and laborious effort'.

Inferno 13   1–108

Not yet had Nessus gained the farther bourne
   Of the Red River, when our course we drew
   To pierce a wood, where path was never worn.
No glad green leaves, but duskiest of hue,
   No fair smooth boughs, but gnarled and bent awry,
   No fruit thereon, but poison thorns there grew.
Ne'er to so rough, so tangled forests hie
   The savage beasts, all cultured lands their hate,
   That 'tween Cecina and Corneto lie.
Here the foul breed of Harpies perching sate,   10
   Who did the Trojans from the Strophads chase
   With dark foreboding of disastrous fate.
Broad are their wings, human their neck and face,
   With taloned feet and feathered paunch, they make
   Lament from off those trees of strangest race.

---

1 *Nessus* the centaur who acted as guide to Dante and Virgil in the preceding canto   9 *'tween Cecina and Corneto* the Tuscan Maremma
10 *Harpies* creatures with women's faces and the bodies of birds of prey; see Virgil's *Aeneid* 3.209ff.

And my good lord, premonishing, thus spake:
    'Know, ere thou farther enter, thou dost stand
    I' the second round, and shalt be, till thou take
Way more tremendous o'er the ghastly sand.
20   Then mark: thy keen-observing eyes shall hail
    Things which to my report may faith command.'
I heard around the shrieks of grievous wail
    From every side, yet saw I not that grieved,
    Wherefore I stayed me, trembling all and pale.
I believe that he believed that I believed,
    Among those stocks so piteous voices came
    Of some that hid to 'scape us unperceived.
Then said my master: 'Gathering if thou maim
    The slenderest rod in which those branches end,
30   Thy present thoughts shall all turn halt and lame,'
With that a little I my hand extend,
    And, as from one large briar a sprout I tore,
    The trunk shrieked out aloud, 'Why dost thou rend
Me thus?' And while it blackened all with gore,
    'Why tear me limb from limb?' – the shrieks renewed –
    'Did never pity's dint thy heart make sore?
Men were we once, who now are stocks of wood;
    Yet might thy hand more mercy deal, I ween,
    Albeit we were the souls of serpent brood.'
40   As from a brand that, lighted while 'tis green,
    Burns at one end, at the other hissing spits
    The wind that seeks a vent the pores between;

---

16 *premonishing* a Latinate word for 'forewarning'; there is no equivalent in
the original   20–21 this mouthful is Dayman's version of words which
mean 'Be very attentive and you will see things that would make you lose
faith in my words [if I merely told you about them].'

23 *that grieved* anyone who was grieving   25 this line 'is a specimen of the
poet's mind too valuable to be diluted. Dante has often the air of a man too
deeply engaged with things to concern himself about words.' [*Dayman's
note*]

E'en thus the splintered branch alike emits
    Both words and blood; whereat as numb with fear
    I stood, my hold the falling fragment quits.
'Could he,' the sage replied, 'have bent his ear,
    Much injured soul, and earlier credence paid
    To that my very verse depainted clear,
Offending hand he ne'er on thee had laid:
    But the' unaccepted truth made me to harden   50
    His heart for deed which doth mine own upbraid.
Yet tell him who thou wert, that he in guerdon
    May for amends refresh thy fame above,
    At his allowed return, and win thy pardon.'
And thus the trunk: 'Lured by thy words of love
    Needs must I speak, and let it not displease
    If, with my story limed, diffuse I prove.
Know, I am he, that whilome kept the keys
    Of Frederic's heart; and as my will inclined
    Locked or unlocked it with so gentle ease,   60
From all besides I veiled his secret mind:
    Too faithful to my glorious task, until
    Forespent I left me vein nor pulse behind.
That public stale who turneth not, but still
    On Cæsar's hostel bends her harlot eyes,
    Pest of each court, and potent aye to kill,
Inflamed all hearts against me; and with lies
    The' inflamed inflamed mine Emperor, till for trust
    And joyous honours, doleful griefs arise.

---

48 *To that my very verse depainted clear* translatorese for 'to what he had never seen except in my poem'; Virgil is referring to the related episode in *Aeneid* 3.22ff.   **57** *limed* stuck fast in   **58** *I am he* Pier della Vigna, a poet and civil servant in the court of the Emperor Frederick II; he killed himself in 1249, having been imprisoned for treachery   **64** *stale* an archaism for 'prostitute'; Dante has the Latinate '*meretrice*' here, partly to characterize della Vigna's preciosity of idiom, very evident at lines 68 and 72 below   **67–8** *Inflamed . . . inflamed inflamed* the verbal play is in the original, wonderfully conveying the relay of courtly rumours

70 My mind, that purposed in her strong disgust
        By death to flee the scorn she so abhorred,
        Against my just self made myself unjust;
    But never broke I feälty's pledged word –
        No, by the new roots of this stem I swear –
        To that my liege and honour-worthy lord.
    And you, if either to the world repair
        Again, uphold my memory in her dues,
        Fallen by the blow that Envy dealt her there.'
    Then silent as he paused: ' 'T were sin to lose
80   Thine hour,' the poet warned me; 'make request,
        Resuming speech, if aught thy fancy choose.'
    Whence I to him: 'Thou rather ask what best
        To thy supposing shall my mind content:
        I cannot speak, such pity wrings my breast.'
    Then he rejoining: 'If with liberal bent
        This man perform the work, O prisoned sprite,
        Thy prayer entreats, may it please thee say how,
            pent
    In yonder knots, the struggling soul so tight
        Is bound, and tell, as haply may be told,
90   If from such limbs it ever disunite.'
    With that the trunk, loud whiffing, thus controlled
        Its windy current for expressive sound:
        'Brief words and few your answer shall infold.
    When the stern spirit from the body's bound
        By her own deed hath rude disseverance got,
        Minos condemns her to the seventh round.
    Within the wood she falls, and place hath not
        Determined, but where Fortune idly throws,
        Like grain of spelt she bourgeons on the spot:

---

85 *with liberal bent* the Italian '*liberamente*' just means 'freely'
86 *sprite* spirit   91 *whiffing* 'to utter with a whiff or puff of air' (*OED*);
Dayman is picking up on the sound of the Italian '*soffiò*'   91–2 the Italian
translates more literally as 'and then that wind was changed into a voice, as
follows:'   96 *Minos* see *Inferno* 5.3–12   99 *spelt* a wheat-like cereal

With tender sprays a wildwood slip she grows;   100
  Then feed these Harpies on her leaves, and
    making
  Woes, make no less a window for her woes.
We, like the rest, our bodies now forsaken
  Shall come to seek; yet none be clad again –
  Justice withholds what self from self hath taken:
Yet hither must we drag them back, and then,
  Each on the thorn of its own shade accurst,
  Shall hang our corpses round the dismal glen.'
      (1843)

FRANCIS SYLVESTER MAHONY
('FATHER PROUT') (1804–66)

Born in Cork, Mahony trained as a Jesuit at seminaries in Paris
and in Rome, where the Abbé Martial Marcet de la Roché
Arnaud found in him all 'the fanaticism, the dissimulation, the
intrigue, and the chicanery' which he took to be characteristic
of the Society of Jesus. Nonetheless, Mahony was soon expelled
from the Society and embarked on a career as a humorous
journalist. The following very loose translation first appeared
in an article for *Fraser's Magazine* written in Mahony's persona
of 'Father Prout', who advances the opinion that *terza rima* is
'not acceptable to our English ear', and proposes instead 'a
lengthened but not unmusical sort of line, in which I think the
old Florentine's numbers might sweep along with something
like native dignity'. Mahony's fourteeners give him ample room
to display his ingenuity but are not much like Dante, either in
meaning or in movement.

The Porch of Hell (Dante) [*Inferno* 3.1–51]

'Seek ye the path traced bye the wrath of God for sinfull
    mortals?
Of the reprobate this is the gate, these are the gloomy
    portals!
For sinne and crime from the birth of tyme dugge was this
    Gulph Infernal.
Guest! let all Hope on this threshold stop! here reigns
    Despair Eternal.'

I read with tears these characters – tears shed on man's
    behalf;
Each word seemed fraught with painful thought, the
    lost soul's epitaph.
Turning dismayed, 'O mystic shade!' I cried, 'my kindly
    Mentor,
Of comfort, say, can no sweet ray these dark dominions
    enter?'

'My son!' replied the ghostly guide, 'this is the dark
    abode
Of the guilty dead – alone they tread hell's melancholy
10   road.
Brace up thy nerves! this hour deserves that Mind
    should have control,
And bid avaunt fears that would haunt the
    clay-imprisoned soul.

---

5 *tears* like much else in this passage, they are Mahony's invention

Mine be the task, when thou shalt ask, each mystery to
    solve;
Anon for us dark Erebus back shall its gates revolve –
Hell shall disclose its deepest woes, each punishment,
    each pang,
Saint hath revealed, or eye beheld, or flame-tongued
    prophet sang.'

Gates were unrolled of iron mould – a dismal dungeon
    yawned!
We passed – we stood – 'twas hell we view'd! – eternity
    had dawned!
Space on our sight burst infinite – echoes were heard
    remote;
Shrieks loud and drear startled our ear, and stripes
    incessant smote.   20

Onward we went. The firmament was starless o'er our
    head,
Spectres swept by inquiringly – clapping their hands
    they fled!
Borne on the blast strange whispers passed; and ever
    and anon
Athwart the plain, like hurricane, God's vengeance
    would come on!

Then sounds, breathed low, of gentler wo soft on our
    hearing stole;
Captives so meek fain would I seek to comfort and
    console:
'O let us pause and learn the cause of so much grief,
    and why
Saddens the air of their despair the unavailing sigh!'

---

14 *Erebus* this classical name for the dark space through which souls passed
on their way to Hades appears nowhere in the *Commedia*.

'My son! Heaven grants them utterance in plaintive
    notes of wo;
In tears their grief may find relief, but hence they
30   never go.
Fools! they believed that if they lived blameless and
    vice eschewed,
God would dispense with excellence, and give
    beatitude.

They died! but naught of virtue brought to win their
    Maker's praise;
No deeds of worth the page set forth that chronicled
    their days.
Fixed is their doom – eternal gloom! to mourn for
    what is past,
And weep aloud amid that crowd with whom their lot
    is cast.

One fate they share with spirits fair, who, when
    rebellion shook
God's holy roof, remained aloof, nor part whatever
    took;
Drew not the sword against their Lord, nor yet upheld
    his throne:
Could God for this make perfect bliss theirs when the
40   fight was won?

31–2 not in Dante   37–9 these angels who sided neither with Lucifer's
revolt against God nor against it are not mentioned in the Bible but derive
from medieval popular tradition   40–1 Mahony's paraphrase here vaults
over six lines of Dante (3.43–8)

The world knows not their dreary lot, nor can assuage
    their pangs,
Or cure the curse of fell remorse, or blunt the tiger's fangs.
Mercy disdains to loose their chains – the hour of grace
    has been!
Son! let that class unheeded pass – unwept, though not
    unseen.' (1835)

ELIZABETH BARRETT BROWNING
(1806–61)

Barrett Browning first translated the opening of *Inferno* 1 in her teens, but the following version, never published during her lifetime, was composed in April 1845. A few weeks later she remarked in a letter to her future husband, Robert Browning, that 'Dante's poetry seems to come down in hail, rather than in rain – but count me the drops congealed in one hailstone'. She was an enthusiastic supporter of the Risorgimento and, like Mazzini, Carlyle and many others, considered Dante to be a visionary forebear of Italian nationalism. *Casa Guidi Windows* (1851), her long poem about the 1848 revolutions, is in a rhyme-scheme closely related to *terza rima*, and suggests that Dante would 'thrill with ecstasy' if he knew of the liberal demonstrations in Florence – although in August 1848 she wrote in a letter to a friend 'the people wants *stamina*, wants conscience, wants self-reverence: Dante's soul has died out of the land'.

Inferno I

All in the middle of the road of life
    I stood bewildered in a dusky wood –
    The path being lost that once showed straight and rife.
Oh words are vain to express that solitude
    Of forest trees, with bristling branches hoar! –
    The terror in the memory comes renewed.

So bitter is it, death were scarcely more! –
    Yet, for the good found in it, I prepare
    To speak the things I suffered and forswore.

10   I cannot tell you how I entered there, –
    For in the moment that I went astray,
    I was too full of sleep and unaware:
But as I reached the mountain-foot, away
    Where all that valley closed, which had distressed
    My heart with consternation and dismay, –
I looked above! – the mountain drew a vest
    Of glory, on its shoulders, from the star
    That guides all other wanderers for the best.
Then, straight, the fear which in my heart did mar
20   Its lake-like calm, that night of piteous case,
    Did grow a little still . . as winds grew far! –
And as one, 'scaped from ocean, in amaze
    Sobs up against the rocks, that refuge give, –
    Then turns back to the perilous deep . . . to gaze, –
Even so my soul that still was fugitive
    Returned to meditate that danger past
    Which never yet was left by soul alive.
And when my weary flesh was soothed at last,
    I climbed the desert on, . . and as I went
30   The lowest footstep was most firm and fast . .
And lo! at that beginning of ascent,
    A panther, light of fetlock, quick of pace,
    Appeared! – her skin with many a spot besprent –

---

9 *suffered and forswore* these words have no equivalent in the original, which just refers to 'the other things I observed there'   17 *the star* the sun, now setting   23 *sobs* E.B.B.'s interpretation of words which mean 'with troubled breath' and could in this context equally refer to choking or panting   32 *panther* medieval commentators interpreted the panther as a figure of lust, the lion who soon appears (45) as pride and the she-wolf (49) as greed   33 *besprent* an archaism for 'sprinkled'; there is no matching archaism in Dante

And would not pass out from before my face,
   But such a hindrance towards my progress, ran,
   That still I turned . . . my footsteps to retrace.

The time was when the morning first began.
   The sun rose upward with the stars that were
   The earliest with him, when God's love for man
Gave motion first to holy things and fair! –   40
   And thus, that lovely beast of purfled skin,
   That hour of dawn, that season debonaire,
Did make me a fair good hope to have and win, –
   Yet not such hope as kept me free from dread,
   When the scene changed and let a lion in!
He came against me with a lifted head
   And with a rabid hunger! . . it appeared
   Air shivered round his mane at every tread.
And straight . . a lean she-wolf came to be feared . .
   Laden, though lean, with lustings infinite! –   50
   Full many a land her starving jaws had seared.
The dread that issued from that latter sight,
   So heavy made my soul, that, overborne,
   I lost the hope of climbing up the height.
As one who gains by commerce, . . when a turn
   Of fortune brings him losses to compute, . .
   In all his thoughts, he can but weep and mourn! –
Even so the beast perturbed me! – foot by foot
   She dodged me where she faced me, and did force
   And drive me downward where the sun is mute.   60

What time I ruined down that headlong course,
   Mine eyes along the gloom, a shape did read,
   One death's perpetual silence had made hoarse.

---

39 *for man* not in Dante   41 *purfled* embroidered; the word is in Milton's
Comus ('purfl'd scarf'); there is no equivalent poeticality in Dante

And when I saw him in that place of need,
  'Have pity on me,' my wailing voice began, –
  'Whoe'er thou art! – or ghost, or man indeed.'
He answered, . . 'No man now, but once a man!
  Of Lombard race my parents did descend, –
  And . . both . . for Country's name . . were Mantuan.
70 I had my birth 'sub Julio,' . . toward the end:
  I lived at Rome, when good Augustus thrust
  No false frail god from altar though he reigned.
I was a poet, and I sang the just
  Son of Anchises, who came out from Troy
  When lofty Ilium's pride was burnt adust.
But thou . . . why turn again to such annoy?
  Why leave to climb the most delightsome mount,
  Which is the source and motive of all joy?'

'What! – art thou, then, that Virgil, and that fount,
80 Which poured a stream of speech so affluent bright?'
  I asked while up my brow the blush did mount –
'O thou of other poets, fame and light! –
  The long appliance and the vasty love
  That made me search thy book, availed me right.
O master . . author . . who my soul didst move
  To loftier ends! – From thee alone I took
  That noble rhetoric which the worlds approve! –
Behold this beast, – the cause that I forsook
  The upward path – Give help, O famous sage! –
90 My veins and pulses thrill beneath her look.'

---

70 *'sub Julio'* in the era of Julius Caesar: Virgil was born in 70 BCE, some
time before Caesar actually came to power, although too late for the dictator
to dignify him as Augustus was to do   80 *affluent* a Latinism for 'flowing';
Dante's *'sì largo fiume'* ('so broad a river') has a Latinizing tinge in the word
used for 'river'   83 *appliance* in the sense of 'application to study'
vasty Dante has only 'great'; E.B.B.'s diction is Shakespearean here
(*1 Henry IV* III.i.52)   87 *which the worlds approve* Dante less boastfully
says 'which has brought me honour'

'Best choose another path of pilgrimage,'
    He answered straightway when he saw me weep, –
    'If thou from hence thy steps would disengage.
Because this beast, for whom I hear thee keep
    Such wailing, . . suffers none to pass this way
    But offers hindrance deep, as death is deep.
Her nature lusts to injure and betray:
    Her ravenous will is never satisfied;
    And most she craves, when gloated most with
        prey.
Full many a beast is wedlocked to her side, –   100
    And more shall yet be – till the Hound arrive,
    Who shall her slay, with tortures multiplied.
HE shall not feed on earth or gold, but live
    By love, heroic virtue, noble lore:
    Feltro from Feltro, shall his country rive.
He comes to save Italia, humbled sore,
    Whom maid Camilla, Turnus with his crown,
    Euryalus and Nisus perished for –
And He will chase the Wolf through every town,
    Until he hath barked her back again to hell,   110
    Whence Envy roused her first to face the sun.

And thee . . I weigh my power to serve thee well,
    If thou canst follow, and I move thy guide,
    And lead thee on along the Immeasurable –
Where thou shalt hear the desperate screeches cried, –

---

91 *pilgrimage* though pilgrims and pilgrimage appear often in the
Commedia, Dante here has simply 'journey'   103 *HE* E.B.B. may have
followed a Protestant tradition which viewed the She-wolf as the Catholic
Church and the Hound as a figure of Luther; she may also have associated
Virgil's prophecy with her own appeal for a 'teacher' to lead the Italian
revolution (*Casa Guidi Windows* 1.795)   105 *Feltro* this line has defeated
commentators ancient and modern; it translates literally as 'and his nation
shall be between feltro and feltro' but there is no consensus as to what a
'feltro' is   107–8 see *Aeneid* 7.803–17; 11.759–835; 9.176–445;
12.697–952

Where thou shalt see the ancient spirits in dole, –
All shrieking for that second death untried!
Where others thou shalt view, upon the whole
Content with fire, because they hope to come
120   At some far hour, to house of blessed Soul.
But if thyself would mount to such a home,
I know a spirit-guide more pure than I,
And I will leave her with thee in my room.
For that imperial King who reigns on high,
Because I spurned his law, . . the later grace
Of guiding toward His city, doth deny.
He reigneth there, who ruleth wide in space! –
There spread his streets! – there, shines his throne
    of fear.
Oh happy soul! elect to heavenly place! –'
130   I answered – 'Poet! I adjure thee here,
By that eternal God thou didst not know, –
To save me from this ill and one more drear!
Now lead me to the place depictured so –
And let me view St. Peter's gate and find
Those spirits in thy speech accounted low . . –'
Then he moved onward, and I trod behind.
        (written 1845)

---

117 *second death* another dark line; the likely meaning is 'who scream
because they suffer the second death', taking 'second death' in a traditional
sense as 'damnation'   118–19 *upon the whole / Content* there is
unfortunately no warrant in Dante for E.B.B.'s 'upon the whole'
123 *her* Beatrice   133 *the place depictured so* this orotundity has no match
in Dante, who refers to 'the place you were just talking about'

HENRY WADSWORTH LONGFELLOW
(1807–82)

Longfellow knew Italian by at least the time he graduated from Bowdoin College in 1825, when he was at once offered the Chair of Modern Languages. In 1834 he moved to Harvard where he formed a 'Dante Club', of which James Russell Lowell and Charles Eliot Norton were members, and soon dabbled in translating the *Commedia*: 'I write a few lines every day before breakfast ... the morning prayer, the key-note of the day' (1843). He began more sustained work after the death of his second wife in 1861; his complete version appeared six years later, to laudatory reviews on both sides of the Atlantic. One obituary suggested that 'there is nothing laboured in Longfellow's translation; the fault is of another kind: we lose, amid all its simplicity the "grand manner," as Mr Arnold would call it' (whether Dante had a "grand manner" to be lost is debatable). Longfellow himself had commented, 'while making it rhythmic, I have endeavoured to make it also as literal as a prose translation'. Longfellow owned what was considered a piece of Dante's coffin: 'think of it', a visitor recalls him saying, 'six hundred years ago the bit of wood in that box touched Dante's bones'. A similar reverence for Dante is manifest in the short poems included below; such attitudes were not unusual among readers of the *Commedia* at this time.

Dante

Tuscan, that wanderest through the realms of gloom,
    With thoughtful pace, and sad, majestic eyes,
    Stern thoughts and awful from thy soul arise,
    Like Farinata from his fiery tomb.

---

1 compare *Inferno* 10.22   4 compare *Inferno* 10.31–36

Thy sacred song is like the trump of doom;
    Yet in thy heart what human sympathies,
    What soft compassion glows, as in the skies
    The tender stars their clouded lamps relume!
Methinks I see thee stand, with pallid cheeks,
    By Fra Hilario in his diocese,
    As up the convent-walls, in golden streaks,
The ascending sunbeams mark the day's decrease;
    And, as he asks what there the stranger seeks,
    Thy voice along the cloister whispers, 'Peace!'
    (1839)

Inferno 4   1–129

Broke the deep lethargy within my head
    A heavy thunder, so that I upstarted,
    Like to a person who by force is wakened;
And round about I moved my rested eyes,
    Uprisen erect, and steadfastly I gazed,
    To recognise the place wherein I was.
True is it, that upon the verge I found me
    Of the abysmal valley dolorous,
    That gathers thunder of infinite ululations.
Obscure, profound it was, and nebulous,
    So that by fixing on its depths my sight
    Nothing whatever I discerned therein.
'Let us descend now into the blind world,'
    Began the Poet, pallid utterly;
    'I will be first, and thou shalt second be.'

---

10 *Fra Hilario* Brother Ilaro of the Benedictine house at Santa Croce del Corvo on the frontiers of Tuscany and Liguria; a fiercely suspected but possibly authentic letter from this monk recounts a meeting with Dante and cites the original Latin opening of the *Commedia*   14 compare the sonnet 'Tanto gentile' (*Vita Nuova* 26)

   1–2 the abruptness and syntactic inversion of this opening match the original

And I, who of his colour was aware,
   Said: 'How shall I come, if thou art afraid,
   Who'rt wont to be a comfort of my fears?'
And he to me: 'The anguish of the people
   Who are below here in my face depicts   20
   That pity which for terror thou hast taken.
Let us go on, for the long way impels us.'
   Thus he went in, and thus he made me enter
   The foremost circle that surrounds the abyss.
There, in so far as I had power to hear,
   Were lamentations none, but only sighs,
   That tremulous made the everlasting air.
And this arose from sorrow without torment,
   Which the crowds had, that many were and great,
   Of infants and of women and of men.   30
To me the Master good: 'Thou dost not ask
   What spirits these, which thou beholdest, are?
   Now will I have thee know, ere thou go farther,
That they sinned not; and if they merit had,
   'Tis not enough, because they had not baptism,
   Which is the portal of the Faith thou holdest;
And if they were before Christianity,
   In the right manner they adored not God;
   And among such as these am I myself.
For such defects, and not for other guilt,   40
   Lost are we, and are only so far punished,
   That without hope we live on in desire.'
Great grief seized on my heart when this I heard,
   Because some people of much worthiness
   I knew, who in that Limbo were suspended.
'Tell me, my Master, tell me, thou my Lord,'
   Began I, with desire of being certain
   Of that Faith which o'ercometh every error,
'Came any one by his own merit hence,
   Or by another's, who was blessed thereafter?'   50
   And he, who understood my covert speech,

Replied: 'I was a novice in this state,
　　When I saw hither come a Mighty One,
　　With sign of victory incoronate.
Hence he drew forth the shade of the First Parent,
　　And that of his son Abel, and of Noah,
　　Of Moses the lawgiver, and the obedient
Abraham, patriarch, and David, king,
　　Israel with his father and his children,
60　　And Rachel, for whose sake he did so much,
And others many, and he made them blessed;
　　And thou must know, that earlier than these
　　Never were any human spirits saved.'
We ceased not to advance because he spake,
　　But still were passing onward through the forest,
　　The forest, say I, of thick-crowded ghosts.
Not very far as yet our way had gone
　　This side the summit, when I saw a fire
　　That overcame a hemisphere of darkness.
70　We were a little distant from it still,
　　But not so far that I in part discerned not
　　That honourable people held that place.
'O thou who honourest every art and science,
　　Who may these be, which such great honour have,
　　That from the fashion of the rest it parts them?'
And he to me: 'The honourable name,
　　That sounds of them above there in thy life,
　　Wins grace in Heaven, that so advances them.'
In the mean time a voice was heard by me:
80　　'All honour be to the pre-eminent Poet;
　　His shade returns again, that was departed.'

---

53 *a Mighty One* Christ, when he descended into Hell to free the Old
Testament worthies　72 *honourable* Longfellow's dwelling on 'honour' and
its cognates (see also 73, 74, 76 and 80) matches Dante's fivefold insistence
on the word

After the voice had ceased and quiet was,
    Four mighty shades I saw approaching us;
    Semblance had they nor sorrowful nor glad.
To say to me began my gracious Master:
    'Him with that falchion in his hand behold,
    Who comes before the three, even as their lord.
That one is Homer, Poet sovereign;
    He who comes next is Horace, the satirist;
    The third is Ovid, and the last is Lucan.   90
Because to each of these with me applies
    The name that solitary voice proclaimed,
    They do me honour, and in that do well.'
Thus I beheld assemble the fair school
    Of that lord of the song pre-eminent,
    Who o'er the others like an eagle soars.
When they together had discoursed somewhat,
    They turned to me with signs of salutation,
    And on beholding this, my Master smiled;
And more of honour still, much more, they did me,   100
    In that they made me one of their own band;
    So that the sixth was I, 'mid so much wit.
Thus we went on as far as to the light,
    Things saying 'tis becoming to keep silent,
    As was the saying of them where I was.
We came unto a noble castle's foot,
    Seven times encompassëd with lofty walls,
    Defended round by a fair rivulet;
This we passed over even as firm ground;
    Through portals seven I entered with these
        Sages;   110
    We came into a meadow of fresh verdure.

---

86 *falchion* sword

People were there with solemn eyes and slow,
  Of great authority in their countenance;
  They spake but seldom, and with gentle voices.
Thus we withdrew ourselves upon one side
  Into an opening luminous and lofty,
  So that they all of them were visible.
There opposite, upon the green enamel,
  Were pointed out to me the mighty spirits,
120 Whom to have seen I feel myself exalted.
I saw Electra with companions many,
  'Mongst whom I knew both Hector and Æneas,
  Caesar in armour with gerfalcon eyes;
I saw Camilla and Penthesilea
  On the other side, and saw the King Latinus,
  Who with Lavinia his daughter sat;
I saw that Brutus who drove Tarquin forth,
  Lucretia, Julia, Marcia, and Cornelia,
  And saw alone, apart, the Saladin.

[In the last few lines of the canto, Dante also sees a group of
great non-Christian philosophers and sages, including Plato,
Aristotle, Euclid, Hippocrates, Avicenna and Averroes.]
  (1867)

---

112 *People* see Aristotle's account of the 'great-souled man', *Nicomachean
Ethics* 4   118 *enamel* a poeticism for 'gleaming'   124 *Penthesilea* queen of
the Amazons; the other names in this and the following four lines are of great
figures from Roman history   129 *Saladin* sultan of Egypt 1174–93, he
captured Jerusalem in 1187; Dante was not always even this complimentary
to Muslims: see *Inferno* 28.28–36

Divina Commedia 1-70

I

Oft have I seen at some cathedral door,
    A labourer pausing in the dust and heat,
    Lay down his burden, and with reverent feet
    Enter, and cross himself, and on the floor
Kneel to repeat his paternoster o'er;
    Far off the noises of the world retreat;
    The loud vociferations of the street
    Become an undistinguishable roar.
So, as I enter here from day to day,
    And leave my burden at this minster gate,   10
    Kneeling in prayer, and not ashamed to pray,
The tumult of the time disconsolate
    To inarticulate murmurs dies away,
    While the eternal ages watch and wait.

II

How strange the sculptures that adorn these towers!
    This crowd of statues, in whose folded sleeves
    Birds build their nests; while canopied with leaves
    Parvis and portal bloom like trellised bowers,
And the vast minster seems a cross of flowers!
    But fiends and dragons on the gargoyled eaves   20
    Watch the dead Christ between the living thieves,
    And, underneath, the traitor Judas lowers!

Divina Commedia, 1-70 These sonnets were first published in Longfellow's
Divine Comedy, where they appeared as prefaces, in the order they are given
here, a pair to each cantica save the last. Comparing the *Commedia* to a
Gothic cathedral was a favourite cliché by Longfellow's time but he is
unusual in the fervid attention he pays to Catholic practices (confession,
prayers for the dead, veneration of the consecrated host)   **18** *parvis* porch

Ah! from what agonies of heart and brain,
    What exultations trampling on despair,
    What tenderness, what tears, what hate of wrong,
What passionate outcry of a soul in pain,
    Uprose this poem of the earth and air,
    This medieval miracle of song!

III

I enter, and I see thee in the gloom
30   Of the long aisles, O poet saturnine!
    And strive to make my steps keep pace with thine.
The air is filled with some unknown perfume;
    The congregation of the dead make room
    For thee to pass; the votive tapers shine;
    Like rooks that haunt Ravenna's groves of pine
    The hovering echoes fly from tomb to tomb.
From the confessionals I hear arise
    Rehearsals of forgotten tragedies,
    And lamentations from the crypts below;
40   And then a voice celestial, that begins
    With the pathetic words, 'Although your sins
    As scarlet be,' and ends with 'as the snow.'

IV

With snow-white veil and garments as of flame,
    She stands before thee, who so long ago
    Filled thy young heart with passion and the woe
From which thy song and all its splendours came;
And while with stern rebuke she speaks thy name,
    The ice about thy heart melts as the snow
    On mountain heights, and in swift overflow
50   Comes gushing from thy lips in sobs of shame.

---

35 *Ravenna* where Dante is buried   41–2 *Although . . . as the snow* quoting
Isaiah 1:18 and alluding to *Purgatorio* 30.85   43–56 compare *Purgatorio*
30.31, 33, 55, 85–91; 31.20

Thou makest full confession; and a gleam,
    As of the dawn on some dark forest cast,
    Seems on thy lifted forehead to increase;
Lethe and Eunoe – the remembered dream
    And the forgotten sorrow – bring at last
    That perfect pardon which is perfect peace.

V

I lift mine eyes, and all the windows blaze
    With forms of saints and holy men who died,
    Here martyred, and hereafter glorified;
And the great Rose upon its leaves displays   60
Christ's Triumph, and the angelic roundelays,
    With splendour upon splendour multiplied;
    And Beatrice again at Dante's side
No more rebukes, but smiles her words of praise.
And then the organ sounds, and unseen choirs
    Sing the old Latin hymns of peace and love,
    And benedictions of the Holy Ghost;
And the melodious bells among the spires
    O'er all the house-tops and through heaven above
    Proclaim the elevation of the Host.   (1867)   70

WILLIAM EWART GLADSTONE (1809–98)

Gladstone knew Arthur Hallam at Eton College, and learned
Italian during a visit to Italy in 1832. Of the words which he
translates below as 'In His Will is our peace' he remarked 'they
cannot be too deeply graven upon the heart'. In 1883 he wrote
'the reading of Dante is not merely a pleasure, a *tour de force*,

---

54 *Lethe and Eunoe* rivers which cause, respectively, the forgetting of sin
and the remembrance of virtue; see *Purgatorio* 31.91–105; 33.112–45
57 *I lift mine eyes* as Dante does often in the *Commedia*; see, for instance,
Paradiso 31.118   60–64 compare *Paradiso* 30.109–17; 31.131; 1.95

or a lesson. It is a vigorous discipline for the heart, the intellect, the whole man. In the school of Dante I have learned a great part of that mental provision (however insignificant it may be) which has served me to make the journey of human life up to the term of nearly seventy-three years'. Paget Toynbee remembers that 'one of the cherished beliefs of his later years' was 'that Dante visited England and Oxford', a superstition common among Oxonians of the time and eventually enshrined in a cartoon by Max Beerbohm (1904). Francesca da Rimini is sculpted on Gladstone's monument at Hawarden.

The Lord's Prayer [*Purgatorio* 11.1–21]

O Father ours, that dwellest in the sky,
    Not circumscribed, but for Thy love intense
    To Thy first Emanations there on high;
Let each and every creature that hath sense
    Praise Thee, Thy name, Thy goodness, as 'tis fit
    They render thanks for Thy warm effluence.
Thy kingdom come; Thy peace too come with it,
    Which, if it come not by Thy gift divine,
    Comes not to us by strength of human wit.
10   As of their wills the angel Powers to Thine,
    Chanting Hosanna, render sacrifice;
    So may we men our human wills resign.
Each day give daily manna from the skies,
    Without the which, in this rough desert place
    He backward slides who forward busiest hies.

---

3 *first Emanations* the original means 'first effects'   4 *that hath sense* the superfluous qualification is not in Dante   6 *warm* the Italian means 'sweet'

And as we pardon each to each, efface
   And blot away, benign, our heavier debt,
Nor hold our ill deserts before Thy face.
Our virtue, weak and easily beset,
   Oh hazard not with the inveterate foe   20
That vexeth sore; but free us from his net.   (1835)

Speech of Piccarda [Paradiso 3.70–87]

Love by his virtue, Brother, hath appeased
   Our several wills: he causeth us to will
But what we have, all other longings eased.
Did we desire a region loftier still,
   Such our desire were dissonant from His,
Who bade us each our several station fill:
A thing impossible in these spheres of bliss
   If whoso dwelleth here, in Love alone
Must dwell, and if Love's nature well thou wis.
Within the will Divine to set our own   10
   Is of the essence of this Being blest,
For that our wills to one with His be grown.
So, as we stand throughout the realms of rest,
   From stage to stage, our pleasure is the King's,
Whose will our will informs, by Him imprest.
In His Will is our peace. To this all things
   By Him created, or by Nature made,
As to a central Sea, self-motion brings.   (1835)

---

21 *net* Gladstone's invention; in Dante our foe is armed with a spur
  1 *Brother* Piccarda is addressing Dante   *hath appeased* Dante's verb is in
the present tense   9 *wis* an archaism for 'know'; Dante's vocabulary here is
not old-fashioned, indeed it draws heavily on then-modish terms from
scholastic theology

ALFRED, LORD TENNYSON (1809–92)

The twelve-year-old Tennyson noted that a passage from *Samson Agonistes* 'puts me in mind of that in Dante, which Lord Byron has prefixed to his "Corsair," "Nessun maggior dolore, Che ricordarsi del tempo felice, Nella miseria"' [*Inferno* 5.121–3] – lines which he later translated in the extract from 'Locksley Hall' printed below. His interest in Dante was fostered by his undergraduate friendship with Arthur Hallam, whom he remembered 'as he lay and read / The Tuscan poets on the lawn' (*In Memoriam*, LXXXIX). Hallam wrote that the *Commedia* gives 'full completeness of form' to 'that idea . . . which represents love as at once the base and pyramidal point of the entire universe, and teaches us to regard the earthly union of souls, not as a thing accidental, transitory, and dependent on the condition of human society, but with far higher import, as the best and the appointed symbol of our relations with God, and through them of his own ineffable essence'. It is apt, therefore, that the poem with which Tennyson mourned Hallam's death should also recollect Dante: *In Memoriam*, he remarked, 'was meant to be a kind of *Divina Commedia*, ending in happiness'; its last line, 'To which the whole creation moves', alludes to the last line of *Paradiso*.

A short poem, written at the request of the Florentines in honour of the six-hundredth anniversary of Dante's birth, addresses the poet as 'King, that has reigned six hundred years, and grown / In power, and ever growest . . .'. In private, Tennyson was on occasion less fulsome: of Dante's style he observed, 'as the English language is much finer than the Italian for variety of sound, so Milton for sound is often finer than Dante . . . What, for example, can be more monotonous than the first lines of the "Inferno" with their "*a-s*"?'

Ulysses [Compare *Inferno* 26.49–142]

It little profits that an idle king,
By this still hearth, among these barren crags,
Matched with an agèd wife, I mete and dole
Unequal laws unto a savage race,
That hoard, and sleep, and feed, and know not me.

I cannot rest from travel: I will drink
Life to the lees: all times I have enjoyed
Greatly, have suffered greatly, both with those
That loved me, and alone; on shore, and when
Through scudding drifts the rainy Hyades   10
Vext the dim sea: I am become a name;
For always roaming with a hungry heart
Much have I seen and known; cities of men
And manners, climates, councils, governments,
Myself not least, but honoured of them all;
And drunk delight of battle with my peers,
Far on the ringing plains of windy Troy.
I am a part of all that I have met;
Yet all experience is an arch wherethrough
Gleams that untravelled world, whose margin fades   20
For ever and for ever when I move.
How dull it is to pause, to make an end,
To rust unburnished, not to shine in use!
As though to breathe were life. Life piled on life
Were all too little, and of one to me
Little remains: but every hour is saved
From that eternal silence, something more,

---

1 *little* Dante's Ulysses is fond of this word; see *Inferno* 26.102, 114, 122
10 *Hyades* a constellation thought to augur rain   **19–21** compare *Inferno*
26.116–17

A bringer of new things; and vile it were
For some three suns to store and hoard myself,
30 And this gray spirit yearning in desire
To follow knowledge like a sinking star,
Beyond the utmost bound of human thought.

This is my son, mine own Telemachus,
To whom I leave the sceptre and the isle –
Well-loved of me, discerning to fulfil
This labour, by slow prudence to make mild
A rugged people, and through soft degrees
Subdue them to the useful and the good.
Most blameless is he, centred in the sphere
40 Of common duties, decent not to fail
In offices of tenderness, and pay
Meet adoration to my household gods,
When I am gone. He works his work, I mine.

There lies the port; the vessel puffs her sail:
There gloom the dark broad seas. My mariners,
Souls that have toiled, and wrought, and thought
        with me –
That ever with a frolic welcome took
The thunder and the sunshine, and opposed
Free hearts, free foreheads – you and I are old;
50 Old age hath yet his honour and his toil;
Death closes all: but something ere the end,
Some work of noble note, may yet be done,
Not unbecoming men that strove with Gods.
The lights begin to twinkle from the rocks:
The long day wanes: the slow moon climbs: the deep
Moans round with many voices. Come, my friends,

30–32 compare *Inferno* 26.97–9   33–43 compare *Inferno* 26.94–6
45–53 compare *Inferno* 26.106, 112–17

'Tis not too late to seek a newer world.
Push off, and sitting well in order smite
The sounding furrows; for my purpose holds
To sail beyond the sunset, and the baths 60
Of all the western stars, until I die.
It may be that the gulfs will wash us down:
It may be we shall touch the Happy Isles,
And see the great Achilles, whom we knew.
Though much is taken, much abides; and though
We are not now that strength which in old days
Moved earth and heaven; that which we are, we are;
One equal temper of heroic hearts,
Made weak by time and fate, but strong in will
To strive, to seek, to find, and not to yield. 70
(written 1833; published 1842)

Locksley Hall 59–86

[The speaker complains, in imagination, to his cousin Amy; he believes she has rejected him and married beneath her own spiritual level for reasons of family prestige.]

Cursèd be the social wants that sin against the strength
of youth!
Cursèd be the social lies that warp us from the living
truth!

Cursèd be the sickly forms that err from honest Nature's
rule!
Cursèd be the gold that gilds the straitened forehead of
the fool!

60–61 compare *Inferno* 26.117, 127–8

Well – 'tis well that I should bluster! – Hadst thou less
    unworthy proved –
Would to God – for I had loved thee more than ever
    wife was loved.

Am I mad, that I should cherish that which bears but
    bitter fruit?
I will pluck it from my bosom, though my heart be at
    the root.

Never, though my mortal summers to such length of
    years should come
As the many-wintered crow that leads the clanging
10   rookery home.

Where is comfort? in division of the records of the
    mind?
Can I part her from herself, and love her, as I knew
    her, kind?

I remember one that perished: sweetly did she speak
    and move:
Such a one do I remember, whom to look at was to
    love.

Can I think of her as dead, and love her for the love she
    bore?
No – she never loved me truly: love is love for evermore.

Comfort? comfort scorned of devils! this is truth the
    poet sings,
That a sorrow's crown of sorrow is remembering
    happier things.

18 *Inferno* 5.121–2

Drug thy memories, lest thou learn it, lest thy heart be
    put to proof,
In the dead unhappy night, and when the rain is on
    the roof.   20

Like a dog, he hunts in dreams, and thou art staring at
    the wall
Where the dying night-lamp flickers, and the shadows
    rise and fall.

Then a hand shall pass before thee, pointing to his
    drunken sleep,
To thy widowed marriage-pillows, to the tears that thou
    wilt weep.

Thou shalt hear the 'Never, never,' whispered by the
    phantom years,
And a song from out the distance in the ringing of thine
    ears;

And an eye shall vex thee, looking ancient kindness on
    thy pain.
Turn thee, turn thee on thy pillow: get thee to thy rest
    again.   (1842)

ARTHUR HENRY HALLAM (1811–33)

When he was thirteen Hallam translated the Ugolino episode
into Greek iambics, and he went on to become a formidable
scholar of Italian. In an essay of 1832 he calmly dismantled
Gabriele Rossetti's theory that the *Commedia* was a tissue
of coded references to a Masonic anti-Catholic conspiracy.
Gladstone remembered, 'I have often heard him complain that
Dante was not properly appreciated even by his admirers, who

---

21 compare *Inferno* 33.26–36   28 compare *Purgatorio* 6.149–51

dwell only on his gloomy power and sublimity, without adverting to the peculiar sweetness and tenderness which characterise, as he thought, so much of his poetry'. In his emphasis on Dante's 'tenderness', Hallam was a child of his time.

A Farewell to the South   269–93
[Compare *Purgatorio* 30.109–45]

[Beatrice speaks]

<blockquote>

Brief was my sojourn here; yet such, that sin
   Shrunk from that boy, as baffled, who adored
   Me as a better nature: nor within
Left I a blank; but with blest tones impower'd
   His soul – blest tones of unexpressive song!
   This was his talisman: by this he soar'd
On pinion, fancy-plum'd, above the throng
   Of dull maligners, what it was to fear
   Unknowing: but to thirst for truth, to long
10 For all that passes not away, to bear
   The spurns of men, this knew he; this from me
   He learnt, while yet my light form flutter'd near,
His visible muse, incarnate poesy!
   Nor when translated hence, by blessed change
   Virtue, and beauty increasing, did I free
His manhood from my sway: albeit to range
   Trackless and guideless led ere he was 'ware
   To anguish; for he trod a pathway strange,
Following false shews of good, which promise fair,
20 Then mock their lovers. Then he turn'd, a child
   Once more in soul, and wept the sinner's tear,

</blockquote>

1–2 compare *Purgatorio* 30.121–3   18–20 *Purgatorio* 30.130–32
20–21 compare *Purgatorio* 31.64; 30.99

To which each heavenly harp in notes more wild
   Of jubilee responds: judge if that hour
   Its might was felt; if Beatrice smiled,
Brightening her brightness.   (1830)

Vita Nuova 20
['Amore e 'l cor gentil sono una cosa']

Love and the noble heart are but one thing,
   So saith the sage in his philosophy,
   And one without the other dares to be
   As much as Reason without reasoning.
Almighty Nature, being amorous, makes
   A King of Love, and of the heart a throne,
   Slumbering whereon his royal rest he takes,
   Now sleeping long, and now awakening soon.
Then in some virtuous maiden graces move,
   Charming the eye, whereat within the heart   10
   Springs a sweet longing for the thing that
      charms.
And this desire such living motion warms,
   That soon it wakes, a spirit of perfect love,
   Nor unresembling is the maiden's part.
         (written c. 1832)

24–5 compare *Paradiso* 30.16–33
   2 *the sage* Guido Guinizelli, a thirteenth-century lyric poet   *philosophy* the
Italian has a word for 'writings'   5 *Almighty* Hallam's addition
6–7 *King . . . throne . . . royal* in Dante, Love ranks only as a 'lord', and the
heart is nothing grander than his 'dwelling-place'   9 *virtuous* Dante writes
'*saggia*' ('wise') here to match the '*saggio*' (which Hallam renders as 'sage') in
the second line   13 *perfect* Hallam supplies the adjective, as he does the
double negative in the next line

ROBERT BROWNING (1812–89)

Browning began to study Italian with the political exile Angelo Cerutti in 1828, and made lengthy visits to Italy in 1838 and 1844 before moving to Florence with his wife, Elizabeth Barrett Browning, in 1846. His imaginative response to Dante was at once profound and tangential, and so is difficult to represent in extracts. The self-revelatory speeches of characters in the *Commedia* were a guide for the development of dramatic monologues such as 'My Last Duchess', the story of which may in part derive from that of La Pia (*Purgatorio* 5); 'The Statue and the Bust', a long poem in *terza rima*, has a root in the episode of Paolo and Francesca. Of the works excerpted below, *Sordello* imagines the life of the thirteenth-century poet whom Dante and Virgil encounter in *Purgatorio* 6, while *La Saisiaz* demonstrates Browning's interest in Dante as a religious teacher.

Sordello 5.580–601

[Sordello prophetically imagines a poem such as Dante will later write.]

What shall I unlock
By song? behold me prompt, whate'er it be,
To minister: how much can mortals see
Of Life? No more than so? I take the task
And marshall you Life's elemental masque,
Show Men, on evil or on good lay stress,
This light, this shade make prominent, suppress
All ordinary hues that softening blend
Such natures with the level. Apprehend
Which sinner is, which saint, if I allot
Hell, Purgatory, Heaven, a blaze or blot,

10

To those you doubt concerning! I enwomb
Some wretched Friedrich with his red-hot tomb;
Some dubious spirit, Lombard Agilulph
With the black chastening river I engulph!
Some unapproached Matilda I enshrine
With languors of the planet of decline –
These, fail to recognize, to arbitrate
Between henceforth, to rightly estimate
Thus marshalled in the masque! Myself, the
    while,   20
As one of you, am witness, shrink or smile
At my own showing! (1840)

From a letter to Elizabeth Barrett [Purgatorio 5.52–7]

... yesterday I was reading the 'Purgatorio' and the first speech
of the group of which Sordello makes one, struck me with a
new significance, as well describing the man and his purpose
and fate in my own poem ...

And sinners were we to the extreme hour;
Then, light from heaven fell, making us aware,
So that, repenting us and pardoned, out
Of life we passed to God, at peace with Him
Who fills the heart with yearning Him to see –
  (1845)

---

13 compare *Inferno* 10.119   14 *Lombard Agilulph* a professed Arian who
became king of Lombardy in 590; not in Dante   15 *river* this owes most to
the river of pitch in *Inferno* 21, though Sordello imagines Agilulph in
purgatory   16 *Matilda* compare *Purgatorio* 33.119, though Sordello
imagines her in the heaven of Venus, which in Dante is where Cunizza,
whom Sordello abducted, appears

One Word More   32–72 [Compare *Vita Nuova* 34]

V

Dante once prepared to paint an angel:
Whom to please? You whisper 'Beatrice.'
While he mused and traced it and retraced it,
(Peradventure with a pen corroded
Still by drops of that hot ink he dipped for,
When, his left-hand i' the hair o' the wicked,
Back he held the brow and pricked its stigma,
Bit into the live man's flesh for parchment,
Loosed him, laughed to see the writing rankle,
Let the wretch go festering through Florence) –
Dante, who loved well because he hated,
Hated wickedness that hinders loving,
Dante standing, studying his angel, –
In there broke the folk of his Inferno.
Says he – 'Certain people of importance'
(Such he gave his daily dreadful line to)
'Entered and would seize, forsooth, the poet.'
Says the poet – 'Then I stopped my painting.'

VI

You and I would rather see that angel,
Painted by the tenderness of Dante,
Would we not? – than read a fresh Inferno.

VII

You and I will never see that picture.
While he mused on love and Beatrice,
While he softened o'er his outlined angel,
In they broke, those 'people of importance':
We and Bice bear the loss for ever.

---

2 *you* the poem is addressed to Elizabeth Barrett Browning
6–8 compare *Inferno* 32.97–9   26 *Bice* Beatrice

VIII

What of Rafael's sonnets, Dante's picture?
This: no artist lives and loves, that longs not
Once, and only once, and for one only,
(Ah the prize!) to find his love a language   30
Fit and fair and simple and sufficient –
Using nature that's an art to others,
Not, this one time, art that's turned his nature.
Ay, of all the artists living, loving,
None but would forego his proper dowry, –
Does he paint? he fain would write a poem, –
Does he write? he fain would paint a picture,
Put to proof art alien to the artist's,
Once, and only once, and for one only,
So to be the man and leave the artist,   40
Gain the man's joy, miss the artist's sorrow.   (1855)

La Saisiaz   207–16

[A poem of religious speculation prompted by the sudden death of Browning's friend Anne Egerton Smith]

                      Why should I want courage here?
  I will ask and have an answer, – with no favour, with no
      fear, –
  From myself. How much, how little, do I inwardly believe
  True that controverted doctrine? Is it fact to which I
      cleave,
  Is it fancy I but cherish, when I take upon my lips

---

32 *an art to others* in Browning's case, this poem's trochaic pentameters, its constant Italianate feminine endings which occur nowhere else in his work

Phrase the solemn Tuscan fashioned, and declare the
    soul's eclipse
Not the soul's extinction? take his 'I believe and I
    declare –
Certain am I – from this life I pass into a better, there
Where that lady lives of whom enamoured was my soul'
    – where this
10   Other lady, my companion dear and true, she also is?
    (1878)

SIR THEODORE MARTIN (1816–1909)

A lawyer and versatile man of letters, Martin was a prolific
translator, mostly from German. His versions of lyrics from the
Vita Nuova were published in 1845, but his translation of the
whole volume did not appear for another seventeen years,
when, in the introduction, he hazarded some reflections on
Dante's private life. 'It seems strange that his love should not
have found its issue in marriage,' Martin wrote, for Dante loved
Beatrice 'as a man loves, and with the passion that naturally
perseveres to the possession of its mistress'. These remarks
caught the attention of Matthew Arnold, who accused Martin
of the 'error' of seeing 'in such a passion as that of Dante for
Beatrice, an affection belonging to the sphere of actual domestic
life' when on the contrary 'the task Dante sets himself is . . . the
task . . . of making the spirit all in all, of effacing the world in
presence of spirit'; in Arnold's view, Martin transforms Dante
'into the hero of a sentimental, but strictly virtuous novel'.
Aptly, Martin's translation was dedicated to his wife, the actress
Helen Faucit.

7–9 compare *Vita Nuova* 42.3; Browning had inscribed a prose version of
these lines on the testament of his wife, who is the 'companion dear and true'
mentioned in line 10

Vita Nuova 41 ['Oltre la spera che più larga gira']

Beyond the sphere that widest rolls above,
    The sigh that issues from my heart is borne,
    Wing'd by a new intelligence, which love
    Infuseth; love with mighty anguish torn.
When it hath gain'd the haven of its ease,
    It sees a lady whom the saints adore,
    So radiant, that the pilgrim spirit sees
    With awe the splendours that around her pour.
It sees her in such wise, that when it seeks
    To tell the tale, at my sad heart's demand,   10
    So deep its words, I understand them not!
Yet of that lady sweet I know it speaks,
    For oft it brings my Beatrice to thought,
    And this, dear ladies, well I understand.   (1845)

SIR THEODORE MARTIN (1816–1909) and
WILLIAM AYTOUN (1813–65)

Like his collaborator, Aytoun was an enthusiast for German literature; he eventually became Professor of Rhetoric at Edinburgh. With Martin he wrote many hugely popular parodies for *Blackwood's Magazine*. That not only *Inferno* 5 but Hunt's version of it (see above) were so recognizable as to be thus minutely guyed shows how domesticated Dante had become in England (he remained so at least until 1881 when 'Francesca di Rimini' [*sic*] was pattered about in Gilbert and Sullivan's *Patience*).

---

1 *sphere* the Primum Mobile   4 *with mighty anguish torn* exaggerated from Dante's *'piangendo'* ('weeping')   6 *adore* Dante does not accord Beatrice an adoration strictly reserved by orthodoxy for God; she 'receives honour' in the skies

Francesca da Rimini   14–23, 53–66

[Francesca, 'an impassioned pupil of Leigh Hunt', meets her
lover at a dance and 'declares the destructive consequences
thus'.]

There's wont to be, at conscious times like these,
An affectation of a bright-eyed ease, –
A crispy-cheekiness, if so I dare
Describe the swaling of a jaunty air;
And thus, when swirling from the waltz's wheel,
You craved my hand to grace the next quadrille,
That smiling voice, although it made me start,
Boil'd in the meek o'erlifting of my heart;
And, picking at my flowers, I said, with free
10   And usual tone, 'O yes, sir, certainly!'

                    *

But when the dance was o'er, and arm in arm,
(The full heart beating 'gainst the elbow warm,)
We pass'd into the great refreshment-hall,
Where the heaped cheese-cakes and the comfits small
Lay, like a hive of sunbeams, brought to burn
Around the margin of the negus urn;
When my poor quivering hand you finger'd twice,
And, with enquiring accents, whisper'd 'Ice,
Water, or cream?' I could no more dissemble,
20   But dropp'd upon the couch all in a tremble.
A swimming faintness misted o'er my brain,
The corks seem'd starting from the brisk champagne,
The custards fell untouch'd upon the floor,
Thine eyes met mine. That night we danced no more!
    (1855)

MATTHEW ARNOLD (1822–88)

Arnold's poetry was little influenced by Dante, partly because the reality of Dante's writing departs so widely from Arnold's cherished notions of style and seriousness, and partly because the sharp actuality of Dante's religion was alien to Arnold. His prose works frequently refer to the *Commedia* and *Vita Nuova*: he thought the *Commedia* to be, with *Paradise Lost*, 'one of only two poetical works in the grand style which are to be found in the modern languages'; in 'The Study of Poetry' (1880) several lines of Dante, notably *'E'n la sua volontade è nostra pace'* [*Paradiso* 3.85], are cited as 'touchstones' of 'high seriousness'.

S.S. 'Lusitania'

I read in Dante how that hornéd light,
Which hid Ulysses, waved itself and said:
'Following the sun, we set our vessel's head
To the great main; passed Seville on the right

'And Ceuta on the left; then southward sped.
At last in air, far off, dim rose a Height.
We cheered; but from it rushed a blast of might,
And struck – and o'er us the sea-waters spread.'

I dropped the book, and of my child I thought
In his long black ship speeding night and day   10
O'er those same seas; dark Teneriffe rose, fraught
With omen; 'Oh! were that mount passed', I say.
Then the door opens and this card is brought:
'Reached Cape Verde Islands, "Lusitania".' (1878)

1–2 compare *Inferno* 26.85–6   3–8 *Inferno* 26.117, 110–11, 133–4, 136–7, 142

CHARLES BAGOT CAYLEY (1823–83)

Cayley studied Italian with Gabriele Rossetti, to whose daughter Christina he soon became close. He published several translations, including a Petrarch in eight volumes. In a bullish preface to his *Divine Comedy*, he distinguishes his rendering of Dante from, among others, that of Cary who, he claims, 'adulterated all [the *Commedia*'s] franker style with the pomp and stiffness of our traditional epic poems' – a half-truth only, for Cary's diction is as often Shakespearean as it is Spenserian or Miltonic.

Inferno 17   79–136

Already mounted I beheld my guide
   Upon the back of that fell reptile, whence,
'Now be thou bold and confident,' he cried.
'By such a staircase must we go down hence;
   Get thou in front, and I between will sit,
That so, the tail may do thee no offence.'
As one who hath so nigh the chilling fit
   Of ague, that with nails already white
He shivers in the shade he shrinks to quit,
10   Such, when those words were uttered, was my fright;
   But shame fell on me from the threats he cast,
Which makes a servant valiant in the sight
Of a good lord. Upon those shoulders vast
   I set myself; I would, but voice no more
Obeyed my thoughts, have said, 'embrace me fast.'

---

2 *reptile* the monster Geryon is not only a 'reptile' (Dante does not have the term), for he has, as is apt to an emblem of deceit, a human face as well as hairy arms

But he that oft had succored me before
   In perilous time, soon as I'd mounted so,
Within his arms enwound me and upbore.
Then to the shape he said, 'Now, Geryon, go;
   Remember what new freight thou dost convey,   20
And make thy circuits large, thy sinking slow.'
As when a bark from haven making way
   Goes backing out, so put forth Geryon there;
But when his form on all sides found full play,
Then stretching out his tail, he turned it where
   His chest had been, and plied it like an eel,
And gathered to him 'neath his claws the air.
No greater dread, I think, did Phaethon feel
   At letting go the reins, through which the round
Of heaven was fired, as lasting proofs reveal;   30
Nor Icarus ill-fated, when he found
   The melting wax displume his loins, when cried
His father, 'On an ill road art thou bound,'
Than mine was, when the air on every side
   I felt, and from my prospect every show
Of substance but the savage beast had died.
He meantime circling and descending slow
   Swam on, but I perceived not that he stirred,
Save by a wind before me and below.
Already 'neath us on the right I heard   40
   That cataract with hideous hurly break,
And cast mine eyes and head down thitherward.
Then feared I more the swoop we had to make,
   For fires I saw, and heard lamentings too,
And shrinking faster to my seat I take.

---

28 *Phaethon* son of the Sun, he crashed his father's chariot: see Ovid's
Metamorphoses 2.47–324   31 *Icarus* his artificial wings melted when he
flew too near the sun: see *Metamorphoses* 8.203–33
45 *take* Cayley here follows Dante's shift into the present tense, as he does
not at lines 37–9

And now I saw, till then had 'scaped my view,
   Our circling and descent, through the great pains
That toward us now from many quarters drew.
Like as a hawk that long on wing remains,
50   But when no bird nor lure appears in sight,
'Alack thou sink'st,' the falconer complains –
Down comes he wearied, and his rapid flight
   Throws in a hundred wheels, and sinks at last
Far from his master, filled with haughty spite;
So with us Geryon to the bottom past,
   Close to the rocky precipice's foot,
And having from himself our persons cast,
Shot off, as arrow from the bow may shoot.   (1851)

CHARLES ELIOT NORTON (1827–1908)

Ruskin remembered Norton as possessing 'the sweetest quiet smile I ever saw on any face (unless, perhaps, a nun's, when she has some grave kindness to do)', and called him 'my first real tutor'. Norton probably learned some Italian from his father, who translated Manzoni's *I promessi sposi*; in the late 1850s he spent two years in Rome, and on his return joined the 'Dante Club' in Cambridge, Massachusetts. His version of the *Vita Nuova*, privately printed in 1859, was in 1867 issued in a uniform edition with Longfellow's *Divine Comedy*. Later in life, Norton wrote a prose translation of the *Commedia* (1891–2) and edited the letters of Carlyle in eleven volumes (1883–91).

Vita Nuova 34

On that day on which the year was complete since this lady was made one of the denizens of life eternal, I was seated in a place where, having her in mind, I was drawing an angel upon

---

1 *this lady* Beatrice

certain tablets. And while I was drawing it, I turned mine eyes
and saw at my side men to whom it was meet to do honor.
They were looking on what I did, and, as was afterwards told
me, they had been there already some time before I became
aware of it. When I saw them I rose, and, saluting them, said,
'Another was just now with me, and on that account I was in
thought.' And when they had gone away, I returned unto my   10
work, namely, that of drawing figures of angels; and while
doing this a thought came to me of saying words in rhyme, as
if for an anniversary poem of her, and of addressing those
persons who had come to me. And I devised then this sonnet
that beginneth, '*The gentle lady*,' the which hath two begin-
nings, and therefore I will divide it according to one and the
other.

*I say that, according to the first, this sonnet hath three parts:
in the first, I say that this lady was already in my memory; in
the second, I tell what Love thereupon did to me; in the third,*   20
I tell of the effects of Love. The second beginneth here: 'Love,
who'; *the third, here*: 'Lamenting they from out.' *This part is
divided into two: in the one, I say that all my sighs went forth
speaking; in the other, I tell how some said certain words
different from the others. The second beginneth here*: 'But
those.' *In this same way it is divided according to the other
beginning, except that in the first part I tell when this lady had
so come to my mind, and this I do not tell in the other.*

First Beginning.
The gentle lady to my mind had come,   30
    Who, for the sake of her exceeding worth,
    Had by the Lord Most High been ta'en from earth
    To that calm heaven where Mary hath her home.

---

16 *divide it* this method of explication, by subdivision and paraphrase of a
text, was widely practised at Dante's time in sermons, commentaries and
theological treatises; Dante applies it exhaustively to several of his poems in
the *Convivio*

Second Beginning.
That gentle lady to my mind in thought
    Had come, for sake of whom Love weepeth still,
    Just at the time when by his powerful will
    To see what I was doing you were brought.
Love, who within my mind did her perceive,
40   Roused himself up within my wasted heart,
    And said unto my sighs, 'Go forth! depart!'
    Whereon each one in sorrow took its leave.
Lamenting they from out my breast did go,
    And uttering a voice that often led
The grievous tears unto my saddened eyes;
But those which issued with the greatest woe,
    'O high intelligence!' they, going, said,
    'To-day makes up the year since thou to heaven
     didst rise.' (privately printed 1859; 1867)

MARGARET OLIPHANT OLIPHANT
(1828–97)

Italy was not a happy place for Mrs Oliphant. In 1859 she travelled to Rome with her husband in vain search of a cure for his consumption; in 1864 her daughter also died there. The following snatches of verse translation are from an introductory handbook on Dante, which was a departure from her usual, remarkably prolific output of popular novels and historical works.

Inferno 8   28–64

Soon as my guide and I were in the boat,
    More deep dipped in the stream than e'er before,
    The ancient prow shot o'er the gloomy moat.

In front of me rose one bedabbled o'er,
   A mass of filth, while o'er the wave we sped:
   'Who art thou here, arrived before thy hour?'
'I come but stay not here,' to him I said;
   'But who art thou, of such an aspect vile?'
   'Thou seest I am one who weeps,' replied
The voice; and I to him, 'With tears and toil,   10
   Spirit accursed, in thy filth remain;
   I know thee, though by foulness hid awhile.'
Then with both hands he clutched the boat amain;
   My master loosed his grasp and cast us free,
   Saying, 'Hence, with other wretches of thy strain!'
Then with embracing arms he turned to me,
   And kissed my face, and said, 'Indignant soul,
   Happy the mother who gave birth to thee!
Proud upon earth was he who bears this dole:
   No gentle deeds lend to his memory grace;   20
   And thus his furious shade has dwelling foul.
Many there be who fill the highest place,
   Kings upon earth, who here like swine shall bide,
   Leaving but scorn and horror in their trace.'
And I: 'Master, within this dismal tide
   Fain would I see him deeply dipped before
   We issue forth upon the other side.'
And he to me: 'Ere we have touched the shore,
   Thou shalt be satisfied; nought should oppose
   To such just wish an answer o'er and o'er.'   30

---

4 *one bedabbled* eventually named at 34 as Filippo Argenti; he was a
member of the Adimari family for whom Dante still has a harsh word in
Paradiso 16.115–20. He was a boss-class Black Guelf (Dante was a White);
some commentators attribute the acrimony of this passage to a specific
grudge Dante had against him but there is no evidence for the supposition
15 *wretches* the Italian means 'dogs'   18 compare Luke 11:27
23 *swine* Mrs Oliphant declines to add, as Dante does, 'in slurry'
25 *dismal tide* the original means 'broth' or 'soup'

A little after such a tumult rose
  Amid those filthy folk, as still to praise
  And magnify our God my thoughts dispose,
'To Filippo Argenti!' loud they raise
  The cry; and that vile spirit Florentine
  Tore himself with his teeth in furious craze.
Thus leave we him with no more words of mine.
       (1877)

Purgatorio 6   61–75

Oh, Lombard soul! how proud and silent thou
  In lofty musing stood, with solemn eyes
  Scarce moving slow beneath thy steadfast brow!
No word he spake; but in such noble guise
  As a reposing lion, on us stayed
  His look, while round we passed, in curious wise.
Then Virgil, drawing near, petition made
  That he would show where best we might ascend.
  To our demand no answering word he said,
But of our country asked, and how might tend
  Our lives. When thus my gentle guide began,
  'Mantua –;' all eager ere he made an end
The spirit turned from where he stood, 'A man,
  O Mantuan! of thy land, Sordello, I.'
  And quick embracing one to th'other ran.

---

14 *Sordello* lyric poet of the first half of the thirteenth century, born, as was
Virgil, in Mantua   15–16 the translation skips 75 lines of diatribe about
contemporary Italian politics

7   1–21

When o'er and o'er this joyful greeting true
  Had been repeated, to remembrance brought,
  Sordello paused, and questioned, 'Who are you?'
'Ere ever on this mountain had been wrought
  By worthy souls to God the high ascent,   20
  I to my grave was by Octavian brought;
Virgil I am: for no impediment,
  Save want of faith, the heavenly state I lost.'
  Thus spoke my guide; and lo! as one intent
On something sudden seen his path that crost,
  Marvelling, believing, doubting still, who cries,
  ''Tis he! nay, 'tis not he,' his being tost
With wonder stood Sordello; then his eyes
  He drooped, and humbly to the Master came,
  Embracing, there where low the suppliant lies,   30
His knees. 'O thou by whom our tongue may claim
  Its highest meed! glory of Latins! praise
  Eternal of the city whence I came!
What grace, what merit, to this height can raise
  Me worthless, that thy noble words I hear?' (1877)

Paradiso 30   19–33

[Dante looks at Beatrice]

> The beauty that I gazed upon excels
>   Not only thought of ours, but well I deem
>   That in no other than her Maker dwells

---

21 *Octavian* the Emperor Augustus, during whose reign Virgil died (19 BCE)
27–8 *his being tost / With wonder* this fine phrase has no equivalent in
Dante

Power to enjoy so pure and full a beam
  Of loveliness. I own me all outdone,
  As never yet was player by his theme,
Be it gay or tragic, overcome;
  For as the sun, that dazzles trembling eyes,
  So all myself melts from my memory, won
10 When but the thoughts of such a smile arise.
  From the first day when I beheld her face,
  Ne'er has my song forsook the high emprize
To celebrate and laud my lady's grace.
  Now must the singing cease: I may not run
  This fair course further, having reached the place
Where artists all must pause, their skill outdone.

  (1877)

DANTE GABRIEL ROSSETTI (1828–82)

Rossetti and his siblings grew up in the shadow of their father
Gabriele's theory, advanced in a series of books, that the *Com-
media* was an esoteric, anti-Papal allegory. As William Michael
Rossetti remembered: 'Dante Alighieri was a sort of banshee in
the Charlotte Street house; his shriek audible even to familiarity,
but the message of it not scrutinized'. In recoil perhaps from
suchlike certainties, Dante Gabriel's interest in the poet focused
rather on the *Vita Nuova* which he translated, together with
lyrics by many of Dante's contemporaries, in his volume *The
Early Italian Poets* (1861), and on the figure of Beatrice, whom
he represented in several paintings, notably *Beata Beatrix*
(1870). T. S. Eliot admitted that 'Rossetti's *Blessed Damozel*,
first by my rapture and next by my revolt, held up my appreci-
ation of Beatrice by many years'; Ezra Pound never tired of the
quasi-Elizabethan idiom into which Rossetti translated Dante's
lyrics (see, for example, his *Canto* LXXXI).

The Blessed Damozel [Compare *Inferno* 2.52–117]

The blessed damozel leaned out
   From the gold bar of Heaven;
Her eyes were deeper than the depth
   Of waters stilled at even;
She had three lilies in her hand
   And the stars in her hair were seven.

Her robe, ungirt from clasp to hem,
   No wrought flowers did adorn,
But a white rose of Mary's gift,
   For service meetly worn;   10
Her hair that lay along her back
   Was yellow like ripe corn.

Herseemed she scarce had been a day
   One of God's choristers;
The wonder was not yet quite gone
   From that still look of hers;
Albeit, to them she left, her day
   Had counted as ten years.

(To one, it is ten years of years.
   . . . Yet now, and in this place,   20
Surely she leaned o'er me – her hair
   Fell all about my face . . .
Nothing: the autumn-fall of leaves.
   The whole year sets apace.)

It was the rampart of God's house
   That she was standing on;
By God built over the sheer depth
   The which is Space begun;
So high, that looking downward thence
   She scarce could see the sun.   30

It lies in Heaven, across the flood
    Of ether, as a bridge.
Beneath, the tides of day and night
    With flame and darkness ridge
The void, as low as where this earth
    Spins like a fretful midge.

Heard hardly, some of her new friends
    Amid their loving games
Spake evermore among themselves
40   Their virginal chaste names;
And the souls mounting up to God
    Went by her like thin flames.

And still she bowed herself and stooped
    Out of the circling charm;
Until her bosom must have made
    The bar she leaned on warm,
And the lilies lay as if asleep
    Along her bended arm.

From the fixed place of Heaven she saw
50   Time like a pulse shake fierce
Through all the worlds. Her gaze still strove
    Within the gulf to pierce
Its path: and now she spoke as when
    The stars sang in their spheres.

The sun was gone now; the curled moon
    Was like a little feather
Fluttering far down the gulf; and now
    She spoke through the still weather.
Her voice was like the voice the stars
60   Had when they sang together.

35–6 compare *Paradiso* 22.134–5   59–60 compare Job 38:7

(Ah sweet! Even now, in that bird's song,
  Strove not her accents there,
Fain to be hearkened? When those bells
  Possessed the mid-day air,
Strove not her steps to reach my side
  Down all the echoing stair?)

'I wish that he were come to me,
  For he will come,' she said.
'Have I not prayed in Heaven? – on earth,
  Lord, Lord, has he not pray'd?   70
Are not two prayers a perfect strength?
  And shall I feel afraid?

'When round his head the aureole clings,
  And he is clothed in white,
I'll take his hand and go with him
  To the deep wells of light;
We will step down as to a stream,
  And bathe there in God's sight.

'We two will stand beside that shrine,
  Occult, withheld, untrod,   80
Whose lamps are stirred continually
  With prayer sent up to God;
And see our old prayers, granted, melt
  Each like a little cloud.

'We two will lie i' the shadow of
  That living mystic tree
Within whose secret growth the Dove
  Is sometimes felt to be,
While every leaf that His plumes touch
  Saith His Name audibly.   90

77–8 Dante bathes, but with Matilda not Beatrice, in *Purgatorio* 31
84 *a little cloud* compare *Vita Nuova* 23.25

'And I myself will teach to him,
 I myself, lying so,
The songs I sing here; which his voice
 Shall pause in, hushed and slow,
And find some knowledge at each pause,
 Or some new thing to know.'

(Alas! We two, we two, thou say'st!
 Yea, one wast thou with me
That once of old. But shall God lift
100 To endless unity
The soul whose likeness with thy soul
 Was but its love for thee?)

'We two,' she said, 'will seek the groves
 Where the lady Mary is,
With her five handmaidens, whose names
 Are five sweet symphonies,
Cecily, Gertrude, Magdalen,
 Margaret and Rosalys.

'Circlewise sit they, with bound locks
110 And foreheads garlanded;
Into the fine cloth white like flame
 Weaving the golden thread,
To fashion the birth-robes for them
 Who are just born, being dead.

'He shall fear, haply, and be dumb:
 Then will I lay my cheek
To his, and tell about our love,
 Not once abashed or weak:
And the dear Mother will approve
120 My pride, and let me speak.

---

111 *white like flame* compare *Purgatorio* 30.31–3

'Herself shall bring us, hand in hand,
   To Him round whom all souls
Kneel, the clear-ranged unnumbered heads
   Bowed with their aureoles:
And angels meeting us shall sing
   To their citherns and citoles.

'There will I ask of Christ the Lord
   Thus much for him and me: –
Only to live as once on earth
   With Love, – only to be,   130
As then awhile, for ever now
   Together, I and he.'

She gazed and listened and then said,
   Less sad of speech than mild, –
'All this is when he comes.' She ceased.
   The light thrilled towards her, fill'd
With angels in strong level flight.
   Her eyes prayed, and she smil'd.

(I saw her smile.) But soon their path
   Was vague in distant spheres: 140
And then she cast her arms along
   The golden barriers,
And laid her face between her hands,
   And wept. (I heard her tears.)   (1850)

---

126 paradisiacal singing is unaccompanied in Dante
138 *she smil'd* compare Beatrice's many smiles, especially *Paradiso* 31.91–3

Vita Nuova 19 ['Donne ch'avete intelletto d'amore']

Ladies that have intelligence in love,
   Of mine own lady I would speak with you;
   Not that I hope to count her praises through,
     But telling what I may, to ease my mind.
And I declare that when I speak thereof,
   Love sheds such perfect sweetness over me
   That if my courage failed not, certainly
     To him my listeners must be all resign'd.
    Wherefore I will not speak in such large kind
That mine own speech should foil me, which were
10   base;
But only will discourse of her high grace
    In these poor words, the best that I can find,
With you alone, dear dames and damozels:
'Twere ill to speak thereof with any else.

An Angel, of his blessed knowledge, saith
   To God: 'Lord, in the world that Thou hast made,
   A miracle in action is display'd,
    By reason of a soul whose splendours fare
Even hither: and since Heaven requireth
20   Nought saving her, for her it prayeth Thee,
   Thy Saints crying aloud continually.'
    Yet Pity still defends our earthly share
    In that sweet soul, God answering thus the
         prayer:
'My well-belovèd, suffer that in peace

---

12 *In these poor words* Rossetti's view, not Dante's; the original reads
'*leggeramente*' ('lightly', 'delicately')   13 *dear* Dante calls the ladies
'*amorose*', perhaps best translated as 'sympathetic to love'   19 modern
editors end the Angel's speech after 'hither', ascribing the rest of lines 19–21
to the Dante who speaks the poem; in the editions to which Rossetti had
access, as in the earliest manuscripts, the speech is not distinguished by
inverted commas at all

Your hope remain, while so My pleasure is,
    There where one dwells who dreads the loss of her:
And who in Hell unto the doomed shall say,
"I have looked on that for which God's chosen pray." '

My lady is desired in the high Heaven:
    Wherefore, it now behoveth me to tell,   30
    Saying: Let any maid that would be well
        Esteemed keep with her: for as she goes by,
Into foul hearts a deathly chill is driven
    By Love, that makes ill thought to perish there:
    While any who endures to gaze on her
        Must either be ennobled, or else die.
    When one deserving to be raised so high
Is found, 'tis then her power attains its proof,
Making his heart strong for his soul's behoof
    With the full strength of meek humility.   40
Also this virtue owns she, by God's will:
Who speaks with her can never come to ill.

Love saith concerning her: 'How chanceth it
    That flesh, which is of dust, should be thus pure?'
    Then, gazing always, he makes oath: 'Forsure,
        This is a creature of God till now unknown.'
She hath that paleness of the pearl that's fit
    In a fair woman, so much and not more;
    She is as high as Nature's skill can soar;
        Beauty is tried by her comparison.   50
    Whatever her sweet eyes are turned upon,
Spirits of love do issue thence in flame,
Which through their eyes who then may look on them
    Pierce to the heart's deep chamber every one.
And in her smile Love's image you may see;
Whence none can gaze upon her steadfastly.

39–40 the relished paradox is Rossetti's   44 *flesh* Dante contrasts Beatrice's
purity not with her physicality but with her mortality ('*cosa mortale*')

Dear Song, I know thou wilt hold gentle speech
  With many ladies, when I send thee forth:
  Wherefore (being mindful that thou hadst thy birth
60   From Love, and art a modest, simple child,)
Whomso thou meetest, say thou this to each:
  'Give me good speed! To her I wend along
  In whose much strength my weakness is made
      strong.'
     And if, i' the end, thou wouldst not be
      beguiled
  Of all thy labour seek not the defiled
And common sort; but rather choose to be
Where man and woman dwell in courtesy.
  So to the road thou shalt be reconciled,
And find the lady, and with the lady, Love.
70 Commend thou me to each, as doth behove.
     (1861; mostly written in the late 1840s)

Vita Nuova 26 ['Tanto gentile e tanto onesta pare']

My lady looks so gentle and so pure
  When yielding salutation by the way,
  That the tongue trembles and has nought to say,
And the eyes, which fain would see, may not endure.
And still, amid the praise she hears secure,
  She walks with humbleness for her array;
  Seeming a creature sent from Heaven to stay
On earth, and show a miracle made sure.
She is so pleasant in the eyes of men
10 That through the sight the inmost heart doth gain

---

63 Rossetti adds a reminiscence of 2 Corinthians 12:9
  9 *the eyes of men* the original is not specific about the gender of Beatrice's admirers

A sweetness which needs proof to know it by:
And from between her lips there seems to move
A soothing essence that is full of love,
   Saying for ever to the spirit, 'Sigh!'
   (1861; mostly written in the late 1840s)

Vita Nuova 26 ['Vede perfettamente onne salute']

For certain he hath seen all perfectness
   Who among other ladies hath seen mine:
   They that go with her humbly should combine
To thank their God for such peculiar grace.
So perfect is the beauty of her face
   That it begets in no wise any sign
   Of envy, but draws round her a clear line
Of love, and blessed faith, and gentleness.
Merely the sight of her makes all things bow:
   Not she herself alone is holier   10
      Than all; but hers, through her, are raised above.
From all her acts such lovely graces flow
   That truly one may never think of her
      Without a passion of exceeding love.
      (1861; mostly written in the late 1840s)

WILLIAM MICHAEL ROSSETTI (1829–1919)

William Michael was subjected to the same early experience of
Dante as his siblings. He recalled that 'the *Convito* [i.e. *Con-
vivio*] was always a name of dread to us, as being the essence

---

7 *envy* the grammar of the original makes clear that no *women* envy her
beauty   11–12 the original is clearer: 'it is not only she herself who looks
beautiful but every other woman is honoured on her account'

of arid unreadableness'; his judgement changed with age, for
among the many works of scholarship which he later produced
is *Dante and his Convito*. The prose parts of the translation of
the *Vita Nuova* credited to his brother are in fact his. He worked
in the excise office, and brought a civil servant's precision to
his rendering of *Inferno*, whose stated aim was 'unconditional
literality in phraseology, and . . . line-for-line rendering'.

Inferno 12   49–96

O blind cupidity, O senseless rage,
Which so dost spur us in the transient life,
And, in the eternal, drench us then so ill!
I saw an ample fosse bent in an arc
Like such one as embraces all the plain,
According as my guide had spoken it:
And centaurs, 'twixt the foot o' the bank and this,
Were running, armed with arrows, as in trace,
As used they go a-hunting in the world.
10   Seeing us coming onward, each one stopped,
And three out of the band disjoined themselves,
With bows and arrows chosen out before.

And one from far cried: 'To what martyrdom
Come ye who are descending from the slope?
Tell it from there: if not, I draw the bow.'

My master said to him: 'We will return
The answer unto Chiron there at hand:
Thy will was always wrongfully so fast.'
He touched me then, and said: 'Nessus is that,
20   Who for the beauteous Dejanira died,

---

2 *transient* literally, 'short'   4 *fosse* ditch

And wrought, himself, the vengeance of himself.
And he in midst, who aims against his breast,
Is the great Chiron, who brought up Achilles:
That other's Pholus, erst so full of rage.
Thousand and thousand round the fosse they go,
Shooting whatever soul protrudeth more
Than its offence assigned it, from the blood.'

We drew anear those rapid animals.
An arrow Chiron took, and, with the notch,
Put back his beard behind the jaws of him.   30

Whenas he had uncovered his great mouth,
To his companions said he: 'Are ye 'ware
The one behind moves that which he doth touch?
So are not wont to do the feet o' the dead.'

And my good lord, who now was at his breast
Where the two natures are associate,
Replied: 'Indeed he's quick, and thus alone
Behoves I to him show the dusky vale:
Necessity constrains him, not delight.
From singing hallelujah one set off   40
Who charged this novel office upon us:
He is no robber, I no thieving soul.
But, for that virtue by the which I move
My steps along this savage road, give one
Of thine to us, to whom we'll be in trust;
That he may show us where the fording is,
And carry this man on his crupper, since
He's not a spirit which can go through air.'   (1865)

---

21 *vengeance* 'by giving Dejanira the poisoned robe which killed his slayer
Hercules' [*Rossetti's note*]   22 *who ... breast* 'this may also mean "who
gazes at his breast"' [*Rossetti's note*]   24 *Pholus* 'another centaur slain by
Hercules, according to Virgil' [*Rossetti's note*]   37 *quick* the original says
'alive' without archaism   40 *one* Beatrice

FREDERICK KNELLER HASELFOOT
HASELFOOT (1829–1905)

Haselfoot was a lawyer who began studying the *Commedia* in 1860. When his translation appeared in 1887, Cardinal Manning praised 'the purity and simplicity' of its language: 'Cary is Latinistic: but your diction is monosyllabic English'. This extract does not strongly support the Cardinal's judgement.

Paradiso 10   52–148

And Beatrice began, 'Thanks, thanks give here
    To the Sun of the Angels, who by grace has brought
    Thee up to this sense-apprehended Sphere.'
Never was mortal's heart with such mood fraught,
    For devout turning to the Deity,
    With all its pleasure to such promptness wrought,
As at these words the impulse rose in me;
    And my love was to Him so wholly knit,
    That Beatrice was eclipsed from memory.
10 At this she smiled so, not displeased at it,
    That, through her smiling eyes' resplendent might,
    My mind from one thought into many split.
I beheld many a live victorious light
    Make us the centre which their circle crowned;
    Sweeter in voice than luminous to sight.
Latona's daughter girt like this around
    We sometimes see, when through the pregnant air
    The thread that makes her zone continues wound.

---

2 *the Sun of the Angels* God   9–10 contrast her vexation when Dante forgets her for other women after her death (*Purgatorio* 31.21–30)

Heaven's Court, whence I return, holds many a fair
    And costly jewel, that may not be ta'en   20
    Out of the realm that they embellish there.
And of these was those luminaries' strain;
    Let him who has not plumes to soar so high,
    Seek from the dumb man tidings thence to gain.
When, singing thus, those burning Suns went by,
    And had whirled round us in gyrations three,
    Even as the stars which to fixed poles are nigh;
Ladies they seemed, not from the dance set free,
    But who in silence halt, on listening bent,
    Till they have caught the new notes' melody;   30
And I heard first words from within one sent: –
    'Since grace's ray, which kindles true love's glow,
    And afterwards by loving gains extent,
Is multiplied and shines within thee so,
    That up that stair it leads thee, up which he
    Who thence descends ne'er fails again to go;
Whoso refused his phial's wine to thee,
    For thy thirst, would have liberty no more
    Than water has, which runs not down to sea.
Thou wouldst know with what plants is flowering
       o'er   40
    This garland; circling amorous to behold
    Her, thy fair source of strength to heavenward soar.
I of the lambs was, of the saintly fold
    Which Dominic conducts, that path to try,
    Where those grow sleek who 'scape from vain
       things' hold.
He who upon my right hand is most nigh,
    My brother was, and Master; of Cologne,
    Albert, is he; Aquino's Thomas I.

---

22 *those luminaries' strain* the original says plainly 'the song of those lights'
31 *one* self-named at line 48 as St Thomas Aquinas   43 *the saintly fold* the
Dominican order   48 *Albert* the Dominican St Albert the Great
(1193–1280)

If thou wouldst have the rest all surely known,
50   Follow my speech by casting round thy sight,
       Up and along the blissful garland thrown.
From Gratian's smile springs that next flaming light;
       Who to one and the other forum lent
       Aid which makes Paradise with pleasure bright.
The other, this our choir's next ornament,
       That Peter was, whose treasure to the share
       Of Holy Church, like the poor widow's, went.
The fifth light, which amongst us is most fair,
       Breathes of such love that all the world below
60   Is greedy to learn tidings of it there.
Within is the high mind where knowledge so
       Profound was placed, that, if the truth be true,
       No second rose, so keen of sight to grow.
Next see the radiance of that taper who,
       In flesh below, had Angels' ministry
       And nature present to his inmost view.
Smiling in the small other light is he,
       Whose advocacy of the Christian reign
       Was lore that served Augustine usefully.
70   Now if thou keepest thy mind's eye in train,
       While following my praise from light to light,
       Thou must in thirst here for the eighth remain.

---

52 *Gratian* a Camaldolese monk, whose *Decretum* (1140) was the basic
textbook of canon law   56 *Peter* the Lombard (died 1160); his *Sentences*
was the basis of academic theology, commented on by many, including
Aquinas himself   58 *The fifth light* Solomon, considered here primarily as
author of The Song of Songs, a book which during the Middle Ages was
thought to describe the love between Christ and the Church
64 *that taper* 'Dionysius the Areopagite', the pseudonymous fifth or sixth
century formulator of negative theology; his work was immensely influential
in the Middle Ages   67 *other light* scholars are undecided between several
candidates, such as St Ambrose, Lactantius, Tertullian, etc.
72 *the eighth* Boethius (*c*.480–526) was imprisoned and died in Pavia where
he is buried in the church of San Pietro in Ciel d'Oro (line 77); Dante
frequently quotes from his *On the Consolation of Philosophy*

Within, by having every good in sight,
    The holy soul is gladdened, which makes clear
    The world's deceit to those who hear it right.
The body it was driven from has its bier
    Down in Cieldauro; and from exile's ban
    And martyrdom it came into peace here.
Further, the flame from the bright spirits scan,
    Of Bede and Isidore and Richard, he   80
    Who was in contemplation more than man.
This one, from whom thy gaze returns to me,
    A spirit's gleam is, to whose serious thought
    Death seemed procrastinating tardily.
Sigier is with this light eternal fraught,
    Who, as he lectured in the straw-named street,
    Syllogised truths of an invidious sort.'
Then as a clock, that calls us when, to greet
    Her spouse with matins that may barb love's
        dart,
    The bride of God is rising to her feet,   90
Draws this and urges on the other part,
    Making 'ting ting' sound in so sweet a tone
    As swells with love a well-intentioned heart;
So to my sight the glorious wheel was shown,
    Moving and rendering voice to voice, in chime
    And sweetness such as nowhere can be known
Save there, where joy endures through endless
        time.   (1887)

---

80 *Bede* English monk and historian (674–735) *Isidore* of Seville, bishop
and encyclopedist (died 636) *Richard* of St Victor, Augustinian prior and
mystic (died 1173) 82–5 *This one . . . Sigier* Siger of Brabant (died 1283),
controversial, indeed condemned, philosopher; Aquinas and he had engaged
in fierce debate but seem to be reconciled among the stars
86 *straw-named street* the Rue de Fouarre in Paris, seat of the university's
school of philosophy 90 *The bride of God* the Church

WILLIAM PATRICK WILKIE (1829–72)

Wilkie was an Edinburgh lawyer. When his translation of *Inferno* appeared in 1862, the *Athenaeum* criticized it for inaccuracy and remarked, apropos of its irregular, unrhymed verse, 'we suspect the manner of the translation is as original as the matter of it'.

Inferno 24   79–151

So we descend along the ridge, and pass
the buttress, which the eighth embankment joins;
and thence the chasm's depths are seen.
   There rolling bands of serpents, so uncouth
and many hued appeared, that even now,
the thought of them doth scare my blood.
   No more let Libya boast of arid sand
engendering stink-snakes, adderdarters, and
spot-vipers, two-heads, and the cobra dire,
10 for pests so hideous and so foul
nor it, nor Ethiopia hot,
nor e'en the Red Sea's strand can show.
   Amid the frightful swarm ran naked shades,
finding no refuge in their wild alarm,
and with no charmèd heliotrope's defence.
   Their hands were tied behind by serpent thongs,
of which the heads and tails past round their loins,
and coiled in knots in front.
   And lo! on one, not far from us,
20 a serpent sprang, and in his neck
inclasped its fangs.

---

15 *heliotrope* a green variety of quartz, thought to cure snake-bites
21 Wilkie omits a line which means 'Faster than any "o" or "i" was ever written, he caught fire'; his versification attempts to convey this speed

That instant he
caught fire and blazed,
at once, to ashes gray;
but hardly had he dust become,
when of themselves his ashes gathered in,
and he stood up restored.
   Thus, sages say,
the Phoenix dies and is reborn
in its five-hundredth year: 30
No herb or grain it picks, but lives on tears
of incense, and amomum balm,
while myrrh and spikenard swathe its fun'ral pile.
   As one who fell, and wits not if
devils possessed and threw him down,
or epileptic spasms wrenched his frame,
and, rising, looks around, confused
and dizzy through the anguish he has borne,
and, looking, sighs, so looked
and sighed the sinner when he rose. –   40
   Eternal Justice, how severe thy law,
which on the doomed such vengeance brings!
   My Guide then asked his name;
and he: 'From Tuscany I fell not long ago,
and this wild gullet gulped me in.
No human, but a bestial life I chose;
mule that I was. Van Fucci I;
a brute, for whom Pistoia was a fitting den.'
   Then I besought the Guide to bid him stay;
and 'Ask,' I said, 'what he atones for here;   50
for once I knew him as a man of rage and blood.'

---

36 *epileptic spasms* Dante has only '*oppilazion*', an erudite Latinism meaning
'obstruction'   47 *Van Fucci* a Black Guelf, whom Dante knew personally;
he was frequently condemned for sacrilegious theft and general brigandage
but escaped earthly justice (he died in 1300 just before the *Commedia* is
imagined to take place)

At this the sinner feigned no vain disguise,
but, cowering, he with abject look,
and burning glow of shame, replied:
   'More pained am I that thou
dost see me in this loathsome place
than I was when first rent from living men;
yet what thou wilt I am unable to refuse:
   'So much degraded here am I, because
60 I robbed the sacristy of all its vessels rich,
and falsely on another threw the blame.
   'But lest thou shouldst rejoice to see me thus,
bear with thee, if thou leave this dark abode,
the things I now foretell:
   'Pistoia first of Neri's thinned;
then Florence other laws and rulers knows;
Mars from the Val di Magra draws a fire
enshrouded close in surcharged clouds,and, with
      impetuous tempest, he
70 in battle rages on Peceno's plain,
where, suddenly, the clouds are split,
and every Bianco lies transpierced.
   'This I have said to torture thee.'   (1862)

CHRISTINA G. ROSSETTI (1830–94)

Unlike her father, sister and brothers, Christina Rossetti did not write scholarly studies or translations of Dante. She attended lectures on the *Commedia* at University College, London in 1878, and traced possible allusions to Dante for Alexander Grosart's edition of the works of Spenser; she produced a brief summary of the poem for *Century Magazine* in 1884. Dante's appearances in her writing are similarly slight and oblique.

---

65 *Neri's* Black Guelfs, enemies of the Whites ('Bianco', line 72)
68 *surcharged* with electricity; Wilkie's meteorological knowledge is more detailed than Dante's   70 *Peceno's plain* near Pistoia

Several of her poems are in Italian; she once wrote to a friend 'I cannot tell you how dear the Italian language is to me, so dear that I will not attempt to compare it with my native English.'

from 'Later Life: A Double Sonnet of Sonnets'

7

To love and to remember; that is good:
  To love and to forget; that is not well:
  To lapse from love to hatred; that is hell
And death and torment, rightly understood.
Soul dazed by love and sorrow, cheer thy mood;
  More blest art thou than mortal tongue can tell:
  Ring not thy funeral but thy marriage bell,
And salt with hope thy life's insipid food.
Love is the goal, love is the way we wend,
  Love is our parallel unending line   10
    Whose only perfect Parallel is Christ,
Beginning not begun, End without end:
    For He Who hath the Heart of God sufficed,
    Can satisfy all hearts, – yea, thine and mine.

10

Tread softly! all the earth is holy ground.
  It may be, could we look with seeing eyes,
  This spot we stand on is a Paradise
Where dead have come to life and lost been found,
Where Faith has triumphed, Martyrdom been
              crowned,
    Where fools have foiled the wisdom of the wise;
    From this same spot the dust of saints may rise,
And the King's prisoners come to light unbound.

1–2 compare *Inferno* 5.121–3

O earth, earth, earth, hear thou thy Maker's Word:
10   'Thy dead thou shalt give up, nor hide thy slain' –
Some who went weeping forth shall come again
Rejoicing from the east or from the west,
As doves fly to their windows, love's own bird
Contented and desirous to the nest.   (1881)

ALGERNON CHARLES SWINBURNE
(1837–1909)

While at Balliol College, Oxford, Swinburne fell in with Dante
Gabriel Rossetti and the Pre-Raphaelites; he became notorious
after *Poems and Ballads* (1866) was denounced for its sensuality
and anti-Christian drive. He was an enthusiast for Mazzini and
the cause of Italian unification (completed in 1870 when the
Papal States were added to the Kingdom of Italy). He considered
'Siena' 'as good as anything I have yet done'.

Siena   181–243

Ah, in this strange and shrineless place,
What doth a goddess, what a Grace,
Where no Greek worships her shrined limbs
With wreaths and Cytherean hymns?
Where no lute makes luxurious
The adoring airs in Amathus,
Till the maid, knowing her mother near,
Sobs with love, aching with sweet fear?
What do ye here?

13–14 in a note, Rossetti appends *Inferno* 5.82–84, which these lines
translate   4 *Cytherean hymns* hymns to Venus, the first of three female
figures whom Swinburne revolves around in this passage   6 *Amathus* site of
a shrine to Venus on Cyprus

For the outer land is sad, and wears   10
   A raiment of a flaming fire;
And the fierce fruitless mountain stairs
   Climb, yet seem wroth and loth to aspire,
Climb, and break, and are broken down,
And through their clefts and crests the town
Looks west and sees the dead sun lie,
In sanguine death that stains the sky
With angry dye.

And from the war-worn wastes without
In twilight, in the time of doubt,   20
One sound comes of one whisper, where
Moved with low motions of slow air
The great trees nigh the castle swing
In the sad coloured evening;
'*Ricorditi di me, che son
La Pia*' – that small sweet word alone
Is not yet gone.

'*Ricorditi di me*' – the sound
   Sole out of deep dumb days remote
Across the fiery and fatal ground   30
   Comes tender as a hurt bird's note
To where, a ghost with empty hands,
A woe-worn ghost, her palace stands
In the mid city, where the strong
Bells turn the sunset air to song,
And the towers throng.

With other face, with speech the same,
A mightier maiden's likeness came
Late among mourning men that slept,
A sacred ghost that went and wept,   40

25–6 '*Ricorditi . . .*' *Purgatorio* 5.133–6 ('Remember me, I am La Pia')
39 *mightier maiden* Italy personified

White as the passion-wounded Lamb,
Saying, 'Ah, remember me, that am
Italia.' (From deep sea to sea
Earth heard, earth knew her, that this was she.)
'Ricorditi.

'Love made me of all things fairest thing,
    And Hate unmade me; this knows he
Who with God's sacerdotal ring
    Enringed mine hand, espousing me.'
50 Yea, in thy myriad-mooded woe,
Yea, Mother, hast thou not said so?
Have not our hearts within us stirred,
O thou most holiest, at thy word?
Have we not heard?

As this dead tragic land that she
Found deadly, such was time to thee;
Years passed thee withering in the red
Maremma, years that deemed thee dead,
Ages that sorrowed or that scorned;
60 And all this while through all they mourned
Thou sawest the end of things unclean,
And the unborn that should see thee a queen.
Have we not seen?   (1868; 1871)

---

41 *passion-wounded Lamb* Christ; Swinburne was most drawn to Christ as a
victim of torture in his Passion   46–9 compare *Purgatorio* 5.134–6; the
addition of 'sacerdotal' to Dante's lines may be meant to imply a parallel
between La Pia's murderous husband and the Pope   55 *she* La Pia
56 *thee* Italy

CHARLES LANCELOT SHADWELL
(1840–1919)

Shadwell taught jurisprudence at Oriel College, Oxford and later became its Provost; he was a close friend of Walter Pater, with whom he travelled in Italy. In the preface to his *Purgatory*, Shadwell notes that *terza rima* 'is not an English metre', and explains that the verse form of his translation 'is that used by Andrew Marvell in his well-known Horatian *Ode to Cromwell*'. This form, he argues, allows him to preserve 'the arrangement into stanzas' of Dante's verse: 'nothing could be more unlike the *Commedia* than the versification of Byron's *Prophecy of Dante*, professing to be written in terza rima, but allowing the break between the sentences to occur at random, at any part of any verse'. Furthermore, 'the change in Marvell's stanza from the eight-syllable to the six-syllable couplet is peculiarly well adapted for introducing a subordinate clause, a reflexion, a simile, an illustration, a parenthetic statement of any kind . . . Such is frequently the use to which Dante puts the last line of a terzina'. (Recent stylometric studies largely confirm Shadwell's views.) Finally, 'there is a resemblance between the language of the two poets. Marvell, like Dante, can produce great effects by the use of very simple and homely words . . . On the other hand, they are alike in their employment, on occasion, of expressions outside the normal poetical vocabulary, as well as of images and ideas which belong to learning and science.' Introducing the translation, Pater remarked that 'for the modern student', living in 'an age of hope', 'the *Purgatorio* should be the favourite section of the *Divina Commedia*'; he found that, appropriately for purgatory, Shadwell's work showed 'all the patience of genius'.

Purgatorio 8

The hour was come that on the sea
Softens the heart with memory,
   The day on voyage sped
   Farewell to friends was said;
Then, if he hear the distant bell,
That seems the dying day to knell,
   Its sound hath power to move
   The new-bound pilgrim's love.
Began I then my ears to close,
And look upon a soul that rose,
   And seemed with outstretched hand
   My notice to demand.
Both palms he joined and upward raised,
And to the East he steadfast gazed,
   As though to God he cried,
   'I care for nought beside.'
'*Before the closing of the day*'
With lips devout I heard him pray:
   His notes so sweetly flowed,
   My soul went all abroad.
The others of that sweet-voiced choir
Followed him through the hymn entire,
   Their eyes devoutly given
   Unto the wheels of heaven.
Turn here, my Reader, turn thy sight
Upon the veil, so fine, so slight,
   'Twere easy now to win
   The secret hid within.

10

20

---

17 '*Before the closing . . .*' the penitent sings the 'Te lucis ante terminum', the
evening hymn sometimes attributed to St Ambrose; Dante quotes it in Latin,
as he does all the liturgical chants in *Purgatorio*   20 *abroad* Shadwell's
touch, along with the implied delight in travel   25 *Turn . . . turn* Shadwell
introduces this repetition, and also doubles the adjectives in the next line

I saw that noble army raise
In silence to the skies their gaze,   30
   Waiting what should befall,
   Pallid and humble all.
And angels twain I saw, that came
Out of the height with swords aflame,
   Swords that had been truncated,
   And of their points abated.
Green, as of leaflets newly born,
The plumage for their raiment worn,
   Drawn after in the wind
   Of their green wings behind.   40
One just above us took his rank:
One lighted on the other bank:
   Between them guarded were
   The people gathered there.
Their fair-haired foreheads I could trace,
But in the brightness of their face
   Was baffled all my sight,
   Quelled by excess of light.
'From Mary's bosom both are sped
'To guard the vale,' Sordello said   50
   'And foil that serpent's guile
   'That shall be here erewhile.'
Not knowing where he should appear,
I turned aside, all chilled with fear,
   To those sure arms, that still
   Could shelter me from ill.

37–40 *Green . . . green* Dante shares with Marvell a fondness for 'green' and
for fresh greenery; he is even more intent on the young leaves than Shadwell
conveys in his beautiful lines: 'green like little leaves just that very minute
born'.   50 *Sordello* the troubadour whom Virgil and Dante meet in
Purgatorio

Once more Sordello: 'Let us go
'Among the mighty shades below,
   'And speak with them: 'twere grace
60   'If they behold thy face.'
But paces three I deem I took
And reached the foot, where one did look
   On me, as though methought
   To know my face he sought.
Dark grew the air: but yet between
His eyes and mine there could be seen
   What late had been concealed,
   But now was all revealed.
Towards me he made and towards him I:
70 Ah! noble Judge, how joyfully
   Then, Nino, could I know
   Thou wast not lost below!
There lacked no salutation sweet
Betwixt us: then did he entreat:
   'When camest thou to this coast,
   'Those distant waters crossed?'
'Oh!' said I: 'Through the place of gloom
'Hither this morning have I come,
   'My second life to gain,
80   'Ere yet the first be ta'en.'
And, soon as they my answer knew,
He and Sordello backward drew,
   As turn in disarray
   Whom sudden fears dismay.
One Virgil sought: the other cried
Unto a soul that sate beside;
   'Up! Conrad, from thy place,
   'Come and behold God's grace.'

---

71 *Nino* Nino di Giovanni Visconti ruled Pisa in 1285 jointly with the
Ugolino who appears in *Inferno* 33; thereafter he was an important Guelf
leader until his death in 1296   87 *Conrad* identified at 157 below

Then to me turning: 'If from Heaven
'This privilege to thee be given   90
   'Of Him, who hides from man
   'His all un-fathomed plan,
'O'er the broad sea when thou art sped,
'Bid my Joanna's prayer be said
   'For me, where grace is lent
   'To pleading innocent.
'Her mother loves me not, I ween,
'Since changed her wimple white hath been:
   'Poor soul, that shall be fain
   'Those weeds to wear again!   100
'Right well may her example prove
'How brief the flame of woman's love,
   'Except by touch or sight
   'It often be relit.
'The viper on the Milan shield
'So brave a burial shall not yield,
   'As had been hers, in ground
   'Gallura's cock had found.'
'Twas thus he spake: and righteous zeal
Upon his front had set its seal,   110
   The measured fervour showing
   Within his bosom glowing.
My greedy eyes to heaven were turned,
Where stars of slowest motion burned,
   As wheel doth slower roll
   Nearer the axle bole.

---

98 *wimple white* a sign of mourning. After Nino died, his wife married
Galeazzo Visconti whose emblem, the viper, is mentioned at 105; 'Gallura's
cock' (108) is Nino's emblem   113 *greedy eyes* it is characteristic of
Shadwell's excellence as a translator that he does not shy away from Dante's
'*ghiotti*' ('greedy')

Then spake my Guide, 'What is't, my son,
'Thou lookest for there?' And I, 'Upon
   'Those torches three I gaze,
120   'That by yon pole-star blaze'
'Those stars thou sawest, those shining four,
'Since morn have sunk 'neath ocean's floor:
   'And these are mounted there
   'Where late the others were.'
And, even as that word was said,
His arms Sordello round him laid,
   With warning finger, 'See!
   'There comes our enemy.'
Upon the dell's unguarded side
130 I looked and saw a serpent glide:
   Haply from such did Eve
   That bitter meat receive.
The evil snake his way was wending,
His head about his body bending,
   The grass and flowers among,
   Like beast with slavering tongue.
Then in an instant from above
I saw those hawks celestial move:
   But in what wise they fell
140   I saw not, nor can tell.
And as by their green wings the air
Was cleft, the serpent fled ascare:
   With even flight the twain
   Turned to their posts again.
The shade, who at the Judge's call
Had joined him, through that onslaught all
   Swerved not a moment's space
   From looking on my face.

---

119 *torches three* a symbol of the three theological virtues, replacing that of the four cardinal virtues mentioned at 121   132 *meat* in the old sense of any sort of food   136 *with slavering tongue* in the original, the beast is preening itself   138 *hawks celestial* the angels of line 33

And he began: 'So may thy will
'With ample wax that candle fill   150
  'Which lights thee, till thou stand
  'On the enamelled strand,
'That crowns the mount, Oh! let thy speech
'Some news of Valdimagra teach,
  'And tell me of her state,
  'For there I once was great.
'There Conrad Malaspina's name,
'That ancient one's, of whom I came,
  'I bore: the love for mine
  'Was showed I here refine.'   160
'Oh! though your lands,' I said 'by me
'Were never seen, yet none there be,
  'In Europe's bounds that dwell,
  'Their fame that know not well.
'The glory of your house of worth,
'Its lords, its country, trumpets forth
  'In tones to reach the ear
  'Of those were never there.
'I swear (so may I reach the skies)
'Your noble race still bears the prize   170
  'Of all that purse or sword
  'To honour can afford.
'Though that false chief the world misdrive,
'Nature and wont such privilege give
  'To thine, they may not stray
  'Out of the perfect way.'

---

157 *Conrad Malaspina* Marquis of Villafranca in the Val di Magra; he died
in 1294   159–60 the original is less clotted: 'For my family I carried the
love which here is being refined'; Dante thought it possible to set too high a
value on family values   173 *false chief* perhaps the devil, perhaps the Pope

'Farewell,' he said 'but in that bed
'Times seven the Sun shall not be laid,
  'The bed by Aries hidden,
180   'With his four feet bestridden,
'Ere this fair thought by stouter nails
'Than aught that comes of others' tales
  'Be fastened in thy brain,
    'So judgment's course remain.'   (1892)

Paradiso 33

[St Bernard prays to the Virgin Mary]

'Maid, Mother, daughter of thy Son,
'Humble, yet high 'bove every one,
  'Predestined to fulfil
  'The everlasting will;
''Tis thou hast given to human nature
'Such nobleness in every feature,
  'His Maker deigned to take,
  'His self himself to make:
'Within thy womb was nursed the fire,
10 'Whereby was kindled Love's desire,
  'To feed the flower's increase,
  'In the Eternal Peace.
'To us within this place above
'Thou art the noonday torch of love,
  'Even as 'mongst those below
  'Hope's lively fount doth flow.

---

178 seven years will not have passed   179 *Aries* the constellation of the ram
  7–8 Shadwell clouds Bernard's meaning, which might more accurately be
rendered 'deigned to make himself its [human nature's] creation'
13–16 St Bernard's contrast is clearer in the original: 'Here you are for us the
noonday torch of charity, and down below, among mortals, you are the
living fountain of hope' – as Aquinas observed, hope is as non-existent in
heaven as in hell

'Lady, so great thy power, that he,
'Who asks for grace of aught but thee,
  'Seeks without wings to fly,
  'His wish to satisfy.   20
'Not he alone who claims thy aid
'Will by thy bounty be repaid;
  'Nay, more, thy goodness there
  'Ofttimes outruns the prayer.
'Mercy and pity both are thine;
'In thee magnificence will shine;
  'And all the creature's grace
  'Is gathered in thy face.
'Now he who from the lowest hold
'Hath seen the Universe unfold   30
  'The spirits every one,
  'Thy eyes to look upon,
'Prays thee for grace to win such might,
'As shall so far uplift his sight,
  'That he may mount above,
  'The height of bliss to prove.
'And I, that ne'er more fiercely burned,
'Till this my vision I discerned,
  'My prayers must pour to thee,
  '(And may they fruitful be)   40
'That thou by prayer will clear away
'All cloud that dims his mortal day,
  'So that the bliss supreme
  'May be revealed to him.
'Wherefore, O Queen, whose will is sure,
'I pray thee keep his longings pure,
  'And guide his steps aright,
  'After so great a sight.

---

28 *in thy face* Shadwell's addition   37–8 the original means 'I never burned
more for the sake of my own vision than I now burn for the sake of his'

'His human will do thou restrain:
'Beatris with her blessèd train
  'Turns her clasped hands on high,
  'My prayer to satisfy.'
The eyes, revered and loved of God,
Fixed fast upon the suppliant showed:
  Showed us how earnest prayer
  Is ever dear to Her.
Then to the light supreme returning,
Far beyond all our power's discerning,
  They passed where our endeavour
  Is barred from following ever.
When I, as duty bade, grew nigher,
To reach the goal of my desire,
  My ardent longings' call
  In me was ended all.
Bernardo then, with beckoning smile,
Bade me look upward for a while;
  Yet of myself I knew
  What he would have me do;
For clearer still my sight became,
And drew me farther through the flame
  Of that sublimest light,
  Which guides itself aright.
Thenceforth my eyes so far could reach
Beyond the power of human speech,
  That sight and memory fail
  To hold the wondrous tale.
As one who dreams, and when 'tis o'er,
The dream returns to him no more,
  While still within his breast
  Remains the thought impressed,

54 *the suppliant* St Bernard of Clairvaux (1090–1153), Cistercian abbot and contemplative, preacher of the second Crusade and tireless ecclesiastical networker; he was known as the '*doctor mellifluus*' on account of his lyrical style

So 'tis with me: that vision will,
Though all but spent, yet trickle still;
 Nor ever from my heart
 Its sweetness may depart.
'Tis thus the Sun unseals the snow;
Thus in the wind the light leaves blow;
 Thus was the Sibyl's lore
 Scattered for evermore.
Thou Light supreme, upraised on high,
Unseen by our mortality,   90
 O let my memory reach
 Somewhat thereof to teach;
And send one sparkle of Thy glory,
To aid me tell the wondrous story;
 And yet leave some behind
 To those of after kind.
For if my mind a little hold,
And somewhat in my verse be told,
 Greater will be the sense
 Of Thy pre-eminence.   100
Then had my eyes been turned away,
Nor dared to face that living ray,
 Bewildered I had been,
 Smit by its radiance keen.
Yet I remember how thereby
I bore that weight to satisfy,
 And make my gaze unite
 With Power infinite.
O boundless Grace, that bade me dare
Upon the Light Eternal there   110
 To fix my eyes, that so
 Its fullness I could know!

---

87 *Sibyl's lore* see Virgil's *Aeneid* 3.443–50

I saw within the depths profound
Love in a single volume bound,
 Which those below disperse
 Throughout the Universe.
Substance was there and accident,
Together in such fashion blent,
 One simple light was all
120 That I can here recall.
And I believe I saw the band,
Whereby the Universe is spanned;
 For as I speak, I feel
 The sense of coming weal.
One moment's sight as long appears
As five-and-twenty hundred years,
 Since Neptune's eyes were stayed,
 Fixed set on Argo's shade.
Even so my mind was there suspended
130 And all immovably attended,
 Whence in its constant gaze
 It grew to fiercer blaze.
For with that light there came such change,
That none elsewhere may ever range:
 To turn aside must be
 Impossibility.
Because the good, our will's desire,
Is there concentred and entire:
 And what is perfect there
140 Defective is elsewhere.

---

115 *those below disperse* in Dante the volume disperses (or more literally
'unbinds') itself 117–20 these lines are densely philosophical and Shadwell
struggles with them; they read more literally: 'entities, attributes and their
relations were so fused together that what I can say about it gives only the
merest glimpse' 128 *Argo's shade* the voyage of the Argonauts took place
in 1223 BCE, according to the usual medieval chronology

Henceforth my speech still more will fail,
To tell again the wondrous tale,
    Even than baby pressed
    Upon his mother's breast.
Yet was there but one single light,
In the live flame before my sight;
    For that can change no more
    From what it was before.
But as my vision stronger grew,
Even as I gazed, one single view   150
    About me ever ranged,
    As I myself was changed.
From the subsistence deep and clear,
In the high light I saw appear
    Three rays, of colours three,
    In one consistency.
As Iris will from Iris reach,
They seemed reflected each from each;
    And all on fire the third,
    By each and either stirred.   160
How weak my speech, how faint, beside
My thought; that too how poor when tried
    'Gainst what I saw, that all
    Would be accounted small.
O Light Eternal, set alone,
Who only to Thyself art known;
    And by Thyself hast won
    Thyself to smile upon!
That Ring by Thee conceived and made,
As in reflected light displayed,   170
    At first my eyes had won,
    Thyself to look upon:

---

157 *Iris* the rainbow   167–8, 171–2 the suggestive parallelism of these lines
is Shadwell's innovation

But soon within Itself It grew,
And to our image changed Its hue;
   Wherefore with fixed intent
   My gaze thereon was bent.
As the Geometer, whose mind
Is set the circle's square to find,
   And yet for all his pain
180   He cannot make it plain,
So was I at that novel sight;
I longed the clue to learn aright,
   How to the circle joined
   The image place could find.
Yet were my pinions all too weak,
Unto such lofty flight to seek,
   Till to my mind it came
   In flash of lightning flame.
Here failed the vision, yet my will
190   As even wheel was driven still
   By Love, that onward bears
   The Sun and all the stars.   (1915)

EUGENE JACOB LEE-HAMILTON
(1845–1907)

On his retirement from the diplomatic service because of ill
health in 1875, Lee-Hamilton went to live in Florence where
he started to write poetry, his most successful collection being
Sonnets of the Wingless Hours. In 1896 he recovered com-
pletely from his illness and soon married; his translation of
Inferno was published in 1898. Although unrhymed, its verse
recalls the hendecasyllabic metre of the *Commedia* because of
its frequent feminine endings (Eliot has a refined version of the
effect in the Dante pastiche of *Little Gidding* II).

Inferno 13 109–51

We were still listening to the trunk intently
  In the belief that it had more to tell us
  When we were overtaken by a noise
Like that which striketh him who heareth coming
  The boar and hunters from his place of lurking,
  And heareth animals and branches crashing.
And, lo, two men, adown the slope to leftwards,
  Naked and torn, were fleeing with such swiftness
  That they were breaking all the forest tangle.
The one ahead: 'Now Death, O hasten, hasten!'   10
  The while the other, who had fain run faster,
  Was crying: 'Lano, thou hadst not such nimble
Legs on occasion of the jousts of Toppo':
  And then, perhaps because his breath was failing,
  He made one heap of self and of a bush there.
Behind them, all the forest was full crowded
  With swarthy bitches, eager and a-running
  Like sleuth-hounds that at last have slipped their
      leashes.
They stuck their fangs into the one who'd fallen,
  And they proceeded bit by bit to tear him,   20
  And then they carried off those aching members.
My Escort took me by the hand thereafter,
  And led me to the bush there that was wailing,
  Through all its bleeding fractures, to no purpose.

---

1 *the trunk* of Pier della Vigna, who has just finished telling his tale
10 *'Now Death, O hasten, hasten!'* the original has an untranslatable string
of urgent elisions and internal rhymes ('*Or accorri, accorri, morte!*')
12 *Lano* perhaps one Ercolano Maconi, said by Boccaccio to be a
spendthrift   13 *Toppo* a battle between Siena and Arezzo in 1288
19 *fangs* 'teeth' was enough for Dante

'O Jacopo,' it said, 'of Sant Andréa,
  What hast thou gained by making me a bulwark?
  What share had *I* in thy nefarious living?'
Then, when the Master stopped and stood above it,
  He said: 'Who wast thou, who from all those tips
      there
30 Dost breathe with blood thy utterance of anguish?'
And it to us: 'O souls that are come hither
  To set your eyes upon the sorry rending
  That thus hath parted these my branches from me,
Collect them at the foot of the sad bush here:
  I once was of the town which for the Baptist
  Changed its first patron; who, for that mere reason,
Will ever with his art now make it wretched.
  And were it not, that at the Arno's crossing
  Some vestige of this presence still remaineth,
40 Those citizens who afterwards rebuilt it
  Upon the ash that Attila had left there,
  Would have performed their labour to no
      purpose.
I made myself a gibbet of my houses.'   (1898)

MELVILLE BEST ANDERSON (1851–1933)

Anderson was a professor of English at Stanford which was,
like several universities in the United States, blessed with a
'Dante circle'. In 1916 he published a pamphlet of verse whose
attacks on the neutrality of the United States in the First World
War hark back to some of Dante's political invectives. When

---

25 *Jacopo* follower of Frederick II and a famous prodigal
  35 *the town* Florence, whose first patron was Mars, the god of war
39 *Some vestige* a fragment of a statue of Mars remained on the Ponte
Vecchio until 1333   41 *Attila* Villani reports a legend that Florence was
sacked by Attila the Hun (d. 453)   43 the canto ends with these words,
leaving Virgil's question unanswered

his version of the *Commedia* appeared, Anderson acknow-
ledged the assistance of Charles Eliot Norton, offered, he says,
'although believing me to be just another "Childe Roland at
the Dark Tower"'.

Inferno 16   106–36

I had a cord that girt my garment in,
   For with it I had once thought requisite
   To take the leopard of the painted skin.
As soon as I had loosed it from me quite,
   To the commandment of my Guide submiss,
   I reacht it to him, coiled and wound up tight
Whereon he turned toward the right, and this,
   A little out beyond the verge, did fling
   Down into that precipitous abyss.
'Now surely it must be that some new thing,'   10
   I said within, 'answer the signal new
   Which thus the Master's eye is following.'
Ah me! how cautious should men be and do
   Near those who witness not alone the deeds,
   But with their wisdom to the thoughts look
      through!
He said to me: 'What I expect must needs
   Come upward soon, and what thy dreams now ask
   Must soon be such that very eyesight heeds.' –
Aye to that truth concealed beneath false mask,
   A man should close his lips, if in him lies,   20
   Lest he, though blameless, should be brought to
      task;
But here I cannot: by the harmonies
   Of this my Comedy, Reader, I swear,
   So may their grace be lasting, that mine eyes

---

3 *the leopard* see *Inferno* 1.42

Saw through the gross and gloomy atmosphere
    A shape come swimming up, of such as be
    To every steadfast heart a thing of fear:
As he returns who sometime dives, to free
    The anchor-fluke, lest vessel come to harm
30   On reef, or aught else hidden in the sea,
Who draws his foot in, and flings up his arm.

17   1-27

'Behold the beast with pointed tail, whose guile
    Doth mountains cleave and walls and weapons
        rend;
    Behold him who doth all the world defile.'
So spoke to me my Leader and my friend;
    And that it come in shoreward beckoned it,
    Near where the trodden marbles make an end.
Then forward came that filthy counterfeit
    Image of Fraud to land its head and bust,
40   But drew not up its tail from out the pit.
Its face was like the face of person just,
    So outwardly benignant was its hue,
    But like a serpent all the rest outthrust.
Paws shaggy to the armpits it had two;
    And many a painted nooselet, many a quirk
    The back, the breast, and both the flanks bestrew.
Never was cloth by Tartar woven or Turk,
    More variously colored, warp and woof,
    Nor yet such tissue did Arachne work.
50   As along shore the wherries lie aloof
    At times, in water part and part on land;
    And as the beaver in his hunt's behoof

---

32 *the beast* later named as Geryon   49 *Arachne* proud of her skill at
spinning, she challenged Minerva to a competition – see Ovid's
Metamorphoses 6.1–145 for the result

Doth yonder 'mid the guzzling Germans stand:
  So lay that worst of beasts along the stone
  That forms the margin fencing in the sand.
All quivering in the void the tail was thrown,
  Twisting aloft the point of it, that bare
  A venomed fork as in the scorpion.   (1921)

DAVID JAMES MACKENZIE (1855–1925)

Mackenzie was Sheriff-Substitute at Lerwick, Wick, Kilmarnock and Glasgow, and author of one book of essays, *Byways among Books*, and a volume of *Poems*. His translation of the *Commedia* was published posthumously.

Purgatorio 23   16–75

As thoughtful travellers, meeting on the way
  some whom they know not, turn about to gaze,
  but do not for this cause their footsteps stay,
So, from behind, more rapid in their pace
  o'ertaking us, and passing, came a throng
  of shades devout who used no spoken phrase.
The eyes of each with hollow gloom were hung,
  their faces pale, so haggard that the skin
  tight to the moulding of the cheek-bones clung.
Nor do I dream that Erisichthon's sin   10
  brought him such expiation, when in dread
  of hunger he was wasted all and thin.

---

1 *travellers* 'pilgrims' in the original   10 *Erisichthon* he was afflicted by hunger for having cut down a tree sacred to Ceres

'These must be they,' within my mind I said,
   'who, mad with hunger, lost Jerusalem
   when on her child the woman Mary fed.'
Each eye seemed like a ring without its gem
   and those who read an OMO in the face
   of men would there distinguish but the M.
Who, ignorant, would imagine that their case
20   arose from that alluring fruit and spring,
   raising desires that on them left this trace?
Already deep I wondered at this thing
   that seemed the cause of their pale meagreness
   and of the scurf that did about them cling,
When lo, from out his hollow front's recess
   a shade cast eyes on me, and with stern gaze
   cried out, 'What grace here lessens my distress?'
Never should I have known him by his face,
   but from his voice did recognition flow
30   that his changed countenance had served to erase.
From this sole spark was sudden lit the glow
   of memory, and in that face so marred
   I did the features of Foresè know.
'Oh, do not gaze on that which has so scarred
   my skin,' he prayed, 'nor at the blots which blight
   my flesh, that on your pitying eyes has jarred.
But tell me truth about yourself. Tell right
   who these are that walk with you. Do not stay
   silent with me: some converse I invite.'

---

15 *the woman Mary fed* during the siege of Jerusalem in 70 CE; Mackenzie
blenches from the exact meaning of the original: 'when Mary stuck her beak
into her son'   17 *OMO* it was widely believed at the time that the word
'*omo*' ('man') could be read in each face: the 'o's formed by the eyes and the
'm' by the superciliary arches and the nose   27 *lessens my distress* there is
no implication of analgesia in the original, which means 'what is this favour
that has been granted me?'   33 *Foresè* Forese Donati, brother of Piccarda
whom Dante will encounter in *Paradiso* 3; he and Dante were friends and
exchanged satirical poems in which Dante mocks Forese's gluttony

'Your face,' I said, 'which once upon a day 40
  I wept in death, now more for pity cries
  and tears, – such awful change does it display.
So, in God's name, declare what agonies
  have stripped you thus, and do not bid me speak,
  for he speaks ill whose mind in wonder lies.'
Then he to me, 'In yonder water seek
  the virtue fallen from the Eternal Mind,
  and in that tree, whence I am wan and weak.
All these, whose song with weeping is combined,
  in hunger and thirst their souls here purify 50
  from greed to which they were too much inclined.
This fruit's sweet scent, wafted as we go by,
  and this fresh spray which falls upon the leaves
  our spirits do with longing sorely try.
Not only once our mind this pain receives
  circling this path, – pain do I say? 'Twould be
  more just to say this wish our pain relieves.
And this desire draws us towards the tree
  and the glad Christ who 'Eli' cried, what time
  His blood the souls of men from sin set free.' 60
  (1927)

GEORGE MUSGRAVE (1855–1923)

Musgrave was a barrister in the Middle Temple. In defence of the verse form of his translation (for which compare the precedent set by Robert Morehead), he pleaded 'since we have no characteristic English measure wherein the lines run *in threes*, there should be no antecedent prejudice against an attempt to apply the most characteristic of all our metres – the *nine-line* Spenserian Stanza – to a rendering of a poem whose verses run in triplets, and, in a surprising number of cases, in *triplets of triplets*'.

---

47 *virtue* in the sense of 'power'   59 *what time* on the cross; see Matthew 27:46

Inferno 23   37–126

[The grotesque demons from *Inferno* 21 and 22 pursue Dante and Virgil.]

So, sudd'n, my Guide, upsnatching me in his arm –
    Just as a mother would upsnatch her son,
When, wak'd by cries of 'Fire,' all in alarm
    (Less thinking of herself than little one)
    She seizes him and flees, nor stops to don
Even the covering of a shift, – down sank
    Right on the hard rock's border, till, anon,
Giving himself to the next Gully's flank,
He, sliding on his back, shot down the pendant bank.

10   Never raced water thro' a conduit faster
    To turn a water-wheel, when rapidest
It shoots towards the paddles, than my Master
    Thus, from the summit of the shelving crest,
    Down-glided, holding me upon his breast,
Not as a Comrade, but as his own Son!
    Howbeit, barely had his feet found rest
Against the Trench's bottom, when upon
The height above They showed: but fear it gave
        him none.

For, by the high decree of Providence,
20   As Ministrants of the FIFTH Torture-place,
None had the power of ever issuing thence.
    Below, we came upon a painted race,
    Who, round and round, with dull slow steps
        did pace,

---

22 *race* the pun is not in the Italian

Weary, bowed down, and weeping. A long cape
   Each wore. Their eyes and all their upper face
Were hidden in deep hoods, made in the shape
Of those that at Cologne the Monkish Brethren drape.

Outside, all gilt to dazzling us they were;
   Within, all lead, that weighed so heavily,
That Frederick's Mantles seemèd by compare   30
   Mere straw to them! O, for eternity
   What weary, weary wearing! Leftward we
Swerved and walked with them, hearing how they
      wept;
   But, 'neath their great gross loads, so tardily
They staggered on, that evermore we kept
New company at our hip, with every step we stept.

Wherefore I spake: 'While now we thus proceed,
   'Strive, Master, if thy keener gaze may reach
'Some Sufferer known to thee by name or deed.'
   Then One, who recognised my Tuscan speech,   40
   Cried after us: 'O stay ye, I beseech,
'Ye who are running on at such a rate
   'Here thro' the dark, for haply I can teach
'The thing thou askest.' Whence to me: 'Now wait,'
My Guide said, turning round – 'then suit to his thy
      gait.'

Halting, I saw Two by their looks bewray
   Great eagerness of mind to reach my side;
Howbeit their burden and the narrow way
   Kept them arear. At length – toiled up – they eyed

---

27 *Cologne* the Italian '*Clugnì*' (though the text is uncertain here) probably
refers not to Cologne but to the great Benedictine monastery of Cluny in
Burgundy   30 *Frederick's Mantles* legend attributed to the Emperor
Frederick II a method of punishment involving lead suits   31–32 Musgrave
introduces the repetition and paronomasia, as again in line 36

50   Silent a while my form, with glance aside,
        Then each to other faced, and, whispering, said:
            'Yon, by his throat, seems never to have died!
        'Or, by what privilege, if both be dead,
    'Go they unmantled here of the ponderous stole of lead?

        'O Tuscan! Thou that comest to the college
            'Of the sad Hypocrites' – to me they said,
        'Who thou mayst be, spurn not to give us knowledge.'
            'By Arno's Beauteous Stream,' I answerèd,
            'In The Great City was I born and bred,
60   'And wear the body I have always holden.
            'But who are ye, adown whose cheeks is shed
            'Such spilth of tears as I have now beholden?
    'And what this punishment that shines on ye so golden?'

        'These orange cowls, under whose weight we wail,
            'Are, oh, so leaden gross,' One answered me,
            'We tremble 'neath them like a creaking scale!
            'Both Jovial Friars, and Bolognese were we,
            'I Catalàno named, Loderingo he;
        'Together chosen by your City, where
70   ''Tis wont to have one only, party-free,
        'To be her peace-preserver. What we were
    'Gardigno's wasted ward doth to this day declare!'

        'Ah! Friars, your crime' . . . I had begun to say,
            But stopt; for lo! a Culprit caught mine eyes
        Cross-fixt, with rivets three, athwart the way;
            Who, when he saw me, in his agonies

---

62 *spilth* spillage   67 *Jovial Friars* or 'Frati Godenti', members of the
Knighthood of the Glorious Virgin Mary, founded at Bologna in 1261
68 CATALÀNO . . . LODERINGO joint governors of Florence in 1266–7
72 *Gardigno's wasted ward* part of Florence, ravaged by a popular rebellion
thought to have been fomented by the two friars

Blew thro' his bush of beard a storm of sighs.
But Friar CATALÀNO forward leant
   And said to me: 'HE WHO TRANSFIXÈD LIES,
   'And over whom thou porest thus intent,   80
'Counselling the Pharisees, said 'twas expedient

'That One Man suffer for the people. Now
   'The bare-strip wretch, transverse upon the way,
   'Must ever feel each Passer's weight, as thou
   'Perceivest. So his CONSORT'S FATHER, yea
   'And EVERY OTHER of THAT COUNCIL, – they
Who sowed such ill for Jewry – in this foss
   Are lying stretcht.' – Then saw I Virgil stay
And gaze with wonder at him on his cross
Thus in vile exile rackt and everlasting loss.   (1893)   90

STEPHEN PHILLIPS (1864–1915)

Phillips was related on his mother's side to Wordsworth, dis-
tantly; Churton Collins saved him from a career in the civil
service by discovering him as a poet. His first book, *Orestes
and other Poems*, appeared in 1884. *Paolo and Francesca*,
written in 1900, was first performed in 1902 and its author was
acclaimed as 'the successor of Sophocles and Shakespeare, and
his royalties rose to £150 a week' (*DNB*). He wrote plays on
Herod (1901), *Ulysses* (1902), *Nero* (1906), etc. Phillips was
not the only writer to theatricalize Dante: between 1825 and
1914 there were more than twenty operas based on *Inferno* 5
alone.

---

77 *bush . . . storm* Musgrave's additions   79 *HE WHO . . .* Caiaphas; see
John 18:14   85 *CONSORT'S FATHER* Annas, the high priest   87 *foss* ditch
89–90 the original says only 'he who was stretched out on a cross so vilely in
eternal exile'

Paolo and Francesca   III.iii.40–91
[Compare *Inferno* 5.127–38]

PAOLO. What is that book you read? Now fades the last
Star to the East: a mystic breathing comes:
And all the leaves once quivered, and were still.
FRANCESCA. It is the first, the faint stir of the dawn.
PAOLO. So still it is that we might almost hear
The sigh of all the sleepers in the world.
FRANCESCA. And all the rivers running to the sea.
PAOLO. What is't you read?
FRANCESCA.   It is an ancient tale.
PAOLO. Show it to me. Is it some drowsy page
10 That reading low I might persuade your eyes
At last to sleep?
FRANCESCA.   It is the history
  Of two who fell in love long years ago;
  And wrongly fell.
PAOLO.   How wrongly?
FRANCESCA.   Because she
  Already was a wife, and he who loved
  Was her own husband's dear familiar friend.
PAOLO. Was it so long ago?
FRANCESCA.   So long ago.
PAOLO. What were their famous and unlucky names?
FRANCESCA. Men called him Launcelot, her Guenevere.
Here is the page where I had ceased to read.
PAOLO. [*Taking book*.] Their history is blotted with new
20   tears.
FRANCESCA. The tears are mine: I know not why I wept.
But these two were so glad in their wrong love:
It was their joy; it was their helpless joy.
PAOLO. Shall I read on to you where you have paused?

---

7 compare *Inferno* 5.98–9

FRANCESCA. Here is the place: but read it low and sweet.
Put out the lamp!   [PAOLO *puts out the lamp.*
PAOLO.   The glimmering page is clear.
  [*Reading.*] 'Now on that day it chanced that Launcelot,
  Thinking to find the King, found Guenevere
  Alone; and when he saw her whom he loved,
  Whom he had met too late, yet loved the more;   30
  Such was the tumult at his heart that he
  Could speak not, for her husband was his friend,
  His dear familiar friend: and they two held
  No secret from each other until now;
  But were like brothers born' – my voice breaks off.
  Read you a little on.
FRANCESCA. [*Reading.*] 'And Guenevere,
Turning, beheld him suddenly whom she
Loved in her thought, and even from that hour
When first she saw him; for by day, by night,
Though lying by her husband's side, did she   40
Weary for Launcelot, and knew full well
How ill that love! and yet that love how deep!'
I cannot see – the page is dim: read you.
PAOLO. [*Reading.*] 'Now they two were alone, yet could not
    speak;
But heard the beating of each other's hearts.
He knew himself a traitor but to stay,
Yet could not stir: she pale and yet more pale
Grew till she could no more, but smiled on him.
Then when he saw that wished smile, he came
Near to her and still near, and trembled; then   50
Her lips all trembling kissed.'
FRANCESCA. [*Drooping towards him.*] Ah, Launcelot!
                       [*He kisses her on the lips.*
            CURTAIN   (1900)

___

51 *Inferno* 5.136

W. B. YEATS (1865–1939)

Yeats had no Italian and admitted in 1917 'I am no Dante scholar and I but read him in Shadwell or in Dante Rossetti'. His sense of Dante was also formed by his study of Blake; his 1897 essay on Blake's illustrations for the *Commedia* espouses some Blakean slants on the poem, as in the claim that 'Dante, who deified law, selected its antagonist, passion, as the most important of sins, and made the regions where it was punished the largest' whereas for Dante passion is not a sin at all, and incontinent appetite (which Yeats mistakes for passion) is the least grave cause of sin. References in Yeats's prose show that he had a wide acquaintance with Dante's works, including, for example, the *Convivio*. Still, Dante for Yeats was rather a cult-figure than a particular reality, though Yeats's ear may have been affected by Dante's rhythms as he heard them through Rossetti (and later through the early work of Pound): note the tendency to hendecasyllables in the first extract, where about one third of the lines have eleven syllables, and the transformative shift to an eleven-syllable line at the end of 'Cuchulain Comforted'.

Ego Dominus Tuus   1–37

Hic.   On the grey sand beside the shallow stream
          Under your old wind-beaten tower, where still
          A lamp burns on beside the open book
          That Michael Robartes left, you walk in the moon,

---

title from *Vita Nuova* 3; Rossetti, in whose version Yeats read the work, translates the relevant passage of Dante's vision: 'I discerned the figure of a lord of terrible aspect . . . Speaking he said many things, among the which I could understand but few; and of these, this: *Ego dominus tuus* ["I am thy master"]'   1 *Hic* Latin for 'this one'   4 *Michael Robartes* a recurrent figure in Yeats's do-it-yourself mythology; he is often associated with esoteric religions

And, though you have passed the best of life, still
   trace
Enthralled by the unconquerable delusion,
Magical shapes.

Ille.   By the help of an image
I call to my own opposite, summon all
That I have handled least, least looked upon.

Hic.   And I would find myself and not an image.   10

Ille.   That is our modern hope, and by its light
We have lit upon the gentle, sensitive mind
And lost the old nonchalance of the hand;
Whether we have chosen chisel, pen or brush,
We are but critics, or but half create,
Timid, entangled, empty and abashed,
Lacking the countenance of our friends.

Hic.   And yet
The chief imagination of Christendom,
Dante Alighieri, so utterly found himself
That he has made that hollow face of his   20
More plain to the mind's eye than any face
But that of Christ.

Ille.   And did he find himself
Or was the hunger that had made it hollow
A hunger for the apple on the bough
Most out of reach? and is that spectral image
The man that Lapo and that Guido knew?

---

7 *Ille* Latin for 'that one'   20–22 Yeats was probably thinking of the
'Bargello' portrait, supposedly by Giotto; both this and the many 'death
masks' of Dante are of dubious authenticity
24 *hunger for the apple* compare *Purgatorio* 23.22–4, 61–75
26 *Lapo . . . Guido* alluding to the sonnet 'Guido, i' vorrei', for translations
of which see the versions by Hayley and Shelley, above

I think he fashioned from his opposite
An image that might have been a stony face
Staring upon a Bedouin's horse-hair roof
30   From doored and windowed cliff, or half upturned
Among the coarse grass and the camel-dung.
He set his chisel to the hardest stone.
Being mocked by Guido for his lecherous life,
Derided and deriding, driven out
To climb that stair and eat that bitter bread,
He found the unpersuadable justice, he found
The most exalted lady loved by a man.
                    (written 1915; published 1917)

Cuchulain Comforted

A man that had six mortal wounds, a man
Violent and famous, strode among the dead;
Eyes stared out of the branches and were gone.

Then certain shrouds that muttered head to head
Came and were gone. He leant upon a tree
As though to meditate on wounds and blood.

A Shroud that seemed to have authority
Among those bird-like things, came, and let fall
A bundle of linen. Shrouds by two and three

---

33 *Guido* Cavalcanti; Yeats may be referring to the Cavalcanti sonnet
translated by Rossetti as 'I come to thee by daytime constantly'
35 compare *Paradiso* 17.58–60
   1 *A man* Cuchulain, the legendary Irish king, who often figures in Yeats's
work; see especially his play, *The Death of Cuchulain*   3 *Eyes stared* for
these animated trees and the 'bird-like things' of line 8, compare *Inferno*
13.4–15, 31–3; Dorothy Wellesley reported that Yeats wrote this poem
first in prose though he always planned to cast it eventually in *terza rima,*
which suggests that he thought of it as a response to Dante's vision of the
afterlife.

Came creeping up because the man was still.   10
And thereupon that linen-carrier said:
'Your life can grow much sweeter if you will

'Obey our ancient rule and make a shroud;
Mainly because of what we only know
The rattle of those arms makes us afraid.

'We thread the needles' eyes, and all we do
All must together do.' That done, the man
Took up the nearest and began to sew.

'Now must we sing and sing the best we can,
But first you must be told our character: 20
Convicted cowards all, by kindred slain

'Or driven from home and left to die in fear.'
They sang, but had nor human tunes nor words,
Though all was done in common as before;

They had changed their throats and had the throats
    of birds.
    January 13, 1939

RICHARD LE GALLIENNE (1866–1947)

Le Gallienne's first book of verse, *My Ladies' Sonnets*, was
privately printed in 1887 and he continued to produce volumes
in the vein of demure amorousness implied by that title (*A
Jongleur Strayed*, *The Lonely Dancer*) as well as successful
romantic novels such as *The Quest of the Golden Girl* (1896);
he contributed to the *Yellow Book* and formed the Rhymers'
Club along with other Nineties luminaries such as Yeats and
Lionel Johnson. He eventually moved to the United States and
then to France, whose government honoured him in 1938 for
From a Paris Scrapbook, 'the best book of the year written
about France by a foreigner'.

Paolo and Francesca 109–171
[Compare *Inferno* 5.127–38]

The world grew sweet with wonder in the west
    The while he read and while she listened there,
And many a dream from out its silken nest
    Stole like a curling incense through the air;
    Yet looked she not on him, nor did he dare:
But when the lovers kissed in Paradise
    His voice sank and he turned his gaze on her,
Like a young bird that flutters ere it flies, –
And lo! a shining angel called him from her eyes.

10   Then from the silence sprang a kiss like flame,
    And they hung lost together; while around
The world was changed, no more to be the same
    Meadow or sky, no little flower or sound
    Again the same, for earth grew holy ground:
While in the silence of the mounting moon
    Infinite love throbbed in the straining bound
Of that great kiss, the long-delaying boon,
Granted indeed at last, but ended, ah! so soon.

As the great sobbing fulness of the sea
20   Fills to the throat some void and aching cave,
Till all its hollows tremble silently,
    Pressed with sweet weight of softly-lapping wave:
    So kissed those mighty lovers glad and brave.

---

2 *he read* in the original, they read together with no gendered distribution of
the roles of reader and listener   6 *in Paradise* Le Gallienne has changed their
reading-matter, for Lancelot and Guinevere were not in Paradise
11 *lost* the word has none of the weight its equivalent carries in Dante

And as a sky from which the sun has gone
    Trembles all night with all the stars he gave –
A firmament of memories of the sun, –
So thrilled and thrilled each life when that great kiss
      was done.

But coward shame that had no word to say
    In passion's hour, with sudden icy clang
Slew the bright morn, and through the tarnished
      day   30
    An iron bell from light to darkness rang:
    She shut her ears because a throstle sang,
She dare not hear the little innocent bird,
    And a white flower made her poor head to hang –
To be so white! once she was white as curd,
But now – 'Alack!' 'Alack!' She speaks no other word.

The pearly line on yonder hills afar
    Within the dawn, when mounts the lark and
      sings
By the great angel of the morning star, –
    That was his love, and all free fair fresh things   40
    That move and glitter while the daylight springs:
To thus know love, and yet to spoil love thus!
    To lose the dream – O silly beating wings –
Great dream so splendid and miraculous:
O Lord, O Lord, have mercy, have mercy upon us.

She turned her mind upon the holy ones
    Whose love lost here was love in heaven tenfold,
She thought of Lucy, that most blessed of nuns
    Who sent her blue eyes on a plate of gold

---

48 *Lucy* St Lucy, a fourth-century virgin martyr from Siracusa in Sicily; she
was not a nun

50 To him who wooed her daily for her love –
'Mine eyes!' 'Mine eyes!' 'Here, – go in peace, they
        are!'
But ever love came through the midnight grove,
Young Love, with wild eyes watching from afar,
And called and called and called until the morning
        star.

Ah, poor Francesca, 'tis not such as thou
    That up the stony steeps of heaven climb;
Take thou thy heaven with thy Paolo now –
    Sweet saint of sin, saint of a deathless rhyme,
    Song shall defend thee at the bar of Time,
60 Dante shall set thy fair young glowing face
    On the dark background of his theme sublime,
And Thou and He in your superb disgrace
Still on that golden wind of passion shall embrace.
        (1892)

LAURENCE BINYON (1869–1943)

Binyon won the Newdigate Prize at Oxford for a poem about
Persephone. From 1893, he worked at the British Museum, first
in the printed books department and then (more congenially,
for he was himself a painter) as assistant keeper of drawings; he
published many art-historical works – on seventeenth-century
Dutch etchings, *Painting in the Far East* (1908), and Blake's
woodcuts and engravings. He planned a huge poetic drama
about Merlin, of which only the first part was completed (*The
Madness of Merlin*, 1947). Pound enthusiastically welcomed
Binyon's *Inferno* in 1934, approving his 'courageous' and
'sound' principle that 'melodious smoothness is not the char-
acteristic of Dante's verse'; Lowell, on the other hand, found

---

63 *golden wind* the wind of *Inferno* 5 is 'dark'

Binyon's diction 'cramped and knotted' with the result that the reader is 'constantly looking at the Italian to discover what Binyon was saying'.

Purgatorio 27   1–114

As when his first beams tremble in the sky
   There, where his own Creator shed his blood,
   While Ebro is beneath the Scales on high,
And noon scorches the wave on Ganges' flood,
   Such was the sun's height; day was soon to pass;
   When the angel of God joyful before us stood.
Outside the flames, above the bank, he was.
   Beati mundo core we heard him sing
   In a voice more living far than comes from us.
Then 'None goes further, if first the fire not sting.   10
   O hallowed spirits, enter unafraid
   And to the chant beyond let your ears cling.'
When we were near him, this to us he said.
   Wherefore I, when I knew what his words meant,
   Became as one who in the grave is laid.
Over my clasping hands forward I leant,
   Eyeing the fire, and vivid to my mind
   Men's bodies burning, once beheld, it sent.
Then toward me turned them both my escorts kind;
   And Virgil said to me: 'O my son, here   20
   Torment, may-be, but death thou shalt not find.

1–5 Dante indicates time on a global clock: it is dawn over Jerusalem; at the extreme West (Spain) midnight; at the extreme East (India) noon; sunset in Purgatory   2 *There* Jerusalem   7 *the flames* the fire which purges the lustful in the previous canto   8 *Beati . . .* Matthew 5:8, 'Blessed are the pure in heart'   12 *let your ears cling* the strained metaphor is not in the original – 'don't be deaf to the singing beyond'   17–18 the syntactic inversion here is Binyon's (as are the inversions at 7, 13, 21, etc.)

Remember, O remember . . . and if thy fear
  On Geryon into safety I recalled,
  What shall I do now, being to God more near?
If thou within this womb of flames wert walled
  Full thousand years, for certainty believe
  That not of one hair could they make thee bald.
And if perchance thou think'st that I deceive,
  Go forward into them, and thy faith prove,
30 With hands put in the edges of thy sleeve.
Out of thy heart all fear remove, remove!
  Turn hither and come confidently on!'
  And I stood fixed and with my conscience strove.
When he beheld me still and hard as stone,
  Troubled a little, he said: 'Look now, this same
  Wall is 'twixt Beatrice and thee, my son.'
As Pyramus at the sound of Thisbe's name
  Opened his dying eyes and gazed at her
  Then, when the crimson on the mulberry came,
40 So did I turn unto my wise Leader,
  My hardness melted, hearing the name told
  Which like a well-spring in my mind I bear.
Whereon he shook his head, saying: 'Do we hold
  Our wish to stay on this side?' He smiled then
  As on a child by an apple's bribe cajoled.
Before me then the fire he entered in,
  Praying Statius that he follow at his heel
  Who for a long stretch now had walked between.
When I was in, I had been glad to reel
50 Therefrom to cool me, into boiling glass,
  Such burning beyond measure did I feel.

---

23 *Geryon* see *Inferno* 17   25 *womb* 'bowels' is closer to the word Dante
uses ('*alvo*')   31 *remove, remove!* the repetitions here (as at 22) are in the
Italian   37 *Pyramus* . . . see Ovid's *Metamorphoses* 4.55–166

My sweet Father, to give me heart of grace,
   Continued only on Beatrice to descant,
   Saying: 'Already I seem to see her face.'
On the other side, to guide us, rose a chant,
   And we, intent on that alone to dwell,
   Came forth there, where the ascent began to slant.
And there we heard a voice *Venite* hail
   Benedicti patris mei out of light
   So strong, it mastered me and made me quail.   60
'The sun departs,' it added; 'comes the night.
   Tarry not; study at good pace to go
   Before the west has darkened on your sight.'
Straight rose the path within the rock, and so
   Directed onward, that I robbed the ray
   Before me from the sun, already low.
I and my sages few steps did assay
   When by the extinguished shadow we perceived
   That now behind us had sunk down the day.
And ere the horizon had one hue received   70
   In all the unmeasured regions of the air,
   And night her whole expansion had achieved,
Each of us made his bed upon a stair,
   Seeing that the nature of the mount o'ercame
   Alike the power to ascend and the desire.
As goats, now ruminating, though the same
   That, before feeding, brisk and wanton played
   On the high places of the hills, grow tame,
Silent, while the sun scorches, in the shade,
   Watched by the herd that props him hour by hour   80
   Upon his staff and, propt so, tends his trade;

---

52 *to give me heart of grace* the original means 'to encourage me'
58 *Venite* Matthew 25:34, 'Come, ye blessed of my Father'
80 *herd* herdsman

And as the shepherd, lodging out-of-door,
　　Watches night-long in quiet by his flock,
　　Wary lest wild beast scatter it or devour;
Such were we then, all three, within that nook,
　　I as a goat, they as a shepherd, there,
　　On this and that side hemmed by the high rock.
Little could there of the outside things appear;
　　But through that little I saw the stars to glow
90　　Bigger than ordinary and shine more clear.
Ruminating and grazing on them so
　　Sleep took me; sleep which often will apprize
　　Of things to come, and ere the event foreknow.
In the hour, I think, when first from Eastern skies
　　Upon the mountain Cytherea beamed
　　Whom fire of love forever glorifies,
A lady young and beautiful I seemed
　　To see move through a plain and flower on flower
　　To gather; singing, she was saying (I dreamed),
100　　'Let them know, whoso of my name inquire,
　　That I am Leah, and move my fingers fair
　　Around, to make me a garland for a tire.
To glad me at the glass I deck me here;
　　But never to her mirror is untrue
　　My sister Rachel, and sits all day there.
She is fain to hold her beauteous eyes in view
　　As me with these hands I am fain to adorn:
　　To see contenteth her, and me to do.'
Already, through the splendour ere the morn,
110　　Which to wayfarers the more grateful shows,
　　Lodging less far from home, where they return,

---

94 *In the hour* just before dawn; 'Cytherea' is another name for Venus, the
morning star　101 *Leah* for the story of Leah and Rachel, see Genesis 29,
30 and 49; the Church traditionally allegorized Leah as the active life and
Rachel as the contemplative　102 *for a tire* as an adornment

    The shadows on all sides were fleeing, and close
       On them my sleep fled; wherefore, having seen
    The great masters risen already, I rose.
    (1938)

G. K. CHESTERTON (1874–1936)

After studying art at the Slade and English literature at London University, Chesterton worked as a journalist, engaging in controversies with figures such as Bernard Shaw and H. G. Wells. He was a libertarian anti-imperialist, or 'Little Englander', who eventually developed his own rubicund form of Catholic orthodoxy (he was received into the Church in 1922), which he promulgated in works of polemic, fantastical novels and, with most popular success, after 1911, in the 'Father Brown' stories. Etienne Gilson called his *St Thomas Aquinas* (1933) 'the best book on St Thomas that has ever been written'.

The Beatific Vision [*Paradiso* 33.49–72]

    Then Bernard smiled at me, that I should gaze
       But I had gazed already; caught the view,
    Faced the unfathomable ray of rays
       Which to itself and by itself is true.

    Then was my vision mightier than man's speech;
       Speech snapt before it like a flying spell;
    And memory and all that time can teach
       Before that splendid outrage failed and fell.

---

1 *Bernard* St Bernard of Clairvaux, who has just completed his hymn to Mary   4 *true* the true light in John 1:9 is Christ, the Incarnate Word
6 *snapt before* the Italian says only that speech 'yields to' such a vision
8 *splendid outrage* a Chestertonian paradox, not in Dante

As when one dreameth and remembereth not
10   Waking, what were his pleasures or his pains,
With every feature of the dream forgot,
          The printed passion of the dream remains: –

Even such am I; within whose thoughts resides
          No picture of that sight nor any part
Nor any memory: in whom abides
          Only a happiness within the heart,

A secret happiness that soaks the heart
          As hills are soaked by slow unsealing snow,
Or secret as that wind without a chart
20   Whereon did the wild leaves of Sibyl go.

O light uplifted from all mortal knowing,
          Send back a little of that glimpse of thee,
That of its glory I may kindle glowing
          One tiny spark for all men yet to be.
          (1915)

WALLACE STEVENS (1879–1955)

Stevens studied French and German at Harvard where he came under the lasting influence of George Santayana; he qualified as a lawyer in 1904 and thereafter worked as an insurance executive. He published his first book, *Harmonium*, in 1923. He maintained the Arnoldian notion that religion is essentially poetical, or a 'fiction' toward which we should nonetheless adopt an attitude of commitment: 'The final belief is to believe

---

16 *happiness* Dante calls the remnant of the vision '*il dolce*' ('the sweetness')
17–20 Dante has the similes of melting snow and the wind which dispersed the leaves on which the Cumaean Sibyl wrote her prophecies (see *Aeneid* 3.443–50) but Dante's point is that as little of the vision remains to him as of the vanished snow or scattered oracles   24 *tiny* not in Dante

in a fiction, which you know to be a fiction, there being nothing else. The exquisite truth is to know that it is a fiction and that you believe in it willingly.' He also noted: 'The time will come when poems like Paradise will seem like very *triste* contraptions.' One poetical contraption he liked was writing in unrhymed tercets, as here or in his *Notes Toward a Supreme Fiction*, as if in wry recall of Dante.

The Hand as a Being

In the first canto of the final canticle,
Too conscious of too many things at once,
Our man beheld the naked, nameless dame,

Seized her and wondered: why beneath the tree
She held her hand before him in the air,
For him to see, wove round her glittering hair.

Too conscious of too many things at once,
In the first canto of the final canticle,
Her hand composed him and composed the tree.

The wind had seized the tree and ha, and ha,   10
It held the shivering, the shaken limbs,
Then bathed its body in the leaping lake.

Her hand composed him like a hand appeared,
Of an impersonal gesture, a stranger's hand.
He was too conscious of too many things

---

1 *first canto* Stevens may refer to *Paradiso* 1, which has a tree, a lake and a dame, though the dame is neither 'naked' nor 'nameless', but he probably remembers Dante through D. G. Rossetti's 'Blessed Damozel'

In the first canto of the final canticle.
Her hand took his and drew him near to her.
Her hair fell on him and the mi-bird flew

To the ruddier bushes at the garden's end.
20   Of her, of her alone, at last he knew
And lay beside her underneath the tree.
    (1942)

EZRA POUND (1885–1972)

Pound studied Italian at Hamilton College as part of his enthusiastic survey of medieval European culture; Dante came to him in the company of Old English, Provençal and medieval French poets. Part of the distinctiveness of Pound's response to Dante lies in his setting the Florentine among his predecessors and contemporaries (particularly Cavalcanti, with whom Pound felt a greater affinity). For example, he disputed Dante's judgement on the troubadour and trouble-maker Bertran de Born (*Inferno* 28.118ff.), bluntly in 'Sestina: Altaforte' (1909) and more acutely in 'Near Perigord' (1915). Pound's first book of poems, *A Lume Spento* (Venice, 1908) takes its title from *Purgatorio* 3.132 and is heavily influenced by what D. G. Rossetti had made of Dante. Pound comments on and cites from Dante throughout his writings, both prose (as in his 1908 book of criticism, *The Spirit of Romance*) and verse (the last *Cantos* are shot through with fragments of *Paradiso*). In 1944 he defined his *Cantos* as 'an epic poem which begins "In the Dark Forest", crosses the Purgatory of human error, and ends in the light, and "fra i maestri di color che sanno"' ['among the intellectual masters'] – that last misquotation or adaptation of *Inferno* 4.131, and the change made to Dante's itinerary (so that

---

18 *mi-bird* unknown to zoology; '*mi-*' is a French prefix meaning 'half-'

Pound's epic ends up triumphantly in what Dante thought of
as limbo), bring out Pound's characteristic de-Christianizing of
the *Commedia*.

[From a Notebook]

It befell that wearied with
　　　　much study
My spirit left for a while
　　　　this corporal
house of life . . . &
journeyed I know not whither
through divers ways
　　　　of strange lights
& mingled darknesses,
Untill after much wayfaring　　　　　　10
I came unto a ruined
gateway, crumbled &
broken, arches, &
wondering what this
might portend
& why no moss or other
green thing was upon
the ruins, &
When sudenly I fell. &
found beneath me broken　　　　　　20
stones, with this much
of inscription:

1–6 compare *Vita Nuova* 42.2–3　　1 *It befell that* echoing Dante's '*avenne
che*', much used in the *Vita Nuova,* for instance at 5.1

> Upon one stone
Per me,
and on another, Dolente
& upon a third, Dolore
Lascete ogni speranza
Then I knew of a truth
> that
it was none other than
Hell gate, whereby
damned souls entered
into eternal grief,
& wherefrom none passed
in all eternity. –
& abashed & would have
turned back,
when one said to me,
'fear not – for high
> omnipotence
by light hath pierced hell
& cast down the keepers
thereof –
Come & see the place
> where hell hath lain
& I 'Who art thou
master that speakest
with such authority' –
& he, 'I am that one
that through the heavens

30

40

50

24–7 *Per me* . . . fragments from the inscription over the Gate of Hell in
Inferno 3.1, 2, 9; they translate as 'through me . . .', 'sorrowful', 'pain' and
'abandon every hope'. The Italian of the fourth is incorrect and should read
'*lasciate*'   33 *eternal grief Inferno* 3.2 ('*etterno dolore*')   34–5 compare
Inferno 27.64–5   38–9 *one . . . Fear not* Virgil tells Dante not to fear at
Inferno 2.49   41 *by light* Pound's adaptation of the 'harrowing of hell' (see
Inferno 4.52–63) to his own Enlightenment purposes   49 *that one* Dante
himself, who takes on here for Pound the role that Virgil played for him in
the *Commedia*

followed Beatrice –
before it was willed that
I leave for ever my earthly
dwelling,'
Whereat I would have
done him reverence, but
he forbade me, saying –
'I am but as the least
          of them that serve,
– Follow –   60
          (written 1906/7?)

Canto XIV

Io venni in luogo d'ogni luce muto;
The stench of wet coal, politicians
. . . . e and . . . . . n, their wrists bound to
          their ankles,
Standing bare bum,
Faces smeared on their rumps,
          wide eye on flat buttock,
Bush hanging for beard,
     Addressing crowds through their arse-holes,
Addressing the multitudes in the ooze,
          newts, water-slugs, water-maggots,   10
And with them . . . . r,
          a scrupulously clean table-napkin

58–60 both the self-deprecation and the command to 'follow' are
characteristic of Dante's Virgil
  1 *Inferno* 5.28 – 'I came to a place deprived of all light'
  3 . . . . *e and* . . . . . *n* though Pound said the names of the individuals
he truncated in *Cantos* XIV and XV were '*not* worth recording as such' and
even that he had forgotten 'which rotters were there', these first two names
are generally identified as David Lloyd George (British Prime Minister,
1916–22) and Woodrow Wilson (President of the United States, 1913–21)
  8 compare *Inferno* 21.139

Tucked under his penis,
            and . . . . m
Who disliked colloquial language,
Stiff-starched, but soiled, collars
            circumscribing his legs,
The pimply and hairy skin
            pushing over the collar's edge,
20   Profiteers drinking blood sweetened with sh–t,
And behind them . . . . . . f and the financiers
            lashing them with steel wires.

And the betrayers of language
            . . . . . . n and the press gang
And those who had lied for hire;
the perverts, the perverters of language,
            the perverts, who have set money-lust
Before the pleasures of the senses;

            howling, as of a hen-yard in a printing-house,
30   the clatter of presses,
the blowing of dry dust and stray paper,
foetor, sweat, the stench of stale oranges,
dung, last cess-pool of the universe,
mysterium, acid of sulphur,
the pusillanimous, raging;
plunging, jewels in mud,
            and howling to find them unstained;
sadic mothers driving their daughters to bed with
            decrepitude,
sows eating their litters,
40   and here the placard ΕΙΚΩΝ ΓΗΣ
                  and here: THE PERSONNEL
                        CHANGES,

---

22 compare *Inferno* 18.35–6   34 *mysterium* the term for 'secret knowledge'
in alchemy, in which 'acid of sulphur' is used (rather than any Catholic
'mysterium')   40 *ΕΙΚΩΝ ΓΗΣ* 'image of the earth'

melting like dirty wax,
        decayed candles, the bums sinking lower,
faces submerged under hams,
And in the ooze under them,
reversed, foot-palm to foot-palm,
        hand-palm to hand-palm, the agents
           provocateurs
The murderers of Pearse and MacDonagh,
        Captain H. the chief torturer;
The petrified turd that was Verres,   50
        bigots, Calvin and St. Clement of
           Alexandria!
black-beetles, burrowing into the sh–t,
The soil a decrepitude, the ooze full of morsels,
lost contours, erosions.

        Above the hell-rot
the great arse-hole,
        broken with piles,
hanging stalactites,
        greasy as sky over Westminster,
the invisible, many English,   60
        the place lacking in interest,
last squalor, utter decrepitude,
the vice-crusaders, fahrting through silk,
        waving the Christian symbols,
. . . . frigging a tin penny-whistle,
Flies carrying news, harpies dripping sh–t through
        the air,

---

48 *Pearse and MacDonagh* executed leaders of the Irish Easter Rising in
1916   49 *Captain H.* Captain J. Bowen-Colthurst was eventually
court-martialled and confined as criminally insane as a result of brutalities
while serving in Ireland   50 *Verres* a corrupt Roman administrator
51 *Calvin* sixteenth-century Protestant theologian *St. Clement* one of the
Greek Fathers of the Church: sainthood is compatible with damnation in
Pound's hell   66 *harpies* compare *Inferno* 13.10–15

The slough of unamiable liars,
        bog of stupidities,
malevolent stupidities, and stupidities,
70   the soil living pus, full of vermin,
dead maggots begetting live maggots,
        slum owners,
usurers squeezing crab-lice, pandars to authority,
pets-de-loup, sitting on piles of stone books,
obscuring the texts with philology,
        hiding them under their persons,
the air without refuge of silence,
        the drift of lice, teething,
and above it the mouthing of orators,
80   the arse-belching of preachers.
        And Invidia,
the corruptio, foetor, fungus,
liquid animals, melted ossifications,
slow rot, foetid combustion,
    chewed cigar-butts, without dignity,
        without tragedy,
. . . . .m Episcopus, waving a condom full of
        black-beetles,
monopolists, obstructors of knowledge,
        obstructors of distribution.
    (1925)

---

73 *pets-de-loup* literally, 'wolf's farts', the term is colloquial French for
'pedants'   81 *Invidia* envy, one of the seven deadly sins

Canto XC   1–57

> Animus humanus amor non est,
> sed ab ipso amor procedit, et
> ideo seipso non diligit, sed amore
>   qui seipso procedit.

'From the colour the nature
            & by nature the sign!'
Beatific spirits welding together
            as in one ash-tree in Ygdrasail.
                    Baucis, Philemon.
Castalia is the name of that fount in the hill's fold,
            the sea below,
                    narrow beach.
Templum aedificans, not yet marble,
            'Amphion!'   10
And from the San Ku 三

孤

            to the room in Poitiers where one can stand
                    casting no shadow,
That is Sagetrieb,
                    that is tradition.

---

epigraph 'The human soul is not love but love flows from it, and the soul
takes delight not in itself but in the love which flows from itself' – from
Richard of St Victor   **1–2** alluding to John Heydon's theory of 'signatures'
by which the visible world may be interpreted as a set of signs of divine
intention   **4** *Ygdrasail* the cosmic ash-tree of Norse mythology
5 *Baucis, Philemon* an old couple who were turned into trees on their death;
see Ovid's *Metamorphoses* 8.611–724   **6** *Castalia* a fountain sacred to
Apollo on Mount Parnassus   **9** *Templum aedificans* 'building the temple'
10 *Amphion* son of Zeus and king of Thebes – the city walls rose to the
sound of his lyre   **11** *San Ku* an inner council in ancient China

Builders had kept the proportion,
             did Jacques de Molay
                    know these proportions?
and was Erigena ours?
20   Moon's barge over milk-blue water
Kuthera δεινά
Kuthera sempiterna
                    Ubi amor, ibi oculus.
Vae qui cogitatis inutile.
             quam in nobis similitudine divinae
                              reperetur imago.
'Mother Earth in thy lap'
                    said Randolph
30   ἠγάπησεν πολύ
liberavit masnatos.
Castalia like the moonlight
             and the waves rise and fall,
Evita, beer-halls, semina motuum,
             to parched grass, now is rain
not arrogant from habit,
             but furious from perception,
                              Sibylla,

---

17 *Jacques de Molay c.* 1244–1314, last grand master of the Order of
Templars   19 *Erigena* the philosopher John Scotus Erigena, *c.* 800–877
21 *Kuthera* Aphrodite δεινά 'terrifying'   22 *sempiterna* 'everlasting'
23 *Ubi . . . oculus* 'where love is, there the eye is also' – a quotation from
Richard of St Victor (d. 1173)   24 *Vae . . . inutile* 'woe to you who think
without purpose'   25–6 *quam . . . imago* misquoted from Richard of
St Victor – 'through which an image of the divine likeness will be found in
us' [*Pound's translation*]   28 *Randolph* John Randolph of Roanoke
(1773–1833), an American statesman who freed his slaves
29 ἠγάπησεν πολύ 'she loved much' – see Luke 7:47
30 *liberavit masnatos* 'he freed his slaves'   33 *Evita* probably Eva Perón,
apparently adduced by Pound as yet another instance of philanthropy
semina motuum 'the seeds of motion'   37 *Sibylla* the oracular priestess of
Delphi

from under the rubble heap
>   m'elevasti
from the dulled edge beyond pain,   40
>   m'elevasti
out of Erebus, the deep-lying
>   from the wind under the earth,
>   m'elevasti
from the dulled air and the dust,
>   m'elevasti
by the great flight,
>   m'elevasti
>   Isis Kuanon
>   from the cusp of the moon   50
>   m'elevasti
the viper stirs in the dust,
>   the blue serpent
glides from the rock pool
>   And they take lights now down to the water
the lamps float from the rowers
>   the sea's claw drawing them outward.
>   (1955)

T. S. ELIOT (1888–1965)

After Shakespeare, Dante was the sharpest and most lasting
influence on Eliot's writing and, unlike Shakespeare, served
Eliot as a deliberately adopted model of style, though Eliot
tended to exaggerate into world-historical antithesis the con-
trasts he saw between the detailed practice of the two writers.
Eliot's first book of poems. *Prufrock and other Observations*,

---

39 *m'elevasti* a Poundian version of '*mi levasti*' at *Paradiso* 1.75, where
Dante is addressing 'the love that rules the skies'; the phrase means 'you
lifted me up'   42 *Erebus* the underworld   49 *Isis* an Egyptian
earth-goddess; she brought Osiris back to life   *Kuanon* Chinese goddess of
mercy

has an epigraph from Dante (*Purgatorio* 21.133–6), as does the first poem in that book, 'The Love Song of J. Alfred Prufrock' (*Inferno* 27.61–6); allusions to Dante persist throughout his poetic life and culminate in *Little Gidding* II (1942). He read Dante at first in the bilingual Temple Classics edition, and may be said to have learned Italian from and for Dante. There are more references to Dante in his *Selected Essays* than to any writer apart from Shakespeare; lines from Shakespeare and Dante appear side by side in three sections of *The Waste Land*, as if dividing the poem between them. In his obituary notice for Eliot, Pound wrote (implying a humbled comparison between himself and Eliot) 'His was the true Dantescan voice'; there seems no good reason to dissent from that judgement.

The Burnt Dancer

sotto la pioggia dell'aspro martiro

Within the yellow ring of flame
A black moth through the night
Caught in the circle of desire
Expiates his heedless flight
With beat of wings that do not tire

---

epigraph *Inferno* 16.6 – 'under the downpour of the bitter torment'; the downpour is the rain of fire which falls in *Inferno* 15 on the 'violent against nature'. Eliot was to return to *Inferno* 15, climactically in *Little Gidding* II
1 *ring of flame* of a candle, probably, but suggesting the infernal circles
3 *circle of desire* though all the zones Dante passes through in the *Commedia* are circles of desire, differing only as that desire is punished, purged or perfected, Eliot may have most in view *Inferno* 5 and *Purgatorio* 26, for the analogy between the moth's fatal attraction to flame and sexual desire is at least as old as Shakespeare (*Merchant of Venice*, II.ix.79)
4 *heedless flight* perhaps recalling *Inferno* 26.125, '*folle volo*' ('mad/witless/ reckless flight')

Distracted from more vital values
To golden values of the flame
What is the virtue that he shall use
In a world too strange for pride or shame?
A world too strange for praise or blame   10
Too strange for good or evil:
How drawn here from a distant star
For mirthless dance and silent revel

O danse mon papillon noir!

The tropic odours of your name
From Mozambique or Nicobar
Fall on the ragged teeth of flame
Like perfumed oil upon the waters
What is the secret you have brought us
Children's voices in little corners   20
Whimper whimper through the night
Of what disaster do you warn us
Agony nearest to delight?
Dance fast dance faster
There is no mortal disaster
The destiny that may be leaning
Toward us from your hidden star
Is grave, but not with human meaning

O danse mon papillon noir!

Within the circle of my brain   30
The twisted dance continues.
The patient acolyte of pain,
The strong beyond our human sinews,

---

14 *O danse* . . . 'O dance my black butterfly'; Christopher Ricks notes that
'*papillons noirs*' are 'dark thoughts'

The singèd reveller of the fire,
Caught on those horns that toss and toss,
Losing the end of his desire
Desires completion of his loss.
O strayed from whiter flames that burn not
O vagrant from a distant star
40   O broken guest that may return not

O danse danse mon papillon noir!
    (written June 1914; published 1996)

The Waste Land
I. The Burial of the Dead (The Waste Land 35–76)

'You gave me hyacinths first a year ago;
'They called me the hyacinth girl.'
– Yet when we came back, late, from the hyacinth
        garden,
Your arms full, and your hair wet, I could not
Speak, and my eyes failed, I was neither
Living nor dead, and I knew nothing,
Looking into the heart of light, the silence.
Oed' und leer das Meer.

34–5 *fire . . . horns* compare *Inferno* 26.85   36 *end of his desire* compare
Paradiso 33.46   38 *whiter flames that burn not* the blessed souls in
Paradiso are frequently described as unconsumed flames; compare the voice
which speaks of the resurrected body in *Paradiso* 14.37–60, especially 52–4
– 'just as a coal which gives out flame is itself whiter than the flame and so its
own shape is not destroyed but can still be seen'

  5–6 compare Dante's response to the sight of Satan, *Inferno* 34.25; Eliot's
notes do not signal this allusion, but then nor do they signal the allusion to
Racine's *Phèdre* (I.iii.275)   8 *Oed'* . . . 'the sea is desolate and empty', from
Wagner's *Tristan und Isolde*, Act 3

Madame Sosostris, famous clairvoyante,
Had a bad cold, nevertheless   10
Is known to be the wisest woman in Europe,
With a wicked pack of cards. Here, said she,
Is your card, the drowned Phoenician Sailor,
(Those are pearls that were his eyes. Look!)
Here is Belladonna, the Lady of the Rocks,
The lady of situations.
Here is the man with the three staves, and here
     the Wheel,
And here is the one-eyed merchant, and this card,
Which is blank, is something he carries on his
     back,
Which I am forbidden to see. I do not find   20
The Hanged Man. Fear death by water.
I see crowds of people, walking round in a ring.
Thank you. If you see dear Mrs. Equitone,
Tell her I bring the horoscope myself:
One must be so careful these days.

    Unreal City,
Under the brown fog of a winter dawn,
A crowd flowed over London Bridge, so many,
I had not thought death had undone so many.
Sighs, short and infrequent, were exhaled,   30
And each man fixed his eyes before his feet.
Flowed up the hill and down King William Street,
To where Saint Mary Woolnoth kept the hours
With a dead sound on the final stroke of nine.

---

22 a frequent sight in Dante's first two *cantiche*   28–9 Eliot indicates the
allusions to *Inferno* 3.55–7 and 4.25–7   31 *fixed his eyes before his feet* a
recurrent posture in Dante, as for example at *Purgatorio* 23.13–15

There I saw one I knew, and stopped him, crying:
    'Stetson!
'You who were with me in the ships at Mylae!
'That corpse you planted last year in your garden,
'Has it begun to sprout? Will it bloom this year?
'Or has the sudden frost disturbed its bed?
40   'O keep the Dog far hence, that's friend to men,
'Or with his nails he'll dig it up again!
'You! hypocrite lecteur! – mon semblable, – mon frère!'
    (1922)

III. *The Fire Sermon* (The Waste Land 292–311)

'Trams and dusty trees.
Highbury bore me. Richmond and Kew
Undid me. By Richmond I raised my knees
Supine on the floor of a narrow canoe.'

'My feet are at Moorgate, and my heart
Under my feet. After the event
He wept. He promised "a new start."
I made no comment. What should I resent?'

'On Margate Sands.
10 I can connect
Nothing with nothing.
The broken fingernails of dirty hands.

---

35 *I saw one I knew* compare the many encounters between Dante and his
acquaintances   42 *hypocrite . . .* from the last line of Baudelaire's 'Au
lecteur' – 'hypocritical reader – my double – my brother'
  2–3 Eliot's note signals the allusion to *Purgatorio* 5.133–4; contrast
Eliot's reticent imitation with Felicia Hemans's expansion of the same lines,
above. Unlike both Mrs Hemans and Swinburne (also above), Eliot recalls
the structure of La Pia's appearance, though he makes her first not last of
three speakers

My people humble people who expect
Nothing.'
          la la

To Carthage then I came

Burning burning burning burning
O Lord Thou pluckest me out
O Lord Thou pluckest

burning   20
     (1922)

Animula

'Issues from the hand of God, the simple soul'
To a flat world of changing lights and noise,
To light, dark, dry or damp, chilly or warm;
Moving between the legs of tables and of chairs,
Rising or falling, grasping at kisses and toys,
Advancing boldly, sudden to take alarm,
Retreating to the corner of arm and knee,
Eager to be reassured, taking pleasure
In the fragrant brilliance of the Christmas tree,
Pleasure in the wind, the sunlight and the sea;   10
Studies the sunlit pattern on the floor
And running stags around a silver tray;

---

title from the Emperor Hadrian's deathbed poem to his own soul – 'Animula
blandula vagula' – translated by Byron as 'Ah! gentle, fleeting, wav'ring
sprite / Friend and associate of this clay!'; the title and first line together thus
form a Dantescan syncretism of pagan and Christian attitudes
1 *Purgatorio* 16.85–8; in this canto, the sin of anger is purged. Dante
worries why 'the world is destitute of every virtue' and it is explained to him
by the penitent Marco Lombardo (who speaks Eliot's first line) that the cause
of evil lies in each individual and not in the stars

Confounds the actual and the fanciful,
Content with playing-cards and kings and queens,
What the fairies do and what the servants say.
The heavy burden of the growing soul
Perplexes and offends more, day by day;
Week by week, offends and perplexes more
With the imperatives of 'is and seems'
20   And may and may not, desire and control.
The pain of living and the drug of dreams
Curl up the small soul in the window seat
Behind the *Encyclopaedia Britannica*.
Issues from the hand of time the simple soul
Irresolute and selfish, misshapen, lame,
Unable to fare forward or retreat,
Fearing the warm reality, the offered good,
Denying the importunity of the blood,
Shadow of its own shadows, spectre in its own
          gloom,
30   Leaving disordered papers in a dusty room;
Living first in the silence after the viaticum.

    Pray for Guiterriez, avid of speed and power,
For Boudin, blown to pieces,
For this one who made a great fortune,
And that one who went his own way.
Pray for Floret, by the boarhound slain between
          the yew trees,
Pray for us now and at the hour of our birth.   (1929)

---

16 *heavy burden* compare *Purgatorio* 31.19   31 *viaticum* 'The Eucharist, as administered to or received by one who is dying or in danger of death' (*OED*)

Little Gidding 78–149

In the uncertain hour before the morning
  Near the ending of interminable night
  At the recurrent end of the unending
After the dark dove with the flickering tongue
  Had passed below the horizon of his homing
  While the dead leaves still rattled on like tin
Over the asphalt where no other sound was
  Between three districts whence the smoke arose
  I met one walking, loitering and hurried
As if blown towards me like the metal leaves   10
  Before the urban dawn wind unresisting.
  And as I fixed upon the down-turned face
That pointed scrutiny with which we challenge
  The first-met stranger in the waning dusk
  I caught the sudden look of some dead master
Whom I had known, forgotten, half recalled
  Both one and many; in the brown baked features
  The eyes of a familiar compound ghost
Both intimate and unidentifiable.
  So I assumed a double part, and cried   20
  And heard another's voice cry: 'What! are *you*
    here?'

---

4 *dark dove* the phrase conjoins the dove of the Holy Spirit with the bombers
which were attacking London in 1942; the episode takes place in the
aftermath of an air raid. The doves of *Inferno* 5 fly in 'dark air'
6 *dead leaves* Dante compares the numerousness of the damned to autumn
leaves in *Inferno* 3.112   12–21 this passage draws searchingly on *Inferno*
15.16–30; the whole section is pervaded by that canto
17 *baked features* compare *Inferno* 15.26, '*cotto aspetto*' ('cooked face')
21 in draft, the allusion to *Inferno* 15.30 was clearer, for at one stage Eliot
named Ser Brunetto

Although we were not. I was still the same,
  Knowing myself yet being someone other –
  And he a face still forming; yet the words sufficed
To compel the recognition they preceded.
  And so, compliant to the common wind,
  Too strange to each other for misunderstanding,
In concord at this intersection time
  Of meeting nowhere, no before and after,
30   We trod the pavement in a dead patrol.
I said: 'The wonder that I feel is easy,
  Yet ease is cause of wonder. Therefore speak:
  I may not comprehend, may not remember.'
And he: 'I am not eager to rehearse
  My thoughts and theory which you have forgotten.
  These things have served their purpose: let them be.
So with your own, and pray they be forgiven
  By others, as I pray you to forgive
  Both bad and good. Last season's fruit is eaten
40   And the fullfed beast shall kick the empty pail.
  For last year's words belong to last year's language
  And next year's words await another voice.
But, as the passage now presents no hindrance
  To the spirit unappeased and peregrine
  Between two worlds become much like each other,
So I find words I never thought to speak
  In streets I never thought I should revisit
  When I left my body on a distant shore.
Since our concern was speech, and speech impelled us
50   To purify the dialect of the tribe
  And urge the mind to aftersight and foresight,

24–5 compare *Purgatorio* 23.43–5   31 *wonder* compare *Inferno* 15.24
37–8 prayer for forgiveness is unknown in *Inferno* (Brunetto Latini is keen
his works should be remembered). These lines mark a pivotal moment in the
passage as Eliot moves from the damned Brunetto Latini to the purged
Arnaut Daniel   40 compare the allegorical animals and their fodder in
Inferno 15.70–76   44 compare *Vita Nuova* 41.11 ('*lo peregrino spirito*')
49 compare *De vulgari eloquentia* 1.11.1

Let me disclose the gifts reserved for age
 To set a crown upon your lifetime's effort.
 First, the cold friction of expiring sense
Without enchantment, offering no promise
 But bitter tastelessness of shadow fruit
 As body and soul begin to fall asunder.
Second, the conscious impotence of rage
 At human folly, and the laceration
 Of laughter at what ceases to amuse.   60
And last, the rending pain of re-enactment
 Of all that you have done, and been; the
  shame
 Of motives late revealed, and the awareness
Of things ill done and done to others' harm
 Which once you took for exercise of virtue.
 Then fools' approval stings, and honour stains.
From wrong to wrong the exasperated spirit
 Proceeds, unless restored by that refining fire
 Where you must move in measure, like a
  dancer.'
The day was breaking. In the disfigured street 70
 He left me, with a kind of valediction,
 And faded on the blowing of the horn. (1942)

HUGH MACDIARMID (1892–1978)

Christopher Grieve began to publish poems in his teens; he
adopted the name 'MacDiarmid' during the 1920s when his
commitment to Scottish nationalism sharpened. At the same
time, he began to write in Scots, as in his long poem *A Drunk
Man Looks at the Thistle* (which has affinities with Dante
too diffusely complex to represent in this anthology). Intensely

---

68–9 compare *Purgatorio* 26.148

'engaged' and excitably learned, he wrote of himself, 'My life has been an adventure, or series of adventures, in the exploration of the mystery of Scotland's self-suppression.'

Dante on the Edinburgh People

In Edinburgh – in Auld Reekie – to-day
Where 99 per cent of the people might say
In Dante's words . . . 'Tristi fummo
Nell'aer dolce che dal sol s'allegra'
    (Sullen were we,
In the sweet air that is gladdened by the sun,
Carrying lazy smoke in our hearts).   (1943)

The Kind of Poetry I Want   670-92

This is the kind of poetry I want
In this world at war when I see
On the Dark Plain (la buia compagna)
'A vast multitude of spirits
Running behind a flag
In great haste and confusion,
Urged on by furious wasps and hornets.
These are the unhappy people
Who never were alive,
Never awakened to take any part
Either in good or evil'
. . . 'che non furon ribelli,
Nè fur fedeli a Dio, ma per sè foro.'

10

3-4 *Inferno* 7.121-2; the lines come from Virgil's account of the souls damned for sinful anger. MacDiarmid's fifth and sixth lines translate the quotation, his seventh translates *Inferno* 7.123
  3 *la buia compagna Inferno* 3.130; the Italian should read '*campagna*'
4-9 *Inferno* 3.52-6, 64-6   10-15 MacDiarmid first translates and then quotes Virgil's words about the 'neutrals' in *Inferno* 3.34-9

(Nor rebels nor faithful to God,
But for themselves!)

A poetry like a glacier caught between the peaks
– A landmark among the high ranges of poetry,
Not hung upon the clouds,
But steadfastly descending to the *Plain*
Where all men can walk and talk and gaze
     and can look upward and forward,   20
Not downward and backward,
On Nature and each other. (1943)

DOROTHY L. SAYERS (1893–1957)

After reading modern languages at Somerville College, Oxford, Sayers worked as an advertising copy-writer, as a teacher, and wrote her celebrated detective novels; she maintained her passion for medieval literature, translating from Old French and Anglo-Norman. She did not read Dante until 1944, under the influence of Charles Williams' *The Figure of Beatrice*, and was at once captivated by the poem – 'I can remember nothing like it since I first read *The Three Musketeers* at the age of thirteen' – and could not, as the saying goes, put it down; she was still translating *Paradiso* when she died (her version was completed by Barbara Reynolds). She published two volumes of papers on Dante in which she often commends him to the modern world as a cure for its ills.

---

16 perhaps influenced by Dante's frequent references to mountain snows
19 *Plain* punning on 'plain' as 'level ground' and 'straightforward, not exalted' of a style, such as that in which Dante wrote the *Commedia*

Purgatorio 12

So, step for step, like oxen in the yoke,
    Beside that burdened soul I held my way
    So long as my kind schoolmaster would brook;

But when he said: 'Now leave him; come, I say,
    Press on; for here must each with sail and oar
    Urge the ship forward strongly as he may,'

I raised me, as good walkers should, and bore
    My body upright, though the thoughts in me
    Remained bowed down and shrunken as before.

10 I'd put on speed and was most willingly
    Following my master's footsteps, he and I
    Showing how fleet of foot we both could be,

When he addressed me: 'Downward cast thine eye;
    For solace of the way, 'twere good thou fall
    To scanning what beneath thy feet may lie.'

And as, to give the dead memorial,
    We trace on many an earthly sepulchre
    Figures that may their living forms recall,

The sight of which will very often stir
20   Men to lament them, memory being still
    Piety's sharpest, or its only, spur:

---

2 *burdened soul* Oderisi, who has pointed out to Dante various notables on
the terrace of pride in the previous canto; he is 'burdened' with the heavy
stones the proud carry for their purgation   3 *my kind schoolmaster* Virgil
brook an archaism for 'tolerate'; there is no equivalent archaism in the
Italian   20–21 the Italian means 'the pricking of memory acts as a spur only
to the pious'

So there, with livelier likeness, due to skill
  Of craftsmanship, I saw the whole ledge graven
  Where, for a road, it juts out from the hill.

Mine eyes beheld there him to whom was given
  The noblest form of any creature made
  On one side fall like lightning down from
      heaven.

Mine eyes beheld Briareus, breast and blade
  Riven by the bolt divine, on the other side
  Lie on the earth, heavy and cold and dead.   30

Mine eyes beheld Thymbraeus, they espied
  Pallas and Mars in arms about their sire
  Viewing the Giants' limbs flung far and wide.

Mine eyes beheld Nimrod, beneath his dire
  High handiwork, look stunned upon the men
  That shared in Shinar his proud heart's desire.

Ah, Niobe, with eyes how full of pain
  I saw thine image on the roadway scored
  Set between seven and seven thy children slain!

25–63 Sayers ingeniously provides an English equivalent for a special,
acrostic effect in Dante: four consecutive tercets begin in the Italian with a
'V' (identical in Dante's script with 'U'), then four with 'O', and a final four
with 'M', spelling out 'UOM' ('man'), the initial letters of the lines of the
thirteenth tercet in the sequence   25 *him* Lucifer   28–33 Briareus and
Thymbraeus were among the giants who fought against the Olympian gods,
such as Pallas and Mars (see *Inferno* 31)   34 *Nimrod* another inhabitant of
Inferno 31, he was punished for trying to build the Tower of Babel on the
plain of Shinar   37 *Niobe* she boasted she was happier than the gods,
principally because she had fourteen children, who all dropped dead as a
result of her boast – see Ovid's *Metamorphoses* 6.146–312

40   Ah, Saul, how fallen, and by thine own sword,
      Didst thou appear, dead on Gilboa, where
      Nor rain nor dew fell everafterward!

      Ah, mad Arachne! I beheld thee there,
      Already half turned spider, on the shreds
      Of that sad web thou wov'st to thy despair.

      Ah, Rehoboam! now there's none that dreads
      Thy face; it threats no more; the chariot flies
      Though none pursue; terror behind thee treads.

      Now showed the stubborn pavement in what wise
50   Alcmaeon made his hapless mother pay
      For that curst gaud, and at how dear a price.

      Now showed it how his sons rushed in to slay
      Sennacherib in the temple where he stood,
      And slew, and left him there, and went their way.

      Now showed it how with carnage all imbrued
      Queen Tomyris made mock of Cyrus, saying:
      'Blood hast thou craved – I'll fill thee full with
          blood.'

---

40 *Saul* the first king of Israel, whom God abandoned because of his
disobedience; he committed suicide after his defeat at the battle of Gilboa
43 *Arachne* she was turned into a spider after losing a weaving contest to
which she had challenged Minerva; see *Metamorphoses* 6.1–145
46 *Rehoboam* the son and successor of Solomon; he was driven from power
by a popular uprising   50 *Alcmaeon* he killed his mother who had betrayed
his father for the sake of a pearl necklace   53 *Sennacherib* an Assyrian king
who oppressed Jerusalem; an angel destroyed his army and he was killed by
his sons   56 *Tomyris* she decapitated Cyrus, who had killed her son, and
then cast his head into a basin of blood with the witticism here reported

Now showed it the Assyrian host's dismaying
   And rout, when Holofernes was undone,
   And showed the grisly relics of his slaying.   60

Mine eyes beheld Troy Town in ashes strown;
   Ah, sacred Ilium, how vile and mean
   Now showed thine image in the carven stone!

What master of the graver or the pen
   Such lines as these, such shading could contrive
   For subtle minds to find amazement in?

The dead seemed dead, the living seemed alive;
   Who saw the fact saw not more clear than I
   Those scenes I trod, leaned down contemplative.

Be proud, then, march with haughty heads held high,   70
   Children of Eve, nor bend them toward the ground
   To see the evil road you travel by!

Farther about the mount our way had wound,
   And more of the sun's course by now was spent
   Than one could judge with faculties thus bound,

When he who all the time alertly went
   In front of me began: 'Lift up thy brow,
   The time is past to go thus ruminant.

Look at the angel over there, and how
   He moves to come to us; look how the day's   80
   Sixth handmaiden resigns her office now.

---

59 *Holofernes* an Assyrian general, killed in his sleep by Judith
62 *sacred* not in Dante   81 *Sixth handmaiden* the day's handmaidens are
the Hours; it is now past noon

Adorn with reverence both thy mien and face,
    That he may joy to speed us up the mount;
    Think that it dawns but once, this day of grace.'

So oft he'd urged me – well I knew his wont –
    Never to waste a moment, that I might
    Scarcely mistake his meaning on that count.

On came the beauteous creature, clothed in white,
    And seeming as he came in countenance
90   A star of dawn all tremulous with light.

He spread his arms abroad, and spread his vans,
    And, 'Come,' he said, 'the stairs are nigh; henceforth
    An easier climb is yours and every man's.'

Glad summons – but with few to prize its worth!
    O human race, born to take flight and soar,
    Why fall ye, for one breath of wind, to earth?

He brought us to the rock's cleft aperture,
    And there he brushed my forehead with his wings;
    Then promised me a journey safe and sure.

100 As, where the road over Rubaconte swings
    Up to the height and the church whose walls
        command
    The city that so discreetly orders things,

The steep grade's eased by steps on the dexter hand,
    Hewn out in times that kept inviolate
    The bushel-stave, and let the audit stand,

---

100 *Rubaconte* a bridge in Florence, leading to the hill on which the church
of San Miniato stands

So is the cliff, which drops precipitate
    Here from the upper cornice, made less sheer,
    Though either side the high rock-walls are strait.

As we turned thither, voices in our ear
    Sang out *Beati pauperes spiritu*:   110
    No tongue could tell how sweet they were to hear.

What different passes these from those we knew
    In Hell! for there with hideous howls of pain,
    But here with singing, we are ushered through.

When by the sacred stair we now again
    Were climbing, lighter far meseemed I trod
    Than I had done upon the level plain;

Wherefore I said: 'Master, what heavy load
    Has slipped from me, so that I walk with ease,
    And scarcely feel fatigue upon the road?'   120

And he: 'When from thy forehead all the P's
    Which, half-effaced and dim, remain there yet
    Are rubbed clean out, as one already is,

Then shall good-will so over-rule thy feet,
    That they will climb, and not be merely strong
    And uncomplaining, but delight in it.'

Then I behaved like one who goes along
    Quite unaware of something on his head,
    Till winks and smiles make him suspect what's
        wrong;

---

110 *Beati* . . . Matthew 5:3: 'Blessed are the poor in spirit'
121 *all the P's* in *Purgatorio* 9.112–14 an angel marks Dante's forehead with
seven letter 'P's, each one standing for '*peccato*' ('sin'); he has just completed
the purgation of pride and so one 'P' has been erased without his noticing

130 And, to make sure, the hand must lend its aid,
     And feels, and finds, for when the doors are shut
     On sight, the touch does duty there instead;

So, with my right-hand fingers all spread out,
     I found those letters only six, which he
     Who bare the keys had on my temples cut;

And, as he watched, my leader smiled at me.   (1955)

ALLEN TATE (1899–1979)

With John Crowe Ransom and Robert Penn Warren, Tate formed the 'Fugitive' group of writers (so called after the magazine they ran from 1922 to 1925), who strove to retrieve what they considered the neglected values of the southern United States. He wrote extensively on politico-literary issues; influenced by the neo-Thomist theologian Maritain, Tate converted to Catholicism in 1950. At his death, he left incomplete a large-scale Dantescan project in *terza rima*, of which 'The Swimmers' and 'The Buried Lake' have been published.

Seasons of the Soul   41–120

To the memory of John Peale Bishop, 1892–1944

> *Allor porsi la mano un poco avante,*
> *e colsi un ramicel da un gran pruno;*
> *e il tronco suo gridò; Perchè mi schiante?*

---

dedication Bishop's reputation as a poet was high in the 1920s; he appears as D'Invilliers in Scott Fitzgerald's *This Side of Paradise*; Tate contributed a 'Personal Memoir' to his *Collected Poems* (1948)   epigraph *Inferno* 13.31–3 ('Then I moved my hand a little forward, and picked a twig from a great thorn bush; and its trunk shouted 'Why do you break me?')

I. Summer

When was it that the summer
(Daylong a liquid light)
And a child, the new-comer,
Bathed in the same green spray,
Could neither guess the night?
The summer had no reason;
Then, like a primal cause
It had its timeless day
Before it kept the season
Of time's engaging jaws.   10

Two men of our summer world
Descended winding hell
And when their shadows curled
They fearfully confounded
The vast concluding shell:
Stopping, they saw in the narrow
Light a centaur pause
And gaze, then his astounded
Beard, with a notched arrow,
Part back upon his jaws.   20

II. Autumn

It had an autumn smell
And that was how I knew
That I was down a well:
I was no longer young;
My lips were numb and blue,

16–20 *Inferno* 12.77–8

The air was like fine sand
In a butcher's stall
Or pumice to the tongue:
And when I raised my hand
30   I stood in the empty hall.

The round ceiling was high
And the gray light like shale
Thin, crumbling and dry:
No rug on the bare floor
Nor any carved detail
To which the eye could glide;
I counted along the wall
Door after closed door
Through which a shade might slide
40   To the cold and empty hall.

I will leave this house, I said,
There is the autumn weather –
Here, nor living nor dead;
The lights burn in the town
Where men fear together.
Then on the bare floor,
But tiptoe lest I fall,
I walked years down
Towards the front door
50   At the end of the empty hall.

The door was false – no key
Or lock, and I was caught
In the house; yet I could see
I had been born to it
For miles of running brought
Me back where I began.

---

43 compare *Inferno* 34.25

I saw now in the wall
A door open a slit
And a fat grizzled man
Come out into the hall: 60

As in a moonlit street
Men meeting are too shy
To check their hurried feet
But raise their eyes and squint
As through a needle's eye
Into the faceless gloom, –
My father in a gray shawl
Gave me an unseeing glint
And entered another room!
I stood in the empty hall   70

And watched them come and go
From one room to another,
Old men, old women – slow,
Familiar; girls, boys;
I saw my downcast mother
Clad in her street-clothes,
Her blue eyes long and small,
Who had no look or voice
For him whose vision froze
Him in the empty hall.   80
        (1944)

61–6 compare *Inferno* 15.17–21   67 compare the paternal/filial vocabulary
of *Inferno* 15 at lines 31, 37, 82–5

BASIL BUNTING (1900–1985)

Bunting objected to military service during the First World War on grounds of Quaker conscience, and was imprisoned for his beliefs (he served in the RAF during the Second World War). He met Pound and his circle in the early twenties, and joined Pound in Rapallo in 1924, later acknowledging 'two living men . . . taught me much: Ezra Pound and in his sterner, stonier way, Louis Zukofsky'. Recognition came overdue to Bunting after the appearance of his 'autobiography', *Briggflatts* (1966). He published translations from Persian, Latin and French.

The Well of Lycopolis   4.1–45

Ed anche vo' che tu per certo credi
che sotto l'acqua ha gente che sospira.

Stuck in the mud they are saying: 'We were sad
in the air, the sweet air the sun makes merry,
we were glum of ourselves, without a reason;
now we are stuck in the mud and therefore sad.'
That's what they mean, but the words die in their
    throat;
they cannot speak out because they are stuck in the
    mud.
Stuck, stick, Styx. Styx, eternal, a dwelling.
But the rivers of Paradise,
the sweep of the mountains they rise in?

---

title see Gibbon, *Decline and Fall of the Roman Empire*, chapter 27
epigraph *Inferno* 7.118–19, translated by Bunting in lines 40–41 below
1–4 *Inferno* 7.121–4   **7** *Styx* one of the rivers of the Greek underworld
8 *rivers of Paradise* see Genesis 2:10–14, but perhaps also referring to the
rivers in the earthly paradise of *Purgatorio* 28.130–31; Bunting notes: 'the
only one of the rivers of Paradise to which we have access on earth, namely
Zamzam, is reported to be brackish'

Drunk or daft hear   10
a chuckle of spring water:
drowsy suddenly wake,
but the bright peaks have faded.
Who had love for love
whose love was strong or fastidious?
Shadow and shadow noon shrinks, night shelters,
the college of Muses reconstructs
in flimsy drizzle of starlight:
bandy, hunchback, dot-and-carry-one,
praised-for-a-guinea.   20

Join the Royal Air Force
and See the World. The Navy will
Make a Man of You. Tour India with the Flag.
One of the ragtime army,
involuntary volunteer,
queued up for the pox in Rouen. What a blighty!
Surrendered in March. Or maybe
ulcers of mustard gas, a rivet in the lung
from scrappy shrapnel,
frostbite, trench-fever, shell-shock,   30
self-inflicted wound,
tetanus, malaria, influenza.
Swapped your spare boots for a packet of gaspers.
Overstayed leave.
Debauched the neighbor's little girl
to save two shillings . . .

muttering inaudibly beneath the quagmire,
irresolute, barren, dependent, this page
ripped from Love's ledger and Poetry's:
and besides I want you to know for certain   . 40
there are people under the water. They are sighing.
The surface bubbles and boils with their sighs.

Look where you will see it.
The surface sparkles and dances with their sighs
as though Styx were silvered by a wind from Heaven.
(1935)

STEVIE SMITH (1902–71)

Stevie Smith had what some would call a quiet life, working
for years as personal secretary to the same publisher, and living
from the age of three with an aunt in Palmer's Green (a suburb
in North London). This is not the impression given in her partly
autobiographical *Novel on Yellow Paper* (1936), which is viv-
acious to the point of mania, and had a deserved success on its
appearance. Her first volume of poems appeared the following
year; her distinctive talent was recognized by the award of the
Queen's Gold Medal for Poetry in 1969. Throughout her life
she puzzled at 'the sweetness and cruelty I have come to think
of as the essence of Christianity'.

At School

*A Paolo and Francesca situation but more hopeful, say in
Purgatory.*

> At school I walk with Elwyn
> Walk with Elwyn all the day
> Oh my darling darling Elwyn
> We shall never go away.
>
> This school is a most curious place
> Everything happens faintly
> And the other boys and girls who are here
> We cannot see distinctly.

---

8 perhaps because in *Inferno* 5 'all light is mute'

All the day I walk with Elwyn
And sometimes we also ride   10
Both of us would really always
Rather be outside.

Most I like to ride with Elwyn
In the early morning sky
Under the solitary mosses
That hang from the trees awry.

The wind blows cold then
And the wind comes to the dawn
And we ride silently
And kiss as we ride down.   20

Oh my darling darling Elwyn
Oh what a sloppy love is ours
Oh how this sloppy love sustains me
When we come back to the school bars.

There are bars round this school
And inside the lights are always burning bright
And yet there are shadows
That belong rather to the night than to the light.

Oh my darling darling Elwyn
Why is there this dusty heat in this closed
        school?   30
All the radiators must be turned full on
Surely that is against the rules?

Hold my hand as we run down the long
        corridors
Arched over with tombs
We are underground now a long way
Look out, we are getting close to the boiler room.

We are not driven harshly to the lessons you know
That go on under the electric lights
That go on persistently, patiently you might say,
40   They do not mind if we are not very bright.

Open this door quick, Elwyn, it is break-time
And if we ride quickly we can come to the sea-pool
And swim; will not that be a nice thing to do?
Oh my darling do not look so sorrowful.

Oh why do we cry so much
Why do we not go to some place that is nice?
Why do we only stand close
And lick the tears from each other's eyes?

Darling, my darling
You are with me in the school and in the dead trees'
50   glade
If you were not with me
I should be afraid.

Fear not the ragged dawn skies
Fear not the heat of the boiler room
Fear not the sky where it flies
The jagged clouds in their rusty colour.

Do not tell me not to cry my love
The tears run down your face too
There is still half an hour left
60   Can we not think of something to do?

---

48 compare *Inferno* 32.40–48   50 *You are with me* Elwyn resembles Paolo,
'this man who will never be separated from me' as Francesca calls him at
Inferno 5.135   *the dead trees' glade* perhaps recalling *Inferno* 13
58 *The tears run down your face* as Paolo's do at *Inferno* 5.140

There goes the beastly bell
Tolling us to lessons
If I do not like this place much
That bell is the chief reason.

Oh darling Elwyn love
Our tears fall down together
It is because of the place we're in
And because of the weather.   (1957)

Francesca in Winter

O love sweet love
I feel this love
It burns me so
It comes not from above

It burns me so
The flames run close
Can you not see
How the flames toss

Our souls like paper
On the air?   10
Our souls are white
As ashes are

O love sweet love
Will our love burn
Love till our love
To ashes turn?

---

title 'in winter' may recall the '*freddo tempo*' ('cold weather') of *Inferno*
5.41   8–10 compare *Inferno* 5.31–3

I wish hellfire
Played fire's part
And burnt to end
20   Flesh soul and heart

Then we could sit beside our fire
With quiet love
Not fear to look in flames and see
A shadow move.

Ah me, only
In heaven's permission
Are creatures quiet
In their condition. (1971)

SAMUEL BECKETT (1906–1989)

James Joyce said to Beckett, some time in the thirties: 'What runs through the whole of Dante is less the longing for Paradise than the nostalgia for being. Everyone in the poem says "*Io fui*" – I was, I was.' There is no record of reply, but Beckett might have answered that, because 'the only true Paradise is the Paradise that has been lost' (*Proust*), the distinction on which Joyce relies is not as sharp as he believed, or hoped. Joyce's remark stayed with Beckett: he quotes it in *Rough for Radio*, II (1976). Dante's influence on Beckett is more profound in his fictions than in his poems, just in the measure that Beckett's prose is more searching than his verse. The second of the poems included here was written shortly after the death of Beckett's father and sometimes referred to by its author as 'The Undertaker's Man'.

25–8 compare *Paradiso* 3.79–85

Alba

before morning you shall be here
and Dante and the Logos and all strata and
          mysteries
and the branded moon
beyond the white plane of music
that you shall establish here before morning

          grave suave singing silk
          stoop to the black firmament of areca
          rain on the bamboos flower of smoke alley
          of willows

who though you stoop with fingers of
          compassion
to endorse the dust   10
shall not add to your bounty
whose beauty shall be a sheet before me
a statement of itself drawn across the tempest
          of emblems
so that there is no sun and no unveiling
and no host
only I and then the sheet
and bulk dead   (1931; 1935)

---

title 'the dawn' (Italian or Latin); probably here, as in Beckett's early stories,
a girl's name   **2** *Logos* the Greek word meaning 'word' or 'concept' or
'power of thought', which St John applies in the opening verses of his gospel
to the Word Incarnate, Christ   **3** *branded moon* Dante and Beatrice discuss
the spots on the moon in *Paradiso* 2; this discussion is discussed in Beckett's
early story 'Dante and the Lobster'   **7** *areca* a kind of palm tree
9–10 see John 8:3–11   **14** *unveiling* contrast the climactic unveiling of
Beatrice at the end of *Purgatorio* 31

Malacoda

thrice he came
the undertaker's man
impassible behind his scutal bowler
to measure
is he not paid to measure
this incorruptible in the vestibule
this malebranca knee-deep in the lilies
Malacoda knee-deep in the lilies
Malacoda for all the expert awe
10   that felts his perineum mutes his signal
sighing up through the heavy air
must it be it must be it must be
find the weeds engage them in the garden
hear she may see she need not

to coffin
with assistant ungulata
find the weeds engage their attention
hear she must see she need not

to cover
20   to be sure cover cover all over
your targe allow me hold your sulphur
divine dogday glass set fair

---

title 'foul tail'; the name of the chief demon in *Inferno* 21   3 *scutal* like a
shield   6 *incorruptible* recalls by reversing 1 Corinthians 15:53
7 *malebranca* 'evil claw'; Beckett makes singular the name for the devils in
Inferno 21 and 22, always plural in Dante   10 compare *Inferno* 21.138–9
12 this line recalls a standard interpretation of the last movement of
Beethoven's last quartet, Op. 135, whose introduction is heard as asking,
'Must it be?' to which the movement is heard to reply, 'It must be'
14 *she* probably calling to mind Beckett's widowed mother
16 *ungulata* equipped with fingernails; perhaps from the '*unghioni*' ('huge
fingernails') of the devil, Rubicante, in *Inferno* 22.41

> stay Scarmilion stay stay
> lay this Huysum on the box
> mind the imago it is he
> hear she must see she must
> all aboard all souls
> half-mast aye aye
>
> nay   (1933; 1935)

W. H. AUDEN (1907–73)

In 1941, when well on his declared way back to the Christian
fold, Auden named Dante, Langland and Pope as the three
greatest influences on his writing, but he mentions Dante rarely
and with no special intimacy or penetration in his prose. His
poems also seem mostly unimpressed by the *Commedia*, with
the evident exception of 'In the year of my youth . . .', un-
finished and unpublished by Auden, which pastiches some
aspects of Dante's style in adept detail as only one who knew
his work well could, though the versification depends rather on
Langland.

'In the year of my youth . . .'   1.16–75, 137–63, 353–432

['The first canto, like the *Inferno*, takes one day. The speaker
falls asleep on a train, and seems to dream of his arrival in a
large city. In the station his old friend Sampson greets him and
proceeds to guide him, that evening, through rich and poor
neighbourhoods, explaining the economic background of con-
temporary social conditions . . . he and Sampson return to their

---

23 *Inferno* 21.105   24 *Huysum* Jan van Huysum, eighteenth-century
flower-painter; the name is used here to refer to one of his works, as in 'a
Degas'   27 recollecting, indifferently, either the boat of the damned in
Inferno 3 or the boat of the partially purged in *Purgatorio* 2, or both

hotel and go to sleep. The second canto, like the *Purgatorio*, begins with ablutions and a journey up a mountain.' (Lucy S. McDiarmid)]

My eyes were opened: we were entering a station,
Our speed was slackening, we had shut off steam.
Under a looming arch of steel
Great as that built by Sir Gilbert Scott
Which to travellers from Derbyshire, dwelling in dales,
Is their first portent of the power of London,
The sliding platforms slowed and stopped.
Descending from carriage I was caught in a crowd,
Schoolboys in shirts, satchel on back,
10   Penclips, sharpeners, and scouters diaries
Bulging the pockets above their hearts,
Daughters of the clergy coming home
Demure from a course of domestic science,
Typists with portfolios efficient and sly
Living by law and the length of a reference
Clerks and murderers and commercial travellers.
I was borne to the barrier by bobbling bowlers,
Swept in a stream of shortened skirts,
Lost among waterproofs and laddered hose.

20   As I gave up my ticket, I was greeted by a cry.
I heard my name and my hand was wrung
By one bareheaded in a windjammer jacket,
Fieldglass locked in a leather case
Slung round his shoulder, and a sun browned skin:
'Sampson' I said and we smiled at each other.

1–7 distantly recall the end of *Inferno* 2 and opening of *Inferno* 3, where entering (2.142), an arch or rather gateway (3.11), and power (3.5) all feature   20–25 compare *Inferno* 1.61–3, which Auden here recalls through Eliot, *The Waste Land* 60–70 (see above)   25 *Sampson* Auden's Virgil-figure is drawn from his friend Gerald Heard, whose theories about civilization and how to save it impressed the poet at this time

'I have not seen nor heard of you
Since we sat all evening by an open window
At a twenty-firster in Tootle's rooms.
Where have you been and what doing
Tell me, since you left the talkative city?'   30
'Just pottering about', he replied, 'but now
Let's get out of this crowd. I've a cab here waiting.
When we reach the hotel we can talk of old times.'
We moved past the bookstall, magazines laid
Like fish on slabs, to the station yard
Where a cabby was standing swinging his arms,
A shadow where giglamps guttered and winked,
Who stopped to salute us and let us in
And away we clattered over cobbled stone.
The windows rattling as the wheels turned   40
Left of the railing up the lighted high street,
A promenade pleasant with plots of grass
Flanking the pavements and planted with trees,
Benches for the leisured; light from the shops
Lit up the leaves on their undersides.
Goods were displayed behind plate glass:
One satin slipper austerely arrayed
On an inky background of blackest velvet,
A waxen sandboy in skiing kit
Dumb and violet among vapourous lamps,   50
While high up in the air in empty space
Five times a minute a mug was filled
Or in ten foot letters time after time
Words were spelt out and wiped away.
But a throng which was passing took them for
          granted:
A multitude, witty, warmed and fed
That glanced at our cab with the gaze of those
Who have paid their allowance to be left alone.
'The fashionable quarter' my friend remarked

*

60   Then I as one in an alien country
      First rehearses the words in his head afraid
      Of a shout of laughter from those sitting at table
      So stammered a question, 'Is it sport or what
      You have settled for to-morrow?' And smiling he
      Pointing to a door said, 'Peckish? Of course.
      Dinner is ready. Let us drift in there.
      Over oyster patties, I'll explain it all.'

      'Here's mud in your eye', he murmured, lifting a glass
      Blown on the Danube, beautiful here,
70   And unfolded a napkin, fuller's delight.
      And we sipped a wine of such a flavour
      Now as I write I also thirst.
      Silver and cutlery shimmered on linen
      Stamped with the mark of that sombre town
      Which fouls the Don still fresh from the moor.
      Waiters scuttled from side to side
      Of the vast hall feeding the valuable people,
      Or as goldfish come to the glass of their tank
      For a second then vanish with a flick of their tails,
80   Interested for a moment in another life,
      Would come to a stop, suddenly still,
      Attentive at table, taking an order.
      Issuing from somewhere an easy tune
      Was making all kinds of memory important
      And in the shaded light of standard lamps
      Clever and sad looked the simplest face.

                              *

---

60 *as one* . . . pastiching such characteristically detailed and psychologically
alert Dantescan similes as at *Purgatorio* 31.64–7   71–2 Dante often has
such turns (though never about food and drink), as at *Purgatorio* 2.112–14
74 *that sombre town* Sheffield, which stands on the River Don and is famed
for stainless steel cutlery; these informative circumlocutions often appear in
the *Commedia*, for example – with conscious humour – at *Purgatorio*
14.16–27   78 compare *Paradiso* 5.100–104

Below us, blue, in a boiler suit
A man was rubbing a rail with a rag
Who looked up staring straight in our faces.
Sampson waved and shouted good evening,   90
But as a dog hurt in an accident lies
Motionless in torture but trembling at a touch
Snaps at him who would help and heal
So did this one frown, his face full of hate,
Laughed and spat and looked away.
'Come', I said, pointing at a clock in the wall
Whose hands made an angle of a hundred and
        eighty,
'Let us see the cathedral. You show the way.'
At the point where we stood an old path divided
Like the arms of a T. We took the right.   100
O human pity in the English heart
Wincing at sight of a surgeon's lancet,
Gripped by the crying of a captured bird,
Shudder indeed at what I saw and tell.
Weep now, howl, till your eyes are full,
That life on one littoral lucky to be
Can make its tittle of eternity so cruel.
The street we traversed with setts was paved
Cracked and uneven as an Alpine glacier,
Wretched and dirty as a run for chickens,   110
Garbage chucked in the gutter and slops
Had collected in the hollows in loathsome pools,
And back to back houses on both sides stretched
A dead straight line of dung-coloured brick.
Here I made certain of a sorrow not
To be forgotten even in the act of love.

96–7 compare such elaborated time-tellings as at *Purgatorio* 9.1ff.
101–104 pity is a core subject of the *Commedia*, and Dante at times makes
such emphatic appeals to the reader's mind or sympathies (for instance at
Inferno 20.19–24)   108 *setts* squared cobble stones

Full as a theatre was that foul thoroughfare
With a great multitude of men and women,
Some sitting like sacks, some slackly standing,
120   Their faces in the glimmering gaslight grey,
Their eyeballs drugged as a dead rabbit's
Or child I saw at a window by want so fretted
His face had assumed the features of a tortoise.
But never murmur nor motion stirred
The inert air as on and on
And on we came, incredulous, beholding,
Sights worse than wounds or [   ]; a human
Forest all by one infection cancelled.
Despair so far invading every fibre
130   Each Sunday had destroyed in them
The private seat of the desire and the intelligence.
Then Sampson broke the silence. 'Nine times
Have the greater part here planted known
The summer's day constricted into winter's
And deeper in disaster must they dig their roots
For none we eye shall ever again
See metal melt nor mould be filled.'
I then, 'What was their occupation?'
And he with the patience of the perfect teacher,
140   Speaking carefully, choosing his pauses,
Walked on unstopping but with slower stride.
'Before the Romans built their rational roads
Riches were found in these surrounding hills
When ore from their bleak sides [   ] scratched
Was smelted by the Britons for its silver and lead
Starting an industry that ever since
As Royal Charters and Rolls record
Has made the hammer honoured here.
And to-morrow the marks of many generations,
150   To this one labour all their lives devoted,
On slope and valley you shall see engraved.
But what time had cherished, a tiddler could undo.

In the year of grace when the German fleet
Scuttled itself at Scapa Flow
And the cad who to scivvies sold his stamps
Was cock of the walk this world was doomed:
For a bargain with the nasal-voiced nation was
        struck
That breathe on the continent whose burning sands
Are furrowed by the tail of the free kangaroo.
They to lend cruisers to keep us still,   160
On newspaper at least, as in Nelson's time
Masters of the seas, the market policemen,
And we in return to take their lead,
Our whole supply at their price to import
With what result you have seen already.
But now let your eyes wake other thoughts
For there ahead is Cathedral rock.'   (written 1932)

C. H. SISSON (1914–2003)

Sisson has the unique distinction for an English poet of having translated both Lucretius's *De rerum natura* and Dante's *Commedia*; among his many other translations are versions of Virgil, Horace, Catullus, du Bellay, La Fontaine and Heine. He described himself as a reluctant poet but overcame that reluctance manfully in half a century of productive work; among his own poems, he identified the long sequence 'In insula Avalonia' (1974) as greatly influenced by Dante (we regret that constraints of space prevent its inclusion). Sisson, like Dante, worked in civil administration and, again like Dante, he adhered to a religious community (in Sisson's case, the Church of England) from much in whose recent conduct he sharply

---

153–4 *In the year* 1919; the German fleet was interned in Scapa Flow, off the north of Scotland, at the end of the war and scuttled by its own crews in June of that year

and painedly dissented. His translation of Dante caused some
surprise on account of its extreme plainness, which was
defended by the critic and poet Donald Davie:

> I think Sisson
> Got it, don't you? Plain Dante, plain as a board,
> And if flat, flat. The abhorrent, the abhorred,
> Ask to be uttered plainly.
> ('Summer Lightning', in *Collected Poems 1971–1983*)

Inferno 18   1–66

There is a place in Hell called Malebolge,
Made all of stone which is the colour of iron,
As is the circle which delimits it.

Right in the middle of the malignant plain,
Opens a well, which is both broad and deep,
The plan of which I will speak of in its place.

The belt which this leaves therefore forms a circle
Between the well and the high, difficult bank,
And the bottom of it has ten distinct valleys.

10   As, when in order to guard the walls,
Ditch after ditch is dug around a castle,
The ground acquires a characteristic formation,

---

1 *Malebolge* Dante invented this name for the eighth circle of hell, where ten
kinds of fraudulence are punished, beginning in this canto with pandars and
seducers; its name translates literally as 'bad pouches', referring to its many
ditches   3 *delimits* the Italian has a plainer word for 'turns around it'
12 *characteristic formation* the original's '*figura*' is less technical – 'contour'
or 'distinct outline' would be equivalents

So was the appearance of the valleys here;
And as, from the doorways of such fortresses,
There are footbridges to the outside bank,

So from the base of the rock emerged projections
Which ran across the embankments and the ditches,
Down to the well where they ended and met.

In this place, shaken from the back
Of Geryon, we found ourselves; the poet   20
Kept to the left, and I followed him.

On the right hand I saw fresh cause for pity,
Fresh torments, and fresh devils, with whips;
With these all the first recess was filled.

Down at the bottom were the sinners, naked:
On one side of the track they came towards us,
On the other, marched with us, but with longer
        strides,

As the Romans, to deal with the great throngs,
In the year of the Jubilee, upon the bridge,
Ordered things so that streams of people could
        pass,   30

And so that on one side they would all face
The castle, and go in the direction of St Peter's;
And on the other go towards the hill.

---

15 *footbridges* picking up Dante's characteristic diminutive in '*ponticelli*'
('little bridges')   19–20 Sisson's syntax matches the word order of the
Italian   20 *Geryon* a monstrous emblem of fraud; see *Inferno* 17.1ff.
29 *the Jubilee* celebrating the year 1300

On both sides, up on the dismal rock,
I saw horned devils with great whips,
Who lashed them cruelly from behind.

Ah, how they made them take to their heels
At the first stroke! And there was nobody
Who waited to have a second or a third.

40   While I went on, my eyes met somebody's;
And I immediately said to myself:
'I am sure that I have seen that man before.'

To look at him the better, I stopped in my tracks:
And my kind master halted with me,
And allowed me to go back a little way.

And that whipped spirit thought that he could hide
By bowing his head; but it availed him little,
And I said: 'O you with the downcast eyes,

If your manner and bearing are not deceptive,
50   You are Venedico Caccianemico:
But what brings you into this stinging mess?'

He said to me: 'I say it unwillingly;
But I am forced to do so by your clear speech,
Which makes me recollect my former world.

It was I who induced the beautiful
Ghisola to do what Marquis wanted,
However discreditable the story may sound.

---

50 *Caccianemico* Dante seems not to have known that he did not die until
1302; a wheeler-dealer in the politics of several North Italian towns, he was
said to have handed over his sister, Ghisola, to the Marquis of Este
51 *stinging mess* the Italian here ('*pungenti salse*') means literally 'piquant
sauces'; its sardonic vulgarity might be translated as 'in such a pickle'

And I am not the only one from Bologna
Who is weeping here; the place is so full of them
That there are not so many tongues learning now   60

To say "sipa" between Savena and Reno;
And if you want authority for that,
Recall to mind how avaricious we are.'

While he was speaking one of the devils struck him
With his long whip, and said to him: 'Go on,
Pimp, you'll make no money from women here.'
(1974)

Inferno 32   70–123

Then I saw a thousand faces there,
Blue with the cold; it makes me shudder
And always will, when I think of those frozen
        shallows.

While we were going onwards towards the centre
At which all weights become a single weight,
And I was shivering in the eternal cold;

Whether it was will or fate or fortune,
I do not know; but, passing among those heads,
I struck one in the face hard, with my foot.

---

61 *'sipa'* Bolognese dialect for *'si'*; 'aye' or 'yeah' might be an equivalent
  2 *blue* Dante has the untranslatable word *'cagnazzi'* which means
'doglike', 'ugly' and 'purple'

10   Weeping, he cried out: 'Why do you tread on me?
      If you have not come to increase the vengeance
      Of Montaperti, why do you molest me?'

      And I: 'My master, now, wait for me here,
      So that, with this one's help, I may clear a doubt;
      After that, make me hurry as much as you please.'

      My guide stood still, and I said to the one
      Who was still uttering frightful imprecations:
      'Who are you, who complain of other people?'

      'And who are you, who go through Antenora,'
20   He answered, 'striking other people's cheeks?
      If I were still alive, I would not stand it.'

      'I am alive, and it may matter to you,'
      Was my reply, 'if you want reputation,
      That I should put your name among my records.'

      And he to me: 'I want the opposite;
      Get out of here and give me no more trouble,
      You do not understand how to flatter here.'

      At that I took him by the scruff of the neck
      And said: 'You'd better tell me who you are,
30   Or I will tear out every hair of your head.'

      Then he to me: 'Even though you scalp me,
      I will not tell you who I am, nor show you,
      Though you stumble on my head a thousand times.'

---

12 *Montaperti* the first hint at Bocca degli Abati's identity (confirmed at 37
below); Bocca switched sides in the strife of Guelf and Ghibelline and at the
battle of Montaperti cut off the hand of the bearer of the Florentine
standard   17 *uttering frightful imprecations* the Italian is less of a mouthful
and means 'was still swearing hard'   19 *Antenora* the second zone of
Cocytus, ninth and lowest circle, where the treacherous are punished

I already had his hair coiled round my hand,
And had pulled out more than one bunch of it,
He yelping, and keeping his eyes lowered;

When another called: 'What is the matter, Bocca?
Isn't it enough for your jaws to chatter,
Without yelping? What devil is biting you?'

'Now,' I said, 'there is no need for you to speak,   40
You filthy traitor; for now, and to your shame,
I will take back a true report of you.'

'Go away,' he answered, 'tell them what you like;
And don't forget, if you get out of here,
The one who had his tongue so loose just now.

The thing he weeps for here is Frenchmen's money;
"I saw," you could say, "that man from Duera,
There where the sinners find it rather cool."

If you are asked who else was here, then say
You had beside you here the Beccheria   50
Who had his throat cut by the Florentines.

Gianni de Soldanier, I think, is further,
With Ganellone and that Tebaldello,
Who opened up Faenza while they slept.'   (1974)

---

47 *that man from Duera* Buoso di Dovera, lord of Cremona, sold out his
Lombard compatriots to Charles of Anjou in 1265   50 *Beccheria* a
treacherous abbot; he was beheaded   52 *Gianni de Soldanier* reputed to
have betrayed his Ghibelline clan for political gain   53 *Ganellone* the
infamous traitor in the *Chanson de Roland*   54 *they* 'it' would be clearer
and closer to the Italian

Purgatorio 17   76–139

We were at the point at which the stairway
Went no further, and we were stuck there,
Just like a ship which has arrived at the shore.

And I listened, to see if I could hear
Anything inside the new circle;
Then I turned to my master, and said:

'My gentle father, tell me, what offence
Is purged in the circle we are in now?
If our feet stop, no need for you to stop speaking.'

10   And he to me: 'The love of the good, defective
Without its duty, is in this place made whole;
Here the idle rower dips his oar again.

But, so that you may understand more clearly,
Pay attention to me, and you will find
Our stay here will yield you some good fruit.'

'Neither creator nor creature was ever,'
He then began, 'my son, without love,
Either natural or rational; you know that.

Natural love is always without error,
20   But the other kind may err, in the wrong object,
Or else through too much or too little vigour.

---

1 *at the point* Dante and Virgil are now on the fourth terrace of the
purgatorial mountain, on which sloth is purged

While it is directed to the primal good,
And keeps to its limits in relation to the secondary,
It cannot be the occasion of sinful pleasure;

But when it is twisted to evil, or seeks the good
With more or with less concern than it ought to have,
The creature is working against the creator.

So you can understand that love must be
The seed of every virtue that is in you
And of every action deserving of punishment.   30

Now, because love can never turn its face
From the well-being of the one who loves,
All creatures are free of hatred of themselves;

And since no being can be conceived as separate
And on its own, apart from the primal being,
Every creature is remote from hatred of him.

It follows, if my demonstration is correct,
That the evil which is loved is that of your neighbour;
And this love starts in three ways, in your dust.

There is the man who, through the suppression of
      his neighbour,   40
Hopes to excel, and for that reason only
Desires to see him cast down from his greatness:

There is the man who fears to lose power, favour,
Honour and glory because of another's success,
And so grieves for it that he loves the opposite:

And there is the man who takes umbrage at injury
So that he becomes greedy for revenge
And such a man must seek to harm another.

These three forms of love are repented of
50   Below us here; now I want you to understand
The other, which seeks good, but not as it ought to do.

Everyone has a confused notion of good,
On which he sets his mind, and which he desires;
And therefore everyone tries to attain it.

If the love which draws you to see or to reach it,
Is idle, then it will happen, here on this cornice,
That after proper repentance, you suffer for it.

There is another good which does not bring
            happiness;
It is not happiness, it is not the benign essence
60   Which is the root and fruit of every good.

The love which gives itself too much to this
Is wept for in the three circles above us;
But as to how the three modes are distinguished,

I say nothing, you can think it out for yourself.'
            (1974)

---

49 *three forms of love* the three misdirections of love which produce pride,
envy and anger, the sins purged on the first three terraces
62 *the three circles above us* the terraces on which, in ascending order,
avarice, greed and lust are purged
62–4 *circles . . . think it out for yourself* the untranslatable rhyme at this
point in the original is discussed in the Introduction

Paradiso 14

Centre to circumference, circumference to centre,
Is how water moves in a circular vessel
Depending on whether you strike from without or
    within.

That was the thought which dropped suddenly
Into my mind, just as the glorious
Life of Thomas became silent again;

It was the likeness which occurred to me
With his speaking and that of Beatrice
Who, when he had finished, was pleased to
    begin thus:

'What he needs, although he does not tell you,   10
Either in words nor, yet, in his thoughts,
Is to get to the root of another truth.

Tell him whether the light with which
Your substance flowers now, will remain with you
Eternally in the manner it is with you now;

If it does remain, tell him how,
When you are made visible again,
It can happen without troubling your sight.'

As, drawn and impelled by an access of gladness,
People who are dancing in a circle   20
Sometimes raise their voices and move more briskly,

---

6 *Thomas* St Thomas Aquinas, who discourses in *Paradiso* 13 on the Trinity
and on the right conduct of human intelligence
17 *made visible again* that is, when the blessed spirits recover their
resurrected bodies at the Last Judgement

So, at this eager and freely offered prayer,
The holy company showed a fresh joy
In their circling and in their marvellous notes.

Anyone who laments that we must die
And go to live above, has not in view
The refreshment that is poured out on us here.

That one and two and three which lives for ever
And reigns for ever in three and two and one,
30   Uncircumscribed, and circumscribing all,

Was sung three times by each of these spirits
With such melody as would itself be
Appropriate reward for any merit.

And I heard in the divinest light
Of the smaller circle a simple voice
Perhaps like that of the angel who spoke to Mary,

Answer: 'As long as this festivity
Of paradise shall last, so long our love
Will shed around us such rays as clothe us.

40   Its brightness is proportionate to its warmth,
The warmth to the vision, and that depends
On how much grace it has beyond its worth.

25–7 though the referents of 'here' and 'there' shift in the *Commedia*, the
Italian at this point clearly means 'A person who laments the fact that we die
here [on earth] in order to go to live up there does not see the cool
refreshment of the eternal rainfall there.' Dante's '*refrigerio*' derives from the
'*refrigerium*' spoken of in the Requiem Mass and is no doubt even more
refreshing than the September rains which end the long Italian summer
28 *That one* ... the Trinity   36 *the angel* see Luke 1:26–33; the 'simple
voice' is that of Solomon

When our flesh, then glorified and holy,
Is put on us once more, our persons will be
In greater perfection as being complete at last:

Because there will be an accession of that light
Which is freely given us by the highest good,
Light which enables us to see him;

In this way the vision must grow clearer,
And the warmth produced by it must grow too,   50
As well as the rays which shine out of it.

But, like charcoal which gives out a flame
And yet glows more brightly than the flame itself
So that it keeps its outline and appearance,

So the radiance which surrounds us now
Will be outshone by the brilliance of the flesh
Which now lies buried in the earth;

Nor will so much light weary us at all;
For the organs of the body will be strong
To everything able to give us pleasure.'   60

One and another chorus seemed to me
So quick and eager to say 'Amen!'
That it was clear they wanted their dead bodies;

Perhaps not just for themselves, but for their
        mothers,
For their fathers and others who were dear to them
Before they turned into eternal flames.

---

62 *Amen!* the highly specific quality of the Italian here is discussed in the
Introduction

And then around us, shining with equal brightness,
Appeared a lustre beyond what was there already,
In the manner of an horizon growing clearer,

70 And as at the first rising of evening,
New objects begin to appear in the heavens
So that they seem to be there, then seem not to be,

I thought that I was beginning to see
Newcomers like the others, making a circle
Outside the other two circumferences.

Oh a true radiance of the Holy Spirit!
How suddenly it appeared and shone
Into my eyes, so that they could not bear it!

But Beatrice showed herself to me
80 So lovely and smiling that her appearance must be left
With those sights which the mind cannot retain.

From this sight my eyes recovered strength
To raise themselves; and I saw I had been translated
With my lady alone to a higher blessedness.

I saw clearly that I had risen higher
By the glancing smile of the star
Which seemed to me redder than ordinary.

With all my heart, and speaking with that tongue
Which is the same in all men, I made to God
90 Such holocaust as befitted this new grace.

---

83 *translated* the Italian is '*traslato*', the only occurrence of the word in the
Commedia, with the root, Latinate sense of 'physically carried over'
86 *the star* the planet Mars   90 *holocaust* in the sense of 'thank-offering'

And the ardour of the sacrifice within me
Was not spent, before I knew that indeed
My offering was accepted and propitious;

For a splendour appeared in two bands
With such radiance and with such red glow
That I said: 'O Helios, who so arrays them!'

As, with its lesser and its greater lights,
The Galaxy spreads its white path between
The poles of the world, and makes wise men reflect;

So those starry bands composed,   100
In the depths of Mars, the venerable sign
Which diameters crossing at right-angles make in
    a circle.

Here what I remember is too much for expression;
For in that cross Christ himself shone
So that I find no fit comparison:

But whoever takes his cross and follows Christ
Will still forgive me for what I leave unsaid
When he sees that that whiteness flashed out Christ.

Meeting together and passing one another,
The lights sparkled brightly as they moved   110
From side to side and up and down that cross:

---

96 *Helios* the Greek god of the sun; the Italian reads 'Eliòs' which makes
clear that Dante is thinking in line with medieval etymology both of 'El'
(Hebrew: 'God') and 'Helios' (Greek: 'the sun')   101 *the venerable sign* a
Greek cross   102 the original is slightly less like a geometry textbook –
'which quadrants make when they join in a circle'   104–8 in the
corresponding Italian lines, Dante uniquely rhymes 'Cristo' with 'Cristo' and
'Cristo'

It is thus that tiny specks may be seen,
Straight and twisted, swift-moving and slow,
Never staying the same, long and short,

Moving through the ribbons of light which sometimes
Appear in the shadow which human skill
And brains procure for our protection.

As rebec and harp with the strings well-tuned
Make a sweet tintinnabulation
120 To one who knows nothing of the notes,

So, from the lights which appeared to me there,
Was gathered on the cross a melody
Which carried me away, though the hymn was
        not clear.

Certainly I could hear it was a song of praise
Because I could make out 'Arise' and 'Conquer',
As one might, without understanding, hear.

I so fell in love at that point
That there had been nothing hitherto
Which had so bound me with sweet chains.

130 Perhaps what I am saying may seem too daring,
When I put second the pleasure from the lovely eyes,
Looking into which my desire reaches rest:

But anyone who considers how the living pledges
Of all beauty worked more the higher we were,
And that I did not turn to look at them,

---

118 *rebec* an early form of fiddle   119 *tintinnabulation* the original has not
'*tintinnabolo*' ('tintinnabulation') but the less fancy '*tintinno*' ('tinkling')
131 *the lovely eyes* Beatrice's

Will be able to excuse what I accuse myself of
In order to excuse myself; and will see that I speak
   the truth;
For here the holy joy is not excluded

Because, as one rises, it becomes clearer. (1974)

JOHN CIARDI (1916–85)

Ciardi was born in Boston of Italian-American stock (he disliked the categorization). He worked vigorously at the diffusion of literature – as a university teacher, poetry editor of the *Saturday Review*, host of a TV arts programme and author of many children's books. His version of *Inferno* appeared in 1954 and sold a million copies in his lifetime; the remaining *cantiche* came out in 1961 and 1970. His popularity declined in the sixties; nonetheless, he co-wrote two volumes of limericks with Isaac Asimov.

Purgatorio 4 88–140

And he: 'Such is this Mount that when a soul
  begins the lower slopes it most must labor;
  then less and less the more it nears its goal.

Thus when we reach the point where the slopes seem
  so smooth and gentle that the climb becomes
  as easy as to float a skiff downstream,

---

139 *clearer* the original has '*sincero*'; the importance of this word to Dante is discussed in the Introduction
  1 *he* Virgil

then will this road be run, and not before
    that journey's end will your repose be found.
    I know this much for truth and say no more.'

10 His words were hardly out when, from nearby,
    we heard a voice say: 'Maybe by that time
    you'll find you need to sit before you fly!'

We turned together at the sound, and there,
    close on our left, we saw a massive boulder
    of which, till then, we had not been aware.

To it we dragged ourselves, and there we found
    stretched in the shade, the way a slovenly man
    lies down to rest, some people on the ground.

The weariest of them, judging by his pose,
20   sat hugging both knees while his head, abandoned,
    dropped down between them halfway to his toes.

'Master,' I said, 'look at that sorry one
    who seems so all-let-down. Were Sloth herself
    his sister, he could not be so far gone!'

That heap took heed, and even turned his head
    upon his thigh – enough to look at us.
    'You climb it if you're such a flash,' he said.

I knew him then, and all the agony
    that still burned in my lungs and raced my pulse
30 did not prevent my going to him. He

---

12 *you fly* not in Dante   22 *Master* at this point in the original, Dante
addresses Virgil as 'O my sweet lord'

raising his head – just barely – when I stood by,
    drawled: 'So you really know now why the sun
    steers to the left of you across the sky?'

His short words and his shorter acts, combined,
    made me half smile as I replied: 'Belacqua,
    your fate need never again trouble my mind.

Praise be for that. But why do you remain
    crouched here? Are you waiting for a guide,
        perhaps?
    Or are you up to your old tricks again?'

'Old friend,' he said, 'what good is it to climb? –   40
    God's Bird above the Gate would never let me
    pass through to start my trials before my time.

I must wait here until the heavens wheel past
    as many times as they passed me in my life,
    for I delayed the good sighs till the last.

Prayer could help me, if a heart God's love
    has filled with Grace should offer it. All other
    is worthless, for it is not heard above.'

32–3 the comment refers to a cosmological explanation which Dante has just
enthusiastically imbibed (*Purgatorio* 4.61–84)   35 *Belacqua* nothing is
certainly known of Belacqua apart from what may be inferred from this
canto – he was a great friend of Dante's, wry, lazy and saved
40 *Old friend* in the original, he calls Dante 'brother', a usual mode of
address in the second and third *cantiche*   41 *God's Bird* this charming
phrase is the product of textual corruption; authoritative editions now
substitute 'angel' for the '*uccel*' which Ciardi translated

But now the Poet already led the way
52   to the slope above, saying to me: 'Come now:
the sun has touched the very peak of day

Above the sea, and night already stands
with one black foot upon Morocco's sands.'   (1961)

Purgatorio 6   1–90

The loser, when a game of dice is done,
remains behind reviewing every roll
sadly, and sadly wiser, and alone.

The crowd leaves with the winner: one behind
tugs at him, one ahead, one at his side –
all calling their long loyalty to his mind.

Not stopping, he hands out a coin or two
and those he has rewarded let him be.
So he fights off the crowd and pushes through.

10   Such was I then, turning my face now here,
now there, among that rout, and promising
on every hand, till I at last fought clear.

There was the Aretine who came to woe
at the murderous hand of Tacco; and the other
who drowned while he was hunting down his foe.

---

53 *the sun* another instance of global time in *Purgatorio*; on the antipodean
Mount of Purgatory it is noon, therefore night descends in the northern
hemisphere down even to Morocco

10 *then* at the end of the previous canto, penitents of the last hour cluster
round Dante asking for his prayers   13 *the Aretine* Benincasa da Laterina, a
judge, murdered by Tacco in revenge for his condemnation of Tacco's
brother and uncle   14 *the other* Guccio da Pietramala, another casualty of
Guelf–Ghibelline strife – he drowned in the Arno

There, hands outstretched to me as I pushed
　　through,
　was Federico Novello; and the Pisan
　who made the good Marzucco shine so true.

I saw Count Orso; and the shade of one
　torn from its flesh, it said, by hate and envy,　　　　　20
　and not for any evil it had done –

Pierre de la Brosse, I mean: and of this word
　may the Lady of Brabant take heed while here,
　lest, there, she find herself in a worse herd.

When I had won my way free of that press
　of shades whose one prayer was that others pray,
　and so advance them towards their blessedness,

I said: 'O my Soul's Light, it seems to me
　one of your verses most expressly states
　prayer may not alter Heaven's fixed decree:　　　　　30

yet all these souls pray only for a prayer.
　Can all their hope be vain? Or have I missed
　your true intent and read some other there?'

And he: 'The sense of what I wrote is plain,
　if you bring all your wits to bear upon it.
　Nor is the hope of all these spirits vain.

---

17 *Federico Novello* murdered about 1290　*the Pisan* a son of Marzucco
degli Scornigiani who was murdered in 1287 on the orders of Count
Ugolino　19 *Count Orso* Orso degli Alberti, another victim of family
hatreds (two of his relatives may be found in *Inferno* 32)　*the shade* of Pierre
de la Brosse, surgeon to the French king; Dante believed he was condemned
to death because of a court intrigue led by Marie of Brabant
28 *Soul's Light* the Italian means only 'O my light'　29–30 compare *Aeneid*
6.376

The towering crag of Justice is not bent,
    nor is the rigor of its edict softened
    because the supplications of the fervent

40 and pure in heart cancel the debt of time
    decreed on all these souls who linger here,
    consumed with yearning to begin the climb.

The souls I wrote about were in that place
    where sin is not atoned for, and their prayers –
    they being pagan – were cut off from Grace.

But save all questions of such consequence
    till you meet her who will become your lamp
    between the truth and mere intelligence.

Do you understand me? I mean Beatrice.
50   She will appear above here, at the summit
    of this same mountain, smiling in her bliss.'

'My Lord,' I said, 'let us go faster now:
    I find the climb less tiring than at first,
    and see, the slope already throws a shadow.'

'The day leads on,' he said, 'and we shall press
    as far as we yet may while the light holds,
    but the ascent is harder than you guess:

before it ends, the Sun must come around
    from its present hiding place behind the mountain
60   and once more cast your shadow on the ground.

---

45 *they being pagan* Virgil is less direct in the original where he says only
that 'the prayer was not joined to God'

But see that spirit stationed all alone
   and looking down at us: he will point out
   the best road for us as we travel on.'

We climbed on then. O Lombard, soul serene,
   how nobly and deliberately you watched us!
   how distant and majestic was your mien!

He did not speak to us as on we pressed
   but held us fixed in his unblinking eyes
   as if he were a lion at its rest.

Virgil, nonetheless, climbed to his side   70
   and begged him to point out the best ascent.
   The shade ignored the question and replied

by asking in what country we were born
   and who we were. My gentle Guide began:
   'Mantua . . .' And that shade, till then withdrawn,

leaped to his feet like one in sudden haste
   crying: 'O Mantuan, I am Sordello
   of your own country!' And the two embraced.

Ah servile Italy, grief's hostelry,
   ah ship unpiloted in the storm's rage,   80
   no mother of provinces but of harlotry!

That noble spirit leaped up with a start
   at the mere sound of his own city's name,
   and took his fellow citizen to his heart:

---

64 *serene* not in Dante   77 *Sordello* troubadour and adventurer, he wrote
amorous and satirical poetry much admired by Dante; he died in 1273

> while still, within you, brother wars on brother,
>   and though one wall and moat surrounds them all,
>   your living sons still gnaw at one another!
>
> O wretched land, search all your coasts, your seas,
>   the bosom of your hills – where will you find
> 90 a single part of you that knows the joys of peace?
>   (1961)

ROBERT LOWELL (1917–77)

Lowell remained faithful to *Purgatorio* 5 over thirty changeable years. 'The Soldier' was published just as he lapsed from the Roman Catholicism to which he had converted in 1941; a last gasp of allusion to Buonconte da Montefeltro's story closes 'Home' in *Day by Day* (1977) where Lowell details his final hospitalization a little over a year before his death. He translated widely and with imperious freedom from several languages and described his aims in *Imitations* (1962): 'I have been reckless with literal meaning, and laboured hard to get the tone. Most often this has been *a* tone, for *the* tone is something that will always more or less escape transference to another language.'

The Soldier

> In time of war you could not save your skin.
> Where is that Ghibelline whom Dante met
> On Purgatory's doorstep, without kin
> To set up chantries for his God-held debt?

---

2 *that Ghibelline* Buonconte da Montefeltro whom Dante meets in *Purgatorio* 5.85–129; his father had appeared in *Inferno* 27.19–132
3 *Purgatory's doorstep* the ante-Purgatory of late repentant souls through which Dante and Virgil pass in *Purgatorio* 1–9

So far from Campaldino, no one knows
Where he is buried by the Archiano
Whose source is Camaldoli, through the snows,
Fuggendo a piedi e sanguinando il piano,
The soldier drowned face downward in his blood.
Until the thaw he waited, then the flood   10
Roared like a wounded dragon over shoal
And reef and snatched away his crucifix
And rolled his body like a log to Styx;
Two angels fought with bill-hooks for his soul.
  (1950)

Brunetto Latini [*Inferno* 15]

(For Lillian Hellman)

And now we walked along the solid mire
above a brook whose fuming mist protected
water and banks from the surrounding fire.
Just as the men of Flanders threw up huge
earthworks to stop the sea that always threatens
their fields and cattle between Ghent and Bruges,
or Paduans along the Brenta spread
out dykes to shield their towns and towers against
spring thawing the Carinthian watershed –
on such a plan the evil engineer,   10
whoever he was, had laid his maze of dykes,
though on a smaller scale, and with less care.

5–7 *Purgatorio* 5.92–3, 95–6   8 *Fuggendo . . . Purgatorio* 5.99 – 'fleeing on
foot and bloodying the plain'   12 *crucifix* this crucifix derives from a very
free reading of *Purgatorio* 5.126–7, where Buonconte says that he made his
own body a cross by crossing his arms on his chest   14 a vivid rendering of
Purgatorio 5.103–8, which Lowell translates more closely in 'Dante 3'
  10 *evil* not in Dante   12 *and with less care* not in Dante

By now we'd gone much deeper underground,
and left the bleeding wood so far behind
I'd have seen nothing, if I'd looked around.
We met a company of spirits here,
trooping below us on the sand. Each one
stared closely at our faces. As men peer
at one another under the new moon,
20   or an old tailor squints into his needle,
these puckered up their brows and glowered. Soon,
I saw a man whose eyes devoured me, saying,
'This is a miracle'. He seized my sleeve,
and as I felt his touch, I fixed my eyes
with such intensity on his crusted face
that its disfigurement could not prevent
my recognizing who he was. 'Oh, Oh,'
I answered groaning, as I stretched my hand
to touch his arm, 'are you here Ser Brunetto?'
30   He answered, 'Do not be displeased, my Son,
if Brunetto Latini turn and walk a little
downward with you, and lets this herd pass on.'
Then I, 'I'll go with you, or we can sit
here talking as we used to in the past,
if you desire it, and my guide permit.'

'O Son,' he answered, 'anyone who stands
still a moment will lie here a hundred years,
helpless to brush the sparks off with his hands.

---

14 *the bleeding wood* of the suicides in *Inferno* 13   16 *here* in the seventh
circle of the 'violent against nature'   27–8 *'Oh . . . groaning* not in Dante
29 *Ser Brunetto* the 'Ser' is a respectful greeting for Brunetto Latini
(1220–94), a Guelf who was exiled in France from 1260 to 1266. His
political activities left him time to translate Cicero and compose his own
works in French and Italian; he was highly esteemed as a rhetorician and
refiner of manners. Only Dante supplies the information that he was a
homosexual.   30 *my Son* only Virgil and Brunetto Latini address Dante as
'son' in hell (the endearment is repeated in the Italian where Lowell repeats it
at line 36)

Move on, I'll follow. Soon enough I must
rejoin my little group of friends who walk   40
with me lamenting their eternal lust.'
Then since I dared not leave my bank and move
over the flames of his low path, I bent
my head to walk with reverence and love.
Then he, 'What brings you here before your day?
Is it by accident, or Providence?
Who is this man who guides you on your way?'
I answered, 'In the world that lies serene
and shining over us, I lost my path,
even before the first young leaves turned green.   50
Yesterday morning when my steps had come
full circle, this man appeared. He turned me round,
and now he guides me on my journey home.'
'O Son,' said he, 'if you pursue your star,
you cannot fail to reach the glorious harbor.
And if the beautiful world, less sinister,
had let me live a little longer, I too
might have sustained your work and brought you
    comfort,
seeing how heaven has befriended you.
But that perverted and ungrateful flock   60
that held the hills with Catiline, and then
descended, hard and sterile as their rock,

---

41 *lust* it is not their 'lust' but their 'woes' or 'hurts' ('*danni*') which are
eternal in Dante   44 *and love* not in Dante   46 *accident, or Providence* in
the original, there is no mention of Providence but only of 'chance or
destiny'; Dante's damned rarely speak directly of God or his operations
47 *this man* Virgil, though Dante for some reason does not answer the
question   50 the original of this line means 'before my age was full' and
does not refer to spring as the events take place at Easter, after spring has
come to Italy   54 *O Son* not in Dante at this point   60 *perverted* the word
Lowell is translating ('*maligno*') has none of the twentieth-century
connotations of 'perverted' and just means 'ill-willed'   60–63 legend had it
that the Romans destroyed Fiesole and then founded Florence with a mixed
population of the defeated Fiesolani and imported Romans

to govern Florence, hate you for the good
you do; and rightly! Could they wish to see
the sweet fig ripen on their rotten wood?
Surely, they've earned their reputation: blind,
fratricidal, avaricious, proud.
O root their filthy habits from your mind!
Fortune will load such honors on your back
70   that Guelph and Ghibelline will hunger for you.
But beat them from the pasture. Let the pack
run loose, and sicken on the carcasses
that heap the streets, but spare the tender flower,
if one should rise above the swamp and mess –
some flower in which the fragile, sacred seed
of ancient Roman virtue still survives
in Florence, that vulture's nest of lies and greed.'
'Master,' I said, 'you would not walk here now
cut off from human nature, if my prayers
80   had had an answer. I remember how
I loved you, sitting at your knees – all thought
fixed on your fatherly and gentle face,
when in the world, from hour to hour, you taught
me how a man becomes eternal. O
Master, as long as I draw breath and live,
men shall remember you and what I owe.
Your words about my future shall remain
with other prophecies I keep to give
a Lady, who if I reach her, will explain.
90   This much I know: If I can bear the stings
of my own heavy conscience, I will face
whatever good or evil Fortune brings.

---

67 *fratricidal* in the original, Latini calls the Florentines 'blind, avaricious,
envious and proud'   70 *Guelph and Ghibelline* the original has only 'one
faction and the other'; for all his political involvements, Dante has only one
use each of the party labels in the *Commedia* (*Paradiso* 6.103 and 107)
74 *swamp and mess* the original is bolder – '*letame*' ('dungheap')
78 *Master* not in Dante   81 *sitting at your knees* not in Dante   84–5 *O /
Master* not in Dante   89 *a Lady* Beatrice

This promise of good fortune has been made
before this; so, let Fortune whirl her wheel
at random, and the peasant work his spade.'

Then Virgil, turning backward with one hand
lifted in wonder, mused at me, and said:
'He who knows how to listen shall understand.'

Dwelling upon his words, I did not stop
eagerly briefing Ser Brunetto, and asked,   100
'Who are the most illustrious in your group?'
And he, 'It's right to know a few of us,
but fitting I be silent on the rest;
our time's too short to squander on such dross.
In one word, we were scholars in our time,
great men of letters, famous in the world
we soiled and lost for our one common crime.
Priscian goes with us on this dismal turf,
and Francesco d'Accorso; you can see,
if you have any liking for such scurf,   110
the man the Servants' Servant chose to serve
him on the Arno, then on the Bacchilione,
where he laid down his ill-extended nerve.
I would say more to you, but must not stand
forever talking, speech must have an end.
I see fresh steam is stirring from the sand,

96–7 *with one . . . wonder* not in Dante   104 *on such dross* not in Dante
108 *Priscian* a sixth-century grammarian, highly respected in the Middle
Ages   109 *d'Accorso* an academic lawyer who held professorships at
Bologna and Oxford   111 *the man* Andrea de' Mozzi, bishop of Florence
('on the Arno') until 1295 and then of Vicenza ('on the Bacchilione')
the Servants' Servant a formulaic title of the Pope's

and men I would avoid are coming. Give
me no pity. Read my *Tesoro*. In
my book, my treasure, I am still alive.'

120   Then he turned back, and he seemed one of those
who run for the green cloth through the green
          field
at Verona . . . and seemed more like the one
who wins the roll of cloth than those who lose.   (1967)

Dante 3. Buonconte
[Purgatorio 5.89, 91–107, 119, 124–7]

'No one prays for me . . . Giovanna or the others.'
What took you so far from Campaldino
we never found your body? 'Where the Archiano
at the base of the Casentino loses its name
and becomes the Arno, I stopped running,
the war lost, and wounded in the throat –
flying on foot and splashing the field with blood.
There I lost sight and speech, and died saying
          Maria . . .
I'll tell you the truth, tell it to the living,
10   an angel and a devil fought with claws for my soul:
You angel, why do you rob me for his last word?
The rain fell, then the hail, my body froze,
until the raging Archiano snatched me,
and loosened my arms I'd folded like the cross.'
          (1973)

117–18 *Give / me no pity* not in Dante   118 *Tesoro* a massive treatise
Latini wrote in French   121–2 *who run . . . Verona* an annual race with a
green banner as its prize
   1 *Giovanna* Buonconte's widow

JOHN HEATH-STUBBS (1918–   )

Heath-Stubbs noted of his translation from *Inferno*, orig-
inally commissioned by the BBC for a translation of the *Com-
media* by various hands: 'The poets who contributed to this
were free to choose their own methods of translating Dante . . .
I did not want to use the Terzarima, which is a very constricting
metre in English . . . Other metres, blank verse, for instance,
seemed to me to have post-Dantesque connotations in relation
to English verse. Then it suddenly came to me that Dante was
after all a medieval poet, and that his nearest analogue in
English literature was perhaps to be found not in Milton . . .
but William Langland. I therefore used a version of the old
English alliterative metre. The effect may strike the reader as
grotesque, but I think I did at least succeed in bringing out
certain features of Dante, which have been lost in other English
translations. I mean a Gothic quality in him, and a kind of
earthiness . . .'

Inferno 6

Then as consciousness came back to my mind which had
    been clouded
  With pity for those cousins, those kinsfolk in their pain,
  Which had astounded me quite and stunned me into
    stupor,
I saw fresh torments there, and fresh tormented
    therewith,
  Around me are ranked there wheresoever I range
  My gaze, or my eyes go, or where they turn back again.

---

1 *as consciousness came back* after Dante has fainted with pity for Paolo and
Francesca at the end of *Inferno 5*   3 Heath-Stubbs expands on Dante's
words, whose meaning is 'which utterly dazed me with sadness'; there are
similar amplifications throughout

I am in the third round's den – deep there is the
    downpour,
  The timeless, cheerless rain, accurs'd and chillily
    falling,
  Which knows no change or renewal in nature or
    quality.
Heavy falling of hailstones, and foul water, and hell's
10   sleet
  Dank through the dark air is continually drenching;
  A filthy stench is from the ground and grievous, that
    takes that falling.
Misformed Cerberus here that both fierce is and fell,
  With his three gullets hideous, houndlike bays
    howling
  Over the people submerged, immersed there in the
    mud.
Blood crimson his eyes are ablaze, black and greasy his
    muzzle
  Both wide is his belly and big, and his hands with
    claws barbed.
  He rends the spirits and wrenches them and rips them
    into quarters.
And the downpour makes them howl dolefully like dogs,
20 With one side seeking still to shelter the other
  Thus writhing and turning, those wretches reprobate.
When Cerberus sighted us, and the great slimy maggot
    saw us,
  He gaped wide his gullets and showed his ghastly
    fangs
  And from stem to stern no limb of him was still.

---

7 *the third round's den* the third circle is given over to the gluttonous
10 *Heavy . . . hailstones* though the pastiche of Langland into which
Heath-Stubbs has translated Dante deploys alliteration as a structural
principle (which the verse of the *Commedia* does not), this alliterative
doublet coincides with a local effect in the original ('*grandine grossa*')
13 *Cerberus* Dante draws on *Aeneid* 6.417–23 for the description of the
infernal watchdog but adds details of his own, such as the pot-belly

My guide then spread out the full span of his grasp,
   Took clods of the clay, whole fistfuls clasping,
   And thrusting he threw them into those ravening throats.
And just as a great dog that growls and barks in his greed,
   Soon as his food he grips, silent he grows,
   Since his instinct and aggression are only to that end,   30
In such manner those foul mouths and filthy muzzles
   Of the rabid devil Cerberus who rants so and roars,
   That those damned souls who hear it are desirous to
     be deaf.
We passed then over those shades pressed down by the
     pouring rain,
   And fetched the soles of our feet on the false show of their
     seeming,
   The baselessness of their being, which assumes the shape of
     a body.
The lot of them lay there on the ground lubberly,
   Saving a single one who raised himself and sat up
   When he saw and perceived us passing on that pathway.
'O you who are here led through the halls of hell'   40
   So he cried out to me 'Recall me if you can;
   You, man who were made before I was unmade.'
And I to him in answer 'The anguish in which you are
   Maybe from my memory and from my mind withholds
     you
   So that it seems to me that I never saw you.
But tell me and teach me too who you are, here in such
     torment
   Down in this dreadful place, such punishment
     deserving:
   Greater there may be and grimmer, yet none so
     disgusting.'
And he to me said then 'Your own city, surcharged
   With bitter envy brimful, so that the bag overflows,   50
   In her I led my lifetime in the light of the clear day.

---

49 *Your own city* Florence

You, native townsfolk, knew me – Ciacco the name was,
    Gluttony was the fault, the foul sin I fell in,
    Wherefore, as now you see, I am soaked in the rain's
        sluice;
And I, a soul here in sorrow, am not alone in this
        sadness;
    Like pain and like penalty here is paid us who suffer
    For sins of the same kind.' He said no word further.
'Ciacco,' I made answer, 'Your misery moves me,
    Weighs heavily on my mind, and would make me to
        weep,
60   But tell me if you can what is cast, and shall come.
For the townsfolk of this town, divided and torn
        asunder,
    Tell me if any be righteous there, and what the root
        and reason
    Why to such division and discord it is doomed.'
Then he to me: 'At length, from long contention and
        lasting
    They shall come to bloodshed and wounds and war;
        and the backwoods party
    Shall drive out the other faction with force and with
        much offence.
This it behoves shall happen, and have place within the
        time
    Of the circling of three suns, then the other side shall
        prevail
    Through the succour of one who now sets his sails to
        every wind.
For a long time they shall lord it with scornful front
70   uplifted,

---

52 *Ciacco* known only by this nickname ('hog')   65 *bloodshed* Ciacco may
prophesy the brawl of 1 May 1300 *the backwoods party* the White Guelfs
66 *the other faction* the Black Guelfs, whose leaders were banished in June
1301   69 *one* probably Boniface VIII, who conspired with the Black Guelfs
to bring about the downfall of the Whites, and Dante's exile, in 1302

Breaking the others down with heavy burdens to bear,
Although overwhelmed they weep, shamefast and
    woebegone.
Two righteous things are to be rated, but their reason goes
    there unheeded;
Arrogance and eager envy with avid avarice also
Are flaming sparks that fire all hearts there as their fuel.'
Completed thus his complaint, plangent and fit for tears,
Made I answer to him then 'More, for my mind's
    enlightenment,
Furnish me further, and favour me with speech;
Tell me where is Farinata now, and Tegghiaio that were
    so noble,
Jacopo Rusticucci, Arrigo, Mosca, and the rest   80
Whose minds were bent on the better course and the
    public benefit?
Where are they now I would know, so to have knowledge of
    them;
For great longing consumes me to learn of their last end,
If Heaven sweetens them now, or Hell, envenomed, holds
    them.'
And he: 'They are blasted among souls more black and more
    blameworthy;
Weighted with different sins, down they have gone to
    the depths:
If you descend so much more you may meet with them
    there.
But when your way you shall wend back to the sweet world
Remember me, I pray, to the minds of men again;
No more shall I speak nor may, no more will answer.'   90
Then his straight eyes he squinted and turned them
    aslant from me,

---

73 *things* a mistranslation; the Italian implies 'two men' who have not been
identified   79–80 *Tell me where* the answer is, in order of naming: in the
sixth circle; in the seventh circle (Tegghiaio and Rusticucci); unknown; in the
ninth pouch of the eighth circle

A little still looked at me, and then at length his head
    slumped,
Then dropped with the others, blinded and blinking in
    the blizzard.
Then said my guide 'No more will he move or wake in
    the mire,
Till that clear sound, and clangour of the Archangel's
    clarion,
The advent of their Adversary who then His power
    advances.
Then each one shall seek once more sadly his sepulchre,
    Refledge himself in his own flesh and his own proper
    form,
And that day hear his doom through eternity
    redounding.'
Thus through the foul mixture and muddle we made
100   onwards
    Through the shadows and the sheets of rain, with slow
    pace shifting,
At leisure touching a little there on the life to come.
'Master,' I said then, 'These torments, will they in time
    Increase more searingly, when is said the great
    sentence,
Dwindle then or diminish, or burn as they do now?'
He said 'Lean on your logic, have you not learned from
    this,
It poses that if anything more of perfection possesses,
The more its potential for pleasure, and for pain
    likewise?
And though they are incapable, this canaille in their
    cursedness,
110   Forever of possessing the pitch of true perfection,
    Needs must after the Judgement they be nearer it than
    now.'
Thus on that street going, our steps we stayed not,
    Touching on many topics which I forbear of telling,

Until we reached that slope where it slants down and
    descends,
Where Plutus we came on plain, the great foe with his
    plunder. (1966; 1988)

Canzone: To the Lady Pietra [Rime 102: 'Amor, tu vedi ben che questa donna']

(from Dante)

O Love, thou knowest well how that this lady
Heeds not thy potency in any season
Though of all other fair it be the lady;
And when she did perceive she was my lady
And shining from my face beheld thy light,
Of cruelty she made herself the lady:
To bear the heart, not of a gentle lady,
But of that breast which proves to love most cold;
So through the season of heat and through the cold
She shows to me the semblance of a lady   10
Made altogether of some beauteous stone
By hand of one who could best carve in stone.

And I, more steadfast-firm than any stone,
Obeying thee for beauty of a lady,
Bear hid in me the mark made by that stone
With which thou smote me as it were a stone
Which thou hadst learned to hate through a long
    season,
Even striking to my heart, where I am stone;

115 *Plutus* the Greek god of wealth; Dante transforms him into a raucous
demon
    title this unidentified 'Lady Stone' is the subject of four lyrics by Dante,
apparently written in the winter of 1296   1 *thou knowest* the archaic
language corresponds to nothing in the original but rather continues D. G.
Rossetti's manner of translating Dante's lyrics

And never was discovered precious stone,
By splendor of the sun or by his light,
Which did possess such virtue and such light
That it might be my aid against that stone,
So that it should not bring me with its cold
To such a pass that I were dead with cold.

My lord, thou knowest that by freezing cold
Water is turned into a crystal stone
In northern regions, where is the great cold;
The very air to element of cold
Is still converted, water being the lady
Of all those lands by reason of the cold:
And so it is that at her aspect cold
The frost comes in my blood at every season;
And thought of her, which shortens my life's season,
Is all converted into substance cold,
Which issues from my eye, the body's light,
Whither first entered the unpitying light.

In her collected is all beauty's light,
Likewise of cruelty runs all the cold
Into her heart, where never came thy light;
For to my eyes so lovely is her light,
Looking on her, I see her in a stone,
And wheresoever else I turn for light;
For me, out of her eyes comes the sweet light
That makes me heedless of each other lady;
Would that she were more piteous a lady
To me, who seek in darkness and in light,
Serving her only, for due place and season,
Nor otherwise would wish to live long season.

Therefore, O power, older than time or season,
Older than motion or the sensible light,
Take pity on me who have such evil season,
And enter now her heart – it is due season:

So shall, by thee, pass forth from her the cold
Which lets me not, as others, have my season;
Should I be overcome by thy strong season,
In such estate, here this most noble stone
Would see me laid within a narrow stone,
Never to rise till end of time and season:
Then shall I see if ever was fair lady
In all the world like to this bitter lady.   60

My song, I carry in my mind a lady
Such that although to me she be of stone,
I am so brave that all men else seem cold,
And dare to fashion even for this cold,
The novelty which through your form shows
        light –
That which was never thought in any
        season.   (1947)

ROBERT DUNCAN (1919–88)

Like Dante, Duncan lost his mother when he was very young;
like Dorothy L. Sayers, he was much impressed by Charles
Williams' *The Figure of Beatrice*. Dante played a major role
in Duncan's distinctive melding of elements from European
tradition with the declared, even declamatory, 'openness' of
form he espoused along with writers such as Olson and Creeley;
he wrote in his *The Sweetness and Greatness of Dante's Divine
Comedy* that 'one of the axioms of a new poetry – "No ideas
but in things" [the phrase is from William Carlos Williams]
– is catholic and in the spirit of Dante.' His *Dante Études*
incorporate, as he noted, parts of 'the Temple Classics transla-
tions of Dante's prose'.

Sonnet 1

Now there is a Love of which Dante does not speak
    unkindly,
Tho it grieves his heart to think upon men
  who lust after men and run
   – his beloved Master, Brunetto Latini, among
   them –
Where the roaring waters of hell's rivers
Come, heard as if muted in the distance,
  like the hum of bees in the hot sun.

Scorcht in whose rays and peeld, these would-be
    lovers
Turn their faces, peering in the fire-fall,
   to look at one another
As men searching for an other
  in the light of a new moon look.

Sharpening their vision, Dante says, like a man
  seeking to thread a needle,
They try the eyes of other men
Towards that eye of the needle
  Love has appointed there
For a joining that is not easy.   (1964)

---

title 'sonnet' is used in the archaic sense of 'a short poem', without
commitment to fourteen lines   3 *run* compare the initial restlessness and
climactic simile – 'like those who run at Verona' – of *Inferno* 15
4 *Brunetto Latini* see *Inferno* 15.22–124   5 *hell's rivers* Virgil names them
and their source in *Inferno* 14.112–20   5–7 compare *Inferno* 16.1–3
   8–14 compare *Inferno* 15.17–21

Dante Études
Book One [De vulgari eloquentia 1.1]

=I=
'We will endeavor,
the word aiding us from Heaven,
    to be of service
to the vernacular speech'

    from 'Heaven' these

'draughts of the sweetest honey-milk',

    si dolcemente

from the language we first heard

    endearments   whisperings

                infant song and reverie   10

a world we wanted   to go out into,

    to come to our selves into,

    organizations in the sound of them
    verging upon meaning,
                upon 'Heaven'

1–4 drawn from the opening paragraph of *De vulgari eloquentia*
6 *sweetest honey-milk* translating '*dulcissimum ydromellum*', the last words
of that first paragraph   7 *si dolcemente* probably quoting from *Purgatorio*
2.113–14 ('he began to sing *so sweetly* that the sweetness still rings within
me')

hermetic talk
into which my range of understandings
was to grow   for love of it

            portents

20   and adults expounding
            controversial doctrines, personal
            science-fictions and
            rules of order

but our own

'is that which we acquire without
any rule'   for love of it
                'imitating our nurses'

                        *

from the beginning,   color
and light, my nurse;   sounding waves
30   and air, my nurse;   animal presences,
my nurse;   Night,   my nurse   .

            out of hunger,   instinctual
            craving,   thirst for 'knowing',

            toward oracular tits.

This,

8–9 compare *De vulgari eloquentia* 1.1.2   **24** *our own* 'language' is to be
understood   **25–7** drawn from the second paragraph of *De vulgari
eloquentia*

being primary,
   natural and common,
being 'milk',

is animal – –

   lungs sucking-in the air, having   40
   heart in it, rhythmic, and,
       moving in measure,
   self-creative in concert

– – and therein,

noble. (1974)

AMY CLAMPITT (1920–94)

Brought up as a Quaker in New Providence, Iowa, Clampitt
moved in the 1940s to New York where she wrote several
novels (as yet unpublished) and worked for Oxford University
Press. She wrote to a friend about a trip to Europe in those
years: 'the minute I crossed the border into Italy at Ventimiglia
– I was free to show excitement, as I'd never quite been any-
where else'. Howard Moss at *The New Yorker* began to publish
her poems in 1978; she produced five books in the fifteen years
which remained to her. In *Archaic Figure* (1987), she has two
poems which view Medusa in a different light from that which
Dante sheds on her in *Inferno 9*.

---

45 *noble* Dante actually claims that our 'mother-tongue' is '*nobilior*' ('more
noble') than any polished, literary language we may later acquire, the prime
example of which for him was Latin

At a Rest Stop in Ohio

Forth from the hand
of God, or, proximately,
the cavern of a westbound

Greyhound, the little
simple soul, at no
great distance still

from its scathed and
shivering first cry,
its gasping first, blind

10   mouthful, here and now
wallows howling, as
though there were no

elsewhere: What ails it?
The dark night of the
little simple soul, without

so much as the resources
to demand to know
Why was I born? is

dark indeed. Bound though
20   it may be for the city
of the angels, snow

---

title 'An infant wailing in a bus terminal, T. S. Eliot's "Animula" and its
sources in the work of Dante and the Emperor Hadrian: this only
momentarily surprising conjunction came out of a reading by Howard
Nemerov, to whose rendering of *Animula, vagula, blandula* the poem owes
its concluding line.' [*Clampitt's note*]   1–2 *Purgatorio* 16.85
4–5 *Purgatorio* 16.88

warnings intervene,
to discommode a mother
ebony of cheekbone

and more than comely
but listless to realign
the warp of history by

more than a snippet, or
forestall, when the wailing
stops, the looming torpor –   30

except from, just possibly,
inside the fragile
ambush of being funny.   (1990)

The Underworld of Dante: Canto IX [Inferno 9]

Seeing me stand there green with fear, my guide,
returning, the more quickly bottled up
the look that told me he was newly worried.

He halted, listening; for through that murk,
that black air's vaporous density, the eye
could hardly venture. 'Surely in the end

we must win out,' he said. 'If not . . .'
A pause. 'Assurances were given. But so
much time, and still no sign of anyone!'

23–5 *a mother . . . comely* compare Song of Songs 1:5
  1 *green* Dante says only 'the colour of cowardice'

10 I heard too vividly how he dissembled,
overlaying what he had begun
to say with words that differed so,

I grew more fearful still – more than,
perhaps, his hesitation warranted,
inferring from it worse than what he'd meant.

'Does anyone,' I asked him then, 'go deep
as this, into this godforsaken hollow,
from that level where the sole penalty

is hope cut off?' 'Rarely,' he answered,
20 'does any of us from that first circle
follow the downward track we travel now –

though I myself once did so, conjured by
the witch Erichtho, whose power it was
to mingle shade with corpse again. My own

remains were not long nude of me before
she summoned me to pass within that wall
and fetch a shade from the abode of Judas –

a circle farther down and darker, more
remote from all that's good, than any other.
30 Oh, I know the way, you may be certain.

---

10 *heard* the original means 'saw'   17 *godforsaken* Dante's adjective means
'sad'   20 *first circle* the Limbo of virtuous pagans, visited in *Inferno* 4
23 *Erichtho* in Lucan's *Pharsalia*, this Thessalian witch brings a dead man
back to life; Lucan's account gives Dante the hint for his otherwise
unprecedented story of Virgil's previous descent into lowest hell

This marsh from which so huge a stench goes up
girdles the doleful metropolis.
Rage will confront us here before we enter.'

What he said next I now forget, my sight
being drawn by then to what appeared
lit up by the infernal glare within

Those towers: three hellish things that had
in form and attitude the look of women,
blood-smeared, greenly garlanded at waist

and temple by a clutch of water snakes,   40
wildly writhing, serpentine-haired,
viperish: such were the Furies.

He who well knew these minions from the
          household
of her who rules where groaning never ends,
named for me one by one the foul Erinyes:

'That is Megaera to the left; the one
who ravens on the right, Alecto; and
between the two, Tisiphone.' He halted,

as each clawed or struck with open palm
at her own person, shrieking so fiendishly   50
I shuddered, and moved closer to the poet.

---

32 *metropolis* the city of Dis, which Dante and Virgil enter at 106ff. below;
Dante calls it only a '*città*' ('city')   37 *three hellish things* Dante draws on
Aeneid 6.570–72 and 7.324–9 for his account of the Furies/Erinyes
47 *ravens* in the original, Alecto 'weeps'   50 *fiendishly* the Italian means
'loudly'

'Call for Medusa: she'll turn him to rock,'
regarding us below, they howled as one.
'What Theseus tried here is not yet paid back.'

'Turn round, and keep your eyes closed. Were
the Gorgon to appear, and you to look,
all chance of our return would be foregone.'

These were the master's words, as his own hands,
not to rely on any act of mine,
60   closed in an outer band about my forehead.

You who are sound of understanding, note,
I say, what trove of doctrine is concealed
beneath the seeming strangeness of this passage.

There came now from about the turbid moat
an uproar such as caused its shores to rumble –
a fracas of confused alarm, as when

a holocaust of torrid gusts, igniting
without check, engulfs a wilderness,
whose snapped limbs' scorched and crackling litter,

70   pulverized, grown irresistible,
drives the animals and those who herd them,
gasping and terrified, alike before it.

---

52 *Medusa* compare Ovid's *Metamorphoses* 4.779ff.
54 *What Theseus tried* he tried to rescue Proserpine from the underworld;
see *Aeneid* 6.392ff.   62 *trove of doctrine* Dante's earliest commentators
debated what this 'trove' is; the question is still open
67 *holocaust* Clampitt relies on one of the word's old senses – 'conflagration'
(from its Greek roots: 'wholly burned'); the forest fire is her invention, for
Dante describes only a hurricane ('a wind impelled by differences of heat')

Uncovering my eyes, my guide said, 'Look
now across that antiquated scum,
to just where the fumes are deadliest.'

As frogs, when the predatory snake
pursues them, vanish, plunging headlong
into the muck, and squat there, hiding,

ruined souls, more than a thousand of them,
I saw in flight from one who, moving dry   80
of foot above the Styx, passed swiftly over.

Repeatedly his left hand fanned away
the rank air from before him – the one
sign he gave at all of being vexed.

Well aware of where this being came from,
it was my guide I turned to now, and at
a sign from him, I offered mute obeisance.

Ah, how terrible in indignation
that one appeared! He held a little rod.
I saw the gate give way, without resistance.   90

I saw him stand there on the horrid threshold.
'O you despised and outcast ones,' he cried,
'why do you harbor such excessive rage?

Why such recalcitrance toward that Will
whose purposes endure unmoved forever,
whom to resist adds to your suffering?

---

80 *one who* an angel   88 *indignation* the original means 'disdain'
92 *outcast* the Italian makes clear that they are outcasts 'from heaven'

What use to butt against what is ordained?
Your watchdog Cerberus still bears those scars
about the neck that are the proof of this.'

100   To the foul thoroughfare he now returned
without a word for us, but with the look
of one who's spurred on by a care beyond

what human thought could possibly encompass.
We moved our steps to pass within, secure
now the angelic words had been pronounced,

and entered without raising any outcry.
Then I, desiring eagerly to learn
the state of those confined in that grim fortress,

cast wondering eyes about me. What I saw
110   was a vast, open desert place, the haunt
of ire and the most dreadful torment.

As where, at Arles, the Rhone goes stagnant, or
in the low-lying precincts of Quarnaro,
past the Italian boundary at Pola,

the burial mounds that crowd those graveyards make,
on every side, a rough terrain: thus was
it here, but far more grievously:

among the mounds the soil was all afire,
so fervently, each tomb appeared to glare
120   hotter than any smelter's craft has need for.

98–9 Cerberus was given his scars by Hercules – see *Aeneid* 6.392–5
102–3 a more literal translation would read: 'like a man who's pressed and
bitten by concerns other than those which occupy the people standing before
him'   109 *wondering* not in Dante

Each lid was up, and from below it came
the groans of one within, whose misery,
thus heard, seemed hardly bearable.

'Master,' I said then, 'what people lie
casketed within those sepulchers,
lamenting without end the end they've come to?'

And he: 'Here lie the greatest heretics
of every sect, with all their followers.
More of them than you would suppose are thus

interred, like next to like, in monuments   130
of varying degrees of burning.' Turning
to the right, we passed between those torments
and the high walls that encircled them.   (1993)

PETER WHIGHAM (1925–87)

Whigham also translated Catullus, Martial and *The Love Poems of the VIth Dalai Lama*. His work on Dante was left unfinished at his death (*Inferno* 1–10 and a fragment of *Inferno* 17 have appeared). In his concise *Do's and Don'ts of Translation* (1982), the fourth maxim reads: '*Don't count the number of syllables in a line, but the time it takes to say them.* A hendecasyllabic line of five or six words will be a lot lighter and take less time to say than a hendecasyllabic line of eleven words. Specifically, a line of Dante will almost invariably contain more syllables, though fewer words, than the same line in English. This has led translators to pad. Time, not number, is the key to equivalence.'

---

126 *without end the end* the play on words is not in Dante

Inferno I   1–30

Life's path half past,
   I came to in a dark forest,
   the road ahead – lost.
With what difficulty attest
   the rigors – harshness – of that wild:
   the thought – and fear's refreshed!
A bitterness falling barely short of dying . . .
   but to explain what good befell *there*,
   I'll tell the rest I descried *there*.
My getting *there* I can't recall,
   crammed so with sleep at the time
   I left that route behind that's rightful.
At length, reaching a hill's first incline
   forming that valley's base
   so fearfully had undermined
My heart, I gazed upwards, saw the rays
   garbing its shoulders from that planet
   that leads all forward by whatever ways.
The fear now was a little quiet
   that had endured in the heart's lake
   through the anguish spent that night.
And, as one breathlessly making
   shore, who escapes the sea,
   and turns on the dire flood a backward look,
My soul still fleeing
   turned to view that strait
   had let no living man go free.
A while for the worn limbs to recuperate,
   then on the desert shore made tracks again,
   ever the back foot holding weight.
      (1985)

8–10 *there* Whigham's triple '*there*' replicates a triple insistence in the
Italian   17 *that planet* the sun

Inferno 3   82–136

And now towards us on a raft there came
  a white-haired old ferryman
  who bawls: 'Woe t' y' all, souls o' shame!
No more skies fer anyone!
  Board here fer t'other shore,
  fer the lasting darkness: ice: flame.
And ye there, soul alive, draw
  back from these dead sort'.
  I stayed, and when he saw
Me stay: 'Another passage, port,   10
  shall beach ye where ye'll land
  by lighter transport brought.'
The Leader: '*Charon*, act goes hand-
  in-hand with will, where this is willed.
  Vex not. No more demand'.
The hirsute jowels fall still –
  that pilot of the livid fen,
  sockets spokes of flame circle.
But the stripped, worn souls listen,
  change color, grind   20
  gums at words dire to them,
Revile God, parents, mankind,
  the hour, place, seed
  of their own birth & of their own kind.
And there the whole breed
  come with loud tears to the grim shoal:
  their meed who God's fear fail to heed.
Charon, demon, eyes coals,
  signals, herds them round,

---

2 *white-haired* this and many other details of Charon's appearance are
drawn from *Aeneid* 6.298–304   16 *fall* Dante's narrative does not shift into
the present tense until line 29 ('herds')   22–4 the rhythm and pace of these
lines are discussed in the Introduction

30   maling'rers thwacking with his pole.
      As leaves in autumn rise, crowding
          one on t'other, till the branch-pole
          scans its spoliation on the ground,
      The sick seed of *Adam* fall
          one on t'other, plunging to the bank,
          as falcons at the falconer's recall.
      Over the dark wave they sank
          from sight; scarce landed
          there, – here fresh rank on rank.
40   Kindly, my Master: 'That band,
          my son, dying in God's ire
          come here from every land,
      Keen to pass beyond the river:
          Heaven's Justice so urges,
          making the feared desired.
      Here no saved souls emerge –
          if by *Charon* you're afflicted
          his intentions judge'.
      He stopped and the dark wide district
50   shook so violently sweat drowns
          me at the terror of it.
      Wind rose from the tearswept ground,
          red lightning flashed.
          All senses bound,

      Fell like a man sleep snatched.   (1985)

---

34 *seed of Adam* the human race   **41** *my son* this is the first time in the
poem that Virgil calls Dante his 'son', perhaps in implicit contrast to the
preceding 'seed of Adam'

ROBERT CREELEY (1926–   )

After dropping out of Harvard, Creeley devoted himself to rearing domestic fowl and writing prose. His friendship with Charles Olson, which began in 1950, concentrated his attention on poetry; he edited the 'flagship' journal *The Black Mountain Review* from 1953 to 1957. He has remained faithful in verse to his early love of storytelling and its 'intimate, familiar, localizing, detailing, speculative, emotional, unending talking that has given my life a way of thinking of itself in the very fact and feeling of existence'. He has treated other poets' works (Mallarmé's, for example) as he here treats Dante's sonnet, as a spring- or sounding-board. Denise Levertov praised his *Pieces* (1968) for its 'absence of perfectionism'.

Guido, i'vorrei che tu e Lapo ed io [Compare *Rime* 52]

Guido,
I would that you, me & Lapo
                              (so a song sung:
                              sempre d'amore . . .)
       were out of this
                     had got to the reaches
of some other wood.

Deadness
         is echo
deadness is memory   10
              & their deadness is
petulant, the song gone
dead in their heads.

---

4 *sempre d'amore* from line 12 of the sonnet which is Creeley's starting point ('and there to speak always of love')   7 *some other wood* perhaps a wood other than the one in which *Inferno* 1 opens

Echo
    is memory
and all that they foster
            is dead in its sound
has no ripeness
could come to its own.

20   Petulance
        is force so contested.
They have twisted
         the meanings & manner
the force of us out of us
left us the faded
       (Who made musick
the sound of the reaches
          the actual wood   (1955)

CHARLES TOMLINSON (1927–   )

Tomlinson has always drawn in his work on strengths from
the west and from the east of these islands. He was early
stimulated by poets in the USA, particularly William Carlos
Williams and Marianne Moore, taking from them, as he says,
'a new sense of confidence and quite literally a new sense of
direction ... [which] replaced my rather wry awareness of
myself as an outsider at home'. He has equally oriented him-
self from the European mainland, translating from, among
many others, Machado, Apollinaire, Ungaretti and Bertolucci.
Henry Gifford, Tomlinson's collaborator on several enterprises
of translation, wrote of their shared aim 'to preserve not the
metre, but the movement of each poem: its flight or track
through the mind. Every real poem starts from a given ground
and carries the reader to an unforeseen vantage-point, whence
he views differently the landscape over which he has passed.
What the translator must do is to recognize these two terminal
points, and connect them by a coherent flight. This will not be

exactly the flight of his original, but no essential reach of the
journey will have been left out . . . Translation is resurrection,
but not of the body.'

Dante, guided by Virgil and Statius, enters the
Earthly Paradise [Purgatorio 27.64–142]

Our path climbed upwards between rock and rock
Until we reached a place in which the sun,
Already low now, faded out before me.
We tried few further steps once we perceived,
I and my sages, that the sun had set
Behind us, taking the shadow with it.
Against the coming of one total dark
Along the horizon's wide immensity
As night extended all its dispensation,
Each of us made his bed across a step: 10
The nature of the mountain took away
The power, not the desire, to clamber on.
As goats that crop their pasture peacefully
Yet were so swift and skittish on the crags
Before they fed, now silent in the shade
While the sun is hot, and guarded by their herdsman
Leaning on his staff, who, leaning, eyes them;
And like the herdsman in the open air
Who watches out the night beside the flock
Wary for beasts, all three of us were then   20

2–3 the Italian means 'in the direction in which I cut off, in front of me, the
rays of the sun which was already low'; i.e. they are walking east
5 *my sages* Virgil and Statius   12 *The power, not the desire* the Italian is
disputed; many editors now prefer a reading which means 'took away the
power and the desire'

Like these – I as a goat and they like him.
Rock rising up on either side of us,
Little was visible beyond its wall,
But through that little I could make out stars
Larger and brighter than in ordinary sky.
While I was ruminating, gazing at them,
Sleep took me unaware, that often brings
Foreknowledge of the things that are to be.
About that hour when Venus from the east
30   First touched the mountain with her ray that seems
To burn with a perpetual amorous fire,
A young and lovely woman gathering flowers
And singing said: 'Know that my name is Leah
And that my hands are fashioning a garland.
Before this mirror I adorn myself.
My sister Rachel never moves from hers
And looks into the depths of her own eyes
Seated there all day. To see contents her,
Only action me.' And now in light
40   That comes before the dawn, to travellers
On their return a grateful sign that they
Are lodged now nearer home, shades fell away
On every side, and with them went my sleep;
And so I rose, seeing my great masters
Already risen. 'The sweet fruit that you seek
Among the tangle of so many boughs
Today will take away your hunger.'
Never did sweetness in whatever gifts
Equal these words that Virgil used to me.

23–4 *little . . . little* though the repetitions in lines 16–18 are Tomlinson's,
here he picks up on Dante's insistence on a favourite word '*poco*' ('little')
26 *ruminating* the joke is also in Dante   29 *About that hour* just before
dawn   33 *Leah* for Leah and Rachel, see Genesis 29, 30 and 49; the sisters
traditionally symbolize, respectively, the active and the contemplative life
40 *travellers* 'pilgrims' in the original

So great was my desire to be above,   50
I felt my pinions grow at every move.
When the whole stair had run beneath our feet
And we had gained the topmost step of all,
Then Virgil fixed his eyes on me and said:
'Son, the temporal fire and the eternal
You have seen, and now have reached a place
Where, of myself, I can discern no further.
I brought you here by force of mind and art;
From now on, let your pleasure be your guide:
You have passed the steep ways and the narrow.   60
Look at the sun that shines against your brow,
Look at the grass, the flowers and the shrubs
Which here the ground produces of itself.
Till those bright eyes whose weeping led me to you
Come to this spot where you can sit at ease
Or wander through this earthly paradise.
Expect no longer word or sign from me.
Your power to choose is upright, whole and free –
The only fault is not to do its bidding:
Firm in yourself I crown and mitre you.'   (1996)   70

W. S. MERWIN (1927–   )

Merwin's prolific career as a poet has been accompanied by a
no less substantial commitment to translation, primarily from
the Romance languages with which he is familiar – he has
published versions of Jiménez, Juavroz and Neruda among
many others – but also from tongues more distant in both space

---

55 *the temporal fire and the eternal* the fires, respectively, of purgatory and
of hell   64 *those bright eyes* Beatrice's; see *Inferno* 2   67 *Expect . . .* these
are indeed Virgil's last words in the *Commedia*; he vanishes at some point
between *Purgatorio* 29.55–7 and *Purgatorio* 30.49, when Dante notices he is
gone

and time, including Japanese and Ancient Greek. He is impelled, he says, by 'a wish to embrace, even through wrappings, poetry that was written from perspectives revealingly different from our own', in which respect 'the great exemplar, of course, was Pound'. While being 'quite convinced of the impossibility of ever really translating *The Divine Comedy* into any other language', Merwin thinks it feasible to approximate phrasing; to find 'convocations of words in another language that will have a comparable thrust and sense', these being 'recognizable elements of verbal order, not verse forms'. This feeling comes through in his version of *Purgatorio*, where the shape of the tercet is marked by irregular assonance rather than by full *terza rima*. Merwin's 'Foreword' notes that 'of the three sections of the poem, only *Purgatory* happens *on* the earth, as our lives do, with our feet on the ground, crossing a beach, climbing a mountain ... Here the times of the day recur with all the sensations and associations that the hours bring with them, the hours of the world we are living in as we read the poem.'

Purgatorio 26

As we went on walking along the edge,
one before the other, many times there
the good teacher said, 'Watch. Learn from my
knowledge.'

The sun struck me above the right shoulder
already with its rays, turning the whole
face of the west from celestial blue to white

and I with my shadow made the flames appear
a deeper red, and I saw it was something
that many shades noticed as we were passing.

---

9 *as we were passing* the sense is rather 'as they were passing'

It was this that started them speaking   10
about me, and to each other saying,
'This body does not look like an illusion.'

Then certain of them came toward me as near
as they could venture while still taking care
not to come out where they would not be burned.

'Oh you that go, not from slowness but rather
perhaps from reverence, behind the others,
answer me who in thirst and fire am burning,

nor am I the only one longing for your
answer, but all these have a thirst for it greater   20
than Indian's or Ethiopian's for cold water.

Tell us how you make of yourself a wall
to the sun, as though you were one who still
had not made your way into the net of death,'

one of them said to me, and I would have made
    plain
to him who I was if my attention
had not been caught by a strange thing I saw then,

for in the middle of the burning path
people were coming facing the other
way so that I stared at them in wonder.   30

Then I see each shade going one way hurry
to kiss each shade going the other way,
not stopping, content with the brief greeting,

---

15 Merwin imitates a double negative in the original   17 *the others* Virgil
and Statius   31 *I see* reproducing a change of tense in the original

as in their dark company ant will touch
ant, muzzle to muzzle, looking perhaps
to learn the way or find out their fortune.

Once they have greeted each other as friends
and before they take the first step onward
each tries to shout louder than the others:

40   those that just came shout, 'Sodom and Gomorrah,'
and the others, 'Pasiphaë enters the cow
to make the young bull charge into her lust.'

Then like cranes, some toward the Riphaean
            Mountains
flying and some toward the desert fleeing
from the frost as others flee from the sun,

one group goes away and the other comes on,
and they return in tears to what they were singing
and to whichever cry is right for them,

and the same ones who had asked me the question
50   came over to me as they had before,
their faces full of their desire to listen.

I for the second time seeing their longing
began, 'Oh souls certain of being
at peace whenever the time for that shall be,

I have not left my limbs, either
green or ripe, back there, but they are with me here
with their own blood and with their jointed bones.

---

40 *Sodom and Gomorrah* see Genesis 18–19   41–2 this union – technical
details of which are given below – engendered the Minotaur; see Ovid, *Ars
Amatoria* 1   43 *the Riphaean Mountains* thought by the Romans to lie in
the north-east of Europe

I am on my way up to be blind no longer.
There above, a lady has won for me
the grace to pass, still mortal, through your world.   60

But so may your greatest longing come to be
fulfilled soon, and that Heaven harbor you
that is most spacious and is filled with love,

   tell me, so I may write it later, who
are you, and who are they in that assembly
that is going away from behind you?'

No different from someone out of the mountains,
amazed, open-mouthed, turning and looking,
      speechless,
on entering, rough and wild, into the city,

   was the way each of the shades appeared to be,   70
but when they were free of their astonishment,
a thing soon quieted in noble hearts,

   'Blessèd are you,' he that had spoken to me
began again, 'who to die better come
to be laden with knowledge of our region.

The offense of the people who are
not coming with us is the one that made Caesar hear
himself called 'Queen' as he passed in triumph.

---

78 *himself called 'Queen'* because of a rumoured intimacy with Nicomedes
Philopator, king of Bithynia; Dante would have found the story in Uguccione
of Pisa.

That is why they shout 'Sodom' when they leave,
80   to reproach themselves, as you have heard, and their
shame adds to the burning of the fire.

Our sin was the performance as both sexes,
but because we did not uphold human law,
pursuing appetite like animals

when we leave them, we call opprobrium
upon ourselves, her name is repeated by us
who was a beast inside the wooden beast.

Now you know what we did and what our guilt is.
Though you may wish to know us each by name
90   there is no time for that, nor could I tell you,

but for your part I will grant your wish: I am
Guido Guinizzelli, purifying myself
already because I repented before the end.'

As the two sons became during the sorrow
of Lycurgus, when they saw their mother again,
I became, without rising to their expression,

hearing my father and the father of others
my betters and whoever has come to use
sweet graceful rhymes of love say his own name,

100   and without hearing or speaking I walked on
a long way, thoughtful, gazing at him,
but because of the fire went no closer.

---

92 *Guido Guinizzelli* Bolognese poet of the mid thirteenth century,
originator of the 'sweet new style' adopted by Dante in the *Vita Nuova*
95 *their mother* condemned for having caused the death of Lycurgus's child,
Hypsipyle was rescued from the hands of the executioners by her own sons
(this rescue is alluded to, darkly by Merwin, more clearly by Dante, in the
next line); see Statius, *Thebaid* 5.72.22

When my sight had feasted enough upon him
I offered my whole self at once to his service
with that earnestness that makes others believe.

And he to me, 'You leave a mark so deep,
through what I hear, and see clearly, in me
that Lethe cannot wash it out nor fade it.

But if it is the truth that you have promised,
tell why it is that your face and speech   110
make it apparent that you hold me dear.'

And I to him, 'The sweet songs of yours
that so long as our present words endure
will make precious the ink in which they were
          written.'

'Oh brother,' he said, 'the one at whom I am
          pointing
with my finger,' indicating a spirit before him,
'was a better workman in the mother tongue:

verses of love and stories of romance,
he was peerless in all of them, and let the fools
          babble
who believe that the Limousin writes better.   120

They attend fashion rather than the truth,
and in that way they make up their opinion
before they give heed to art or reason.

---

117 *a better workman* Arnaut Daniel, Provençal troubadour of the twelfth
century, whose highly wrought '*trobar clus*' poems Dante imitated in his
'*rime petrose*'   120 *the Limousin* Giraut de Bornelh, another troubadour,
active in the early thirteenth century

That was the way many did with Guittone,
shout after shout all giving the prize to him
until the truth overcame most of them.

Now if so vast a privilege is yours
that you are free to walk on to the cloister
in which Christ is the abbot of the college

130   recite to Him there a Paternoster for me,
insofar as we need one in this world
where the power to sin is ours no longer.'

Then, it may be to make room for another
who was close to him, he vanished through the
          fire
like a fish going into the deepest water.

I moved forward a little toward the one
who had been pointed out and said to him
that my wish had made a welcome for his name.

Freely he began to speak to me:
140   'Your courteous question gives such pleasure to me
that I will not and cannot conceal myself from you.

I am Arnaut who weep and go singing.
With anguish of mind I see my old folly
and with joy see before me the hoped-for day.

---

124 *Guittone* an Aretine poet of the generation before Dante's, perhaps more
of an influence on him than he cared to admit; the harsh judgement here
echoes that in *De vulgari eloquentia* 2.4.8   131 *insofar as we need one* souls
in purgatory have no need of the verses which guard against temptation and
evil, as *Purgatorio* 11.19–24 explains   140–47 'in the original Arnaut's
speech is in Provençal' [*Merwin's note*]

Now I beg of you by that power
that is leading you to the top of the stair,
while there is time remember how I suffer!'

Then hid himself in the fire that refines them.   (2000)

DEREK WALCOTT (1930–   )

Born and schooled on St Lucia, Walcott began publishing his
poetry at the age of eighteen. After teaching at various colleges
in the West Indies during the fifties, he founded the Trinidad
Theatre Workshop which he directed until 1976. He won the
Nobel Prize in 1992 for his many plays and poems. Walcott
compares himself with very distinguished predecessors: 'I hap-
pen to have been born in an English and a Creole place, and
love both languages . . . It is mine to do what other poets before
me did, Dante, Chaucer, Villon, Burns, which is to fuse the
noble and the common language, the streets and the law courts,
in a tone that is true to my own voice, in which both accents
are heard naturally.' He describes the shape of *Omeros* as
'Roughly hexametrical with a terza rima form. It's like a combi-
nation of a Homeric line and a Dantesque design.'

Omeros   58

I

Up heights the Plunketts loved, from Soufrière upwards
past that ruined scheme which hawsers of lianas
had anchored in bush, of Messrs. Bennett & Ward,

---

1 *Plunketts* a retired expatriate British Army major and his wife, Maud (see
Omeros 5.1) *Soufrière* a town on St Lucia near a volcanic crater with
sulphur springs   3 *Bennett & Ward* nineteenth-century English
entrepreneurs who ran a sulphur mine which failed (see *Omeros* 10.2)

the blind guide led me with a locked marble hand as
we smelt the foul sulphur of hell in paradise
on the brittle scab crusting its volcano's sores

and the scorching light that had put out Lucia's eyes
seared mine when I saw the Pool of Speculation
under its horned peaks. I heard the boiling engines

10   of steam in its fissures, the deep indignation
of Hephaestus or Ogun grumbling at the sins
of souls who had sold out their race, the ancient forge

of bubbling lead erupted with speculators
whose heads gurgled in the lava of the Malebolge
mumbling deals as they rose. These were the traitors

who, in elected office, saw the lands as views
for hotels and elevated into waiters
the sons of others, while their own learnt something
      else.

Now, in their real estate, they lunged at my shoes
to pull me down with them as we walked along
20   shelves
bubbling with secrets, with melting fingers of mud

---

4 *blind guide* Walcott's Virgil-figure is a compound of Homer, a bust of that
poet, and Seven Seas, a former sailor who has lost his sight (*Omeros* 2.2)
7 *Lucia* fourth-century Sicilian virgin martyr, after whom Walcott's native
island is named; she is often depicted with her eyes in a dish though there is
no specific legend which explains this tradition
11 *Hephaestus or Ogun* both blacksmith-gods, who typically have their
forges in volcanoes   14 *Malebolge* the vast and pitted eighth circle of
Dante's hell where the fraudulent are punished   15 *These were* a common
turn of phrase in Dante; see for instance *Inferno* 7.46

and sucking faces that argued Necessity
in rapid zeroes which no one else understood
for the island's profit. One had rented the sea

to offshore trawlers, whose nets, if hoisted, would
    show
for thrice the length of its coast, while another thief
turned his black head like a ball in a casino

when the roulette wheel slowed down like his clicking
    teeth
in the pool's sluggish circle. It screamed in contempt
that choked in its bile at black people's laziness   30

whenever it leapt from the lava and then went
under again, then the shooting steam shot its price
from a fissure, as they went on making their deals

for the archipelago with hot, melting hands
before the price of their people dropped. The sandals
led me along the right path, around the fierce sands,

round the circle of speculation, where others
kept making room for slaves to betray their brothers,
till the eyes in the stone head were cursing their tears.

III

The stone heels guided me. I followed close behind
through the veils of stinking sulphur, filthy and frayed,
till I was as blind as it was, steering with one hand

35–6 *The sandals / led me* Dante has similar locutions about Virgil's feet; see
for instance *Inferno* 23.148   39 *the stone head* see *Omeros* 2.3 and 56.1
    1–4 compare *Purgatorio* 16.1–13; the terrace of envy is apt to the literary
'backbiting' which now follows

in front of my face, beating webs from my forehead,
through the fool's gold of the yellow rocks, the thin sand
running from their fissures. But in such things, the guide

needs the trust of the wounded one to begin with;
he could feel my doubt behind him. That was no good.
I had lost faith both in religion and in myth.

10   In one pit were the poets. Selfish phantoms with eyes
who wrote with them only, saw only surfaces
in nature and men, and smiled at their similes,

condemned in their pit to weep at their own pages.
And that was where I had come from. Pride in my craft.
Elevating myself. I slid, and kept falling

towards the shit they stewed in; all the poets laughed,
jeering with dripping fingers; then Omeros gripped
my hand in enclosing marble and his strength moved

me away from that crowd, or else I might have slipped
20   to that backbiting circle, mockers and self-loved.
The blind feet guided me higher as the crust sloped.

As I, contemptuously, turned my head away,
a fist of ice gripped it from the soul-shaping forge,
and it wrenched my own head bubbling its half-lies,

crying out its name, but each noun stuck in its gorge
as it begged for pardon, willing to surrender
if another chance were given it at language.

---

10 *the poets* though there are many poets in the *Commedia*, they have no
enclosure specifically reserved to them   16 contrast the decorous welcome
given Dante by the poets of *Inferno* 4   23–32 compare and contrast *Inferno*
32.70–108

But the ice-matted head hissed,
                                    'You tried to render
their lives as you could, but that is never enough;
now in the sulphur's stench ask yourself this question,   30

whether a love of poverty helped you
to use other eyes, like those of that sightless stone?'
My own head sunk in the black mud of Soufrière,

while it looked back with all the faith it could summon.
Both heads were turned like the god of the yawning
      year
on whose ridge I stood looking back where I came from.

The nightmare was gone. The bust became its own
      past,
I could still hear its white lines in the far-off foam.
I woke to hear blackbirds bickering at breakfast.   (1990)

GEOFFREY HILL (1932–   )

In his 1986 Clark Lectures, Hill considered the reciprocity in
Dante of 'the assertive rebellious will' and 'the judging imagina-
tion'. References to Dante have been more frequent in his recent
work (see, for example, *The Triumph of Love* CXXXV and his
essay in Peter S. Hawkins and Rachel Jacoff (eds.), *The Poets'
Dante*, listed above in 'Further Reading'). *The Orchards of
Syon*, a sequence of seventy-two 24-line poems, takes its title
from a fifteenth-century Englishing of St Catherine of Siena's
Dialogo.

---

39 *blackbirds* they appear first at a breakfast-time in *Omeros* 2.2 and
perhaps convey for Walcott some of the airy relief Dante feels on seeing stars
again at the end of *Inferno*

The Orchards of Syon

XXVI

Dantean eclogues. Relentless, a toothed
mill-wheel baptizes the mill-race. Invisibly
made evident, the wind shapeshifts, towers
in self-turned glassy sheenings. Lofted
swarms build, dark as locusts. *Where are you*
    fróm?
I said. He said, *La nostra madre comune.*
Saltmarsh or creek-mire where ochre-
and umber-rendered verdure becomes tinder
in a dry spell. Unforgettable
10   doctrine, *Matrona*: engage with my contrite
heart of anger. All things are possible.
The spirit materializes; once for all
we know its oratory. So moving
to the one outcome I fancy this light

---

1 *Dantean eclogues* Dante wrote two Latin eclogues around 1319 in reply to
a verse-letter from a Bolognese academic (called, with an odd half-aptness,
Giovanni del Virgilio) who urged him to stop wasting his considerable talents
on Italian and turn his hand to Latin. Dante is thought to have sent his
critical admirer ten *canti* of the *Paradiso* to show what could be done with
what the first eclogue calls 'the words of comedy of which he [del Virgilio]
disapproves, whether because they sound clichéd on women's lips or because
the Castalian sisters are ashamed to receive them'
5 *Where are you fróm* the shades in the *Commedia* are regularly keen to find
out someone else's birthplace or declare their own
6 *La nostra madre comune* 'the mother we all share', probably meaning the
earth; compare *Purgatorio* 11.63, where Omberto Aldobrandesco regrets
that family pride made him forget that we all have a '*comune madre*'
7–9 perhaps pastiching the off-the-peg purling stream of Dante's first
eclogue, 11–17 (Hill's 'umber' may come jokily from Dante's '*inumbrat*')
10 *Matrona* a married woman, wife, matron (Latin); the word is used in
high-flown Italian, but not in the *Commedia*

fantastic carries itself as completion
somewhere that I am not. Ions emote
to make and break aeons; yet still I mourn
yoú, my sister, as for a dead twin.
Terra madre, Terra incognita,
this is the end I imagine, but who   20
first said we were finished?
Who said, to think about nothing is not
nihilism but superfluity –
just to break even with you in despair?

LVII

Reading Dante in a mood of angry dislike
for my fellow sufferers and for myself
that I dislike them. Dante is exact
in these conferrals. The words of justice
move on his abacus or make a sudden
psst psst like farrier's hot iron on horn.
The small blue flame of the glass votive lamp
that jibs in the funnelled air at the right
hand of Mary Mediatrix is his also.
From this distance the many barbed divisions   10
between Purgatory and Hell appear blurred.
You could step across or shake hands. Logic
is fierce, though at the last less feral
than mock-logic that destroys many.
Sensuous is not sensual, but such knowledge
increases with sensuality – *psst psst* –
hissing and crying out, the final throes.

---

19 *Terra madre, Terra incognita* mother earth, an unknown land (the first
phrase is Italian, the second Latin)

Messaline – FRÉNAUD – *la vulve*
insomnieuse – ever-working valve-part
20   unsightly, blood-gravid. Look, Virgin
of Czestochowa, shelterer
from the black rain, look, ser Brunetto
whom Dante loved, look, Farinata: the sun
moves a notch forward on the great wheel.   (2002)

ALAN MASSEY (1932–   )

Massey's book *The Fire Garden* (1986) includes translations
from Rudel and Arnaut Daniel. Embarking on Dante, he found
'the stark impossibility of making a faultlessly literal rhyming-
and-metrical translation' to be a stimulus rather than a deter-
rent: ' "Difficulty is our plough", as Yeats wrote'.

18–19 *Messaline . . . insomnieuse* Hill quotes from André Frénaud's poem,
La Sorcière de Rome (1973), lines 406–8 of which translate as 'And the
Virgin Mary, happening to meet Messalina, / the insomniac vulva, / kissed
her on the forehead and blessed her.' Frénaud commented that the passage
concerns 'attempts at a synthesis or unification of contrary elements' – hence
its relevance to Hill's poem, especially his lines 10–12. (Messalina, wife of
the emperor Claudius, had a reputation for sexual voracity.) Hill puns from
'vulve' to 'valve', a cardiac valve imagined to be as tireless as Messalina.
20–21 *Virgin / of Czestochowa* said to have been discovered by Saint
Helena in the fourth century, this Byzantine 'Black Madonna' (probably
thirteenth- or fourteenth-century) is revered by five million visitors a year at
the Polish monastery of Jasna Gora   22 *black rain* the phrase is sometimes
used of the rain which fell on Hiroshima and Nagasaki after they were
bombed *ser Brunetto* see *Inferno* 15, especially 79–87
23 *Farinata* see *Inferno* 10   23–4 *the sun . . . the great wheel* compare
Paradiso 33.144–5 ('*rota . . . sole*')

Paradiso 22

Aghast, I turned aside to her, with just
   That instinct shown by a little child who scurries
   Always back to somebody he can trust;
She, as a reassuring mother hurries
   To calm her pale and breathless one, to heal
   With her familiar voice his little worries,
Said: 'Don't you know yet? Didn't I reveal
   That this is heaven, where all is holiness,
   And righteous anger privilege of zeal?
Their great cry shook your heart; then how much
      less   10
   You could unshaken bear their sacred song,
   Sustain my smile, you may begin to guess.
If you had understood their wrath at wrong,
   The retribution, too, you would have seen
   Which they and you shall witness before long.
The sword of heaven severs quick and clean
   As God wills, neither late nor early – save
   To those who await it, fearful or serene.
But leave such thoughts; turn to the truly brave,
   The many hero-saints you shall meet here   20
   If you'll look where I say.' My lady gave
A sign; I saw, as if one pearl-like sphere,
   A hundred smaller spheres which magnified
And beautified each other, tier on tier.

---

1 *Aghast* in the last lines of the previous canto, the blessed souls cry out like
thunder in indignation at the corruptions of the Church *her* Beatrice
15 *before long* Beatrice predicts Dante will see this unspecified '*vendetta*'
('vengeance') '*innanzi che tu muoi*' ('before you die')
19–20 *truly brave . . . hero-saints* both phrases translate '*illustri spiriti*'
('illustrious spirits')   22 *as if one pearl-like sphere* not in the original

As one who, fearing spiritual pride,
   Bites back the question he yet burns to ask,
   I waited, still and silent, with my guide.
The brightest pearl took on itself the task
   Of satisfying hunger unexpressed;
30   Advancing, came in these terms to unmask:
'If you could see what burns within our breast
   As well as I – pure charity – then you
   Would pour out all your thoughts without arrest.
Since you are not forthcoming, listen to
   My answer, though your question be unspoken,
   And so shall you with less delay win through.
In days long past, Cassino's hill was woken
   To impious sacrifices, pagan cries;
   Inveterate wrong and error were not broken
40   Till I took to the summit of that rise
   The name of One who brought to us below
   The truth that yet uplifts us to the skies.
Such grace shone down on me, suffused me so,
   That all the neighbouring townspeople quit
   The foolish ways that lead the world to woe.
These others, all contemplatives, were lit
   By the same fire, which brings forth sacred flowers
   And sacred fruits; the cloister nurtured it
In all these holy ones, brothers of ours:
50   Here is Macarius, Romualdus here:
   The monastery kept their steadfast hours.'

---

25 *fearing spiritual pride* the original is less specific – 'afraid of going too far'   37 *Cassino's hill* Monte Cassino, about halfway between Rome and Naples, where St Benedict founded the mother-house of the Benedictines in the sixth century   38–9 these lines more literally translate as 'that mountain ... was populated on its summit by a deluded people, inclined to evil' 45 *The foolish ways* ... the Italian is more severe: 'the impious cult which seduced the world'   50 *Macarius, Romualdus* respectively, the founder of oriental monasticism (d. 404) and Romuald, a reformer of Benedictinism (d. *circa* 1027)   51 *hours* rhyme impels Massey to a free rendering; the original says the monastery kept their '*cor*' ('heart')

I said to him: 'Since you have met my fear
   With pure affection, and in your fellow-fires
   The self-same warmth and kindliness appear,
I grant such holy charity requires
   That my confidence grow, much as the sun
   Compels the rose to bloom as he desires.
I'll ask – and tell me when it shall be done,
   Father, I pray you – whether I may see
   Your face unmasked, as you look to that One.'   60
And he: 'My brother, your desire shall be
   Gratified *there*, in the last sphere of all,
   Fulfilment of all these others, as of me.
There, everything we thought beyond recall
   Returns to us, perfected, true and sweet,
   With all we still desire. Since not in thrall
To space or time, eternity is complete:
   Each part is where it was. Stealing from sight,
   Our ladder leads there: try it with your feet!
The patriarch Jacob saw it reach a height   70
   You cannot yet conceive when, in his dream,
   It rose, dressed with God's angels, to the light.
But no one sees it now. My people seem
   Too weak to climb our ladder, and my Rule
   Is yellowing waste paper, ream on ream;
The abbey is a ruin, and the school
   A sty; the cowl, our sign of holiness,
   Only a sack stuffed with decaying gruel.
God is not mocked, and He will no more bless
   The extortion of the usurer's tight fist   80
   Than what misleads our monks to the caress

---

60 *as you look to that One* not in the original, where Dante also qualifies his
request with 'if I have the capacity for such a grace'   **64–6** these eloquent
lines render one and a half Italian lines very freely – 'there every desire is
perfect, ripe and entire'   **69** *try it with your feet* not in the original
71 *You cannot yet conceive* not in the original   **79** *God is not mocked* not
in the original

Of folly. Every gift the Church has kissed
   Is for the needy, asking in God's name –
   Not for the libertine, the nepotist!
Our earthly flesh is weak, falls into shame
   Too easily from many a good beginning:
   From new-sprung oaks poor acorns ever came.
Peter in poverty found all his winning,
   Francis in pure humility, and I
90   In prayer and abstinence an end of sinning;
But hold those starting-points with a clear eye
   Against what followed, and you cannot fail
   To note the fall, the darkening of the dye.
Nevertheless, recall the Jordan; hail
   The flight of the Red Sea, which God decreed:
   Think of those miracles; let hope prevail.'
Benedict spoke; and I watched him recede
   To join his fellow-saints. Together merged,
   As in a whirlwind that most holy breed
100   Swept upward on the stair. My lady urged
   Me with a sign to follow; I obeyed,
   My will suspended as her own will surged;
No journey here below was ever made
   So rapidly, as though by gift of wings,
   For actions there are like our thoughts, unstayed.
Reader, may I remember well such things
   And, though I beat my breast, weep for my sins,
   Relive the triumph our devotion brings,
For quickly as in and out of white fire wins
110   A finger I found myself within the bright
   Constellar miracle we call the Twins.

---

97 *Benedict* Dante does not name St Benedict in this canto   102 the original
means 'so did her energy ["*virtù*"] conquer my nature'
107 *though I beat my breast* Massey's 'though' is misleading – it is *because*
Dante repents that he hopes he may return eventually in reality to the
Paradise he at present imagines

O glorious stars, O virtues filled with light,
  You brightnesses wherein I recognise,
  Such as they are, my own prowess and right,
It was in your division of the skies
  The all-engendering sun-god rose and set
  When Tuscany first opened to my eyes;
And when, by a mercy I remember yet,
  I entered on the high all-moving wheel,
  It was the self-same region that I met.   120
Beneath your house of glories, then, I kneel:
  Grant my soul the grace of inspiration
  To bring her task, completed, to its seal.
'You are so close to ultimate salvation,'
  Beatrice said, 'that your eyes must be keen.
  Look down then: see how much of the creation
By holy providence I have put between
  This starry realm you are in and that place
  You were in; then, enlightened by the scene,
Joy in your heart, once more you'll turn your face   130
  Toward the triumphant host you'll see advance,
  Rejoicing, through the ringed ethereal space.'
The seven spheres, held in my single glance,
  Revolved below; I saw this tiny world
  And, wondering at its insignificance,
Could only smile. The man whose thought is hurled
  The farthest from it should be counted wise;
  His judgment who considers it with curled
Lip, the soundest. Looking again, my eyes
  Rested on the resplendent moon, now free   140
  Of shade that once defeated all surmise;

---

112 *O virtues filled with light* in the original, the Gemini are addressed as
'lights pregnant with great energy ["*virtù*"]'
116 *the all-engendering sun-god* the original is more circumspect – 'he [the
sun] who is father of every mortal life'   133–4 the original means 'with my
gaze I returned through every one of the seven spheres'   134 *tiny* not in the
original

My sight sustained the sun's ferocity
   As though he were no brighter than the stars;
   Nearby, the gods Venus and Mercury
Swam in their spheres; between Saturn and Mars
   Great Jupiter majestically steered,
   Tempering those excessive avatars.
All seven in their magnitude appeared,
   In speed of revolution through the air
150   And in what just relation they are sphered.
The little floor that maddens us was there:
   Gemini showed me every stream and spur
   As I was sped with that eternal Pair.
I turned again to her sweet eyes, to her.   (1996)

TOM PHILLIPS (1937–   )

After graduating from St Catherine's College, Oxford, Phillips
trained at the Camberwell School of Arts and Crafts. In 1966,
he produced *A Humument*, a complex reworking of W. H.
Mallock's 1892 novel *A Human Document*, on which he draws
again in his Dante. He writes about his searching illustrations
to the poem: 'I felt that most illustrated versions merely re-
peated, however skilfully, the action and circumstances that the
poet already so vividly describes: they concentrate on the
poem's exterior events as if Dante's subject matter were only
people writhing about in the gloom . . . instead of the human
soul in crisis as it faces the world in all its painful perplexity.
The *Inferno* is Europe's harsh masterpiece of eschatology:

---

151 *floor* the Italian '*aiuola*' is usually translated as a 'threshing-floor'; the
world 'makes us . . . fierce' ('*ci fa . . . feroci*') because we squabble over its
harvests; Dante may also have been thinking of the divine threshing, the
separation of wheat from chaff, as mentioned in Matthew 3:12 and
Luke 3:17   152 *stream and spur* the original reads '*da colli alle foci*' ('from
the hills to the river-mouths'), another of Dante's favourite water-journeys to
the sea

magnificent descriptions alternate with bleak but moving con-
frontations with the range of Man's baser potentialities;
through these we come to know Dante's own beliefs, trials and
visionary hopes.'

Inferno 21

From bridge to bridge discussing in this way
yet further things, of which my comedy
is not concerned to sing, we went along,
and reached the topmost point to stop and view
the next of Malebolge's cavities,
its next ravine of ineffectual tears,
where quite uncanny darkness met my eyes.
As in the Venice Arsenal they boil
the sticky tar in wintertime to caulk
the leaks in unsafe ships, since that is when   10
they cannot put to sea, and so instead
some build a brand-new boat and some fill in
the ribs of older and much-travelled craft,
some hammer at a prow and some a stern,
some fashion oars, yet others twine their ropes
while others patch a mainsail or a jib;
so here below, though not by means of fire
but by divine mechanics, viscous pitch
boiled up and smothered all the banks like glue.
I stared at it, but stared at nothingness   20
except for bubbles rising, as it boiled
and bellied up and sank back in a mass.
While I was straining hard to see below,
my guide exclaimed, 'Now watch out there! Watch
    out!'
and stretched to pull me back from where I stood
towards himself. At which I turned around
like any man who can't resist a glimpse

of something he should be escaping from
yet, struck by sudden terror, loses nerve
30   and does his looking while he runs away.
And there behind me coming up the ridge
I saw a jet-black demon at full pelt.
And what a wild fantastic sight he was!
And with what sharp alacrity he moved
those light and nimble feet and outstretched wings!
His pointed shoulders proudly bore aloft
a sinner by both thighs, securely fixed
with claws sunk in the tendons of his feet.
He shouted from our bridge, 'Hey Malebranche,
40   here's one of Santa Zita's aldermen!
You stick him under, I'll go back for more;
there's plenty of them back in his home town,
where every single one's a racketeer,
except of course Bonturo. That's the place
where "no" becomes "o.k." for ready cash.'
He flung him down below and then sprang back
along the rocky ridge with speed enough
to beat an unleashed hound pursuing thieves.
The sinner sank, then bobbed up buttocks first
50   as demons shrieked from underneath the bridge,
'The Sacred Face! Why, what's it doing here?
The swimming here's not like the Serchio!
Unless you want a taste of our sharp hooks
you'd better not break cover from the pitch!'

---

33 *fantastic* not in Dante   39 *Malebranche* 'evil claws'; Dante coined the
name for this particular squad of demons   40 *Santa Zita* a housemaid
whose relentless piety earned the devotion of her fellow citizens in Lucca; she
died in 1272 and had not yet been canonized in the poem's 1300
44 *Bonturo* Bonturo Dati, a powerful leader of the popular faction in Lucca,
he was still alive in 1324; the 'except of course' is, of course, sarcastic
51 *Sacred Face* a Byzantine crucifix revered, then as now, in the cathedral at
Lucca; it is made of black wood, hence the outrageous implied comparison
of the icon to the buttocks of the surfacing sinner   52 *Serchio* the river near
Lucca

They spiked him with a hundred prongs and cried,
'Your little caper's going underground,
so try your swindling while you're lying low!'
Like cooks they were, that make their kitchen-boys
poke back the bits of meat inside the pot
with forks, to stop them floating to the top.   60
My friendly master said, 'To make quite sure
that no-one will suspect your presence here
crouch down behind this rock to give yourself
some kind of cover; don't be frightened now,
whatever outrage I'm subjected to:
there's nothing that I can't take care of here;
I've had rough dealings of this kind before.'
He then went on beyond the bridge's end
and having reached the sixth dividing bank
he needed to put on his bravest front   70
for then, with all the rush of frenzied dogs
who hurl themselves on some poor mendicant
as soon as he attempts to stop and beg,
they hurtled out from underneath the bridge
and set upon him, brandishing their hooks.
He shouted, 'Now, no mischief, anyone.
Before you start to prod me with your forks,
let one of you come forward: hear me out
and then decide if you should grapple me.'
They all cried out, 'Right, Malacoda, go.'   80
And one stepped forward while the rest stood still.
He said, 'How will he benefit from this?'
'Now Malacoda, do you really think
you'd see me come this far,' my master said,
'despite all your defences, still quite safe,
without divine intent and fate's accord.

---

67 *before* see *Inferno* 9.22ff.   80 *Malacoda* 'evil tail'; Phillips notes that he
did not try to English the demons' names because the results of previous
attempts have been 'generally quite feeble'

Make way, for up in heaven it is willed
that I must show a stranger this wild road.'
This so deflated all that blustering pride
90   his fork slipped from him, falling to the ground.
He said to them, 'This man must not be harmed.'
My leader called to me, 'You there, crouched down,
curled up amongst the boulders of the bridge;
it's safe again for you to join me now.'
So I emerged and hastened to his side.
The devils jostled forward in a bunch
and I was scared they wouldn't keep their word,
as once some soldiers that I'd seen were scared
when, marching from Caprona under truce,
100   they saw themselves ringed round by enemies:
I drew as close towards my leader's side
as possible, not letting out of sight
their faces, which were not encouraging.
They brought their forks down lower. 'Why don't I
just nick him in the arse?', suggested one;
and one agreed, 'Yes, let him have it, there.'
The demon who'd been talking with my guide
whipped round immediately at this, and said,
'Leave Scarmiglione, you leave off',
110   and then announced to us, 'You can't go on
much further by this route; the sixth bridge lies
all smashed to pieces in the pit below.
So if you really want to push ahead,
then carry on along this ridge. Quite near
another archway will provide a route.

---

99 *Caprona* a castle belonging to Pisa which the Tuscan Guelfs took in
1289; Dante may have participated in its siege
109 *Scarmiglione* 'tousle-top'

Just yesterday, and five hours on from now
twelve hundred years had passed, plus sixty-six,
since this road here collapsed into a heap.
I'm sending out some members of my troop
in that direction so that they can check   120
if anyone is coming up for air.
Go with them; they'll not do you any harm.
Step forward Alichino,' he began,
'and Calcabrina, and Cagnazzo too;
and Barbariccia, you lead the ten.
Then Libicocco, Draghignazzo, you,
and Ciriatto with the tusks as well
with Farfarello, Graffiacane, yes
and crazy Rubicante, go and scout
around the boiling glue. Make sure this pair   130
are safe until the next bridge that you'll reach
which runs from ditch to ditch without a break.'
'Oh, Master, I don't like the look of this!
Why don't we just go on alone,' I said,
'without an escort if you know the way?
for this arrangement's hardly what I'd choose.
If you're as watchful as you've always been
you must have noticed how they grind their teeth
and how they threaten danger with their brows.'
But he, 'Believe me, there's no cause for fear   140
and let them grind away just as they please;
it's only for the poor fools stewing there.'

116–18 it is now 7 a.m. on Holy Saturday 1300; Dante measures the interim
between this now and noon on Good Friday 34 CE, when the earthquake
marking Christ's death broke the infernal bridge (Dante follows his
understanding of Luke 23:44–6 Luke in timing Christ's death at noon). The
fictional dating of the *Commedia* depends entirely on this demonic reference
123–9 more devils with emblematic names, such as 'dirty dog', 'pigface', and
so on   142 *the poor fools stewing there* Dante calls them more laconically
'*li lessi dolenti*' ('the boiled mourners')

They wheeled off to the left along the dyke,
but first they made, by squirting out their tongues
between their teeth, a sign towards their chief,
who with his arsehole blew the bugle call.   (1985)

PETER DALE (1938–   )

As his earlier translations of Villon and Laforgue show, Dale
has particularly interested himself in the matter of translating
poetic form. He describes the initial impetus which set him
going on the *Commedia* as follows: 'In writing a short book
on rhyme-technique, having criticized the opening rhymes of
several versions of the first canto of the *Comedy*, I felt obliged
to risk my neck in a footnote with an attempt of my own out
of a sense of fairness. But terza rima is a running rhyme and
you haven't really achieved it until at least the end of the
canto. So, this version is perhaps one of the longest footnotes
in history.'

Paradiso 15   13–135

As through the pure and tranquil sky there slips,
   From time to time, a sudden flaming trace
   So that a fixed gaze glances up, then dips,
From what appears a star changing its place,
   Except that where it lit no star is gone,
   And that its light endures but little space –
So, from the horn extended right, and on
   To foot of that same cross, a star was seen
   To shoot in this constellation that so shone.

7–9 at the end of the previous canto the blessed souls in the heaven of Mars
form, by synchronized soaring, the shape of a cross; one soul now makes its
way from an arm of that cross towards Dante at its base

The gem, not leaving from its ribbon's sheen,   10
   Along the radiant strip towards me made,
   Like fire behind an alabaster screen.
With selfsame tenderness Anchises' shade
   Greeted his son (if we grant our greatest muse a
   Measure of credit) in Elysium's glade.
'O sanguis meus, o super infusa
   Gratia Dei – sicut tibi, cui
   Bis unquam coeli janua reclusa?'
Thus that light; so I marked his words to me,
   Then at my Lady looked again; and twice   20
   I was amazed, first there, now here to see,
For such a smile was shining in her eyes
   I thought that I had touched with mine the bound
   Of grace to me, and of my paradise.
A joy to see the sight and hear the sound,
   The spirit added to his opening things
   I did not comprehend because profound,
Nor did he hide by choice his offerings
   But by necessity for his thought flew
   Beyond the range of mortal reasonings.   30
Yet when love's ardent bow relaxed and drew
   Within the range of our mentality,
   The first thing that I understood came through:
'Blessèd be Thou, Thou One-in-Three
   Who art so greatly courteous to my line!'
   And then continued clear enough to me:
'A clear, long-cherished hunger in which I pine,

16–18 'O blood of my blood, O superabundant outpour of God's grace, for whom has heaven's gate ever been opened twice as it has been for you?' The speaker is Dante's great-great-grandfather (though this only slowly becomes apparent and he does not name himself for a further 106 lines). As the allusion at line 13 suggests, Dante elaborately aligns this meeting with that of Aeneas and the shade of his father, Anchises, in *Aeneid* 6; the words of affiliation – '*sanguis meus*' – are taken from Virgil (*Aeneid* 6.835), the rest of the Latin is Dante's

Drawn from the reading of the mighty tome
Where neither black nor white to change incline,
40   You have assuaged, my son, in this my home
Of light from which I speak to you. All thanks
To her who gave you wings to reach this dome.
You judge that all your thoughts are not as blanks
But come to me out of the Primal Thought,
As from the unit five or six-fold ranks.
And so you do not ask why I am wrought
To greater joy than others at this feast,
Nor who I am, nor why you have been sought.
You judge correctly for the greatest and least
50   Of spirits in this life gaze in that glass
Where, ere you think, you spread your thought
      uncreased.
But so that sacred love may come to pass –
In which I gaze unendingly – that lends
This thirst and sweet desire, be not sparse
Of word but voice the longing that now pends;
Sound forth your wishes, bold and confident,
And joyously. My answer, decreed, attends.'
I turned to Beatrice who heard of my intent
Before I spoke, and granted me a sign
60   That made my wings expand for their ascent.
'Once the Primal Equality chose to shine
On you, an equal weight was made between
Wish and performance in your every design,
Because the Sun that poured on you its keen
Warmth and its light has such equality
All similes fall short of what they mean,'

---

38 *the mighty tome* God's mind   42 *her* Beatrice   45 the original of this
line is no easier to understand, but the sense is that someone who grasps the
mathematical concept of 'one' will also see that all other numbers can be
derived from the unit; similarly, because Cacciaguida is in tune with God's
primal mind, he can 'derive' from that mind all other thoughts, including
Dante's   60 the original means 'gave wings to my desire', the desire to
question his ancestor; Dante, though enskied, has only metaphorical wings

I'd started. 'Yet will and means in men must be –
　　For reasons clear to you – suited much less,
　　And fledged upon their wings unevenly.
And therefore I, a mortal, feel the stress   70
　　Of this imbalance, and only in my heart
　　Give thanks for the fatherly welcome you express.
I can and do entreat you at the start,
　　O living topaz, gem in this coronet,
　　Tell me your name before you must depart.'
'O leaf of mine – who gave delight when yet
　　Only expected here – I am your root.'
　　This was the first answer that I met.
He added, 'He from whom your kindred bruit
　　Their name – who has a hundred years or so   80
　　Circled the Mount, the first tier of the route –
Was son to me, your grandfather's father, know.
　　It is befitting now your prayers should spare
　　Those years of toil he has to undergo.
Florence, within its ancient bounds, from where
　　She still hears tierce and nones, reposed as yet
　　In peace, sober and chaste, serene and fair.
There was no bracelet then, no coronet;
　　No embroidered gowns; no girdle's sway
　　That strikes the eye before the person met.   90
Those days the daughter's birth caused no
　　　　dismay
　　To fathers; on the bride's side and the groom's,
　　Both age and dowry in due measure lay.
No mansions were deserted to the glooms;
　　Sardanapalus had made no arrival
　　To show what acts may be indulged in rooms.

---

76 *leaf* the Italian has '*fronda*' ('branch')　　81 *the Mount* of Purgatory;
Dante somehow misses his great-grandfather on the terrace of pride, the first
'tier' of the mountain　　86 *tierce and nones* liturgical hours, marked by bells
95 *Sardanapalus* an Assyrian king, notorious for racy living

Montemario was unpassed by your rival,
    Ucellatoio which, as it has surpassed
    In rising, shall surpass in ruin's deprival.
100   Bellincion Berti have I seen to cast
    Leather and bone about him, and his wife
    Turn from her mirror plain-faced, shamefast.
I've seen dei Nerli's and del Vecchio's life
    Content with hide tunic, untrimmed of lace,
    And at the flax and spindle each one's wife.
Ah, happy clan! secure of their burial place!
    And none was left deserted in her bed
    Because of France and those it drew apace.
One watched the cradle, spoke and often said
110   The soothing words that first put such delight
    Into a mother's and a father's head.
One, drawing threads from the distaff, would recite
    And tell her household of the Trojan tale,
    Of Fiesole, and Rome in all her might.
A Chianghella, a Lapo Salterello'd avail
    As great a marvel then, as now might stir
    A Cincinnatus or Cornelia, on your scale.
To such a restful, so fair a life in her,
    To such a citizenship, so loyal in aim,
120   To such a kindly inn for the traveller,
Mary gave me with loud cries on her name,
    And there, within your ancient baptistry,
    Cacciaguida, and a Christian I became . . .'
        (1996; revised 2002)

97–9 Cacciaguida, like many grand old men, has a stilted way of putting
things; his mouthful here means 'Florence had not yet outstripped Rome in
wealth and power (as it will soon outstrip Rome in decline)'   100 he lists
examples of noble families who were not debauched (and who were all
Guelfs)   102 *plain-faced* the original less ambiguously says 'without having
painted her face'   115 *Chianghella* . . . debauched members of the
fourteenth-century Florentine jet set *avail* the Italian means 'would be
thought'   117 *Cincinnatus* . . . noble Romans   121 *Mary* invoked by his
mother in the agony of childbirth   123 *Cacciaguida* apart from what Dante
reveals or suggests here, we know of Cacciaguida only that he died before 1189

SEAMUS HEANEY (1939–   )

In *The Redress of Poetry* (1995), Heaney wrote: 'There is nothing extraordinary about the challenge to be in two minds.' He has met and made that challenge throughout his extraordinary career, which culminated in the award of the Nobel Prize in 1995. The earlier work has as a generative conflict his sense that 'Ulster was British, but with no rights on / The English lyric' (*North*, 1975); more recently, he has been gravelled into song by 'two often contradictory commands: to be faithful to the collective historical experience and to be true to the recognitions of the emerging self' (1985). A keen involvement with Dante marks this second phase: 'What I first loved in the *Commedia* was the local intensity, the vehemence and fondness attaching to individual shades, the way personalities and values were emotionally soldered together, the strong strain of what has been called personal realism in the celebration of bonds of friendship and bonds of enmity. The way in which Dante could place himself in an historical world yet submit that world to scrutiny from a perspective beyond history, the way he could accommodate the political and the transcendent . . .' (1985).

Ugolino [*Inferno* 32.124–39; 33.1–90]

We had already left him. I walked the ice
And saw two soldered in a frozen hole
On top of other, one's skull capping the other's,
Gnawing at him where the neck and head
Are grafted to the sweet fruit of the brain,
Like a famine victim at a loaf of bread.

---

1 *him* Bocca degli Abati, who has been denouncing some of his fellow traitors   5 *sweet fruit* not in the Italian

So the berserk Tydeus gnashed and fed
Upon the severed head of Menalippus
As if it were some spattered carnal melon.
10   'You,' I shouted, 'you on top, what hate
Makes you so ravenous and insatiable?
What keeps you so monstrously at rut?
Is there any story I can tell
For you, in the world above, against him?
If my tongue by then's not withered in my throat
I will report the truth and clear your name.'

That sinner eased his mouth up off his meal
To answer me, and wiped it with the hair
Left growing on his victim's ravaged skull,
20   Then said, 'Even before I speak
The thought of having to relive all that
Desperate time makes my heart sick;
Yet while I weep to say them, I would sow
My words like curses – that they might increase
And multiply upon this head I gnaw.
I know you come from Florence by your accent
But I have no idea who you are
Nor how you ever managed your descent.
Still, you should know my name, for I was Count
30   Ugolino, this was Archbishop Roger,
And why I act the jockey to his mount
Is surely common knowledge; how my good faith
Was easy prey to his malignancy,
How I was taken, held, and put to death.

---

8 *severed head* the original has only 'temples'   9 Heaney supplies the melon
and the simile   10 *shouted* Dante does not raise his voice in the original
13 *any story* Dante stipulates there must be good reason for any complaint
he will relate   16 *clear your name* Dante does not make this promise
31 *jockey to his mount* touched up from the original which means 'I will tell
you why I am so close to him'

But you must hear something you cannot know
If you're to judge him – the cruelty
Of my death at his hands. So listen now.

Others will pine as I pined in that jail
Which is called Hunger after me, and watch
As I watched through a narrow hole   40
Moon after moon, bright and somnambulant,
Pass overhead, until that night I dreamt
The bad dream and my future's veil was rent.
I saw a wolf-hunt: this man rode the hill
Between Pisa and Lucca, hounding down
The wolf and wolf-cubs. He was lordly and
     masterful,
His pack in keen condition, his company
Deployed ahead of him, Gualandi
And Sismundi as well, and Lanfranchi,
Who soon wore down wolf-father and wolf-sons   50
And my hallucination
Was all sharp teeth and bleeding flanks ripped open.
When I awoke before the dawn, my head
Swam with cries of my sons who slept in tears
Beside me there, crying out for bread.
(If your sympathy has not already started
At all that my heart was foresuffering
And if you are not crying, you are hardhearted.)

They were awake now, it was near the time
For food to be brought in as usual,   60
Each one of them disturbed after his dream,

41–2 *bright . . . overhead* not in Dante   44 *the hill* the Monte di San
Giuliano   51 *hallucination* not in Dante, because Ugolino has every reason
to think his dream prophetic rather than delusive   53–4 *my head / Swam* this
cliché is not in Dante

When I heard the door being nailed and hammered
Shut, far down in the nightmare tower.
I stared in my sons' faces and spoke no word.
My eyes were dry and my heart was stony.
They cried and my little Anselm said,
'What's wrong? Why are you staring, daddy?'
But I shed no tears, I made no reply
All through that day, all through the night that
    followed
70   Until another sun blushed in the sky
And sent a small beam probing the distress
Inside those prison walls. Then when I saw
The image of my face in their four faces
I bit on my two hands in desperation
And they, since they thought hunger drove me to it,
Rose up suddenly in agitation
Saying, 'Father, it will greatly ease our pain
If you eat us instead, and you who dressed us
In this sad flesh undress us here again.'
80   So then I calmed myself to keep them calm.
We hushed. That day and the next stole past us
And earth seemed hardened against me and them.
For four days we let the silence gather.
Then, throwing himself flat in front of me,
Gaddo said, 'Why don't you help me, father?'
He died like that, and surely as you see
Me here, one by one I saw my three
Drop dead during the fifth day and the sixth day
Until I saw no more. Searching, blinded,
90   For two days I groped over them and called them.

---

62 *nailed and hammered* the original does not have the superfluous 'and
hammered'   70 *blushed in the sky* Heaney substitutes this metaphor for a
different effect in the original – Ugolino hears the way out ('*uscio*') being
nailed up and implicitly contrasts his imprisonment with the sun's freedom of
movement when it 'came out' ('*uscì*')   82 in the original, Ugolino asks 'Ah,
hard earth, why did you not open [to swallow us]?'

Then hunger killed where grief had only
  wounded.'
When he had said all this, his eyes rolled
And his teeth, like a dog's teeth clamping round a
  bone,
Bit again into the skull and again took hold.

Pisa! Pisa, your sounds are like a hiss
Sizzling in our country's grassy language.
And since the neighbour states have been remiss
In your extermination, let a huge
Dyke of islands bar the Arno's mouth, let
Capraia and Gorgona dam and deluge   100
You and your population. For the sins
Of Ugolino, who betrayed your forts,
Should never have been visited on his sons.
Your atrocity was Theban. They were young
And innocent: Hugh and Brigata
And the other two whose names are in my song.
    (1979)

Station Island   II

I was parked on a high road, listening
to peewits and wind blowing round the car
when something came to life in the driving mirror,

---

91 the original says more plainly, and more ambiguously, that 'hunger was
stronger than grief'   96 *Sizzling* Heaney introduces a pun on the original
which says 'the lovely country where the *"si"* ["yes"] is heard'; in line 70,
'blushed' similarly picks up on the sound of Dante's word *'uscío'* ('came
out')   100 *Capraia and Gorgona* islands in the Arno estuary near which
Pisa stands   101 *your population* the original is more meticulously
genocidal: 'drown every single person in you'   104 *Theban* Thebes was
known for its atrocious crime statistics

someone walking fast in an overcoat
and boots, bareheaded, big, determined
in his sure haste along the crown of the road

so that I felt myself the challenged one.
The car door slammed. I was suddenly out
face to face with an aggravated man

10   raving on about nights spent listening for
gun butts to come cracking on the door,
yeomen on the rampage, and his neighbour

among them, hammering home the shape of things.
'Round about here you overtook the women,'
I said, as the thing came clear. 'Your *Lough Derg
      Pilgrim*

haunts me every time I cross this mountain –
as if I am being followed, or following.
I'm on my road there now to do the station.'

'O holy Jesus Christ, does nothing change?'
20   His head jerked sharply side to side and up
like a diver surfacing,

then with a look that said, *who is this cub
anyhow*, he took cognizance again
of where he was: the road, the mountain top,

4–7 compare the sudden appearance of Statius in *Purgatorio* 21.4–12
15 *the thing came clear* though his name is delayed in the Dantescan manner
(until line 63), the figure now becomes identifiable as William Carleton
(1794–1869). The child of Irish-speaking, Catholic farmers in County
Tyrone, Carleton became both Protestant and vehemently anti-Catholic in
the 1820s (hence 'turncoat' in line 32); after 1839, he produced many novels.
He made the Lough Derg pilgrimage in his youth and cavilled at its papist
superstitiousness in his 'Lough Derg Pilgrim' (1829); Heaney thought of him
as 'a sort of [County] Tyrone Virgil'

and the air, softened by a shower of rain,
worked on his anger visibly until:
'It is a road you travel on your own.

I who learned to read in the reek of flax
and smelled hanged bodies rotting on their gibbets
and saw their looped slime gleaming from the sacks –   30

hard-mouthed Ribbonmen and Orange bigots
made me into the old fork-tongued turncoat
who mucked the byre of their politics.

If times were hard, I could be hard too.
I made the traitor in me sink the knife.
And maybe there's a lesson there for you,

whoever you are, wherever you come out of,
for though there's something natural in your smile
there's something in it strikes me as defensive.'

'I have no mettle for the angry role,'   40
I said. 'I come from County Derry
born in earshot of an Hibernian hall

where a band of Ribbonmen played hymns to Mary.
By then the brotherhood was a frail procession
staggering home drunk on Patrick's Day

in collarettes and sashes fringed with green.
Obedient strains like theirs tuned me first
and not that harp of unforgiving iron

---

30 the line may owe something to the gruesome account of disembowelment
in *Inferno* 28.25–7   31 *Ribbonmen* an early nineteenth-century nationalist
secret society to which Carleton belonged for a while   *Orange* the Protestant
order, founded in 1795 and still potent   42 *Hibernian* a more respectable
successor to the Ribbonmen

the Fenians strung. A lot of what you wrote
50   I heard and did: this Lough Derg station,
flax-pullings, dances, summer crossroads chat

and the shaky local voice of education.
All that. And always, Orange drums.
And neighbours on the roads at night with guns.'

'I know, I know, I know, I know,' he said,
'but you have to try to make sense of what comes.
Remember everything and keep your head.'

'The alders in the hedge,' I said, 'mushrooms,
dark-clumped grass where cows or horses dunged,
60   the cluck when pith-lined chestnut shells split open

in your hand, the melt of shells corrupting,
old jampots in a drain clogged up with mud –'
But now Carleton was interrupting:

'All this is like a trout kept in a spring
or maggots sown in wounds –
another life that cleans our element.

We are earthworms of the earth, and all that
has gone through us is what will be our trace.'
He turned on his heel when he was saying this

70   and headed up the road at the same hard pace.
          (1984)

---

49 *Fenians* a terrorist organization, founded in 1858 to fight for the
independence of Ireland   **55** *I know, I know* . . . perhaps recalling climactic
repetitions in the *Commedia* as at *Purgatorio* 30.56–7 and 73 or *Paradiso*
27.22–3   **67** *We are earthworms* taking off from and transforming
Purgatorio 10.124–6   **69** *He turned on his heel* a characteristic action at the
end of Dante's encounters (see, for example, *Inferno* 9.100 and 15.121)

ROBERT PINSKY (1940–   )

Since 1997, Pinsky has been Poet Laureate of the USA and Consultant in Poetry to the Library of Congress. His *Inferno* is written in a muted *terza rima*, because, in Pinsky's words, 'though we call it a form, verse is physical, and in this sense the sounds of a poem are its body. By devising *terza rima* as the body for a poem about the fates of souls and bodies, Dante added an expressive element as well as a kind of movement. His variations in tone and idiom – from direct to elaborately rhetorical, for example, or from high to low – have an emotional truth that moves in counterpoint with the current of interlocking rhymes . . . The goal [of Pinsky's rhyme-scheme] is to make enough of a formal demand to support the English sentence, but not so monstrous a demand as to buckle it, or to mangle the particularly delicate gestures English syntax and idiom make as they accomplish work another language might perform with inflected endings.'

Inferno 28

Who could find words, even in free-running prose,
　　For the blood and wounds I saw, in all their horror –
　　Telling it over as often as you choose,

It's certain no human tongue could take the measure
　　Of those enormities. Our speech and mind,
　　Straining to comprehend them, flail, and falter.

---

2 *in all their horror* not in Dante　　4 *human* not in Dante
5 *Of those enormities* the original means 'of so much'

If all the Apulians who long ago mourned
　　Their lives cut off by Trojans could live once more,
　　Assembled to grieve again with all those stained

10　By their own blood in the long Carthaginian war –
　　Rings pillaged from their corpses poured by the bushel,
　　As Livy writes, who never was known to err –

And they who took their mortal blows in battle
　　With Robert Guiscard, and those whose bones were
　　　　heaped
　　At Ceperano, killed in the Puglian betrayal,

And the soldiers massacred in the stratagem shaped
　　By old Alardo, who conquered without a weapon
　　Near Tagliacozzo when their army was trapped –

And some were showing wounds still hot and open,
20　Others the gashes where severed limbs had been:
　　It would be nothing to equal the mutilation

I saw in that Ninth Chasm. No barrel staved-in
　　And missing its end-piece ever gaped as wide
　　As the man I saw split open from his chin

---

8 *Trojans* used here to stand for 'Romans' who claimed descent via Aeneas
from Troy   10 *long Carthaginian war* the second Punic war (218–201 BCE)
11 *Rings pillaged . . .* the original less vividly says that the war 'made such
high spoil heaps of rings'   14 *Robert Guiscard* Norman invader of Italy in
the late eleventh century   15 *Ceperano* a battle in the struggle between the
Angioni and the Svevi (1266–8)   17 *Alardo* Alard de Valery, counsellor to
Charles of Anjou, King of Naples (1266–85) who defeated the Hohenstaufen
at Tagliacozzo in 1268   22 *Ninth Chasm* the ninth of the ten subdivisions
of Malebolge, reserved for schismatics and troublemakers; 'Chasm' is
Pinsky's aggrandizement of the original's 'pouch'

Down to the farting-place, and from the splayed
　　Trunk the spilled entrails dangled between his
　　　　thighs.
　　I saw his organs, and the sack that makes the bread

We swallow turn to shit. Seeing my eyes
　　Fastened upon him, he pulled open his chest
　　With both hands, saying, 'Look how Mohammed
　　　　claws   30

And mangles himself, torn open down the breast!
　　Look how I tear myself! And Alì goes
　　Weeping before me – like me, a schismatic, and cleft:

Split open from the chin along his face
　　Up to the forelock. All you see here, when alive,
　　Taught scandal and schism, so they are cleavered
　　　　like this.

A devil waits with a sword back there to carve
　　Each of us open afresh each time we've gone
　　Our circuit round this road, where while we grieve

Our wounds close up before we pass him again –   40
　　But who are you that stand here, perhaps to delay
　　Torments pronounced on your own false words to
　　　　men?'

---

30 *Mohammed* Dante may or may not have believed the then-widespread
calumny that Mohammed was an apostate cardinal who founded Islam out
of disappointed spite when he failed to be elected Pope
30–32 *Look . . . tear myself* Pinsky doubles the violence of the original:
'Now see how I lacerate myself, see how deformed Mohammed is'
32 *Alì* Mohammed's son-in-law and the fourth caliph; after his death in
661 CE, Islam split, with Alì's followers forming the Shia branch
33 *schismatic* not in Dante

'Neither has death yet reached him, nor does he stay
   For punishment of guilt,' my master replied,
   'But for experience. And for that purpose I,

Who am dead, lead him through Hell as rightful guide,
   From circle to circle. Of this, you can be as sure
   As that I speak to you here at his side.'

More than a hundred shadows were gathered there
   Who hearing my master's words had halted, and
50   came
   Along the trench toward me in order to stare,

Forgetting their torment in wonder for a time.
   'Tell Fra Dolcino, you who may see the sun,
   If he wants not to follow soon to the same

Punishment, he had better store up grain
   Against a winter siege and the snows' duress,
   Or the Novarese will easily bring him down' –

After he had lifted his foot to resume the pace,
   Mohammed spoke these words, and having spoken
60   He stepped away again on his painful course.

Another there, whose face was cruelly broken,
   The throat pierced through, the nose cut off at the
       brow,
   One ear remaining, stopped and gazed at me,
       stricken

---

53 *Fra Dolcino* leader of the Apostolic Brothers, one of many extreme
reformist sects in the late-thirteenth-century Church; he and his followers
were starved out of their camp in the mountains near Novara by papal forces
and Dolcino burned at the stake (June 1307)
61 *whose face was cruelly broken* not in Dante

With recognition as well as wonder. 'Ah, you,'
  His bleeding throat spoke, 'you here, yet not eternally
  Doomed here by guilt – unless I'm deceived, I knew

Your face when I still walked above in Italy.
  If you return to the sweet plain I knew well
  That slopes toward Marcabò from Vercelli,

Remember Pier da Medicina. And tell   70
  Ser Guido and Angiolello, the two best men
  Of Fano: if we have foresight here in Hell

Then by a tyrant's treachery they will drown
  Off La Cattolica – bound and thrown in the sea
  From their ships. Neptune has never seen, between

Cyprus and Majorca, whether committed by
  Pirates or Argives, such a crime. The betrayer
  Who sees from one eye only (he holds a city

Found bitter by another who's with me here)
  Will lure them to set sail for truce-talks: then,   80
  When he has dealt with them, they'll need no prayer

For safe winds near Focara – not ever again.'
  Then I to him: 'If you'd have me be the bearer
  Of news from you to those above, explain –

---

70 *Pier da Medicina* we know nothing of him, though the early
commentators retail many unsubstantiated rumours
71 *Guido and Angiolello* they were said to have been treacherously drowned
on the orders of the Malatesta lord of Rimini   77 *Argives* Greeks
The betrayer the same Malatestino denounced in lines 71ff. The 'city' is
therefore Rimini; the 'another' is identified in lines 88–92. The mangled
attributions and suspect identities of this passage read, and may be meant to
read, like the double-talk of 'intelligence services' engaged in wary trading

What man do you mean, who found a city bitter?'
    Then he grasped one shade near him by the jaw,
    And opened the mouth, and said, 'This is the
        creature,

He does not speak, who once, in exile, knew
    Words to persuade Caesar at the Rubicon –
90 Affirming, to help him thrust his doubt below,

"Delaying when he's ready hurts a man."'
    I saw how helpless Curio's tongue was cut
    To a stub in his throat, whose speech had been so
        keen.

One with both hands lopped off came forward to
        shout,
    Stumps raised in the murk to spatter his cheeks with
        blood,
    'Also remember Mosca! I too gave out

A slogan urging bloodshed, when I said
    "Once done it's done with": words which were seeds
        of pain
    For the Tuscan people.' Then, when he heard me add,

100 '– and death to your family line,' utterly undone
    By sorrow heaped upon his sorrow, the soul
    Went away like one whom grief has made insane.

---

92 *Curio's* Caius Curio, the people's tribune, switched allegiance from
Pompey to Julius Caesar whom, near Rimini, he urged to cross the Rubicon,
thereby precipitating the civil war of 49–46 BCE   96 *Mosca* Mosca dei
Lamberti, sometimes 'credited' with starting Florence's internecine strife by
urging in 1215 the murder of Buondelmonte regardless of consequences
('Once done it's done with'); a century later, the repercussions of this murder
were still not done with

I stayed to see more, one sight so incredible
    As I should fear to describe, except that conscience,
    Being pure in this, encourages me to tell:

I saw – and writing it now, my brain still envisions –
    A headless trunk that walked, in sad promenade
    Shuffling the dolorous track with its companions,

And the trunk was carrying the severed head,
    Gripping its hair like a lantern, letting it swing,   110
    And the head looked up at us: 'Oh me!' it cried.

He was himself and his lamp as he strode along,
    Two in one, and one in two – and how it can be,
    Only He knows, who so ordains the thing.

Reaching the bridge, the trunk held the head up high
    So we could hear his words, which were 'Look well,
    You who come breathing to view the dead, and say

If there is punishment harder than mine in Hell.
    Carry the word, and know me: Bertran de Born,
    Who made the father and the son rebel   120

The one against the other, by the evil turn
    I did the young king, counseling him to ill.
    David and Absalom had nothing worse to learn

107–8 *sad promenade . . . companions* the original is plainer: 'walking as the
others walked in that sad flock'   119 *Bertran de Born* Provençal poet and
bully-boy, he encouraged Henry II's son to rebel against him (and wrote a
beautiful lament when the son died as a result of taking his advice), as
Achitophel counselled Absalom to rebel against his father, David (see
2 Samuel 15–18)

From the wickedness contrived by Achitophel.
  Because I parted their union, I carry my brain
  Parted from this, its pitiful stem: Mark well

This retribution that you see is mine.'   (1994)

CLIVE WILMER (1945–   )

After graduating from King's College, Cambridge, Wilmer lived
in Florence and Padua; his first book of poems, *The Dwelling
Place*, appeared in 1977. He has edited Ruskin, Dante Gabriel
Rossetti and William Morris; their concern for the religious
aspect and social responsibilities of artistic practice persists in
his work, though much sobered in expression.

      Sestina [*Rime* 101: 'Al poco giorno e al gran
                  cerchio d'ombra']

      I have come now to the long arc of shadow
      And the short day, alas, and where the hills
      Whiten, the colour gone from the old grass;
      Yet my desire is constant in its green,
      It has so taken root in the hard stone
      That speaks and hears as if it were a woman.

      Similarly this miracle of woman
      Stays frozen like the deep snow left in shadow:
      For she is no more moved than is a stone
      By the sweet season – that which warms the hills
      Turning the whiteness of them into green
      And decking them in wild flowers, herbs and grass.

Sestina another of the four poems about the 'Donna Pietra', Dante's
equivalent of the 'Dark Lady' of Shakespeare's sonnets

When her hair is garlanded with woven grass,
She draws the mind away from other women:
She braids the rippling yellow with the green
So beautifully, Love lingers in their shadow –
Love, who confines me here between low hills
More stringently than mortar binding stone.

Her beauty holds more power than precious stones
And nothing remedies – not herb nor grass –
The hurt she gives: so over plain and hill
I have fled, my one need to escape that woman,
But from her eyes' clear light have found no shadow
By mountain, wall or leafage dense with green.

There was a time I saw her dressed in green
In such a way she could have made a stone
Feel the great love I bear her very shadow;
I desired her, therefore, in a field of grass –
As much in love as ever any woman
Has been – and ringed about by lofty hills.

But rivers will flow back and climb their hills
Before this wood, which is both damp and green,
Will at my touch catch fire – as fair women
Are known to do; and I would sleep on stone
My whole life long and go feeding on grass
Only to see where her dress casts a shadow.

Whenever hills cast their blackest shadow,
With lovely green she makes it, this young woman,
Vanish, as stones are hidden in the grass.   (1985)

PETER READING (1946–   )

Born in Liverpool, Reading studied and later taught at that city's College of Art. His work often combines 'found' material with ostentatious structuring, as in *C* (1984), which starts with the note 'Incongruously I plan 100 100-word units'. *Perduta Gente* cuts the *Commedia* together with estate agents' ads, outraged letters to the press, what look like pages torn from a derelict's notebook, and the Lamentations of Jeremiah.

Perduta Gente   p. 29

These who have never lived, blind lives so mean they
            envy all others,
        caitiffs whose deep-wailing plaints,
        horrible outcries, hoarse sighs,
Even in duff weather I'd rather do a
            skipper than stop there –
        trouble with kiphouses is
        vermin and no privacy.
piercing the starless air, dark-stained, dolent;
10   *when I remember,*
        terror still bathes me in sweat –
        their thunderous outbreathing of woe.
Hundreds of beds and the blankets is never
            changed off the last one –
        crabs, you can pick up like that.
        No fucking plugs in the sinks.

Perduta Gente 'lost people'; the phrase occurs in the inscription over the gate of hell (*Inferno* 3.3)   1–4 *Inferno* 3.64; 3.46–8; 3.22; 3.26
9–12 *Inferno* 3.23; 1.6

> *From the tormented Sad, sigh-troubled breath a-*
> *rises around them,*
> *crowds that are many and great,*
> *children and women and men.*   20
> Bloke in the next bed to me (I could see him)
>   pissed in his pillow
> then he just slep on it wet.
> Some on em masturbates, loud.
> *Let us not speak of them, merely observe and*
> *silently pass by.* (1989)

STEVE ELLIS (1952–   )

Before he set out on his own translation of *Inferno*, Ellis pro-
duced his acute study of earlier English responses, *Dante and
English Poetry, Shelley to T. S. Eliot* (1983). He stresses that
Inferno 'abounds in striking idiomatic expressions, vivid
homely details and comparisons, and dialect terms and phrases,
not only from Dante's native Florence but from other Italian
regions as well'; he has tried to match this quality in the original
by drawing on the speech of his native Yorkshire: 'this transla-
tion is bonded within a particular speech-community, and my
objection to other available versions of the poem might be
summed up in the belief that they employ no particular language
at all: rather an odd mix of the bookish and the self-consciously
demotic, a strange hybrid that lives nowhere off the page (nor
frequently indeed even on the page)'.

17–20 *Inferno* 4.29–30   25–6 *Inferno* 3.51

Inferno 11

Right on the lip of a deep bank,
   or curve of great broken rocks
   we arrive, with hordes below us
in worse pain; and it's so bad,
   the stink the great abyss exhales,
   that we draw back to the cover
of a huge tomb, chiselled, I see,
   with: 'I guard Pope Anastasius,
   lured by Photinus from the truth.'
10   'We ought to delay our descent
   till we're used to this dire smell
   a little; then it won't bother us.'
So my guide. 'Can we use our time
   so it won't be wasted?' I ask,
   and he: 'I'm thinking that too.
My son, you've three lesser circles
   rimmed by these rocks,' he begins,
   'narrowing like those we've left.
They've all got evil spirits inside:
20   but so the sight's enough for you
   hear why and how they're kept.
Every evil that earns heaven's hate
   has injustice as its end, an end
   that uses force or fraud to hurt;
as fraud is man's particular sin
   God hates it more, so bottommost
   the fraudulent are, in most pain.

---

3 *we arrive* Dante's narrative is at this point in the past tense
8 *Anastasius* Dante follows the tradition that Anastasius II (Pope from 496
to 498) was struck down by God for admitting to communion Photinus, who
held the heretical view that Christ was only human

The violent are in the first circle;
    but because force has three targets
    the circle is built in three rings: 30
at God, at oneself and at others
    violence can aim, at the person
    or the possessions, as I'll explain.
You have death or physical harm
    inflicted on others, or their goods
    can be smashed, stolen, extorted;
so murder and all unlawful assault,
    robbers, ransackers, all are damned
    in the first ring, in various groups.
Men can be violent to themselves   40
    or their own goods; so ring two
    is where this type repents in vain,
the self-remover from your world,
    the fritterer who wastes his means,
    crying where he should be happy.
Then there's violence to the deity,
    the heart's denial or open curses
    or abusing nature and its gifts;
so the badge of the smallest ring
    marks Sodom and Cahors, also those   50
    who insult and disparage God.
Fraud, gnawer of every conscience,
    this works in two different cases,
    where trust is, and where it's not.
This latter case means the murder
    of the natural bond of love only;
    so the second circle's the lair

---

28 *first circle* the first, that is, of the three circles they still have to visit
which, as they have already passed through six, is seventh in the sum total
50 *Sodom and Cahors* 'abusers of nature, named for the cities of Sodom
(sexual malpractice, see Genesis 18–19) and Cahors in southern France
(famous for its great number of usurers in the Middle Ages)' [*Ellis's note*]

of hypocrisy, flattery, enchantment,
   counterfeiting, thieving, simonists,
60   pimps, swindlers, crap like this.
The other means the disregarding
   of natural love, but added to this,
   the further love that creates trust;
so the smallest circle, that point
   of all the universe, where Dis sits,
   traitors are there, tortured always.'
I say, 'Master, your explanation
   is totally clear, and your division
   of this abyss and all its residents.
70 But tell me: those in that marsh,
   those thrashed by the wind or rain,
   those cursing, meeting head on,
why aren't they in this fiery city
   and hurt here, if they annoy God?
   Why their situation if they don't?'
He says, 'Why do your wits wander
   out of their normal way so much?
   Or what's your mind got hold of?
Don't you remember those words
80   in your Ethics, treating thoroughly
   the three dispositions heaven rejects,
incontinence, behaving like beasts
   and malice? And how the first
   offends God less, is less to blame?

---

65 *Dis* a Roman name for the god of the underworld, used by Dante as an
alternative for 'Satan'   68 *totally clear* Ellis brings out the chatty
fulsomeness of the original (*'assai chiara . . . assai ben'*)
73 *this fiery city* the city of central hell, which they enter in *Inferno* 9
80 *your Ethics* Aristotle's *Nicomachean Ethics*; Virgil's exposition shows
that, like Dante, he understands Aristotle through Aquinas's commentary

If you digest this judgement well,
    and recall those who are above
    undergoing the torments outside,
you'll see why they're kept apart
    from this evil bunch, also why
    the divine hammer is less cruel.'   90
'O sun that clears up every mist,
    your clarifying delights me so much
    I enjoy doubt as much as knowing.
But go back a little,' I tell him,
    'to where you say usury is a sin
    against God's gifts: untie that knot.'
'Philosophy notes more than once,'
    he replies, 'if you understand it,
    how nature's realm takes its course
from the divine mind, and its art: 100
    if you examine your Physics well,
    you'll find early on in the book
that your arts as far as possible
    follow her, as students to teacher:
    so they're like God's grandchildren.
Recall Genesis from the beginning,
    where she and they are the means
    that humanity is to live and grow;
but the usurer takes another way,
    slighting nature and her follower   110
    and putting his hopes elsewhere.

86–7 the denizens of hell's outer circles where lust, gluttony, avarice and
wrath are punished   101 *your Physics* Aristotle again   102 *early on* in
Book II of the *Physics*   104 *her* Nature   106 *Recall Genesis* 'man was
originally put in the Garden of Eden "to dress it and keep it" (Genesis 2:15);
he was later ordered to labour "in the sweat of [his] face" (3:19). Usury tries
to avoid the divine imperative whereby existence is sustained through the
partnership of nature and human industry.' [*Ellis's note*]

But come now, it's time to leave;
   the Fish glitter on the horizon,
   the Bear is right over Caurus
and over there we can climb down.'   (1993)

ROBIN ROBERTSON (1955–   )

'The Wood of the Suicides' is from Robertson's second book, *Slow Air*. The soul whom Dante presents as the third-personal object of his vision is here strikingly re-imagined as a first-person narrator.

The Wood of the Suicides

after Dante (Inferno, Canto XIII)

Beyond the barking of the damned in the red river, before the phosphorus sand: another dark wood. A tangle of thorn and bitter leaves, torn at by women with the feet of birds; perched there in the barren trees they dismember and defile.

A descant rises under their shrieks and the batter of wings: a low, encroaching moan of grief. The groans of millions fill the ruined wood.

113–14 'Pisces immediately precedes Aries (where the sun at present is, see [*Inferno*] 1.38) in the zodiac; the twelve zodiacal signs each rise over the eastern horizon at two-hourly intervals, so the dawn of Easter Saturday is not far away. The Great Bear lies in the north-west, above the Caurus, or north-west wind.' [*Ellis's note*]

   1–2 compare *Inferno* 12.100–102, 14.28–39   2 *another dark wood* like the '*selva oscura*' of *Inferno* 1.2   2–3 *A tangle of thorn . . . bitter leaves* compare *Inferno* 13.4–7   3 *women with the feet of birds* the Harpies of *Inferno* 13.10

Two men have come amongst us:
sight-seers; voyeurs. One takes
the twig of my finger in his hand   10
and snaps the bone.
The pain is sudden, and remote.
I am run through by flame.
The stump starts to sweat and sputter,
like a green reed half-in,
half-out of the fire,
one end burning, the other bubbling
air and sap and blood, whistling,
spitting out
words: 20

'You know now what I am.
                    Like you, poet,
I was expelled from my own land; but unlike you
I could look no longer on what I saw
and killed what hurt me.
I closed my own eyes.
And for this crime
I was banished from my body;
it lies in the upper ground
while my soul was tossed like a seed   30
                    Like you, poet,
these creatures come
to rest in my limed branches,
destroying them:
giving pain, and giving pain a voice.

---

8 *Two men* Dante and Virgil   9–20 compare *Inferno* 13.31–45   13 *I* in
the *Commedia*, the speaking tree is identifiable as Pier della Vigna,
Chancellor to Frederick II, who committed suicide when he had been accused
of treachery, imprisoned and blinded   28–44 compare *Inferno* 13.94–108

They say that on the final day
I can claim my skin,
but being self-killed
can never wear it.
I will drag it down here
– as the butcher-bird –
and skewer my body
on my soul's thorn.

You have heard my story and can leave,
as you leave all the lost.
I made my home my hanging-tree.
Now let me drop.'   (1996; revised 2002)

40

---

47 *Inferno* 13.151

List of Editions

Melville Best Anderson, *The Divine Comedy of Dante Alighieri: A line-for-line translation in the rime-form of the original* (New York: World Book Company, 1921).

Anon, *The Museum: or, The literary and historical register* (London: R. Dodsley, 1746), p. 57.

Matthew Arnold, *The Poems of Matthew Arnold*, ed. Kenneth and Miriam Allott (2nd edn, London: Longman, 1979).

W. H. Auden, 'In the year of my youth . . .', ed. Lucy S. McDiarmid, *Review of English Studies*, 29.115 (August 1978), pp. 281–312.

Samuel Beckett, *Collected Poems in English and French* (London: John Calder, 1977).

Laurence Binyon, *The Divine Comedy* (rev. edn, London: Agenda Editions, 1979).

Henry Boyd, *The Divina Commedia of Dante Alighieri: Consisting of the Inferno – Purgatorio – and Paradiso* (3 vols., London: T. Cadell jun. and W. Davies, 1802).

Elizabeth Barrett Browning, *Hitherto Unpublished Poems and Stories, with an Inedited Autobiography* (2 vols., Boston: Bibliophile Society, 1914).

Robert Browning, *The Poetical Works of Robert Browning*, ed. Ian Jack et al. (Oxford: Oxford University Press, 1983–).

— *The Brownings' Correspondence*, ed. Philip Kelley, Ronald Hudson and Scott Lewis (Winfield, Kansas: Wedgestone Press, 1984–).

Basil Bunting, *The Complete Poems*, ed. Richard Caddel (Oxford: Oxford University Press, 1994).

Charles Burney, *A General History of Music from the Earliest Ages to the Present Period* (4 vols., London: printed for the author, 1776–89).

George Gordon, Lord Byron, *The Complete Poetical Works*, ed. Jerome H. McGann and Barry Weller (7 vols., Oxford: Clarendon Press, 1980–93).

Henry Cary, *The Vision; or, Hell, Purgatory and Paradise, of Dante Alighieri* (3 vols., London: Taylor and Hessey, 1814).

Charles Bagot Cayley, *Dante's Divine Comedy: The Vision of Hell: Translated in the Original Ternary Rhyme* (London: Longman, Brown, Green, and Longmans, 1851).

Geoffrey Chaucer, *The Riverside Chaucer*, ed. Larry D. Benson (3rd edn, Oxford: Oxford University Press, 1988).

G. K. Chesterton, *Collected Poems* (London: Burns, Oates & Washbourne, 1927).

John Ciardi, *The Divine Comedy* (New York: W. W. Norton, 1977).

Amy Clampitt, *Collected Poems* (London: Faber and Faber, 1998).

Robert Creeley, *The Collected Poems of Robert Creeley 1945–1975* (Berkeley: University of California Press, 1982).

Peter Dale, *The Divine Comedy: A Terza Rima Version* (London: Anvil Press Poetry, 1996; revised 2002).

John Dayman, *The Divine Comedy of Dante Alighieri: Translated in Terza Rima* (London: Longmans, Green, and Co., 1865).

Robert Duncan, *Roots and Branches* (New York: New Directions, 1969).

— *Dante Études* (Canton, New York: Institute of Further Studies, 1974).

T. S. Eliot, *Inventions of the March Hare: Poems 1909–1917*, ed. Christopher Ricks (London: Faber and Faber, 1996).

— *The Complete Poems and Plays* (London: Faber and Faber, 1969).

Steve Ellis, *Hell* (London: Chatto and Windus, 1993).

James Ford, *The Divina Commedia of Dante Translated into English Verse* (London: Smith, Elder & Co., 1870).

Joseph Garrow, *The Early Life of Dante Alighieri Together with the Original in Parallel Pages* (Florence: Felix Le Monnier, 1846).

William Ewart Gladstone, *Translations by Lord Lyttleton and the Right Hon. W. E. Gladstone* (London: Bernard Quaritch, 1861).

Thomas Gray, *Thomas Gray and William Collins: Poetical Works*, ed. Roger Lonsdale (Oxford: Oxford University Press, 1977).

Arthur Henry Hallam, *The Writings of Arthur Hallam*, ed. T. H. Vail Motter (New York and Oxford: Modern Language Association of America and Oxford University Press, 1943).

Sir John Harington, *Ludovico Ariosto's* Orlando Furioso *Translated into English Heroical Verse* (1591), ed. Robert McNulty (Oxford: Clarendon Press, 1972).

Frederick K. H. Haselfoot, *The Divina Commedia of Dante Alighieri Translated Line for Line in the Terza Rima of the Original* (London: Kegan Paul, Trench & Co., 1887).

William Hayley, *An Essay on Epic Poetry; in Five Epistles to the Reverend Mr Mason (1782)*, ed. Sister M. Celeste Williamson, SSJ (Gainesville: Scholars' Facsimiles & Reprints, 1968).

Seamus Heaney, *Field Work* (London: Faber and Faber, 1979).

— *Station Island* (London: Faber and Faber, 1984).

John Heath-Stubbs, *Collected Poems 1943–1987* (Manchester: Carcanet New Press, 1988).

Felicia Hemans, *The Works of Mrs Hemans; with a memoir of her life, by her sister* (6 vols., Edinburgh and London: William Blackwood & Sons and Thomas Cadell, 1839).

Thomas Heywood, *The Hierarchie of the blessed Angells. Their Names, orders and Offices. The Fall of Lucifer with his Angells* (1635) (repr. New York and Amsterdam: Da Capo Press and Theatrum Orbis Terrarum Ltd, 1973).

Geoffrey Hill, *The Orchards of Syon* (London: Penguin, 2002).

Frederick Howard, Earl of Carlisle, *Poems by the Earl of Carlisle* (London: J. Ridley, 1773).

William Huggins in *The British Magazine, or Monthly repository for gentlemen & ladies* (London: James Rivington & James Fletcher, & H. Payne, 1760), p. 266.

Leigh Hunt, *The Poetical Works of Leigh Hunt*, ed. H. S. Milford (Oxford: Oxford University Press, 1923).

John Keats, *The Poems of John Keats*, ed. Miriam Allott (corrected edn, London: Longman, 1975).

— *The Letters of John Keats*, ed. Hyder Edward Rollins (2 vols., Cambridge, Mass.: Harvard University Press, 1958).

Walter Savage Landor, *The Poetical Works of Walter Savage Landor*, ed. Stephen Wheeler (3 vols., Oxford: Clarendon Press, 1937).

Eugene Jacob Lee-Hamilton, *The Inferno of Dante* (London: Grant Richards, 1898).

Richard Le Gallienne, *English Poems* (London and New York: Elkin Matthews and John Lane at the Bodley Head and The Cassell Publishing Company, 1892).

Henry Wadsworth Longfellow, *The Divine Comedy of Dante Alighieri* (3 vols., Boston: Ticknor and Fields, 1867).

— *Longfellow's Poetical Works* (London: George Routledge and Sons, 1879).

Robert Lowell, *Poems 1938–1949* (London: Faber and Faber, 1950).

— *Near the Ocean* (London: Faber and Faber, 1967).

— *History* (London: Faber and Faber, 1973).

Charles Lyell, *The Poems of the Vita Nuova and Convito of Dante Alighieri* (London: C. F. Molini, 1842).

Sir David Lindsay, *The Monarche and other Poems of Sir David Lyndesay*, Part 1, ed. John Small (2nd edn, revised, London: Early English Text Society, 1883).

Hugh MacDiarmid, *Complete Poems*, ed. Michael Grieve and W. R. Aitken (2 vols., Manchester: Carcanet New Press, 1993).

David James Mackenzie, *The Vision: or, Inferno, Purgatorio and Paradiso of Dante Alighieri* (London: Longmans, Green and Co., 1927).

Francis Sylvester Mahony, *The Reliques of Father Prout* (2 vols., London: James Fraser, 1836).

Sir Theodore Martin, *The Vita Nuova of Dante* (London: Parker, Son, and Bourn, 1862).

— and William Aytoun, *The Book of Ballads*, ed. Bon Gaultier (London: W. S. Orr and Co., 1855).

Andrew Marvell, *The Poems & Letters of Andrew Marvell*, ed. H. M. Margoliouth (corrected edn, 2 vols., Oxford: Clarendon Press, 1952).

Alan Massey in *Agenda*, vol. 34, nos. 3–4 (*Dante, Ezra Pound and the Contemporary Poet*), pp. 40–51.

Thomas Medwin and Percy Bysshe Shelley, *Shelley: Poetical Works*, ed. Thomas Hutchinson, corrected by G. M. Matthews (2nd edn, Oxford: Oxford University Press, 1970).

John Herman Merivale, *Poems Original and Translated* (2 vols., London: William Pickering, 1838).

W. S. Merwin, *Purgatorio* (New York: Alfred A. Knopf, 2000).

John Milton, *Of Reformation Touching Church-Discipline in England: and the Causes that hitherto have hindered it*, in *Anti-Prelatical Tracts*, ed. H. M. Ayres, C. L. Powell and F. A. Patterson, vol III.1 of *The Works of John Milton* (New York: Columbia University Press, 1931).

— *John Milton's Complete Poetical Works Reproduced in Photographic Facsimile*, ed. Harris Francis Fletcher (4 vols., Urbana: University of Illinois Press, 1943–8).

James Montgomery, *The Poetical Works of James Montgomery* (4 vols., London: Longman, Orme, Brown, Green, and Longmans, 1841).

Thomas Moore, *Moore's Poetical Works Complete in one Volume* (London: Longman, Brown, Green and Longman, 1843).

Robert Morehead, *Poetical Epistles: and specimens of poetical translation, particularly from Petrarch and Dante* (2nd edn, Edinburgh and London: Archibald Constable and Co. and Longman, Hurst, Rees, Orme, and Brown, 1814).

George Musgrave, *Dante's Divine Comedy: The Inferno or Hell* (London: Swan Sonneschein & Co., 1893).

Charles Eliot Norton, *The New Life of Dante Alighieri* (Boston: Ticknor and Fields, 1867).

Margaret Oliphant Oliphant, *Dante* (Edinburgh: William Blackwood and Sons, 1877).

Thomas Love Peacock, *The Works of Thomas Love Peacock*, ed. H. F. B. Brett-Smith and C. E. Jones (10 vols., London: Constable and Co., 1924–34).

Robert Peterson, *Galateo of Maister John della Casa, Archebishop of Beneventa. Or rather, A treatise of the manners and behaviours, it behoveth a man to use and eschewe, in his familiar conversation, now done into English* (1576; repr. New York and Amsterdam: Da Capo Press and Theatrum Orbis Terrarum Ltd, 1969).

George Pettie, *The civile Conversation of M. Stephen Guazzo, written first in Italian* (London: Thomas East, 1586).

Stephen Phillips, *Paolo and Francesca: A Tragedy in Four Acts* (London and New York: John Lane, 1900).

Tom Phillips, *Dante's Inferno* (London: Thames and Hudson, 1985).

Robert Pinsky, *Inferno of Dante: a new verse translation* (London: J. M. Dent, 1996).

Ezra Pound, *The Cantos of Ezra Pound* (4th edn, London: Faber and Faber, 1987).

— '[From a Notebook]', transcribed in Stuart Y. McDougal, 'Dreaming a Renaissance: Pound's Dantean Inheritance', in George Bornstein (ed.), *Ezra Pound Among the Poets* (Chicago: University of Chicago Press, 1985).

Peter Reading, *Perduta Gente* (London: Secker and Warburg, 1989).

Jonathan Richardson, *A Discourse on the Dignity, Certainty, Pleasure and Advantage, of the Science of a Connoisseur* (London: W. Churchill, 1719).

Robin Robertson, *Slow Air* (London: Picador, 2002)

Charles Rogers, *The Inferno of Dante Translated* (London: J. Nichols, 1782).

Samuel Rogers, *Italy, A Poem* (London: T. Cadell and E. Moxon, 1830).

William Roscoe, *The Life of William Roscoe, By His Son* [Henry Roscoe] (2 vols., London and Edinburgh: T. Cadell & W. Blackwood, 1833).

Christina G. Rossetti, *The Complete Poems of Christina Rossetti*, ed. R. W. Crump (3 vols., Baton Rouge: Louisiana State University Press, 1979–90).

Dante Gabriel Rossetti, *The Poems of Dante Gabriel Rossetti* (Oxford: Oxford University Press, 1913).

William Michael Rossetti, *The Comedy of Dante Allighieri, Part 1 – The Hell* (London: Macmillan and Co., 1865).

Thomas Sackville, Earl of Dorset, *The Mirror for Magistrates*, ed. Lily B. Campbell (Cambridge: Cambridge University Press, 1938).

James Sanforde, *Hours of Recreation, or Afterdinners; which may aptly be called the Garden of Pleasure* (2nd edn, London: H. Bynneman, 1576).

Dorothy L. Sayers, *The Comedy of Dante Alighieri the Florentine: Cantica II: Purgatory* (Harmondsworth: Penguin, 1955).

Charles Lancelot Shadwell, *The Purgatory of Dante Alighieri (Purgatorio I–XXVII): An Experiment in Literal Verse Translation* (London: Macmillan and Co., 1892).

— *The Paradise of Dante Alighieri: An Experiment in Literal Verse Translation* (London: Macmillan and Co., 1915).

Percy Bysshe Shelley, *The Bodleian Shelley Manuscripts*, vol. VI, ed. Carlene A. Adamson (New York: Garland Publishing Inc., 1992).

— *Poetical Works*, ed. Thomas Hutchinson, corrected by G. M. Matthews (2nd edn, Oxford: Oxford University Press, 1970).

— *Shelley's 'The Triumph of Life': A Critical Study*, ed. Donald H. Reiman (Urbana: University of Illinois Press, 1965).

— 'Voi che 'ntendendo il terzo ciel movete' in Timothy Webb, *The Violet in the Crucible: Shelley and Translation* (Oxford: Clarendon Press, 1976), pp. 292–3.

C. H. Sisson, *The Divine Comedy: A new verse translation* (Manchester: Carcanet New Press, 1980).

Stevie Smith, *The Collected Poems of Stevie Smith* (London: Allen Lane, 1985).

Edmund Spenser, *The Faerie Queene*, ed. A. C. Hamilton (London: Longman, 1977).

Wallace Stevens, *The Collected Poems of Wallace Stevens* (London: Faber and Faber, 1984).

Algernon Charles Swinburne, *The Poems of Algernon Charles Swinburne in Six Volumes*, vol. 2, *Songs Before Sunrise* (London: Chatto and Windus, 1904).

Allen Tate, *Poems* (Chicago: Swallow Press, 1961).

Alfred, Lord Tennyson, *The Poems of Tennyson*, ed. Christopher Ricks (2nd edn, 3 vols., London: Longman, 1987).

Charles Tomlinson in *Agenda*, vol. 34, nos. 3–4 (*Dante, Ezra Pound and the Contemporary Poet*), pp. 38–9.

Derek Walcott, *Omeros* (London: Faber and Faber, 1990).

Peter Whigham, *A Dante Portfolio: A translation in progress* (San Francisco: Red Hill Press, 1985).

William Patrick Wilkie, *Dante's Divina Commedia: The Inferno* (Edinburgh: Edmonston and Douglas, 1862).

Clive Wilmer, *Selected Poems 1965–1993* (Manchester: Carcanet Press, 1995).

Ichabod Charles Wright, *Dante* (London: Longman, Orme, Brown, Green, and Longman, 1845).

W. B. Yeats, *The Poems*, ed. Daniel Allbright (London: J. M. Dent, 1990).

Table of Translated Passages

Purgatorio

RIME

VITA NUOVA

CONVIVIO

Acknowledgements

Grateful thanks are due to Curtis Brown Ltd for permission to reproduce the extract from 'In the year of my youth . . .' by W. H. Auden; to Calder Publications for 'Alba' and 'Malacoda' by Samuel Beckett; to the Society of Authors for the extract from Laurence Binyon's translation of *Purgatorio* 27; to Bloodaxe Books for the extract from 'The Well of Lycopolis' by Basil Bunting; to A. P. Watt for 'The Beatific Vision' by G. K. Chesterton; to W. W. Norton & Company, Inc. for the extracts from John Ciardi's translations of *Purgatorio* 4 and 6, from *The Divine Comedy* (1977), copyright © the Ciardi Family Publishing Trust 1954, 1957, 1959, 1960, 1961, 1965, 1967, 1970; to Faber and Faber for 'At a Rest Stop in Ohio' and 'The Underworld of Dante: Canto IX' by Amy Clampitt; to the University of California Press for 'Guido, i'vorrei che tu e Lapo ed io' by Robert Creeley; to Anvil Press Poetry Ltd for the extract from Peter Dale's translation of *Paradiso* 15; to New Directions Publishing Corporation for 'Sonnet 1' by Robert Duncan; to Faber and Faber for 'Animula', 'The Burnt Dancer' and the extracts from *Little Gidding* and *The Waste Land* by T. S. Eliot; to Random House for Steve Ellis's translation of *Inferno* 11; to Faber and Faber for 'Ugolino' and the extract from 'Station Island' by Seamus Heaney; to David Higham Associates for 'Canzone: To the Lady Pietra' and the translation of *Inferno* 6 by John Heath-Stubbs; to The Penguin Group for the extracts from *The Orchards of Syon* by Geoffrey Hill; to Faber and Faber for 'The Soldier', 'Brunetto Latini' and 'Dante 3. Buonconte' by Robert Lowell; to Carcanet Press Ltd for 'Dante on the Edinburgh People' and the extract from 'The Kind of Poetry I Want' by Hugh MacDiarmid; to Alan Massey for his translation of *Paradiso* 22; to the Wylie Agency for W. S. Merwin's translation of *Purgatorio* 26; to Tom Phillips for his translation of *Inferno* 21; to J. M. Dent (Orion) for Robert Pinsky's translation of *Inferno* 28; to Faber and Faber for *Canto* XIV and the extract from *Canto* XC by Ezra Pound; to Omar S. Pound and Mary de Rachewitz, courtesy of Peggy L. Fox, for the extract from a notebook by Ezra Pound; to Bloodaxe Books for the extract from *Perduta Gente* by Peter Reading; to Macmillan Publishers for 'The Wood of the Suicides' by Robin Robertson; to David Higham Associates for Dorothy L. Sayers' translation of *Purgatorio* 12; to Carcanet Press Ltd for C. H. Sisson's translations of *Inferno* 18 (extract), *Inferno* 32 (extract), *Purgatorio* 17 (extract) and *Paradiso* 14; to the estate of James Mac-Gibbon for 'At School' and 'Francesca in Winter' by Stevie Smith; to Faber and Faber for 'The Hand as a Being' by Wallace Stevens; to Farrar, Straus and Giroux, LLC, for the extract from 'Seasons of the Soul' by Allen Tate; to Charles Tomlinson for 'Dante, guided by Virgil and Statius, enters the Earthly Paradise'; to Faber and Faber for the extract from *Omeros* by Derek Walcott; to Carcanet Press Ltd for 'Sestina' by Clive Wilmer; to J. M. Dent (Orion) for 'Cuchulain Comforted' and the extract from 'Ego Dominus Tuus' by W. B. Yeats.

Every effort has been made to trace or contact all copyright holders. The publishers will be glad to make good any omissions brought to their attention.

Index of Translators and Poets

PENGUIN CLASSICS

LA VITA NUOVA (POEMS OF YOUTH)   DANTE

'When she a little smiles, her aspect then
No tongue can tell, no memory can hold'

Dante's sequence of poems tells the story of his passion for Beatrice, the
beautiful sister of one of his closest friends, transformed through his
writing into the symbol of a love that was both spiritual and romantic. *La
Vita Nuova* begins with the moment Dante first glimpses Beatrice in her
childhood, follows him through unrequited passion and ends with his
profound grief over the loss of his love. Interspersing exquisite verse with
Dante's own commentary analysing the structure and origins of each
poem, *La Vita Nuova* offers a unique insight into the poet's art and skill.
And, by introducing personal experience into the strict formalism of
Medieval love poetry, it marked a turning point in European literature.

Barbara Reynolds's translation is remarkable for its lucidity and
faithfulness to the original. In her new introduction she examines the
ways in which Dante broke with poetic conventions of his day and
analyses his early poetry within the context of his life. This edition also
contains notes, a chronology and an index.

Translated with a new introduction by Barbara Reynolds

PENGUIN CLASSICS

THE DECAMERON   GIOVANNI BOCCACCIO

'Ever since the world began, men have been subject to various tricks of Fortune'

In the summer of 1348, as the Black Death ravages their city, ten young Florentines take refuge in the countryside. They amuse themselves by each telling a story a day for the ten days they are destined to remain there – a hundred stories of love, adventure and surprising twists of fate. Less preoccupied with abstract concepts of morality or religion than earthly values, the tales range from the bawdy Peronella hiding her lover in a tub to Ser Cepperallo, who, despite his unholy effrontery, becomes a Saint. The result is a towering monument of European literature and a masterpiece of imaginative narrative.

This is the second edition of G. H. McWilliam's acclaimed translation of *The Decameron*. In his introduction Professor McWilliam illuminates the worlds of Boccaccio and of his storytellers, showing Boccaccio as a master of vivid and exciting prose fiction.

Translated with a new introduction and notes by G. H. McWilliam

PENGUIN CLASSICS

THE BOOK OF THE COURTIER
BALDESAR CASTIGLIONE

'The courtier has to imbue with grace his movements, his gestures, his way of doing things and in short, his every action'

In *The Book of the Courtier* (1528), Baldesar Castiglione, a diplomat and Papal Nuncio to Rome, sets out to define the essential virtues for those at Court. In a lively series of imaginary conversations between the real-life courtiers to the Duke of Urbino, his speakers discuss qualities of noble behaviour – chiefly discretion, decorum, nonchalance and gracefulness – as well as wider questions such as the duties of a good government and the true nature of love. Castiglione's narrative power and psychological perception make this guide both an entertaining comedy of manners and a revealing window onto the ideals and preoccupations of the Italian Renaissance at the moment of its greatest splendour.

George Bull's elegant translation captures the variety of tone in Castiglione's speakers, from comic interjections to elevated rhetoric. This edition includes an introduction examining Castiglione's career in the courts of Urbino and Mantua, a list of the historical characters he portrays and further reading.

Translated and with an introduction by George Bull

PENGUIN CLASSICS

LIVES OF THE ARTISTS VOLUME I
GIORGIO VASARI

'In this painting of Leonardo's there was a smile so pleasing that it seemed divine rather than human'

Giorgio Vasari (1511–74) was an accomplished painter and architect, but it is for his illuminating biographies that he is best remembered. Beginning with Cimabue and Giotto in the thirteenth century, he traces the development of Italian art across three centuries to the golden epoch of Leonardo and Michelangelo. Great men, and their immortal works, are brought vividly to life, as Vasari depicts the young Giotto scratching his first drawings on stone; Donatello gazing at Brunelleschi's crucifix; and Michelangelo's painstaking work on the Sistine Chapel, harassed by the impatient Pope Julius II. The *Lives* also conveys much about Vasari himself and his outstanding abilities as a critic inspired by his passion for art.

George Bull's introduction discusses Vasari's life and influences, and the political and historical background of sixteenth-century Florence. This volume also includes notes on the artists by Peter Murray and a list for further reading.

'The most influential book about the history of art ever written'
New York Review of Books

A selection translated by George Bull, with notes on the artists by Peter Murray

PENGUIN CLASSICS

LIVES OF THE ARTISTS VOLUME II
GIORGIO VASARI

'Enterprises endowed with virtue and talent ... never pause or rest till they have reached the height of glory'

In his *Lives of Artists of the Italian Renaissance*, Giorgio Vasari (1511–74) demonstrated a literary talent that even outshone his outstanding abilities as a painter and architect, revealing both a deep understanding of human nature and perceptive responses to great works of art. Through character sketches and anecdotes he depicts Piero di Cosimo shut away in his derelict house, living only to paint; Giulio Romano's startling painting of Jove striking down the giants; and his friend Francesco Salviati, whose biography also tells us much about Vasari's own early career. Vasari's original and soaring vision, and his acute aesthetic judgements, have made him one of the most influential art historians of all time.

In his introduction, George Bull discusses Vasari's life and works, and his development as an artist. This edition includes notes on the artists by Peter Murray and suggestions for further reading.

'It is his unfailing enthusiasm for art, his delight in artists and their artistic temperament, and his sensitivity, which make his books so valuable'
The Times

A selection translated by George Bull with notes on the artists by Peter Murray

PENGUIN CLASSICS

DON QUIXOTE MIGUEL DE CERVANTES

'Didn't I tell you they were only windmills? And only someone with windmills on the brain could have failed to see that!'

Don Quixote has become so entranced by reading romances of chivalry that he determines to become a knight errant and pursue bold adventures, accompanied by his squire, the cunning Sancho Panza. As they roam the world together, the ageing Quixote's fancy leads them wildly astray. At the same time the relationship between the two men grows in fascinating subtlety. Often considered to be the first modern novel, *Don Quixote* is a wonderful burlesque of the popular literature its disordered protagonist is obsessed with.

John Rutherford's landmark translation does full justice to the energy and wit of Cervantes's prose. His introduction discusses the traditional works parodied in *Don Quixote*, as well as issues surrounding literary translation.

'John Rutherford ... makes *Don Quixote* funny and readable ... His Quixote can be pompous, imposingly learned, secretly fearful, mad and touching' Colin Burrow, *The Times Literary Supplement*

Voted greatest book of all time by the Nobel Institute

Translated with an introduction and notes by John Rutherford

PENGUIN CLASSICS

PARADISE LOST   JOHN MILTON

'Better to reign in Hell, than serve in Heav'n ...'

In *Paradise Lost* Milton produced a poem of epic scale, conjuring up a vast, awe-inspiring cosmos and ranging across huge tracts of space and time. And yet, in putting a charismatic Satan and naked Adam and Eve at the centre of this story, he also created an intensely human tragedy on the Fall of Man. Written when Milton was in his fifties – blind, bitterly disappointed by the Restoration and briefly in danger of execution – *Paradise Lost*'s apparent ambivalence towards authority has led to intense debate about whether it manages to 'justify the ways of God to men', or exposes the cruelty of Christianity.

John Leonard's revised edition of *Paradise Lost* contains full notes, elucidating Milton's biblical, classical and historical allusions and discussing his vivid, highly original use of language and blank verse.

'An endless moral maze, introducing literature's first Romantic, Satan'
John Carey

Edited with an introduction and notes by John Leonard

PENGUIN CLASSICS

DEAD SOULS NIKOLAI GOGOL

'It's not a question of the living. I've nothing to do with them. I'm asking for the dead'

Chichikov, a mysterious stranger, arrives in the provincial town of 'N', visiting a succession of landowners and making each a strange offer. He proposes to buy the names of dead serfs still registered on the census, saving their owners from paying tax on them, and to use these 'souls' as collateral to re-invent himself as a gentleman. In this ebullient masterpiece, Gogol created a grotesque gallery of human types, from the bear-like Sobakevich to the insubstantial fool Manilov, and, above all, the devilish conman Chichikov. *Dead Souls*, Russia's first major novel, is one of the most unusual works of nineteenth-century fiction and a devastating satire on social hypocrisy.

David Magarshack's introduction discusses Gogol's plan for a novel in three parts, tracing Chichikov's progress from sin to redemption, and tells how Gogol destroyed part of the manuscript in the grip of madness. The surviving sections, volume one and a fragment of volume two, are translated here.

'Gogol was a strange creature, but then genius is always strange'
Vladimir Nabokov

Translated with an introduction by David Magarshack

PENGUIN CLASSICS

RESURRECTION   LEO TOLSTOY

'In the very depths of his heart, he knew that he had behaved so meanly, so contemptibly, so cruelly'

Serving on a jury at the trial of a prostitute arrested for murder, Prince Nekhlyudov is horrified to discover that the accused is a woman he had once loved, seduced and then abandoned when she was a young servant girl. Racked with guilt at realizing he was the cause of her ruin, he determines to appeal for her release or give up his own way of life and follow her. Conceived on an epic scale, *Resurrection* portrays a vast panorama of Russian life, taking us from the underworld of prison cells and warders to the palaces of countesses. It is also an angry denunciation of government, the upper classes, the judicial system and the Church, and a highly personal statement of Tolstoy's belief in human redemption.

Rosemary Edmonds's fine translation is accompanied by an introduction discussing how *Resurrection* relates to Tolstoy's own spiritual development and how the scope and depth of the book are even more ambitious than his other works.

Translated with an introduction by Rosemary Edmonds